HEALER

HEALER

DR PRATHAP CHANDRA REDDY
and the
TRANSFORMATION
of INDIA

PRANAY GUPTE

PORTFOLIO
PENGUIN

PORTFOLIO
Published by the Penguin Group
Penguin Books India Pvt. Ltd, 11 Community Centre, Panchsheel Park,
New Delhi 110 017, India
Penguin Group (USA) Inc., 375 Hudson Street, New York, New York 10014, USA
Penguin Group (Canada), 90 Eglinton Avenue East, Suite 700, Toronto, Ontario,
M4P 2Y3, Canada (a division of Pearson Penguin Canada Inc.)
Penguin Books Ltd, 80 Strand, London WC2R 0RL, England
Penguin Ireland, 25 St Stephen's Green, Dublin 2, Ireland (a division of Penguin Books Ltd)
Penguin Group (Australia), 707 Collins Street, Melbourne, Victoria 3008, Australia
(a division of Pearson Australia Group Pty Ltd)
Penguin Group (NZ), 67 Apollo Drive, Rosedale, Auckland 0632, New Zealand
(a division of Pearson New Zealand Ltd)
Penguin Books (South Africa) (Pty) Ltd, Block D, Rosebank Office Park, 181 Jan Smuts
Avenue, Parktown North, Johannesburg 2193, South Africa

Penguin Books Ltd, Registered Offices: 80 Strand, London WC2R 0RL, England

First published in Portfolio by Penguin Books India 2013

Copyright © Pranay Gupte 2013

ISBN 9780670086801

Typeset in Sabon by R. Ajith Kumar, New Delhi
Printed at Replika Press Pvt. Ltd, India

'I admire Dr Prathap Chandra Reddy greatly, because he returned to India despite the enormous opportunities and prospects that he had in the United States. The contribution he has made in emphasizing preventive care and ensuring a parallel stream of high-class research in all the hospitals that he has established sets a benchmark which I hope others will be inspired to emulate. I believe this book, authored by Pranay Gupte, a distinguished journalist-intellectual, is a justifiable contribution to this entrepreneur who has excelled in whatever he has undertaken, most notably by bringing up institutions of high excellence and world-class professional standards in the field of medical science in India.'

Dr Rajendra K. Pachauri, Chairman, Intergovernmental Panel on Climate Change (recipient of the 2007 Nobel Peace Prize)

'Dr Reddy built Apollo Hospitals from the ground up to provide state-of-the-art, high-grade medical diagnosis and treatment in India. He has grown his business model effectively and professionally over time. His model has been noticed and emulated in other countries in the developing and developed world. In the years I have interacted with Dr Reddy, he has always remained humble, affable and extremely down to earth, ready to help and assist and worry about the details later. Dr Reddy is a role model for many in terms of serving the nation in a sustainable, effective manner. He has been respected for imparting professional medical care to many, many Indians and his contribution deserves to be recognized. I'm pleased that Pranay Gupte has written this major biography of an icon.'

Ratan N. Tata, Chairman, Tata Trusts

'I heartily commend Dr Reddy for two achievements. Since good health is a pre-requisite for human development, I have always believed that apart from education, health care is the biggest driver of India's journey towards becoming a developed nation. Given the diversities in our society, India needs to pursue multiple models of health care. However, the common denominator in all these multiple paradigms has to be the commitment to both quality and compassion in the service of patients. In its own category of health care business, the Apollo chain of hospitals has earned its reputation by showing this commitment in abundant measure. Dr Reddy's other exemplary achievement is women's empowerment in Indian business. His four daughters Preetha, Suneeta, Shobana and Sangita who have helped him so ably in building and running his enterprise have shown that professionally well-qualified and capable women can be equal to their male counterparts in any enterprise, especially in the enterprise of health care.'

Mukesh D. Ambani, Chairman and CEO, Reliance Industries Limited

'I have always looked to Dr Reddy for advice on health-related matters for my family and friends. He has the rare ability to provide comfort and the reassurance of a personal overview despite the myriad pressures that weigh on him while leading such a large enterprise. He has indeed endeared himself to many with his characteristic humility and compassionate demeanour. Not many have the ability to pursue their dreams and create a legacy that enriches the lives of millions. Dr Reddy is doubly blessed – to be able to create this inspiring legacy and also to receive the gratitude of the millions he and his institutions have served.'

Y.C. Deveshwar, Chairman, ITC Limited

'Dr Reddy is one of the giant figures of post-Independence India whose contributions to improving health care have been invaluable. At a personal level, I am always touched by his warmth and affection, and also by his continuing goodwill towards everyone who comes in contact with him.'

Kamal Nath, Union Minister for Parliamentary Affairs and Urban Development

'The Greek God Apollo was the God of heavenly light, illuminating the soul of man. Apollo Hospitals have provided a similar yeoman service for health care, touching the poorest of the poor and providing quality service to all patients. The spirit behind this is a man, a visionary ahead of his times. Dr Prathap Chandra Reddy is innovative, seeking to provide solutions for health care which will endure. He believes that health care must provide accessible and affordable solutions for ordinary people. He has in the past and will in the future lead from the front. Apollo Hospitals and Dr Reddy are synonymous – they both represent excellence and passion for service.'

Kapil Sibal, Union Minister for Law and Justice, Communications and Information Technology

'Dr Reddy is a visionary who has transformed the medical landscape in India and made it more accessible and affordable to common people of the country.

He founded Apollo Hospitals, the success of which is a topic of a Harvard Business School case study. Today, the Apollo Group is the reference point for peers in the industry. At this age also, he is continuously working towards his vision of making India a health care destination of the world. A great social change agent and a great human being, he is a true asset for this country. I am confident that his legacy will be there forever.'

G.M. Rao, Chairman, GMR Group

'Dr Reddy is a trendsetter in setting up private health care institutions in India and has paved the path for others to follow. His hospitals attracted the best non-resident Indian doctors; thus, he reversed the brain drain and brought talent back to India. I think that the private sector's involvement is majorly responsible for creating a paradigm shift in the Indian health care scenario. India has over 750 corporate hospitals. Apollo Group hospitals perform more major surgeries than any other facility in the world. This is the true testimony to the quality and consistency of health care that private sector involvement can bring to India.'

G.V.K. Reddy, Founder and Chairman, GVK Group

'Dr Prathap C. Reddy's story is that of a unique, extraordinary leader who combines in himself the ingredients of a pioneer and a pathfinder, commanding enormous respect, affection and admiration. He is a thought leader and nation-builder in the critical health care sector, and this book is a must-read.'

Tarun Das, Senior Mentor, Confederation of Indian Industries

'Apollo Telemedicine Services is a very wonderful contribution to the health care of the people who live in rural villages, and I hope that people all over the world will follow Dr Reddy's lead, because if they do, the benefits of hi-tech medicine can go to everyone and not just to people who live in big cities.'

William Jefferson Clinton, forty-second President of the United States

'The most striking thing about Dr Prathap Reddy is the sheer breadth of his vision for Apollo and for his country and the values on which it is based. Over the last thirty years he has not only enhanced the lives of millions by providing them with health care but enriched India and the world with research, education and innovation. Apollo is now one of the great health care companies of the world and he one of its great health leaders.'

Lord Nigel Crisp, House of Lords, British Parliament, and former CEO of the National Health Service

'As diagnostic imaging continues to improve, as surgical tools become increasingly refined, and as the techniques are improved through experience, the effect on patient care and recovery stands to improve. The adoption of minimally invasive surgery will surely spread into fields where they have not yet even been attempted. I commend Dr Reddy and Apollo Hospitals for such adoption of state-of-the-art techniques in surgery.'

His Highness Sheikh Nahayan Mabarak Al Nahayan, Minister of Culture, Youth and Community Development, United Arab Emirates

'Though I have known about Padma Vibhushan Dr Prathap Chandra Reddy for a long time, I was pleasantly surprised to learn more about his wisdom and commitment from his daughter Mrs Sangita Reddy during the inauguration of Apollo Sugar Clinic at Muscat. I was amazed to know about Dr Reddy's foresight, which helped him revolutionize the medical landscape of such a large and diverse country like India. Dr Reddy's vision for the future of health care and his dedication to the cause of clinical excellence is very inspiring and this gives a lot of pleasure and assurance to all of us who are partnering him in countries away from India. I wish Dr Reddy a very healthy and long life and may he continue to steer the Apollo Hospitals Group steadily with his dynamism and foresight.'

His Highness Shihab bin Tariq Al Said, Chairman, Seven Seas Group, Muscat, Sultanate of Oman

'To bring affordable world-class health care to India with easy accessibility and quality has remained the aim of the Apollo Group. India's health care system is developing at a high speed. It is very essential to keep pace with the technological advances and latest research going on in the world. I appreciate the contribution made by Dr Prathap C. Reddy to health care in India.'

Narendra Modi, Chief Minister, Gujarat

'I had met Dr Prathap Chandra Reddy for the first time when I went as a youngster to Apollo, Chennai, to meet my father, who was admitted there. We come from the same district in Andhra, and that is something we have in common. I have seen Apollo grow and I can attribute its success to the sheer dedication and leadership of Dr Reddy. It was his grand vision that enabled millions of Indians to have access to high-quality health care. Dr Reddy has raised the benchmarks and set new milestones that will take some time for anybody else to surpass. I am happy that his facility Apollo Hospitals, Hyderabad, sparked the development of large hi-tech hospitals – and Andhra Pradesh is now the health care capital of India.'

N. Kiran Kumar Reddy, Chief Minister, Andhra Pradesh

'Dr Reddy has been a pioneer of the private health sector in the country. He has made it globally competitive and is responsible for making India the destination for the health needs of the developing countries. Having established hospitals of international reputation, he has also contributed to the development of telemedicine in the country. His visionary approach in the sector has taken telemedicine to the common man. While Dr Reddy may belong to Andhra Pradesh, he actually belongs to the world – such is the stature of his thought process and the global goodwill that he has created with the inimitable brand Apollo in the world. I am happy that we both come from Chittoor district and share progressive ideas for the development of the country.'

Nara Chandra Babu Naidu, President, Telugu Desam Party and Leader of the Opposition, Andhra Pradesh Legislative Assembly

'Dr Prathap Chandra Reddy has transformed the concept of health care in India. In many ways, we can demarcate health care in India as before Apollo and after. Sitting upon such laurels, the man himself is childlike, effervescent and joyful. His irrepressible enthusiasm at eighty is to be seen to be believed. He is a devout being and a visionary entrepreneur, a true blessing for the nation.'

Sadhguru Jaggi Vasudev, Founder, Isha Foundation

'Dr Reddy is a visionary who brought telemedicine to rural areas, enabling multitudes of people to have easy access to health care, filling their lives with much-needed healing. He is lauded by numerous people both in India and abroad. He has enriched and enhanced the lives of a large number of people. Our *mangalasasanams* are always with him and his family to serve the needy with much more advanced medical technology, to see smiles on the faces of the needy.'

Sri Chinna Jeeyar Swami, Founder, Vedic University

'Dr Prathap Chandra Reddy has brought a new dimension of care to health care in India. His approach is totally people-oriented: People First! By combining that approach with the best in medical technology, Dr Reddy has shown that India need not be a "Third World" country when it comes to health care.'

Bakul Rajni Patel, former Sheriff of Mumbai

'The mutual regard, respect and affection between two of India's illustrious sons, the former President of India R. Venkataraman and the Founder Chairman of India's first corporate hospital Dr Pratap C. Reddy, was a joy to witness and behold. Having had the pleasure of being associated with the birth and growth of Apollo Hospitals over the years, Shri Venkataraman took every opportunity he got to commend the vision, the entrepreneurial zeal and the able leadership of Dr Reddy. When he inaugurated the Apollo Hospital in Hyderabad on 27 August 1988, he called it a "generational leap" in hospital care. President Venkataraman said, "The Apollo Group has overcome numerous handicaps. Some entrepreneurs break down under pressure. But I can say that Dr Reddy has done more than just 'go on'. He is an exemplar not only to health care professionals but to all entrepreneurs." It was President Venkataraman's dream that Apollo grow from strength to strength to establish many such centres of excellence throughout India, a dream that Dr Reddy has been fulfilling not only for his friend and guide but for all Indians across the length and breadth of the country.'

Lakshmi Venkataraman Venkatesan, daughter of former Indian President R. Venkataraman

'Dr Reddy's name is synonymous with consistent, high-quality health care, as this biography makes clear. His many innovations – including the Apollo hospital system – have transformed the face of medicine in India and touched countless lives worldwide. When I visited Apollo Hyderabad in 1990, I was favourably impressed by its modern facilities and the morale of its personnel.

Since that time, Apollo has become one of the world's leading hospital systems, and India has emerged as a growing market for international patients. I salute Dr Reddy for his ongoing contributions to this progress, and I applaud his vision, courage, compassion and pioneering spirit.'

Dr Denton A. Cooley, MD, Founder, Texas Heart Institute, Houston

'I have known Dr Prathap Chandra Reddy since 1997. He has really accomplished his vision for health care. When I first came into health care in 1997 as CEO of GE Healthcare I had the opportunity to meet Dr Reddy and was struck by his passion and unwavering determination to make a difference in health care. He has been a global pioneer in so many ways, and I've admired his willingness to go after the big challenges in health care and to leverage technological advances to build a world-class, transnational health care system. I am delighted that Pranay Gupte has written this major biography.'

Jeffery Immelt, Chairman and CEO, General Electric

'As insurance and reinsurance experts we truly understand risks on a global and local scale. But this knowledge only creates value when it can be adapted to the needs of local clients. Thanks to Dr Reddy we were able to combine our expertise with his profound knowledge of the Indian health care sector. We feel privileged to have him as Chairman of the Board in our important joint venture. His influence and guidance continue to be critical also for the future success of Apollo Munich Health Insurance.'

Dr Nikolaus von Bomhard, Chairman of the Board of Management of Munich Re

'Dr Reddy is recognized worldwide both as a highly skilled cardiologist and as a visionary medical innovator. In reflecting upon the success of the Mayo Clinic, Dr William Mayo observed, "If we excel in anything, it is in our capacity for translating idealism into action." Dr Reddy and the Apollo Group reflect that same commitment to innovation and to translating idealism into action.'

Dr John H. Noseworthy, MD, President and CEO, Mayo Clinic

'I have had the great privilege of knowing Dr Prathap Chandra Reddy for over forty years, since my early childhood days and predating Apollo Hospitals.

Dr Reddy's belief that health care in India can be the very best in the world led to the creation—and fuelled the growth—of Apollo Hospitals. Dr Reddy's entrepreneurial ingenuity in pursuing his belief has improved the quality of lives of millions by healing the sick, educating those unaware about caring for their health, and broadening health care access to the underprivileged. Through his amazing mix of foresight, insight, passion and compassion, he has radically transformed health care in India and other countries. Dr Reddy's purposeful journey to reshape India's health care system is an instance of the positive impact that can be achieved by thinking boldly and remaining persistent to a noble cause that concerns the health and well-being of people.'

Arun Rai, PhD, FAIS, Regents' Professor, Georgia State University

'Out of ignorance, my parochial assumption was that US medicine had little to learn from India. How wrong I would prove to be, and it was my eventual good friend Dr Reddy who opened my eyes to the unique sophistication and efficiency of Indian health care, the product of a modern revolution that he personally helped foster through his founding of the Apollo Hospitals Group. Dr Reddy and I have much in common. We both did residency training at Harvard and at least for a while were practising physicians in the United States. More importantly we are both physician innovators and entrepreneurs. As the inventor of the CyberKnife and image-guided therapeutic radiation, my most important innovations were technology- and surgical procedure-based. I have been fortunate in life to see my ideas benefit several hundreds of thousands of patients and their families. In contrast, Dr Reddy's great innovations were grounded in developing ever more efficient processes for organizing and delivering cost-effective health care to the enormous and largely poor population of a great emerging nation. His ambitions and drive have clearly benefited, and often saved the lives of, many millions of patients to date, with millions more being served every year. I have been rightfully proud of my own accomplishments in life and there are not many men that I envy. However, when I think of the positive impact that Dr Reddy has had on so many patients, I am envious, but only in a way that inspires me to try even harder to help even more patients in the future.'

Dr John R. Adler, Jr, MD, Dorothy and T.K. Chan Professor, Stanford University, and Editor-in-Chief, Cureus.com

This book is for Dr Prathap Chandra Reddy and Sucharitha Reddy
for welcoming a stranger into the innermost sanctums
of an extraordinary family.

And for N. Ram and Mariam Ram, who created the opportunity.

Contents

Allan E. Goodman

'I SWEAR BY APOLLO . . .'

As I heard my daughter and her husband take the Hippocratic Oath at their medical school graduation, I looked around at the faces of their classmates. While I knew that most were American citizens, it was also clear that many had parents who originally came from somewhere else. Increasingly, we are a nation of immigrants again and benefit greatly from attracting the best and brightest to our universities from all over the world. Today, nearly two-thirds of all science and engineering graduates in the United States are from India and China, and over 25 per cent of our medical residents are graduates of foreign medical schools.

No one knows how many go back. And when my children refer their patients to a cardiologist from India, an ophthalmologist from China, an oncologist from Egypt, an obstetrician from Ghana or a dermatologist from Italy, you have to wonder if there are enough

Dr Allan E. Goodman is President and CEO of the Institute of International Education (IIE), a not-for-profit educational and cultural exchange organization based in the US that, among other activities, administers the Fulbright Programme.

doctors to treat the people back home.

The Institute of International Education, where I serve as president, has fostered the international exchange of education and ideas since 1920, and has also done an annual census of international student and scholar mobility to and from the United States. Today, over 750,000 internationals are enrolled in US higher education institutions, with China and India being the leading countries from where international students come. Together they account for about one-third of the United States's total international student enrolment. There is, however, no systematically collected data on who stays beyond this period of their education, or, more importantly, who returns to their home countries after a year or more of experience here in their chosen professions. We do hear that thanks to globalization these days, brain gain is increasingly common.

But in Dr Reddy's era, it was not. And this makes his odyssey and this book – *Healer* – so compelling for someone in my field.

Pranay Gupte is writing about the difference that a single individual can make in an area very much in the news in America and around the world. How are we going to care for the ill and vulnerable in our societies? And where does the role of the private sector end and the government's begin? Can there be practical and cost-effective partnerships? And what should societies do to develop and retain both their domestic talent and that which comes to us from abroad?

Healer also begs the question of what obligations any of us in the fields of medicine or education owe to solving problems beyond our borders. When do we speak up to our students and interns and urge them to consider returning to practice in their home countries? Or, if our hospitals benefit from the talents of people from particular places, what can we do to loan them our staff to develop local capacity? A good example is the global health service corps, named Seed Global Health, created by two US physicians to enable medical professionals to serve abroad. If it had been around when Dr Reddy was starting out, he might well have applied to join. One of the founders is an alumnus of the Fulbright Programme which the Institute has the honour to administer on behalf of the Bureau of Educational and

Cultural Affairs at the US Department of State. The other is a former Assistant Surgeon General of the United States. His spouse is an internist, born in Ghana.

The late Senator J. William Fulbright once observed that international education 'transforms nations into people'. So does Dr Reddy, as these pages will show. In almost every chapter there is a reminder that the human touch is important to the ill and poor, as it is essential to healing. That staff have names. And that no CEO can hope to succeed if she or he thinks it is their own needs and status that matter most.

For America and the world, India is a really big country that has got to work. Indian medicine and hospitals have to work especially well because its problems, especially in the area of public health, are not its alone: they can impact the larger world easily because of its large population. And India is important also because many of the low-cost and scalable solutions to the world's public health problems have emerged within the country. Dr Reddy's odyssey shows all of us how this dream can become a reality.

Of course, it also, as we say, 'takes a village'. One thing you will learn from reading this biography is that everyone can play a part in making everybody better. As Rabindranath Tagore observed when he accepted the Nobel Prize for Literature:

> The spirit of India [is to] comprehend all things with sympathy and love. We must go deeper down to the spirit of man and find out the great bond of unity, which is to be found in all human races. And for that we are well equipped. We have inherited the immortal works of our ancestors, those great writers who proclaim the religion of unity and sympathy in saying: he who sees all beings as himself, who realizes all beings as himself, knows truth. This has once again to be realized, not only by the children of the East but also by the children of the West.

So *Healer* has much to teach us all.

As I write this foreword, the world we share is becoming

increasingly polarized. Dr Reddy's story gives us all a measure of hope that it need not be so and that, indeed and ironically, an international education may be the best investment any of us have to realize the fundamental truth to which Tagore's voice and Dr Reddy's example beckon us still today.

The Seven Hills of Tirupati

TO ENTER THE INNERMOST sanctum of Lord Venkateshwara's shrine at the ancient temple of Tirupati in southern India's Andhra Pradesh is to be transported into an indefinable zone of spirituality. It almost doesn't matter if you are a believer in God or not, and it doesn't matter whether you believe that the deity's blessings have affected the lives of millions of people over several centuries. No matter where you come from, no matter what your background and no matter what your faith, you inevitably feel a powerful force emanating from Lord Venkateshwara in the narrow confines of the sanctum.

As I stood in the gold-covered sanctum, I felt that I was also tapping into the collective energy of millions of devotees who'd visited Tirupati for more than a thousand years. One isn't allowed to stay very long in the shrine because the Brahmin priests good-naturedly but efficiently keep the lines of worshippers moving, speaking in English, Tamil, Telugu and Hindi; some 200,000 visitors come to Tirupati every day. But there was a couple in front of me who had been permitted to stand in front of Lord Venkateshwara for longer than most. They had been coming to Tirupati since their respective childhoods – indeed, before some of the current priests were even born, and before the temple complex was developed – and this was, after all, a very special occasion.

It was the occasion of Dr Prathap Chandra Reddy's eightieth birthday in February 2013, and I had been invited to join him and his large family on a pilgrimage to Tirupati, one of the holiest Hindu shrines in India. We'd taken a private jet from Chennai, a mere hundred miles away, to the small but modern airport at Tirupati, and then driven in a small caravan of cars up the hills to the actual temple complex itself. As we drove up the steep grades, I could see devotees trekking up the seven Tirumala hills towards the Venkateshwara temple, which is at an elevation of nearly 1,800 metres.[1] The hills form one of the oldest rock formations on our planet.

In the shrine, both Dr Reddy and his wife Sucharitha had their eyes closed in deep prayer. I was there at the end of nearly a year of following them around India for this biography. Although the Reddys had previously allowed me to join them in prayers at small mandirs, or shrines, at their homes in Chennai, Hyderabad and New Delhi, I had never observed them together in what clearly seemed to be a deep trance. I wondered what was going on in their minds.

When I put that question to both of them afterwards, each responded, separately, and in exactly identical words, 'Just thanks. Nothing more than thanks to the Almighty for everything that He has given us.'

---

1 The Tirumala Hills are about 16 sq. km in area. They comprise seven peaks, representing the seven heads of Adisesha – one of the primal beings of creation in Hinduism – thus earning the name Seshachalam. The seven peaks are called Seshadri, Neeladri, Garudadri, Anjanadri, Vrushabhadri, Narayanadri and Venkatadri. The temple is on Venkatadri (also known as Venkatachala or Venkata Hill), the seventh peak. The presiding deity of the temple is Lord Venkateshwara, a form of the Hindu god Vishnu. The temple lies on the southern banks of Sri Swami Pushkarini, a holy water tank. The temple complex comprises a traditional temple building, with a number of modern queue and pilgrim lodging sites. The temple, with assets of nearly $1 trillion, is the richest pilgrimage centre, after the Sree Padmanabhaswamy Temple in Thiruvananthapuram in Kerala, of any faith, and the most-visited place of worship in the world. It is visited by about 50 million people annually, while on special occasions and festivals, like the annual Brahmotsavam, the daily number of pilgrims shoots up to 500,000.

I thought that their responses demonstrated rare humility in two of the best-known figures in contemporary India. Dr Reddy later told me that he never asks God for any favours. Every prayer, whether at Tirupati or at home or at any number of the hundreds of temples that he and Sucharitha have visited across India, the only word that is repeated over and over again is, 'Thanks!'

They have plenty to be thankful for, although Prathap Chandra Reddy's stunning success in creating India's first private-sector hospital system was surely the result of relentless dedication and smart political manoeuvring to change the health care landscape of a country characterized by mass poverty and inadequate health facilities.

Much as I tried during the Tirupati trip to get Dr Reddy to claim some sort of personal credit for transforming India's health care landscape, he stubbornly refused to do so. At a time when other people of his age contemplate retirement, read books they missed out on earlier in life or settle in ashrams, Dr Reddy challenges what other people think and do. During one of our conversations in Tirupati he pointed out that India planned to spend $1 trillion over the next five years on building infrastructure. But what about the $250 billion that was needed, at the very minimum, to meaningfully tackle the growing scourge of heart problems, cancer, diabetes and infectious diseases? Public funding is unimaginably inadequate. 'Health care in India has no godfather. The government is not paying proper attention to the health care needs of India. What is a nation minus health care?' he said.

This isn't a criticism of government policy as much as it is an expression of sadness and disappointment. Dr Reddy has a tremendous amount of energy and puts it to use whether in the business of Apollo Hospitals or generally helping the people of India get better. He is never satisfied with the accomplishments of Apollo and he doesn't rest on his laurels. 'I'm always asking myself, "What more can we do? How fast can we do it? What will it take to generate greater awareness of good health and personal well-being?"' Even in Tirupati, I saw him vigorously go around and ask priests and devotees if they'd had preventive health check-ups. He would move from shrine to shrine within the temple complex at a clip that left me – a much younger man – somewhat winded.

So I asked him: 'Where does your energy come from?'

No matter how often he's been asked questions like this before, Prathap Chandra Reddy has developed the art of responding as though it were the first time that he'd heard the query.

'Where does my energy come from? Faith. All of us have this universal capability but only a few excel either because they don't know or do not want to do the work. We all have unqualified built-in strength. You can use several things to help you achieve your potential – meditation and yoga are helpful and I use them whether to overcome a major obstacle or to think in a new way. Regardless of our own convictions there is always some higher power. If you believe in God, the higher power is God. If you don't believe in God, the higher power is a creator. Faith helps drive all action. I believe in the three Ps: Purity – that your motivation is not for yourself; Persistence – working hard and continuously on problems; and Patience. Faith fortifies people in different ways. I don't discount the efforts that my colleagues and I have made over the years. But ultimately, there's a higher power that has blessed us. I truly believe that.'

He has perhaps been blessed more than most. He was blessed because he was born into a loving family in the small village of Aragonda in Andhra Pradesh, where his parents placed great value on education and good deeds. He was blessed when a mysterious stranger rescued him at Tirupati after six-year-old Prathap had tumbled into a cascading waterfall. He was blessed with sterling friends at medical school. He was blessed with medical associates such as Arcot Gajaraj, M.K. Mani, M.R. Girinath and Major General C.S.V. Subramanyam, and a professional accountant named V.J. Chacko, who helped him develop and reinforce Apollo Hospitals from the beginning. He was blessed with finding an extraordinary woman to be his spouse: Sucharitha Reddy of Khammam village in Andhra Pradesh. He was blessed with four daughters – Preetha, Suneeta, Shobana and Sangita – who turned out to be able leaders at Apollo. He was blessed with sons-in-law who had careers independent of Apollo but who loved him as they would their own fathers. He was blessed with ten grandchildren who now constitute the next generation of Apollo's stewardship. He was blessed with a loyal staff. He was blessed with legions of friends in politics, business and practically every sector of society – not only in India but also across the world. He was blessed with an ability to size up situations, and to apply foresight in coming up with solutions to social and health care problems. He was blessed with curiosity. He was blessed with a remarkable ability of relating to people and making them feel that he truly cared about their problems. He was blessed with a sense of humour that helped him diffuse thorny encounters with difficult people. He was blessed with an ability not to badmouth others – even those who considered themselves bitter competitors. 'We cannot grow on the failure of others but on our own strengths,' Dr Reddy told me. He was blessed by a perception that he never compromised on his integrity. 'He was blessed by being born in India – because Dr Reddy was born in a country that truly needed his skills and enterprise at a critical moment of national development,' Dr Rajendra K. Pachauri, the environmentalist and chairman of the Intergovernmental Panel on Climate Change that was awarded the 2007 Nobel Peace Prize (along with former US vice president Al Gore) told me in New Delhi.

But in my view, Prathap Chandra Reddy was blessed most of all by an unflinching faith in his own ability to get things done despite overwhelming odds – and always smile in the face of adversity. He was blessed with a determination to pay any price, and to go to any length, to achieve his objectives for the public good. He was blessed with the ability to keep his doubts – if indeed there were any at all – to himself, and not to burden others with tales of his inner turmoil, which surely there must have been regardless of his regimen of prayer and chanting. He was blessed with an emollient personality, one that made every encounter matter because the recipient of his attention felt that Dr Reddy truly listened to him or her. He was blessed with a rigorous sense of ethics, one that could be understanding of people's character flaws but that also made it clear that certain kinds of behaviour – especially in the professional world – were simply unacceptable. He was blessed with the deep belief that medicine was a high calling, one that should never be abused or exploited.

Did all these blessings emanate from Lord Venkateshwara?

Possibly. But as we left Tirupati on that chilly February day I asked Prathap Chandra Reddy for his definition of God, and he said something that intrigued me: 'You just have to look through a microscope at the millions of cells that form the human body. Who else but a higher power could have created such a mechanism? You may not want to call that higher power "God" – but it is a higher power. The human body is valued at $7 trillion. But, in truth, how can you put a value on anything that a higher power has created?'

It wasn't quite a definition of 'God'. But to me, at least, what Prathap Chandra Reddy said certainly offered an insight into how he viewed the miracle of life. He is a man of faith; he is a physician who became a businessman in order to better pursue his vision for the betterment of life for the growing millions of a rapidly changing India. So when he looks into that microscope, he sees and senses things that most of us cannot even begin to imagine. Perhaps even more than Tirupati or any other house of worship, it is the microscope that is his conduit and connection to a higher force.

INTRODUCTION

Healer

PRATHAP CHANDRA REDDY LOOKS and acts like the experienced doctor that he is. He is a handsome man with exquisitely polite manners. When I first met him many years ago, I felt that, had he wanted to, he could have been in the movies. If you were planning to produce a film for which a tall, greying, debonair, kindly and reassuring person were needed to play the role of a physician, it's a safe bet that the casting director would send someone who looked like Dr Reddy. He is, in fact, someone who can be called – in today's parlance – a metro-male. That is to say, he can carry himself with authority and empathy in almost any culture, attired suitably – and perfectly – for that environment, and totally capable of immediately grasping the idiom and ethos of that society.

If you were to accompany the real-life Dr Reddy on his daily rounds at any of the fifty-odd Apollo Hospitals that he established in India starting 1983, you'd find that the concern he conveys to patients isn't out of any movie script. Those patients represent a microcosm of contemporary India. They range from peasants to presidents, and they hail from cities to hamlets. And more and more, they also come from well beyond the boundaries of the country.

Over the course of a year, as I followed Dr Reddy around India for this book, I was struck by how much compassion he could summon for patients. I never got the feeling that Dr Reddy – a cardiologist by training – was putting on some sort of show because there was a writer tagging along. I was convinced that with every patient he reached deep into a reservoir of genuine empathy, and of professional scrutiny. He made every patient feel that, during the encounter, the patient was the only person who mattered in Dr Reddy's universe. I thought that such focus was remarkable; I'd rarely witnessed such a connection before.

On one occasion, Dr Reddy discovered that a patient could not be accommodated on a hospital operating table at Apollo Chennai because of the man's weight – nearly 340 kilos – so he personally phoned the bed manufacturer and asked that a larger table be delivered forthright. And when Dr Reddy calls, everyone listens. After all, he employs nearly 70,000 people in more than fifty hospitals; Apollo is one of India's largest purchasers of medical equipment. It is also the most valuable health care services company in the country with market capitalization of over $2.7 billion.

I was struck by the extent to which Dr Reddy would personally inquire after a patient's well-being even after he or she had been discharged from Apollo. By underscoring that he personally cares for the thousands of patients who are treated at Apollo, Dr Reddy is setting an example to even the most experienced of physicians that it's not only the care that counts, but also the aftercare. It is an example that physicians well beyond India's precincts might do well to emulate. At a time when doctors in many societies – and certainly in the West – are often criticized for their commercialized and sometimes indifferent attitude towards patients, Dr Reddy is a man for whom medicine and compassion come well ahead of making money.[1] Dr Reddy is a stickler for punctuality and expects his doctors to keep their appointments with patients in a timely fashion. He asks, 'Why should the patient wait for you? Our patients always come first.'

Simply put, the man is sui generis. He is indeed a 'Healer'.

---

1 I don't mean to suggest that Dr Reddy doesn't value money. Of course he does. His net worth, according to Forbes, is nearly $700 million.

When I started work on this book, I had two key questions: What prompted this doctor – who had studied in the best of colleges in India, trained in the best of institutions in England and the United States and upon returning to his motherland, developed a flourishing medical practice – to challenge the strong prevalent belief that advanced health care could only be in the government domain? And what gave him the strength to face all the difficulties and obstacles that were inevitable in attempting to make such a revolutionary change?

When I put these questions to Dr Reddy, his eyes turned misty. He composed himself, and then said:

'I can never forget that image, though it happened over three decades back. The stunned look on the faces of a young woman and her two small children, whose very world had come tumbling down that moment. Her husband was my patient at HM Hospital in Chennai, which I had joined after my return from the United States. The patient was a thirty-eight-year-old man with constant chest pain, which was just not responding to medicines. I knew a credible surgical programme to treat this was available in the US. Actually I had even fixed up an appointment for his surgery at the Texas Heart Institute. But he could not raise the $50,000 that was required, and therefore he could not go. He came to the hospital one evening complaining of severe chest pain, and unfortunately passed away the next day.

'I wondered sadly, "How many more are going to lose their loved ones, just because they do not have the money to go abroad for getting treated? And more importantly, why should it at all be necessary to go out of India to get medical care?" And then some inner voice told me, "You have to do something about it, and you can do it." On that day, I resolved that I would create a health care infrastructure in India that would offer the best of what was available in the world and make it affordable to most. Apollo Hospitals is the result.'

That conversation with Dr Reddy took place one afternoon over a lunch consisting of dishes from his native Andhra Pradesh that his wife, Sucharitha, had prepared at his home in Chennai's tree-lined Bishop Garden neighbourhood. I then asked Dr Reddy how he kept

up his punishing schedule of tending to Apollo's patients and also
to the business of Apollo.

This is what Dr Reddy told me, speaking slowly in his sonorous
voice:

> At the end of the day, when you see smiling faces and you are
> satisfied that you have given your best to help people, that is what
> keeps you going. I truly enjoy what I do. There is no 'secret' to the
> way I work. It's simply passion. I never claim our success as my own.
> Our success is the sum total of the dedicated enterprise of each and
> every member of the Apollo family. That is why I make it a point
> to meet as many Apollo family members as possible every day of
> the week, and every week of the year. Even when I am travelling,
> I stay in touch with my colleagues. And I always am in contact
> with our patients – whether through daily rounds of the wards, or
> by telephone. I call it offering the human touch; our patients say
> it is reassurance provided by a chairman who also happens to be
> a physician himself.
>
> Whatever it is, I truly believe that medicine's curative value is
> enhanced when the physician and other institutional personnel
> give personal attention to patients. I believe that patients aren't
> simply numbers – medicine is a matter of people, and that means
> paying special attention to people's feelings, anxieties, trepidations,
> worries and hopes. It also must mean paying special attention to
> their aspirations for leading a healthy, productive life in a disease-
> free society.

It has not been a smooth ride for him. Apollo has had its share of
travails – left-wing ideologues who resisted the introduction of the
private sector in India's health care system; powerful politicians, some
of whom expected handsome gratuities in exchange for much-needed
permissions for the hospitals, and who were stunned when Dr Reddy
turned down such demands, albeit in such a manner that no umbrage
was taken; bureaucrats who put antiquated rules above common
sense; competitors who tried to raid Apollo's roster of world-class

physicians; disaffected doctors who whispered about inconsistent management practices; staff members who chafed at the discipline and dedication that Dr Reddy emphasized at all times; and patients who complained about some physician or the other.

It has also not been easy for Dr Reddy because, as Jagannath Ramaswamy – a well-known veteran of the Indian advertising world – told me in a conversation in Chennai, 'I would unhesitatingly label health care among the toughest products to handle. This is where creative invention helps. At Apollo Hospitals, however, hyperbole has always been a strict no-no. The advertising objective invariably was more to educate the public rather than gain business. This strategy has worked. Look at where Apollo is today.'

In researching this book, I was struck by the expanse of Dr Reddy's experiences and how he has brought Apollo to its position of preeminence. From the first hospital in 1983 in Madras,[2] to the second in Hyderabad in 1988, the Apollo Speciality Hospital in Madras in 1993 and the fourth institution in Delhi in 1996, Apollo marked the evolution of industry-shaping legislative and administrative changes as well as industry-defining moments in funding patterns and corporate structure. Educational institutions, health-access initiatives and other group companies formed the integrated health care enterprise that Apollo is today.

Consider the changes that flowed from Dr Reddy's initiatives. Among them: India's pathetic casualty departments gave way to clean efficient emergency departments that functioned round the clock; an organ donation bill was passed enabling cadaver transplants; health insurance was introduced in India; new technology introduction in health care was now becoming commonplace; investments in the private sector health care industry grew sharply thanks to key legislative changes – in essence significantly increasing the reach of advanced health care and making it affordable to all across the country.

---

2 Madras was officially renamed Chennai in 1996. All references to the city in this book earlier to that year use the original name.

The noted philosopher and the inspiration behind the Isha Foundation, Sadhguru Jaggi Vasudev, says: 'Dr Prathap Chandra Reddy has transformed the concept of health care in India. In many ways, we can demarcate health care in India as before Apollo and after. Sitting upon such laurels, the man himself is childlike, effervescent and joyful. His irrepressible enthusiasm at eighty is to be seen to be believed. He's a devout being and a visionary entrepreneur, a true blessing for the nation.'

In view of such encomiums, I wondered how Dr Reddy kept himself anchored to his fundamental role as a 'healer'. I asked him: How do you convey your competence to patients?

His response: 'By creating in them a continuing belief that there are people – Apollo people – who care 24/7, and that there's a system that works.'

That belief is earned: it is not fostered easily in men and women more accustomed to the unresponsiveness they encounter in many of India's institutions of public service, particularly hospitals. It is also reinforced when a medical facility provides thoughtful aftercare to patients because a founder like Dr Reddy insists.

He also happens to be a thoroughly decent man who isn't impressed by his own success – he is in fact one of the most decent and likeable figures I have known in public life since I entered international journalism in 1968. Whether it's a ward boy at a hospital, the chief minister of one of India's twenty-eight states, the head of one of the country's seven union territories, or a visiting dignitary from overseas, Dr Reddy engages the person with an egalitarian warmth and curiosity. He is a man of endless questions – which is why it's often difficult to interview him, because he's always asking questions of his interviewer. In fact, this reversal of roles can be unsettling at times for a writer.

It can also be unsettling when the subject of a biography is modest to a fault. Repeatedly during our interviews, Dr Reddy kept attributing Apollo's successes to his colleagues. 'I realize that one book cannot possibly include the names of all six thousand of our doctors, and seventy thousand other members of the Apollo family,' he said at one point. 'But by acknowledging the contributions of at least a few, I am personally expressing my gratitude to all those who have made Apollo's growth possible. I also think it's important to acknowledge the millions of patients who have placed their trust in our hands.

'When the first Apollo hospital opened in 1983, I told the assembled staff – there were 700 of us then – how impressed I was by the richness of ethnic and geographical and professional diversity,' Dr Reddy continued. 'I spoke to them about the trust that patients would place in us. And I told them how important it would be to perform beyond our patients' expectations. That's why I always ask of myself, and why I always urge my colleagues to ask of themselves, "Have we done enough?"'

Indeed, that was a question that I asked myself during the writing of this book: Have I done enough to include all the vital elements of this legendary man's life? What started off as a conventional biography became, in effect, a sweeping saga of a vast country's health care transformation triggered by the ideas and passion of one man.

Tempting as it was for me to write a hagiography of a man who is one of India's few living icons, prudence – and journalistic judgement – suggested that I refrain from adulation. There are enough people out there who sing hymns about Dr Reddy every day, and even more who compose glowing letters of appreciation and admiration. I do not question the authenticity of their affection for him. Nor do I doubt that Dr Reddy enjoys such affection. He has, after all, earned it. But he doesn't solicit praise; he elicits it.

So *Healer* isn't a hagiography. Call it, if you will, a biography as a travelogue. It is an author's year-long journey through the life of a man who changed the health care landscape of India, examining also the lives of some of those who have worked with him. This is not an institutional or corporate biography of Apollo Hospitals. Although Dr Reddy and his family gave me all the cooperation I needed, this is not an 'authorized biography' either. That would have been another book entirely. There are many ways to write a biography, and some other writer might have approached Dr Reddy's story differently. But I chose to tell his story in a style that I was most comfortable with, always keeping in mind not only the professional readership but also – perhaps even more importantly – the everyday audience whose lives have been impacted for the better on account of the transformation that Dr Reddy brought about in health care. I also wanted to ensure that my book adhered to the historical record, particularly when it came to transformative legislative changes that Dr Reddy initiated. I felt that it would be essential to include legitimate criticisms. A large institution such as Apollo also attracts accusations, and so I had to exercise caution and judgement in sifting through them.

I felt that readers would be curious to know more about this remarkable man. I felt that an anecdotal biography would turn up special insights. I also felt that since Dr Reddy had helped create 'stars' in the constantly evolving field of medicine, it would be useful to sketch mini-profiles of some of those doctors and medical personnel. Of course, Dr Reddy has helped develop the careers of thousands of such 'stars', and it would be impossible to narrate the stories of every one of them, people whom he and his four daughters call 'the unsung heroes of medicine and of Apollo'.

I chose to examine the experiences of some people who were close to Dr Reddy, especially as he went about establishing Apollo. What has struck me about Dr Reddy is how much he honours the contributions of such doctors and others – and how much he downplays his own role in Apollo's development.

'We are a team,' he told me, 'we are always a team. No one man could have created and sustained Apollo. From Day One, our total footprint was in the very best health care that could be offered to patients – and in preventive health care. It all happened because we simply didn't give up, no matter what the obstacles were. Nowadays, of course, there are many others in the private-sector health care industry. We are not Massachusetts General, or Sloan-Kettering, or Johns Hopkins or Mayo Clinic. But believe me, none of them is what Apollo is today in our total health footprint. Apollo will continue this journey of transforming the form and delivery of health care. We led the journey in India. And the journey continues. You can take my word for it.'

It is that remarkable journey on which Dr Prathap Chandra Reddy embarked some thirty years ago that convinced me to write this book. Dr Reddy was convinced at the outset of his journey that a fundamental transformation in health care was required. He speaks frequently of delivering health care from the bottom up; and yet to break through at the top, many changes were needed including the ability to establish corporate health care, an overhaul of tax and investment rules, a responsive government, eliminating or liberally relaxing import restrictions so that the very best medical equipment could be brought to India, and the ability to retain top talent and entice medical professionals to return home.

Dr Prathap Chandra Reddy began his special phase of life at the age of fifty, when many professionals are more concerned with preparing for their retirement than starting a new career, let alone an ambitious enterprise in a country where – at least when Dr Reddy started Apollo – any new business meant exercising enormous will, displaying tact, and tending to the delicate egos of mandarins and politicians. As Vineeta Rai, a distinguished member of the Indian Administrative Service (IAS), told me in a conversation, Dr Reddy truly introduced the concept of tertiary, or super-speciality, health care in India. Until he established Apollo, hospitals in India were mostly in two categories: those run by the government or municipalities, and those operated by private charities or trusts.

Dr Reddy persuaded scores of physicians of Indian origin who had settled abroad to return to their homeland to practice medicine. Indeed, Indira Gandhi, who unabashedly expressed admiration for Dr Reddy, once told a parliamentarian: 'Dr Reddy has reversed the brain drain and brought talent back to India.'[3]

---

3 The Indian government says that more than 3,000 graduates of Indian medical schools leave the country annually to seek employment abroad, mostly in Europe and the United States. Some 22 million people of Indian origin live and work abroad. Of these, more than 300,000 are physicians. On an average between 300 and 400 doctors of Indian origin who live abroad are in Apollo's data bank. Some 85 per cent are from the United Kingdom and Ireland, and the rest are from Australia, New Zealand, the

One has to just look at the list of the consultants at any of the Apollo hospitals to see that the statement is true. The number of specialists who have returned from prestigious and lucrative positions in Britain and the United States is a testament to the ethics, working atmosphere, opportunities and motivation that the institution built by Dr Reddy offers. Richard M. Cashin Jr, founder and managing partner of One Equity Partners, found that out one day. He told me of the time that Dr Reddy was visiting New York. 'He was falling asleep with jet lag one afternoon, so I suggested going for a walk. We headed over towards Central Park. After a while, we came across some young men of Indian origin. They recognized Dr Reddy, introduced themselves as specialist doctors, and asked for a job in India. They already had good jobs in America, but they all said that their mothers were driving them crazy, insisting that they return to India before their kids became too Americanized. Until Apollo, they didn't have an option in India with high-end labs and medical equipment to pursue their careers. For them, Apollo was their only way to have the career that they trained for and keep their mothers happy. US-trained Indian doctors are a huge asset that Dr Reddy has made available to India by building Apollo.'

Perhaps Dr Reddy wasn't surprised that those Indians in New York recognized him. But surely he was taken aback one day in 2011; he was walking by the Churchill Hotel near Portman Square in London when a man using a walker stopped him.

He was Nigerian and said, 'You must be that Dr Reddy from Apollo?'

Dr Reddy said, 'I am. How did you know?'

The man was in his mid-fifties and told him that he had had a stroke and fallen. His left arm and hand and both legs were impaired. He was brought by plane on a stretcher from Nigeria and stayed at Apollo Chennai for a month. And here he was walking on the London streets. He had received extensive physiotherapy and told

---

Middle East and from other European countries. A few are from the United States. About 120 physicians of Indian origin migrate to Apollo every year.

Dr Reddy it was the personal care that made all the difference and that he could not have got better medical care or attention anywhere else in the world.

Dr Reddy later told me: 'This is the way that all our patients should feel. They may go to better-known destinations but they will not receive better health care. So many people worldwide are without the best care. Some don't even have care. There is a huge gap, and it still remains. We have not even met today's challenges let alone those of the twenty-first century.'

Still, there's general agreement that Dr Reddy's vision has dramatically changed Indian health care.

'India today is a sought-after destination for high-end medical care by patients the world over,' says Dr Anupam Sibal, Apollo's Group Medical Director. He continues, 'Every Indian physician who went overseas aspired deep inside to be able to come back to his or her roots and serve his country, given the right opportunity. It was this aspiration of thousands of Indian physicians like me who went overseas that Dr Reddy has fulfilled by giving us the opportunity to be part of this health care revolution he has led. Instead of seeking the Indian health care revolution from a distance, we got an opportunity to be a part of it. He always thinks big and he always thinks differently. He is respected by the medical community for his foresight, his compassion for patients and his humility. He is always receptive to new ideas and has given wings to many an idea that saw great heights. Indian health care has to keep up the momentum of the revolution that Dr Reddy has ushered. It is possible only through an enhanced focus on health care education. As more health care infrastructure comes up, the limiting factor shall be health care personnel. We need to have more and more medical colleges, nursing schools and paramedical educational courses to be able to meet our growing need of health care manpower to heal the global citizen.'

When he was planning Apollo in 1981, Dr Reddy and his colleagues devised what reputed institutions the world over now call the 'Iron Triangle'. Its components: 'Quality, Affordability, Accessibility'. He lives by it; he also expects that his associates do so. That mantra is at the heart of Apollo's very being, but clearly Dr Reddy isn't satisfied with just a mantra. As he points out:

'We need to provide a much larger vision. No time is more right than the present to take a giant leap and bring India to the forefront of global health care services. What would I describe as a "disappointment" in this bittersweet journey? We are not going as fast as we could, and to add to our woes we have an increasing disease burden, like the lifestyle diseases, coupled with the ageing population. The government, hospitals and health care providers need to work together, push ourselves and together prosper. We need to be relentless about this; health is in our hands and so is health care.'[4]

What Dr Reddy expresses so succinctly contains the very essence of the future of global health care. Long-term sustainability is the key to that future. In conversations with him, I discovered that he not only possessed solutions to pressing health care problems; more, he stressed the significance of implementing those universally applicable solutions.

Dr Reddy elicits a tremendous amount of respect from his associates, and not just because he's Apollo's founder and chairman. Some weeks before his death in July 2013, Professor N. Rangabashyam, one of India's leading gastrointestinal surgeons, told me that Dr Reddy's peers admired him for – among other things – the opportunities that he has created for specialists to advance their practice through incorporating and advancing high technology in medicine.

Over tea one afternoon in New Delhi, Dr Vijay Madan – a physician who later became a senior member of the IAS, and is now Director General of the powerful Unique Identification Authority of India – said to me, 'They respect him not only because he's one of their own – a doctor – but also because he's a very, very good doctor. Even today, at the age of eighty, Dr Reddy keeps up with the literature in cardiology. I often wonder where he finds the time!'

People marvel at the Niagara of ideas that flows from Dr Reddy.

---

4   Interview with Parita Dholakia in 2010.

One afternoon in Chennai, I met with Konijeti Rosaiah, the Governor of Tamil Nadu, at Raj Bhavan, a sprawling compound where deer wander on rich green lawns shaded by a variety of trees. 'Ever since I've known Dr Reddy, he's always coming up with new plans for improving health care,' Governor Rosaiah – who once served as chief minister of Andhra Pradesh – told me. 'He simply doesn't stop. And those ideas are all practical. For him, health care is the art of the possible.'

I did not quite expect to write this book. It wasn't that Dr Prathap Chandra Reddy was a subject I hadn't tackled before. Indeed, I'd written a couple of newspaper articles more than a decade ago about the renowned cardiologist from Aragonda village in Chittoor district of Andhra Pradesh. Chittoor, of course, is famous for the Tirupati, Kanipakam and Sri Kalahasti temples, among others. It would be no hyperbole to say that Chittoor is now almost as famous for the network of the schools and hospitals and clinics that Dr Reddy has built.

When I first wrote many years ago about Dr Reddy, it was his fame that fascinated me. Men and women in the limelight, particularly those in politics and public life, have long intrigued me. What drives these people? Is it ego, is it the quest for power, is it a sense of destiny, is it a desire to serve the public, is it a determination to change the polity, or is it something else? Is there an 'X factor' at work, something spiritual that most observers cannot quite discern, let alone capture? Could it be that leading figures in the public sphere tap into a special 'force'? Such fascination had led me to write biographies of Indira Gandhi and her son and successor Rajiv Gandhi. They were both assassinated, martyrs to the cruel politics of ethnicity.

Politicians, of course, aren't the only people in the limelight. There are businessmen whose stories are larger than life – such as the late Dhirubhai Ambani, the founder of the Reliance Group, who started off in life as a petrol pump attendant in Aden and went on to build an industrial empire.[5] There are actors like Amitabh Bachchan,

---

5 Dhirubhai Ambani, who died from complications after a stroke on 6 July

Shah Rukh Khan and Rajinikanth, whose film careers have been impossibly enduring. There's Anita Anand of Delhi who's fought vigorously at international organizations for women's rights and for global sustainable economic development for decades. There are a handful of writers like historian Ramachandra Guha, storyteller Shobhaa Dé, political and economic analyst Gurcharan Das, the diplomat-turned-politician Shashi Tharoor, and management guru Ram Charan – a special favourite of Dr Reddy's – who churn out bestseller after bestseller over a long period of time. What sustains these people? Determination is a key characteristic of such strivers, to be sure. But what is it that makes them so durable?

These questions were apparently also on the mind of my long-time friend and journalistic mentor N. Ram, formerly editor-in-chief of India's distinguished newspaper *The Hindu*. He phoned me from his home in Chennai in early 2012 to ask if I'd be interested in writing a biography of Dr Reddy. Ram said that this was as good a time as any to tell the Reddy story: Dr Reddy would turn eighty on 5 February 2013, and Apollo Hospitals would mark its thirtieth anniversary on 18 September of the same year. In the thirty years since its founding, more than 35 million patients had been treated at Apollo's hospitals; the number of daily footfalls exceeded 140,000.[6]

In India, of course, Dr Reddy is scarcely an unknown entity – there have been hundreds of articles on him and Apollo in the media, most of them laudatory, a few of them questioning his emphasis on private enterprise. But there hadn't been an authoritative book on his life and times.

2002, and Dr Reddy were friends. Whenever the latter travelled to Mumbai, the two of them would meet in a private suite at the Oberoi Towers and spend hours chatting about the tough business conditions in India. 'You just have to be persistent,' Ambani would tell Dr Reddy.

6   According to Apollo's physicians, its hospitals daily conduct around 60,000 laboratory tests, handle 3,000 emergency cases, process 2,200 admissions, carry out 800 CT scans, do 400 MRIs, administer 700 dialyses, undertake 800 major surgeries – including forty cardiac operations – and perform four major organ transplants.

I told Ram that this surprised me. But he averred that a story of Dr Reddy and Apollo Hospitals, set against the backdrop of a rapidly changing India and its unmet health care and social needs, would be a worthwhile enterprise. The thirty years of Apollo's existence more or less coincided with the thirty years of India's liberation from socialist shibboleths that had held back its economic growth since independence from the British in 1947.

Moreover, Dr Reddy is widely regarded as a national treasure. He is revered across the country. The Government of India has honoured him with its second and third highest civilian honours: the Padma Bhushan in 1991 and the Padma Vibhushan in 2010.

Much of the material in *Healer* is drawn from more than two hundred first-hand interviews with the major players cited in the book, including Dr Reddy and his family. Most people were happily cooperative, sometimes to a fault. I often had to remind people that I was looking for anecdotes and insights about Dr Reddy, and not just fulsome praise.

Healer is a blend of anecdote, reportage, analysis and narrative. This is the story of one man who set out to revolutionize the unaddressed health care needs of the world's largest democracy. It is a tale of manoeuvring through difficult bureaucratic and complex medical systems. It is a tale not without accounts of failings within Apollo, and certainly of some questionable dealings in India's economic and health care systems. But I dare say that, perhaps more than most private-sector institutions in India, Apollo has managed to put in place an administrative structure that delivers affordable health care through increased efficiency.

I hope that this book will also give readers an insight into the nature and future of medical care in India. I hope, too, that readers – particularly abroad – will better understand the complexities of doing business in India as a result of reading this biography. The fact that Dr Reddy was successfully able to navigate his way through the labyrinthine Indian system offers testimony to his acuity, his ethics, his resilience and his persistence.

His is an inspirational story. It is a salutary tale of how

overwhelming difficulties can sometimes be overcome with what Dr Reddy calls his 'Three Ps' – Purity, Patience and Persistence. To these I would add 'faith'. I have observed Dr Reddy at prayer – he prays several times a day, as do his family members – and it's quite apparent how much strength he seems to draw from spiritual values. When His Holiness the Dalai Lama called Dr Reddy a 'Karmayogi', he was right on the mark. When the philosopher Sri Sri Ravi Shankar said that Dr Reddy changed people's attitudes toward health care throughout India, he was right on the mark. When Prime Minister Indira Gandhi said that Dr Reddy would transform Indian health care and strengthen its people, she was right on the mark. When Prime Minister Rajiv Gandhi said that Dr Reddy was an 'enabler', he was right on the mark.

How did Dr Prathap Chandra Reddy help transform India's health care landscape? The creation of Apollo was the first step, after he'd returned home to India in 1970 after nearly a decade in the United States. He lost a thirty-eight-year-old patient in Madras because the man could not mobilize the resources for a heart bypass operation in America. He was not able to save his own father, Raghava Reddy, who suffered from a brain haemorrhage, or his mother, who succumbed to cervical cancer. He could not save his dear friend Kumara Raja Muthiah, who died of a sudden heart attack. Lodged in Dr Reddy's mind is the thought that had Apollo been in existence then, the lives of all of them could conceivably have been saved. It is a powerful, atavistic thought, and it continues to drive him to continually search for better technologies and more sophisticated systems to improve health care in India.

That thought has engendered in Dr Reddy a relentless focus on how health care is delivered in a country of more than a billion people, most of them poor. He transformed health care by generating widespread awareness of a simple, sensible method – that prevention is better than cure. He did it by building a system in urban and rural areas; more hospitals and clinics are in the pipeline. He did it by building training colleges for nurses, and schools for children in rural areas in the belief that education about health care should be part of the curriculum from an early stage – and that perhaps more students would want to go on to choose medicine as a career in a developing country such as India.

In the course of Dr Reddy's thirty-year journey, he has truly transformed India's health care landscape. Transformation, by definition, presupposes an unprecedented change of paradigms in one or all of the following attributes – scale, character, genre or value. When Apollo started in 1983, it was Dr Reddy's belief, his charisma and his power to carry the team with him that gave life to what was essentially a vision.

He actualized that vision with a deep abiding spiritual faith, and he did it with a self-confidence that motivated hundreds to join him in a venture that had seemed impossible – the creation of a nationwide hospital system in the corporate sector. 'I took others with me,' Dr Reddy said to me. 'I emphasized that the true Apollo spirit is: If anything that can be done in the field of medicine anywhere in the world, we can do it better.'

Dr Reddy recognized that India seemed well on its way to becoming the world's fourth largest economy, after the United States, China and the European Union. Business constituencies in America and elsewhere perceived exponential growth opportunities in a place that Winston Churchill had once dismissed as a land of fakirs.

It can be certainly said that the vision of Dr Prathap Chandra Reddy of Aragonda has been durable. Thirty years ago, when he started Apollo Hospitals, he named it Apollo after the Greek god of medicine, music, light, law and prophesy.[7] Today, it has grown into one of the world's largest among such networks. And it is growing, both in size and in market value.

One afternoon in Chennai, over a cup of steaming coffee with the celebrated astrologer D. Nagarajan in his modest two-room apartment, I heard an intriguing story of how Apollo Hospitals came to be adopted as a name by Dr Reddy.

---

7 Suneeta, the second of Dr Reddy's four daughters, came up with the name Apollo. She had initially wanted a Sanskrit or Telugu name, but it would have been too unwieldy or unpronounceable for most people.

'He came to me quite excited about the name that he'd just registered – Apollo Hospital Enterprises,' Nagarajan said. 'I immediately sensed that the name wouldn't work, and I told him that.'

Dr Reddy's face fell. 'What can I do now?' he said. 'I've already registered that name.'

Nagarajan did some quick numerological calculations.

'Rename it "Apollo Hospitals",' he told Dr Reddy. 'Add an "s" to Hospital. You will see how your business will grow into many hospitals.'

And so Apollo Hospital became Apollo Hospitals. That was three years before the first Apollo facility was inaugurated in Madras in 1983. Dr Reddy's wife, Sucharitha, told me separately that well before her husband established Apollo, Nagarajan had read her hand and predicted that Dr Reddy would launch an enterprise that would benefit millions.

I hope that this book will reach a large cross-section of people just as Apollo Hospitals has. While it is factual and therefore should appeal to those connected to the health care sector, the story of transforming Indian health care should actually appeal to everyone who's interested in the drama of post-Independence India's development.

'While issues such as poverty elimination have long been bandied about by the nation's leaders, health care hasn't been a significant part of the political conversation. Health affects a society's productivity. Health care must be a priority for India,' the industrialist and shipping magnate Shashi Ruia told me.

In writing this book, my challenges were: How do I share the business story so it will appeal to entrepreneurs, especially young men and women? How do I stay consistent to the theme of healing and caring so that everybody is moved? And how do I include developments in technologies so that patients will find hope, and people at large are inspired by Apollo's story? How best to explain policy-making in India?

And the final challenge was: How do I depict the fact that Dr Reddy, Apollo Hospitals and the health care sector in India are intrinsically intertwined?

There have been many who have followed since Dr Reddy opened
the first Apollo Hospital in Madras in September 1983, some of
them quite successful. [8] Dr Reddy has often said that he welcomes
competition because India's health needs are so formidable that even
more providers are needed. Preetha Reddy, his eldest daughter and
Managing Director of Apollo Hospitals, told me, 'Chairman Reddy has
always encouraged individuals to invest in health care and often says
that India needs many more Apollos.' She made a strong reference to
the thousands of professionals that Apollo has on board – all of whom,
in her words, are 'pivotal in making Apollo scalable and sustainable'.

Some competitors have even let it be known informally that they
would hope to some day buy out Apollo, even though the equity
structure in the organization is such that Apollo is likely to stay in the
Reddy family for the foreseeable future. Dr Reddy's four daughters
– Preetha, Suneeta, Shobana and Sangita – are all key executives at
Apollo, and have been lauded for their talents. His ten grandchildren
are increasingly assuming leadership roles. There will be continuity at
Apollo in offering access to high quality clinical care – and affordable
care. 'Where else in the world can you get such top-class medical
treatment at such low cost?' Rakesh Jhunjhunwala, the billionaire
Mumbai-based investor and financier, told me.

Say this for Dr Reddy: as with other remarkable entrepreneurs
like Dhirubhai Ambani, he had foresight, of course, and he had a
compelling vision. But, far more than most of his contemporaries,
he took a great risk in an industry at a time when everybody advised
him otherwise. When he embarked on establishing Apollo, almost no
one – with the exception of his wife Sucharitha, and the astrologer
Nagarajan – thought that Dr Reddy would succeed.

Dr Reddy said to me, 'People would tell me, "You are foolhardy.
Why are you giving up a successful cardiology practice to start
something that's never been done before in India, a corporate-sector
hospital system?"'

8 I was amused to see some of Apollo's competitors present at Dr Reddy's
   eightieth birthday celebrations in Chennai. He had graciously invited them.

Well, as the record shows, Dr Reddy carried on nonetheless. And the people who invested in Apollo at the very outset became very wealthy indeed. Those who could have invested but didn't surely rue their reservations.

His is a tale of how one man, against all odds, overcame financial, bureaucratic and systemic difficulties. It is a tale that young, would-be entrepreneurs of today might do well to study. It is a story, plainly put, of grit and nerve and willpower.

This is what India's leading industrialist Mukesh Ambani told me: 'I have a hunch that, true to the name, Dr Reddy wanted to accomplish an Apollo-like dream in the field of medicine in India. How else can one explain the fact that an enterprise that began with a single 150-bed hospital in Chennai in 1983 has now grown into one of the largest health care providers in Asia with over 8,500 beds at more than fifty hospitals in India and abroad? Paraphrasing the famous words of Neil Armstrong, the first astronaut to land on the moon "That's one *small step* for man, one giant leap for mankind" I would say that the one small but steadfast step that Dr Reddy took thirty years ago has now become a giant leap for the private sector-led world-class health care in India.

'I heartily commend Dr Reddy for two more achievements. Since good health is a prerequisite for human development, I have always believed that apart from education, health care is the biggest driver of India's journey towards becoming a developed nation. Given the diversities in our society, India needs to pursue multiple models of health care. However, the common denominator in all these multiple paradigms has to be the commitment to both quality and compassion in service of patients. In its own category of health care business, the Apollo chain of hospitals has earned its reputation by showing this commitment in abundant measure.

'Dr Reddy's other exemplary achievement is women's empowerment in Indian business. His four daughters – Preetha, Suneeta, Shobana and Sangita – who have helped him so ably in building and running his enterprise, have shown that professionally well-qualified and capable women can be equal to their male counterparts in any enterprise, especially in the enterprise of health care.'

Finally, Dr Reddy's story is the tale of a heroic struggle that continues. The story of the 'Healer' is by no means complete. It is a story that encompasses contemporary history. As India rockets into the second decade of the twenty-first century, it could be said that what Dr Prathap Chandra Reddy set into motion thirty years ago is gathering even more velocity, especially in the private sector. And that is good news.

The not-so-good news – and it has nothing to do with Dr Reddy – is that in order to keep up with the growing demand for better health care, India will need to add at least 100,000 new hospital beds annually for the next ten years. Right now, India has around 400,000 doctors, 800,000 nurses and some 2.5 million other personnel in the medical industry. The country needs at least to double the number of doctors, have three times the number of nurses and four times the number of paramedics to take care of the present population alone.[9] If the health care industry – especially in the private sector – is strengthened, it has the potential to be among India's biggest employers. Part of Apollo's strategy has been to expand its structural capacity – what's known as 'greenfield projects' – to better meet the country's growing health care needs.

---

9 According to estimates by the Task Force on Medical Education for the National Rural Health Mission, as of 2009–10, India had approximately 300 medical colleges admitting 34,595 students annually. India needs to open 600 medical colleges (at an average of 100 seats per college) to meet the global average of doctors. Moreover, India produces 30,558 medical graduates every year while there are only 12,346 postgraduate seats available in various courses of all medical colleges, according to the Central Bureau of Health Intelligence. According to the *Economic Times*, there are only 620,000 physicians in the country, against a requirement for 1,300,000 – a staggering shortage of just over 50 per cent, according to the 2010 World Health Statistics report. India has less than one doctor for a thousand people (0.6) as compared to China (1.4 doctors per thousand). In absolute numbers, the US – whose population is a fourth of India's – has more doctors than India.

Every successive Indian government has promised the much-needed sizeable increase in spends on health care. But unfortunately when it comes to actual allocations, health care seems to lose its priority. Now that Dr Reddy's efforts have dramatically opened up private-sector participation, the nation as such is bound to benefit substantially if a responsive government steps up its efforts in addressing the primary health care needs and simultaneously provides encouragement to the private sector to focus on tertiary care. Measures such as according infrastructure status to health care can have a far-reaching favourable influence on the country's health system. So will streamlining the bureaucratic processes involved in managing and regulating health care.

'The government has to give us infrastructure – not for a day, not for six months, there has to be long-term infrastructure, policies that are sustainable so that we can then also plan accordingly,' Yusuf Hamied, founder of the pharmaceutical giant Cipla, told Firstpost.com. 'In health care there are five ministries involved – chemicals and fertilizers, finance ministry, law ministry, health ministry, commerce ministry – there is no nodal body. Who do you go to for infrastructure or for advice or anything?'

Keshav Desiraju, a member of the IAS and secretary of the Department of Health and Family Welfare, told me in New Delhi that India's twelfth Five-Year Plan has committed Rs 287,000 crore to health care; states provide Rs 350,000 crore, or 60 per cent of the overall expenditure on health care. 'The government recognizes that substantial spending is needed to make a dent in the country's disease burden,' Desiraju, a grandson of the late President Sarvepalli Radhakrishnan, said. 'Clearly, we don't have public resources to meet that disease burden. But there's also the question of the capacity to spend what's already allocated to health care.'

Does that faze Dr Reddy?

'It can be done if we have the collective will, the resources, and the guts,' he says simply.

Guts?

My all-time favourite writer, Ernest Hemingway, was asked by

Dorothy Parker when she was interviewing him for a profile for the *New Yorker*, 'Exactly what do you mean by "guts"?'

Hemingway replied, 'Grace under pressure.'

Prathap Chandra Reddy could well have uttered that memorable phrase. But, of course, he doesn't need to characterize himself as a man of guts. Why would he? How many people have been able to accomplish what he has, especially in an economic environment that was so dogmatically resistant for so many years to private-sector involvement in health care? And how many people could be so utterly modest about their achievements?

It is that modesty, that decency in Dr Reddy that I find so endearing – which has made writing this book even more difficult because it has meant pursuing a central question: What made the 'Healer' the man he is?

CHAPTER ONE

15 February 1969 – The Letter

THE VILLAGE PATRIARCH WROTE to his son in America five or six times a year, and he always made it a point to send good wishes to Prathap on his birthday. The letter always arrived from India on or around the son's birthday, 5 February. But this year, Dr Prathap Chandra Reddy, a cardiologist at Missouri State Chest Hospital in Springfield, had not heard from his father, Raghava Reddy, who lived in the small village of Aragonda in Chittoor district of India's southern state of Andhra Pradesh. He was slightly disappointed, to be sure, but he wasn't alarmed. Postal services between India and the United States, even by air mail, weren't exactly reliable.

In those days there was no e-mail. International telephone calls were spotty, and had to be placed through indifferent operators. There was no certainty that even the so-called 'lightning calls' – the ones supposedly with priority, and hence involving higher charges – would get through, let alone not be disrupted. So written correspondence was the best way for the son to stay in touch with his father. It had been that way since Dr Reddy had left India on 2 March 1963 to accumulate experience, first in Britain and then in the United States.

He had never been abroad before. The scene at Madras airport was chaotic. There was no air conditioning. There seemed to be more mosquitoes than people in the dilapidated building. Relatives of passengers jostled with one another to bid farewell, and officials utterly failed to keep any semblance of order. The aromas of idlis and vadas and sambar – South Indian delicacies – suffused the terminal, as well wishers reached into tiffins to extract savouries to feed their departing loved ones.

In that crowd, Prathap Chandra Reddy stood out on account of his height, his striking looks, and his elegant light brown bush shirt and dark brown sharkskin trousers. He was, in fact, always fastidious about his attire, ordering custom-made shirts, jackets and trousers from India Silk House, a leading clothier in Madras.

But as he prepared to board the Air India Boeing 707 to London – the flight would first make a brief stop in Bombay – Dr Reddy felt anything but comfortable. The flight would certainly be a novel experience, and one that naturally spawned some anxiety. He had already begun missing his parents, Raghava and Shakuntala Reddy. He missed his seven siblings and many cousins with whom he'd grown up in Chittoor. He missed the Ardhagiri Temple of Lord Hanuman, in Aragonda, which he often visited with his family. He missed the many friends he'd made at Stanley Medical College (SMC) and in the six years since his graduation. He would be travelling alone: his wife Sucharitha would join him in London towards the end of May after Dr Reddy had ensured that they would have adequate housing abroad. Two of their four daughters, Suneeta and Shobana, would follow in December; and the two other daughters, Preetha – the oldest – and Sangita – the youngest – would come from Madras the following year. Preetha was already well into her schooling in Madras, and Sangita was deemed too young to travel with her parents.

On this morning, they had all come to Madras airport to see him off. Raghava and Shakuntala Reddy were there. So were Prathap's elder brothers, Subramanya and Krishnamurthy. There were family retainers from Aragonda.

The previous day, they had all visited Kapaleeshwar Temple in the Mylapore section of Madras. The temple was believed to have been built in the eighth century by the Pallavas. It was dedicated to Lord Shiva, known by one of his many names, Kapaleeshwar.

The statue of his wife, Parvati, was also situated in the temple and known as Karpagambal. Dr Reddy recalls that, although he'd been to the Kapaleeshwar Temple many times, he nevertheless marvelled how it demonstrated a typical Dravidian architectural style, where the *gopuram* stands out on the street on which the temple lies. It has two entrances. Apart from Shiva, the temple houses other shrines that are dedicated to lords such as Ganesha, Murugan and Shani Bhagvan. It also contains images of *vahana*s like the elephant, the bull, the bandicoot, the goat – and a golden chariot. The gods and goddesses sitting on the vahanas are brought around the temple with the devotees playing music. The deities are offered four pujas daily.

Prathap's mother, Shakuntala, had brought him a gift that she thought would be useful for his journey abroad. It was a blue-and-green trunk with a safety lock. But the son thought that the trunk would be a bit too bulky to carry, so he took it to the shop where Shakuntala Reddy had bought it and exchanged it for a brown leather suitcase. By the time he and his parents had packed it with Prathap's clothes and other belongings, the suitcase could hardly be closed.

As he spent time with his family on the day before his departure for London, Dr Reddy thought about his childhood in Aragonda.

'Don't you think that I was a boisterous child?' he suddenly asked his mother.

'Not boisterous, but mischievous,' Shakuntala Reddy said with a smile, offering no special elaboration.

Prathap recalled that he and his brothers and cousins would rise early and go diving at a nearby well. They called it 'well diving' – and it was, actually, a dangerous thing to do. The well's walls were about thirty feet high, and the boys had a good time and would dive in over and over. Had their parents known about this practice, they would surely have put an end to it.

The fact that Prathap Chandra Reddy would be leaving for London the next morning wasn't exactly reassuring for his parents, although, of course, they wished him well. In those days, graduates of Indian medical schools – at least those who could afford it – often pursued postgraduate studies abroad after putting in mandatory residencies at domestic hospitals. Britain was the favoured destination, of course, on account of the long ties of Empire between that country and India. Prathap Chandra Reddy had received his MBBS on 14 April 1957 from Stanley Medical College in Madras.[1]

As he prepared to board his flight, Dr Reddy thought about how his father – a village headman – had somehow never quite comprehended the fact that his son had become a full-fledged physician. In fact, no one from the Reddy family had attended his graduation. Prathap had hit upon an idea: espying booths that had been set up by enterprising photographers, he headed for one featuring the famous firm of G.K. Vale. He had his picture taken, resplendent in a black cap and gown, and brandishing his newly minted medical diploma. He ordered several copies. When he returned to Aragonda village and gave his mother a copy of the photograph, she was so overjoyed that she gave him a fistful of rupees.

The episode engendered yet another idea in Prathap: each time he would give his graduation photograph to a relative, he did so with a slightly expectant expression. The recipient would inevitably fork over some cash as a way of expressing his felicitations. Dr Reddy used that modest fortune to entertain his friends at a Chinese restaurant in Madras, and at the beach. He also went on a two-week tour of Andhra Pradesh and Tamil Nadu, visiting temples and meeting friends. He went to Cochin to attend the wedding of a classmate from medical school, Dr Padmanabhan. Prathap was on his own, and went about having as much fun as he possibly could.

As Prathap Chandra Reddy was about to board his flight, one particular episode involving his father came to his mind. He was visiting Aragonda one afternoon. A local police superintendent also happened to be paying his respects to Prathap's father that day. Raghava Reddy casually waved towards his son, and said to the

---

1 MBBS stands for Bachelor of Medicine and Bachelor of Surgery. Technically, these are two separate degrees, but are usually treated as one. An MBBS in India is the equivalent of the MD degree in the United States.

police official, 'There's my son. He's not in agriculture or business or anything like that. He's studying medicine.'

Prathap was amused. He had received his medical degree nearly four months earlier. He quietly reminded his father of that fact.

'Manchiti, manchiti,' Raghava Reddy said in Telugu. 'Very good, very good.'

That sort of terseness did not suggest indifference on the father's part. But he was a man of few words. His letters to his son were always brief. Dr Reddy was always conscious of the fact that his father hadn't particularly wanted his son to go into medicine. Raghava Reddy, a wealthy man, hoped that Prathap Chandra Reddy would enter business or engineering – not the least because Prathap's elder brothers, Subramanya and Krishnamurthy, had declined to do so for reasons that weren't entirely clear to anyone, perhaps not even to themselves. In fact, Krishnamurthy fancied himself as a man of the proletariat: he once organized a strike of students, for which he was promptly tossed out of Voorhees College in Vellore, and he never told anyone about it until many years later; he was never to graduate. Prathap was also convinced that his older siblings were more intelligent than him and he knew that Raghava Reddy would have really wanted them to travel to Germany to acquire engineering degrees. He particularly regretted that Krishnamurthy never quite created a career for himself.[2]

Dr Reddy would later recall: 'Our parents always wanted us to excel, and so they spared no effort in giving us the best possible education. They never said so, but I suppose our father and mother must have been disappointed.'

On 15 February 1969, when Dr Reddy opened the customary blue aerogramme from his father, he was startled. The letter was handwritten by his father in Telugu, their native language. Usually,

---

2 Dr Reddy told me that Krishnamurthy had such a prodigious memory that, whenever he was asked by his elders to recite stanzas from the Bhagavad Gita, a vital part of the epic Mahabharata, he could easily declaim all 700 verses without faltering.

Raghava Reddy's epistles were dictated to one of his *karanam*s or aides, who carefully took down what he had to say to his son.

Also, there was not a word about the son's birthday in this letter. This is a rough translation of what Raghava Reddy wrote:

> I am so happy, as is your mother, that you and the family are doing well in America. We feel great joy each time we hear from you about the work that you are doing. But keep in mind your duty to your *desam* and *samajam*.[3] Just think if you come back, how many more people can benefit from your training abroad? How many more people can regain good health?

Dr Reddy paused after he read his father's words. Then he turned to his wife Sucharitha and said, 'Well?'

'We should go home,' Sucharitha Reddy said without hesitation.

Their daughters were too young to protest.

Dr Reddy looked at his wife again. They had, after all, spent nearly a decade away from India, and these had been good years. They had lived in London, and then in Worcester, Massachusetts and Boston, before settling in Springfield, Missouri. They had made many friends all over the United States. They had become affluent. Their daughters liked living abroad. Sucharitha Reddy was popular in their neighbourhood, especially with children, because they savoured her cooking, especially the homemade gulab jamuns and other Indian sweetmeats. The Reddys were welcome everywhere, and were a fixture on the social scene. Did they really want to give up all that? Raghava Reddy had never directly asked his son to come home. But to Prathap Chandra Reddy, the message was clear: his father wanted him back in India.

Sucharitha Reddy also sensed that subtext in Raghava Reddy's letter. She didn't say it at the time, but she understood that Prathap Chandra Reddy had a filial obligation to return to India.

'We are going home,' she said to her husband.

---

3 Country and society, respectively.

And so it was that, on 12 January 1970, Prathap Chandra Reddy, Sucharitha Reddy and their four little daughters were back in Madras for good. Preetha had returned to India for her schooling in July. Dr and Mrs Reddy and the other three daughters and one nephew (Rahul) packed for their journey home to India. After they'd left Springfield on 19 December 1969, they drove around the United States for some sightseeing, and then flew to London where Dr Reddy bought train tickets for the family. They gave themselves a two-week holiday in Britain, France, Italy and West Germany.

The tickets and hotel stays had been arranged by a New York entrepreneur named Gopal Raju. Years earlier, Raju had approached Dr Reddy for a loan, and the latter had given him some money. He never asked Raju to return the loan. Raju parlayed that loan into a successful travel agency, and later founded a weekly newspaper, *India Abroad*, in 1970, the first of a number of publications that he launched. When Raju handed the Reddys the tickets, Prathap Chandra Reddy quietly assumed that, for Gopal Raju, it was giveback time.[4]

After enjoying themselves in Europe, the Reddys got back to India from Rome. In Rome, Dr Reddy had met a man named Dr Ravindranath, with whom he became lifelong friends. Dr Reddy had hoped to take his family to the Vatican for the Christmas celebrations, but no train tickets had been available from Paris. Instead the family visited Monaco on Christmas Eve. They got to Italy a few days after Christmas.

With the return to India, a new chapter in their lives had begun. None of them could have possibly imagined what an extraordinary adventure it would be. Prathap Chandra Reddy could not have possibly anticipated that within just thirteen years, Dr Reddy would be a household name in India because of Apollo Hospitals.

He could not have anticipated that his beloved father Raghava Reddy would not live to personally witness his son's monumental success.

---

4 Raju told me in New York well before his death how grateful he was for Dr Reddy's generosity.

'To this day, every time I speak at a function, every time that I am addressing a group of my colleagues at an Apollo Hospital in India, I always see my father seated in the first row,' Dr Reddy says. 'And every time I look at my father, there's a soft smile on his face. I know that he's there; I know that my father and mother are watching. And I hope they know that I've tried to be a good son.'

CHAPTER TWO

Can You Go Home Again?

WHEN DR PRATHAP CHANDRA Reddy told me about the circumstances leading to the return of the Reddy family to India in 1970, it occurred to me that he could well have been alluding to one of my favourite novels, *You Can't Go Home Again* by the great American writer Thomas Wolfe. The phrase 'you can't go home again' has entered American speech to mean that once you have left your native town for a sophisticated metropolis you can't return to the narrow confines of your previous way of life and, more generally, that attempts to relive youthful memories are always bound to fail.

So could the Reddys really go back home again?

One afternoon in Chennai, I asked this question of one of the family's closest friends, Dr Meena Muthiah. She's Tamil Nadu aristocracy, the Kumara Rani of Chettinad, one of the southernmost regions of the state.[1] Dr Muthiah is an educator and author, and widely regarded as one of India's foremost authorities on Tanjore paintings. She first met Prathap Chandra Reddy in 1952, when he was at the Stanley Medical College, and she was in her second year studying economics and history at Queen Mary College, also in

---

1 Dr Muthiah told me that there are barely 126,000 people of Chettinad descent left in the world, most of them in the West.

Madras. Her husband, Kumara Raja Muthiah, was also a close friend of Dr Reddy's. The husband and wife were introduced to Dr Reddy by his cousin Pavana, who now lives in Los Angeles.

Kumara Rani – everyone calls her that – received me at her sprawling seaside house, decorated with antiques from Chettinad, which was once part of the ancient Pandya kingdom some 2,000 years ago. Dozens of her own elaborate Tanjore paintings were mounted on the walls. Among the images and statues of gods prominently displayed in her living room were Lord Ganesha and Nataraja, the dancing Shiva who is her family's main deity.

'Would Prathap and Sucharitha return home to India from America?' Kumara Rani said, as if amused by my question. 'Of course they would. There was no doubt in my mind. I'm sure that Prathap had promised his father even before leaving India that he would come back home again after acquiring experience abroad. I don't think his father really expected that Prathap would live permanently anywhere but in India. To understand Prathap you have to understand the strong family ties that bind the Reddys of Andhra Pradesh and Tamil Nadu. There was no way that Prathap would have abandoned India.'

The India that Sucharitha and Dr Prathap Chandra Reddy would be returning to would be a bigger country demographically than the one that they had left in 1963. It was natural that there would be significant changes in governance and society. India's burgeoning population growth had given rise to chaotic cities: the country added some eighteen million people each year, the equivalent at the time of a new Australia annually.

Madras, one of the densest cities in the south with a population of 3 million, after all, wasn't Springfield, which had barely 150,000 people at the time. The Reddys had become accustomed to the tidiness and orderliness of American cities, and the generally strong civic sense of Americans. Would they find India stifling? Would their daughters be comfortable? Having been exposed to leading-edge practices in cardiology in the United States, what sort of facilities could Dr Reddy expect in his native country?

'It won't be the same in India as it was in Springfield – the facilities, the friends and parties,' Dr Reddy said to his wife one day after they'd made the decision to move back.

'Yes, I know, we have lived in India before,' Sucharitha Reddy replied tartly but with her usual pinch of humour. 'Besides, if you don't like it back in India, you will always have a job waiting for you in America,' she added.

When the Reddys had left India, the country's population was 439 million. In 1970, it had risen to 546 million. Jawaharlal Nehru, the Kashmiri patrician and freedom fighter, had been India's prime minister in 1963, a position he had occupied since India's independence from the British Raj on 15 August 1947. John Fitzgerald Kennedy of Massachusetts had been President of the United States, having narrowly defeated Richard Milhous Nixon of California in the elections of November 1960. Nehru died in New Delhi on 27 May 1964 at the age of seventy-four, the consequence of a stroke he'd suffered some months earlier; Kennedy had been assassinated in Dallas, Texas, on 22 November 1963; he was forty-six. Dr Reddy had met both Nehru and Kennedy, men he'd admired, men whom he called 'heroes'.

By the time the Reddys returned home, the health care situation in India hadn't significantly changed for the better since they had left in 1963. Although India, since Independence, had eliminated smallpox, had established 11,500 primary health care centres, trained 250,000 government paramedics and some 300,000 private sector midwives and nurses, the annual mortality rate was still around 15 per thousand. Moreover, India was grappling with the continued presence of malaria and tuberculosis and also had to deal with afflictions of the developed world such as diabetes, heart disease and cancer.

Friends of the Reddy family in the United States weren't entirely pleased that they would be leaving Springfield for India. Nevertheless, their friends in Springfield feted the Reddys. One special friend was a pathologist, Dr David Gorelick, who threw several soirees for the Reddys. Meanwhile, Dr Reddy continued his medical routine, arriving at the hospital around 8 o'clock in the morning and leaving for his modest three-bedroom home at 5 o'clock in the evening. He would watch the evening network news – it was usually Walter Cronkite on CBS, or Chet Huntley and David Brinkley on NBC – with his family, have dinner, and then go back to the hospital.

On some evenings, Dr Reddy would play chess or bridge with friends, a practice he continues to this day. Dr Reddy would also participate in special exhibition chess games, where the pieces were a foot high. Was he a champion? 'I did quite well,' he says with an impish smile. Three days a week, he would play a vigorous game of tennis. At least two or three times a week, Dr Reddy would receive calls requiring him to visit cardiac patients at the hospital well after midnight. But then, as now, his energy seemed boundless. He even continued his practice of occasionally going to races in New York City and New Hampshire. Dr Reddy, accompanied by Sucharitha, went to races at Aqueduct in New York and the Kentucky Derby in Louisville.

'Racing is not just about the horses. It's about the people around,' Dr Reddy would often say to friends who asked about his interest in horses. After his return to India, he became a noted racehorse owner, and was a familiar figure at all the important races at the Madras Race Club, founded in 1777, the oldest institution of its kind in India. Its longtime chairman, Dr M.A.M. Ramaswamy – who is also head of the huge Chettinad Group of companies – told me that he always found Dr Reddy's enthusiasm 'infectious', and his knowledge about the equine world 'extremely impressive'.

As news spread in their Springfield neighbourhood that the Reddys would be leaving for India, local children stepped up their visits to the Reddy home for snacks. In addition to Indian goodies, Sucharitha Reddy was known for her delicious pizzas, pies and chocolate cakes.

'Will we get these in India?' one of her daughters, Suneeta, asked.

Other friends elsewhere in America also bade fond, if sad, farewells: friends such as the great heart surgeon Denton A. Cooley of the Texas Heart Institute in Houston. Dr Cooley had become famous for the first clinical implantation of a completely artificial heart. Dr Cooley told Dr Reddy that he understood the latter's desire to be back in India, where the country's health care needs were mounting. Many years later, well after Apollo Hospitals had been established, Dr Cooley would visit India and marvel over what his friend had accomplished.

Dr Reddy knew that one of the toughest farewells would be with Dr Charles E. Brasher, medical director and superintendent of the Missouri State Chest Hospital in Springfield, where he had flourished. Not a man usually given to butterflies in the stomach, Dr Reddy nonetheless felt trepidation as he approached Dr Brasher. As propitiation, he brought with him a small ivory replica of the Taj Mahal.

Predictably, Dr Brasher seemed shocked that Dr Reddy would want to leave the hospital. 'The biggest present that you could give me would be to take it [the Taj Mahal replica] back and stay. And, I promise you, I will visit the real Taj with you one day,' he said.

'This is not a decision to stay or not to stay, or whether we like it here or don't like it here. It's a decision we made on account of our parents – our parents have wished it, and there's something in it if they have wished it. And we felt that it was the right thing to do,' Dr Reddy said.

As he spoke to Dr Brasher, Dr Reddy thought to himself, 'How do I explain my emotional bond with my father? How do I explain the Indian tradition of listening to one's parents? I am a man of science. How do I explain my special inner connection with my parents?'

Although the Reddys had decided in February 1969 that they would return to India, it took them several months to wrap things up in America. Dr Reddy flew to New York to meet with Indian shippers who specialized in sending household goods back to India. The only possessions they decided to leave behind in Springfield were the potted plants.

They also left behind a four-door Ford Deluxe car that Dr Reddy had bought for his father. Raghava Reddy had seen pictures of the left-hand-drive automobile, and had expressed a liking for it. The son promised that he would get the blue-and-gold car for his father. He even offered to have the manufacturer change it to a right-hand-drive, since traffic in India was the opposite side of the road. But Raghava Reddy insisted that he wanted a left-hand-drive vehicle. The New York shippers – who included two strapping Sikhs – promised that the car would be dispatched by ship and delivered in 'tip-top shape' to Madras within a few months.

When the Reddys landed in Madras, Kumara Raja and Kumara Rani were inside the airport terminal to receive them and to help them with customs. They seemed surprised that the Reddys weren't carrying much baggage with them.

'We've shipped everything,' Dr Reddy said to them.

Outside the customs enclosure, Dr Reddy saw his parents, Raghava and Shakuntala Reddy. He immediately went up to them and, in the traditional Indian style, bowed and touched their feet.

'I am here, Father,' Dr Reddy said, as Raghava Reddy beamed uncharacteristically.

He then hugged his mother. 'We need your blessings,' Dr Reddy said to Shakuntala Reddy.

'You already have those in plenty,' she said.

Dr Reddy's brother, Krishnamurthy, seemed a bit dour. 'Have you really given serious thought to moving back to India?' he said to Prathap.

Dr Reddy didn't think that the question warranted a response. After all, they had already returned to India, hadn't they?

A few days after their arrival, Dr Reddy called on one of his old medical college professors, Dr Rathinavel Subramaniam, to pay his respects. The professor wasn't encouraging.

'Go back to America,' he said. 'You won't even make a hundred rupees here.'

Dr Reddy was speechless for a moment, then recovered his wits sufficiently and said, 'I have not come back to make a hundred rupees. I just came for my parents.'

Meanwhile, Kumara Raja and Kumara Rani had arranged for the Reddys to stay at an apartment in Madras's Adyar neighbourhood. The place was fully furnished.

Twelve days after Dr Prathap Chandra Reddy, Sucharitha Reddy and their daughters moved to Madras, Kumara Raja suffered a massive heart attack. By the time Dr Reddy got to the Muthiahs' palace, Kumara Raja was dead. He was forty years old.

And in March, Raghava Reddy died of a cerebral haemorrhage in Aragonda village, on the very day that his son was at Madras customs getting the Ford Deluxe car cleared for his father. He was sixty-two years old.

It was not an auspicious homecoming for the Reddys.

CHAPTER THREE

The Funeral

AT 11 O'CLOCK ON the morning of 12 March 1970, exactly two months to the day from when Dr Prathap Chandra Reddy and his family returned home, he was at the customs enclosure at the Madras port. Dr Reddy was admiring the 1969 four-door Ford vehicle that he'd ordered specially for his father. As the New York shippers had promised, it had arrived undamaged.

Dr Reddy was in conversation with a local customs agent about how much duty he'd have to pay for the car. Suddenly, he heard a commotion. Another customs agent, a man named Raja Rao, rushed up to Dr Reddy.

'Come to my office,' Rao said, 'there's an urgent call for you.'

Dr Reddy assumed that it was some medical emergency and that the call had come from HM Hospital, which he'd joined soon after his arrival in Madras. There were no mobile phones or pagers in those days.

The call was indeed from HM Hospital, and it was from Dr Reddy's secretary, Pattamal.

'You have to go immediately to Aragonda,' she said. 'Your father is in a serious condition.'

'What happened?' Dr Reddy asked in Tamil, the secretary's native language.

'I don't know,' Pattamal said. 'But you must go at once.'

Dr Reddy got into the Chevrolet saloon that Kumara Raja and Kumara Rani had obtained for the family, and first drove to the apartment on Sir C.P. Ramaswamy Road that they'd moved into. He spoke to his wife Sucharitha, and they gathered their daughters and drove at breakneck speed to Aragonda.

There were no highways – the roads were narrow. The journey took nearly three hours. Dr Reddy kept saying to their driver, 'Go faster, go faster.'

As they were entering the village, a couple of residents recognized Dr Reddy.

'No, no, your father is not here. You must go to the district hospital,' a man said in Telugu, the language of the region.

Dr Reddy later recalled, 'No one said anything other than that he was very serious. When I walked into the room, I knew that he was not with us any longer. They had kept giving him oxygen – because at that time there were no respirators – but it was clear. I touched him and he was unresponsive, beginning to be cold to the touch. I checked his eyes, the lids had been closed and I pulled them back. His pupils were dilated.'

That morning, Raghava Reddy had risen before dawn as usual. After performing his ablutions and prayers, he had got into one of the olive-coloured Jeeps that he had purchased from the British Army after World War II. He loved to drive himself, and the driver rode shotgun. They went a distance of about eight kilometres towards a thirty-acre plantation of sugarcane and mangoes that the family owned in Aragonda.

Raghava Reddy stopped at the edge of the plantation. He and the driver got out. Two relatives, a man and his wife, to whom Raghava Reddy had gifted five acres of the land, greeted Reddy. The couple looked after the entire plantation for the Reddy family.

They had walked no more than fifty metres when he grabbed his head and said in Telugu, 'The pain is too much. My head is bursting.'

Even as he uttered those words, Raghava Reddy collapsed to the ground.

The woman held Raghava Reddy's head on her lap. Her husband spotted a public transport bus hurtling down the dusty road, and waved it to a stop.

Passengers emptied the bus so Reddy could be put aboard – but some people stayed on the bus because they wanted to be with the patriarch. The bus turned around and, without any further stops to pick up passengers along the way, went directly to the district hospital. The journey took about forty minutes. This was about 10 o'clock in the morning.

By the time Dr Reddy arrived from Madras, his mother Shakuntala was already at the hospital. 'Everyone was crying. My sisters Vanajakshi, Leela and Sushila were there. The fourth sister, Madhavi, lived a fair distance from Aragonda, so she wasn't there. Hundreds of villagers had started coming to the hospital. My father, after all, was the village patriarch, and he was greatly respected,' Dr Reddy would later recall.

Raghava Reddy had been a victim of a cerebral haemorrhage. He had seemed in excellent health even that morning. He would always rise early and go on horseback to wake up his farm labourers at their dormitories, and then return to his house for the morning puja and ablutions. He would take his first cup of strongly brewed coffee at 8 o'clock, a routine he'd observed since he was eighteen years old.

Father and son had spoken just a few days before, and Dr Reddy had taken great pleasure in informing Raghava Reddy that the Ford Deluxe he'd coveted would be with him shortly.

When he saw his father at the Chittoor District Hospital, Prathap Chandra Reddy was devastated.

'I really felt broken,' he recalled. 'Here I was, a doctor, and yet I could do nothing for my own father when he needed it most. I thought to myself, "What are you worth if you could not help? If you could not help your own father?" Had I asked him how he was doing? Did I suggest a preventative check-up? Did I say, "Daddy, let me check your blood pressure?" Even a month before his death, if I had insisted that his blood pressure be checked, perhaps I could have done something to save his life. I was a cardiologist, and I could not even save my own father.'

Prathap Chandra Reddy felt, perhaps for the first time in his life, totally helpless. 'I was inconsolable,' he said.

One person who was constantly at his side was Poornachandra Reddy, his cousin, who tried to comfort Dr Reddy.

He and his siblings took Raghava Reddy's body back to the family house. After washing the body and dressing their father in the traditional attire of a long white coat and dhoti, they preserved the body on ice; a white sheet of cotton covered the entire body except for the head.

Members of the family, friends and those who knew Raghava Reddy would pass by the platform, touch his feet, join hands in a namaskar, and pray. A fire of charcoal was made and kept burning in the room. Many visitors brought flowers and placed them on the body.

'I and my sisters and brothers took turns sitting with my mother, trying to comfort her. Hers was the biggest loss. She kept saying, "Why did you take him, God? Why not me?"' Dr Reddy recalled.

As he looked at his father's body, Dr Reddy vowed, 'I will live up to whatever you had in mind for me.'

He almost said those words out loud, as though his father were listening, but then he realized that Raghava Reddy was dead.

According to Hindu tradition, the funeral service would have been conducted the same day. But Madhavi, the fourth sister, was driving down from a considerable distance, and she wouldn't reach Aragonda until very late that evening. So the funeral service was scheduled for the next morning.

'Hundreds of people waited to see him and be with us. He was known for his fairness. People would come and present their cases to him, he listened and then decided – and there was no dispute. The whole village became a great place of sadness,' Dr Reddy recalled.

As he waited for the funeral service to start, Dr Reddy inevitably thought of the loss that the family had suffered. How does one ever replace a family's patriarch? In the image that memory summoned up, Raghava Reddy usually wore a yellow dhoti and a cream shirt. He frequently wiped the tears of others on his shirtsleeves.

'I came back home because my father had wanted me to come back,' Dr Reddy thought to himself. 'I wanted to please him. Now whom am I going to please?'

A funeral pyre made of different kinds of wood was constructed near a rivulet not far from the family house. Raghava Reddy's body was washed again, and a fresh set of clothes was put on him. The body was put onto a new, lightweight platform made of bamboo. The men of the family gathered around the stretcher, lifted it up on their shoulders and began to walk to the pyre. The eldest brother carried a mud pitcher of water on his shoulder. Subramanya began walking around the pyre carrying the pitcher. Hindu women generally do not attend funerals. But Shakuntala Reddy and her four daughters walked some distance towards the pyre before returning to the house.

The body was put on the pyre. Dry, raw rice was put in Raghava Reddy's mouth, along with some ghee, or clarified butter. Subramanya circled the pyre three times. Each time a hole was made in the pot and the water flowed on to the ground. After he completed this ritual, he lit a torch from the charcoal fire and set fire to the pyre. Everyone watched for several hours as the fire burned.

Everyone was crying. The entire family, villagers and many important people were there, along with district collectors and senior police officials. Elders from four or five other villages were also present. Everyone felt part of the Reddy family that morning. After the funeral pyre had completely burned out, Prathap Chandra Reddy and his relatives went back to their house.

Two streets in the village had been closed and local villagers had built shelters with bamboo tops for shading and poured fresh sand on the street. It was here that the thousands of visitors from around the Chittoor district sat, ate, slept and wept for Raghava Reddy.

The brothers and sisters went back the next day to the site of the funeral pyre and said their prayers. On the third day, they performed a puja and each family member took some of the ashes, made a mound and poured milk into the ashes. Then they went home again.

On the eleventh day after Raghava Reddy had been cremated, a venerable Brahmin priest whose back was bent with age performed the final rites. Despite his age, the priest exuded an aura of spirituality. Part of that aura emanated from the local belief that the priest had experienced some miraculous revelations. The service and prayers lasted nearly two hours. Afterwards, the villagers sang songs in honour of Raghava Reddy. They sang songs about Raghava Reddy's bravery, his astuteness, about how he was respected. They sang about his decisiveness, they sang about how he controlled the peace and welfare of the village, and they sang about how fair he was. They sang about how powerful a man he was, a man whose knowledge was extensive. They sang about his profound wisdom.

'It left an impression for years,' Dr Reddy recalled to me many years later. 'They would also sing in other villages. And if my older brother Subramanya heard about it, he would send a carriage for those villagers to bring them to Aragonda so that our family and local villagers could hear those songs.'

Even children came to the ceremony. Later, they all had food. Raghava Reddy had liked wild boar very much and so that was served along with two kinds of chicken and eggs and curry. It was the tradition after a death that no food be cooked in the house until the third day. Neighbours had brought food to the Reddy house during this time. It was, clearly, a gesture of affection from the people of Chittoor.

To this day, nearly five decades after Raghava Reddy's funeral, whenever Prathap Chandra Reddy sees anyone in Aragonda village from those days, someone who'd brought food to the Reddy house, he stops and talks to them.

The sadness that he and the Reddy family experienced that year would continue well into the future. But few who were present at Raghava Reddy's funeral on 12 March 1970 knew that Shakuntala Reddy herself did not have much longer to live.

She was being treated for cervical cancer at Christian Medical College (CMC) in Vellore. By the end of the year Shakuntala Reddy would be dead. There would be yet another funeral in the Reddy family.

When Prathap Chandra Reddy reflects about the events of 1970, he inevitably thinks of how he lost three people he was closest to within the space of a few short months: his friend Kumara Raja Muthiah Chettiar, his father Raghava Reddy, and his mother Shakuntala Reddy. He stills feels the desolation: they were there once, and then they were gone.

And he cannot help thinking to himself, 'If I had Apollo Hospitals then, I could have saved their lives.' But, of course, the creation of Apollo was more than a decade away at the time.

CHAPTER FOUR

The Hills of Aragonda

IN THE DAYS AND months following the funeral of Raghava Reddy in March 1970, there was inevitably a great deal of reflection in the village of Aragonda about the patriarch who was no more. More than four decades later, as I researched this biography, I discovered that there were aspects of Raghava Reddy's character and mien that seem clearly present in Dr Reddy – the personal discipline, punctuality, an insistence on doing things right, forthrightness, the spontaneous concern for the welfare of others, spiritual values, a desire to encourage education for all, and the readiness to help those in distress.

His widow, Shakuntala, kept up her practice of ensuring that everyone who came to the family home was properly fed. Despite her illness, she supervised the kitchen, even as she made frequent trips to Christian Medical College in Vellore for her treatment. In Aragonda, Shakuntala Reddy was sometimes referred to as Annapurna, the Hindu goddess of food. She would frequently tell her children that *annadaan*, or feeding people, wasn't an act of charity but an obligation. Prathap's wife, Sucharitha, was similarly involved in extending the family's hospitality to all visitors.[1] The four daughters

---

1 Sucharitha Reddy is an accomplished cook and the author of two culinary books. The author can personally attest to the excellence of her cooking.

also helped, as was to be expected.[2]

Raghava Reddy's death was mourned deeply, of course, but the people of Aragonda and members of the Reddy family celebrated his life through songs. They recounted individual experiences of his wisdom and acuity, or of the calm feeling they obtained by simply being in his proximity. As his physician-son himself would in years to come, Raghava Reddy had touched the lives of everyone he met, making them feel that they mattered as human beings in their own right. That is why, among other things – and not only because he was Aragonda's patriarch – villagers came to him for counsel, they approached him with details of personal and property disputes. So respected was he, and so formidable in his bearing, that no one actually stood in front of him as they addressed Raghava Reddy: people stood to his side and spoke in soft, hushed tones. And they almost always went away satisfied that he had given them a thorough hearing and that the solutions he had suggested were fair.

In every home, there was the feeling of loss, a sense that a great man had gone away prematurely from their midst, that he would be irreplaceable. The villagers of Aragonda remembered Raghava Reddy's tall, upright physique, how he rode his horses with natural grace, how he frequently stopped to ask people about how they were doing, how he drove his Jeeps to his farms, how he carefully inspected the mango, sugarcane, coconut plantations and paddy fields, how he patted the backs of agricultural labourers in appreciation for their work.

---

2 The hospitality of the Reddys continues to this day as Prathap and Sucharitha host receptions and parties for family members, villagers, and Apollo employees who are, in fact, regarded as 'family'. In late 2012, Dr Reddy donated a school for children in Aragonda set up in honour of his grandfather Muniswamy Reddy. More than 5,000 guests were fed from the family's kitchens. On another occasion in June 2012, the Reddys welcomed large crowds at a reception in Aragonda following the wedding of granddaughter Upasna Kamineni – daughter of Shobana and Anil Kamineni – to film star Ram Charan Teja. Over 60,000 fans came to see the couple. Needless to say, all guests were amply fed.

They also remembered his love of the Hindu epics, the Ramayana and the Mahabharata, and of the Vedas and Puranas. They recalled how he would encourage street shows in Aragonda village where amateurs, including local schoolchildren, enacted episodes from these epics and scriptures.

They remembered, too, how Raghava Reddy always stuck to his vigorous daily schedule. They remembered how after the day's work, he would ride to Chittoor in his horse cart to play cards at the local officers' club. Raghava Reddy spoke only Telugu and Tamil, but no English; his playing partners were judges, district collectors, engineers, the superintendent of police, and an occasional Englishman or two who'd be visiting from Madras or Hyderabad. These games would often go on past eight o'clock, and Raghava Reddy almost always won and later distributed all his winnings among his workers. After the card games, he would occasionally go to the home of his sister Parvatamma in nearby Kattamanchi for a meal, and then return to his own home to sleep for a few hours. He would rise just before 5 a.m., and start his daily routine in Aragonda.[3]

While Raghava Reddy remained anchored to his role as the family patriarch, his younger brother Narasimha Reddy attended to the family's finances. He kept accounts, and doled out monthly amounts for household expenditures. Prathap and his siblings especially cultivated Narasimha because it was he who gave them pocket money. Another brother of Raghava Reddy's, Raja Reddy, was the family disciplinarian. 'Every day, without fail, he would administer a good beating to us boys,' Prathap says. 'He needed no reason for this other than the fact that he automatically assumed we were being mischievous or disregarding our studies. And if he ever caught us doing something bad – like consuming too many sweets – then his beatings would be even more hard.'[4]

---

3 The author is indebted to Dr Bala Showri Reddy, an eminent writer in Hindi and Telugu, for providing some of these details.

4 Raja Reddy became a wealthy businessman through his trade in mangoes, jaggery and textiles. He was also the largest supplier of coal to Madras.

His uncles are especially remembered by Prathap Chandra Reddy when he recalls his childhood days spent in Aragonda, and how his forefathers were landlords; his uncle Raja Reddy had donated a school, and brought electricity to the village a decade before Raghava Reddy's demise.

Prathap Chandra Reddy is also conscious of his lineage. Raghava Reddy's father, Muniswamy Reddy, was Aragonda's revered patriarch; he and his wife Lakshmamma had four sons: Raghava, Narasimha, Anjaneyulu and Raja.[5] They also had four daughters: Tulasamma, Parvatamma, Krishnavenamma and Ratnamma. When Prathap was growing up, at least fifty siblings and cousins in Aragonda surrounded him. There were a dozen cooks in and around the house, catering to almost every whim. Cattle, sheep and chicken roamed in the vicinity.

The word 'Aragonda' means a half-mountain in Telugu. The Ramayana legend has it that when Hanuman was summoned to assist Lord Rama's brother Laxman, who had been wounded grievously in a battle against the Lankan king Ravana who had abducted Rama's wife Sita, he went to the Himalayas to fetch life-saving herbs. He found those herbs on Sanjeevani mountain, but as he flew over Aragonda, a part of the mountain fell to the ground to form what came to be called Aragonda. That may explain why a temple dedicated to Hanuman was built in Chittoor district.

When he was growing up in Aragonda, Prathap Chandra Reddy, his brothers and his cousins would visit the Hanuman temple on weekends. Adjacent to it was a freshwater lake that seemingly never dried up, not even during the scorching summers that characterize the area. The lake's waters were reputed to possess medicinal properties, and the boys enjoyed their swims. Afterwards, servants from the family home would show up with hampers filled with delicious curries and steaming idlis. A good time was had by all in those days in Aragonda.

---

5 Raghava and Shakuntala Reddy had three sons: Subramanya, Krishnamurthy and Prathap Chandra, and four daughters: Vanajakshi, Leelavati, Sushila and Madhavi.

The village of Aragonda sits in a valley, in an area known for coconut, mangoes, sugarcane and jaggery, rice, tamarind and peanuts. There are tall coconut trees, and mostly one-storey houses. The streets are now paved. And there are little eateries and barber shops. Everyone has a mobile phone nowadays, of course.

Chittoor district was far less developed in Raghava Reddy's days than it is now. His physician-son has helped establish schools – including an English-medium institution – a nursing college, and a hospital with full telemedicine connectivity to all Apollo hospitals. Then US President Bill Clinton, while on a visit to Hyderabad on 24 March 2000, inaugurated the world's first satellite-enabled telemedicine hospital in Aragonda.

There are highways in Chittoor now. Where once it took more than three hours to drive to Aragonda from Chennai, you can now make the trip comfortably in less than two hours. To drive from Chennai to Aragonda, you take a four-lane highway to Chittoor, and then drive another 20 kilometres to Aragonda through heavy green forests, through banana-leaf gardens, coconut and neem trees, populated with monkeys.[6] Chittoor city is not so rural and its houses are dotted with DTH dish antennas, and even thatched roofs on brick buildings. The average literacy rate for Chittoor district is above 72 per cent; males have a higher literacy percentage than women, especially in rural areas. Chittoor is also home to a deer forest. And in nearby Kanchipuram in Tamil Nadu, brides and their families from across India come to select from the exquisite silk saris that are woven there.[7]

The Reddy house, made of brick and limestone, is very large. The doors are made from Burma teak, considered valuable and prestigious. At the time of Diwali, the auspicious Hindu festival of lights each year, the house is whitewashed. As with several generations

---

6 Chittoor is an amalgamation of two words, Chit (small) + oor (town or 'dense forest') in Telugu.

7 Kanchipuram, or Kanchivaram, saris can sometimes cost as much as the equivalent of $1,000 apiece.

of Reddys, Prathap Chandra Reddy and his siblings could have chosen to stay on in Aragonda; they would most certainly have led comfortable lives there as agriculturists.[8]

'Father had divided up the possessions and the middle brother – Narasimha Reddy – received the house,' Dr Reddy says. 'It should have gone to the eldest brother's family by our tradition, but my father gave it instead to Narasimha Reddy because his daughters were still unmarried at the time. It was our ancestral home. I was the last child of my generation who was born there – but all had lived there.'

'Father and mother alone lived on the top floor,' he continues. 'The other fifty or so cousins also lived in the house. There were so many of us, many sleeping in the great hall and many others outside on the terrace. Of course, at that time there were no indoor toilets —a small shed was built in the back with open pits.'

Prathap Chandra Reddy was a mischievous boy. He would often mooch cigarettes from his father's room, and smoke them secretly. After giving up the habit later, Dr Reddy today calls cigarettes 'killer sticks', and frowns on anyone smoking in his vicinity.

For several hours, starting at four o'clock in the afternoon, the children in the Reddy family received special teaching on the open

---

8 Apollo Hospitals started a new health insurance scheme – Family Health Plan (FHP) – in Aragonda in 2000. Under this scheme, individuals have to pay one rupee per day as premium for 365 days; a family of five have to pay Rs 2.50 per day and a family of seven Rs 3.50 per day. The insured persons are eligible for Rs 30,000 for inpatient treatment. The total number of beneficiaries in Year One was 2,000. Most people could afford this but for the few who could not, one month later Dr Reddy paid the premium and ensured the entire village had a 'Passport to Health'. The claims ratio in one year was below 10 per cent but subsequently grew to over 12 per cent. This was still a lower number than many of the other rural insurance schemes. These numbers gave FHP a good idea of rural insurance financing and formed the basis of the Arogya Bhadratha scheme of the Andhra Pradesh Police and subsequently the Yesheswani Insurance scheme in Karnataka. This was indeed the first time that rural health insurance was instituted in India. The scheme was the forerunner of subsequent national and state community health insurance schemes.

terrace at the house by a tall, fair-skinned Brahmin tutor, Venkoba Rao. They were made to study maths and grammar. The tutor would only consume peanuts and lemon juice, and the only exception he made was for the coffee that Prathap's mother made especially for him. In three years, Venkoba made his students fully conversant with multiplication tables and with Wren & Martin, the classic text on high school English grammar.

Before the schooling the children would play, walk, cycle, swim, dive and secretly drive Raghava Reddy's old Jeeps. They would surreptitiously roll a vehicle down a hill so that the engine made no noise. Then one of the boys – usually Prathap – would work the ignition, and the children would be off on a joyride.

Among the 'culprits' was Poornachandra Reddy, one of the cousins who lived, played and studied with Prathap, first in Aragonda and later in Chittoor. He and Prathap were best friends although each had very different ambitions. Poorna retired in the 1980s and Prathap is still opening new hospitals and launching new products. When Prathap organized a party for Poorna's eightieth birthday in 2013, the old friends embraced and sat together clasping each other's hands. The laughter and stories did not stop, the camaraderie the same as always. After the party Poorna said, 'He is the same as when we were boys, warm and affectionate. No matter how famous or important or successful Prathap becomes, he is my friend as always, he's my brother.'

The children did not especially look forward to Venkoba Rao's tutorials: he was a strict teacher who often rapped them on their knuckles with a ruler if they made mistakes. To put it mildly, the children tested Venkoba's patience.

Dr Reddy sometimes looks at his knuckles all these many years later and smiles, as if recalling the fact that, of all the Reddy children, he was the one who received the most number of raps on the knuckles after his cousin Vimla.

In fact, sometimes in the evening if Prathap's mother was angry at him for something he'd done and the possibility of punishment awaited him, he would show her his knuckles and say, plaintively,

'But look at my hands, I have already been punished today.' The mother would then reward Prathap and the other children with extra pooris; Dr Reddy told me that he was a voracious consumer of these deep fried puffs, sometimes eating as many as eleven at one sitting.

But Venkoba's discipline proved useful when Prathap moved to Kattamanchi village near Chittoor to complete his high school studies. His aunt Parvatamma lived there, and Prathap boarded with her family. He received his secondary-school certificate from Chittoor High School, and tried to figure out what he was going to do with the rest of his life.

It was not a question for which answers came easily. Raghava Reddy wanted Prathap to join the family business immediately, but he also wanted his son to continue his education – especially since the other two sons hadn't advanced much in college.

'Going to Madras made sense for me,' Prathap Chandra Reddy recalls. 'After all, that was where fun was to be had.'

CHAPTER FIVE

The Road from Chittoor

PRATHAP CHANDRA REDDY HAD become a tall, strapping man, and he was raring to go out in the world and get further education. By now, Aragonda – and Chittoor district – seemed to have become much too confining for someone who was keenly aware that there was a bigger world out there. After all, Prathap had been exposed to that world – at least through word of mouth – by various visitors who had stayed at the three-room guest bungalow adjacent to Raghava Reddy's house. These visitors included important administrators such as collectors of the elite Indian Civil Service (ICS) who'd been assigned to the district and whose first port of call would inevitably be the home of the patriarch.[1] Various Englishmen would stop by, too.

From these visitors, Prathap heard all about what was going on in that larger world outside of Chittoor district – stories of India's

---

1   The Indian Civil Service was the precursor of today's Indian Administrative Service (IAS). About 850 candidates are finally selected each year out of the nearly 550,000 (2010 data) who apply for the IAS, but only a rank in the top eighty guarantees an IAS selection – an acceptance rate of 0.025 per cent, which makes it one of the most competitive selection processes in the world. When India became independent, there were 980 British – and some Indian – officers serving in the ICS. Today there are about 6,000 civil service officers in India.

independence struggle against the British, and stirring tales of leaders such as Jawaharlal Nehru and Mahatma Gandhi – but his focus was far more local, about the good times that could be had in Chittoor. In time, Prathap was to meet Nehru and Gandhi and other men and women who helped drive out the British after their 200-year rule of India, and he was to meet scores of other important leaders from all over the world. Years later, he would have the pleasure of welcoming many of them – such as President Bill Clinton.

When independence came, Prathap Chandra Reddy was in the tenth standard. He can still hear the firecrackers that were set off that day, and he can still recall that Raghava Reddy joked about the loud noise. I asked him if he was aware at the time of the great suffering that occurred during the partition of British India into Islamic Pakistan and secular India. 'No, that wasn't something that too many of us followed,' he said. Dr Reddy wasn't being indifferent: growing up in South India, where communal strife between Hindus and Muslims were uncommon, Partition for young Prathap would not have been the life-changing experience that it was for more than 12 million people in India's North and East. And because Raghava Reddy wasn't especially interested in politics, the Indian struggle for freedom from the British was rarely the subject of conversation in the Reddy home in Aragonda.

For the visitors who came to Aragonda in those days in the 1930s and 1940s – and even later – meeting Raghava Reddy was always deemed a special privilege, not the least because he belonged to the Justice Party.[2] The family's hospitality was legendary, and so people looked forward to scrumptious meals at the Reddy home. 'The Reddys were always wonderful hosts – they knew how to make their guests feel like royalty,' Dr Bala Showri Reddy told me. 'Little wonder that their contemporary involvement in the health care and hospitality sectors is a success.'

The quarters in the 'officers' bungalow' in Raghava Reddy's

---

2 The Justice Party, established in 1917, was officially known as the South Indian Liberal Federation in the Madras Presidency of British India. It was considered the main rival to the Indian National Congress.

compound were comfortable, and servants were constantly in attendance. And there was the implicit prestige attached to the belief that, somehow, by meeting Raghava Reddy the visitors had received his blessings. His goodwill and benevolence were always sought after. So were his knowledge of local history, and his familiarity with the special characteristics of local ethnic groups.

Among those groups, the Reddys of Andhra Pradesh were always considered extraordinary.[3] Visitors learnt that the Reddy community had a history of successful farming, and its members – such as Raghava Reddy – had a special affinity for leadership. The Reddys could trace their ancestry back to ancient times, when they were rulers and warriors. Visitors to the Reddy household – then and now – were not surprised to learn that where there was an infrastructure project, or something in irrigation, education and construction, the chances were that a Reddy was involved.[4] My friend Santosh Reddy – himself a successful entrepreneur based in Hyderabad – notes that Reddys tend to be natural leaders, and that Reddy women 'are strong women – whether they are in the family business or minding the home, Reddy women always play a part in decision making.' Dr Reddy told me several times during the course of my research for this biography that he considered his wife Sucharitha his closest friend, and that he did not take a single major decision without consulting her.

Prathap Chandra Reddy mulled over which college he should enter in Madras. Among young people in those days, the three main colleges in that city had been given cheeky designations: Presidency College, founded in 1840 – first as a school, and later upgraded to college status – by the British, was termed an institution of 'gentlemen' because of the insistence on etiquette and proper manners; Loyola College, founded in 1925 by Reverend Francis Bertram, SJ, a French Jesuit priest, had the reputation of being an especially tough institution, presumably because of the rigorous personal discipline and academic demands imposed on students in the Jesuit tradition; and the oldest institution,

---

3   The history of the Reddys is examined in a subsequent chapter of this book.
4   Source: The Reddy Society.

Madras Christian College, founded in 1837 by a Scottish missionary, Reverend John Anderson, was termed an institution of 'graduates' – presumably because its reputation was that every student who enrolled also wound up not failing. And Pachiappa College was known as an institution of rowdies.

In those years, high school ended in the tenth standard, so students were required to enrol for two years of college leading to an intermediate diploma – after which they could decide whether and where to pursue further studies. In view of his easygoing nature, and his inclination for favouring fun over books, Prathap Chandra Reddy decided that he would go to Madras Christian College.[5]

As he mulled over his choice of college, two incidents from his childhood strangely popped up in Prathap's mind.

One was the time when, at the age of six, he contracted tetanus. Prathap was rushed to the Chittoor district hospital. There he was treated by a physician named Mohammed Ibrahim. Many years later, the two men ran into each other in Chennai, where Dr Ibrahim had risen to a high position in government.

'Dr Reddy, do you realize that you would not be here had it not been for me?' Dr Ibrahim said, as the two men recalled the tetanus episode.

Ever quick on the uptake, Dr Reddy smiled and said, 'Dr Ibrahim, do you realize that you wouldn't be here either had it not been for me? Had I died of tetanus, my villagers would have killed you.'

It was, in fact, not long after Prathap's recovery from tetanus that the Reddy family decided to make a special pilgrimage of gratitude

---

5 Prathap Chandra Reddy had actually hoped to enter Presidency College, but although he topped the entrance examination in Chittoor district, he was denied entry to Presidency because the government had just instituted a quota system for Madras Presidency (which then included Andhra Pradesh). Prathap's candidacy, he likes to joke, was among India's first casualties – a medical term – of the quota system, which in later years became controversial, albeit in a different political and social context. After initially attending Madras Christian College, he transferred to Presidency College, where he studied for just four months before moving on to Stanley Medical College.

to Tirupati. Raghava Reddy, who ordinarily did not accompany the family on pilgrimages, went along this time, as did Prathap's mother, Shakuntala. His brother Narasimha along with his wife Krishnamma, Prathap, Poornachandra, Vimla, and several servants were all there. Everyone shaved their heads, as per tradition, and then went to a nearby waterfall for ritual bathing – known as *papanasanam*, which in Telugu means cleansing of sins – before entering the inner shrine.

Suddenly, Narasimha Reddy shouted, 'Where's Prathap?'

It appeared that young Prathap had fallen into the waterfall, and had been swept away.

But even before that shock had registered, a stranger showed up. He was carrying Prathap in his arms. The boy was drenched.

Relieved that Prathap was alive, nobody thought of asking the stranger how he had rescued the boy. When Raghava Reddy and the family members looked around, the stranger was gone.

'I am convinced to this day that I was saved by Lord Balaji. How else to explain that episode? Who was that man? I have no recollection whatsoever of being swept away in the waterfall. The next thing I knew, I was back with my parents and family,' Dr Reddy told me.

'Do I feel blessed? Yes.'

When Prathap recounted this episode to friends at Madras Christian College, they would be riveted. Some of them told me years later that there had been a divine purpose in the saving of Prathap – so that, in years to come, he would himself save lives, he would become the 'Healer'.

But as he enrolled at Madras Christian College, healing lives was the furthest thing on his mind. Having fun was.

He was impressed by the sprawling green 365-acre campus in Tambaram, on the outskirts of Madras. He took long walks. He ran to ensure that his enormous appetite did not result in excessive fat. He played tennis. Prathap was assigned to all-male quarters at Bishop Heber Hall, one of the three on-site hostels (the other two being Selaiyur and Saint Thomas Halls).

Although Prathap Chandra Reddy wasn't an exceptional student, he was generally considered bright. But he was known even more for being an effervescent personality. People at Madras Christian College enjoyed being around him. He was tall, he had good looks, and he made people laugh with his witty remarks. He was, as everybody would say, a lover of life and laughter.

That meant he would want to be at the beach in Madras, where the fun was. Prathap Chandra Reddy was always the man who caught everyone's eye.

Back at Madras Christian College, Prathap particularly caught the eye of the Reverend A.J. Boyd, the principal (he served from 1938 to 1956). Boyd made it a point to know each student's name (after they had made just one appearance before him, Boyd had the phenomenal ability to remember the names of 3,000 students); he also made it a point to follow each student's academic progress – or lack thereof. Boyd seemed especially pleased that Prathap Chandra Reddy enjoyed Shakespeare. Prathap also seemed to like chemistry – and when he recalls his days at Madras Christian College, he wonders if the urge to become a doctor was engendered in him during chemistry classes. Prathap was at the top of his class.

Still, Boyd summoned Prathap one day. He expressed disappointment that the lad hadn't been doing as well academically as he had the potential to do. Boyd reminded Prathap who his maternal uncle was – Sir Cattamanchi Ramalinga Reddy, who had been knighted by the British in recognition of his contributions to the academic world. The uncle was founder of Andhra University. He had graduated with distinction from Madras Christian College.

'You must understand that you come from Sir C.R. Reddy's family,' Boyd told Prathap. 'So think about this: Is your name going to be remembered here, like that of your uncle, or is it going to be rubbed out?'

Dr Reddy told me much later, 'It was that talk with Boyd that really fired me up. I was absolutely determined to do well academically.' He soon started topping all his examinations. Boyd thought that Prathap would make a good chemist.

But years afterwards, Dr Reddy recalled to me that the very same Boyd had advised another student of Madras Christian College to become a doctor, and not discontinue his studies. The student had wanted to be a soldier. 'You'll make a much better doctor than a soldier,' Boyd told the young man.

That student's name was Krishnaswamy Sundarji. He disregarded Boyd's advice. And in time, General Sundarji became one of India's most decorated soldiers, and Chief of the Army Staff.

One day, not long after his own talk with Boyd, Prathap Chandra Reddy went to meet his uncle to pay his respects. The old man was a lifelong bachelor, and he and Prathap's father, Raghava Reddy, were not exactly on talking terms, reportedly because of differences over India's education priorities. Raghava Reddy had felt that agricultural education needed to be prioritized. Sir Cattamanchi, who had studied at Cambridge University after Madras Christian College, felt that for Indians while liberal arts education was needed, a focus on science was also required.

Before Prathap could tell his uncle about the 'chat' that Boyd had had with him, the old man began talking about his concern that the newly independent country was being hamstrung by infighting within the ruling Indian National Congress. The subject of division of states was especially sensitive. It is indeed an irony that the original logic of state formation based on the language of the area is getting diluted with demands for further division of these states being raised with predictable regularity these days.

Jawaharlal Nehru and Vallabbhai Patel – both of whom Dr Reddy recalls with pride – would have been pained by today's shrill debates on new divisions of India's states.

CHAPTER SIX

Into the Movies?

PRATHAP CHANDRA REDDY MAY not have liked the directness with which A.J. Boyd spoke with him about his academic work at the time, but, looking back, he acknowledges that the conversation was a life-changing episode.

'I hope you won't end up as a mere police officer,' Boyd said to Prathap, words that grated on the young man.

They grated because Prathap had become particularly fond of Boyd, and not only because of the interesting way in which he taught Shakespeare to the students of Madras Christian College. Boyd would assign a seat to each of the 250 students in his classroom, and would be quick to spot absentees. It was a class that Prathap did not like to miss.

Then there were the after-hours activities that endeared Boyd to his students.

Every evening at 6.30, Boyd would invite a few students to his quarters for tea; at 8 o'clock another set of students would be asked to join him for dinner. Boyd's own family had stayed behind in their native Scotland, and so he relished the company of students during off hours. Prathap would be among those whom he'd invite frequently for these repasts.

Each time, a thick fruitcake would be served. 'You mean we are supposed to eat all of this?' Prathap would ask, actually looking forward to consuming the confection.

Boyd invariably smiled. 'In your case, I wouldn't worry – eat as much as you wish.'

Boyd knew that Prathap was a runner. So no matter how many calories he consumed, the young man's build always stayed lithe. Boyd himself was tall, nearly six feet – almost as tall as Prathap – and had a strong physique. Prathap does not recall Boyd himself eating the fruitcake. In fact, Boyd ate rather lightly.

During those tea and dinner sessions, Boyd would ask students about their parents, and what they hoped to do after college.

'Did your father and mother advise you to study hard?' was a question that Boyd habitually posed. Naturally, each student nodded vigorously.

The parents of many of those students would sometimes visit Madras Christian College. Shakuntala Reddy came a couple of times, but Raghava Reddy never did, perhaps out of displeasure that Prathap hadn't joined business, or that he hadn't travelled to Germany to study engineering as had been expected of him and his brothers Subramanya and Narasimha. (In later years, Raghava Reddy did visit Prathap at Stanley Medical College, but only once and that, too, only briefly.)

Like other students, Prathap rose at 6.30 in the morning and studied at the library until 8.30, when classes began.

When Boyd seemed to challenge Prathap about the direction in which his life was headed, Prathap tore up his monthly train pass of one and a half rupees that he'd used to travel daily to Marina Beach. That was done with a dramatic flourish that seemed to surprise Boyd.

'You might want to try your hand at agriculture,' Boyd said to Prathap, alluding to the Reddy family business in Aragonda. 'Wouldn't it be nice if you went into business?'

Had Prathap Chandra Reddy continued at Madras Christian College, he would have been on track after the initial two years to obtain a bachelor's degree in commerce. But Prathap told Boyd that he wanted to go to Presidency College instead; it offered a wider array of subjects.

Prathap would miss his trips to the beach, of course. Those daily jaunts from the campus of Madras Christian College into the city took at least thirty minutes each way. Time just flew while Prathap and his friends were having fun. He was aware that the gates of Heber Hall, his dormitory, would be promptly closed at 8 p.m. Equally importantly, the college mess would also be closed at that same hour.

'My friends kept a window open for me so that I could sneak in,' Dr Reddy recalls. His room during his first year at Madras Christian College was on the ground floor, so climbing in wasn't a problem. But he was moved to a second-floor room in his second year, which meant that Prathap needed to summon athleticism in order to climb back into his quarters.

If Boyd was offended by Prathap's decision to apply to Presidency College, he did not show it.

Perhaps Boyd did not take offence because of his liking for Prathap. Not only was he pleased that the young man had taken a shine to Shakespeare, Boyd was also impressed by the fact that Prathap had volunteered for the National Cadet Corps (NCC).

Each year, the students who'd volunteered would take a train to Trichy in March, at the conclusion of the academic year. The Indian Army had set up a camp for the NCC cadets, and the boys would be up at the crack of dawn for a daily ten-kilometre run during the ten days that they'd spent at the camp. Because of the regular running that he'd done on the Madras Christian College campus, these daily exercises came easily to Prathap. He attended the NCC camps in Tiruchirappalli. Assuming that the authorities would recognize his natural leadership skills, he was a tad disappointed to be assigned the somewhat menial task of polishing shoes. 'That certainly taught me humility,' Dr Reddy recalls. 'No one should be above any kind of labour. All labour has its own dignity.'

Prathap was assigned to Platoon C of the four NCC units. In the first year, Captain Suri of the army headed the camp; Captain Narayanan, also of the army, headed the camp the next year. At the end of the ten-day period, students were awarded certificates. Even though Prathap's Platoon C was regarded as the weakest, the students of Madras Christian College won the overall medal for best performance at the NCC camp.

This pleased Boyd no end. He travelled to the camp himself for the ceremony. He wore a uniform, and smartly saluted the cadets. 'I am proud of you,' Boyd told the students. 'I am sure that your parents are also very proud of you.'

Dr Reddy would later tell me: 'Those NCC camps helped instil a lot of discipline in us boys. Whenever I take my daily walks, I still remember those runs. And so I try and walk more briskly.'

After two years at Madras Christian College, Prathap applied to Presidency College and was accepted, although there was a delay of nearly three months for technical reasons. When Prathap informed his uncle Narasimha Reddy – the family bursar – the latter was delighted. Of the colleges in Madras at the time Presidency was considered the most prestigious. Presidency College in Chennai is one of the oldest government arts colleges in India. It is one of the two Presidency Colleges established by the British in India, the other being the one in Kolkata.

To pay for the fees, Narasimha Reddy immediately sent across a thousand rupees to the college warden as a security deposit. He also ensured that Prathap received fifty rupees each month: the hostel and food fees were twenty-five rupees; ten rupees were meant for Prathap's personal expenses; and the remaining fifteen rupees were designated by Narasimha Reddy as miscellaneous expenses.

Prathap's peers considered him a natural leader, a source of jokes and good cheer. This was true both during his short stint at Presidency College and during the five years he spent at Stanley Medical College. When Prathap reported to Stanley Medical College for his hostel assignment, he was in for a rude shock. While he had grown accustomed all along to having a single room, he now had to share one.

His roommate was a fun-loving character named Kodanda Ramiah. The word about him was that he liked being in college so much that he arranged to fail every course so that he could continue being at Stanley Medical College.

Among Kodanda's friends were N.T. Rama Rao (widely known as NTR, he would later become a Telugu film superstar with a huge following and would subsequently found the Telugu Desam party and become the chief minister of Andhra Pradesh) – and Kanta Rao. Neither was a student at SMC, but both participated in the Shakespeare plays that were staged at the college. Both had prodigious appetites, and Prathap would arrange for mounds of spicy biryani for them. NTR also insisted on mango pickles. Through a friend, three bottles of brandy would be snuck into the campus.

NTR keenly aspired to get into movies, which he proceeded to do. When his friend H.M. Reddy made his first film, *Voddu Anta Dabbu* (which roughly translates as 'When Money Starts Coming, You Don't Need It'), Prathap Chandra Reddy was invited to a celebratory party.

His father, Raghava Reddy, became upset when he heard from Aragonda villagers that his son had been seen at the party, having a good time. Prathap received a letter from his mother.

'My advice would be to stay away from your father for a while. He's very angry with you,' Shakuntala Reddy wrote.

Why did Raghava Reddy object? Because the same villagers who'd told him about Prathap's presence at NTR's party had somehow suggested that the son had entered the movie world. His son as a movie actor? Never![1]

And what if Prathap *had* wanted to enter the movies when he was a student? After all, he had the looks, he had the voice, and his friends NTR and Kanta Rao would surely have welcomed him as a leading man. Did the thought occur to him?

Dr Reddy's answer: 'No, of course not.'

So why attend NTR's parties?

'The idea was to go out and have fun. We were all young then. Why not have fun? What harm was there in having fun?'

---

1 Interestingly, many decades later, one of Dr Reddy's granddaughters, Upasna Kamineni, married a star of the Telugu film industry, Ram Charan Teja.

But I sometimes wonder what a career in Indian films would have been like for Dr Reddy. Maybe NTR would have produced a film titled *Doctor*, and maybe Prathap Chandra Reddy would have played the role of a cardiologist.

Instead, he got to be a physician in real life.

CHAPTER SEVEN

Becoming a Doctor

PRATHAP CHANDRA REDDY MAY not have made it into the movies, but he gets the star treatment wherever he goes in India. He is, after all, the founder of the ubiquitous Apollo family of hospitals. At airports, people come up to him and greet him effusively. Sometimes they offer him flowers. Aboard aircraft, cabin crews fuss over him. He doesn't seek any special treatment – quite the contrary: people are surprised that Dr Reddy engages them in conversation, mostly asking them questions about their circumstances. He wears his fame very lightly indeed.

It's not that Dr Reddy doesn't enjoy films, although he told me once that had he watched more Hindi movies his own command of that language would have been better. When he was at Stanley Medical College, he went to a nearby theatre to watch *The Million Pound Note*, a 1954 comedy starring Gregory Peck, some fifty-one times.

I asked Dr Reddy: 'Fifty-one times? What was so special about that film?'

He didn't have a persuasive response. But later I obtained a DVD of *The Million Pound Note* and now I think I understand why Prathap Chandra Reddy might have subconsciously wanted to see it over and over again. It's a tale of the implausible becoming possible; although

I doubt that at the time Prathap Chandra Reddy had anything more in mind than enjoying himself as young men might. He grins when asked about all the fun he had in those youthful, carefree days.

But what really made Prathap shift from Presidency College to Stanley Medical College? After all he was having quite a bit of fun at Presidency, too. Was one part of his mind turning restive? Was it a mere degree that he was looking for? Or was there a calling he was destined for? Was there a mega role that he was meant to perform which could bring about a sea change in a growing India? Could one influence have been the visit along with his mother to Dr S.T. Achar, a leading paediatrician who also practiced general medicine in Madras (though trained in paediatrics, Dr Achar would often visit Aragonda and consult Shakuntala)? 'I hope my son also becomes like you one day,' Prathap's mother had said to Dr Achar, a comment that her young son heard.

Apart from this passing reference, medicine, or for that matter no specific profession, was not suggested or identified by his parents for him. But enough hints were given that something better than his brothers – who shunned higher education and never left the precincts of Chittoor and Vellore – was expected of Prathap. So was it at that chance visit to a doctor's clinic that the idea of a life in medicine was subliminally implanted in the mind of the young Prathap Chandra Reddy? Was it that which propelled him to Stanley Medical College and which set him on a purposeful path to a career of medicine and medical entrepreneurship? Was it that visit with Dr Achar that placed young Prathap on a course which in time would transform the very way in which health care was looked at and delivered in our country?

One afternoon in Chennai, I met Dr Ramaswami Venkataswami, one of India's most distinguished plastic surgeons and a classmate of Prathap Chandra Reddy.

One of his more abiding memories of their days at Stanley Medical College concerned plays that students put on. One role that Dr Venkataswami especially recalls is that of the Tamil nationalist poet, Subrahmanya Bharathi, which he enacted as part of the Stanley

Medical College theatre group in 1955. Prathap wasn't in that play, but always showed up to cheer his friends; he was the college's arts secretary.

'This young man was conspicuous by his attire and presence,' Dr Venkataswami said of Prathap Chandra Reddy. 'Even in college, he used to wear a suit and tie. He was always very easygoing. I could see that he was highly intelligent – but I can't say that Prathap was hardworking. He was fond of making puns. But one good thing about Prathap was that he never gossiped. Yes, he laughed a lot – but he laughed with people, not at them. He always struck me as optimistic, someone who had great faith in himself and who encouraged others.'

Ramaswami Venkataswami's background was very different from that of Prathap Chandra Reddy's. The latter came from a prosperous agricultural family. But Venkataswami hailed from a poor farming family in the village of Kothaneri near Virudhunagar – a town known for being the birthplace of Kumarasami Kamaraj, a leader of the Indian National Congress, and later chief minister of Tamil Nadu. His father, V.R. Ramasami, was an ardent nationalist who often told his two sons, 'Never work for the British!'

Venkataswami attended his village school in his early years, and then transferred to middle school in nearby Gopinaickenpatti at the suggestion of a local teacher. One very hot day, Venkataswami heard a lot of commotion outside the school. Prime Minister Jawaharlal Nehru's motorcade had ground to a stop outside because Nehru's automobile had broken down. Nehru stepped out of his car, greeted the students and chatted with them while his car was being fixed. Venkataswami still remembers how fresh the rose on Nehru's lapel seemed even though the heat was stifling.

From Gopinaickenpatti, Venkataswami went on to complete high school at an institution known as the Ramakrishna Mission Vidyalaya in Coimbatore. Mahatma Gandhi had laid the foundation stone of the school in 1934. Nehru and virtually all major leaders of the Indian freedom movement visited the school while Venkataswami was a student there. It was in 1951 that the young man joined Stanley Medical College, a lovely campus of mango and plane trees, and rolling lawns. These were later demolished to make way for a new building. 'Such a shame,' Dr Reddy says.[1]

The irreversible alteration of the bucolic aspects of old Madras is a matter of regret to men and women of Dr Reddy's generation, and certainly those who attended Stanley Medical College with him, like Venkataswami.

While Venkataswami was applying himself to his studies, Prathap Chandra Reddy would show up just about everywhere but in class. This particularly infuriated a professor named Ramamurthy.

Prathap hadn't attended Ramamurthy's classes for three months. When he finally turned up one day, the professor was livid.

'Get out of my class,' the professor screamed. 'Get out now!'

Prathap continued to be seated. This enraged the professor even more.

'Get out! I don't want to see your face ever again!' he said, this time in Tamil.

'I am not Tamilian,' Prathap said coolly. 'Could you please repeat yourself in English this time?'

The professor came across and grabbed Prathap's hand.

'Out,' he said. 'Out! Now!'

'Why ask me to get out? You could have simply marked me absent,' Prathap said to Professor Ramamurthy.

'I am the professor here, not you. I don't have to explain anything to you,' the professor thundered, as other students quietly chuckled.

Prathap rose from his seat, which was at the front of the classroom. He went and sat down in an empty chair at the back of the room.

---

1 Stanley Medical College is steeped in a history that goes back to the days of the East India Company. In 1835, the Company set up a medical school in a small building in north Madras to conduct a two-year 'hospital dressers' course for the 'natives'. Slowly, this school grew in stature and on 27 March 1934, the institution was renamed Stanley Medical School, after the then Governor of Madras Presidency, Sir George Fredrick Stanley. It was upgraded to a regular medical college in 1938; SMC is now affiliated to the Tamil Nadu Dr MGR Medical Sciences University. Stanley has produced some of India's finest doctors.

The next day, and every day thereafter during the academic term, Prathap would come to Professor Ramamurthy's class and sit at the rear. The professor seemed clearly upset, but he said nothing.

At the end of the term, Professor Ramamurthy took his revenge. He gave Prathap a 'zero' in the final exam. This added six months to his course. That meant that he would lose almost a year in medical school. It would take Prathap Chandra Reddy five years to receive his MBBS from Stanley Medical College instead of the typical four-and-a-half years.

Did he regret that?

'What for?' Dr Reddy told me. 'I was having fun. I was myself. I was a free spirit.'

Part of the fun that Prathap Chandra Reddy was having at Stanley Medical College involved organizing student events of all sorts. He was class representative, and his peers looked to him for ideas on enhancing their campus experience. Decades later, some of these classmates would join Dr Reddy at Apollo Hospitals.

'He was a born leader, no question about it,' says Dr S. Kalyanaraman, a classmate and a man who went on to achieve great fame as a neurosurgeon, initially through his association with Dr Balasubramaniam Ramamurthi, a globally renowned neurosurgeon and a pioneer in neurosurgery in India. As with Dr Venkataswami, Dr Kalyanaraman was to join Dr Reddy at Apollo, helping transform India's health care landscape.

As he spoke, Dr Kalyanaraman smiled and looked around his office, which is lodged in a two-storey house in a quiet Chennai residential neighbourhood. Its walls are decorated with pictures of various Hindu deities such as Lord Ganesha, Lakshmi (the goddess of wealth) and Saraswati (the goddess of knowledge). In the anteroom of the office, there are pictures of more deities, and there are photographs of various swamis and contemporary holy men.

'I'm not much of a believer in aptitude and all that stuff that people say marks a person. But I'll say this for Prathap Reddy: he possessed an aptitude for creativity,' Dr Kalyanaraman said presently. That creativity wasn't necessarily confined to academics. Some of the innovative events he had organized as the college's arts secretary clearly demonstrated that. For example, it was evident in a unique form of humour that Prathap devised during his second year at SMC. The senior students all wore white coats, and led a procession in which everybody – but particularly first-year students – was required to carry human bones from cadavers that the college received. The students faithfully followed Prathap's lead: they were under the impression that this procession was some sort of requirement for first-year students.

Then the first-year students were led into a college auditorium and told that the dean would address them. Prathap had persuaded a friend who was a professional makeup artist from the Tamil movie industry to come to SMC and work his craft on him, making Prathap appear much older than he was. The idea was that he should look like a college dean. The professional did a very good job. He coloured Prathap's hair grey and applied makeup in such a manner that Prathap, who was in his early twenties, now looked at least forty years older.

When he walked into the auditorium, the first-year students respectfully stood up. Prathap spoke to them for ninety minutes on a variety of things, including 'rules of behaviour' that would apply to them at Stanley Medical College.

Among these rules were:

'You should pray to your parents every single day for sending you to this college.'

'You should pray to your senior colleagues so that they will share their wisdom with you, and be nice to you.'

'You can wear what you wish on campus. But once a month, the boys must wear dhotis to class.'

'Some of you boys went to all-male intermediate colleges before coming to SMC. Now listen: we have very strict rules about mixing between the sexes here. When you are outside the classroom, boys are not allowed to even shake hands with girls. But when you are in the classroom itself, you can do anything you wish. We will not object.'

The students listened to him with dropped jaws. They all sprang from conservative backgrounds where such talk – let alone suggestive behaviour – would be considered out of the question.

Then came Prathap's pièce de resistance.

'Once every term, we will give you an exam. You will be allowed to cheat while taking it.'

After his 'lecture' was over, Prathap told the students that a treat lay in store for them. He and two female friends, Kripamayi and Krishnakumari – who also were to become doctors – had arranged for a buffet of North Indian food. Dishes included chicken and pork, which startled the first-year students, most of whom hailed from South India; virtually none of them had ever sampled the grease-heavy non-vegetarian cuisine of North India.

A couple of days later, Prathap Chandra Reddy walked into the dining hall. He carried his trademark yellow tin of cigarettes: he was a conspicuous smoker in those days. The first-year students, still believing him to be the dean, stood up respectfully again. They still hadn't figured out Prathap's joke.

Prathap's friends loved his sense of humour. One extremely close friend was Dante Mathuranayagam, whose personal distinction was that he'd failed anatomy thirteen times.

When a professor chided Dante for not answering a question in class, Dante said to him: 'I paid you money to teach, but you haven't paid me to answer.'

Sometimes Prathap Chandra Reddy's creativity kicked in for a good cause too. One day, Prathap approached Ramaswami Venkataswami and said, 'I have a great idea.'

'What's that?' Venkataswami said, casually brushing off lint from the immaculate white khadi trousers and half-sleeved shirt that he wore every day.

'Let's organize a medical exhibition for the public,' Prathap said, slightly distracted by his friend's attention to his attire. 'What do you want to be? A physician or a politician?' he said, partly in jest but alluding to the fact that Mahatma Gandhi had made it de rigueur for Congress politicians to wear khadi.

Prathap's idea was to use assorted SMC buildings to illustrate how the human body worked. They would demonstrate the impact of various diseases on people. None of the dozen or so medical colleges in India at the time had thought of putting on such a show.

The exhibition would require some thirty thousand rupees for creating stands and for other preparations, a large amount in those days. Prathap Chandra Reddy and Ramaswami Venkataswami went to meet the SMC principal, Dr Ananthanarayana Iyer. They had grown to like him, and thought that since he was also a professor of anatomy he would be enthusiastic about the proposed exhibition.

'No, we don't have the money,' Dr Iyer said, clearly unhappy that he had to turn down the request of his enterprising students.

The young men were dejected. But one of the classmates, Vathsala, who belonged to the TVS Group, which was well known in Madras and Madurai,[2] stepped in and helped raise 15,000 rupees. And Prathap managed the rest.

Prathap and his friends went about setting up the medical exhibition. It was late March, and the academic term was about to end. Many students had already gone home for the annual two-month break. But about a hundred students stayed behind to assist Prathap and the exhibition organizers. Prathap sent off telegrams to students who'd gone home urging them to return to SMC for at least five days, the planned duration of the exhibition.

The opening was scheduled for a Saturday morning. Prathap and his friends were certain that hundreds, if not thousands, would show up. Only ten people came; they were mostly relatives of students.

Instead of being despondent, Prathap decided to show some initiative in the face of adversity, a quality that was to characterize his career again and again in subsequent years. Even to this day, college friends such as Dr Venkataswami say that Prathap Chandra Reddy

---

2 From its beginnings at the turn of the twentieth century, the $4 billion TVS Group has grown to become a large player in the automotive industry. The TVS family members over generations have continued to have a close rapport with the Reddys.

was always resourceful, always quick on his feet to find solutions to problems.

Prathap felt that the exhibition needed the support of the local media. He had once met an entrepreneur named Sivasailam Anantharamakrishnan, who'd acquired the erstwhile *Madras Mail*. So Prathap, Vathsala and Kripamayi jumped into a taxi and went to the newspaper's offices in Anna Salai. Anantharamakrishnan wasn't there, but Prathap persuaded the paper's editors that the SMC exhibition was the first of its kind in India and that the *Madras Mail* should assign a reporter to cover it.

'I leave it up to your reporters' judgement – they should write about our exhibition only if they feel it to be worthwhile,' Prathap said. Implicit in what he said was the notion that the students might go across to rival newspaper *The Hindu* in order to obtain coverage if the *Madras Mail* editors balked.

What the *Madras Mail* editors hadn't realized was that Prathap Chandra Reddy knew full well that offices of *The Hindu* and the *Indian Express* were nearby and that he planned to visit the editors of those papers as well. Prathap knew Gopalan Narasimhan, whose family owned *The Hindu*, and who, at the time, served as manager of the newspaper. Narasimhan wasn't on the premises when Prathap and his friends stopped by.[3]

Meanwhile, the *Madras Mail* editors dispatched a reporter and a photographer to Stanley Medical College. They gathered enough material by 1 o'clock and rushed back to newspaper headquarters in order to meet the 4 o'clock deadline for the evening edition of the paper. That edition's front page carried a prominent feature on the medical exhibition.

The next day, Sunday, at least a thousand people came to the SMC

---

3 Both of Narasimhan's sons served as editors-in-chief of *The Hindu*: N. Ravi, the youngest son, from 1991 to 2003, and the oldest son, N. Ram, from 2003 to 2012. Narasimhan's younger brother, G. Kasturi, was editor of *The Hindu* from 1965 to 1991. Kasturi, whom I interviewed in Chennai for this book, died in 2012.

campus for the exhibition. So did representatives of *The Hindu* and the *Indian Express*, chagrined no doubt that they'd missed out on what was a big story for Madras, while their rival, *Madras Mail*, gloried in its coverage. On Monday, the number of visitors rose to two thousand. On Tuesday, three thousand people came. The papers carried pictures of people lining up to pay the modest entrance fee to the exhibition.

Even students who had already returned to their homes dashed back to volunteer. An SMC student who would explain aspects of the human anatomy manned every exhibit. Professors got into the spirit and also joined their students at exhibits. The SMC principal, Dr Ananthanarayana Iyer, seemed to take special pride in talking about anatomy, his subject. Each time he passed Prathap Chandra Reddy or Ramaswami Venkataswami, he would pat them on the back.

Prathap said to himself, 'I wonder what Principal Iyer is thinking now. Did he think that we wouldn't succeed? Would he have helped us with the cash had he had it?'

A stall that Prathap Chandra Reddy was particularly proud of was one where the blood pressure and blood sugar of visitors were checked.

'You must get regular health check-ups,' Prathap would go around telling everyone at the SMC exhibition. 'Prevention is better than cure.'

He did not know it at the time, but after Apollo Hospitals had been established in 1983 early health check-ups became one of Dr Reddy's main exhortations.

Another stall that was always crowded was the one where savouries were sold. A restaurant on nearby Broadway Road supplied the food. Realizing that he needed to set an example, Prathap always paid for the snacks that he bought for himself and his friends.

The medical exhibition had been originally scheduled to run for five days. But popular response was so overwhelming that its duration was extended to ten days. 'It was an enormous success, but it wasn't easy,' Dr Reddy recalls.

When Prathap and his friends tallied the proceeds, they found that the exhibition had made a profit of almost 100,000 rupees – a colossal sum in those days. What to do with the money?

'Let's donate it to a village,' Prathap said. 'We'll go there and dig wells, and teach people about hygiene and good sanitation.'

They came up with a name – Alamathi village in nearby Thiruvallur district. Stanley Medical College offered the students a bus, which bumped and groaned its way over unpaved roads connecting the thirty kilometres to the village.

There the village headman greeted the students with great warmth, in the Tamil tradition. His wife immediately gave them a meal. The medical students had wanted to first talk about the importance of boiling potable water, and maintaining proper sewage disposal. But it would have seemed rude to have not eaten lunch at the very start of their visit.

'We nearly choked,' Dr Venkataswami recalls. 'The sambar had so much salt in it that it was impossible to consume. But the headman and his wife and a dozen of their relatives were watching us closely. They kept bringing mounds of rice, and buckets of sambar.'

Prathap and his friends set up a health check-up facility in the village. It is maintained to this day by Stanley Medical College. Other medical colleges, following the lead of SMC, soon 'adopted' other villages in the region. Tamil Nadu and Andhra Pradesh today have among the best health care facilities in India.

Non-governmental organizations (NGOs) have also accelerated their involvement in establishing health check-up clinics. Krishnamohan Ramachandran, formerly India national head for training and talent of Ogilvy & Mather, has created an NGO in a small village called BL Shed, about thirty kilometres from Kodaikanal. A full-time nurse staffs a medical clinic, and every Friday a doctor from a Kodaikanal hospital drives for the day to provide full check-ups for villagers. More than three hundred villagers are served by Krishnamohan's clinic each month.

That figure may seem miniscule in view of India's demography, but Krishnamohan points out that hundreds of NGOs such as his are springing up all across the country. When I discussed Prathap

Chandra Reddy's idea of a medical exhibition at Stanley Medical College, Krishnamohan smiled.

'If he were in advertising and marketing, he would have been hailed as a genius for his creativity,' he said. 'To me, creativity involves anticipating a need. That's what Prathap Reddy did back in his college days. And he's certainly shown creativity on a much larger scale in conceiving and building Apollo Hospitals.'

After the enormous success of the medical exhibition at Stanley Medical College, other educational institutions in the area sought to host similar shows. Madras Medical College was one such institution; it had more funds than SMC. Prathap Chandra Reddy, displaying his tendency to avoid confrontation and instead seek collaboration, came up with a solution: the colleges would each sponsor medical exhibitions every alternate year. His recommendation seemed to please everybody.

Many years later, Dr Reddy would tell me: 'Students, especially smart students at medical colleges, tend to be hyper-competitive. But you know what? Health care has its own huge challenges. Why compete when you can collaborate? I learned early that it's far better to smile and do your job well, than snarl and fail miserably.'

CHAPTER EIGHT

Gandhiji, Chachaji and Rajaji

DURING THE TWELVE MONTHS that I travelled around India with Dr Prathap Chandra Reddy for this book, I often asked him why he decided to become a physician. I'd heard many people ask him the same question. Neither they, nor I, quite received a full answer. Maybe it's a particular perception on my part, but I've long believed that people consciously or subconsciously decide early how they will spend the rest of their life. Still, did a career in medicine just 'happen' for Dr Reddy?

So one afternoon in March 2013, as we were flying to New Delhi from Chennai, I asked him if there had been a decisive moment when he decided to become a doctor. Had there been a moment when someone said something that spurred him to a life in medicine and, later, medical entrepreneurship?

There hadn't been such a moment, Dr Reddy said, especially because the Reddy family had had no tradition of producing physicians. Indeed, when he decided to apply to Stanley Medical College he could have asked for help from a leading Madras educator named D.S. Reddy. Reddy could have eased his entry. But Reddy was also a friend of Raghava Reddy's, and Prathap was concerned that had Reddy mentioned his plans to his father, Raghava Reddy would have nixed them. Becoming a doctor wasn't exactly what Raghava

Reddy had in mind for his son; he would have preferred Prathap to be a business graduate.

But ambition had begun to crystallize in Prathap Chandra Reddy's mind during his two years at Madras Christian College. At the very least, pursuing commerce, or just a Bachelor of Science degree, wasn't what he'd intended.

Years later, when he was a resident at Madras Medical College, Dr Rathinavel Subramaniam, a well-known surgeon and professor, would say to Dr Reddy: 'All doctors have to have a purpose in life. That purpose is to heal the largest number of people they can possibly reach.'

But well before that episode, his father Raghava Reddy and mother Shakuntala subtly nudged Prathap during the years that he was completing high school. They did not, of course, suggest any particular career. But when Dr Reddy thinks back to those years, he realizes that his parents were clearly anxious that he should make something of himself in life.

His mother's message seemed to be that high accomplishments were expected of Prathap.

'Whenever she spoke to me, she would hug me, placing her hand on my head in a gesture of blessing,' Dr Reddy recalls. 'I always felt a whole new energy, an electric current. I believe to this day that she infused me with a sense of purpose.'

His father was much more blunt.

'I hope you won't come back to Aragonda and take up the plough,' he said to Prathap.

But there was more to it in the use of the term 'take up the plough'. That term suggested not a position of a landowner but that of an ordinary farm labourer. It wasn't that Raghava Reddy looked down on such labourers or that he didn't value their work; after all, he employed scores of them. The term, however, implied that only someone without much education, or from a poor background, would want to be tilling the fields of Aragonda.

When Prathap Chandra Reddy was coursing along at Stanley Medical College, some of these memories would occasionally spring up.

He would visit Aragonda every couple of months to meet his parents, not just to demonstrate his love for them but also, however implicitly, to reassure them that he was receiving a proper education in Madras.

During those visits, the doting mother would slip some money into Prathap's pockets. The money was intended not for his education – that was already taken care of by Raghava Reddy's brother Narasimha – but for personal expenses.

Raghava Reddy also sometimes gave Prathap a few rupees. But he would add, in humour: 'You don't need money from me because I know that your mother has already given you plenty of it.'

And Shakuntala Reddy would say, in mock horror, 'Yehmandi!' The Telugu word, denoting respect, was how she always addressed her husband. (Raghava Reddy called his wife by her proper name, Shakuntala.)

On one of those visits home, Prathap suddenly recalled an incident involving Mahatma Gandhi. The year was 1942, the Quit India movement was on in full force. Prathap was nine years old. Gandhi had come to Chittoor to give a speech urging Indians to step up their efforts to rid India of its British rulers.

The rally was held at a cinema hall in Chittoor, Gurunath Talkies. But it seemed that the local police – whose commander, naturally, was a Briton – hadn't given official permission for the rally.

Prathap was in the crowd, and the moment Gandhi appeared on the dais, everyone kept shouting, '*Gandhi-ji ki jai!*'

The police swooped down on the crowd. Several people were arrested, among them thirty children – including Prathap. They were taken to a police station opposite Prathap's school.

Prathap's paternal grandfather, Muniswamy Reddy, heard the news and rushed to the jail in his horse buggy from Aragonda. 'If the boys didn't have the sense not to be at the rally, didn't you have the sense to realize that you had arrested children?' he shouted at the police officers.

He was so highly respected that the police immediately freed Prathap and his friends. But the boys' woes weren't over. Back at their school, Principal Daniel walloped each one of them with his cane.

Later that day, Srirama Reddy, Prathap's maternal uncle, consoled the boys. He told them to go to his house, where delicious food had been laid out for them. It turned out that Srirama Reddy was a staunch supporter of Gandhi's Indian National Congress.[1] He had obviously been thrilled that Mahatma Gandhi had come to Chittoor, and was distressed that his nephew and the other schoolchildren had been taken into custody.

Although Prathap and his friends were not politically engaged – they were far too young to be part of the Indian freedom movement – some of them joined the Rashtriya Swayamsevak Sangh, a Hindu nationalist movement.[2] It was on a lark, and there was nothing political to joining the RSS on Prathap's part. He would regularly attend drills, where fitness exercises were emphasized.

Then came news, on 30 January 1948, that Nathuram Godse, a former member of the RSS, had assassinated Mahatma Gandhi as he was on his way to a prayer meeting at Birla House in New Delhi. A crowd set upon Prathap and his young friends while they were engaged in a drill.

'We got beaten up severely,' Dr Reddy recalls.

Of course, neither he nor any of his friends had anything to do with the Hindu extremists who were displeased with Gandhi's efforts to prevent British India's partition into two countries, Islamic Pakistan and secular India. The assassin Godse belonged to a fringe element.[3]

---

1 Srirama Reddy would later become an active politician in Andhra Pradesh.
2 The RSS was founded in 1925 by K.B. Hedgewar, a revolutionary and a doctor from Nagpur, as a socio-cultural group meant to counter British colonialism in India and suppress Muslim separatism. The group became an extremely prominent Hindu nationalist organization in India. By the 1990s, the RSS had established numerous schools, charities and clubs to spread its ideological beliefs. The RSS was banned by the British authorities, and then thrice by the Indian Government after Independence – in 1948 after the assassination of Mahatma Gandhi, then during the Emergency (1975–77), and again after the demolition of the Babri Masjid in 1992.
3 The assassination of Mahatma Gandhi is superbly reconstructed in *The Men Who Killed Gandhi* by Manohar Malgaonkar; I would also recommend *Freedom at Midnight* by Larry Collins and Dominique Lapierre.

In subsequent days, Prathap and just about everyone else in Chittoor followed the news by radio as the nation mourned. Prathap would visit the home of his aunt, Parvatamma, where a large radio set seemed to be on all the time, blaring broadcasts from All India Radio (AIR), the government network, including Jawaharlal Nehru's memorable address about India's loss which started with the famous words: 'The light has gone out of our lives.'

It would be an irony that, not many years later, Prathap Chandra Reddy would meet Nehru and invite him to address students in Madras. Prathap was already active in student-union activities at Stanley Medical College then, and when he heard that Nehru would be in Madras he asked the office of the state Governor, Sri Prakash, if he could get an appointment with the prime minister.

So Prathap went to the Governor's official residence. He sat briefly in a well-appointed waiting room, and was then asked to enter another room where Nehru was receiving visitors. Prathap thought about the fact that Nehru was a passionate advocate of education for India's children and youth, believing it essential for India's future progress. He knew that Nehru had also outlined a commitment in his five-year plans to guarantee free and compulsory primary education to all of India's children.[4]

'What do you want?' Nehru said, without any pleasantries.

'Sir, students of all twenty-one colleges in Madras would like to hear you speak to them,' Prathap said, not fazed by the prime minister's directness.

He then told Nehru – who was often called Chacha-ji (Uncle), especially by young people – that he headed the student union at Stanley Medical College. This seemed to annoy the prime minister.

'What union? Why are you students disturbing your lives through such activities? You should concentrate on your studies,' Nehru

---

4 In later years, Nehru's government oversaw the establishment of many institutions of higher learning, including the All India Institute of Medical Sciences, the Indian Institutes of Technology and the Indian Institutes of Management.

said. It occurred to Prathap that for a self-professed Fabian socialist, Nehru's stand against student unions was unusual, at the very least.[5]

'Sir,' Prathap said, 'the unions are just a way to see how we students could help one another. This isn't about any agitation.'

'All right,' Nehru relented. 'I'll consider coming. You keep in touch with me. But don't spoil your lives by forming unions.'

In the event, the prime minister accepted the invitation that had been extended to him by Prathap Chandra Reddy. But Prathap felt that Stanley Medical College did not have a space large enough to accommodate the thousands of students and others who'd surely turn up to hear Nehru speak.

So he approached his friend Habibullah Badsha, who was leader of the student union at Presidency College. Badsha agreed that the grounds at Presidency were more spacious.[6]

And so Jawaharlal Nehru showed up at Presidency College and spoke before a crowd estimated at more than five thousand, mostly comprising students. Prathap Chandra Reddy welcomed the prime minister, and then Badsha rose to make a more formal introduction. But Nehru seemed impatient. Before Badsha could say more than a few sentences, Nehru stood up and reached for the microphone.

He spoke for about forty-five minutes about the need to widen education in India, which had been independent for only a few years. There wasn't much – if anything – that Nehru said about health care in India. Consider this extract: 'To be in good moral condition requires at least as much training as to be in good physical condition.'

---

5 It could well have been that the prime minister suspected that the Madras students were perhaps conspiring to get him to deal with the Modified (or New) Scheme of Elementary Education. Critics had dubbed it the *Kula Kalvi Thittam* (Hereditary Education Policy). This proved to be an abortive attempt at education reform introduced by the Madras chief minister C. Rajagopalachari in 1953.

6 Many years later, Badsha, who was to become a prominent lawyer, was among the first people to serve on the board of Apollo Hospitals. He and his wife Shyamala became great friends with Prathap Chandra and Sucharitha Reddy.

What he said was not exactly memorable – except, perhaps, for one line that Prathap Chandra Reddy remembers to this day: 'You shouldn't grow up to become clerks.'

In my view, that remark constituted an unintended irony on Nehru's part. Between 1947 (when India obtained independence from the British) and 1964 (when Nehru died), India came to be reviled as a nation of clerks, or babus in the vernacular. This was because the administrative apparatus at national and state levels had bloated to a point where the government became the country's biggest employer. According to various estimates, the number of clerks in government in India today exceeds 10 million.

In my previous books on India, I have written that Jawaharlal Nehru, as prime minister, focused on heavy industry, engineering and technology. He established the Indian Institutes of Technology. And yet he failed to build primary schools, health clinics and rural roads to educate the poor and provide decent health care in India's poverty-stricken hinterland.

Both Jawaharlal Nehru and Prathap Chandra Reddy were to transform the landscape of India. In Nehru's case, the transformation was in politics and economic development. Dr Reddy introduced the concept of professionally run private-sector hospitals, and – in my view and that of many others – proved to be no less a transformational figure than India's first prime minister. I also venture to add that in the long term, Dr Reddy's contribution to India's health care system may be far more enduring than what Nehru did for the Indian polity as prime minister. Nehru's adherence to socialist dogma retarded India's economic growth for decades, and his statist ideology still lingers in some influential political quarters.

Prathap was obviously delighted that the Nehru speech in Madras received a great deal of popular and media attention. In those days, media coverage of the prime minister tended to be largely uncritical, and overwhelmingly adulatory. Prathap did not share his own disappointment that Nehru's oration could have been more stirring. After all, the prime minister was addressing thousands of young people, the very constituency that would, in a few short decades, become India's majority.[7] Perhaps Nehru was simply tired that day; within a decade, he would be dead after suffering a debilitating stroke.

Prathap decided that he would now approach C. Rajagopalachari, then chief minister of Madras, to address the students at Stanley Medical College. He first consulted with his friend Ramaswami Venkataswami, who was the general secretary of the Stanley Medical College students' union. After all, Rajaji was a living legend: he was the first Indian to serve as the country's Governor General, after Lord Louis Mountbatten; he had been active in the Indian freedom movement; he was a lawyer by training, and an educator by vocation; some of his books, particularly his retellings of the Ramayana and the Mahabharata, were enormously popular.

College union president Dante Mathuranayagam and Prathap also reminisced about how they had got other luminaries to come to Stanley Medical College to meet with and speak to students. The dignitaries included Sir Alexander Fleming, the Scotsman who discovered penicillin, and Dr Pietro Valdoni, a noted orthopaedic surgeon from Italy. Among political figures that came to SMC were Conjeevaram Natarajan Annadurai, founder of the DMK, and Surendra Mohan Kumaramangalam, the veteran Communist leader. Also visiting Stanley Medical College was Sir Arcot Lakshmanaswami Mudaliar, who was to be the longest-serving vice chancellor of Madras University.

So inviting C. Rajagopalachari to SMC would be in keeping with a fine tradition that Prathap Chandra Reddy and his colleagues had established.

Accompanied by his friend Dante Mathuranayagam, Prathap went to Rajagopalachari's nondescript home in the Mylapore section of Madras. They drove in a bright red Jaguar sports coupe – license plate X120 – that Mathuranayagam owned. He came from a distinguished family of physicians – both his parents were well-known doctors, and Mathuranayagam, who wasn't a particularly industrious student,

---

7 Today, more than 65 per cent of India's population of 1.2 billion is under the age of thirty.

later surprised his friends by obtaining prestigious medical degrees in London.

On this day, Madras was warm and humid, even though it was December, a month when the southern climate tends to be kinder than the rest of the year. Rajagopalachari came to the door himself, and led the young men to his living room, where the most conspicuous decoration was a large stand groaning under the weight of Tamil and English books.

Rajagopalachari, of course, knew his visitors by name. He was friends with Dante Mathuranayagam's parents, Dante Sr and Florence. And, as chief minister of Madras, he'd travelled to Chittoor, where Prathap's family constituted the stuff of legend and history.

Dante started to tell Rajagopalachari about the history of Stanley Medical College when Prathap tapped his forearm. Of course Rajaji would have known all about the SMC. In fact, years earlier, in 1938, he'd met with Sir George Fredrick Stanley, the British parliamentarian after whom the college had been named.

'What can I do for you?' Rajagopalachari asked in his gravelly voice.

The students told the chief minister that they wanted him to address their colleagues on what was called Old Stanleans' Day, normally held at the end of January.

Rajagopalachari agreed to attend, and wound up spending more than an hour on campus. There had already been considerable buzz about the fact that Prathap and Dante had persuaded the chief minister to come.

'Imagine,' students would say, 'the former Governor General himself is coming.'[8]

---

8 Chakravarti Rajagopalachari hadn't been Governor General of India for some time – Nehru had appointed him India's home minister before he returned to Madras to assume the chief minister's seat – but everyone still called him Governor General. He was the first and only Indian to serve as Governor General of India, and the last person to hold the post (Warren Hastings was the first Governor General of India, serving from 1773 to 1785). India formally became a secular republic in 1950, and the Governor General's post was replaced by that of President of India.

Rajagopalachari was welcomed from the dais by Dante and Venkataswami. Then the students put on a performance of Indian classical dance, notably Bharata Natyam. After that, the chief minister was treated to a skit in Tamil. He watched as students showed how doctors flippantly 'examined' patients. It was, to put it mildly, a naughty skit, and Prathap wondered if the chief minister would be displeased. But Rajagopalachari seemed to be enjoying himself thoroughly. Prathap saw that the chief minister laughed more loudly than almost anyone else.

When Rajaji rose to address the students, it was a bit anticlimactic after the preceding entertainment.

'We need to better understand one another's roles in society,' Rajagopalachari said. 'I am happy to note than Stanley Medical College is turning out fine doctors. Our bodies are our temples, and you doctors are the priests of those temples.'

Then, turning to Prathap Chandra Reddy, the chief minister said: 'If I'm ever sick, I will come to you for treatment. I hope you will accept me as your patient.'[9]

After Rajagopalachari completed his brief speech, Prathap Chandra Reddy went up to the dais to deliver the traditional vote of thanks.

'I thank you, sir,' Prathap said. 'I thank you. I thank you. I thank you.'

Probably for the first time in his life – and most certainly the last – Prathap Chandra Reddy was at a loss for words.

As he led Rajagopalachari to his car, the chief minister said to him, 'Come to my home at 6 o'clock tomorrow morning. I have something to tell you.'

Prathap, again accompanied by Dante Mathuranayagam, showed up at the Rajagopalachari home at 5.45 a.m. The chief minister asked

---

9 Many years later, when Dr Reddy was in private practice as a cardiologist, Rajagopalachari indeed came to him for treatment at HM Hospital. He died on 25 December 1972, eleven years before the first Apollo Hospital opened in Chennai.

Dante to wait while he took Prathap into a private study.

'You are such a good organizer. That was a fine event yesterday. You were going to make a speech, weren't you?' Rajaji said. 'But you froze. Now this is what I want you to do. When you go back to your hostel, go into the bathroom, look into the mirror, and make that full speech.'

That's exactly what Prathap Chandra Reddy did. Never again in life would he ever falter in the hundreds of speeches that he was to make, nearly all of them extemporaneous.

Years later, when Apollo Hospital was inaugurated in Madras on 18 September 1983, among the guests was Dante Mathuranayagam and his wife. They had both become skilled physicians, and they had come to wish Dr Reddy well. The founder had made a moving speech in the presence of President Zail Singh, who had come to inaugurate the first of Apollo's fifty-plus hospitals.

At one point after the inaugural ceremony, Dr Dante Mathuranayagam took Dr Reddy aside. He whispered into his ear: 'Remember that day when the Governor General came to Stanley? You have come a long way since then, Prathap.'

CHAPTER NINE

Shakuntala

AS HE LOOKED AT the large gathering of luminaries, friends, relatives, colleagues and everyday people who had gathered for the inauguration of Apollo Hospital in Madras on 18 September 1983, Dr Prathap Chandra Reddy thought to himself: 'I wish they could have been here. How I wish they could have been here.'

'They', of course, were his father, Raghava Reddy, and his mother, Shakuntala Reddy. Both had passed away thirteen years prior to the inaugural of Apollo Hospital; they had died within months of each other in 1970 shortly after Dr Reddy and his family returned to India at the implicit behest of his father.

He had been close to them both. Raghava Reddy particularly favoured Prathap and his younger sister Sushila. She often sat on his lap as a child. So did Prathap when he was a little boy.

But Shakuntala Reddy absolutely doted on her youngest son. To please her, Prathap sometimes went out and bought make-believe trophies – tin cups, really – and showed them to his mother.

'See? I won these in a competition,' he would tell his mother. And she would hug him.

To this day, Dr Reddy cannot say with certainty whether his mother actually believed him, or simply indulged him. After all, Shakuntala Reddy never asked Prathap just what were the competitions where he won these 'trophies'.

One of Prathap's older brothers, Krishnamurthy, sometimes jokingly said to him: 'Amma forgets that she has other children too.'

And Sushila – Raghava Reddy's pet – would say to Prathap: 'She doesn't even ask me how I am, but she always hugs you.'

To which Prathap would invariably respond: 'That's because you get so much attention from Father. Why do you need more?'

While Prathap was at Stanley Medical College, his mother would often say to her husband: 'Poor fellow, I hope he's eating well.'

And Raghava Reddy would retort: 'What "poor fellow"? I'm told that he practically eats up everything in the mess. Besides, there's all that food you send him.'

His reference was to the wild boar that Prathap loved. At least once a month, Raghava Reddy would shoot some local wild boar with his English double-barrelled rifle. Shakuntala Reddy would then cook the meat and pack it carefully. A special bus would come by the Reddy home in Aragonda, and the parcel would be delivered to Prathap Chandra Reddy at his hostel in Madras.

Prathap always welcomed that delivery. So did his friends. Prathap made sure that everyone got to share the wild boar. The contents of Shakuntala Reddy's parcel would be consumed within days, and then everyone would await the next consignment from Aragonda.

But the students didn't necessarily have to wait for another month to sample Shakuntala's food. Every few weeks, she would travel to Madras for shopping, sometimes accompanied by her daughters Sushila and Madhavi. They would cook for Prathap and his friends, and the food would be sent to SMC. Shakuntala knew how fond her son was of good food: indeed, the mess offered three categories of food, and Prathap had signed up for the highest – and most expensive – category because it offered non-vegetarian dishes.

Shakuntala's shopping was more for relatives back home in Aragonda or in Chittoor. Raghava Reddy was well aware that his wife rarely bought anything for herself, and this pleased him because he – like her – always held that it was better to give things to others. Prathap Chandra Reddy recalls occasions during his childhood when his mother boarded a bus to Kanchipuram where she would shop for Kanjeevaram saris. As always, she would later give away those coveted silk saris to her daughters, relatives and friends.

They always stayed at the home of a man named Sundaram Pillai, a native of Aragonda who had run away from a tyrannical father and established himself in Madras as a businessman. He exported a fabric known as 'Bleeding Madras', which was made of artificial dyes. After washing, the fabric's colours ran into each other, creating an appealing effect. Pillai had joined up with a Marwari businessman whom everyone called 'Sethji'. Because the Reddy family had always treated him well during his Aragonda childhood, Sundaram Pillai insisted that whenever anyone from the family came to Madras, they should stay at his house with his wife and three children.

'You are my only relatives,' Pillai would say to Shakuntala and her daughters. 'I have no world other than you.'

His house happened to be quite close to Stanley Medical College, and Shakuntala would sometimes visit the campus. She would casually inspect Prathap's quarters: her real purpose was to find his tins of Wills cigarettes, which she would then throw away. Prathap's mother did not approve of smokers, even though her own husband was one.

I asked Dr Reddy one day if he'd send gifts to his parents from Madras. 'It wasn't customary in those days to send gifts,' he said. 'The best gift that my parents expected from me was to visit them frequently in Aragonda.'

Sometimes Prathap would be so caught up in campus activities – and in his social life – that he'd skip a visit or two. Invariably, when he next went to Aragonda, Raghava Reddy would express displeasure over his son's failure to visit his parents more frequently.

The visits became even more infrequent after Dr Reddy and his family went to the United States in 1963. From that year until 1970 – when they returned for good to India – Prathap came back to India only once. That was in December 1967, when Dr Reddy went to Bombay for a three-day medical conference. Afterwards, he spent a week with his parents and other family members in Aragonda

and Chittoor. He also made it a point to see Kumara Raja Muthiah
Chettiar and Kumara Rani Meena Muthiah in Madras; his eldest
daughter Preetha had been staying with them much of the time that
her parents were in the United States.

'We did not have children of our own, so Prathap and Sucharitha
allowed us to informally adopt Preetha,' Kumara Rani told me during
a conversation in Chennai in March 2013.

As Kumara Rani tells the story, it happened like this: after Preetha
Reddy was born on 28 October 1957 in Hyderabad – a little under
nine months after Prathap and Sucharitha were married in Hyderabad
on 1 February 1957 – the proud parents brought her to Madras to
the Chettiar home.

'When I saw that baby, I said to Sucha, "Can I bring up this
baby?" And Prathap said, "Of course you can bring up the baby."
They didn't take it seriously, but I did. In South India we have this
custom that if you help bring up someone else's baby, then you will
also have your own baby,' Kumara Rani said.

She had tried to have a child of her own. Kumara Rani told me
that she often consulted a noted obstetrician and gynaecologist in
Bombay, Dr Vithal Nagesh Shirodkar, proponent of the Shirodkar
cervical cerclage – but to no avail. She poured all her love and
generosity into helping raise Preetha, and to this day Preetha Reddy
calls both Kumara Rani as well as her natural mother 'Mummy'.

In 1963, the year that Dr and Mrs Reddy left for America, Preetha
Reddy was enrolled at Church Park Convent School in Madras, and
later at Rosary Matriculation School in Santhome, which her sisters
Suneeta, Shobana and Sangita also attended after their return from
the United States in 1970.[1]

While her sisters were with their parents in America, Preetha
Reddy spent most of her early years in Madras. She visited her

---

1   All four Reddy daughters were born before Dr Prathap Chandra Reddy and
    Sucharitha Reddy went abroad: Preetha on 28 October 1957 in Hyderabad,
    Suneeta on 3 April 1959 in Madras, Shobana on 27 November 1960 and
    Sangita on 8 July 1962.

grandparents in Aragonda; and, of course, her presence always made Shakuntala Reddy ecstatic.

During that period, 1963 through 1969, Preetha spent a year in Massachusetts with her parents when Dr Reddy was at Worcester City Hospital and then at Massachusetts General Hospital. Later, Kumara Raja and Kumara Rani took Preetha to Springfield, when Dr Reddy was at Missouri State Chest Hospital. While they were in Springfield, Kumara Raja decided to go on a tour of South America. Kumara Rani and Preetha returned to Madras by plane, travelling via Japan. Was Preetha's love of travel shaped in those years? In time, she would become an accomplished amateur photographer – her skills easily on par with most professionals, according to a Chennai photo specialist A.K. Rajkumar – and, of course, her position as Apollo's managing director would take her to many places around the world.

Kumara Rani recalls that one day in 1953, while still at Stanley Medical College, Prathap Chandra Reddy had yet another idea about getting students of various educational institutions in Madras to cooperate with regard to social and other programmes. At the time, she was secretary of the Queen Mary's College student union, and both she and her husband had become close friends with Prathap.

Prathap approached his friends Ramaswami and Dante again. 'Let's form a Madras City College Union,' he said. 'This would enable us to collaborate on various student activities including cultural festivals.'

Venkataswami and Mathuranayagam were both initially cautious, not the least because they knew that the president of the student union was a brilliant young man named T. Aravindakshan who felt very proud of his organization's activities. They did not want him to feel upstaged in any way.

Prathap came up with a solution: Aravindakshan – who would later become one of the most eminent lawyers in Chennai – would be named president of the city union. Kumara Rani would serve as secretary. And Prathap, of course, would churn out ideas for programmes from behind the scenes, along with his friends Venkataswami and Mathuranayagam.

It was a solution that pleased everybody – and especially Shakuntala Reddy, who was delighted to see her beloved son's popularity rise in Madras. In her mind, Prathap had 'arrived'.

At the same time, however, her motherly instincts drove her to wonder if Prathap was paying a tad too much attention to his social life at the expense of his studies. Among Prathap's friends and classmates were several Tamil Brahmins – or TamBrams, as they are popularly known[2] – including many like Dr S. Kalynaraman who later joined Dr Reddy at Apollo Hospitals.

I should say here that, over the period of five decades that I've been an author and journalist, I've found the Reddys to be among the least ethnicity-conscious people I've met. At almost all Apollo Hospitals, for example, there's a shrine on every floor dedicated to a different world religion so that patients and their visitors can pray. When Dr Reddy makes his daily rounds of Apollo Hospitals in whichever city he happens to be in, he bows his head and joins his hands in front of whichever deity happens to be on that floor.

'Health care has no class, caste or community,' Dr Reddy once said to me. He counts among his closest friends men and women from every religion and creed.

That was why I was surprised to hear the following story that Dr Reddy told me one day over breakfast at his home in New Delhi's New Friends Colony.

It was during one of his visits to Aragonda during his time at Stanley Medical College that Prathap decided to tease his mother.

'Amma, I've decided to marry,' Prathap said.

Shakuntala Reddy looked pleased, and smiled.

'But I've decided to marry a Muslim girl,' Prathap continued, mischievously.

---

2 Tamil Brahmins count among their ranks scholars, bureaucrats and entrepreneurs. There's a perception that TamBrams constitute the majority of Tamil Nadu's population of 73 million. But in fact, Tamil Brahmins comprise less than 6 per cent of the state's population. Their influence – in India and in the Indian diaspora worldwide – far exceeds their demographic numbers.

He had expected his mother to be cross with him. Instead, she said, 'I don't care if you don't marry a Reddy girl. But try and marry a Hindu girl, at least. Anyway, you will always do the right thing. We will celebrate, no matter what.'

The Reddys were actually highly regarded in Chittoor's Muslim community. Every Eid, Raghava Reddy would go to the homes of his Muslim friends, bearing gifts. In turn, he would be invited to partake of feasts.

That spirit of communal harmony still continues in Chittoor. And it is very much a part of the Reddy family tradition.

It may even explain why – like his father and mother – Prathap Chandra Reddy has never affiliated himself with the politics of ethnicity in India. He often says that while he is at ease in the company of politicians of all persuasions, he doesn't like politics.

Maybe that's why in the course of researching this book, I couldn't find anybody in political and social communities who disparaged Dr Reddy. He's not perceived as a political man who takes sides – although his political instincts and his ability to size up people are as sharp as those of the most experienced politician. Representatives of several parties have offered him political appointments – and even tickets to run for parliament – and he's always declined those invitations.

'What do I need politics for?' Prathap Chandra Reddy said to me.

That was about as politically savvy a statement as I've ever heard in all my long years of covering politics.

CHAPTER TEN

The Autumn of the Matriarch

PRATHAP CHANDRA REDDY HAS few regrets in life – he considers himself a blessed man – but one regret does come up frequently in conversations with him. It is that his father Raghava Reddy and his mother Shakuntala did not live to see the inauguration of Apollo Hospitals. Would the institution he created have been able to save them – if only Apollo had existed when they passed away in 1970? That isn't a question anyone can answer with certainty; but I'm convinced that it will always remain in a private zone of Dr Reddy's mind.

'My mother shaped and brought out the softer side in me,' Dr Reddy says. 'She always encouraged me, in her own quiet way. I learnt from her that one was obliged to do something meaningful in life.'

In India, the mother figure is especially venerated. Dr Reddy's regard and respect for women for all ages is heartfelt. I have no doubt that it springs from the values that Shakuntala Reddy imbued in him. As a child, he saw how much respect his father showed towards his mother. Prathap also saw that his father treated his sons and daughters with equal fairness.

His mother led by example and showed him the best way to relate to others was with tenderness. She wanted little for herself, preferring to provide for others. Dr Reddy says, 'You always give lessons not by teaching or beating but by showing. Amma was like that. She taught by her works.'

But Amma was not beyond occasionally punishing the naughty Prathap when he was a little boy. The intention, of course, wasn't to hurt him – it was just Shakuntala's way of expressing displeasure. Prathap would promise never to repeat whatever crime he'd been found guilty of – until the next time. 'She always felt bad about punishing us for being naughty,' he recalls. 'But she also realized that, as a mother, she couldn't leave all the disciplining to our father.'

One day in Hyderabad – where she lives – I asked Shobana Kamineni, the third of Prathap Chandra and Sucharitha Reddy's four daughters, about her own upbringing. Shobana looks after Apollo's growing chain of pharmacies, and also its insurance business, and research and consumer projects.

Shobana said that growing up in the Reddy household was 'both challenging and delightful'. She, along with her older sister Suneeta and younger sister Sangita, spent their early years in the United States. Dr Reddy, as a father, was always known for his discipline and was quick to take action when he felt academic and extracurricular activities were not going as well as they should. She was the most mischievous – most certainly taking after him – and acknowledges that she has his fire. Dr Reddy, in turn, describes Shobana as 'adventurous and bold'. These are compliments; and of course, each daughter has her own strengths that Dr Reddy recognizes and respects.

'His engagement with us was always intense,' Shobana says. 'He made sure that he knew what we were doing and that he spent real quality time with us. Our parents set excellent examples of activity for us. They would drive us around the United States so that we could learn about America's history. They also injected in us a sense of optimism about life. Dad has fantastic people management skills. For example, he made it evident that he expected each one of us to perform some act of goodness every day, howsoever insignificant it may be. It sort of forced us to do something, so that when he would ask with such eagerness, "What good thing did you do today?" we would really have something to relate. We were sure he would not have been angry if we did not have anything to report, but would have been perceptibly disappointed. And that is the last thing any of us would want. Even today he often starts off his conversation with the same question not just with us, but with many others too. What higher motivation can you think of to constantly improve one's performance? My sisters and I always make sure that we have some good news to tell him.'

However, within a few months of their return to India in early 1970, Dr Reddy would have to share sad news with his daughters.

When they arrived at Madras Airport on 12 January 1970, both Raghava and Shakuntala Reddy were waiting. They'd last seen their son in 1967, when he had come to India to attend a conference. Prathap's two older sisters, Vanajakshi and Leelavati, also came to the airport. His youngest sister Madhavi came to Madras the next day. His brother Subramanya was present at the airport too.

The father was on top of the world. The mother was exuberant. After touching their feet in the traditional Hindu style indicating respect towards one's elders, Dr Reddy looked at his parents and said, 'I came back because you asked me.'

Raghava Reddy stayed for two nights in Madras that time – usually his visits lasted only a day if he had any business – but Shakuntala Reddy stayed for nearly a week at the three-bedroom apartment in the Madras neighbourhood of Adyar that Kumara Raja and Kumara Rani had arranged for the Reddys.

'I still remember how my mother's face was glowing. And for the first time ever, I was able to present my parents with gifts,' Dr Reddy recalls.

Dr Reddy knew that his father was fond of fine writing instruments. He was especially enamoured of Parker pens, so he'd bought a high-end one for Raghava Reddy. Prathap also knew that his father liked watches, and so he'd got his Springfield physician-friend Dr David Gorelick to help pick out an Omega Speedmaster Professional, the same model that Neil Armstrong wore when he landed on the moon with fellow astronaut Edwin 'Buzz' Aldrin on 20 July 1969.[1]

While Prathap presented the watch to his father, the kitchen utensils that Sucharitha Reddy had acquired for her mother-in-law were still on a cargo ship. The Reddys' household effects wouldn't arrive for another week or so.

The celebrations in the Reddy family were to be short-lived however: Kumara Raja Muthiah Chettiar died suddenly of a heart attack on 24 January; he was only forty years old. Then two days later, Dr Reddy – whose apartment did not have a phone connection – was asked to come to Chettinad House in Madras to take a call from Aragonda. It was a family retainer named Venkamiah on the line.

'You must come at once,' he told Dr Reddy. 'Amma has been taken to the hospital.'

Shakuntala Reddy had been admitted to Christian Medical College Hospital in Vellore, not far from Madras. No one had thought of consulting her physician-son beforehand.

Dr Reddy and Sucharitha got into a Fiat that the Muthiahs had lent them. They left their four daughters in the care of Kumara Rani.

At CMC, Dr Reddy met with the hospital's chief radiation oncologist, Dr Padam Singh. The physician had a grave expression.

'You are a doctor, so let me tell it to you straight,' Dr Singh said to Dr Reddy. 'You mother has cervical cancer. It's already at stage four, and it's not curable. We've been giving her chemotherapy and radiation. But it's a difficult situation.'

Dr Reddy could scarcely believe what he was hearing. He broke down.

His mother was the world for him. Now that world was collapsing. As a physician he knew that stage four cervical cancer meant that Shakuntala Reddy's days were numbered. How could this be?

---

1 Dr Reddy had visited the Lyndon B. Johnson Space Centre of the US National Aeronautics and Space Administration (NASA) in Houston that same year. An Indian scientist there presented him with a tie clip, which also doubled as a two-way microphone – a novelty in those days.

Apparently his mother hadn't told anyone that she'd been in pain, and even her daughters did not figure out that she was gravely ill and that she would bleed almost constantly. Perhaps the cancer could have been cured if diagnosed earlier, but Shakuntala had been too shy to discuss her symptoms. Even today, many women rarely complain if they experience pain and excessive bleeding.

Before he went to see his mother, Dr Reddy thought to himself, 'What am I going to say to her? Whatever words we use with our parents, there's nothing that really describes the equation that a son has with his mother. Why didn't I come back home months ago? Perhaps I could have detected her cancer, and perhaps she could have received treatment earlier.'

Shakuntala Reddy looked very pale on her hospital bed, and she extended her hand to her son when he entered her room.

'Tell me that I am going to be well again,' Shakuntala Reddy said to him. 'Did the doctor say that I will be all right?'

But she could tell from her son's expression that life was never going to be the same for them again.

They kept Shakuntala Reddy at CMC for a few more days, and then Dr Reddy and his father took her back to Aragonda. In March, Raghava Reddy died of a cerebral haemorrhage.

Prathap Chandra Reddy wanted to take his mother back to CMC for more treatment after his father's death.

'For whom should I live?' Shakuntala Reddy said.

'Father is gone – and that's all the more reason you should be with us. Now we have only you,' the son said.

But the cancer had advanced to her lungs and bones. Shakuntala Reddy was in severe pain. Prathap Chandra Reddy said to himself, 'She doesn't deserve such suffering. What did she ever do to harm anyone? She always helped people, she fed people with her own hands – and now she gets such pain in return?'

It was the son in him emoting. As a physician, Prathap Chandra Reddy understood that perhaps it would be best if God took his mother, regardless of the incalculable loss that her death was certain to bring to the family.

One morning in early June, Dr Reddy received a phone call from Aragonda.

'Mother has left this world,' was the short message in Telugu.

Prathap Chandra Reddy had been expecting such a call. Still, he said to himself, 'I wish I had been at her side when she passed away.'

Sucharitha Reddy had also been expecting the news. In a moment that only a husband and wife can share when confronted by loss, she said to Dr Reddy: 'I know that nobody can replace Amma.'

She didn't have to say anything more.

The funeral of Shakuntala Reddy was held the next day in Aragonda. Hundreds of villagers came, not only from Aragonda but also from around Chittoor district. Few people expected that there would be two deaths in the Reddy family within months of each other. While Raghava Reddy was respected because he was the patriarch, Shakuntala Reddy was revered for her overwhelming kindness.

As the flames of the funeral pyre rose towards the sky, Prathap Chandra Reddy said to himself, 'Amma, you gave me all that love. You gave me all your blessings. And I couldn't even save your life.'

Shakuntala Reddy's ashes were immersed in India's holy rivers, the Ganges, the Yamuna and the Cauvery. Villagers were fed after the ten-day mourning period was over. The Reddy family wanted Shakuntala to be remembered with joy and not grief.

Perhaps the eventual setting up of Apollo Speciality Hospital, with its focus on cancer care, was Prathap Chandra Reddy's way of ensuring that her passion for doing good to others continued, something that would be helpful to people and touch their lives, something that would honour Shakuntala Reddy in the way that she had extended her benevolence to thousands of people over the years.

CHAPTER ELEVEN

The Road to Apollo

WHEN HE RETURNED TO India in January 1970, the establishment of Apollo Hospitals may not have been among Prathap Chandra Reddy's objectives. His first goal was to create a first-rate cardiology practice in Madras. Apollo Chennai evolved from that practice, and out of the first Apollo hospitals emerged what is now a multi-billion-dollar enterprise that includes hospitals, clinics, pharmacies, an insurance company, and other businesses.

There were many steps along the way, of course, many hurdles, many animosities from potential competitors, and many bureaucratic barriers that Dr Reddy had to push against. But on the journey, he never wavered in his determination and will to achieve his personal and professional objectives.

In his personal life, Dr Reddy was keen to raise his four daughters with the utmost sophistication, giving them the best possible education and the widest exposure to the world. He was, after all, a Reddy.

I asked Gunapati Venkata Krishna Reddy – founder and chairman of the conglomerate GVK – whether there was a special quality about the Reddys of Andhra Pradesh that explained the success of people like Dr Reddy.

'The Andhra entrepreneurs have an appetite for taking risk

because there is a strong safety net in the community,' he told me. 'They score on market knowledge. There is a lot to learn from within the community in today's times. You learn while working together and educate one another. There is a lot of collaboration. This coupled with hard work and clarity of direction helps the Andhra entrepreneurs be so successful. Dr Reddy is driven by the zeal to bring about a transformation through his endeavours.'

That his endeavours would include launching Apollo Hospitals on 18 September 1983 could scarcely have occurred to Prathap Chandra Reddy as he watched the flames from his mother's funeral pyre on that terribly sad spring day in Aragonda village in 1970.

Almost exactly twenty years after his mother's death, after the first hospital had been built in Madras, and a second one in Hyderabad was opened, Dr Reddy received an unexpected visitor. It was the radiation oncologist who had treated Shakuntala Reddy in 1970 at Christian Medical College in Vellore, Dr Padam Singh.

Dr Singh had retired by then, and was living in Bangalore. He happened to be visiting friends in Madras. He called Dr Reddy, who invited him for a tour of the Madras hospital and, of course, for a multi-course meal.[1]

After the repast, Dr Singh said, 'All this makes me so happy. You've done all this – but have you forgotten your mother's illness?'

Dr Reddy thought the remark to be odd. Did Dr Singh really think that a son would ever forget his mother's fatal illness? It then occurred to him that Dr Singh was trying to indicate that although Apollo had developed into a tertiary-care institution, offering a variety of specialities such as oncology, cardiology, neurology and kidney transplants, it did not yet have a full-fledged hospital that combined the three main elements of cancer treatment: medical, surgical and radiation therapy.

---

1 A multi-course meal is part of the Reddy tradition. In more than a year of following Dr Reddy and his family members around for this book, I was never once served a meal that consisted of just one course. If you asked for a cup of tea, it invariably came with at least three varieties of savouries.

That encounter with Dr Singh set off a chain of events that resulted in the setting up of Apollo Speciality Hospital[2] in Madras, which was inaugurated on 30 September 1993, and establishments in other Indian cities where state-of-the-art cancer care is available.[3] It resulted not only in Apollo becoming one of the leading cancer care facilities in India, but also in various other private-sector hospitals replicating what Dr Reddy had created.

When Dr Reddy gets an idea, he typically follows up immediately with several moves that would help achieve his objective. For example, after his meeting with Dr Padam Singh, Dr Reddy flew to Houston to see his old friend Dr Denton A. Cooley. Perhaps Dr Cooley, a cardio-vascular surgeon whom Dr Reddy calls 'my guru in medicine', might come up with ideas for an Apollo cancer centre.

Dr Cooley was pleased to learn about the rapid progress that Apollo Hospitals had made since its founding in 1983. And he indeed had ideas for the cancer centre that Dr Reddy planned to start. Dr Cooley introduced Dr Reddy to a physician named Charles A. LeMaistre, who was president of the MD Anderson Cancer Centre at the University of Texas.

Dr LeMaistre and his associates showed Dr Reddy around. The latter was impressed by the state-of-the art facilities including high-end machines that the centre had for radiation therapy used in the treatment of cancer patients. That visit to MD Anderson reinforced Dr Reddy's conviction that Apollo should have a cancer speciality hospital, that it should be staffed by the best and brightest doctors, and that it should provide patients with the best treatment available anywhere else.

Such an ambition wasn't unrealistic. Apollo had already developed a brand. There were well-known people in business, the arts and academe who insisted on being treated only at Apollo Madras. The minister

---

2   The facility, on Mount Road, was originally called Apollo Cancer Hospital.
3   Apollo Speciality Hospital, Chennai, India's first super-speciality hospital, offers advanced tertiary care in oncology, orthopaedics, neurology and neurosurgery, head and neck surgery and reconstructive and plastic surgery.

of state for tourism, K. Chiranjeevi, a former superstar of Telugu films (and now, of course, father-in-law to Dr Reddy's granddaughter Upasna), says that whenever his father-in-law, Allu Ramalingaiah – himself a superstar who played comic roles in Telugu movies – felt even slightly unwell, he wanted to be taken to Apollo. Why?

'Because of Dr Reddy,' Chiranjeevi told me in a conversation at his apartment in the Hauz Khas area of New Delhi. 'He wouldn't take any medication unless Dr Reddy had approved it. He always said that Dr Reddy not only had great hands as a doctor, he had a great heart.'

By the time that Dr Padam Singh met Dr Reddy in Madras in 1990, Apollo's founder had already hired several top oncologists, including Dr Ramesh Nimmagadda, from Vijayawada, Andhra Pradesh, who was working in Canada at the time. He was among those who helped develop Apollo into one of the best cancer-care centres in the world.[4]

Some of the most influential names in the world of oncology – the branch of medicine that deals with tumours, including study of their development, diagnosis, treatment and prevention – are associated with Apollo. They include Dr Vijay Anand Reddy, Dr Harsh Dua, Dr Jose Easow, Dr Umanath Nayak and Dr S.V.S.S. Prasad. In cancer treatment a patient is normally seen by an oncologist, a surgeon and a radiation specialist.[5]

The presence of these doctors on Apollo's rolls offers testimony to Dr Reddy's determination in creating world-renowned cancer hospitals, and utilizing the latest available equipment.

---

4 By 1990, when Dr Padam Singh met Dr Reddy, Apollo Hospitals Enterprises had set up a comprehensive 250-bed hospital, with an emphasis on speciality and super-specialties in more than fifty departments, at Greams Road in Madras, equipped with best available facilities at that time. In acknowledgement of its excellent facilities and its highly trained consultants, Apollo Hospital, Madras was recognized for imparting training to doctors for the examination of Fellow of the Royal College of Radiologists (FRCR) in Britain.

5 Dr Arcot Gajaraj was a leading radiation specialist who was one of the four pillars contributing to the establishment of Apollo Hospitals.

Dr Vijay Anand Reddy said: 'When PET-CT scan, a revolutionary diagnostic tool, was introduced in the United States, it was big news. I came to know that Chairman Reddy was planning to order it, and as usual all the Apollo centres were after him to place it in their facilities. I went to Chairman and requested it too. He said, "I have enormous faith in you and your team, you will get it." That was fascinating news, and we got the first PET-CT scan machine with an on-site cyclotron at Hyderabad; it was the first in Asia.'

Elaborating on the subject of Dr Reddy's keenness to incorporate high-tech in Apollo's operations, Dr Vijay Anand Reddy added: 'Once I met Chairman at the Ganesh Temple at the entrance of Apollo Hyderabad. Chairman as usual asked me, "How are things?" Hesitantly, I said, "Sir, I think we need a low-end Linac machine for Hyderabad." Chairman said, "Why are you asking for a low-end machine, you deserve the best. I will give you the best." Within a week, I got an e-mail from the Chennai office that Chairman had ordered TX, the first and the best machine in the country, for Hyderabad. What more encouragement can one expect?

'A couple of years back, Chairman met my wife Dr Shashi at Apollo Hyderabad and said good things about me. What better compliment can you dream of? Getting such a compliment from a legend is a dream come true and that too, to my wife.'

On another occasion, Dr Reddy was addressing the Hyderabad doctors and said, 'Please start group practice with sub-specialities, work together, share the income, you will excel.' This was very inspiring for them; they formed teams in oncology, against the wishes of some individuals.

'It has been six years since we started group practice,' Dr Vijay Anand Reddy said. 'We are thoroughly enjoying it. We have excelled in every aspect – there is amazing harmony, great quality, excellent outcomes and exceptional patient satisfaction.'

———

Dr Ramesh Nimmagadda's story illustrates Prathap Chandra Reddy's ability to attract top-notch physicians to Apollo – among other things by pledging to obtain for them medical equipment that could be the best available anywhere. Dr Nimmagadda had specialized in oncology in Canada. By 1984, he wanted to return home to India. He travelled to Madras to meet Dr Reddy, about whom he'd already heard a great deal from fellow physicians in North America who had invested in starting up Apollo. Dr Nimmagadda joined Apollo in February 1985. He's still there, twenty-eight years later.

'Am I surprised by Apollo's growth?' Dr Nimmagadda said in a conversation with me. 'Well, back in 1985 I wouldn't have envisioned how far Dr Reddy would take the institution. But back then I hadn't reckoned on his sheer determination, his vision and his foresight. He always wants to create confidence in the medical fraternity. He's never imposed his will on doctors. Rather, his way is to always ask us what's needed to better service our patients.'

So when Dr Reddy asked the oncology team what would be needed to develop a world-class cancer centre, the first thing that came up was that Apollo would need a separate building. This happened a few years later. Apollo Speciality Hospital started operations in 1993, and was formally inaugurated in 1995 by then prime minister H.D. Deve Gowda.

This hospital was meticulously built and grew to be the largest private cancer facility equalling the best oncology facilities anywhere in the world. It began with 100 beds. Today, it is a 250-bed hospital with state-of-the-art technology including Linac, CyberKnife and radiosurgery and has a very competent team of medical, surgical, radiation oncologists and physicists.[6]

---

6 A linear particle accelerator (often shortened to Linac) is a type of particle accelerator that greatly increases the velocity of charged subatomic particles or ions by subjecting the charged particles to a series of oscillating electric potentials along a linear beam line. Linacs have many applications: they generate X-rays and high-energy electrons for medicinal purposes in radiation therapy, serve as particle injectors for higher-energy accelerators, and are used directly to achieve the highest kinetic energy for light particles (electrons and positrons) for particle physics.

Says Dr Reddy: 'I always acknowledge members of this team for their outstanding work: those who have completed 580 BMT, the radiation oncologists who have completed 1,000 CyberKnife treatments, doctors who performed the most difficult oncology surgery.'

In 2012, a team of urologists, oncologists and colorectal specialists did robotic oncology surgeries at Apollo. Apart from Chennai, similar facilities of Apollo are now available in seven other cities, treating thousands more people. As the single largest private oncology institute at global standards, Apollo will soon be adding on the Proton with an investment of Rs 400 crore (the equivalent of about $75 million) for a single piece of equipment. Apollo has received patients not only from India but also from overseas who use the institution's cancer-care programmes.

Every cancer hospital in the Apollo system conducts a tumour board meeting on a weekly basis. Every month, a tumour board meeting is held through video conferencing with participation from all cancer hospitals to ensure the best possible care for patients.[7]

'There is absolutely no comparable institute in the world which does this,' Dr Reddy says. He points to a team from HCA International that visited India with the objective of franchising HCA international oncology care and outpatients clinics.

'They visited our cancer hospital, interacted with various specialists and later had lunch and a discussion with me. Michael Neeb, CEO of HCA International, said that he was amazed with the tremendous work that we are doing. He went to Delhi the following day, visited our facility there and had more than an hour's discussion with Dr Anupam Sibal,' Dr Reddy says. 'Neeb mentioned that it was rare to find a hospital anywhere in the world following such strict monitoring. He noted that our system has helped Apollo to continuously deliver excellent care and live up to the trust of patients. They were so pleased with Apollo putting up

---

7   Every Tuesday, a video meeting is also held with medical executives from Apollo hospitals around the country.

the Proton, which none of the British institutes have done. Also, the CyberKnife in Chennai was started much earlier than the one they bought in Britain.'

Apollo introduced several high-technology machines at the cancer hospitals, as well as at its other facilities. 'Dr Reddy was always on the lookout for the latest in technology – and he spared no effort in getting Apollo the very best that was available in the world,' Dr Raja Thirumalairaj, a senior oncologist, said. 'For Dr Reddy, the patient is first – so he has always brought the best.'

One such machine was a high-dose Selectron, which was manufactured in Holland. It was, in effect, a high-energy accelerator used to give radiotherapy directly to the cancerous tumour while ensuring that the impact on surrounding tissues was minimized. Dr Reddy looked around India for doctors familiar with the Selectron machine, but couldn't find any.

'Why don't we ask the Europeans?' he said one day to a senior doctor at Apollo.

The physician was surprised. In those days, it was unheard of for foreign physicians to be invited to come and work in India.

'This certainly will be unique,' the Apollo doctor thought.

Dr Reddy came up with the name of a man in Budapest: Dr Janos Stumpf, who had made a name for himself in radiation treatment, particularly for the spine.

Both Dr Reddy and some Apollo doctors wondered if Dr Stumpf would be fluent enough in English in order to work in India.

'Why don't we call him and check?' Dr Reddy said.

So Malathi Manohar, Dr Reddy's executive assistant, placed a call to Dr Stumpf. He answered the phone himself. And, as Dr Reddy and various Apollo physicians were to discover, Dr Stumpf spoke English well. The radiation oncologist is still at Apollo all these many years later.

A highlight of Apollo's cancer-care facility was when bone-marrow transplants were performed starting in September 1994. A young woman named Shilpa suffered from relapsed leukaemia. The procedure was so successful that Shilpa, who now lives in the United

States and is the mother of twin daughters – has been in perfect health since her bone-marrow transplant.[8]

Another highlight was when Apollo cancer surgeons performed an umbilical-cord blood transplant on a boy, drawing fresh blood from another boy. Still another achievement was when an eight-year-old Ugandan boy came to Apollo with a rare blood problem in 2007.[9] 'We got frozen cells in liquid nitrogen from a donor in the United States through the National Marrow Donor Programme,' Dr Jose Easow recalls. 'Today, many hospitals in India are doing such transplants. But Dr Reddy was always a pioneer – Apollo has shown the way for other cancer hospitals.'

'When I look back at the twenty-eight years that I've been at Apollo, the main thing that comes to my mind is that Dr Prathap Chandra Reddy gave me an opportunity to make a life for my family and myself in our own country,' Dr Nimmagadda says. 'I was doing well abroad. But I don't think that I would ever have received this kind of consistent support and encouragement anywhere else.'

I asked one senior physician what he thought to be the 'secret ingredient' of Dr Reddy's way with people. I did not tell him that just days before our conversation, Dr Reddy himself had said to me that doctors were generally the most difficult people to handle.

This was his response to my question: 'I have always said that the handling of super-specialist doctors is like handling ballerinas and divas. Handling one ballerina is tough. Can you imagine dealing with hundreds of doctors who have proved that they are the best in their business? I think that Dr Reddy respects their individual accomplishments: he never really interferes with your work. I think he just knows that if he trusts his doctors, they will in turn never let him down.'

---

8 An interesting fact: for bone marrow transplants, physicians don't need material from the same sex and the same blood type as the patient. Surgeries from donors' cells are known as allogeneic transplants. The patient's own cells are called autologous.

9 Apollo gets patients from more than 120 countries each year.

In March 2009, Apollo Speciality Cancer Hospital installed Asia Pacific's most advanced and India's first CyberKnife. 'The CyberKnife at Apollo Speciality Cancer Hospital, Chennai is now set to offer treatment access to millions of patients diagnosed with cancer in India every year. We are working towards a goal of making all types of cancer curable,' Dr Reddy said during the clinical inauguration of the CyberKnife, initiated with Dr John Adler of Stanford University, known as the 'Father of the CyberKnife', consulting the first patient scheduled to undergo treatment.

He added, 'With the launch of CyberKnife, Apollo Speciality Cancer Hospital joins the global league of hospitals equipped to provide 360-degree cancer care.'[10]

'I am particularly grateful to Dr Reddy's help in bringing a relatively advanced technology like image-guided radiosurgery to the great Indian subcontinent,' Dr Adler said. 'Although a cardiologist by training, Dr Reddy's innate instinct for recognizing important new medical technology clearly drove the decision at the Apollo Speciality Hospital in Chennai to acquire a very expensive medical instrument like the CyberKnife. Without Dr Reddy's support and entrepreneurial willingness to take risks (and believe in a young fellow entrepreneur), this would never have happened. Because of his courage thousands of Indian as well as foreign patients have since benefited from the non-invasive ablation which the CyberKnife enables. More recently I have turned my entrepreneurial energies towards transforming peer-reviewed scientific journals, thereby hoping to remove significant ongoing barriers to medical publishing. Once again my good friend

---

10 The CyberKnife® is a frameless robotic radiosurgery system used for treating benign tumours, malignant tumours and other medical conditions. Dr John R. Adler, of Neurosurgery and Radiation Oncology at Stanford University, and Peter and Russell Schonberg of Schonberg Research Corporation invented the system. The Accuray Company headquartered in Sunnyvale, California makes it. The CyberKnife system is a method of delivering radiotherapy with the intention of targeting treatment more accurately than standard radiotherapy. Dr Adler is also vice chairman of Varian Medical Systems, the world leader in manufacturing devices and software for treating cancer.

Prathap Reddy quickly stepped up and supported my fledgling journal, Cureus.com. No words can adequately express my gratitude to Dr Reddy for assisting me again and again to recognize my own dreams, and in doing so, help so many patients worldwide.'

'Apollo is a world leader in medical care,' Dr Adler said, adding that he was confident about Apollo's durability and sustainability as a major global health care institution.

Apollo Speciality Cancer Hospital has treated more than a million patients. While observing the twentieth anniversary of its founding in late September 2013, Dr Reddy reaffirmed the institution's commitment to bringing greater awareness, improved care and innovation in detection and treatment of cancer.

Which, of course, brings up the question of the next generation of Apollo leaders. What sort of equation will the system's doctors have with them?

A senior oncologist said: 'Over the last thirty years Dr Reddy has developed a distinct culture of excellence and discipline. There's a great deal of confidence that people have in the Reddy daughters.'

That sentiment also came from the industrialist and shipping magnate Shashi Ruia, who told me that 'Apollo is in very good hands with Dr Reddy's daughters'.

Ruia said that he first met Dr Reddy in 1974 at HM Hospital, where his mother Chandrakala Ruia was being treated. Later, Dr Reddy also treated Shashi's wife, Manju, for a bronchial infection. 'They both became great fans of Dr Reddy,' Ruia said.

'He's a very warm person, the relationship evolved from that of doctor–patient to a lasting friendship,' he told me in Mumbai.

'Even back then Dr Reddy was speaking of plans to put up private hospitals to address the growing health care needs of the nation,' Ruia said. 'To be frank, it seemed to me somewhat improbable and out of context at the time. Private hospitals were not on the scene. But Dr Reddy spoke with great conviction. He would talk about the importance of health care for societies. He had a charismatic personality. One could notice how important people were drawn to him.'

Shashi Ruia – whom I've known since the early 1990s when I made a documentary on him, his brother Ravi and their Essar Group for public television in the United States – spoke of the importance of private-sector hospitals.

'Given the vast expanse of our country, it would be impossible for the government to provide tertiary health care by itself,' he said. 'If you go to any district hospital, you will see large numbers of people waiting for medical attention. It's very painful to watch. We need sustained intervention, and private-sector hospitals can offer that, provided of course the government ensures the necessary stimulus and support. We need a proper systematic approach to health care, and the government is simply not focused. You need well-organized and well-managed institutions like Apollo.'

He said he was particularly pleased that Apollo was widening its reach into India's rural areas. Ruia's own foundation runs rural health camps, which serve some 240,000 people annually.

'But so much more needs to be done in health care,' he said. 'That's the need of India today – so much more needs to be done.'

CHAPTER TWELVE

The Reddy Rules

BOTH SHASHI RUIA AND Dr M.R. Girinath, one of India's leading cardio-thoracic surgeons, aver that Dr Prathap Chandra Reddy introduced and sustained a 'certain culture of excellence and discipline' at Apollo. 'Dr Reddy always wants everyone to aim to be the best; second-best simply isn't good enough for him,' Dr Girinath told me. 'He truly believes that if anything good is being done in medicine anywhere in the world, we at Apollo can do it better.'

Dr Reddy's belief is widely shared beyond the hospitals' precincts. Sucharitha Reddy says that his insistence on world-class medical standards, in fact, preceded the creation of Apollo Hospitals in 1983: in the seven years that he spent in the United States, he quickly absorbed what these days are called 'best practices'. After Dr Reddy returned to India from America in 1970 and then joined HM Hospital in Madras, he quickly gained a reputation as being a stickler for discipline and detail.

Three physicians who had joined Dr Reddy at HM Hospital – and who are still with Apollo – recall those early days. They are Dr Satyabhama Narayanamurthy, medical director of Apollo Hospitals in the Chennai region; Dr Uma Nataraja, a senior consultant in internal medicine; and Dr Udhaya Balasubramaniam, director of preventive medicine. Malathi Manohar, who first showed up for treatment for typhoid, became Dr Reddy's executive assistant, a position she holds to this day.[1]

The two-storey HM Hospital was so small that it could scarcely qualify as anything more than a nursing home. It billed itself as a 'heart and lung clinic'; diagnostic facilities were housed on the ground floor, and in-patient rooms on the first. Most of Dr Reddy's renowned current-day practices originated here, and so did many of his most loyal patients. HM Hospital – named after a man named Dr H. Mehta – was located on St Mary's Road in the Abhiramapuram section of Madras, which was quite upmarket and home for affluent people of the time like the noted industrialist, Dr N. Mahalingam, chairman of the Shakti Group, a $1.2 billion conglomerate. The paper baron, Rajkumar Menon, also lived nearby: he has been an independent board director of Apollo Hospitals since its legal formation in 1979.

The famous Tamil comedian Nagesh, known as the Jerry Lewis of India, lived almost diagonally across from the hospital. He was quite fond of the hospital staff, and was known to personally offer umbrellas to nurses as they walked past his gate on hot summer days.

Dr Satyabhama had graduated from medical school in Pondicherry, and moved back to Madras soon after her marriage to a lawyer named Narayanamurthy. The husband took note of HM Hospital, went there and met Dr Reddy, asking if the doctor would be interested in meeting his wife. Dr Reddy needed a temporary replacement for a doctor who was going on maternity leave and said yes. The fresh graduate immediately joined and has stayed with Dr Reddy since.

'I was a little scared at first. Dr Reddy had such a big personality – but he immediately put me at ease,' Dr Satyabhama says. 'The nursing home was fresh and new, very clean and bright. We had a six-drawer cupboard in which we kept patient records. After ten years, it became a thirty-drawer cupboard with over 30,000 case records. It was very busy. Not only did ordinary citizens come but also foreign

---

1 Malathi's institutional memory is extraordinary. She can recall virtually every day of the more than forty years that she has spent working with Dr Reddy.

consulate staff, business people, families, and movie stars.[2] We had no marketing. The overflow of patients was all just word of mouth. I remember one of my first patients had jaundice with encephalopathy and seeing what we did for him was very satisfying.'

Dr Reddy shared his dream of starting his own hospital with colleagues such as Dr Satyabhama. In fact, an architect's drawing of the first Apollo hospital was prominently displayed in the waiting area of HM Hospital, and used to be the cynosure of attention for staff members who never dreamed that the Madras facility would be just the first in the sprawling Apollo empire. They didn't know how Dr Reddy would do it but had faith in him. That drawing still hangs in the foyer of Dr Reddy's office at Apollo Chennai – almost as a reminder to people of the power of dreams.

The other doctors emulated his behaviour and learnt that he truly meant it when he said 'the patient comes first'.

'There was always more and more to do, new developments every day, of course. On one occasion we had been monitoring a patient who was very sick: he had many complications following a heart attack. His blood pressure was falling and his heart rate was feeble. The patient became increasingly unstable and we defibrillated him many times. Dr Reddy was leaving the hospital. I called out to him and he immediately came back to help stabilize the patient. When you see the kind of commitment that Dr Reddy has, all the attention for this one life, it rubs off on you,' Dr Satyabhama recalls.

She and her colleagues kept long hours: they would report to work at 7.30 a.m., and broke for lunch for about an hour around 1.30 p.m. Then work resumed and most doctors – including Dr Reddy – stayed till 9 p.m. Technically, the doctors weren't required to work more than twelve hours a day. But such was their dedication – and their loyalty to Dr Reddy – that they put in longer hours.

---

2 In those days, Madras was the main centre for the production of films in Tamil, Telugu, Malayalam and Kannada. Now, of course, Hyderabad has sprung up as a production centre as well. But what Indians call 'Tollywood' remains centred in Chennai.

When asked what made the most difference in patient care, Dr Satyabhama says, 'It was personal commitment. Don't lose your cool. Be objective. Don't panic. Always do what is best for the patient. Dr Reddy opened the door and we all saw the potential. He is very committed to a strong health care system for India. And, we can be the Mayo Clinic or Johns Hopkins for Asia and beyond. When you see the result of your care, you cannot go back, you must go forward. That is what Dr Reddy taught us from the very beginning.'

'The heart of India is in our hands,' Dr Satyabhama says. 'This concept was the seed which germinated into this huge tree called Apollo. Always the heart is the most romantic of our entire being and it can kindle many a great emotion. Maybe the loss of that young man due to a massive heart attack way back in the late 1970s brought the dormant force within Dr Reddy's heart to wake up and conceive this hitherto untried concept of private corporate health care in India, of creating institutions of international standards within reach of Indians. Though Apollo soon emerged as a great multi-speciality tertiary care institute, still "the heart" remains its principal focus, leading to the "Billion Hearts Beating Campaign", a burning desire to wipe out heart disease from our country.

'We have many true stories which make us almost believe our cardiac surgeons are gods, who are the only people who can stop the heart and restart it at will, next only to God. For example, we can never forget the pregnant woman who had a near cardiac arrest in her second trimester, had a stent placed in her totally occluded left side coronary artery, went on to complete her term and deliver a healthy boy. Or the thirty-eight-year-old labourer from Tiruvannamalai, truly Lord Shiva's abode, who came from that distance with a ruptured left main artery into our operating room, and was saved by our team of doctors. The stories are endless. Happiness abounds in our patients' lives as well as ours. No wonder Dr Reddy goes on starting heart hospitals all over.'

Mohan Guruswamy, a former Secretary in the ministry of finance, and a well-known economist and social commentator, is among those who endorse Dr Satyabhama's belief about the transformation that Dr Reddy brought about in India's health care industry.[3] Moreover, the Harvard-educated Guruswamy says he has no hesitation in terming Dr Reddy a 'pioneer'. His daughter Menaka Guruswamy – who was a top student at Harvard Law School – practices at the Supreme Court in New Delhi, and is a lawyer for the Reddys.

'Apollo set the standard, the benchmark, and now other companies are copying what he did, including using pastel colours in their logos. That was Apollo and now all the other hospitals have followed,' Guruswamy said during a conversation in Hyderabad. 'A pioneer is not an ordinary individual. He or she goes about life thinking of the future. He has to be an entrepreneur in the best sense of the term, a public-relations consultant, a financial engineer, a troubleshooter and a fixer in order to manage his breakthroughs. Everyone then follows the path created by such pioneers. Dr Reddy brought structure, attitude and social acceptance to health care and to health insurance.'

Dr David L. Levy is among those who endorse this view, characterizing Dr Reddy as one of the authentic pioneers in global health care. He received his medical degree from McGill University in Canada, and is now with PriceWaterhouseCoopers – one of the world's foremost consulting firms – as its global leader for health care, based out of New York. He is a tall, lean man with a broad forehead who keeps fit by running daily.

I met him at the sidelines of the annual meeting of the Asian Development Bank in New Delhi in early May 2013, where he was moderating a panel on health care. 'The international narrative is that there's a huge potential in health care that's not been met,' Dr Levy said. 'Dr Reddy has done a remarkable job in developing private sector hospitals. But for such a huge country, India spends

---

3 Mohan Guruswamy was inducted into the ministry of finance from outside the Indian Administrative Service in 1998, with the rank of full Secretary. Among his predecessors was Nitin Desai, who was similarly inducted from outside the IAS, and was also a distinguished economist.

less than anyone else on health care. India's dilemma is how to do much more with much less.'

Dr Reddy has talked frequently about these health care deficiencies both globally and in India. Dr Levy told me that, given the enormous challenges, perhaps the best way for countries to provide better health care would be through public–private partnerships, a solution that was also advocated by Montek Singh Ahluwalia, deputy chairman of India's Planning Commission, in a conversation with me in late 2012 at his New Delhi office in Yojana Bhavan.

'We like Dr Reddy because of his constant efforts to come up with creative solutions to India's health care problems,' Ahluwalia, an acclaimed economist who was earlier with the World Bank, told me. 'He has shown that entrepreneurship is the key to implementing those solutions. He is an extraordinary risk taker, and his record at Apollo shows that taking risks and developing new models in health care in a timely manner paid off.'

Preetha Reddy, Dr Reddy's oldest daughter – and managing director of Apollo Hospitals – told me: 'I have often heard Chairman say that entrepreneurship is not just a behavioural trait but a willingness to embark on a journey. His journey of over four decades, especially ever since he returned to India from the United States, has been incredibly exciting.'

And, as can be expected, Dr Reddy's record of that journey is also envied; entrepreneurs who opened up medical facilities in the private sector since Apollo's founding in 1983 have sought to replicate his success: there are now more than 3,000 private-sector hospitals in India, nearly 400 of them in Chennai alone. But it's far tougher to replicate the 'rules' that drove that success.

One morning in New Delhi, an old friend of the Reddy family, Palaniappan Chidambaram, neatly summed up those 'rules' for me. I met him at his office in North Block, part of the massive sandstone complex built by Sir Edwin Lutyens during the British Raj. Driving up Raisina Hill to Chidambaram's office, it was hard not to be in awe of the sheer magnificence of the area, and to imagine the vast sweep of history it has witnessed.

Chidambaram, of course, is India's finance minister, his third stint in this powerful post. His corner office on the first floor of the ministry of finance is almost the size of a tennis court, and on its walls are two striking paintings of Mahatma Gandhi and Jawaharlal Nehru. There is a long rectangular conference table. There are numerous desk phones, although Chidambaram is almost constantly on his mobile device. I had met him on earlier occasions, including at a Bharata Natyam dance recital in Chennai by his daughter-in-law, Dr Srinidhi Chidambaram, a physician who works at Apollo Hospitals as head of its international patients programme. But this was the first time that Chidambaram and I discussed Dr Reddy. It was clear that Chidambaram held him in very high regard indeed – after all, he had known him since his childhood in the aristocratic Chettiar community in Tamil Nadu.

'Our families have known each other for quite some time,' Chidambaram said, with a healthy glow on his face that surprised me – I'd expected him to seem more tired since he'd just returned from a lengthy trip to Japan and East Asia, such travel being part of 'selling' to potential investors the benefits of being engaged with a $1.4 trillion economy. Chidambaram, whose parliamentary constituency is Sivaganga in Tamil Nadu, frequently spends his weekends at his Chennai home.

'When I was growing up, your main doctor was the general practitioner. He was the one who referred you to a specialist, if it were necessary,' Chidambaram said. 'The idea of treating a human being in a multidisciplinary manner under one roof in the corporate sector – that concept was really introduced by Dr Reddy when he started Apollo. He was a pioneer in corporate hospitals. He believed in the idea, and he applied in India what he'd learned during his stay in the United States. He had a remarkable faith in his ability to create the corporate sector in India's health care.' He noted that there were now many others who had followed Dr Reddy and had succeeded.

Lest he be thought of as dismissing the public sector's contribution to health care in India, Chidambaram quickly pointed out that the government has 'dramatically increased the number of seats' in the country's 345 medical colleges.[4] He also pointed to the fact that public-sector hospitals were increasingly diversifying their medical specialities. He emphasized that smallpox had been abolished in India, and polio virtually so. And he noted the success of the government's renewed mass-scale immunization campaign.[5]

It was all very well to cite progress in health care, but I wanted to know the downside. So I asked Chidambaram about his worries concerning the health care industry. He was surprisingly candid.

'Outlays are fine, but outcomes are worrying,' Chidambaram said. 'And this is purely a function of governance. The formula? Outlays plus governance equals outcomes. Things are improving, but we aren't quite there yet.'[6]

In this context, Chidambaram returned to his assessment of Dr Prathap Chandra Reddy's emphasis on performance. In effect, the finance minister was spelling out what I call the 'Reddy Rules'.

'Dr Reddy believes – as do I – that there's no such thing as the Indian way of doing things,' Chidambaram said. 'That's all too often (the excuse) for accepting shoddy results and behaviour. What Dr Reddy did was to instil critical values such as punctuality, efficiency,

---

4   More than a million students compete each year for 40,000 seats at these medical schools. The government has established quotas for students from economically and socially backward constituencies, a move that has proved controversial.

5   Apollo Hospitals launched an adult immunization project in April 2013 titled 'Apollo Protect'. The campaign focuses on encouraging vaccinations for the adolescent and adult population and it will be driven across the group's integrated health care network of over fifty hospitals, 1,500 pharmacies, 100 clinics, four cradle hospitals, day surgery centres, occupational health centres, telemedicine centres and patient information centres across the country.

6   The India 2013-14 budget that was unveiled by Finance Minister P. Chidambaram on 28 February 2013 called for a total expenditure of $304 billion. Of this amount, $37.4 billion was allocated to defence, and $12 billion for education. The health care allocation was $6.88 billion, or 2 per cent of the government's overall expenditures – grossly inadequate to meet even the country's primary health care needs.

ethics, attention to detail, cleanliness, and total focus on patients among his colleagues and employees at Apollo. From the very start, he was particular about establishing such high standards. And you'd be surprised how much they've been absorbed by Apollo personnel.'

Actually, I wasn't surprised. I had seen for myself over a period of a year the institutional discipline and values that Dr Reddy had instilled at Apollo, what many observers have termed 'thinking big' on Dr Reddy's part. Shrinivas Pandit, a management expert who has studied Dr Reddy's work at Apollo, says: 'The creative foray, however, is not only in thinking big, or putting bricks, mortars, and hospital staff together and leveraging the post-product. It is more in providing quality service of immeasurable dimensions, which captures the heart of patients. It means making available a continuous attention process built on "tender loving care" – TLC, as Dr Reddy calls it. Whether it is receptionists, ward boys, nurses or doctors, they will be treating patients, poor and rich, with these cardinal values. This is a difficult call but the staff at Apollo have taken it.'[7]

A few days later, in a conversation at his home in New Delhi, Union health minister Ghulam Nabi Azad told me that he had always been impressed by the emphasis that Dr Reddy put on the care and aftercare of Apollo patients. He said that he often had conversations with Dr Reddy about the issue of public–private partnerships in India's health care scenario. He said that compared to three decades ago, progress in health care had been significant.

Suresh Kochattil, a communications strategist who's been associated with Apollo in Hyderabad and who speaks widely on corporate performance, echoed that sentiment: 'To understand what Dr Reddy has done for India, look at the time he began. There was little health care technology in the country but he fought to be able to import key pieces of medical equipment. There was no quality service. Now, Indian hospitals led by Apollo achieve some of the highest results in the world, better even than those of famous hospitals

---

7 *Nurturing Leader* by Shrinivas Pandit, New Delhi: Tata McGraw-Hill, 2007.

in the West. Dr Reddy has extremely high standards. He brought in a culture of accountability to the Indian health care field. Before Reddy and Apollo, accountability didn't exist. People went to the hospital when they were unwell but they had no expectations of the kind of care that they would receive. The value proposition in health care was essentially created by Apollo.'[8]

Staff members at Apollo's competitors such as Fortis, Medanta and other institutions are also clearly mindful of the kind of system that Dr Prathap Chandra Reddy instituted. One day in mid-2012, I went to meet Shivinder Mohan Singh at the swanky new Fortis Hospital in Gurgaon, just outside New Delhi. Shivinder is managing director of Fortis Healthcare.

'There's no question that Dr Reddy has set a standard in India for health care and its delivery,' Shivinder said.

It is to the credit of Dr Reddy that such encomiums come unsolicited from several who are his business competitors.

A few months later, in February 2013, Shivinder and Malvinder turned up as invited guests at Dr Reddy's eightieth birthday celebrations in Chennai. I was seated right behind them, and I could see them listening intently to him as he spoke about Apollo's future and how there was so much more to be done to meet India's health care needs. I was next to Dr K.C. Mehta, the well-known orthopaedic surgeon at Apollo Ahmedabad, who had recently operated on Sucharitha Reddy's knees.

Dr Mehta and I looked at each other and smiled in silent agreement that no wonder Dr Reddy was considered the undisputed leader of health care in India.

---

8 Suresh Kochattil, formerly with the *Times of India*, advises Apollo on communications issues. He now also works with the Apollo Foundation.

CHAPTER THIRTEEN

Sucharitha

THE FAMILY IS AT the heart of everything that Dr Reddy does, and he is always very eloquent and expressive about his parents, wife, daughters and grandchildren.

I once asked him who his best friend was. It was a question whose answer I'd already guessed, but I wanted to hear it anyway from Dr Reddy.

'My wife Sucharitha,' he said. 'She is my best friend. I don't take any major decision without consulting her. I always trust her judgement.'

His daughter Sangita added: 'Our mother is the rock of the family, she's the nucleus. Her judgement is always on the mark.'

It was Sucharitha's judgement that had prompted Dr Reddy to leave behind a flourishing medical practice at Missouri State Chest Hospital in Springfield, and return home to India after he had received that life-changing letter from his father, Raghava Reddy, on 15 February 1969. When her husband informed her in 1978 that he wanted to develop Apollo Hospitals, it was Sucharitha who encouraged him, no matter what her private worries.

'For me, those were tense times,' Sucharitha Reddy told me. 'My husband is a man who's always trying to do something creative. And his ideas are often ahead of their time. But he would always share his thoughts with the family and in return invariably got our full support.'

Sucharitha Reddy is not as much an extrovert as her husband, and one gets the feeling that she doesn't like publicity. But on the several occasions that I saw her with Dr Reddy at public events, the impression I got was of an elegant couple who simply looked good – and comfortable – with each other. What also struck me was the effort she made to converse with everyone who'd greet her, and the smiles she left in her wake. What impresses most people is her genuine warmth. The amalgam of her regent upbringing and her innate humility is evident in her self-confidence. She is not overwhelming as a person, but deeply caring. There isn't a scintilla of condescension in her. She is as much at ease with the highest nobility as she is with the common man on the road.

Sucharitha Reddy is also known for going out of her way to look out for the well-being of everyday people in Chennai. One day in 1975, she was driving through the city when she spotted a young man pushing a cart loaded high with boxes. He worked for a hostel in Adyar, a neighbourhood in the southern part of the city. He was sweating heavily in the heat and humidity. Sucharitha asked her driver to stop, and offered the man a bottle of water. But she got the impression that he couldn't hear her.

The man's name was V. Ramaiah, and indeed he had a severe hearing problem; it was a condition that ran in his family, and his hearing had deteriorated during childhood to the point where he was virtually deaf. Sucharitha obtained his details, and asked him to come to HM Hospital, where Dr Reddy worked at the time. Dr Reddy then called a noted ENT specialist, Dr V.S. Subramaniam, to see if he could assist Ramaiah. Dr Subramaniam, who was affiliated with Lambert Clinic, said that he was booked up for three years.

However, within a few days, the ENT specialist called Dr Reddy and said that an opening had occurred and he would see Ramaiah. He operated on the right ear first, and then, six months later, on the other ear. He also prescribed a hearing device, which Ramaiah wears to this day.

Ramaiah is just one example. Hundreds like him have been

the beneficiaries of Sucharitha Reddy's passion to care for the less fortunate. In very many cases it has not been just temporary help but also a lifelong vocation.

Dr Reddy not only paid for Ramaiah's operations, but also hired him to work at HM Hospital. Later, when Apollo Madras opened in 1983, Ramaiah moved there to become an ECG technician. Now he's at Apollo Tondiarpet. 'I have never known anyone as generous as Dr and Mrs Reddy,' Ramaiah told me in Tamil, which his son Dinesh translated into English. 'Because of them I got my hearing back – and I got a lifetime job,' he said, adding that his colleague M. Mahalingam – also a veteran of Apollo – provided incalculable collegial help.

When I spoke to Mahalingam – who had joined HM Hospital in 1973 – he said that he has never got over the solicitude that Dr and Sucharitha Reddy have shown him. 'Their feelings are genuine,' Mahalingam said in translated Tamil. 'I have always been the beneficiary of their generosity and love. I am a simple man, but that doesn't matter to the Chairman and Mrs Reddy. In their eyes, everyone is equal, and everyone gets treated with equal respect and dignity.'

Another man who remains a steadfast admirer of the Reddys is Dr K.R. Gangadharan, director of the International Federation of Ageing, and founder of Heritage Hospitals in Hyderabad. He had been working as manager of industrial relations at Hindustan Motors in Madras when a recruiter from a placement agency suggested that he meet Dr Reddy, who was about to open Apollo Hospital in September 1983.

'I remember meeting Dr Reddy in the canteen of the hospital on a Sunday,' Gangadharan told me, noting that his encounter with the founder was just a couple of weeks before the formal opening of Apollo on 18 September.

It was a brief conversation, and Dr Reddy hired him to run the personnel department, since that's where Gangadharan's experience lay.

'From the moment I met Dr Reddy, he seemed an inspiring figure,'

Gangadharan said. 'There was charisma, certainly, but there was something more – an unusual ability to immediately get you to accept his vision for health care.'

He eventually rose to become a general manager for operations at Apollo Chennai.

Gangadharan was also impressed by the fact that Dr Reddy liked to encourage the hiring of women; he felt that qualified women needed to be given the right opportunities to make a contribution to the economy, especially in health care. Gangadharan hired a woman named Mary Ann Joseph in housekeeping services; but when he promoted her to be manager of that department on account of her outstanding performance, there was criticism from some quarters.

'Dr Reddy was completely supportive of my decision,' Gangadharan said. 'He trusted my judgement – which was borne out by the fact that Mary Ann proved to be a superb manager. That's among Dr Reddy's great qualities – he doesn't second-guess you. When he's satisfied that you've been doing a good job, he trusts you implicitly and explicitly.'

It is no coincidence that apart from Dr Reddy's daughters who are all managing their specific portfolios as members of the Board, many of the top managers in Apollo including a few CEOs are women who have proved to be highly efficient professionals.

'The Apollo experience was a defining one for me,' Gangadharan said. 'Dr Reddy and Mrs Reddy are peerless. I keep in touch with them, and it's as if all those years since I left Chennai for Hyderabad never happened. I will always feel part of the Apollo family – the Reddys make you feel very special.'

This 'making one feel special' experience was echoed by quite a lot of people. That a guest at the Reddy home would have to have something to eat and drink was taken for granted. But what was surprising was that the servants were asked to make sure that the driver of the guest too got something to eat. And if this happened to be around a regular mealtime, a full meal would be served. Sucharitha is also known throughout the Apollo family for bringing home-cooked meals for the staff.

Sucharitha Reddy's passion for serving the society goes much beyond the bounds of religion. For example, for years she has been cooking an elaborate lunch on Christmas day and serving it in the orphanage in a church at St Thomas Mount.

People who've known them from the day of their marriage, 1 February 1957, say that the couple always seemed 'made for each other'. That may well be the case, but Dr Reddy likes to joke that he married above himself. There's more than humour to that. Sucharitha Reddy, like Prathap Chandra Reddy, hails from Andhra Pradesh (she is from Nagulavancha in Khammam district). But Sucharitha's father, Sitaram Reddy, was a *deshmukh*, and considerably wealthy.[1] He and his wife Shakuntala had seven children (the same number as Raghava and Shakuntala Reddy). Sitaram Reddy died relatively young, and Sucharitha's mother and other relatives were responsible for her upbringing.

The cultural differences between the backgrounds of Sucharitha Reddy and Dr Prathap Chandra Reddy were significant. He's an 'Andhra Reddy', a Rayalaseema Reddy from Chittoor, which is closer to Bangalore than to Chennai, and has a salubrious climate. The Chittoor Reddys have traditionally emphasized education in their families. Chittoor used to be part of the old Madras state, run by the British. People were prone to factional fighting; feuds sometimes lasted generations. Chittoor has the famous Tirupati Temple, of course, and the Rishi Valley School, where admission is highly coveted.

Sucharitha comes from Khammam, which is in the Telangana

---

1 Deshmukh was a historical title given to a person who was granted a territory of land in certain regions of India, specifically Maharashtra, Andhra Pradesh and Karnataka. The deshmukh was in effect the ruler of the territory, as he was entitled to the collected taxes. It was also his duty to maintain the basic services in the territory, such as police and judicial duties. It was typically a hereditary system. The title of deshmukh provided the titled family with revenues from the area and the responsibility to keep the order. The deshmukh system was feudal, and was mostly abolished after India's independence in 1947.

part of Andhra Pradesh, and is economically more backward than Chittoor.[2] It's a predominantly forested district. Telangana was ceded to the British in 1840 by the Nizam of Hyderabad. Landlords in Telangana had large estates, and the culture was far more feudal than in Chittoor. Some estates in Telangana were heavily infused with the Hyderabadi Nizam culture. The men were raw-boned and hefty, yet exceedingly courteous; Reddy women from Telangana have traditionally been determined and strong-willed.

Sucharitha Reddy came from a far more privileged – and far wealthier – background than Prathap Chandra Reddy. She hails from a zamindar family from Nagulavancha. Zamindars were landlords and their mansions were generally large, spacious homes built of stone and teak wood, with a wraparound porch and rooms leading off from a large central courtyard, although this varied with the region. The mansion was a part of a vast estate as in the case of Nagulavancha where the walls around the mansion were fifty feet tall. The entrance into the mansion was by two huge gateways or doors. Each door required several personnel to open or close them.[3]

The Nagulavancha zamindars were known for their generosity and philanthropy. Today a school and junior college stand in their name. The ancestors also built a temple, which is used by all the villagers. The family owned cars and horses. There were several maids who tended to all the personal needs. All pulses, grains and vegetables and fruit were grown on the estate. Large kitchens equipped with three cooks served meals for all the workers and inmates, which was up to fifty members for each meal. Food was an important tradition of the daily routine and the family strongly believed that the way to the heart is through the mouth. But it didn't stop with that; they also believed that offering food to the hungry was the best service one could render.

Besides her younger sisters Vijayalakshmi and Veena, Sucharitha

---

2   Telangana supporters want it to be India's twenty-ninth state.
3   During a visit to Khammam, Prime Minister Indira Gandhi stayed at Sucharitha Reddy's ancestral home.

has an older sister Hemalatha, who lives in Hyderabad. Her brother Narendra lives in the United States, as do Vijayalakshmi and Veena. Another brother, Upender, is based in Hyderabad and has his own security firm. A third brother, Surender, was president of Apollo Hyderabad until his death in 2010.

'I know my aunt as the most generous and loving individual I have ever come across,' one of Sucharitha's nieces, Lakshmi, says. 'It is this love and affection that I strongly believe is the cause of us coming together as one strong family with rich cultures and values. Whether it is the religious values or a sense of deep affection, the roots come from my aunt.'

Sucharitha Reddy herself told me that she strongly believes in the 'supernatural power of prayer'. When the ground was broken for Apollo Madras, there were reports that a snake had been seen. It was Sucharitha who insisted that the Krishna Mariammian temple that was built on the grounds should have an open pit where such a snake would always find a dish of milk at night. The priests at the temple told me that they often find the dish empty in the morning.[4]

Sucharitha is well versed in the ancient scriptures, and knows Sanskrit, the language in which most Hindu rituals are conducted. For pujas at their homes, Sucharitha invites Brahmin priests from Tamil Nadu, Karnataka, Kerala and, of course, Andhra Pradesh.

'What are your favourite temples?' I asked Sucharitha.

She smiled sweetly. 'You'd have to fill three or four pages of your notebook if I started giving you the names,' she said. But besides Tirupati and the temples of Trichy, she cited Muktinath, a Vaishnavite temple in the Himalayas, and the Varadarajaswamy temple in Kanchipuram. Sucharitha said that she'd visited all of the 106 Vaishnavite temples – in fact, she and Dr Reddy had to take a helicopter to go to Muktinath

---

4   In Hindu mythology, the snake primarily represents rebirth, death and mortality, due to its casting off its skin and being symbolically 'reborn'. Over a large part of India there are carved representations of cobras or *naga*s, or stones as substitutes. To these food and flowers are offered and lamps are burned before the shrines.

because of the treacherous terrain. 'The trip took two hours each way, and the passengers were so scared,' Sucharitha said.

An intriguing question is: how was it that Sucharitha and Prathap married across this cultural and geographical divide?

Like her siblings, Sucharitha Reddy received her early education from tutors who came to their big family home. But when she was eight years old, it was decided that Sucharitha should attend St Ann's Convent in Hyderabad, which was about 200 kilometres from Khammam.

'I felt that I was in a different world from my village,' Sucharitha told me about St Ann's. 'That's where I got to learn about Christianity. That's where I learned that all faiths should be respected.'

She was to stay at St Ann's for only three years. The agitation over whether the Nizam of Hyderabad would agree to join the newly formed independent country of India worried Sucharitha's family. Sucharitha joined a school in Madras started by Durgabai Deshmukh, a prominent social activist, and run by the Andhra Mahila Sabha. Sucharitha still recalls that both Durgabai Deshmukh and the school principal, a woman named Jamunabai, were strict disciplinarians. She recalls that students lined up in a guard of honour whenever political leaders such as Jawaharlal Nehru, Sardar Vallabbhai Patel, Sarojini Naidu, Rajkumari Amrit Kaur and Rajendra Prasad visited the school. They had all been colleagues of Durgabai Deshmukh during India's freedom struggle.[5]

By the time Sucharitha turned eighteen, her mother felt that it was time for her to get married. The daughter had already enrolled in a women's college that was located on the grounds of one of the Nizam's seventeen palaces in Hyderabad.[6] The classrooms

---

5 Durgabai Deshmukh's husband, C.D. Deshmukh, served as finance minister in the government of Prime Minister Jawaharlal Nehru.

6 Nizam-ul-Mulk was the title of the native sovereigns of Hyderabad state (now divided into the states of Andhra Pradesh, Karnataka and Maharashtra on a linguistic basis) since 1724, belonging to the Asaf Jah dynasty. Seven Nizams ruled Hyderabad over two centuries until Indian independence in 1947. The Asaf Jahi rulers were great patrons of literature, art, architecture, culture, jewellery and rich food.

were big, [7]and Sucharitha recalls that the gardener was especially attentive to ensuring that the large lawns and flowerbeds were maintained well. The fragrance of jasmine permeated the college. Because it was a women's college, a 'purdah' system was followed. That meant any time a car drove up and male visitors got out, two women would shield the college students with a large silk cloth that they held in front of them. 'We called the college "the dungeon",' Sucharitha says, more in humour than anything else. All the while, her mother Shakuntala was searching for a suitable husband for her daughter.

'In those days they never told us anything about such efforts,' Sucharitha says.

It turned out that a maternal uncle, Manmohan Reddy, had come to know Prathap Chandra Reddy through mutual friends. Prathap was in his final year at Stanley Medical College in Madras then. Manmohan Reddy brought Prathap to Hyderabad. It was all a plot to get him to meet Sucharitha.

Given his acuity, it's difficult to believe that Prathap didn't figure out that something was afoot. He was, after all, considered highly eligible. 'He cut a dashing figure,' Sucharitha's younger sister Vijayalakshmi told me during a conversation in Chennai. 'Prathap always dressed well. He was tall, and he projected energy. It would be fair to say that parents of many girls of marriageable age were interested in him.'

On the day that Prathap came to Hyderabad, Hemalatha Reddy – who was Sucharitha's older sister – said to Sucharitha, 'Let's go see a film.'

Any opportunity to leave the college precincts was always welcome. So Sucharitha went with her sister to a movie hall, Lakdi Ka Pul.[8] Audiences used to be segregated in those days, and Prathap didn't actually get to meet Sucharitha. It was only during

---

7 The building had been used as a residency at one point during the British Raj.

8 The movie hall still exists in Hyderabad, although it's been considerably modernized since the time that Sucharitha Reddy was at college.

the intermission of the highly acclaimed film, *Tenali Ramakrishna*, that Prathap actually got a glimpse of his future bride.[9] She was descending a staircase, and he saw her reflection in an ornate mirror. He thought, 'She is very beautiful, like a princess.'

The next day, Kishen Reddy – Hemalatha's husband – and Prathap drove up to Sucharitha's college in an Austin car. Sucharitha says that she was surprised that Kishen came, but that she was too shy to ask why. The ride lasted barely fifteen minutes. Sucharitha wore a starched cotton coloured sari. She and Prathap talked briefly, and Kishen asked Prathap about his family in Aragonda.

'That's when I suspected that something was going on,' Sucharitha Reddy told me.

When the men dropped Sucharitha off, Prathap handed over a magazine produced by Stanley Medical College. He had contributed an article to it, and the magazine had published a picture of him.

Her sister Vijayalakshmi, who read the article along with Sucharitha, immediately started teasing her: 'You saw the boy, you saw the boy!'

That was in August 1956. No one had asked Sucharitha's opinion of Prathap, nor did she volunteer it. After that, unbeknownst to her, members of her family and those of Prathap's started exchanging visits. Sucharitha's family dispatched two estate managers to check out Prathap's family and their status in Aragonda. The men gave a highly positive report to Sucharitha's mother, Shakuntala.

The marriage ceremony was fixed for 1 February 1957.[10] Between

---

9 *Tenali Ramakrishna* was a 1956 Telugu and Tamil bilingual film based on the story of Tenali, court-poet of Sri Krishna Deva Raya, emperor of the Vijayanagara Empire. The film was produced and directed by B.S. Ranga, and N.T. Rama Rao played the role of the emperor. Another friend of Prathap's, A. Nageshwara Rao, played the role of Tenali. The film was based on a play written by C.K. Venkataramaiah, also a friend of Prathap Chandra Reddy's.

10 The marriage rituals of the Reddys commence with a promise made by the two families to each other that a wedding will be honoured. After speaking with an astrologer, a particular day and time are arranged for the marriage

the times that Sucharitha and Prathap had first met and their wedding, they hadn't had the chance to speak to each other. 'He sent me a greeting card for New Year's Day 1957,' Sucharitha recalls.

But she received visits from several of Prathap's relatives and friends, including his cousin Pavana. 'It's customary for families in our community to send emissaries to meet the prospective bride and bridegroom,' Sucharitha says. 'And it's all taken in good spirit. Everybody is welcomed warmly.'

Reddy weddings typically lasted at least seven days during those years. But Sucharitha says that her marriage went on for just about three days.

'And even that was a strain for me,' she says. 'I wasn't used to so many people. Thousands of villagers from all over Khammam came for the festivities.'

One day, not long after the wedding, Sucharitha asked her husband, who was six years older than her, 'How come you never married a doctor?'

Prathap replied, 'I never wanted to.'

When Sucharitha went to her in-laws' home in Aragonda for the first time, they fussed over her. Prathap's uncles and aunts engaged her in conversation, and made sure that she was always well looked after.

'They made me feel very much at home, they were all very affectionate,' she recalls. 'Prathap's father was extremely sweet to me. His mother gave me lots of bangles – she herself was very fond of bangles.'[11]

---

ceremony and both parties generate written contracts. These contracts are then put in yellow cloth bundles along with betel nuts, turmeric, fruits and betel leaf. These in turn are blessed by an officiating pujari. A Telugu marriage comprises ceremonies, rituals and rites that are filled with symbolism and rich meaning. These are conducted in a similar way to most Hindu marriage rites, with a stress on spirituality. The wife has an esteemed position in all the ceremonies. Source: The Reddy Society.

11 Bangles are one of the most important ornaments that an Indian woman wears. For married women, bangles are considered a significant sign of their 'suhaag'. They are thought to bring good fortune and sound health for the husband.

The cuisine in Aragonda was different from that of Khammam: it was heavily influenced by the proximity of Tamil Nadu. But Sucharitha never had any problems with Chittoor food, which was significantly less spicy than that of her own region. And as always, her attire reflected her background and upbringing: Sucharitha wore jewellery, and starched cotton coloured saris. She had a regal presence, even though she was still a teenager. She looked and moved like the princess that Prathap thought she was when he first caught a glimpse of her in that mirror in the Hyderabad movie theatre.

But in Madras, where she and Prathap shared a small apartment in the Adyar neighbourhood, life wasn't as comfortable. For one, Sucharitha did not know how to cook. In fact, she didn't cook for her family until 1963, when the Reddys, now parents of four daughters, moved to Worcester, Massachusetts.[12]

'Prathap was such a good person to put up with this,' Sucharitha Reddy told me, alluding to the fact that Dr Reddy loved hearty meals that, at the time, he didn't necessarily get at home.

He had started his internship at Madras General Hospital, and therefore needed to spend a lot of his time with patients. Sucharitha's mother would visit her from time to time, and provided the couple with a cook, and also an ayah, or nanny, after Preetha was born in Hyderabad on 28 October 1957. 'The presence of the cook and the ayah made it easy for me,' Sucharitha says.

Her three other daughters – Suneeta, Shobana and Sangita – arrived in the next five years.

And less than a year after the youngest daughter, Sangita, was born on 8 July 1962, Dr Prathap Chandra Reddy would leave for Britain to pursue postgraduate studies. Neither he nor Sucharitha had been abroad before, and the couple knew that they were going to have wholly alien experiences.

---

12 In time, Sucharitha Reddy would go on to write acclaimed cookbooks. *Nostalgia Cuisine*, which contains recipes from Telangana, went through several printings. Her latest book, *Joyful Cuisine*, is scheduled for publication in 2013.

In effect – although neither Dr Prathap Chandra Reddy nor Sucharitha knew it at the time – that journey abroad to Britain and then to the United States was the genesis of the Apollo story. In time, the story would propel Dr Reddy to global fame and certainly make him and Apollo household names in India. In time, Dr Reddy would be hailed and applauded by his countrymen for changing the health care landscape of India by introducing and strengthening the corporate health care sector. In time, Sucharitha Reddy would be widely known for her extraordinary hospitality, her authorship of cookbooks, and for the exquisite way in which she raised her daughters, each of whom is a recognized leader not only at Apollo but also in the medical industry.

But in the year of that journey, 1963, the Reddys could not have possibly seen that far into the future.

CHAPTER FOURTEEN

London Spring

WHEN DR PRATHAP CHANDRA REDDY left for London for postgraduate studies[1] on 2 March 1963, Sucharitha Reddy stayed behind in Madras

---

1 In all developed countries, entry-level medical education programmes are tertiary-level courses, undertaken at a medical school attached to a university. Depending on the university, entry may follow directly from secondary school or require pre-requisite undergraduate education. Programmes that require previous undergraduate education (typically a three- or four-year degree, often in science) are usually four or five years in length. Hence, gaining a basic medical degree may typically take from five to eight years, depending on jurisdiction and university. Following completion of entry-level training, newly graduated medical practitioners are often required to undertake a period of supervised practice before full registration is granted, typically for one or two years. This is referred to as an 'internship'. Speciality training usually begins immediately following completion of entry-level training. Hence, a physician often does not achieve recognition as a specialist until twelve or more years after commencing basic medical training—five to eight years at university to obtain a basic medical qualification, and up to another nine years to become a specialist. Dr Reddy already possessed an MBBS degree from Stanley Medical College, and had nearly six years of residency at various institutions, including Madras General Hospital. Although he travelled to London for 'postgraduate studies', he was, in effect, going for yet another residency. He did not become a specialist in cardiology until some years later when he was practicing in the United States.

to ensure their four daughters were looked after until such a time that they could join their parents. There were plenty of Reddy relatives in and near Madras – including Sucharitha's sisters – and both Kumara Raja and Kumara Rani Muthiah Chettiar also made the necessary arrangements for the well-being of the girls.

Dr Reddy flew by Air India in a Boeing 707, in those days perceived as one of the most modern commercial airliners. In London he booked himself at the Savoy, a grand Edwardian building. He had heard a great deal about London's most famous hotel, one that opened for business in 1889. Monet and Whistler painted the city from their rooms here, and Chaplin and Astaire practiced their acts on the hotel roof. Dr Reddy hadn't known that a room at the Savoy would cost him £10 a night.

He hadn't expected to pay this sort of tariff. So after spending a night at the Savoy, he moved to the YMCA International, where he was required to pay only one bob[2] a night, breakfast included. But he discovered after returning to the facility after a short walk that £70 had been stolen from his wallet. He called a family friend, a tobacco trader, who came across a couple of days later and gave him £100. (That money actually came from Narasimha Reddy back home in Aragonda; through Narasimha, Raghava Reddy had made sure that his son wouldn't be lacking for money while abroad.)

When Dr Reddy reported the theft to the police, they grilled him in such a manner that he was made to feel as though he'd purloined his own money. The police even kept back his Indian passport. The thief was never caught; the robbery was almost surely an inside job.

What to do now? He called his classmate from Stanley Medical College, Dr Kripamayi, and her husband Veera Reddy, also a physician. They lived in Birmingham.

'Don't move,' Kripamayi told Prathap. 'Wait for fifteen minutes, then go to a bank that's opposite the YMCA. There's only one bank in that locality. We have an account in that bank. They will give you

---

2 'Bob' was the slang for a shilling. Twenty shillings made a pound.

some money. Then take a train to Birmingham. But you will have to produce your passport.'

Dr Reddy thought to himself, 'Passport? What passport?' The London police had retained it. So he spoke to the officers and explained that he needed his passport in order to collect funds from the nearby bank. They seemed to balk, which irritated Prathap: he hadn't eaten all day. But eventually the police returned Dr Reddy's passport.

After collecting some £50 from the bank – where officials were more polite than the policemen, but only just – Dr Reddy went to the Euston train station and caught a train to Birmingham. The journey took about two hours, and Prathap was delighted at being reunited with his friends.[3]

He spent the weekend in Birmingham, enjoying their company and wolfing down home-cooked dishes from his native Andhra Pradesh. Then early on Monday morning, Dr Reddy took a train back to London and reported to Guy's Hospital. He carried with him a reference letter given by a noted orthopedic surgeon and leprosy specialist at Christian Medical College in Vellore, Dr Paul Brand. He also carried a letter that Dr Brand had given for Dr Sheila Sherlock, a noted liver specialist.[4] Dr Reddy met with the superintendent at Guy's Hospital.[5] For a weekly salary of £7, he would be made *locum registrar* on a short-term basis. This meant that Dr Reddy was always on call.

---

3 At Stanley Medical College, Prathap Chandra Reddy and his closest friends were known as the 'Reddy Gang'. In addition to Prathap, there was Kripamayi, Krishna Kumari, Padmanabhan, Dante Mathuranayagam, Venkataswami, Arcot Gajaraj and Parthasarathy.

4 When Dr Sherlock started her medical career, little was known about liver disease. Her work helped establish hepatology as a medical speciality. In years to come, doctors at Apollo Hospitals would often consult Dr Sherlock's research on liver disease.

5 Thomas Guy, a publisher of unlicensed Bibles who had made a fortune in the South Sea Bubble, founded the hospital in 1721. It was originally established as a hospital to treat incurables discharged from St Thomas's Hospital. Guy's Hospital has expanded over the centuries.

He was given a dingy one-room apartment in the hospital complex. When he informed the authorities that his wife would be joining him soon, one official said to Dr Reddy: 'If you are lucky, we will allot you two rooms.' But there was no charge for the accommodations, or for the food.

He quickly made friends among Britons and Indians alike. Some of the Indian doctors he'd met then would later become investors in Apollo. Dr Reddy has a phenomenal memory, and he rarely forgets names and faces. Surely he was making mental notes on everyone he met. Many of the friendships he made in Britain endure to this day. He also quickly picked up the ins and outs of the institution's procedures. Dr Reddy had been transferred to St Olave's Hospital within weeks of joining Guy's Hospital because St Olave's needed more doctors on constant call.[6] His physician-friends of Indian origin shared their experiences with him, noting that there was an implicit bias against people of colour in British society. An attitudinal hangover from the British Raj?

Dr Reddy himself experienced no such bias. Perhaps his gregariousness and curiosity about other people insulated him from cultural resistance. One friend, an Irishman named Dr Richard O'Donohue, would accompany him to a nearby pub where they'd guzzle warm English beer. (Of Dr O'Donohue in Britain and Dr David Gorelick in the United States – whom he was to meet later in Springfield, Missouri – Dr Reddy says that they were outstanding friends, the kind that lift you up and ones you want to keep always.) Dr Reddy and Dr O'Donohue also went to greyhound races, including those at Hackney Wick Stadium. Did he bet? Did he win? Dr Reddy smiles at such questions. 'Yes, we did bet. But I recall losing twenty or thirty pounds at those races.' His uncle Narasimha Reddy would send his nephew money regularly – perhaps a total of £100 between March and the end of June 1963, a not inconsiderable sum in those days – but it's doubtful that the strict disciplinarian would have

---

6 St Olave's Hospital was a general hospital serving the Rotherhithe area of London until its closure in 1985.

continued subsidizing his nephew had he known that Prathap would wager some of that money at races.

Meanwhile, Dr Reddy saw that several Indian doctors at Guy's Hospital and at St Olave's were studying for an entrance examination that would get them into a hospital in the United States. Some of them told disheartening stories about how strict the American exams were, and how they had repeatedly failed.

Then one day Dr Reddy remembered that he had applied for that very exam while he was still in Madras. And so he sent a telegram to the examination authorities; they were based in Philadelphia. He wanted to know if he'd been accepted for the exam.

He received a telegram back saying that he was indeed registered for the US examination. They had, they said, been trying to get hold of him in Madras. He was instructed to take the telegram to the exam and it would serve as his 'entrance hall ticket'.

Dr Reddy sat for the exam and received another telegram saying that he had passed. Later on, he received a letter about his appointment at Worcester City Hospital, one of several that had been interested in him. He took both the letter and the telegram when he applied for his visa at the United States Embassy in Grosvenor Square. He recalls being impressed by the building, which was designed by the Finnish-American modernist architect, Eero Saarinen, and by the large gilded aluminium 'Bald Eagle' by Theodore Roszak, which had a wingspan of 10 metres. The letter and telegram were both needed because it was customary for visas to be granted only in one's home country but Prathap was in London and not in India. An exception was made for him and his visa was granted.

He was anxious to convey the news to his wife. Prathap Chandra Reddy missed Sucharitha, and he certainly missed his daughters. He would call them as often as he could, but international calls weren't easy to make in those days, and connections would be frequently cut off. He counted the days until her scheduled arrival towards the end of April.

When Sucharitha Reddy arrived in London, Dr Reddy's friends and colleagues immediately noticed how his spirits perked up.

They also noticed how elegant the couple looked – Prathap in his suit, always with a neatly knotted tie, and Sucharitha always in exquisite cotton saris. They also noted that Sucharitha loved going to the theatre, but that she usually went by herself: Dr Reddy was constantly required at the hospital. He went for one play, a musical in London's West End.

Prathap Chandra Reddy and Sucharitha began preparing to travel to the United States. Raghava Reddy had arranged for tickets on an Air India flight to New York from London. Dr Reddy worked at the hospital until the last day of his contract.

On 2 July 1963, two days before the US Independence Day, the Reddys arrived in America.

'I was only looking forward to expanding my professional horizons,' Dr Reddy told me years later. 'After all, America was where all the leading-edge research in medicine was being mostly done. I also had the self-confidence that I possessed the skills that would serve me well in American hospitals. Sucharitha and I were looking forward to making new friends. We also felt that the American experience would be good for our small daughters – it would expose them to new people and new cultures. And an American education would help them later in life.'

But life takes strange and unexpected turns. Exactly twenty years later, on Independence Day, 1983, Dr Reddy would visit America to meet with doctors of Indian origin who lived there to assure them that the institution in which they had each invested between $5,000 and $10,000 would formally be opened on 18 September that year.

As he watched the Independence Day fireworks in Springfield, Missouri – where he had worked, among other places – that summer evening in 1983, Prathap Chandra Reddy could scarcely contain his elation. It seemed to him that the imminent opening of Apollo Hospitals was being celebrated. And, really, of course it was.

CHAPTER FIFTEEN

Coming to America

THE AIR INDIA FLIGHT that Prathap Chandra and Sucharitha Reddy had boarded in London landed at New York's Idlewild airport on a sunny afternoon on 2 July 1963.[1] During the seven-hour flight, Sucharitha kept talking about their four daughters, and how she wished they'd been with them on the flight. She wondered aloud how the girls would have liked the flight: 'Would they be restless? It's such a long flight. Would they have been happy? Would they try to run up and down the aisles?'

'Well, we're in mid-air right now, so I can't see how our girls can join us,' Dr Reddy said, in a humorous attempt to allay his wife's anxiety.

The Reddys found the international arrivals terminal in New York almost as chaotic as the airport in Madras, and a startling contrast to London's Heathrow airport where things seemed to be well organized.

'Welcome to the United States,' an immigration officer said to them, after stamping their passports. He cast an appreciative glance

---

1 Dedicated as New York International Airport in 1948, the airport was more commonly known as Idlewild Airport until 1964, when it was renamed after John Fitzgerald Kennedy, the thirty-fifth president of the United States, who was assassinated on 22 November 1963.

at Sucharitha's sari. Indian visitors to America were still a rarity in those days, and women in saris were rarer still.

Outside the customs enclosure, a man carrying a placard was waiting for the Reddys. The hand-painted sign bore their names. He was a local travel agent who Worcester City Hospital had arranged to pick them up. He got them and their luggage into a van and drove into Manhattan's Port Authority Terminal on West 42nd Street where he put them on board a bus for Worcester. He asked if they had money for the bus tickets and Dr Reddy said, 'Yes, we have.' Nevertheless, the man gave him the $10 the hospital had sent for their transportation.

The Reddys had wanted to spend a day or two in New York to take in the sights, but the hospital officials did not consider that possibility for the young couple. In any case, the hospital wanted Dr Reddy to begin as soon as possible. About the only glimpse they got of the great metropolis was of the Empire State Building as they were being driven to the bus station.

Both Prathap and Sucharitha were filled with joy. They were in America, a land of hope and dreams and one of which they had heard so much about. Except for missing their daughters and other family members, they looked on their trip as a bright, new adventure and both were very excited.

The bus stopped for the passengers to have a meal at a Howard Johnson's and they got their first glimpse of hot dogs. Sucharitha had only the French fries.

The couple was also impressed by the highway system that linked New York to Worcester; the 300-km journey took about four hours. Dr Reddy did not realize it at the time, but in a few years he would be practicing medicine at Boston's Massachusetts General Hospital, one of the most famous medical institutions in the world. He could not have possibly anticipated that a few years after that, some of the top surgeons at Mass General would visit the institution that Dr Reddy created in 1983, Apollo Hospitals.

As they rode in the bus towards Worcester, Prathap Chandra Reddy felt what he later termed a 'lurking tension, despite our elation at being in America'. That was, of course, natural: he had never been to America, a land renowned for its leading-edge research in medicine, and for its hi-tech hospitals. Would he be up to the task? That's when his innate self-confidence kicked in. Of course he would do well. He rationalized to himself that he did not have to face any examination, nor an interview. He already had a job. 'We are in this giant island called America,' he thought to himself. 'We are going to make the best of it.'

The day after arriving in Worcester was free for Dr Reddy; the hospital gave him a day to get settled. The day after, a Thursday, was 4 July, Independence Day, but Dr Reddy had to work even though it was a national holiday.

When the Reddys arrived in Worcester, they were pleasantly surprised to find that the hospital had allotted them a three-bedroom apartment in a two-storey house. They were given the ground floor, with a patch of green in front and a slightly larger lawn at the back. The Reddy family loved the backyard and later planted tomatoes that were so abundant they could not eat them all. They shared them with neighbours, friends and colleagues at the hospital. They cared for the rose bushes that Sucharitha had planted, and also planted other flowers of their own choosing, carefully placing the seeds in the ground, watering and grooming them. The colours were usually bright, reminding them of home in India and chosen at random by looking at the pictures on the front of the seed packets.

A couple of days after they'd arrived in Worcester, Prathap Chandra Reddy and Sucharitha went to a grocery store in their neighbourhood to buy supplies for their home. They ran into a woman named Mrs Knight.

'You're new here,' the woman said. 'Welcome to Worcester! You are going to like it here.'

Mrs Knight turned out to be a social worker. She began inviting the Reddys to her home, and it was through Mrs Knight that the newcomers started making friends. Sucharitha and Mrs Knight became very close. Sucharitha also became close friends with another woman named Mrs Stoddard, and with the wife of a Pakistani doctor at Worcester City Hospital. When Prathap Chandra Reddy first met Mrs Knight he was surprised that she knew all about the children and was eager to meet them.

The Reddys were a curiosity in Worcester. There were very few South Asians in the area at the time.

'People asked about our families,' Sucharitha recalled. 'They seemed fascinated that ours had been an arranged marriage. They were also surprised at how well we adjusted to life in America.' Occasionally someone would ask about Sucharitha's bindi with curiosity.

'Is that a bloodstain on your head?' one woman asked Sucharitha, who patiently explained the significance of the bindi.

There were also questions about Indian culture, a subject that Sucharitha loved to discuss.

At that point in her life, Sucharitha Reddy did not know how to cook or how to drive. She resolved to learn both.

'I started with dal and rice,' Sucharitha told me. 'Even today, my husband teases me that my hand was abundant.' She learned by trial and error, and in time she became a great cook. Soon, neighbourhood children would make a beeline for the Reddy home because among the Indian dishes she made were gulab jamuns.

When asked for his opinion about her cooking, Prathap Chandra Reddy would encourage Sucharitha by saying, 'Good, but could be better.' (This is the same mantra he uses at Apollo, ever striving for excellence.) He actually was a fussy eater, and therefore quite difficult to cook for. He acknowledges that people would 'tremble' at his sometimes petulant behaviour at home in reaction to a dish he didn't like. On a trip to the store one day, he bought his wife an apron with a bib and said, 'Wear it or you will stain your saris.'

As Sucharitha developed her culinary skills, she wished that her daughters were there with her so that she could feed them.

'Oh my God, I missed them so much,' Sucharitha Reddy told me. Suneeta and Shobana came to Massachusetts in 1964, and Preetha and Sangita in 1965. 'I spoiled them,' Sucharitha said. 'But they were all good girls, and we wanted the best for them.'

Suneeta and Shobana arrived in the US in December 1964 and Dr and Mrs Reddy drove to JFK airport to meet them. The stewardess escorted the girls off the plane to be greeted by their parents but the girls would not look at them, especially not at Dr Reddy. They were angry at having been left behind in India, and full of anxiety themselves, even though they were not able to describe their feelings in such a fashion. When the girls showed no reaction to the parents, the stewardess thought that they did not recognize them and repeatedly said, 'These are your parents. This is your dad.' After some time in the car and extra cuddling, the girls warmed up and the ride home to Worcester turned out to be joyful and fun.

Daughters in tow, Dr Reddy first stopped off at the emergency room of Worcester City Hospital to see how things were. Struck by the cool temperatures in America, the family joke used to be that the whole country was air conditioned.

And then when they reached home, the parents and girls were greeted with a wonderful surprise: their friends, including Mrs Knight and Mrs Stoddard, and the upstairs neighbours, had decorated the outside of the Reddy house with Christmas lights. The inside of the house was decorated with a Christmas tree and lights and other holiday decorations. They had even thought of gifts for the girls and gave each a doll and some ice skates that they could use on rinks, or even outdoors if they could brave the winter.

As word spread about Sucharitha's culinary talents, local residents started to invite the Reddys over. The expectation was that the guests would bring along some Indian dish, and the hosts were rarely disappointed. These friends seemed intrigued by the fact that Sucharitha always wore saris, never Western attire. Sucharitha started to offer cooking classes for the women of Worcester.

'My husband made friends very easily – he had a natural talent,' Sucharitha said. 'He was full of life. He would play cards, and he would go to the races up in New Hampshire's Rockingham Park. I was pleased that he quickly developed his own circle of friends.'

Sucharitha Reddy was less pleased that her husband continued to smoke. She herself was – and remains – a teetotaller and non-smoker. Whenever she complained about his smoking habits, Dr Reddy would say, 'I will stop, Sucha, don't worry.'

He did stop for two years but when a tornado caused much destruction he stopped at the local store, bought a pack of cigarettes and started smoking again. It wasn't until well after the Reddys returned home to India in 1970 that Prathap Chandra Reddy finally quit smoking for good: in fact, he gave up cigarettes in 1982, the year before the first Apollo hospital opened in Madras.

It was her husband who taught Sucharitha how to drive. They'd bought a second-hand grey Dodge. The sign in the window at the dealership read, 'Own this car for $30'.

Dr Reddy went in and asked, 'What does this mean?'

The representative from a local bank who occupied a seat at the dealership said, 'What do you do?'

'I'm a doctor,' Prathap Chandra Reddy said.

'Where?'

'Worcester City Hospital.'

'How much do you make?'

'$700 a week.'

'Go home, go to work and come back tomorrow afternoon.'

This would be Prathap's first background and credit check. When he came the next day, Dr Reddy was told, 'You don't have to pay the $30, remit just $10 per month.'

And so it was that the Reddy family had a 'new, old car', as Dr Reddy puts it. Later they purchased a dark green Ford Galaxy when the old Dodge gave out after a trip to Niagara Falls.

'Dad and Mom had taken us to see *The Sound of Music*,' Shobana recalls. 'I helped pick out our first new car, that dark green Ford Galaxy. When we sold it before returning to India, we had gone to see the movie *The Love Bug*. That night we went back to the car lot to say goodbye to the car again.'

Sucharitha picked up driving in three days. On the fourth day, she passed her driving test and became the proud possessor of a

Massachusetts driving license.[2]

She also began to learn about computers, which were extremely basic in those days; Sucharitha says that she became quite proficient in typing and handling correspondence. 'I was bored, and had a lot of time on my hands,' she says.

Sucharitha applied for work at a local bank, and obtained a job that paid $2.50 an hour. It was to be her first and last job ever.

'My husband never asked me how much I earned – but everything I made would be spent on the children,' Sucharitha told me.

She would return home around 8 o'clock in the evening, when Dr Reddy would return as well from Worcester City Hospital.

At the hospital, Dr Reddy displayed his typical frenzied dedication to work. 'I had thoughts about how different the Western world would be,' he told me, 'and I was right. There was a whole range of new innovation, technology. I was not startled but I would use the term that I was not let down. I was impressed by the use of the latest equipment, and the facilities were good.'

Occasionally Dr Reddy would have disagreements with officials at Worcester City Hospital. Just after he was designated as chief resident but before assuming the position, he fought with the administration to let them set up an intensive care unit (ICU) but they didn't agree on the grounds that there was no money available. Dr Reddy had seen an ICU at Mass General and knew that ICUs were literally lifesavers. One day the city commissioner's brother-in-law needed intensive care after a major heart attack. He died due to the lack of ICU facilities.

When local newspapers asked the reason for his death, Dr Reddy said that if the hospital had had an ICU they could have saved the brother-in-law. An ICU could have given them the opportunity to defibrillate the heart, provide adequate monitoring and better medical dosage. His statement made quite a splash, and within a month the hospital installed six beds in a brand new ICU unit. Two doctors –

---

2 In later years, Sucharitha Reddy would even drive in India, where every ride was a challenge on account of the clangourous conditions and the total disregard of Indians for road discipline.

including Dr Reddy – and three nurses spent three days for special training in ICU procedures at Mass General. Years later, Dr Reddy would recall that the episode convinced him to become a cardiologist.

Dr Reddy also engendered other innovations at the hospital. He would conduct mock drills for doctors. He would make frequent inspections of in-patient wards. He even paid close attention to the hospital's billing procedures.

But Prathap Chandra Reddy was already yearning for bigger responsibilities, even though he had been made chief resident at Worcester City Hospital. The custom was that residents had to move out, either into a fellowship or a speciality programme, or set up their own practice after a certain period of service.

Clearly, the time had come to make a move for an ambitious man like Dr Reddy – and he was determined to make that move. Indeed, to say that Dr Reddy has a strong personality is an understatement. He is not what Americans call a 'glad hander', with loud laughter and bright, eager handshakes empty of meaning. He does, however, have a presence. It precedes him wherever he is and lingers after his departure. While he's typically gregarious, Dr Reddy also projects a quiet dignity. He would never, for example, thump people on their backs. A pat of appreciation, maybe, but nothing that would make the recipient wince.

He's quite firm in his opinions and ideas but certainly open to suggestions and well-thought-out proposals. He was that way at home, too. Sucharitha Reddy told me that although her husband was a strict disciplinarian he could be persuaded to a different point of view.

Dr Reddy commands the room and is not shy about expressing his opinion or reacting to that of another. Recalling their time in the United States, Sucharitha said that occasionally when something had not gone the way he wanted, Dr Reddy could be quite challenging.

'His eyes flash and he roars his disapproval. When he does this I call him the "lion king", as he stalks through his territory. Everyone trembles and then, just as suddenly, peace returns to the forest,' Sucharitha said.

The daughters agree and wonder if perhaps he was indulged as a youth. Shobana says, 'Mom has always been very patient with him but I am sure there would have been times when she might have wanted to roar back. Of course I cannot imagine her or anybody else attempting to do that.' And Suneeta adds, 'Yes, this is very like Dad. Of course, if his roars are at the hospitals or about health care, they don't so easily subside. Everyone definitely pays attention.'

Everyone in the Reddys' circle in Worcester started to pay attention to where Dr Prathap Chandra Reddy might go next. But they were certain of three things: he would land himself a good position; he would make his mark at a new hospital in short order; and that Sucharitha Reddy and her daughters would become immensely popular in their new community. That was the kind of perception that people had of the 'lion king' and his pride.

CHAPTER SIXTEEN

From Massachusetts to Missouri

BUT WHERE TO MOVE TO? Worcester City Hospital, after all, had offered Dr Prathap Chandra Reddy his first opportunity to practice medicine in the United States. He had been made chief resident in 1964, just about a year after arriving in America. Being at the hospital had opened doors to all sorts of friendships in medicine and beyond.

The people of Worcester had welcomed him and Sucharitha without reservations. The Reddys had become especially close to a dentist, Dr Louis Angelo Ricciardelli, and his wife Josephine, both of Italian descent.[1] They enjoyed Josephine's cooking so much that, as Dr Reddy would tell me years later, 'I was never again able to go to an Italian restaurant because I always remembered Jo's cooking.'

Still, Dr Reddy had crossed thirty, he was ambitious, and he was anxious to expand his medical experience. The residency period at Worcester City Hospital would soon end. There was the possibility of joining St Vincent's Hospital, which was also in Worcester. There were overtures from the 827-bed North Shore Jewish Medical Centre

---

1 Robert Ricciardelli, their son, came to India in June 2012 along with his mother to attend the wedding in Hyderabad of Dr Reddy's granddaughter Upasna Kamineni to Ram Charan Teja. His father couldn't attend because he had suffered a stroke.

in New Hyde Park, on Long Island, New York. A hospital in New Haven, Connecticut, also expressed interest in getting Dr Reddy on board, as did one in Rochester, New York.

But now Dr Reddy had set his sights on Massachusetts General Hospital in Boston. He had already chosen cardiology and he felt that Mass General would be just the right kind of place for him.[2]

When Dr Reddy applied in 1965 to Mass General for residency and a fellowship, he was informed that there were no open slots. That came as a disappointment, to be sure. But serendipity has always played a role in Prathap Chandra Reddy's life. Many years later, during a conversation I had in New Delhi with his friend Lord Swraj Paul of Marylebone, Lord Paul told me: 'Hard work and enterprise are important to becoming successful. So is spotting the right opportunity. But ultimately you have to have luck on your side.'

Dr Reddy doesn't like the word 'luck' because it suggests a kind of passivity. But serendipity manifested itself when he received a call from Professor Lee at Mass General asking him to come over. It was the same Professor Lee who had earlier informed Dr Reddy that there were no openings at the hospital. Why would the professor want to see him now?

He wanted to meet Prathap Chandra Reddy because, as it so happened, one of the physicians who'd been given a slot at Mass General found himself drafted into the military. Those were the years of the Vietnam War, and thousands of young men were being inducted into the armed forces.[3]

That physician was Robert McKay. When he met Dr Reddy at

---

2   In those days cardiology was still in its nascent stages. Dr Reddy felt that precisely because cardiology was a field that wasn't sought after, he could make important contributions. He was prescient.

3   The number of total service members in the United States was 8,744,000 between 1964 and 1975. Of those, 3,403,000 were deployed to Southeast Asia. From a pool of approximately 27 million, the draft raised 2,215,000 men for military service during the Vietnam era. It has also been credited with 'encouraging' many of the 8.7 million 'volunteers' to join rather than risk being drafted. Only men were drafted at the time.

Mass General, one of the first things he said to him was, 'Ah, you are Professor Lee's favourite!'

Favourite or not, the fellowship at Mass General fetched Dr Reddy a stipend of just $1,500 a month. But it required him to spend the entire day at the vast hospital. Dr Reddy also obtained an evening job at Waltham Hospital; it paid $25,000 annually. This meant that Dr Reddy spent the day at Mass General, starting at 7 a.m., came home for dinner around 6 o'clock, and went to work at the Waltham facility thereafter. His work 'day' would end well past midnight. Saturdays and Sundays were particularly busy. Dr De Domenici became a mentor, as did other senior physicians.

At Mass General, Prathap Chandra Reddy quickly developed a reputation not only as a highly energetic physician but someone who was extremely insightful about diagnoses. One particularly challenging case involved a patient who had been brought in with severe stomach pain and had been treated for just that. But then the patient began coughing up blood. Dr Reddy did an analysis and diagnosed that the man had an amoebic liver abscess, which had ruptured into the lung.

'Everyone looked at me with astonishment,' Dr Reddy recalls.

His diagnosis was based on the fact that the patient had served in the United States Army in the Philippines, and had contracted an amoebic illness there.

Dr Reddy enjoyed his time at Mass General because of the opportunities for gathering experience. The collaborative style of the specialist was new and interesting to observe. Doctors discussed cases over lunch, in the hallway and knowledge was shared freely.

'You could sit at any table you wished, and even if the doctors there were much more senior you could bring up your case,' Dr Reddy said.

Years later, he tried to institute this system at Apollo; but the Indian class and seniority systems being what they are, senior physicians didn't necessarily prefer to mix at mealtimes with their juniors. Yet he persists and some units at Apollo are ensuring this powerful culture of Mass General is emulated.

Dr Reddy sometimes cites Dr Paul Stelzer, the Co-Director of the Heart Valve Centre and a senior surgeon in the Department of Cardiothoracic Surgery at Mount Sinai Medical Centre in New York.

'The most unique aspect of being a doctor is that it involves caring for people and not just things. Every person has special concerns about health, family, work, illness, and a host of other concerns that enter into the picture when medical treatment is required,' Dr Stelzer told him. 'In the time-honoured model of history and physical examination the patient will almost always reveal the diagnosis in the history but it requires that someone ask the right questions and listen to the answers. A relationship of trust must be established for a person to speak honestly and thoroughly about such problems and the attitude and approach of the physician is crucial to establishing this trust. There is a big difference between the doctor who stands at a distance, never makes eye contact, cuts people off and just orders tests, and the doctor who sits down at the bedside, holds a trembling hand, smiles into the anxious eyes of the patient and offers hope. Often the patient is asked to do some very difficult things and endure painful treatments to get back to health. The personal touch and concern of the physician is incredibly powerful in motivating people to do these things. Having the privilege and the responsibility of helping other human beings in such a way is what gives such powerful depth of meaning to being a doctor.'

This is a Reddy credo – and he always reminds Apollo physicians, particularly the younger ones, how essential it is that they *listen* to patients.

Back in Boston, did Dr Reddy feel that his exceptional work invited jealousy on the part of colleagues?

'If it did, he never mentioned it,' Sucharitha Reddy said. 'He never brings his problems home. Once in a while, when I could sense that he was upset about something, I would say to him, "Things will change".'

One particular episode provided to be a boon for Dr Reddy. In 1964, he attended a conference of the Cardiological Society of North

America, where Dr Reddy was introduced to the world-renowned cardio-vascular surgeon Dr Denton A. Cooley. One of Dr Reddy's senior colleagues, pointing to him, said to Dr Cooley: 'This is one of my brilliant boys.'

Dr Cooley and Dr Reddy kept in touch regularly. 'I knew that he'd given me the liberty of asking for his help and advice at any time,' Dr Reddy said.

Their association proved mutually beneficial. After he'd returned to India in 1970 and started working at HM Hospital in Madras, Dr Reddy had occasion to refer numerous patients – including chief ministers, prime ministers and captains of industry – to Dr Cooley at the Texas Heart Institute, which he'd founded in Houston. In February 1990, Dr Reddy proudly hosted Dr Cooley at Apollo Hyderabad and told him how much of an inspiration he'd been to him during his time in the United States.

Recalling the Hyderabad visit in a letter sent to Sangita Reddy on 8 August 2012, Dr Cooley said: 'The facility and personnel at the hospital were impressive, and your father was justifiably proud of their record for cardiac surgery . . . Dr Reddy was actively involved with the Apollo Group and played an active role for the hospital at Hyderabad and also in the entire plans for Apollo hospitals throughout India. These institutions have improved importantly the level of health care in his native country. His leadership has been evident and is highly commendable.'

Even as Dr Reddy was meeting luminaries such as Dr Cooley at medical conferences around America, he and Sucharitha felt that they were starting to fit into Waltham, which was a suburb of Boston. They would always celebrate Diwali, the Hindu festival of lights, and invitations to their home were coveted by Indian physicians in the area – not the least because of the variety of dishes that Sucharitha would prepare. In the games that the children played, Shobana – even though she was the third-born of the four Reddy girls – was almost always the most assertive. 'She loved to play the leader,' Dr Reddy recalls. In the Ramayana that the Reddy daughters staged one Diwali,

Shobana insisted on playing the lead character of Lord Rama; her sisters had to settle for other roles.[4]

Sucharitha recalls that the seven small lakes in the area enthralled her. The children loved watching the rabbits playing there. Dr Reddy – who was always conscious about fitness – would go jogging, even when it snowed.

His daughters, although still very young, were starting to sense their father's commitment to medicine. Was that how they first developed the work ethic that would characterize their own professional lives in the years to come at Apollo?

In a conversation with me in Hyderabad in late 2012, Sangita Reddy – Apollo's executive director – said: 'There was no question that our father thrived in the environment in America. Despite his schedule, he had boundless energy. As his daughters, we couldn't help but be impressed by how hard he worked. And yet he always had time for us. He would ask about our homework. And he could be quite strict. His temper sometimes flared, but it would subside just as quickly.'

Sucharitha Reddy would take her daughters to museums in and around Boston. They enjoyed their mother's explanations of American history, so much of which had formed in New England. They also loved the dolls that she bought for them. Dolls made by Madame Alexander were particular favourites.[5]

'The dolls were costly but very interesting. They were beautifully

---

4 Diwali is a celebration of Lord Rama's triumphant return to his rightful kingdom of Ayodhya after long years of exile, culminating in a battle to the death with Ravana, the king of Lanka.

5 In 1923, Madame Beatrice Alexander Behrman founded the Alexander Doll Company and began to fulfil her dream of creating beautifully handcrafted play dolls for children. Her vision was founded on her unwavering belief that dolls should engage the imagination and contribute to a child's happiness and understanding of the world. Over the decades, great works of literature, the arts, and the different cultures of the world became the inspiration for many of her creations. Ninety years later, the company she founded upholds this dream by creating award-winning dolls that continue to delight generations of children and collectors all over the world.

crafted with a lot of detail. One day the girls were both quiet and giggling. I knew that some special activity was underway and went to check on them. As I turned the corner, I heard a "snip, snip, snip" and saw that the dolls were getting haircuts. They were not good haircuts either. They had spiked hair and uneven lines,' Sucharitha remembers with a smile.

Even back then in Waltham, the daughters – and his own medical colleagues – noticed Dr Reddy's constant efforts to gain clinical knowledge through his work at the hospitals and through extensive reading. And in Dr Reddy's own mind, there arose a question for which there was no immediate answer: 'Why is it that Indians, especially doctors, do so well abroad but not back home in India?'

The economist and social commentator – and former Secretary in India's finance ministry – Mohan Guruswamy offered the answer to me many years later during a conversation in Hyderabad about Dr Reddy. 'India never had an enabling environment for entrepreneurs,' Guruswamy said, noting that the Industries Act of 1951 required all businesses to get a license from the government before they could launch, expand or alter their product strategy. 'Nehru adhered to his own brand of Fabian socialism, and was deeply suspicious of capitalism – although not necessarily of specific capitalists who contributed to the coffers of the Congress party. Similarly, Indian doctors who'd settled overseas – and particularly in the United States – felt that they would not be very welcome in the country's government hospitals. In any case, these hospitals had nowhere near the kind of equipment and "best practices" that these doctors were accustomed to in the West. Dr Reddy, of course, would change the environment for the practice of hi-tech medicine in India through Apollo, and he would persuade Indian doctors abroad to return home.'

But all that was to come in the distant future. Right now, Prathap Chandra Reddy was wondering where he'd go from Waltham. As it happened, officials at Missouri State Chest Hospital invited him to fly down to Springfield for an interview. He took an Eastern Airlines flight to St Louis from Boston, and then a commuter aircraft to Springfield.

'The job is yours if you want it,' one of the hospital administrators told Dr Reddy.

Dr Reddy liked the atmosphere at Missouri State Chest Hospital. Among the first physicians to befriend him was Dr David Gorelick. Another was a neurologist of Chinese descent, Dr Wong. Dr Reddy recalls, 'Wong was a brilliant neurologist; David Gorelick and I used to tease him often but he always took it sportingly.'

Some of Dr Reddy's colleagues tried to figure out the nuances of Indian culture. A physician friend of Dr Reddy asked Sucharitha why she never called him by his first name, whereas Prathap would always call her 'Sucha' or 'Darling'. Sucharitha's response: 'There's a belief in Hinduism that if a wife calls her husband by his name, then the life span for both of them comes down.'

Sucharitha's mother, Shakuntala, visited the Reddys once during the years that they were in the United States. Shakuntala would also travel to Portland, where her younger daughter Vijayalakshmi lived. (Another daughter, Veena, was later domiciled in Oklahoma, but that was after the Reddys returned home to India in 1970. A son, Narendra, lived in Chicago.) The Reddys themselves took their daughters by car around the United States, to places such as the Grand Canyon, Yellowstone and Mt Rushmore. These were lengthy trips, but they reinforced the closeness between the Reddys and their daughters. Through those trips, the daughters were learning things about their parents.

Years later, Suneeta Reddy had this to say about her mother: 'My mother taught me that I should be an independent person in spite of my dominant father. She learned this, too, as his strong personality as a husband could overshadow her. Her independence is clear in that she is a free thinker. She has a deep belief in God. Her ability to show kindness to every human being is always a beacon to me. It is in the Vedas, everything is a part of God and we must respect all human beings. It is her mixture of religion and actions that show who she really is. For example, it is okay to criticize an action but not the person.'

Recalling those years in the United States, Preetha Reddy told me:

'Dad was a very tough disciplinarian. He was fun but tough and it was hard to get away with anything. One time he said that as naughty as I was, it was only one-tenth of his own behaviour growing up. We loved our weekend picnics and excursions and all of us liked playing in the lovely green grass, it felt like a carpet.'

The Reddy family didn't have much money when they were in the United States, but the daughters remember feeling lavished with love. 'Mom saved as much money as she could. Then she would go to Woolworth's[6] and buy us wonderful treats. There were always surprises under the bed. We would get dolls and dresses and other toys. Mom taught us tolerance and patience and how to live. Moving to the US and then back to India required a lot of adjusting. Her focus on spirituality was very helpful in dealing with the stress. She also gave us a strong understanding of generosity and a rich and deep level of graciousness. Our friends in the US recognized this in her, and it stays with me,' Preetha said.

Dr Reddy's spirituality also impressed his daughters. 'Daddy gets a lot of strength from the Vedas and the Mahabharata. Both he and Mom would relate to us excerpts from these epics. I have often thought that Dad's singleminded focus and discipline in his personal and professional aims was so similar to that of Arjuna. Arjuna, one of the five Pandava brothers was a superb archer. When seeking the hand of Draupadi he and the others were challenged to shoot out the eye of a fish that had been put on a rotating wooden wheel. Arjuna was able to accomplish this seemingly impossible task. He was asked how he was able to do it and replied, "I saw only the eye." Daddy has that ability – to clearly focus on his goal. His goal was better health care for India. There are other characteristics that Daddy exemplifies: leadership, integrity, strength and wisdom,' Preetha added.

Her sister Shobana has similar fond recollections of the time that the Reddys spent in America. 'Our father's engagement with us was always intense. He made sure that he knew what we were doing and that he spent real quality time with us. Our parents set excellent

---

6 A variety store now out of business.

examples of activity for us,' Shobana told me. 'As we were growing up, we saw that his discipline was immense. He would go to the puja room every morning and pray. Mother was consistently religious and spiritual. You know how couples that have been together a long time often begin to look and act alike; this is what happened with our parents. As time passed, Dad became more spiritual, devoting more time to prayer. He always used to meditate and as children we saw him change and become more and more spiritual. Initially, it was my mother who taught us the spiritual rituals and slowly, Dad's leadership took over.

'In later years, when we went through very difficult phases, such as when he was building Apollo Chennai, Dad began to pray more for guidance. It was like hitting rock bottom with everyone saying to quit and questioning his dream. His prayers were for direction. Dad doubled down when the problems with Chennai arose and said, "Let me build another hospital" in the middle of these huge problems. He meditates for an hour every morning. It absolutely does motivate one to do more with meditation and prayers when you see the example set by your parents.

'In India, it is a very big responsibility to build a temple. This is because you are creating an obligation for the generations that come after you to keep up the temple and care for its people. Our father goes every day to the temple, no matter where he is, and gives large sums to whoever is there. One day I was with him and there was a young girl selling flowers and he gave me a thousand-rupee note with a finger to his lips and motioned that I should give it to the girl. I slipped it onto her plate and we walked away. I don't think she had any concept of the gift because all of her coins were small.'

When the family lived in the US, they would take cross-country road trips with Dr Reddy driving and Mrs Reddy as navigator. Each child was always encouraged to keep a journal of what they saw and learnt. Their parents felt that taking notes would enhance their ability to observe, and to be aware of the details of their environment.

'When we lived in the US, there were not many Indian children and so people were curious about us and the way that we lived,'

Shobana said. 'We studied at private Catholic schools and later in India, in convents. I remember that we had a school survey of some kind and it asked that everyone check the box that indicated his or her religion. We didn't know what that was and asked Mom. She explained it to us. Of course, there was no box for "Hindu". Preetha brought a sari to school and demonstrated Indian dancing. The students had natural curiosities. Only now have people begun narrowing down religion. But we were brought up to respect all faiths during our days in America.'

Dr Reddy always felt that India – and Indians – was often misunderstood in America during those years. 'Some Americans thought – and some of them still think – that India is centuries behind the West, that there are only villages in India. In Springfield, missionaries came forward to help Indians by going to the Subcontinent, but some of them also spoke badly about Indians.'

During their Springfield years, the Reddys lived in Mount Vernon, a small town not far from Missouri State Chest Hospital. Vijayalakshmi Reddy, Sucharitha's younger sister, told me that the Reddys often visited relatives in different parts of the United States. In 1967, she and her family lived 500 kilometres north of Mount Vernon in Steelville, Illinois, another small town.

'On a December morning after I saw my husband off to his office, we were hit by a fierce tornado,' Vijayalakshmi remembers. 'My son Rahul, who was eight months old, and myself were thrown into a cornfield. I was unconscious. We were very badly injured and it is a great miracle we survived. Prathap bawa, Sucha akka and the kids drove and came to the hospital where we were admitted. They stayed with us for days, in spite of his busy work schedule, until we were in a stable condition. This is only one of the instances where they took care of us. He was always there for us and for the extended family and friends. They are like parents to us – although he is only ten years older than me. They are great role models and great souls. You can always count on him, he has a special quality that would make him stand out and make a difference in the world. He always took the needy under his wing, which helped him in later years in the health care business.' When Vijayalakshmi was pregnant, she went to Massachusetts for the birth. The child was Rahul. They stayed several weeks in Massachusetts, and later on Rahul went back to India with the Reddys when they moved home in January 1970.

Preetha Reddy says, 'Dad's own medical experiences have taught him to endure physical pain.' Dr Reddy has never been known to complain about his own ailments, which include diabetes (which he has controlled carefully through a strict regimen of diet, exercise and medication). In April 2013 Dr Reddy fell and broke his humerus just after landing at Dubai International Airport. He decided to fly back to Hyderabad for surgery, refusing to take any pain medication. As he arrived in the early morning hours he said, 'They will not do surgery now. I am going home so that the staff can rest.' At 10 o'clock, he arrived at the hospital emergency area and was met by many well-wishers from the staff – and a wheelchair. Dr Reddy refused the wheelchair. He prayed and then walked to the CAT scan unit and afterwards to his room to await the surgery.

Her aunt Vijayalakshmi, recalling the time when Prathap Chandra Reddy first met her older sister Sucharitha (Vijayalakshmi was thirteen then), said, 'I was awed by his intelligence and his unique quality of paying attention and listening to young and old. When you talk to him he will make you feel that you are the most important person, this is one of the great qualities that helped him so much in the health care business. He started the business with the least resources and against a million odds. His success can be attributed to the extraordinary qualities he is blessed with – he is very intelligent, kind, humble, generous and very charismatic. Sucha akka is a pillar of strength, and she is his good luck charm.

'Could I have predicted back in those days in America that Prathap bawa would become such a huge success? Well, maybe I couldn't have predicted how Apollo would come into existence, but there was no doubt in my mind that he was destined for great things in life.'

But neither she, nor anyone else, could have had any idea at that time of the price that Prathap Chandra Reddy would have to pay to achieve great things through Apollo.

CHAPTER SEVENTEEN

From Missouri to Madras

PRATHAP CHANDRA REDDY AND Sucharitha decided in mid-February 1969 that they would return to Madras from Missouri. That life-changing letter from Raghava Reddy had reached them on 15 February, and its implicit message that the son should come home again was the clincher.

But it's rare in life that one event, or one development, triggers something as major as a life-changing move from one country to another. During the course of writing this book, I sometimes wondered if that letter from Raghava Reddy to his son was the only factor that determined his return home.

'We had talked on and off about how the girls should grow up in India,' Sucharitha Reddy told me, when I asked her about her father-in-law's epistle. 'They loved America – we would take them strawberry-picking and sightseeing. They had plenty of friends. But the hippie movement had started in America, and privately my husband and I worried that young people were becoming increasingly influenced.[1] We also wanted our daughters to grow

---

1 The hippie subculture in the United States was originally a youth movement that arose during the mid-1960s and spread to other countries around the world. The word 'hippie' came from 'hipster', and was initially used to

up surrounded by Indian culture. My mother was also keen that
we come back.'

Sucharitha hadn't been back to India since she'd left Madras in
April 1963, although Dr Reddy had briefly visited Bombay for a
medical conference in 1967.

About the decision to return to India, Sucharitha told me: 'We
always reasoned that if India didn't work out for us, we could always
go back to the United States.'

Dr Reddy told me, 'We took a trip to the West Coast and both
Sucha and I were horrified at what we saw in California. The
teenagers and young adults were openly doing drugs and displayed
other behaviour that we did not want our daughters to follow.'

Some of the wives of Indian physicians in the Springfield area
envied the fact that the Reddys were going home. Clearly, not all of
them enjoyed being in America as much as the Reddys did. But not
all of them had immersed themselves as thoroughly as Sucharitha
in reading American history as well as contemporary literature, and
in keeping up with social trends. The tendency among many Indian
spouses was to stick to their own community, and their major pastime
was socializing or talking about Indian movies.

'How lucky you are to go back,' one Indian friend said to
Sucharitha.

The daughters initially didn't seem keen on returning to India.
America had proved a lot of fun for them. Sangita Reddy told me of
an episode when, in order to just wander in their neighbourhood,
she and her older sister Shobana climbed out of the window of
their room and started walking down the tree-lined road. It was
early evening. When Dr Reddy and Sucharitha discovered that their
daughters were missing, they got into their car and drove around to

---

describe beatniks who had moved into New York City's Greenwich Village
and San Francisco's Haight-Ashbury district. Hippies created their own
communities, listened to psychedelic rock, embraced the sexual revolution,
and some used marijuana and LSD. Hippie fashions and values had a major
effect on culture, influencing popular music, television, film, literature, and
the arts.

find them. It didn't take long. When they got back home, both girls received severe reprimands.

'But in all our growing-up years, our parents never laid their hands on us,' Sangita said. 'Sometimes just a frown was enough to convey their displeasure at our errant behaviour.'

Knowing that their time in the United States was now limited, the Reddys decided they would explore as much of the country as possible with their daughters. They had already taken their daughters around the country during all the years that the family had been in America, but this would be the farewell tour. For more than fifteen days, they drove around in their Ford. At times Sucharitha had to caution her husband not to drive so fast.

'We covered the complete West,' Sucharitha recalls, noting how delighted their daughters were seeing the big expanse of the Grand Canyon and the Badlands National Park in South Dakota.

Her daughters kept asking questions about what life would be like back in India. Would they get the same standard of schooling as in America? (Of course, the oldest daughter Preetha was already exposed to Indian education, since she spent much of her time in Madras under the wings of Kumara Raja and Kumara Rani Muthiah Chettiar.)

But even as they were preparing to return to India, Dr Reddy kept up his frenetic schedule at Missouri State Chest Hospital. His daughters recall how he would prepare slides for lectures, and do practice runs in their living room. Sucharitha would feed the girls in the living room as they watched their father's slides.

When they got to Madras – after two weeks in Europe – one of the first things that the daughters remarked was, 'All the time it's Indian food. We don't get pizzas any more.'

And so it was that Sucharitha Reddy started preparing pizzas, pecan pies (the pecans would be brought from the US) and spaghetti at home. Then there was the chocolate cake that she baked every day for the girls. Soon, word spread throughout the neighbourhood that if you wanted really fine American-style food, then the place to go to was the Reddy home. Friends of the Reddy girls, including the children of the many diplomatic homes in the Bishop Garden area, would swarm their home in the afternoons after school. There was always a crowd of young people. To this day, young people are attracted to Dr Reddy and Sucharitha, and the couple thoroughly enjoy being with them.

The Reddy daughters also noticed how particular their parents were about cleanliness both at home and at HM Hospital, where Dr Reddy had started his cardiology practice.

Dr Reddy told his daughters whenever they came to the hospital, 'Tell me anything that's not good. We will change it.'

Shobana asked, 'What about the good things, Dad?'

Dr Reddy replied, 'The good things are for people to enjoy and to help in healing. The bad things do not contribute to healing. But they tell us what to change.'

He encouraged his daughters to always carry paper and a pencil. One of the daughters, during a visit to the hospital, told her father, 'People are saying good things about you. But the hospital's bathrooms are smelly.' Needless to say, the 'smelly bathrooms' were immediately cleaned, and a regimen of new training and a more frequent schedule for housekeeping staff was implemented.

The girls would also ask patients about their experience at HM Hospital. 'Dr Reddy wants to know,' was the line they used.

'Even though we were young girls, our father always made it a point to hear us out,' Shobana later recalled. 'He had – and still has – the ability to make everyone feel important.'

In fact, Sangita and Preetha at one point wanted to be doctors like their father. But Dr Reddy came down against the idea.

'No,' he told them, 'you'll bring the hospital home with you. No doctor ever truly finishes his work. It's always round-the-clock.'

He had no idea that years later all four daughters would be at Apollo – not as physicians, of course, but nevertheless working pretty much around the clock. But even in those early days after returning to Madras, the daughters would come to Dr Reddy's clinic on Sundays to talk to patients. It would prove to be, however subconsciously, great training in market research. When they chatted amongst themselves, the topic would often be the hospital.

As Prathap Chandra Reddy, Sucharitha and their four daughters settled into the routine of life in Madras, their relatives surged to help them. Some of them also recalled the early years when Prathap first met Sucharitha Reddy in Hyderabad.

Veena Reddy, a younger sister of Sucharitha's, told me: 'Their return home brought back all sorts of feelings and memories. Sucha was only eighteen years old when she married Prathap. He was still at Stanley Medical College. (Prathap had graduated from medical college and got married in the same year.) He was adapting to the Deccan culture, learning the dialect, and so on. Right from the beginning we knew that he had a strong backbone – that backbone was none other than my sister Sucha. She supported him throughout his great endeavours. Our beloved mother Shakuntala Devi looked upon him with pride. She reserved a favourite corner of her heart for him. Sucha continues to be a role model for her younger sisters, Vijayalakshmi and me. Her exemplary role as a sister and mother is unconditional. She extends healing powers through her kind words and compassion. Sucha and Dr Reddy complement each other.'

Veena Reddy then told me about the day that her older sister got married: 'On the busy morning of her wedding Sucha made the time to braid our hair and get our attire ready. I could not bear anyone else braiding my hair other than Sucha. Sucha to this day makes her younger sisters have the best attires. She constantly touches people's hearts with such actions. We grew up in a conservative family. Our social horizons expanded when my brother-in-law came into our family. He treated us to movies and dining out. When they returned to Madras, they picked up right where they'd left off when they went to America in 1963. We were all once again caught in their social swirl.'

A woman named Malathi Manohar was definitely not part of that social swirl. Born and brought up in Rangoon – a number of Tamils had settled there for jobs and trade – she returned to Madras in 1965 to complete her studies at Church Park Convent, and took a number of courses in order to qualify as an office professional. She was enrolled in a computer-training programme at a company called TI Cycles of India, when she contracted what was later diagnosed as typhoid. At first, she was treated at home by a family physician, Dr Bobji – whose wife had previously worked for Dr Reddy – but when the fever wouldn't subside, another physician friend, Dr Jayanti Rama Rao, took Malathi to HM Hospital.[2] Dr Reddy had by now set up practice at HM Hospital. [3]

'Don't worry, you are going to be all right,' Dr Reddy said to Malathi. Even though she was in a delirious state, Malathi noticed how well groomed Dr Reddy was in his dark blue suit. In fact, she later learned that he rarely doffed his jacket.[4] 'It later struck me that perhaps Dr Reddy didn't remove his jacket in those days because he had no time,' Malathi said. 'He was like a whirlwind – he would be everywhere all at once at the hospital.'

She wound up spending two weeks as a patient at HM Hospital. Dr Reddy would come by regularly to check up on her, as would Dr Satyabhama. By that time, Malathi had already met a food technologist named K. Manohar, who'd graduated from Adyar Catering College and went on to work in almost every aerated beverage company in Madras – starting from Coca-Cola in the '70s, and encompassing everything in between: Spencer's, Gold Spot, Cheers, Kickapoo, Double Cola. Eventually he became the factory manager when Frooti started their factory in Sriperumbudur. Manohar, in fact, accompanied the physicians who brought Malathi to HM Hospital.[5]

---

2 Dr Bobji and Dr Jayanti Rama Rao both later joined Dr Reddy at Apollo Hospital in Chennai; Dr Bobji became head of Apollo's blood bank.

3 HM Hospital closed in 1998.

4 Dr Reddy wears suits six days of the week, and dresses casually only on Sundays. Of course, he wears traditional dhotis and long-flowing kurtas when he prays at home, at traditional ceremonies, or when he visits temples.

5 K. Manohar and Malathi would be married on 8 December 1974. Dr Reddy, Sucharitha and their daughters came to the wedding, as did many of Malathi's colleagues from HM Hospital. 'I'm sure that my father sought Dr Reddy's approval to marry my mother,' says Kishore Manohar, the couple's son, who works as a brand consultant in Chennai. On 1 May 1996, K. Manohar suffered a severe heart attack. He died even before the ambulance could reach the hospital. Every year on 1 May, Malathi and Kishore remember K. Manohar with a celebration of his life, and not with grief.

On one visit, when Dr Reddy saw Malathi very distressed, he asked her, 'What's worrying you?'

'It's my work. If I don't return with a medical certificate I might lose my job. And I really can't afford to.'

Dr Reddy smiled at her in his usual reassuring way.

'Don't worry. If you have a problem at work you can always apply here,' he said.

'But Doctor, I've no idea about medicine. I can't even spell diarrhoea,' Malathi said.

'Don't worry, I still can't spell phlegm,' Dr Reddy retorted, chuckling.

Malathi formally joined HM Hospital on 17 September 1972. It would take her two hours on two different bus routes each way to get to work and back. The only equipment in her office was a battered Swedish typewriter, a Halda.[6] Malathi still remembers the hospital's five-digit telephone number: 72236.[7] She also remembers that Dr Reddy exclusively used British-made Jack Wills pens – which had thick nibs – with which to write out prescriptions. No other doctor at the hospital was allowed to borrow these pens.

Malathi's responsibilities included meeting and greeting representatives of firms that manufactured medical equipment and pharmaceuticals. They would leave mounds of pamphlets with her. And then there were stacks and stacks of files that Dr Reddy himself generated. He would dictate every afternoon to Malathi, spelling out medical terms, and she was expected to maintain files on patients in a timely and orderly fashion. After Malathi had typed out reports or letters, Dr Reddy insisted on reading each sheet before signing it. Within months, some 30,000 files had accumulated, and metal filing cabinets were brought in to accommodate them; each alphabet was assigned a drawer. A woman who'd worked for Dr Reddy earlier,

---

6   Hemingway fans might remember that in the 1940s, the writer switched to Halda typewriters from the Connecticut-manufactured Royal typewriters.

7   As with many Indian cities, Chennai has since progressed to six-digit, then seven-digit, and now eight-digit telephone numbers.

Esther Hall, had cautioned Malathi that he did not tolerate slackness or laxity on the part of anyone who was employed at HM Hospital. 'It's his way of bringing to India what he learned in America,' Esther said to Malathi. 'Patients always come first for Dr Reddy.'

As he dictated his reports and letters, Dr Reddy would pull out cigarettes and, as Malathi recalls, would 'smoke just a few puffs and throw the cigarette away. He never smoked them to the end.' He would simultaneously consult that day's racing forms, which would be produced – and still are – by the Madras Race Club. Horse racing was, and remains, a passion for Dr Reddy.[8]

A man named Rangaswami Ramakrishnan talked about Dr Reddy's passion for racing. Ramakrishnan is known to everyone as 'RK'. He is a tall, engaging, open man, very similar to Dr Reddy. When you meet him, even a non-racegoer like me immediately thinks, 'Yes, I would like to go to the races with you!' He has great charm and radiates the joy of life.

He is a director of TVS Motor Company, which is one of India's top manufacturers of two- and three-wheelers; RK is also a director of the Shriram Group. He is a leading retailer of international sofa brands such as Natuzzi, Stressless, Koinor, Becker HTL, branded in India under the name 'Simply Sofas'.

He and Dr Reddy have been fast friends for nearly five decades after being introduced by a mutual family friend from college. The men immediately took to each other.

'The "vibes" between us were just right. At twenty-six, I was the youngest person to ever be named a steward of the Madras Race Club. We had shared interests, mostly about horses,' RK said. 'Prathap was an ardent racegoer and we eventually co-owned several horses, maybe

---

8 Dr Reddy still loves horses. But he's in racing for the fun and social enjoyment, not for gambling. He owns three thoroughbreds: What's Up, Snooze You Lose and Spring Delight. Sucharitha Reddy comes along for important races, always wearing Indian clothes. Dr Reddy's best horse was Red Orchid; he doesn't race any longer. The brown show horse is now in Hyderabad. It won many prestigious awards in Hyderabad and people are always delighted to see him.

ten or twelve. He would always tease me about the names I chose for
the horses: King Maker (there were a lot of politicians in the clubs),
Class One, Rolling Plan, Place in the Sun (Dr Reddy's first horse),
Rio Grande (an expensive but not talented horse).[9] None were super
champions, except Prathap's Red Orchid. That horse was particularly
strong but unfortunately losing a major race broke his spirit.'

RK and Prathap shared information on which horse might win
each race and why they thought so. According to RK, 'Neither of
us was in it for the gambling. We loved the sport of it and Prathap
especially liked seeing the horses run. He would often come out early
to the paddocks and see the horses exercise, talk to the jockeys and
stable boys. He would do this at whichever club he visited – Madras,
Hyderabad or the Bangalore Turf Club – before he got too busy.'

The race clubs would stage major races for Pongal (the South
Indian harvest festival), Christmas and New Year. On these occasions
you could meet everyone who was anyone – horse owners, celebrities,
politicians, bureaucrats, business owners, and even the casual
racegoer was welcomed. In the '70s and '80s everyone dressed to
go to the races, with women beautifully attired and the men in suits
and ties. 'It was something special to everyone. I remember one
Pongal when our horse lost and Prathap was very sporting and took
it in his stride saying, "We'll blame it on the jockey,"' said RK. To
Dr Reddy and RK their racing experiences were wonderful days, full
of such fun. The Who's Who in racing and in Madras were all at the
club. Even men much older were always happy to welcome RK and
Dr Reddy, and teach them what they knew.

Prathap's racing silks were pink and white. RK had two different

---

9 Some of the other horses were named Justice, Conscience Keeper, Rule of
   Law, Don't Ask, Yes Sir, Welcome Sir, Thank You Sir, and OK Sir. How are
   racehorses named? According to Rick Bailey of Kentucky's Jockey Club,
   there is an approval process whereby the owners of the thoroughbreds submit
   the names, and the Jockey Club runs a check for phonetics, duplication, etc.
   There is a limitation of eighteen characters, and there are permissions to be
   sought if someone wants to name a horse after a person. The same process
   applies at horse clubs all over the world, including India.

sets, one black, and red squares for the DMK party. 'When I was with the Janata Party my colours were green, orange and white. Rio Grande ran in the Golconda Derby and he was running so poorly that I said, "Prathap, the horse may come last. Let us hope he finishes the course." When the race was over, Prathap turned to me and said "RK, you were wrong, he came in second to last!"' RK said.

It was good clean fun. Dr Reddy was always invited by the Maharaja of Kashmir to sit in his box at the racecourse in Bangalore. These enclosures were places to be seen, and members of high society vied for invitations.

RK was well known in Madras and served as chairman of the great Madras Race Club for three consecutive years. During that time because RK wanted to appear neutral he had no horses or colours. At twenty-seven, RK was named Sheriff of Madras. It was a largely ceremonial position and the young RK was granted an aide-de-camp by the government. The ADC wore the liveried white uniform with a wide bright red sash and accompanied RK everywhere he went, not so subtly announcing that the sheriff was coming whether it was for a school opening or to welcome visitors and ships. It opened a lot of doors.

He was the youngest member of parliament, in the Rajya Sabha – the Upper House – at the age of thirty-three. In 1983 when RK was chairman of the Turf Authorities of India, the Indian Turf Invitation Cup was run at the Guindy Race Course in Madras. There was not even standing room for this premier occasion. Dr Reddy brought an important visitor from the US, a legislator. He warmly introduced RK to the guest saying, 'Here is the dynamic young man who heads this club and made all this possible. And, mind you, he is a senator!' The American seemed startled at the relative youth of the man who headed such a major racing organization.

'Prathap has enormous social graces, an innate know-how in relating to people,' RK said. 'These are no artifices. It was his vision and discipline that brought about Apollo. He delegates and trusts people to do the job. And, he knows when they don't because he is meticulous about follow-ups. On a personal level, he has no airs and will see anyone. He is a man who's naturally fun-loving, and who appreciates others who share that characteristic.'

Richard M. Cashin Jr, founder and managing partner of One Equity Partners in New York, possesses that characteristic. He recalled for me the time when he showed up in Chennai for a business meeting with Dr Reddy.

'We met Dr Reddy and his merry band of daughters, each gracious and smart, and were immediately nervous about making business proposals. These are some of the hardest working people of commerce with deep sector expertise we'd ever met. We held our breath and tried a few ideas like – offer to put 10,000 pharmacies in Indian railway train stations where Apollo could guarantee the medicine and provide primary care with a nurse practitioner; buy the mining industry hospitals with their substandard practices and troublesome labour. But Dr Reddy kept saying that Apollo should continue to do what made them the best health care group in the country, and that anything else would be a mistake – hard to argue with that.

'Maybe the funniest thing that happened to me in India was at a big cocktail party on a veranda overlooking Chennai. For some reason, I decided to sing "*16 tons*" – the American mining song. Standing between two women with fabulous rings on, I sang:

'*If you see me coming, better step aside*
A lot of men didn't and a lot of men died.
(Then I lifted the bejewelled hands of the women beside me)
I've got one fist of iron and the other of steel
And if the right one don't get you, then the left one will!'

———

Dr Reddy's accessibility, his willingness to meet people from all walks of life, and his evangelism on behalf of Apollo, was something that struck a man named Mecca Rafeeque Ahmed on a pleasant evening in Madras more than thirty years ago.

Ahmed, chairman of the Farida Group – whose 10,000 employees produce finished leather goods for the global market – was told about Dr Reddy by a mutual friend, Habibullah Badsha, a leading Madras lawyer.

'Dr Reddy is planning to establish a corporate-sector hospital here,' Badsha said. 'Let's meet him. You will enjoy getting to know Dr Reddy. Come along with me.'

Badsha and Ahmed went to Dr Reddy's home at Bishop Garden, where they sat in his garden.

'I must admit that, for some reason, I was a little unsettled at the beginning,' Ahmed told me. 'But Dr Reddy was completely relaxed, and he put me at ease. He talked about his vision for Apollo, and how he saw the future of health care in India. I was quite impressed. As a businessman, I recognized the depth in his concept.'

As he and Badsha left the Reddy home, Ahmed turned to his friend and said: 'You brought me to the right person. I am impressed by Dr Reddy's vision and his personality. We will invest.'

Ahmed immediately sent two lakh rupees to Dr Reddy. His investments to date are forty lakh rupees. Moreover, he agreed to be a charter member of Apollo's board, along with Badsha. Both men are still on the institution's board of directors.

'One has to admire how Dr Reddy overcame hurdles, how he pushed ahead with his vision,' Ahmed said. 'We stood behind him all the way. As a businessman, I know that when new things are suggested, some people object. But Dr Reddy always seems to find a way to get around those objections. He's very clear in his mind that buildings and ideas aren't enough to create an enduring institution. He understands the human factor. He persuaded so many doctors to return home to India from abroad. He has a remarkable way of persuading people to join his vision. The entire Apollo system is energized by his presence. He makes us proud.'

Ahmed's wife, Sabiha Banu, shares that pride. She received treatment at Apollo, as did Ahmed's uncles. They were particularly struck by the aftercare at the hospital.

An Apollo board member with whom Preetha and Dr Reddy interact closely is Khairil Anuar Abdullah, an independent director from Malaysia. He is chairman of Pantai Holdings Bhd in Kuala Lumpur.

After a recent board meeting at Apollo headquarters in Chennai, Abdullah said: 'There was a fair amount of robust debate in the board meeting about the best way to use technology to make health care affordable and accessible to more people. The so-called learning curve happens faster at Apollo than anywhere else I have seen.'

'Comparing between private health care providers can be a case of comparing apples with oranges. The apples are the price and the oranges are the care. Apollo's focus is to provide quality health care,' he said. 'Many Apollo hospitals are JCI accredited, which comes with implicit commitments to follow best practices. Best practices are not cheap; there are large numbers of Indians and expatriates who would not have had access to top-level health care if it were not for Apollo. Many of the middle classes work now in multinationals or are attached to a large corporation and those groups have arrangements for care with Apollo.'

He also touched on the succession issue, one that several other directors such as N. Vaghul also brought up in conversations with me.

'Dr Reddy and Apollo are addressing a serious succession plan that will keep things running smoothly with a leader that might expand its business model. The company wants to expand in metro areas, at the same time building reach hospitals and clinics for the underserved. A good hub-and-spoke network of hospitals will help Apollo do that. Expanding from acute care to wellness will burnish the Apollo brand, which will be good for investors,' Abdullah said.

————

Apollo's Reach hospitals are examples of expansion into rural regions in India where health care is desperately needed. The Reach concept was unveiled in Chennai on 5 September 2008 by Prime Minister Manmohan Singh at the Indian Institute of Technology. Also present were Chief Minister M. Karunanidhi of Tamil Nadu, and Union ministers P. Chidambaram and Anbumani Ramadoss.

'I was among the people who convinced Dr Reddy to come home,' the prime minister said. 'The Reach Hospitals will start a new era in health care history in India.' Karunanidhi quoted a poem in Tamil to the effect that when Dr Reddy came towards you, 'The moment we hear his steps we know it's Dr Reddy; the moment he touches us, we feel better.'

The first Reach hospital itself was inaugurated in Karimnagar, Andhra Pradesh, by Chief Minister Rajasekhara Reddy on 19 September 2008. Dr Prathap Chandra Reddy flew in by a helicopter but couldn't fly back since he kept talking to the doctors and missed the take-off deadline. The airport had no facility for night take-offs.

'We drove back in my husband Vishweshwar's new Audi and reached home in the early morning hours,' recalls Sangita Reddy. 'Almost all the way home he planned on how every one of India's 520 district headquarters must have a "Reach Hospital". Either directly or indirectly we must make sure this happens. It will create the much needed access to quality health care.'

The 'Reach' concept received the G-20 award for sustainable health care in 2012.

Sangita Reddy told me: 'Reach – rural access to equitable quality health care – was our way to improve on the Aragonda model and create a new layer of health access. We re-engineered the design, modified air-conditioning, and reworked electrical plans, all to ensure cost effectiveness. We then reworked the process and the doctor engagement model to ensure buy-in and quality in these inaccessible locations.'

I spoke to Dr K. Hariprasad, CEO of Apollo Hospitals Central Region, about the Reach hospitals. A large, kindly man who always seems to wear a worried expression, he's based in Hyderabad and is in overall charge of the project.

'Some 70 per cent of the population in India lives in semi-urban and rural areas. Some 25 per cent of families in India classify as at the Base-of-Pyramid (BOP – defined as those who spend less than $70 per month on goods and services) and 85 per cent of these families reside in non-metro areas whereas a major proportion of tertiary health care infrastructure is located in metros,' Dr Hariprasad told me. 'This means that a large chunk of the population has no or little access to quality tertiary health care.'

The concept of Reach hospitals bridges this gap by making quality and affordable tertiary health care accessible to these BOP individuals. The strategy leverages technology to make available services like telemedicine, specialist second opinion services and mobile health care for better management of diseases and health alerts.

———

While he treated his staff kindly and was amiable towards all patients, Dr Reddy was also a strict disciplinarian – traits that would also be amply evident after Apollo had been launched. He put in more than twelve hours at work every day, and he was pleased when his physicians would too. Dr Udhaya Balasubramaniam and Dr Uma Nataraja – who'd joined him and Dr Satyabhama – well remember the punishing schedule at HM Hospital.

Dr Udhaya was the third doctor hired by Dr Prathap Reddy to help in his cardiology practice when he worked at HM Hospital.[10] She and her husband, Dr K.A. Balasubramanian – a chemical engineer – had returned to India after five years in Canada. A classmate of hers at Madras Medical College, Dr Manon V. Rajah, was working as Dr Reddy's assistant. When Dr Raja wanted to take a two-week vacation at her home in Malaysia, she asked Dr Udhaya to substitute for her.

The offer suited Dr Udhaya very well as her husband was setting up a new plant in Trichy and she did not have any particular interest in moving there. She was still looking for her place in medicine in India. Until this time, Dr Udhaya and her husband were living in

———

10 Dr Udhaya, Dr Uma, Dr Satyabhama and Malathi Manohar are among the initial HM Hospital colleagues who are still with Dr Reddy at Apollo Hospitals. Others include Mrs Usha in the front office at Apollo Chennai, and Mahalingam and Ramiah in the ECG department.

their hometown of Tirupur; she could stay with her aunt in Madras for the two weeks while she would work with Dr Reddy.

It was 1973 and Dr Reddy was already a very popular physician, probably the most popular in Madras. 'Once a person became his patient, they never wanted to leave,' said Dr Udhaya. His practice was growing every day and he needed help in screening and examining the patients. So when, at the end of two weeks, Dr Udhaya went to say goodbye to him, Dr Reddy said that he would be happy if she could continue. Since her husband's work would continue full pace in Trichy for at least six months, she agreed. Forty years later Dr Udhaya is still with Dr Reddy at Apollo. It turns out that her late husband didn't mind commuting to Madras and they set up home in the seaport city.

Dr Reddy had just started doing what he referred to as 'Master Health Checkups' and wanted Dr Udhaya to oversee the programme. 'He conceived the idea and named it: primary health tests for everyone, all conducted in one place – it was a masterstroke and it was just the kind of activity I was interested in. Incidentally preventive health checks are now globally prevalent,' says Dr Udhaya. Today she is the director of Preventive Medicine for Apollo Hospitals Group.

She's a very systematic person, organized and able to have a broad overview of activities and planning and also to direct staff in executing the day-to-day flow required when people are getting many different kinds of tests done, each requiring a different time frame. Apollo Chennai does between 250 and 300 health check-ups each day.[11]

When Dr Reddy started the Master Health Checkup, a typical test cost five rupees – less than a dime in today's terms and less than a dollar even in those days. A total health check-up cost Rs 250 (in 2013, the cost is Rs 5,900). At that time Dr Reddy didn't envision

---

11 On an average, the Chennai region accounts for 110,000 checks per year and the five other major Apollo centres – Delhi, Hyderabad, Bangalore, Kolkata and Ahmedabad – for around 84,000; along with the rest of the group, between 250,000 and 300,000 health check-ups are being done every year according to Dr Udhaya.

the need to copyright the name. Other hospitals have copied his idea and the name he chose. That's why the Master Health Checkup is now called the Apollo Personalized Health Check and covers a complete health screening: blood pressure, blood work including tests for sugar, cholesterol, kidney, liver function, lung and heart, ECG, abdominal ultrasound, gynaecology and dietary counselling followed by a comprehensive review by a senior physician. Rightly recognizing that the importance of preventive health checks can only increase in the future, Apollo has formalized an 'Apollo Future Health Check' which includes a set of personalized and predictive tests using new parameters like validated genetic risk markers. These would help an individual to modify behaviour and lifestyle and acquire control over his/her future health.

In the days at HM Hospital, Dr Reddy wanted more doctors to look after three kinds of patients – those who were in hospital, those who were walk-in outpatients and those who came for a master health check-up. Dr Manon was first physician, then Dr Satyabhama, then Dr Udhaya, followed by Dr Uma, also a general practitioner.

Dr Reddy's ideas were new to the country and he rapidly set his practice apart by setting up the first centre to check cardio fitness and also allergy testing and immunology. That programme tested for allergic reactions to dust mites, pollen, hair of cats and dogs, and food items. The doctors would do the test in Madras and then a lab in Delhi would prepare the antigens that they would administer. 'It was such a new programme but won early acceptance,' Dr Udhaya says.

Dr Udhaya still has the notebook in which appointments were written beginning in 1983. This was before computers and online programmes were ubiquitous. She also has a notebook in which the total health checks are tallied year by year. 'In the beginning, we didn't have many patients who were aware of the health checks but once we got started, our growth was phenomenal. In 1983, we did 320, in 1984, the number was 3,113 and in 1985, there were 4,839,' she says.

Dr Udhaya's 'ownership' of Apollo Health Checks is apparent: 'As a person and as a physician it is very gratifying to know that in some way you are helping another person. By bringing good health to an individual, we are also helping the family. Of course, we are very pleased when we can prevent disease.'

Apollo gets a significant number of health check-ups for pre-employment testing. One such was a twenty-six-year-old woman. In the clinical exam, Dr Udhaya felt a small nodule in the woman's thyroid and further tests including a CT scan revealed a very early stage cancer that was treated successfully surgically. Afterwards, the woman reapplied for the job and was hired.

Through Dr Reddy's emphasis on the root causes of diabetes and heart disease and early detection, preventive health care is not only saving millions of lives, it is easing the financial burden for citizens across India. People who are not well either can't work or do not work at their highest level, Dr Udhaya says. 'I'm very sentimental about the check-ups. Dr Reddy was the perfect mentor and leader. He has always given a lot of freedom, allowing us to do what was best for the patients, the programme, and the hospital. I made rounds with him every day, doing work-ups, getting his opinions and so forth. We would talk about what was needed and I could ask him directly for new initiatives. He would sanction them on the spot. For example, as our patient load increased, I proposed a new X-ray and a second ultrasound machine just for the health check-ups. He sanctioned them without question,' she remembers. 'Dr Reddy not only gave us freedom to act, he gave us a long rope. With that freedom came responsibility to do the very best and all of us recognize this.'

She mentions many of Dr Reddy's personal characteristics but the top two are trust and personal warmth. 'He and Mrs Reddy really have treated us as family, whether it is a sweeper or a senior consultant. There is no prejudice and they do not withhold affection. I remember when my son was born, Dr and Mrs Reddy came to the house to see the baby. Some twenty-six years down the line, both of them were very much there to bless the couple when my son got married at a place which is 500 kilometres from Chennai. One wouldn't normally expect that of someone so senior.'

At HM Hospital, Dr Reddy would talk to his colleagues about the sorry state of health care in India. In those days, there were only two kinds of hospitals: ones run by the government, and others run by charities or missionaries. In view of the fact that India was adding 18 million people to its population each year – the equivalent at the time of the entire population of Australia – the country's supply of hospital beds was woefully short. 'One of the main challenges for the health care sector is the shortage of beds. The population-to-bed ratio is about one bed for 1,050 people. In the United States it is one bed for 250 people, the Japanese are luxurious with one bed for 85 people. Our challenge is to maintain a ratio of at least one bed for 300 to 400 people,' was how Dr Reddy put it.[12]

He was also starting to talk more and more about the diseases that afflicted Indians the most. 'We are the diabetic capital of the world, the heart disease capital of the world, the cancer capital of the world, and of infections. These four have become a huge set and the way they are increasing is phenomenal. So, we need to have a programme: how do we bring awareness of this, how do we do preventive check-ups, and how do we increase the facilities for people who have these illnesses?'[13]

It was that sort of commitment to patients that strengthened Dr Reddy's reputation as the 'doctor to see' in Madras. From everyday people to celebrities, they came – and, as Dr Uma puts it, 'Everybody received the same degree of careful attention and polite treatment. Everyone was made to feel by Dr Reddy that he personally cared about them – which, of course, he did.'

The celebrities included film stars such as Sivaji Ganesan and Gemini Ganesan, Jeetendra, Sridevi, Rajinikanth, the comedians V.K. Ramaswamy, Manorama and Nagesh, Cho Ramaswamy, Amitabh Bachchan, Anil Kapoor, Prem Chopra, Vyjayanthimala Bali,

---

12 This has become almost a mantra for Dr Reddy.
13 Dr Reddy used more or less these very words in a televised interview on CNBC India on 1 February 2013 – almost forty years after he first started talking about India's health care needs.

Sowcar Janaki (who was present at the eightieth birthday celebrations of Dr Reddy in 2013), and M.G. Ramachandran and Jayalalithaa (both of whom later became chief ministers of Tamil Nadu). Dr Reddy soon came to be known as the 'Doctor to the Stars'. In fact, the young Jayalalithaa was so impressed by Dr Reddy's Ford that she bought it from him.

One of the stars of Telugu cinema, K. Chiranjeevi, would later tell me: 'Dr Reddy has a unique ability to inspire loyalty and to enthuse people. He was born with those gifts.'

The Reddy daughters set an example by coming in to donate blood. Sucharitha Reddy often sent homemade food to the hospital for the staff. Pongal, a dish made out of rice, was a special favourite for breakfast. During the Muslim festival of Eid, delicious mutton biryani would be dispatched. And when Dr Reddy travelled – especially abroad – he always brought chocolates back or trinkets for staff members. 'His thoughtfulness was remarkable,' Dr Udhaya recalls. 'I could cite other instances of his thoughtfulness and courtesies – Dr Reddy always stood up no matter who came into his office. It's a practice he has kept up to this day.'

Dr Reddy encouraged patients from every community in Madras to come to HM Hospital. He also urged top companies in Madras to send their personnel – and they responded fulsomely. M.A.M. Ramaswamy of the Chettinad Group – and the reigning raja of racing in Madras – was a patient, and sent his colleagues to HM Hospital, as did N. Mahalingam of the Shakthi Group. Other companies that sent patients included Larsen & Toubro, the TVS Group, Amalgamations, Parry & Co, Lipton, ITC and the Union Bank of India. Patients also came from various foreign consulates located in Madras, especially those of the United States, Great Britain and West Germany.[14]

Dr Reddy and Sucharitha, along with their daughters, took great pains to ensure that the staff at HM Hospital was treated like family

---

14 Many of these patients – both individuals and companies – remain loyal to Dr Reddy and Apollo Hospitals.

members. During Diwali, the Reddys sent sparkling saris from Benares for female staffers. Sometimes, there were games associated with the dispatching of these saris. If a staffer selected a particular sari, she was entitled to a second one as well; if another – obviously more expensive – sari were chosen, then the recipient got just that sari.

Kishore Manohar – Malathi Manohar's son – still remembers how on Diwali day, his father and mother would ride on a red Vespa scooter to the Reddy home, 'Temple Trees', at 19 Bishop Garden Avenue. They would stop off first at the Chola Hotel to buy packets of mithai. There would be lots of food, priests would chant hymns, and in the evening there would be displays of fireworks.

In the early 1980s, before Apollo Madras had started operations, Kishore's father had a major cardiac event and had to be rushed to HM Hospital. The rooms might not have been elegant but they were clean and organized, and there was the best and most modern equipment, and there was always Dr Reddy, the ever-attentive cardiologist. Whenever Kishore came to HM Hospital, his mother would elbow him, and pointing towards Dr Reddy, say to her son, 'Ask for his blessings.'

And Dr Reddy would invariably say to Kishore, 'Hello, young man!'

Such encounters would occur often because young Kishore spent many holidays at the hospital. The Madras of those days was far less bustling than it is today. It was in fact a quiet little city known for its peaceloving, industrious, cricket-crazy people. Entertainment comprised a visit to the Marina Beach or a trip to the movies and the whole city used to be tucked in bed by 8 p.m. Business development was largely unheard of and hospitals were the usual 'white buildings with bed pans and a distinct smell of iodine'. It was notorious for lack of potable water, and people like the Manohars would store water in large oil drums whenever it rained. When they decided to acquire a house, Dr Reddy helped arrange a loan for them.

No wonder everybody became excited when Dr Reddy let it be known in 1979 that he was planning his own hospital. A Madras architect named P.S. Govind Rao, who had never designed a hospital before, was retained to come up with a sketch. Incidentally, he misspelt the name Apollo as 'Appollo'.[15]

The colour sketch still hangs in the foyer outside Dr Reddy's office at Apollo Chennai. It still elicits an occasional chuckle from Prathap Chandra Reddy. Back then, three decades ago, who would have believed that the sketch would become a reality – that is, who other than Dr Reddy and Sucharitha? And, of course, P.S. Govind Rao.

'I just knew that Dr Reddy would make it happen,' Govind Rao told me. 'Was I being optimistic back then? Perhaps. But I've been proven right, have I not? I always believed in Dr Reddy's ability to get things done.'

———

Part of being in Apollo's upper leadership echelon means participating in public events, as the Reddy daughters well know. At Hyderabad's Radisson Blu, the Federation of Indian Chambers of Commerce & Industry (FICCI) had arranged for Shobana Kamineni, the executive director of new initiatives for Apollo Hospitals Enterprises, to interview the management consultant Devdutt Pattanaik on stage. Shobana and her sister Sangita are active members of industry organizations such as FICCI and the Confederation of Indian Industries (CII).

Pattanaik is a doctor by training and once worked at Apollo Health Street, which provided outsourced IT solutions to enhance patient

---

15 The assignment proved lucky for the architect. Although he was already accomplished by the time he designed Apollo Madras, P.S. Govind Rao became even more of a distinguished architect over the years. Among his accomplishments are Apollo Colombo, Temple Towers (Nandanam), Temple Steps (Chinna Malai), Fagun Mansion, Shivalaya Buildings, Hotel Savera, Stella Maris College and AVM Rajeswari Kalyana Mandapam. He was also instrumental in the design of the revolving globe with the AVM logo for the studio in Vadapalani. Govind Rao has designed about 2,000 houses, farmhouses and retreats across the country. He is also the architect of a dozen theatres, temples, IT complexes, apartment blocks and townships.

care by focusing on financial management and business capabilities. Now Pattanaik is the Chief Belief Officer for the Future Group, an Indian retail conglomerate. He often speaks about mythology and about work ethics, and is also a prolific writer. We must look at our work and our lives in a way that is different from the West; work is hard only when you're doing something you don't love, he said.

Shobana Kamineni says that views about mythology and its relevance to today's business are important, noting that, 'Somehow over the years the society has lost it. We hope that people will reconnect and understand our great mythology and its many sources. Whether it's to do with business or to do with family life or you mix it all together . . . what we need today is to have more belief and we have to have more trust, more integrity.'

Suneeta Reddy also has strong views on the overall health care ecosystem. She is equally concerned about the ominous correlation of health demands and a rising population with high cardio-vascular disease, diabetes, cancer and obesity rates.

'The country needs entrepreneurship and growth in manufacturing, agriculture and the service sector. For growth to be sustainable, we must create vibrant business models. We have every opportunity to manufacture our own consumer goods, which in turn will provide jobs in many sectors from labour to transportation to fuel and even health care. The right kind of entrepreneurship is needed. It's not just about cheap labour and quotas, it's about business opportunities,' she says.

What was the one thing of which she is particularly proud?

'There are several in my career,' she says. 'One is the money that we raised for Apollo and for thirty years we've flourished in business. Personally, I've experienced quite a few bumps and even had to sell some businesses, but I got back on my feet again. It does hurt you but I'm very proud that I have had the courage to get up and start running.'

It has indeed been an interesting run for Suneeta and her sisters – not to mention their parents – from Missouri to Madras.

CHAPTER EIGHTEEN

The Transformation of India

WHEN I MENTIONED TO P.S. Govind Rao, the architect who had come up with the original sketch for Apollo Madras, that Dr Prathap Chandra Reddy's ambition to establish his own multispeciality hospital in the private sector was not necessarily shared by many at the time, he challenged me.

'Why do you say that?' he said. 'There were a lot of people who believed totally in Dr Reddy. They may not have said it openly, but people were convinced that a first-class hospital with state-of-the-art technologies was needed in Madras. And they were convinced that if anyone could make that happen, it would be Dr Reddy.'

Govind Rao had been a patient at HM Hospital, and had built many homes and was the most sought-after architect for residential dwellings in southern India. As a matter of fact, that's exactly why Govind Rao was selected to design the hospital. Dr Reddy and his daughter Shobana searched for an architect who was not bound by convention. Moreover, Dr Reddy wanted a fresh new approach to hospital design just as he wanted the same for health care in India.

When Govind Rao said he knew nothing about building hospitals but was open to new and absorbing ideas, Dr Reddy and Shobana agreed that he would be the best architect for the new hospital. The one thing Govind Rao knew was that a world-class hospital such as the one Dr Reddy had in mind would be very costly.[1]

Govind Rao had come to know from Dr Reddy about the land on Greams Road that Dr Reddy had bought for Rs 2,200,000,[2] and where he planned to build his multispeciality hospital.[3] 'So I requested him to let me come up with a sketch,' the architect told me. 'One of the things that I discussed with Dr Reddy and his daughter Shobana – she always called me Govindrao Uncle[4] – early on was how we could build a hospital where the distance between the entrance and access to a doctor could be kept to a minimum for the patients. I was familiar with the government hospitals of those days, where you had to walk and walk along dingy corridors before you reached your doctor's office. In my view, the people most responsible for the welfare and comfort of patients are doctors and the architects who build hospitals.'

---

1 It took Dr Reddy more than two years to raise the initial capital. Initial investors included Dr Prathap C. Reddy & Associates, various doctors of Indian origin in the United States and Britain, P. Obul Reddy, Dr G.V. Chelvapilla, T.M. Joseph, Habibullah Badsha, Rajkumar Menon and S.R. Jiwarajka. The initial equity in Apollo was Rs 3 crore, and debt was Rs 6 crore. Apollo's leading investors now include: Dr Prathap C. Reddy and family, and associate companies, Integrated Healthcare Holdings (Khazanah Group), Oppenheimer Funds, Newton Investment Management Limited and Fidelity Management & Research Co. Limited. Apollo's market cap, as of 4 June 2013, was $2.52 billion, with 139,125,159 shares outstanding.

2 Dr Reddy told me that a friend had suggested that he could make a quick profit by selling that land for one crore rupees, instead of building the hospital. Eventually, Apollo Madras cost Rs 12 crore to build; Apollo Hyderabad cost Rs 40 crore; and the Indraprastha Apollo Hospital in New Delhi cost Rs 200 crore.

3 When Dr Reddy used the term 'multispeciality hospital', Govind Rao and Malathi Manohar found it a tongue twister. Today, both laugh about it – but they still find the term to be awkward to articulate.

4 Govind Rao frequently refers to Dr Reddy's daughters in conversation, characterizing them as 'talented', 'dynamic' and 'extremely capable'. They, in turn, clearly hold him in high respect, and demonstrate warmth towards him. Sucharitha Reddy, who is an avid gardener, appreciates the fact that the architect himself cultivates bonsai plants, and that he maintains a small art gallery featuring his own paintings on Mount Road in Chennai.

One afternoon in May 2013 at the Apollo corporate office in Chennai, Dr Reddy told me the story of how he came to acquire the plot. After he was advised against acquiring a Ramada Hotel property, Dr Reddy found out about a plot of nearly two-and-a-half acres on Greams Road in central Madras, a choice location indeed, one that was just off the main thoroughfare of Mount Road. An auction had been scheduled for 10 October 1979 at Cochin House by a firm called Murray & Company. Bids were due by 3.30 p.m. that day.

Dr Reddy consulted his astrologer and numerologist, D. Nagarajan.

'How much are you willing to pay?' Nagarajan asked Dr Reddy.

'Between seventeen and eighteen lakh rupees,' Dr Reddy said.

Nagarajan did some calculations, and suggested a figure of Rs 1,740,002.

Dr Reddy sent his sealed bid to Cochin House by 10.30 a.m. It proved to be the winning bid.

During the architectural stage of Apollo, Govind Rao evolved what he calls the 'magic cube' concept: the elevators would be installed in the middle of the building so that patients and their visitors could readily access any part of a particular floor. He applied the same concept to Apollo's hospital in Hyderabad, which he designed some years after the one in Madras. 'Dr Reddy gave me a free hand,' the architect says. 'And some of the doctors who worked abroad also contributed ideas.'

As there weren't any hotels nearby where relatives of patients could stay, Dr Reddy came up with the idea of constructing Sindoori Hotel – named after his granddaughter (Suneeta's daughter Sindoori, the Reddys' first grandchild) – and Govind Rao proceeded to design rooms that could accommodate three beds each.[5]

Some critics carped that the hospital's corridors were too wide.

---

5   As Apollo Madras grew, the building housing Sindoori Hotel was converted into an adjunct of the hospital itself. Since hotels have proliferated in the neighbourhood, out-of-town patients' relatives rarely have problems in finding accommodation now.

However, Dr Reddy had seen the necessity of wide corridors that could accommodate the smooth and timely flow of hospital beds, equipment, medical, food and housekeeping carts plus the flow of patients and their families and friends. Every second counts in a hospital, and Dr Reddy wanted to eliminate any obstacles to the best care. He knew that it was critical for the hospital to plan for medical emergencies and increased demand – and the wide corridors were a necessity for that.

When M.G. Ramachandran, then the chief minister of Tamil Nadu, was hospitalized at Apollo Chennai, the police had enforced tremendous security. Two cordons were thrown around the hospital, making it difficult for even genuine patients to come in to the hospital. Crowds amassed outside the hospital, blocking even the road to the hospital.[6]

Another unique feature at Apollo Madras and Hyderabad was the inclusion of ramps within the hospital to expedite services and patient flow.

Apart from the Apollo facility in Madras, Govind Rao built the Reddys' home in Bishop Garden. He also designed the family home of Mohan Guruswamy, the former Secretary in the finance ministry. Just as Govind Rao and Dr Reddy occasionally discussed the sorry state of India's health care sector, Guruswamy himself reflected independently on the issue. At that time – in the mid- to late 1970s – the government provided 85 per cent of the total medical care in India.

Though in the government-run hospitals, there were special wards for the elite, politicians and top-level bureaucrats often went abroad even for simple operations. When Mohan Guruswamy needed to

---

6 M.G. Ramachandran – known widely as MGR – was a popular actor in Tamil films. After he entered politics, he became chief minister of Tamil Nadu on 30 June 1977. He died on 24 December 1987 in Madras. His death sparked off frenzied rioting all over Tamil Nadu. The violence during the funeral alone left twenty-nine people dead. This state of affairs continued for almost a month. Around one million people followed MGR's remains; around thirty followers committed suicide; and countless people had their heads tonsured.

be operated on for appendicitis, he was given special treatment at Osmania General Hospital – not the least because his father N.K. Guruswamy was a member of the IAS.[7] When Mohan's mother Saraswati was diagnosed with a brain tumour in the 1970s and had to be rushed to Osmania Hospital, the government facility flew in a well-known neurosurgeon, Dr Balasubramaniam Ramamurthi, from Madras to attend to her.

'Had my father been just a clerk, my mother and I would have wound up in the hospital's general ward,' Guruswamy says. 'The Indian equivalent of the nomenclatura of the erstwhile Soviet Union in those days – the ruling class, mostly privileged politicians, purportedly elected to serve the public and the bureaucrats, euphemistically called public servants – didn't have to worry about health care. Its members had it good. Everybody else didn't. It was mindless conformation to a peculiar sort of Indian-grown socialism.'[8]

That socialism spawned strange peculiarities. If you ordered a government-manufactured Maruti car in those days, you had to wait for as long as eight years to get delivery – unless you were a politician, of course. You wanted a gas supply to your home? Nothing less than a recommendation from your local member of parliament would suffice. Getting a telephone connection was almost equally difficult.[9] Virtually all utilities, not to mention health care, were government monopolies.

---

7 N.K. Guruswamy was the first member of the Board of Revenue of Andhra Pradesh in the early 1970s, with the rank of Chief Secretary.

8 According to Mohan Guruswamy's estimates, India currently has 23.5 million government employees at the federal level. They are all entitled to lifetime benefits provided by the Central Government Health Scheme.

9 The telecommunications sector was thrown open to private operators in the 1990s. India now has more than 1 billion wireless and landline subscribers. By the end of 2013, an estimated 97 per cent of the population of 1.2 billion will have phone connections. Landline subscribers total 31.53 million (as of May 2012), and cell phone subscribers nearly a billion. The telecommunications system in India is the second largest in the world, after China. Competition has caused prices to drop and calls across India are some of the cheapest in the world. The competition has forced the landline services to become more efficient too.

Then there was the License Raj, which spawned the much-derided 'Hindu rate of growth'.[10] At one point after Guruswamy returned to India from studies at Harvard University, friends would ask him, 'Why have you come back? Do you really want to put up with all the nonsense here?'

The License Raj continued even after Dr Reddy had set up Apollo Madras. One day he visited the office of a government official in New Delhi to discuss the purchase of the first ever CT scanner in India.

'Why do you want this technology?' the supercilious official said.

Dr Reddy replied: 'If your child had an accident, wouldn't you want the very best treatment?'

This wasn't a stray occurrence. For every item of the 370 pieces of medical equipment that Apollo Madras needed, Dr Reddy had to go through the same process. Twelve applications to be filled and that many babus – the widely used Indian term for bureaucrats – to be met. So much so that Dr Reddy had to spend every Thursday and Friday in Delhi for several weeks running before he got the necessary clearances.

This clearly demonstrates that no official was too low for Dr Reddy to go and see in the cause of Apollo. If mixing with the political leaders and their mandarins was what it took to advance the cause of health care in the private sector, Dr Reddy would not hesitate to do so. He strongly believed that the power of his will would enable him to overcome any barrier that came between him and the public good.[11]

---

10 The term 'Hindu rate of growth' was coined by Raj Krishna, who taught at the Delhi School of Economics. It suggests that the low growth rate of India, a country with a high Hindu population, was in sharp contrast to high growth rates in other Asian countries, especially the 'East Asian Tigers', which were also newly independent. This meaning of the term, popularized by Robert S. McNamara – then president of the World Bank – was used disparagingly and has connotations that refer to the supposed Hindu outlook of fatalism and contentedness.

11 Dr Reddy told me that during the stressful period leading up to the building of Apollo Madras, he listened to music and did yoga exercises regularly. He

Dr Reddy recalls a related incident. D.R. Mehta of the Jaipur Foot[12] fame, once came to visit a patient admitted in Apollo Chennai. While he was admiring the excellent facilities in the hospital, Dr Reddy wryly informed him about the dozens of applications and the numerous visits he had to make to Delhi before it was made possible to import the equipment he was admiring now. D.R. Mehta, who was the director general of Foreign Trade at that time, asked for the list of the equipment. Later under his instructions these were removed from the list of medical equipment that required an import license. Dr Reddy reflects, 'I am happy that at least now people will not have to go through the struggles I had to for importing necessary equipment.'

Shobana Kamineni told me: 'He's fond of saying "Belief is Power". He has always believed in himself since he was a young boy. He always says, my brothers were smarter but they let that be enough. I wanted to be something better. He was the first person to come up from his village. He had the smarts – great intelligence. Just a few years after starting the Apollo project, our father could understand finance, could understand strategy, understand HR and all those intricate aspects of management that eluded everyone else in the room. So no one was talking down to him; and there's this elite sharpness about him – he's smart, sharp, possesses the ability to think naturally. All these are his great qualities. Who would have imagined anyone breaking through the barrier of government domination of

---

quit smoking in 1982. He would climb stairs instead of taking elevators. And he would go for walks: often, he would ask his driver to stop the vehicle a mile or so ahead of his destination, and go on foot the rest of the way. To this day, Dr Reddy is remarkably attentive to his personal fitness. 'Worry produces excessive adrenalin,' he told me, 'and puts tremendous strain on the resting heart.' Through his fitness regimen, Dr Reddy can lower his heartbeat to 50 from 65.

12 D.R. Mehta was fitted with an artificial leg after a gruesome accident. He set up Bhagwan Mahaveer Viklang Sahayata Samiti (BMVSS) in Jaipur in 1975, which has emerged as the largest organization for the handicapped in the world, providing prosthetics popularly known as the Jaipur Foot and other aids for free.

the health care industry back in the late 1970s when Dr Reddy began thinking of starting Apollo?'

Mohan Guruswamy says: 'Dr Reddy's brilliance is especially noteworthy when considered against the backdrop of the bleak years when his idea germinated, and of the hard conditions that made pioneering impossible, when brilliance was being drowned by mediocrity and anything that flew away from the socialist mindset was viewed with suspicion.'

The economy was bleak, and India's economic prospects were bleaker. The government crushed initiatives; it made people scramble all the time. It wasn't until 1991 under Prime Minister P.V. Narasimha Rao that the License Raj slowly began loosening. By that time, Dr Reddy had already been through rings of fire and had managed through charm, discretion and surprising business acumen to start Apollo Hospitals. He had already gone through days and nights of daunting challenges, and he had triumphed.

'It's really all about taking on daunting challenges and making it happen,' Mohan Guruswamy says. 'Dr Reddy dreamt big at a time when he wasn't allowed to dream big. The real transformation here has been that private medical care now accounts for almost 70 per cent of medical expenditures in India. Improved care also had its impact on improved drugs and pharmaceuticals. That laid the seeds of the pharma boom in India. He had a catalytic effect on everything.'[13]

'The story of how Dr Reddy attracted medical talent from abroad back to India is also fascinating to me,' Guruswamy says. 'He gave these doctors the option to come back and serve their communities. When new doctors come, you create a new culture of competence and care. I believe that the availability of highly improved medical services, apart from giving us a better image overseas, also raised the expectations of people. No detail was beyond his view: before Apollo,

---

13 In a separate conversation with the author in New Delhi, Kiran Majumdar-Shaw also credited Dr Reddy with being the spark for the pharmaceutical industry in India. Her company Biocon, among others, supplies drugs to the nearly 2,000 pharmacies run by the Apollo Group across India.

hospitals usually had a hideous green for their walls; Dr Reddy brought in pleasant shades of pastel that proved soothing, mood enhancers in an emotionally difficult environment like a hospital.'

Guruswamy, whose views are highly sought after by universities in India and abroad – and even in India's government, no matter what its hue – not the least on account of his directness, says: 'Just look at how Dr Reddy inspired changes that have cut across all sectors such as education, the institutes of management, centres of excellence. Apollo has bootstrapped other institutions to a higher level. I've never felt more optimistic for India. Our Apollo hospitals can compete with the best in the US.

'Dr Reddy knew that medical care had to come into the twenty-first century with a revolution of ideas, not just machines. He paid great attention to detail. He broke every rule in the world. This is the same as Dhirubhai Ambani who built the world's largest polyester fibre company. When the government wouldn't let him import a second line, he brought it in as spare parts and put it to work. He challenged the government when it did not provide the encouragement, when he wanted to use all his capacity. He redefined the word "innovator".'

Nitin Desai similarly emphasized Dr Reddy's role as an innovator who went against the grain. I have known Desai for many years: his younger brother Shitin Desai was a classmate of mine at St Xavier's High School in Bombay in the early 1960s, and went on to be the executive chairman of DSP Merrill Lynch in India. Nitin Desai, a man widely known for his prodigious intellect, was Secretary in the government Department of Economic Affairs, and an advisor to the Planning Commission. He taught at the London School of Economics and served for many years as Under Secretary for Sustainable Development at the United Nations. When I spoke to him in New Delhi in October 2012, he was about to be named as president of Oxfam International.

'Dr Reddy is an example of thinking in a different way,' Desai said to me, as we sat in the lounge of the India International Centre in the heart of New Delhi, a gathering place for the city's intellectual, media and political elite. 'He was truly a pioneer. You've got to give him his due, he pushed and he kept pushing so that health care would be accessible. Look now at all the hospitals that have come up. It is very difficult to put a value on the vision that Dr Reddy had. He was a visionary to provide quality in health care, speed, and access . . . and he keeps doing it.'

Desai added: 'We are a nation of young people, and 70 per cent of our population is below the age of thirty. We can empower them with education and good health. Again, Dr Reddy recognized this, and he took action.'

Equally important was education and access to employment for women, who constitute 52 per cent of India's population of 1.2 billion, Desai told me.

'The transformation of women in Indian society is well underway, of course, and will also contribute to our strength,' he said. 'Old rules and traditions are fading and there are some excellent chief executives who are women. You have only to look at Dr Reddy's daughters, and other women leaders like Kiran Majumdar-Shaw.'

Some weeks after I'd spoken with Nitin Desai, I met with Kiran Majumdar-Shaw, the billionaire founder and chief executive officer of Biocon. Like Guruswamy, she talked about how Dr Reddy – a longtime friend – had changed the face of medical technology in India. 'His thought leadership is very modern. And the future that he sees for the health care sector is technology-driven,' she said. 'When I look at Dr Reddy, I see him as a father figure – not just for myself and the health care industry, but also for our country. He's somebody whom I admire because he's a transformational character.'

She told me the story of how Vijay Mallya, the liquor tycoon, invited Dr Reddy in 1990 to join hands with him in building a hospital in Bangalore. Even though the flamboyant Mallya – who shared Dr Reddy's passion for racehorses – promised that their joint venture would be humongous, Dr Reddy's instincts later persuaded him not to proceed with the arrangement. Mallya went ahead anyway, and later reportedly faced a number of management and other problems. There is general agreement that Mallya simply did not have the same standing in the medical industry as Dr Reddy. Dr Reddy, after all, had made Apollo a brand that resonated internationally.

Majumdar-Shaw paused, then continued: 'Who are the people who made India a global brand of excellence, and not of poverty? Who are the people who said, "We don't have to go around saying that we are poor, that we have no resources"? Who are the people who built their businesses under unimaginably difficult conditions and against all odds?

'Prathap Chandra Reddy is certainly one such person. When historians write about the builders of modern India, he will certainly be placed high on that list. Is it too much to call him an icon? Well, what else would you call him?'

In the early years, Apollo faced several obstacles and went through hardships that most health care providers who came into the sector in recent years would not have experienced.

Dr Reddy was very keen to invite Dr Sujoy B. Roy, the first head of the cardiology department at AIIMS, to join Apollo.

'Sujoy, I want somebody like you. People think that I'm nobody because I'm in private practice,' Dr Reddy said to Dr Roy at one point.

'Prathap, I get your message,' Dr Roy said.

A few weeks later, when Dr Reddy was in Los Angeles to raise funds from investors, someone told him, 'Sir, Dr Roy went to Mauritius on a holiday, and he passed away.'

This was devastating news because Dr Reddy not only admired Dr Roy, but he liked him personally. He believed that having a physician of Dr Roy's stature would enhance Apollo's reputation at a critical stage. Of course, never one to be stymied by setbacks, Dr Reddy went right ahead and built a first-rate health care infrastructure at Apollo.

When I asked Dr Reddy about this, he said, 'Yes, with great pleasure I do accept that I had a vital role to play, but it was also luminaries like the late Prime Minister Indira Gandhi who brought about changes in legislation and helped me in introducing high-end tertiary care that was unavailable for our people prior to 1983 – and that was the genesis of Apollo Hospitals Chennai.'

Similarly, Dr Reddy is highly complimentary about Pranab Mukherjee, currently President of India. Mukherjee has held several important ministerial portfolios, including that of finance.

'He championed so many significant changes in the country – each leading to transformational impact in India,' Dr Reddy said. 'The very first support that I would cite is the urgent assistance that he extended in 1981. At that point, there was tremendous scarcity of steel and cement and that was holding up the construction of Apollo Madras. Pranab Mukherjee was so impressed with our project that he sanctioned an allotment of 500 tons of steel at the price of Rs 1,850 per ton and 1,500 bags of cement at the highly subsidized government price of Rs 18 – the market price for each item was at least three times more.[14]

'The second support which I would refer to is that although R. Venkataraman, as finance minister, granted corporate status for Apollo and allowed listing of the company, he could not succeed in amending the existing rules for hospital funding. In a meeting regarding funding for hospitals I distinctly recall an incident wherein Pranab Mukherjee spoke to the then Economic Secretary, R.N. Malhotra, in my presence and said, "I will be an ineffective finance minister if I don't do this. He [Dr Reddy] will go to the prime minister who is convinced that Dr Reddy will bring international doctors and establish world-class health care in our country."

'Malhotra grabbed my hand and took me to his room. I had to wait for just a while before he came back and placed in my hand a "Letter of Order" which stated that Indian banks henceforth would be allowed to fund 50 per cent and the balance could be sought in foreign exchange for import of equipment. This along with several other major initiatives helped us to commission the first hospital in Chennai.'

In his last annual budget for 2011–12 presented in 2011 before he

---

14 Incidentally, for building his own house around the same time, Dr Reddy had bought steel and cement at market prices.

became the President of India, Pranab Mukherjee gave a major fillip to health care, by moving preventive health checks to the Negative List of Service Taxes.[15]

Dr Reddy recalls with great satisfaction the opportunity he got to show his appreciation for all that Pranab Mukherjee had done. Once, when Mukherjee held no cabinet post and wanted to visit Tirupati, Dr Reddy organized everything, starting from a car to meet him at the airport, take him to Tirupati and have a wonderful darshan. On his return Mukherjee stopped by Dr Reddy's house to be treated to a sumptuous tea by Sucharitha Reddy. His grateful parting words were: 'Dr Reddy, you helped my heart fill with the wonderful darshan of Lord Balaji. Now your wife has made sure that my stomach is full too.'

Dr Reddy recalled: 'When I asked Prime Minister Indira Gandhi to inaugurate the Madras hospital, she very kindly suggested, "You should ask the President to inaugurate, as they all feel that I have already done a lot for Apollo." I was not too happy that she sent me up to the President, but then the joy that I experienced on 18 September 1983 at the launch of Apollo Hospital Madras, India's first corporate hospital, took away the entire pain and problems equivalent to the million bricks of Apollo and turned my institution

---

15 For a couple of decades now, the government has been charging Service Tax (payable on any service rendered and accepted). There is a notified list of services that attract this tax. Over the years, this list has got progressively enlarged. But there were always some highly specialized or uncommon services which one could claim were not in the taxable list. The government then came up with another strategy. They notified what was called a 'Negative List'; unless the service offered was in the 'Negative List', it would be taxable. In the 2011–12 Union budget, preventive healthcare services were included in the 'Negative List'. This would mean a substantial saving of over 12 per cent in costs to the patient. Also, deductions introduced on income tax included Rs 5,000 for preventive health checks; an increase from 100 per cent to 150 per cent of capital expenditure for new hospitals with more than 100 beds; an increase from Rs 15,000 to Rs 20,000 on medical insurance premium paid by senior citizens; and an increase from Rs 40,000 to Rs 60,000 with respect to specified diseases for senior citizens.

into a temple of health. On that momentous day, President Zail Singh, who had allotted twenty minutes for the inauguration function, spent an hour and fifty minutes and repeatedly said, "An American hospital is here."

'With Giani Zail Singhji's blessings and the consummate commitment of all the people who joined me – the doctors, nurses, technologists, the maintenance team, housekeeping and all other supporting staff who have come from different backgrounds, religions, academics and even from different states – they all stood with me and assured that they would be committed to Apollo in bringing world-class health for our people and took a vow that their service to the patients who would come to our hospitals would be the same as one that they would give to their own kith and kin.

'In the last thirty years, this team Apollo has grown from 670 to nearly 70,000; it has achieved innumerable medical marvels for our people and has been instrumental in creating more than fifty hospitals. In each discipline they have surpassed the world standards,' Dr Reddy told me.

Among Dr Reddy's admirers is Dr Shivinder Singh Sidhu, a member of the IAS who served as Health Secretary under Prime Minister Indira Gandhi, and later as Governor of Goa, Manipur and Meghalaya. He also served a three-year term as Secretary General of the International Civil Aviation Organization, before which he was a troubleshooter for Prime Minister Indira Gandhi in Punjab during the time of the Khalistan agitation.

Dr Sidhu invited me to his apartment on Hailey Road in New Delhi for tea one afternoon in June 2013. His Man Friday, Ishwar, served a brew laced with ginger that soothed a sore throat I'd developed.

He reminisced about how both Indira and Rajiv Gandhi had been supporters of Dr Reddy's vision for better health care in India.

'Why can't we create a health care facility in India that compares with the very best that the world has to offer?' Indira Gandhi once said to Dr Sidhu, according to the latter. She told him that Dr Reddy's plans for the private sector Apollo Hospital Madras deserved full support.

'Dr Reddy always had a reputation for improving the health care system of India,' Dr Sidhu told me. 'And he had a reputation for being straightforward and scrupulous. That mattered a lot with Mrs Gandhi.'

'What also mattered to me was that Dr Reddy was always respectful of the government's decision-making processes, even if he faced a lot of hurdles,' Dr Sidhu said. 'I believe that the IAS has some very smart people and, with an occasional exception or two, they act in the public interest.'

Like Dr Sidhu, Keshav Desiraju believes that the IAS brings a strong element of continuity and discipline into the decision-making process. Desiraju serves as Secretary of the Department of Health and Family Welfare. I went to see him at Nirman Bhawan in New Delhi, a sprawling complex of nondescript buildings that house various units of the Ministry of Health and Family Welfare. I had earlier interviewed his minister, Ghulam Nabi Azad of Kashmir, who'd spoken highly and affectionately of Dr Reddy. But the minister also left me with the impression that his personal priority was less about private sector hospitals than developing government institutions.

Desiraju, who's enjoyed a sparkling career in the IAS, has a reputation of speaking his mind, and he certainly did so during our interview in his office. Behind his curved desk hung a black-and-white picture of Mahatma Gandhi. There was a large TV set mounted on one wall. On a coffee table in front of the sofas on which we sat there were nicely arranged fresh roses.

'I feel very firmly that the delivery of health care is a public responsibility,' he said. 'That doesn't mean the private sector doesn't have a role. Statistics are thrown around that 80 per cent of expenditure in health care is in the private sector – but these need to be looked at very carefully. I have no ill-will towards the private sector. But there's enough evidence – both anecdotal and data-based – that public facilities in health care are preferred.'

'I see my job as strengthening and building the public sector,' Desiraju, a handsome bespectacled man with a stylish haircut that highlighted his deep-set eyes, said to me. 'This means meeting the resource gap. And while we've had some success with the infrastructure gap, we still need more facilities and medical personnel in more and more locations around India, particularly in rural areas. The big issue in tackling non-communicable diseases such as diabetes, cancer and heart disease is that they need early diagnoses and long-term maintenance.'

Desiraju pointed out that the great divide in health care in India was at two levels: between urban centres and villages, and between the South and the North.

'Our cities are well supplied as far as hospitals go, but the villages are not,' he said. 'How someone in South Delhi or South Mumbai – both relatively affluent areas – reacts to the availability of good health care is very different from what you'd get in a village.'

'And a very big challenge is that the northern states – unlike the southern states – suffer badly from an absence on the ground of enough doctors and other medical personnel. You need a qualified medical person at some level – you cannot expect that only community-care centres will provide adequate medical services,' Desiraju said.

He also reflected on the Planning Commission's new mantra of 'public–private partnerships' in health care.

'The Planning Commission is gung-ho on public–private partnerships – but where is the partnership?' Desiraju said. (Perhaps this is the reason why Apollo is redefining these arrangements as 'public–private–people partnerships'.)

But he acknowledged that Dr Reddy – through Apollo Hospitals – had brought an important focus on maintaining high standards of accountability at health institutions. 'The complaint about government-run institutions is that they are poorly maintained, with many having an uncared-for look,' Desiraju said. 'To Dr Reddy's credit, he recognized the significance of a well-functioning institution, one that's marked by good management.'

CHAPTER NINETEEN

Making the Dream Happen

IT'S UNLIKELY THAT IN the late 1970s when he was planning Apollo Hospitals Prathap Chandra Reddy gave much thought – if indeed any thought at all – to the possibility that one day he would be regarded as an iconic figure of India. But one day, while he was still at HM Hospital in Madras, he did indeed think of the fact that Indian medical facilities badly needed technological upgrading.

That meant setting up a cardiac care unit. Initially the CCU had just two beds but it was fully equipped with all the diagnostic and monitoring devices such as EKG machines, defibrillators, monitors and even a treadmill. It was in this unit that HM Hospital launched its first preventative programme for heart care and also gave stress tests to the patients. Its emphasis was on diagnostic and preventative care and in a small, yet significant way it was the forerunner to Apollo's 'Billion Hearts Beating' campaign.

One day Dr Reddy went to meet a man named T.S. Narayanasami, who was branch manager of the Union Bank of India on Chamiers Road in the city's Nandanam section. Dr Reddy maintained an account at that branch for the unit of HM Hospital he ran; the unit was known as the Heart and Lung Clinic. Narayanasami was a very young man – only twenty-one years old, as it turned out. Typically, people didn't get to be branch managers of banks in those days until they were in their early thirties. If Dr Reddy was surprised at the banker's youth, he didn't show it.[1]

It also turned out that Narayanasami was not a banker by training, but a physicist who'd received his bachelor's degree from Vivekananda College in Madras. The banking job was available, and young Narayanasami had taken it. Dr Reddy and Narayanasami hit it off well – although the doctor thought that the banker's brand of tea, not Dr Reddy's favoured brew, was far too robust and its consumption far too frequent – and their chat resulted in a loan of Rs 100,000 that enabled HM Hospital to buy a treadmill with telemetry. It was to be the first machine of its kind in India. For a cardiologist like Dr Reddy, to have a treadmill at his cardiac facility made sense.

'But the fact that Dr Reddy was already thinking of how to incorporate technology in hospitals suggested to me that here was a man who had a vision of bringing better health care to India,' Narayanasami told me in a conversation many years later in Chennai. 'I realized that he had foresight. Even to this day, whenever we meet, Dr Reddy reminds me that I made it possible for him to acquire that first treadmill.'

The two men also discussed Dr Reddy's plans to build his own hospital. Narayanasami sat in on the initial meetings convened by Dr Reddy about raising capital, among other things through an IPO (initial public offering). 'It was purely his foresight and commitment that made the Apollo dream come true,' Narayanasami says. 'The self-confidence and enthusiasm that he demonstrated back then were remarkable – as was his sense of humour. Dr Reddy still retains those qualities. He hasn't changed.'

In the event, it wasn't Narayanasami's Union Bank but Indian Overseas Bank that took the lead position in the consortium that raised the funds for Apollo Madras. At the same time, there were

---

1 Narayanasami became a distinguished banker. His posts included chairmanships of Andhra Bank, Indian Overseas Bank and the Bank of India; he was also executive director of Punjab National Bank. He currently sits on the board of Dr Reddy's Indraprastha Apollo Hospital in New Delhi.

plenty of sceptics. Mohan Guruswamy recalls that leading journalists questioned how for-profit institutions such as Apollo might serve the ordinary Indian. Many years later, a well-known writer named Shobha Warrier asked Dr Reddy in Chennai: 'Is it not true that only the elite in India can avail the facilities that you offer in the Apollo Hospitals? Is it not true that the ordinary citizens of India cannot afford to treat themselves here?' Dr Reddy's response was: 'You just go and look at the people in the lobby. Do they look like the elite of India? They are all ordinary citizens of India. I am a man with a human heart.'

Dr Reddy's new office where he planned Apollo consisted of a small room, about 300 sq. ft, above a garage at HM Hospital. It was divided into two sections, one for the doctor and consultants, the other for the support team. It was in this small space that the plans for the big idea of Indian health care came together. After about a year and a half, the office moved to a slightly larger location near where he and Mrs Reddy now live in Bishop Garden. The occupants had a youthful, perhaps even naïve enthusiasm for the project. If it worked as anticipated, then India would move into the modern era of health care.

When he began his efforts towards establishing Apollo some thirty-five years ago, Dr Reddy had two main problems. The first was the labyrinthine Indian bureaucracy – the License Raj – and the second was money. But Dr Reddy had a big heart and the vision to achieve. He didn't think too much about spending the money but he was always thinking of how to get it. When it came to spending, if it was necessary for quality construction and equipment, then Dr Reddy approved the expense. The only criterion for approval was that the expenditure was really needed to build the best hospital and to provide the best of patient care.

Govind Rao and Associates, the architects, had created a cardboard model of the hospital, which focused everyone's attention on the task at hand. The drawings were approved and then came another roadblock when a nearby institution, the Asan Memorial School, said that the hospital would be detrimental to the health of its children. School officials succeeded in temporarily blocking construction. Discussion was held on how to handle the waste, and parents and politicians were concerned that it would pollute the environment. There was a very real possibility that the Apollo project would be a failure even before it started.[2]

Dr Reddy may have had many things on his mind, but failure wasn't one of them. 'Urban land ceiling problems consumed more than eighteen months. Numerous applications had to be made to import medical equipment and the process was cumbersome. The concept of a corporate hospital was new in India, and we certainly had our share of challenges,' he told me in a conversation in late 2012 at his office in Hyderabad, which was decorated with statues of Lord Ganesha and Lord Venkateshwara.

'I needed the government's blessings for bringing hospitals into the corporate sector, and allowing us to go public and issue shares, so I went to see Charan Singh, who was then India's prime minister. He also held the finance portfolio at the time,' Dr Reddy told me. Liberalization hadn't been brought into India's economy at that time, and even though Charan Singh was an economist by training himself, he disapproved of Indian entrepreneurs borrowing from abroad.

The famously crabby Charan Singh took one look at Dr Reddy's application, tore it up, and reportedly tossed it into the wastebasket.

What to do now? Again, Dr Reddy had the benefit of serendipity. It so happened that Indira Gandhi staged a political comeback in 1980 and became India's prime minister again. She had first suggested to Dr Reddy that perhaps he should build Apollo Hospital in either Andhra Pradesh or Karnataka, states that her Congress party controlled. But then she relented, and agreed that Madras would be an appropriate location, her closest aide, R.K. Dhawan, told me years afterwards at his home in New Delhi. Dhawan also recalls that one time when Dr Reddy went to see Indira, Chief Minister Tanguturi Anjaiah of Andhra Pradesh was waiting outside the prime minister's

---

2 The issue was finally resolved in the Madras courts in favour of Apollo
`   Hospitals.

office. It was the very same T. Anjaiah who had insisted that Dr
Reddy start a hospital in Andhra Pradesh.[3]

After Anjaiah had met with Indira, he came towards Dr Reddy,
took his hand and led him out of the building. He wanted him to
come to Hyderabad, where Dr Reddy had already started thinking
of building a second Apollo hospital. 'It is after all your home
state,' Anjaiah said. 'Come to Hyderabad and I will ensure you are
facilitated by our government in every way.'

He did indeed live up to that promise and offered Dr Reddy seven
acres in the heart of the city at Sanjeeviah Park.

Dr Reddy's brother-in-law, Surender Reddy, suggested that he go
to meet Umapathy Kamineni, Commissioner of Hyderabad and a
highly regarded member of the IAS.[4]

'If I were you, I wouldn't touch it,' Kamineni said, adding that
some regulations would be violated if Apollo Hospital were to be
raised on the property.

Meanwhile, Surender Reddy had identified several other properties.
One was a thirty-acre plot in Jubilee Hills, a place filled with huge
boulders. Dr Reddy climbed the terrain. Surender, meanwhile, kept
ruing, 'Why did I ever show him this place?'

Dr Reddy liked the plot, and he wanted Apollo Hyderabad to be
built in Jubilee Hills. Many considered this decision crazy but today
the Apollo Health City is a testament to that vision. Union Minister
A.P. Sharma came to lay the foundation stone on 27 August 1988.

Perched on the highest point in the city, Apollo Hyderabad abuts
a very old mosque, which they say many years ago housed a famous
hakim. People from all over the Deccan came to him for healing.
Maybe it was the vibrations at this place of healing that drew Dr
Reddy.

---

3 Anjaiah was the chief minister of Andhra Pradesh from 1978 to 1983. His
   wife is a patient of Apollo. He unfortunately passed away in 1986 before
   Apollo Hyderabad was opened.
4 Many years later, Kamineni's son Anil was to marry one of Dr Reddy's
   daughters, Shobana.

As with Anjaiah and Dhawan, Dr Reddy found a great ally in G.K. Moopanar, a powerful Congress leader from Tamil Nadu who was known to have turned down high-ranking cabinet positions several times. Indira Gandhi once offered him the defence minister position, and he refused to take it. Like K. Kamaraj – the former chief minister of Tamil Nadu – Moopanar was known as the 'kingmaker'. He would take Dr Reddy to Indira's residence on Safdarjung Road. Moopanar would stand in front. 'Reddy, Reddy,' he would say to Dr Reddy, beckoning him so that the physician got a chance to meet her. And Indira would invariably say, 'I believe you have something to say to me.'

Years later, Moopanar's son, G.K. Vasan – a member of Prime Minister Manmohan Singh's cabinet – told me that his father always held Dr Reddy in high regard because 'he was genuinely a people's person – Dr Reddy liked meeting people and finding out about their needs.'

Vasan recalled that his mother Kasturi had been operated on at HM Hospital for an intestinal obstruction, and that Dr Reddy supervised her stay 'day and night'.

'It was a very risky surgery – but she got her life back,' Vasan told me over coffee at his home in the Alwarpet section of Chennai, a leafy neighbourhood where a number of movie stars and politicians also live. 'I was very young back then, but I can still recall how Dr Reddy was attentive to each and every patient. That's when our families became very close.'

Moopanar was persuaded that Dr Reddy's vision for a private-sector hospital was indeed viable. 'My father was very happy to help Dr Reddy achieve his vision,' Vasan said. 'He was particularly impressed by Dr Reddy's integrity, and how determined he was in the face of all kinds of resistance to his hospital project. In the Rajiv Gandhi years, the prime minister himself often said that India should become a medical destination, and he supported Dr Reddy's efforts.'

Dr Reddy and Moopanar would meet in Chennai or at the Western Court in New Delhi, where the Congress leader stayed. (Moopanar stayed at Western Court for thirteen years, and Vasan has been staying at the same quarters for the last twelve years.) His position as General Secretary of the All India Congress Committee made him a very influential figure indeed; he was a troubleshooter for both Indira Gandhi and Rajiv Gandhi. Moopanar sold hundreds of acres of his own family property in order to help the Congress party in Tamil Nadu.

'My father was also impressed by the fact that Dr Reddy had the remarkable ability to be persuasive,' Vasan said. 'He did not try to bulldoze people into accepting his ideas. His presentations were carefully prepared; my father often said how thorough Dr Reddy was in explaining the Apollo concept to anybody who cared to listen. He walked them through his ideas until they were convinced of their validity. And my father was impressed by the fact that Dr Reddy had focus. It was his intensity about the need for good health care for India that impressed my father. It also impressed Prime Minister Indira Gandhi.'

To this day, Dr Reddy speaks warmly and respectfully of Indira Gandhi. She recognized his total dedication to improving health care in India. And he credits her with expediting developments in health care. 'She made it very clear that she liked the Apollo concept,' Dr Reddy told me. 'Indira Gandhi was responsible for giving birth to my concept.'

'Prime Minister, the rich can afford to go abroad for treatment,' Dr Reddy said to Indira during one of their first meetings, 'but what about ordinary Indians? They deserve the best treatment here in their own country.'

At that time, Chief Minister M.G. Ramachandran of Tamil Nadu was putting roadblocks before Apollo Madras. Indira instructed C.R. Krishnaswamy Rao,[5] the Cabinet Secretary, to write to MGR about the hospital. In effect, Rao wrote to MGR, 'Your government should help Dr Reddy to bring a hospital to our country. The prime minister wonders what objections you have to such a worthy objective.'

---

5 C.R. Krishnaswamy Rao, who belonged to the Andhra Pradesh cadre of the IAS, died in Chennai on 12 February 2013 at the age of eighty-six.

Whenever Dr Reddy went to meet MGR at his home or office subsequently, the latter would pretend to be asleep.

So nothing happened for three months. One day, Indira Gandhi asked Dr Reddy to come to her office in Delhi. Dhawan said she was aware of what had happened.

'Nothing has happened so far with the hospital?' The prime minister said to Dr Reddy. Then, turning to C.R. Krishnaswamy Rao, she said: 'Can you do anything about this?'

Rao wrote a letter to MGR, saying that it would be appreciated if MGR gave his approval by 31 March. Dr Reddy went to Satara on 29 March to meet the Shankaracharya. The swami told him, 'Everything is over, permission is given.'

On an earlier occasion, Dr Reddy had met with the Shankaracharya before starting Apollo Hospitals. He asked the Paramacharya (the elder Shankaracharya) three questions: 'Can I do it? Will I do it? Should I do it?' The reply he got was: 'Why do you keep asking? You were born to do it. You will do it. You should do it.'

Dr Reddy caught a train to Hyderabad from Satara. He arrived in the city on 31 March, and then flew to Madras. Everybody he encountered at HM Hospital said, 'The CM wants to meet you.'

MGR had invited him home for breakfast.

Dr Reddy told Sucharitha: 'This is a man who doesn't want me to open my mouth. Now he wants to feed me.'

When Dr Reddy arrived at the chief minister's home, MGR was full of warmth. He'd been writing something at a desk next to the dining table. The heavily laden table was groaning with all sorts of aromatic dishes.

'Come, come, come,' MGR said.

Dr Reddy recalls that several mutton dishes were served, and that he ate some of them, along with idlis.

'Why do you have to go all the way up to the top?' MGR said to Dr Reddy, in a veiled reference to the fact that he'd received Indira Gandhi's letter via Rao. 'We can settle these things among ourselves. It's nice that you are putting up a good hospital.'

Then MGR added: 'We'll go to the Secretariat. And we'll get the paper signed. It will take ten minutes.'

When they reached the Secretariat, MGR's secretary said: 'This will take more than ten minutes. About forty-five minutes.'

As it happened, it was the day Anjaiah arrived in Madras to sign a document with MGR detailing the sharing of the waters of the Krishna river – the Telugu Ganga – between Tamil Nadu and Andhra Pradesh.

When Anjaiah deplaned at the airport, he was quite upset that only a single motorcycle escort had been sent for him. By the time Anjaiah reached the government bungalow where he was being put up, he was seething with anger.

He felt so insulted that he declared that he would return to Hyderabad without attending the document signing ceremony.

Dr Reddy, who was with the Andhra chief minister, could sense his anger and told him that Sucharitha had prepared a number of his favourite dishes, and that the Reddys expected him for lunch at their home. But Anjaiah said that the food should be sent to an Andhra government bungalow on the Andhra side of the border.

'Sucha didn't call you for food,' Dr Reddy told Anjaiah. 'She called you to visit our home.'

Finally, Anjaiah agreed to come to the Reddy home, not the least because he was personally very fond of Dr Reddy and Sucharitha.

Even as he and Dr Reddy were talking at the Reddy home – with several ministers having gathered in the living room – the phone rang. It was MGR.

Dr Reddy said to Anjaiah: 'At least please take his call.'

'Mannichidu Iyya,' MGR said to Anjaiah in Tamil, which roughly translates into, 'Please forgive me.'

Anjaiah replied brusquely, 'All right, I will come this evening.'

He went to the signing ceremony. However implicitly, Dr Reddy had helped in ameliorating the clash of two huge political egos.

MGR later told Dr Reddy: 'Whatever I've done, you've done a bigger thing.' At the ceremony, both MGR and Anjaiah praised each other.

That ability to resolve problems between people has been a major characteristic of Dr Reddy's all his life. He doesn't like confrontations. Even when people disagree with him, he is able to mollify them. And he's able to convince others of the value of his vision for Apollo – and how that vision can benefit the nation.

'Dr Reddy had remarkable foresight – and remarkable persistence,' M.R. Sivaraman, the former Revenue Secretary and India's Executive Director at the International Monetary Fund, said. 'He should be proud of his accomplishments. Dr Reddy had a way of getting others to see his vision not only for Apollo but also for health care in India.'

Ghyanendra Nath Bajpai, former executive chairman of the Life Insurance Corporation of India, supported Sivaraman's view of Dr Reddy. He said: 'Dr Reddy is very persistent, which isn't common to people. He demonstrates persuasive leadership. He will get his team around him. He's willing to listen. He will find ways to navigate around problems. That helped when it came to dealing with India's bureaucracy. In India, pioneering is very difficult. But he created a successful model. That went a long way towards persuading officials that Dr Reddy was acting in the national interest, and not just on behalf of Apollo.'

Also in 1980, Ramaswamy Venkataraman, a Tamil lawyer and politician, became minister of finance in the Indira Gandhi administration.[6] Decisions affecting a ministry rarely went to the prime minister directly unless their resolution had national ramifications. Venkataraman's daughter, Lakshmi Venkataraman Venkatesan, recalls being present at a meeting between the two men: 'I heard my father's advice to Dr Reddy, "I have seen in you the spirit, the talent and the capability to achieve your goals. Leave aside the problems as I am sure you will find the solutions."' It was Venkataraman who gave permission for Apollo to become a corporate entity.

---

6 Ramaswami Venkataraman later became President of India, serving from 20 August 1982 to 27 July 1987. He died on 27 January 2009, just after his ninety-eighth birthday. Earlier, he had his heart surgery done at Apollo, and recovered fully.

Becoming a corporate entity was one thing; being one was entirely
another matter. That meant money. 'Babudom intervened here, too,'
Dr Reddy said. 'A joint secretary in the finance ministry put up
resistance because hospitals weren't included in the institutional list
for funding. I made no fewer than two dozen pilgrimages to New
Delhi and Mumbai.'

After long meetings, endless cups of coffees, and urgency disguised
as appeals to the target's conscience and desire to expedite progress in
India, Dr Reddy was finally given permission to borrow 50 per cent
from Indian banks, and the rest from foreign institutions. Apollo's
first loan came from Indian Overseas Bank – the first time that the
bank funded a hospital. It wouldn't be the last time, of course. There
are more than a thousand corporate-sector hospitals in India today,
and most of them have little difficulty getting loans from banks. Most
of today's corporate hospitals enjoy easy access to private equity
funding and are able to scale up a lot faster.

Senior government officials who were involved in the decision-
making process at the time say that they appreciated the fact that
Dr Reddy respected them and did not attempt to circumvent
procedures. After all, he was a friend of Prime Minister P.V.
Narasimha Rao – who also hailed from Andhra Pradesh – and Dr
Reddy could have easily gone to the prime minister to get the job
done. Indeed, Narasimha Rao later chuckled and asked Dr Reddy
why he had put himself through such a grind instead of coming
directly to the prime minister. But it would have been uncharacteristic
on Dr Reddy's part to use his personal friendships in such a manner.

'He was always pukka, especially with regard to his balance
sheets,' Sivaraman told me at his home in the Mylapore section of
Chennai, opposite the 2,000-year-old Kapaleeshwar Temple. 'People
might disagree about the concept of corporate-sector hospitals, but
no one, not a single soul, could ever challenge Dr Reddy's personal
integrity. He has proven how important his contribution has been
to health care in India.'

Finance Minister Venkataraman asked Dr Reddy to approach

the Industrial Development Bank of India.[7]

IDBI said they thought the 'project was very unique and that they would like to fund it,' according to Dr Reddy. 'Venkataraman was visiting Madras; he asked me to get there towards the end of his day, at around eight o'clock, to sign on the permission. But in between, someone in the department of banking had written on the permission document that funding the project would invite severe criticism. So Venkataraman had a blank face and told me this can't be done. "You meet me in Delhi in a week," he said.'

During that week, there was a Cabinet shuffle, and Venkataraman was made the defence minister, and the current President of India, Pranab Mukherjee, took charge as finance minister.

The current prime minister, Manmohan Singh, was the Governor of the Reserve Bank of India at the time.[8] Dr Reddy was asked to wait for the finance minister's verdict: 'Indira Gandhi (the prime minister) had approved it, he (the banking Secretary) said, "Let's see what the minister will say."' The elusive letter of permission came at last; the finance minister had allowed Apollo to borrow 50 per cent from banks in India and 50 per cent in foreign exchange for import of medical equipment.

But it did not end there. Dr Reddy had to go for credit authorization to the Reserve Bank of India. In the meantime, the credit authorization officer had changed. 'He said, "Why should I turn the wheel fully to give you permission?"'

Dr Reddy was disheartened. He was at the airport, heading back

---

7 At the time, IDBI was constituted under the Industrial Development Bank of India Act, 1964, as a Development Financial Institution (DFI). It was regarded as a public financial institution and continued to serve as a DFI for nearly forty years, till 2004. Its chairman and managing director at the time was S.S. Nadkarni, whom Dr Reddy admires very much indeed. In an interview in late 2013, one of Nadkarni's successors, Dr Kamalaksha U. Mada, told me how much he admired Dr Reddy's scrupulous dealings with IDBI and other banks.

8 Singh was RBI Governor between 1982 and 1985.

to Madras, when he bumped into the then minister of civil aviation, A.P. Sharma, at the airport.

'Sharma suggested that he and I go to Delhi right away and knock on Pranab Mukherjee's door. It was 11.15 at night when we reached Mukherjee's residence. I told Pranab Mukherjee: "Tomorrow the deputy governor[9] is going for two weeks to the United States. My whole project will be derailed." He said to me, "It will be done." And he asked me to get to the Reserve Bank building at noon the next day.'

Dr Reddy took the first flight to Mumbai. The monsoons were in full force, delaying him by forty-five minutes. He reached the RBI building at 12.45 p.m., and heard someone say, 'Who's Dr Reddy? Who's Dr Reddy?'

Dr Reddy went into the official's chamber and looked on as the credit authorization officer signed on the permission document permitting Apollo to raise funds from banks and foreign exchange, and said: 'You know why I am doing this.'

'Finally my ordeal of cutting through layers of bureaucracy and red tape to get permissions to build a state-of-the-art hospital ended,' Dr Reddy said. 'Then I received a call from the finance minister, saying: "You were not there at 12.00." He was keeping track.'

Dr Reddy said, 'Rain. The whole city is flooded.'

Pranab Mukherjee said, 'Are you happy?'

Dr Reddy said again and again, 'Yes, sir.'

Some years later, after Sivaraman became Revenue Secretary in the ministry of finance, he had occasion to deal with Apollo business.[10]

---

9 A man named Amitav Ghosh who later served as Governor of the RBI for a short period.

10 Sivaraman's father M.S. Ramanathan, who was with Andhra University, came to know Dr Reddy through his boss and mentor O. Pulla Reddy, ICS. Ramanathan was to become one of the shareholders in Apollo. Sivaraman himself had once visited Dr Reddy at HM Hospital to get a complete health check-up. In later years, both his parents received treatment at Apollo Chennai. His wife Nalini's brother, Dr A. Ganapathy, and his spouse Dr Vijaya Ganapathy, are both highly respected physicians at Apollo Chennai.

The Revenue Secretary's post is of great significance in the government, because it is he who prepares the draft of the tax proposals for the annual government budget. Those proposals are included in the speech that the finance minister traditionally delivers in Parliament in late February or early March each year, which is shown to the prime minister in the stealth of the night before public unveiling. In addition to the finance minister and his chief economic advisor, only the finance secretary and the revenue secretary are present at this meeting, which is usually held at the prime minister's residence. Every tax proposal in the budget has to be signed off by the revenue secretary before it can be shown to the finance minister and then the prime minister. Sometimes the prime minister offers suggestions – usually predicated on existing political exigencies – and then the budget's final version is taken to Parliament.

Dr Reddy was seeking elimination of various conditionalities in the import of medical equipment at concessional rates of duty. But opposition came from some quarters in the health ministry. Undoubtedly there were questionable doings in the process that affected the import of modern equipment by Indian hospitals.

'I was trying to run world-class hospitals, and people were obstructing me from importing modern equipment,' Dr Reddy said.

According to finance ministry records, Sivaraman was asked to see his boss, Manmohan Singh, who was finance minister at the time in the government of Prime Minister P.V. Narasimha Rao[11] – this was in 1995 – and explain the situation.[12]

The finance minister was fully supportive of Dr Reddy. But Manmohan Singh also said it would be desirable if the reduction or elimination of import duties on life-saving equipment got the

11 Manmohan Singh is widely considered the architect of the liberalization of India's economy, which started during the administration of Prime Minister P.V. Narasimha Rao. Singh became India's prime minister in May 2004.
12 Keshav Desiraju, Secretary in the department of health and family welfare, told me in an interview that even if he had wanted to proceed unilaterally with the proposal, Finance Minister Manmohan Singh would have involved the top officials of the ministry, especially the Revenue Secretary.

endorsement of important constituencies. The highly respected Sivaraman told him that he would form a committee consisting of doctors from medical institutions such as the All India Institute of Medical Sciences (AIIMS). These doctors were only too glad to join the committee and offer suggestions for medical equipment that should be exempted from import duty. When some dentists heard about the committee's work, they too made their own list and gave it to Sivaraman.[13]

Despite the influence of what is generally termed as Delhi's 'secretary panchayat', the final word in making recommendations to the finance minister such as the lifting of import duties was the prerogative of the Revenue Secretary. Manmohan Singh agreed that life-saving equipment that used to be imported annually at the time by hospitals would be exempt from import duty.[14]

Amarnath Verma, then the Principal Secretary to Prime Minister P.V. Narasimha Rao, was also a strong supporter of Dr Reddy's – and said as much. Verma was considered to be one of the behind-the-scenes driving forces of the economic liberalization that was being carried out by Narasimha Rao and Manmohan Singh. Such support helped counter critics within the government bureaucracy who had opposed the lifting of the import duty on medical equipment.

Keshav Desiraju told me that however sympathetic cabinet ministers or even the prime minister might be to issues that are brought to their attention, 'Ministers are respectful of civil servants' opinions.'

---

13 These conversations and transactions are included in official records.

14 Finance Minister Manmohan Singh, in his 1995–96 budget speech, told Parliament on 15 March 1995: 'For promoting health care, last year I had simplified the import duty structure on medical equipment, exempted many types of life-saving equipment from payment of duty, and abolished the certification procedure for availing of the exemption for charitable hospitals. In order to help manufacture and maintenance of medical equipment, I am extending the benefit of full exemption from import duty to all parts of exempted life-saving and sight-saving equipment. Some crucial spare parts of other dutiable medical equipment such as populated PCB will attract an import duty of 15 per cent. I am also proposing to fully exempt linear accelerators, which are vital for the treatment of cancer patients . . .'

The creation of Apollo had a multiplier effect. 'Dr Reddy was a true pioneer in every sense of the term,' Dr Devi Shetty, a well-known cardiac surgeon and founder of the Narayana Hrudayalaya in Bangalore, told me in a conversation. 'He opened the door for the rest of us who followed him into the private sector in health care.'

Dr Shetty – who trained at Guy's Hospital in London – noted that Dr Reddy has encouraged fellow clinicians and several organizations in starting up hospitals in the country. 'His life's journey has been emblematic of the fact that in health care, it is more about collaboration than competition,' Dr Shetty said.

———

Loans alone wouldn't suffice to get Apollo started. Prathap Chandra Reddy needed to float shares, for which he needed government permission.

'In Bombay they laughed when I said I wanted to list the share,' Dr Reddy said.

'But by then Dr Reddy had acclimatized himself to people laughing at his plans and their disparaging comments,' according to journalist Shweta Punj.

One of the first people whom Dr Reddy contacted about raising capital in the markets was an influential Bombay-based financier named Bhupen Dalal. Dalal, a lanky, amiable man, ran a company called CIFCO and was considered a whiz kid of Dalal Street[15] – the equivalent of New York's Wall Street. He was not initially impressed.

A common friend, S.V.S. Raghavan, had introduced Dalal to Dr Reddy on the telephone about an IPO for Apollo Hospitals. 'I immediately turned it down with a remark, "How can hospitals make

---

15 In the 1990s, Bhupen Dalal became embroiled in a securities controversy involving a financier named Harshad Shah. No charges were brought against Dalal, but Shah was first found guilty and then acquitted. Shah died in December 2001 of a massive heart attack.

money? It is always charity,"' Dalal told me about Dr Reddy's idea for a for-profit hospital.

'Dr Prathap Reddy tried convincing me that a corporate hospital was like a service industry. He said that he had thought of me since I had successfully managed the East India Hotel [what is now Trident Hotel at Nariman Point in Mumbai] public issue without any bank or financial institution support. I shared the conversation with my colleague Kamlesh Gandhi. His reaction was: "Let us do something new." The Apollo Hospital was the first corporate hospital wanting to tap the capital market. So I invited Dr Reddy for a meeting at my office in Mumbai. He gave a presentation that completely convinced me to take up the assignment. The presentation was so carefully prepared. I was even more impressed by the charm of the person behind the concept. After the presentation, I was convinced that a corporate hospital was a viable business model and that it would succeed, particularly in the hands of a person like Dr Reddy.'

How did Bhupen Dalal go about raising capital? 'We decided that we would ask the team of brokers who were with us in all the earlier issues to come forward. Our tactic was that if we asked them for a donation to a hospital, they would give it readily. Their answers were "Yes!" We then asked them to participate in underwriting anywhere between Rs 100,000 and Rs 500,000 each. Thus the issue was tied up at a party on my terrace garden in the office that very evening.'

But raising capital can be a laborious process. The first part involved convincing the underwriters. Later there was a host of procedures such as applying for permission to the Controller of Capital Issues. There was the drafting of the prospectus, and there were stock exchange formalities.

The real challenge, however, lay in marketing the Apollo shares, whose face value was ten rupees. Press conferences had to be organized. Once the prospectus was filed, meetings with brokers and potential investors were scheduled. It was necessary to tap the non-resident Indian market to obtain subscriptions.

'I got hold of a directory of all doctors in Britain,' Bhupen Dalal told me. 'I marked Indian-sounding names – and avoided names that could be both Indian or other nationalities. My office did some blind mailing.'

Dalal and Dr Reddy then went on a trip to the Gulf. They visited wealthy individuals and financial institutions in the United Arab Emirates, Qatar, Kuwait and Bahrain. Dalal could not obtain a visa for Saudi Arabia, so Dr Reddy went there by himself.

Dr Jetti Geeta Reddy, currently minister for major industries in the Andhra Pradesh government, was working as a gynaecologist in Saudi Arabia at the time. She fondly remembers hosting Dr Reddy and inviting her colleagues over to her home for dinner to hear the Apollo pitch. She calls herself part of the Apollo family. She and her husband, Dr Ramachandra Reddy, not only invited colleagues to their home to hear Dr Reddy, they also invested $5,000 – despite the fact that they had planned to start their own nursing home.

Apart from such 'road shows', Dr Reddy and Bhupen Dalal met many doctors in Britain individually and solicited $5,000 each from them. [16] Most of these physicians were quizzical – if only because the concept of a corporate-sector hospital in India was totally new to them. Dr Reddy's second daughter Suneeta – who is joint managing director, and looks after finance at Apollo – recalls: 'Our father used to travel from one city to another in the United States, meeting groups of Indian doctors and explaining his vision.'[17]

Like Bhupen Dalal, Dr Reddy's presentation, and the brochure that he distributed, impressed these potential investors.[18] But they

---

16 Among those who invested in establishing Apollo were hundreds of Indian doctors, including doctors living in the United States, and doctors in Britain. Their average investment was $5,000.

17 That vision, as it translated into reality, went something like this: Apollo Hospitals, Madras, was the first hospital to go public in 1983, offering 12.96 lakh shares. It raised Rs 1.7 crore. For expansion, it went for a rights issue in 1984 and mopped up Rs 1.50 crore. It took eighteen months for Dr Reddy to find a piece of land for the first hospital and to get the necessary approvals. Securing licenses to import the medical equipment for the hospital itself took two years.

18 Dr Reddy credits his four daughters – who were still in school and college at the time – with preparing a lot of the initial presentation material. 'They

had some misgivings in the beginning as Dr Reddy planned to invest heavily in state-of-the-art technology. Some of the savvy investors wondered if he would succeed by buying the best against calculating the returns. 'There were a continuous number of impediments[19] and some of the NRIs began to ask for their money back. Dr Reddy would always tell them to wait, assure them that acceptance and approval were coming, and he would ask for just a little more time. Most agreed to wait,' Dalal said.

However, as soon as the company started making profits, the doubts of these investors evaporated. They became convinced that Apollo would succeed. Dalal believes that Apollo's success has been a combination of several factors. One is that Dr Reddy tried to introduce professional hospital management practices to Indian health care. A second is that the ambience, systems and flow of treatment for patients attracted people. Third, Dr Reddy insisted on high-quality doctors because he wanted his hospital to be the very best. He knew it would not succeed otherwise.

T. Subbarami Reddy, a member of the Rajya Sabha from Andhra Pradesh – and former chairman of the Tirupati Temple Trust – told me in a conversation in New Delhi that there was a fourth factor that contributed to Dr Reddy's success. 'We Reddys are risk takers. We

---

prepared the hospital brochure so well that when I took it abroad people were surprised to see such good quality material from India,' Dr Reddy said.

19 In 1979, when Apollo Hospitals was incorporated, the health care industry was a fragmented mass of hospitals. There were government hospitals, missionary hospitals and those run by not-for-profit trusts. In tertiary care, some renowned hospitals like Bombay Hospital and Breach Candy in Bombay and Sir Ganga Ram Hospital in New Delhi had made a mark, having come into existence in the 1950s. Jaslok Hospital in Bombay then also made its mark. Earlier, Christian Medical College in Vellore had established a stellar reputation. As Rama V. Baru, professor at the Centre of Social Health and Community Medicine, Jawaharlal Nehru University, puts it, 'Health care was a confused mass. Though there were several renowned hospitals which were keen to improve their own clinical excellence, none thought of spreading out to different geographies and replicating the model as Apollo did.' Sources: Various, including Apollo website.

are aggressive by nature and a dominating force both politically and agriculturally. As a natural offshoot, Reddys are successful business barons as well. No one in his right mind would have taken the risks that Dr Reddy took in the late 1970s. But he was a Reddy – full of self-confidence, brimming with energy. He had a vision. He knew – and I knew – that it was only a matter of time before he succeeded in creating Apollo,' Subbarami Reddy said, dressed in an impeccably tailored long shirt, khadi jacket and tight trousers. His drawing room featured many portraits of leading Indian political figures such as Gandhi, Nehru, Indira and Rajiv. 'Dr Reddy works all the time – that's another Reddy trait. He wants things done today – today, not tomorrow.'[20]

'So am I surprised by Dr Reddy's success?' Subbarami Reddy said. 'Of course not. There was never any doubt in my mind. His greatness lies as a strong leader of a strong institution and as an able organizer.'

Bhupen Dalal mirrored his thoughts. 'The growth of the last thirty years can be said to be phenomenal, but I am not surprised,' he said. 'Dr Reddy has always been a charming personality, and coupled with his passion for health care and meticulous planning, he did not find any difficulty later in raising monies. After all, nothing succeeds better than success.'

I asked Bhupen Dalal: 'What, in your view, are the financial risks associated with investing in Apollo?'

His response: 'None whatsoever. The business model is robust and I feel Dr Reddy will succeed very well in spreading his wings in India as well as overseas. He has a good management in place, with his four daughters fully on the ground. He is a genuine nation builder.'

When I mentioned to Dr Reddy that Bhupen Dalal – an initial sceptic – had characterized him as a 'nation builder', he demurred. Then he quoted from one of his favourite management gurus, Ram

---

20 T. Subbarami Reddy hails from one of the first Reddy families from Nellore to enter the construction business — fifty years ago, with the Nagarjuna Sagar dam. The family's business interests now span hotels, films, construction, power, highways, infrastructure, sugar and chemicals.

Charan, who said during a speech in Chennai: 'No nation ever got built without entrepreneurship. It's the entrepreneurs who are able to have a vision, who have the tenacity and the energy to build the enterprises and that's how a nation is built.'

The ability to persuade and to bring people around to his point of view has been a characteristic of Prathap Chandra Reddy's since his youth. To bureaucrats he would point out the sore need for more hospital beds in a demographically growing India – and the fact that beyond providing basic primary health care, the government simply didn't have the wherewithal or the manpower to offer tertiary care. To public intellectuals and other influencers of public policy, Dr Reddy would point out that by the year 2030 India would have a retiree population of 500 million – out of a projected national population of 1.6 billion, the world's largest such cohort. Who would give them the appropriate health care? Dr Reddy often says, 'We are the disease capital of the world for diabetes and heart problems. The United Nations estimates that the cost of this disease burden by 2020 will be $500 billion annually in India.'

A man named Anil Thadani was convinced that Dr Reddy was the right man to provide such health care for Indians. In the early '90s he was running a private equity investment business that was part of the worldwide Schroder Ventures Group. His mandate was to look for interesting investment opportunities throughout the Asia-Pacific region. Thadani had started his private equity investment business in 1981 and through the decade of the '80s had become a major investor in the hospitality sector, principally hotels and tourism.

In 1989, Thadani's group decided to divest the vast majority of its hospitality interests because of a concern as to the amount of real estate exposure it had with these investments. It was at this time that Thadani started to think about what the next 'big' investment theme would be for this region.

'After some very basic diligence, we came to form a view that health care would provide an interesting investment theme,' Thadani told me from Singapore, where he is now based. 'Our thinking was largely based on a simple premise that the vast majority of health care in Asia was public health care; private health care was largely undeveloped. We felt that the demand for private health care would increase as the disposable incomes of the Asian population increased. As people became more affluent, they would look for private health care. In addition, we were attracted by the defensive nature of health care; we felt it was less susceptible to the economic swings that were commonplace in Asia.'

There had been no private equity investment in health care until that time; the common view was that only doctors understood health care – and doctors generally did not make good businessmen so health care was not considered something one could easily invest in. Furthermore, it was very difficult to find a health care business to invest in as the vast majority of private health care was practised like a cottage industry with private practitioners setting up small clinics to see their patients.

Sometime in early 1994, Anil Thadani was introduced to Dr Reddy. At that time, the Indraprastha Apollo Hospital in Delhi was under construction and Dr Reddy, upon learning of Thadani's interest in health care, offered his group a 25 per cent equity interest in that hospital.

'When I first met Dr Reddy, I could not help but be impressed with his presence and his confidence. He struck me as a person with a mission that he was passionate about. Instead of simply accepting his offer to invest in the Delhi hospital, I decided to probe a little further to see if I could get him to tell me what his larger game plan was. Something told me that I may have met the entrepreneur doctor that I had been looking for,' Thadani said.

Over the next several months, he and Dr Reddy met many times; Thadani was fascinated by Dr Reddy's sense of purpose, and by his vision to build a world-class health care business in India.

'The more time I spent with him, and the more I listened to his plans, the more impressed I was with his passion and his clarity of thought on the subject. In my mind, I was certain that this was the health care business that we had been looking for,' Thadani said.

At the time, there had been no foreign private equity investment in India by anyone, and there had been no private equity investment in health care anywhere in Asia. 'And here we were thinking about making a private equity investment in India, in health care! I can think of at least one seasoned private equity investor who thought we were mad,' Thadani said, chuckling.

During their various meetings and discussions, Thadani and his colleagues gained a much better understanding of how Dr Reddy's operations were structured. He had a private management company, called Indian Hospitals Corporation Limited (IHC), which would manage the hospitals that he built. The actual hospitals themselves could be owned by other investors or indeed partly by IHC and partly by other investors.

'We suggested to Dr Reddy that we would be interested in partnering him in realizing this dream of creating a world-class health care enterprise in India but that we wanted our interests to be perfectly aligned with his and, as such, we were also interested in investing in IHC, his private company. When I first thought about asking him about investing in IHC, I felt that he would resist this but to my very pleasant surprise, Dr Reddy immediately saw the logic of what we were suggesting. He readily agreed to give us a stake in IHC and we also agreed that, at some time in the future, we would look to merging the hospital-owning entities with IHC to create an integrated health care enterprise, which we felt would be very well received by the investing public,' Thadani said.

'Since everything seemed to be going well, we commenced our usual due diligence process on the existing business. It was our first investment in India (indeed the first foreign private equity investment in India) and the first investment in health care, so we proceeded quite cautiously and drilled down quite deep with probing questions about Apollo's affairs. We were very pleasantly surprised to find, not only Dr Reddy, but the entire family, very open and cooperative and they went out of their way to help us gain an understanding of their business and their plans for the future. The more we delved, the more impressed we were and the more certain I was that we had found an excellent business partner,' he added.

A key aspect of the due diligence process was that it was by no means one-sided.

'While we were attempting to understand Apollo's business, Dr Reddy was evaluating us to try and determine whether we would, in fact, be acceptable business partners for his enterprise. His idea of due diligence went well beyond the usual reference checks,' Thadani told me. 'I can remember having to attend a very hot prayer session in a temple where we were surrounded by fire and, not anticipating this, I had showed up in a suit! I think I lost a few pounds by the time the session was over. On another occasion, I was introduced to Dr Reddy's astrologer – D. Nagarajan – and had to spend a full session with him as he evaluated my suitability as a potential partner of Apollo and of Dr Reddy. Fortunately, not only did I pass muster, but I also distinctly remember the astrologer giving Dr Reddy a prediction of a glorious future for our partnership together. With the benefit of hindsight, I now realize how right he was. At the time, all I could think of was how this holy man could have nixed our whole investment, and months of work, if he had decided, in his wisdom, that I was not a suitable partner.

'Our diligence proceeded smoothly, as fortunately did his on us, and soon after, we documented our investment and became shareholders in both the Indraprastha Apollo Hospital in Delhi and in IHC. We invested a total of approximately $15 million for our stake in these two businesses and Dr Reddy invited my partner and me to join the board.'

Over the nine years or so that Thadani's company held this investment, it had an excellent relationship with Apollo and all of the members of the Reddy family who, he says, 'were so active in and passionate about the business'.

Several years later, in 1999, Thadani made his second health care investment in Parkway Holdings in Singapore. Parkway was the leading health care player in Southeast Asia.

'I felt that there was opportunity to put two plus two together and perhaps get five! I was already on the board of Apollo, so I invited Dr Reddy to join the board of Parkway, where I was the chairman.

We managed to do a couple of joint ventures together with the two companies, the most notable of which was the Apollo-Gleneagles hospital in Calcutta,' Thadani said.

'Our stake in Apollo was held in a fund, which had a finite life of ten years; before we could successfully realize additional synergies between the two businesses, our fund came to the end of its life and we had to, sadly, sell our stake in Apollo. Financially, it was one of the best investments we had ever made. I was sad to sell it because I was convinced that it had a long way to go – this has, of course, been borne out by actual events as Apollo has gone from strength to strength. The greatest benefit, of course, has been the relationship we built up with Dr Reddy and the whole Apollo family, a close relationship that endures to this day.'

There is no doubt in Anil Thadani's mind that Dr Reddy was the key player in bringing about fundamental change in the quality of, and the manner in which, health care services were provided in India.

'By building world-class health care infrastructure, he has been able to attract the best medical talent – Indian doctors practicing in the West – to return to practice in their native country. Apollo alone has been responsible for the repatriation of hundreds of Indian doctors who have returned from the US and the UK to practice in India,' he said.

'It was not that long ago that the general view abroad was that you could get sick if you travelled to India; today medical tourism is a growing business in India and patients from the West come to India for treatment because it is of high quality and affordable. The West now comes to India to get well! That is one of the important legacies of Dr Reddy and Apollo,' Thadani said.

Like Anil Thadani, Rakesh Jhunjhunwala was highly impressed with Dr Reddy the very first time that he met him. The investor based his trades, in part, on the business model of a company, its growth potential, and its potential for longevity. He factored in heavily the competitive ability, scalability and management quality of the enterprise. The entrepreneur, according to Jhunjhunwala, made an invaluable difference to his expected investment returns. 'Believing in the vision and the beliefs of the entrepreneur and evaluating risks that may not be perceived by the entrepreneur are key success factors for a trader,' Jhunjhunwala told me.

The year was 1992, and Dr Reddy was in Bombay raising money for the cancer hospital. Dr Reddy was making a presentation at the Oberoi Hotel at Nariman Point. Jhunjhunwala had begun to take interest in the health care industry, where the private sector's role was still nascent.

'I'd heard of Apollo Madras because a number of my relatives had gone there for treatment,' he said. 'They had had very good experiences. But I am a born capitalist. I look to make profits. Until Dr Reddy came along, there was no concept of profitability in hospitals in India. He was the father of corporate health care, a pioneer who did what others said was impossible to do.'

There were about fifty people at that presentation, and Jhunjhunwala says that after he heard Dr Reddy, he thought to himself, 'This man is a born entrepreneur. He has such a clear vision of what he wants to do.'

On the basis of Dr Reddy's presentation, Jhunjhunwala bought a 5 per cent stake in Apollo, or 2,500,000 shares, at Rs 20 per share – or Rs 10 face value, plus Rs 10 premium. In 2001, Jhunjhunwala sold his shares for Rs 300 each, netting a profit of Rs 280 per share. Had he held on to his Apollo shares until 2013, he would have made even higher profit because the price went up to Rs 1,072 per share in May. But by then perhaps it didn't matter to Jhunjhunwala. He had already become a billionaire.

'Dr Reddy is very loyal to people,' Jhunjhunwala told me from his Mumbai base. 'It's been almost a decade since I sold my shares in Apollo, but he still invites me to every function. It's very rare to see such loyalty these days. And let me also tell you this: Dr Reddy will be remembered not only for Apollo but also for what he has done for health care. We have an exploding middle class in India, and Dr Reddy created a model health care system that benefits everybody.'

After Dr Reddy's struggle with money and legalities, there was one more problem. It was the scarcity of cement and steel. At that time, these were sold on a quota basis and the allotment made to Apollo was already used up. This cost a lot in interest and cost overruns. Here again, Dr Reddy drew on his growing network of friends in political and business circles. In answer to my question as to how he overcame the many obstacles, Dr Reddy recalled what his friend Dhirubhai Ambani, the great industrialist, had once told him: 'It's all a matter of relationships. No matter what business you are in, you must develop and sustain friendships. If you remember to stay in touch with people, they will remember you at your time of need.'

One friend happened to be Narendra Kumar Salve of Maharashtra – better known as N.K.P. Salve – who also happened to be a minister in the Union cabinet; his wife had been a patient of Dr Reddy's. Dr Reddy approached him, and Salve in turn referred Dr Reddy to the then minister of steel, Pranab Mukherjee – and the quotas that were due to Apollo Madras were expedited. [21]

I met Salve at his New Delhi home just three weeks before his death on 1 April 2012 at the age of ninety-one. Dr Pushi Changulani, a veteran physician at Indraprastha Apollo Hospital, was looking after him. He sat in a padded chair, with a blanket across his legs. A large picture of Indira Gandhi dominated his bedroom. He was too ill to talk much, but smiled when I mentioned Dr Reddy's name. An avid cricket fan and administrator, Salve was watching a game on TV. As I bade him farewell, Salve said, faintly but distinctly, 'Doctor Reddy.'

It was a touching moment. Salve and Dr Reddy had known each other for decades, and I so wish that I had met him before for this book. He would have had so many memorable stories to tell about how Prathap Chandra Reddy went about making the Apollo Dream

---

21 'Pranab Mukherjee never delayed anything,' M.R. Sivaraman told me. 'No matter what his portfolio – steel, finance, etc. – he acted quickly if he was persuaded about the soundness of a project.'

Raghava Reddy

Shakuntala Reddy

Prathap Reddy as a
young man

Wedding of Prathap and
Sucharitha

Prathap and Sucharitha
just after their marriage

With Sucharitha and the
four children

At the Grand Canyon with
Sucharitha

With Dr Denton Cooley

Construction
site for Apollo
Hospitals
Madras

Inauguration of Apollo
Hospitals Madras by
President Giani Zail
Singh on 18 September
1983

Prime Minister
Indira Gandhi visits
Apollo Madras on
16 October 1984

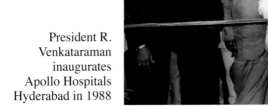

President R.
Venkataraman
inaugurates
Apollo Hospitals
Hyderabad in 1988

With Rajiv Gandhi on
16 January 1991

With G.K. Moopanar
(fourth from left) and
others in the early
days of Apollo

With Mother Teresa

At his office at HM
Hospital, Madras

At his office at
Apollo Madras,
soon after its
opening

At his office at
Apollo Chennai
today

With Tamil Nadu chief minister J. Jayalalithaa at the inauguration of the Apollo Centre of Excellence at Kotturpuram

With Tamil Nadu chief minister K. Karunanidhi at the inauguration of Apollo Speciality Hospitals Madurai

With Delhi chief minister Sheila Dikshit at the inauguration of the Bone Marrow
Transplant Unit at Apollo Indraprastha New Delhi

In 2005, Apollo Indraprastha becomes the first Indian hospital
to be accredited by JCI

At the inauguration of Apollo Bengaluru in 2009 with President Pratibha Patil

A new landmark – the completion of 10,000 beating heart surgeries at Apollo

With Prime Minister Dr Manmohan Singh during the latter's visit to
Apollo Hospitals

With former leader of the Opposition L.K. Advani and Gujarat
chief minister Narendra Modi

US President Bill Clinton inaugurates the Apollo Telemedicine facility at Aragonda in 2000

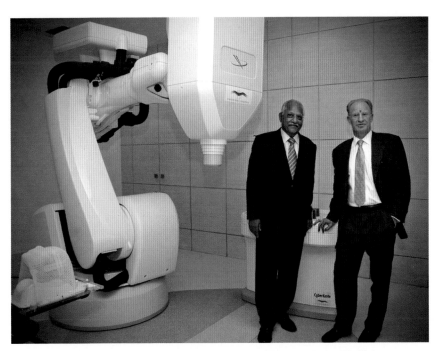

With Prof. John Adler, known as the 'father of CyberKnife'

Twenty-fifth anniversary celebrations of Apollo Chennai

With some of the doctors who are part of the Apollo family

Dr Reddy and Sucharitha Reddy with His Holiness the Dalai Lama in Delhi

With his four daughters – (L to R) Sangita, Shobana, Suneeta and Preetha

With a four-month-old infant from Nigeria after her surgery

With a young patient

At the Krishna Mariamman Temple in the Apollo Chennai campus

At the puja on the occasion of Dr Reddy's seventy-fifth birthday in February 2008

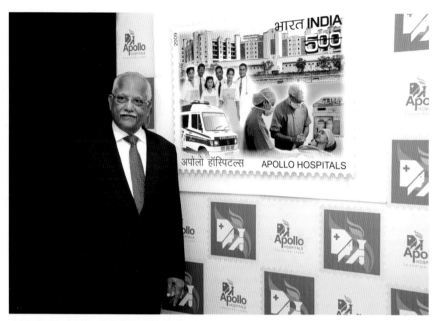

A stamp honouring Apollo Hospitals issued in 2009 by the Indian Postal Service

Receiving the Padma Vibhushan from President Pratibha Patil in 2010

happen. When I heard of his death, I thought to myself, 'At least he lived long enough to see how Apollo succeeded. At least it happened in his lifetime.'

CHAPTER TWENTY

In the Arena

IN THE OLD DAYS – which is to say, when he was at HM Hospital, and then after the opening of Apollo Madras in 1983 – Dr Prathap Chandra Reddy would typically come to the premises at seven o'clock in the morning and spend ten to eleven hours at work.

These days, he prudently breaks up his workdays into tranches: he wakes up at 5 o'clock at his home in Bishop Garden, meditates and then comes to the balcony to have a half-cup of tea that Sucharitha brings to him, prays for an hour with Sucharitha, eats a simple breakfast of guavas, melons and idlis, washed down with 'miracle juice' – a mix of apple, beetroot and carrot – and then arrives at the hospital around 9.30 a.m. He visits the Krishna Mariamman temple[1] just behind the main hospital building, and then makes the rounds of various wards before going to his ground-floor office. Lunch is taken around 1.30 p.m., sometimes at home but usually at Apollo's headquarters in the nearby Prestige Palladium building with executives and family members; and then after a short rest Dr Reddy is in his corporate office receiving visitors and chairing meetings until

---

1 In Hindu mythology, Mariamman is generally regarded as Lord Krishna's sister. In southern India, she is worshiped as a goddess who brings rain, and who cures the sick.

6 p.m. Thereafter, thrice a week, he goes to Madras Club for a game of bridge with old friends. Dinner is almost always at home with Sucharitha. Dr Reddy is in bed by 10.30 p.m.[2]

Such a schedule, followed faithfully day after day, would be punishing for anybody. But I am struck by how fluidly Dr Reddy, now in his eighty-first year, goes through the hours. In more than a year of observing him for this book, I never once heard him complain about exhaustion or any physical ailment, even though I was aware that he would suffer back spasms from time to time. Whether he's in Chennai or Hyderabad or Delhi or anywhere else, he scrupulously sticks to a rigorous schedule, including his prayers. Personnel at hotel rooms in various countries have become accustomed to seeing Dr Reddy perform morning pujas in his room.

While such a schedule requires enormous self-discipline, I think it goes beyond that. I believe that Dr Reddy's daily engagement across the spectrum flows from a special passion that, in turn, is wired into his DNA. Surely it's that passion that explains how he built the vast Apollo organization, how he dealt with the initial challenges, and how he navigated the multitude of troughs and successes with equanimity.

That equanimity may explain part of the Reddy story, but not all of it. After all, Dr Reddy didn't just build a hospital company. He made Apollo into one of the world's foremost integrated health care groups. It is a fascinating story of building and nurturing a business model. The more I delved into the story, the more I became intrigued with the thought that there had to be something more to it than Dr Reddy's DNA. The thought persisted through the initial stages of this book.

I raised the question of Dr Reddy's success with his third daughter, Shobana Kamineni, during a conversation we had in Apollo's

---

2   There are rarely exceptions to this 'rule'. One exception that I know of was on 2 January 2013 on the occasion of the sixtieth birthday of his daughter Suneeta's husband, Dwarakanath. Dr Reddy was so enthralled by the outdoor celebrations at the Reddy family beach house in Chennai, so taken with the music, and so captivated by conversations with the diverse crowd of youngsters and seniors, that he stayed until almost midnight.

boardroom in Hyderabad. Shobana is a sports enthusiast and squash player. Tall like her three sisters, the first word that came to my mind when I met her was 'striking'. Here's what Shobana said to me:

'I can think of many people who came from a small background and created something larger than life – but my father's story has a slightly different twist because it's not just about making good but also about doing a lot of good. There's a whole social purpose beyond it, and not in a saintly way. I don't think Dad is a saint by any stretch of the imagination and he would hate to be called one too. I think his life shows the ability of the human being to really evolve; any young person looking at his career can say, "This could be me". Everyone has that potential. Dr Reddy always says "Belief is Power", and so he loves to empower people with his big vision – sometimes people realize that vision, and sometimes they don't. But I can say this: no one has regretted adhering to his values or following his vision. Over the years, Apollo has grown to be more than Dad as Chairman. He represents a philosophy and way of thinking that will still be here whether he is physically present or not. The DNA is always here and he is larger than life. Maybe we four can be likened to apostles. So we are completely equipped to handle the future.'

Still, something kept tugging in my mind. I knew that I was missing a critical element that would help explain Prathap Chandra Reddy's extraordinary success in life. And then it came to me in a flash: Sucharitha Reddy, his wife since 1 February 1957.

During my long career in journalism and writing, I have seen many couples that enhanced each other's lives, but it's fair to say that I can think of few other couples that have so enriched each other's existence as Sucharitha and Prathap Chandra Reddy have. It goes well beyond co-dependency – it's co-nourishing.

I asked Shobana about her mother – it didn't seem appropriate to ask directly what impact Sucharitha might have had on Dr Reddy's career – and I figured that somewhere in her response I would find the magic key.

'From my mother we learned tolerance,' Shobana said. 'You can't put up with a person like my father without it. You can't be selfish and self-centred, and she's a person who has been a great support to him. He can't function independently if he has to think about where he has to get his clothes from or what he has to eat – she takes him away from that. Now if Dad travels alone she worries. So from her I learned tolerance and respect for what you do in your family life and a huge amount about how you can combine religion with being good. At the time when I was growing up, I thought it was boring and was kind of rebelling against it. But I'm kind of growing and it's become part of me now. I see that even in my children, in all the grandchildren, this regard for respect, for religion, for doing good.'

From her parental family Sucharitha Reddy learned early about the power of prayer. She's a devout believer. She believes that one's husband is next to God. She won't go anywhere without telling Dr Reddy where she's going. Their bonding is remarkable. For example, whenever Dr Reddy travels, he will stop off at home first in order to perform a brief puja with Sucharitha. Throughout their life together, she's been known for looking after guests – including people working for Apollo.

So was there an extra-dimensional aspect to medicine, and to leadership, that most of us are clueless about? I put the question to Dr Alok Ranjan, a neurosurgeon at Apollo Hospital in Hyderabad. He is a slim, very fit man, not yet fifty, and he hails from a family of accomplished bureaucrats and teachers in Bihar. He was always a brilliant student, and was at the top of his class at Christian Medical College in Vellore. He then practiced medicine in Britain before Dr Reddy hired him in 1999 for Apollo Hyderabad.

Since he knew the human brain intimately, I thought that it might be useful to get Dr Ranjan's view of the neurons that fire the intellect, and perhaps an intangible spiritual force that animates genius.

'There is a supreme power and we are nowhere close to understanding it,' he said. 'And we certainly can't understand fully one creation of the supreme power – the brain. I am completely fascinated by that. I can explain conditions that can be seen in a scan, which is the amount of brain a person possesses. But the question is – one of the most fascinating ones – why some people are tangibly smart and others are not. For instance, by looking at the way a person looks or by looking at the brain can we say whether a person is smart? You cannot. If we take a section of a monkey's brain and a human brain, they look very similar. The growth anatomy is the same. So basically we're down to those two aspects of neurons and how they are connected. Are they the same neurons or different neurons and so on? Basically there must be something very fascinating – what makes something so superior in one faculty and not so superior in another faculty.

'If I could go back to my own experience, my brother does not talk much but he can take care of himself. We can go somewhere and five years later he can lead me to the same place. His directional sense is phenomenal. It also gives you the opportunity to see that every individual can be brilliant at something. The trick is to find where the brilliance is.'

Dr Reddy has just that – the ability to find each person's brilliance.

'It would be incredible to study Dr Reddy's brain,' Dr Ranjan said. 'He began Apollo when he was already fifty, at an age when mental powers are supposed to start deteriorating. But in his case, his sharpness and acuity kept increasing. There was something happening in his brain that gave him added stimulus. As a neurosurgeon, the question that fascinates me is: "What was that factor?"'

In 2002, Dr Ranjan established the first department of neurosurgery in Hyderabad and, in 2003, the department of neurology was established under the guidance of Dr Subhashini Prabhakar. The unusual thing was that they were independent consultants, and not paid salaries by the hospital. Training of residents soon started and finally by 2013, out-trained residents were able to join the group as independent neurosurgeons.

'That was the time we were keen to introduce clinical research in the system. I was told to go to see the highly publicized stem cell therapy at Seoul because we were only keen for clean and fruitful research. We finally decided to establish our own research facility at Hyderabad. This journey finally proved that Dr Reddy could envisage things so many years in advance,' Dr Ranjan told me.

'Neurosurgeons and cardiothoracic surgeons are notorious for their "God syndrome". This required a shift in mindset. It required a nudge from Dr Reddy and his four daughters. Thus came the idea of the centres of excellence, or COEs. He chose six departments for COEs: cardiology and cardiothoracic surgery, orthopaedics, neurosciences, emergency medicine, cancer and transplant medicine – leading to the acronym CONECT. It was a huge task,' Dr Ranjan said. 'Each COE had a guiding mentor from the organization. With one idea, more than 150 out of 2,000 neurosurgeons and neurologists were able to interact with each other. Good practices were shared. Second opinions were taken, and not only because patients wanted that.'

He added: 'Apollo Hospitals gets a great mix of patients. Of course we have the trust of the affluent section of society but 60 per cent of patients come from the lower socio-economic strata. Actually with our full participation in government-sponsored medical schemes a fair share of patients are poor. But the system never differentiates patients as those who can afford treatment and those who can't. There is a uniform standard of care; the nurses and doctor ratio is the same; the care facility in the operation theatre is the same; food and housing needs are similarly taken care of. This comes as a great paradox for many.'

———

Dr E.C. Vinaya Kumar is one the senior consultants specializing in ENT; his contributions in the field of cochlear implant surgery have been phenomenal. Setting up of the first cochlear implant clinic in South India, establishing SAHI (Society to Aid the Hearing Impaired) to directly benefit rural children with impaired hearing, convincing the government of Andhra Pradesh to include cochlear implant surgery as part of the Rajiv Aarogyasree Scheme are among his several noteworthy achievements which have led to his recognition as a leading ENT surgeon in the country. 'But what has given me immense satisfaction,' says Dr Vinaya Kumar, 'is the over 700 cochlear implant surgeries I have done. Incidentally, I am told that this the largest number in Andhra Pradesh. In every case it added a meaning to the child's life. And without Apollo's support in general and our Chairman's support in particular, this would not have been possible.'

In recognition of its yeoman work, SAHI was presented philanthropy honours by Cochlear Asia Pacific and the Ministry of Disability Services, Government of New South Wales, Australia on 1 March 2013 at Sydney.

'How does Dr Reddy spend billions for a proton radiation machine not available in this part of Asia, and even in Australia, on one hand, and support charitable foundations for cochlear implants and hundreds of paediatric heart surgeries on another? How does he manage to get expensive machines like the CyberKnife and Novalis TX and at the same time help in government-run schemes? How is he able to run such huge expenditures on one hand and loathe to throw out some hard-working personnel who may not be needed in the organization to cut down the cost?' Dr Vinay Kumar said. 'It is because he has never allowed his computer brain to interfere with things that are close to his heart. That's why everyone in the organization loves him. Can a big man be so humane? You have the answer.'

———

One morning in March 2013, Dr Reddy seemed uncharacteristically concerned. His friend Rangaswami Ramakrishnan was having a cardiac procedure done in the catheterization lab. He and Ramakrishnan, who's popularly known as 'RK', have known each other more than four decades.

The procedure began and Dr Reddy decided to walk around the hospital before returning to the catheter lab. Just exiting his office created a stir. The hospital was overflowing with patients and their attendants, families and friends. Many people recognized him and wanted a word or blessing. Passing staff members stopped and greeted him and he, in turn, talked with them. Dr Reddy does not rush away or nod a cursory hello. There is always recognition of the other person. He stopped and prayed before an image of Lord Ganesha. This one was above a plaque acknowledging the first Founder's Day of the hospital in 1986.

In the emergency room, which had the usual high number of patients, a young man appearing in his early thirties was on a gurney just inside the door. He was wearing a soft cast on his lower left leg and had several family members with him. The patient had been referred by another doctor, and would be admitted for treatment at Apollo Chennai.

'Hello, young man, what's wrong with you?' Dr Reddy said.

'I think that I have fractured my leg, sir,' the patient said. 'It was previously fractured and now, it may have another fracture on the side. I think it is going to require an operation.'

Dr Reddy said, 'Who is taking care of you? Who is your doctor?'

He listened to one of the staff members who offered the information, then said to the young man, 'Don't worry. I will speak to your doctor and our team will make you well.'

In an adjoining room, there was another patient, accompanied by three family members. The patient had been intubated and couldn't talk. He had an advanced case of COPD (Chronic Obstructive Pulmonary Disease) and had been treated at home. On this day, he took a turn for the worse and became very sick. His family talked intensely to Dr Reddy, who leaned in and offered a soft touch of his hand, and kind words to the patient and his elderly father.

As Dr Reddy walked towards the catheter lab, he was approached by relatives of other patients, and also by staff members. He stopped for a word or two with everyone.

Dr Reddy and my research colleague Twilla Carolyn Duncan – a Texan transplanted to New York – entered a narrow rectangular room with a large viewing window so that they could see the entire lab. There was a desk, a couple of chairs, a microphone and a bank of monitors showing the details of the procedure. Dr Reddy leaned over and pushing the button on the microphone said, 'Hello, RK. I am here. All the best.'

The monitor displayed images of RK's heart from different angles. 'We could see the blockages and understand why this patient, Dr Reddy's friend and fellow horseracing enthusiast, was in for a procedure,' Twilla said later.

The cardiologist Dr Samuel Matthew Kalarickal is the director of Interventional Cardiology and Cardiac Catheterization Laboratories at Apollo Hospitals. He is world famous, and when he can take a short break in the procedure he steps into the viewing room to discuss the patient's treatment with Dr Reddy. Dr Matthew said that he was using three stents, not two, and that in a few months they would dissolve into carbon dioxide and water.

Dr Reddy bade farewell with one last word to the patient that he would see him the next day. He said, 'Another doctor would have only put two stents or sent the patient for surgery but Dr Matthew is able to see the future need. This is why he is apart from other interventional cardiologists. He is very gifted with his hands.'

In the hallway, Twilla saw Dr Satyabhama, the director of medical services and one of the doctors who joined the group when Dr Reddy launched Apollo in 1983. Dr Reddy stopped to say hello to her and to Dr K. Chidambaranathan who is the head of the department of radiology. The radiology department is extremely active and held in very high regard for the skills of its doctors. There are twenty-three doctors on staff and they are active 24x7. Now hospitals in Europe want radiologists from Apollo to read their scans, mammograms, MRIs and ultrasounds. This new programme is called teleradiology and hospitals worldwide believe it will revolutionize the number of readings that can be given in any one day. Using digital transmission and high definition screens, the radiologists can see much more clearly than ever before, making for better and more accurate analysis. At Apollo Chennai, the radiologists read and send a written report of each procedure within two hours of the test. This is a remarkable feat by modern medical standards.

Later that day I asked Sucharitha Reddy if, some thirty years ago when her husband started planning for Apollo Madras, she would have anticipated how much the business would grow, and how acclaimed it would become for its medical record and innovations. Could she have imagined that Apollo would be all about transforming health care in India?

'I told him, "For you to start will take time – but you must push ahead,"' Sucharitha Reddy said. 'I knew that he had the talent and experience, and that he was a strong-willed man. I thought that he would build a good hospital with perhaps 100 beds, with good facilities. Our focus was never on growing the hospital into such a big business. The most important thing is the journey. The outcome is not in our hands. We must only concentrate on doing good every day. And I am always there to support him.'

Sucharitha Reddy, for example, could not have imagined that a day would come when Apollo Hospitals would perform heart and lung transplants. Would anyone have imagined back in 1983 that Dr Reddy and Apollo would take the lead in getting cadaver transplants approved and Tamil Nadu would become the Indian state that had the most cadaveric donations? Many of these cadavers come in as the result of motorcycle accidents. 'Helmets are required but few are worn and enforcement is rare because of the lack of political will,' said Dr Anand Ramamurthy, a key member of Apollo Chennai's liver transplant programme.

The appointment with Dr Ramamurthy had been scheduled for 12 noon but medical emergencies don't wait. It was nearly 4 p.m. by the time he showed up; he had just completed a liver transplant from a forty-two-year-old male casualty of a traffic accident in Coimbatore to save the life of a thirty-eight-year-old ex-alcoholic male whose liver was almost completely destroyed from the effects of excess drinking.

The call had come during the night and a team was dispatched to retrieve the organ. In transplants, time is of the essence, so while those harvesting the organ were on their way to and from Coimbatore, the team in Chennai began preparing the recipient. Minutes after the commercial flight carrying the life-saving liver landed, the transplant team began its incision. Eight hours later the recipient had a new opportunity of life.

Anand Ramamurthy was born in Tamil Nadu and trained at Maulana Azad Medical College and Sir Ganga Ram Hospital, both in Delhi. His father and Dr Reddy were friends. In 2006 Dr Reddy told the father, 'I want your son to work for me.' He had heard that the young Ramamurthy was an excellent surgeon. As a boy, Anand Ramamurthy had heard of Dr Prathap Reddy and when he met the chairman for the first time Dr Reddy said, 'I want your father's genes in Apollo with me.' He encouraged the young doctor to experience more surgeries and innovative techniques, which Dr Ramamurthy did at King's College Hospital in London.

'I wanted to learn how to adapt Western systems to Indian needs and that time was very useful for me. I also saw many more cases and gained experience in multi-organ transplants,' Dr Ramamurthy said. 'Before King's College Hospital I had never seen a cadaver liver transplant so it was excellent to participate in a mature programme. I remember thinking that the entire programme ran very smoothly; it was all deceptively easy except – it wasn't easy at all. It was the result of hard work. Dr Julia Wendon ran the liver ICU at King's College and her thoroughness made all the difference.'

Dr Ramamurthy joined Apollo Chennai in 2008 when Dr Anand Khakhar, the head of the Liver Transplant Centre, was looking for a partner. They became an excellent team but they weren't the only members of the team: cardiologists, nephrologists, nursing, anaesthetists, and laboratory technicians – each one was critical to the survival of patients. Programmes at other hospitals had often failed because the people backing up the surgeons didn't have the vision necessary for comprehensive care. They didn't understand what it takes to perform such complicated surgeries.

There was scepticism among some doctors and patients as to whether a liver transplant programme would be successful. Patients were often encouraged to wait until the last moment before seeking a transplant but this was not good because the sicker they are the more risk there is, leading to a less successful surgery.

Initially Dr Ramamurthy travelled extensively to meet and educate other doctors, explain the Apollo system, counsel and reassure patients, and instil confidence in the transplant processes. Apollo physicians participated with the Indian Medical Association and other professional groups to disseminate knowledge and spread awareness of the possibilities and outcomes. More doctors began to refer patients; the Tamil Nadu government helped out by increasing awareness for the general public.

The life of a transplant surgeon isn't easy, particularly at Apollo. There are odd hours, long hours, little sleep and constant vigilance to keep up a world-class programme. 'We've got to maintain our eminence in this transplant programme and offer unique, innovative treatment. We must do this all the while increasing accessibility and affordability. The commitment of our team is remarkable, the staff often sleeping in the changing room just so that they are near to critical patients,' Dr Ramamurthy said.

'The Apollo gastroenterology team has a personal incentive to have a strong international programme where we train medical personnel and support staff. We can make a big impact in Bangladesh, Sri Lanka and Africa using our knowledge to improve their health care. This is an example where people were sceptical about possible success. There are many countries whose economies are poorer than India. Chairman Reddy is a global citizen and wants us to contribute where we can. It can also be financially beneficial for Apollo – if even a small fraction of patients from these countries visit our hospitals we will be flooded,' Dr Ramamurthy said.

The office of his direct boss, Dr Anand Khakhar, is a relative oasis of peace in Apollo's bustling Sindoori Block building in Chennai. He is the programme director of the Centre for Liver Disease and Transplantation, and a transplant and hepatobiliary pancreatic surgeon. It is easy to recognize his thorough, disciplined manner; his liver transplant patients are put at ease by his emollient manner and compassionate counselling.

He joined Apollo in 2007 after graduating from M.P. Shah Medical College in Jamnagar, and after advanced training in London, Ontario and New York City. When asked why he chose to come back to India after having open doors in the United States, he replied, 'Your home is your home. India is my cultural identity and that is superior to a foreign environment where cultural interaction is limited. I knew that my family and I could have a fuller life at home.'

Dr Khakhar had developed expertise in pancreatic and living donor transplants and desired to join a hospital that could provide these extremely essential services. There was nothing like it in South India at the time and so he inquired at several hospitals about their interest and facilities.

Apollo had had experience with transplants and knew it was more complicated than that. Dr Reddy told Dr Khakhar that the hospital was licensed and could be geared up on short notice. But he added: 'I don't think we are prepared for it just now. Please make me a report with details from the medical side, the infrastructure needed, how to organize the programme and the aftercare, the staffing necessary.'

Then, after drafting the report that Dr Reddy had wanted, Dr Khakhar received a call from the chairman. He invited the surgeon to sit with him for three days. Dr Khakhar was surprised to see that Dr Reddy had not just read the report, but also thoroughly studied it. 'There were questions in the margins, exclamation points, underlines, questions marks . . . all about the nitty-gritty of what I proposed. The business element was addressed, how much would it cost for the hospital and for the patients. He asked for more of my inputs and I asked for his. I realized that while he was asking me, as the project person, for information, he was also assessing what kind of individual I was. Was I capable of being given the responsibility for the patients and for the Apollo name and commitment? Did I have the cognitive ability to perform the surgery and lead the department? It was very reassuring.'

At the end of Day Three, Dr Reddy wrote a simple one-line endorsement on a piece of paper and gave it to Dr Khakhar. It said: 'You are appointed as team leader for liver transplants.'

It took a while for some of the Apollo team to commit wholeheartedly to the programme. Some persons felt out of the loop because they were not consulted and yet were expected to execute the infrastructure needed. Chairman Reddy and Managing Director Preetha Reddy gave the finances and space; but some organizational resistance continued until it was clear that there was no retreating on Dr Reddy's resolve. Apollo Madras was launching a new aggressive liver transplant programme in 1995 that would provide the best of care for South India.

'Dr Reddy selects people who can fly with him. He wants people with rocket fuel and not gasoline. He is a constant example of thinking for the future, not just how to eliminate traffic jams today but to expand the road for tomorrow. If we choose not to follow or to be penny-wise and pound-foolish, we fail to do justice to Chairman Reddy's vision,' Dr Khakhar said.

Technically, liver transplants are the most demanding because of all the feeder and filter issues, the mega factors of cleaning the blood of toxins and maintaining healthy tissues. According to Dr Khakhar, 'There is no compromise on patient care. The selection criteria are strictly medically based. A patient cannot "jump the line". Chairman Reddy has never asked us to favour anyone. He doesn't want politics involved in medical decisions and leaves it up to the surgical team to assess patient status and make judgement calls as necessary. The milieu during surgery is hostile and the surgical challenges are second to none. It requires attention to surgical nuances. I could not look myself in the eye in the mirror if my decisions were not medically based.'

The Apollo success rate in liver transplants is quite high: 90 per cent. Success rates in marginal patients is 88 per cent and it is 92 per cent for those patients whose liver disease is not as pronounced. These rates are among the highest in the world, better than Bellevue, Mount Sinai and Columbia-Presbyterian in New York City. Dr Khakhar acknowledges that many of the US teaching hospitals work under more strenuous conditions because they are always pushing the envelope in terms of volume, outcome, research, money and aggressive procurements of livers. In 2013, 35 to 40 per cent of liver transplants were from living donors, and 60 to 65 per cent were cadaveric at Apollo Chennai. It was through the work of Dr Reddy and Apollo that harvesting from cadavers was brought up.

Dr Khakhar believes that the greatest challenge to the transplant programme will be growing at an appropriate pace and incorporating more kidney and multi-organ transplants. Logistics, organization, infrastructure and manpower will all need to be effectively managed.

'Chairman Reddy is the backbone of Apollo and his support is critical to our success,' Dr Khakhar said.

The belief that Dr Prathap Chandra Reddy is the 'backbone' of Apollo is shared throughout the system. One of Dr Reddy's oldest friends was Professor N. Rangabashyam, a noted gastrointestinal surgeon and recipient of the Padma Bhushan, India's third highest civilian award, for performing the first gastroenterology surgery in India.[3] Professor Rangabashyam and Dr Reddy shared similar characteristics. They are tall, calm, energetic, invigorating, inviting, smart and dedicated to the health care of Indians.

The men knew each other casually from their college days but did not keep in contact during their early years as practicing physicians. Dr Rangabashyam was in Scotland and Dr Reddy in the United States. In the mid 1970s Dr Rangabashyam learned that his old friend had joined HM Hospital in Madras and began referring patients to Dr Reddy for a cardiology fitness review.

The men would occasionally meet at the Madras Racing Club with their wives. Both enjoyed socializing, had similar values and interests and many common friends. They enjoyed the adventure found in horse racing. 'From the beginning, it was clear that Prathap had the capacity and knowledge to be both an excellent physician and a man who knew how to use business to benefit others,' Dr Rangabashyam said. 'He understood the fundamentals of business and that it was necessary to provide health care services for a wide area. He had contacts in a wide business circle and even if the businessmen did not want to invest in Apollo, they could refer their friends and NRI doctors.

---

3   Dr Rangabashyam died in his sleep in mid-July 2013.

'At that time, there was no such thing as a full health check-up. Dr Reddy was the first to use a Master Health Check. It was an eye-opener that detected illness in those who had no symptoms or in people who did not recognize the symptoms. This would include diabetes, irregular heart rate, high blood pressure and so forth. It had great impact. I had opened a small clinic and when my patients needed surgery I sent them to Dr Reddy for pre-operative testing.'

Neither doctor had an interest in politics and both paid a price for not catering to politicians and their whims or requests for money. For Dr Reddy this meant delays in getting licenses and so forth. For Dr Rangabashyam, it meant not receiving the professional appointments he had earned.

When asked about the criticism that some journalists and medical professionals have directed at Apollo, Dr Rangabashyam said, 'Many people come up in life by shooting others down rather than contributing. They would not try to access the mango orchard if there were no mangoes, if the trees had not been cultivated and well tended. Why did these critics not plant their own orchard? Dr Reddy should be proud of the contribution he made to health care and for poor people. He is a man who you can trust.'

Both Dr Reddy and Dr Rangabashyam believed that the Indian government and Indian businesses can do more to improve health care in the country. They both emphasized educating the population as to the importance of hygiene. India is a study in contrasts. The professor said, 'Curative medicine is not the answer for the great masses. It is prevention and disease control. Apollo has extended beyond its specialities to help in the education and with vaccinations. We have many controllable diseases. We must teach the children, ban child labour, educate and socialize them.'

These are the sorts of words that his friend Dr Prathap Chandra Reddy would like to see resounding even more in India's medical arena.

Dr Reddy emphasizes that the key ingredient in health care is the personal attention and qualifications of persons who attend to the patients. Medical colleges and hospitals around the world are now taking note of the fact that technology isn't the only thing that drives success in health care. Dr Reddy and Apollo have practiced the 'high-tech/high-touch' philosophy since Apollo Chennai opened in 1983.

This is critical to Apollo's relationship with its patients. Dr Reddy stresses preventative health care and proper diagnosis. These two elements are extremely important in a country with such a huge population at risk.

Apollo's Personalized Health Checkup is one example where technology and touch meet. But the Apollo approach goes beyond the formal physical exam. Dr Reddy's philosophy is that each physician should not only perform routine tests such as pulse or heart rate, blood pressure and temperature but also go beyond to the kind of thorough examination that physicians once gave. That, he believes, is a missing element in treatment.

'Lower tech tests such as EKGs and breathing or pulmonary tests, CT scans and MRIs are all excellent tools. But it is also important for a physician to know how to perform a basic thyroid examination, look at the tongue for abnormalities, check reflexes, listen to the lungs, palpate the spleen and look at pupils, not to forget breast, rectal and other examinations,' Dr Reddy said.

Dr Reddy also knows that it is important to listen to what a patient is saying. A good doctor can get a 'head start' on diagnosis by getting basic background details that are not covered in a sophisticated test. Another characteristic that Dr Reddy has is the willingness to touch a patient and in that simple, caring gesture form a person-to-person bond that carries its own healing properties. Indeed, when Apollo Colombo opened, Sri Lankans often remarked how impressed they were by the fact that Apollo's physicians actually listened carefully and spent as much time as was needed with them.

Preetha Reddy, Managing Director, and Sangita Reddy, Executive Director, Operations at Apollo, both spend time on hospital floors visiting patients and talking with their families and friends. The phrase 'Apollo family' applies in more ways than one. It's true that all staff from the ward boys and housekeeping to the heads of department and most senior surgeons are 'family'. There is a constant emphasis on communication and well-being, and each floor has at least one 'Namaste' greeter who visits patients several times a day.

Not long ago, Dr Reddy received high praise for the way Apollo hospitals are run from one of India's leading industrialists, G.V.K. Reddy, founder, chairman and managing director of GVK, a diversified business conglomerate with interests in energy, resources, airports, transportation, hospitality and life sciences sectors; he has established GVK as a key infrastructure player in Indian and global markets. Realizing India's huge growth potential and the need for a strong foundation of infrastructure to sustain this growth, Reddy pioneered the development of infrastructural projects by setting up India's first independent power plant in Andhra Pradesh in 1997.

'Dr Reddy, Apollo's rooms are so good and the food is so delicious that patients don't want to leave,' he said to Apollo's founder.

One day at Hyderabad's Apollo Health City, Sangita Reddy shared an elevator with a small-framed but extremely bright-looking person. His name was Dr Vallivayal Rajgopal.

Dr Rajgopal, a specialist in urology, had left Britain more than twenty-four years ago to join Apollo Hyderabad. Sangita asked him the simple question that she had asked many physicians across the system: 'What made you leave a lucrative position and come back?'

With no hesitation Dr Rajgopal said, 'As a doctor we look for two things: an ability to practice good medicine with the infrastructure we need, and an environment that enables it. At Apollo I was able to fulfil my love for medicine and further my love for my country and larger family.'

Sangita says that the same sentiment has been expressed by hundreds of doctors across the eco-system in the Apollo family. Of the more than 72,000 people in the Apollo system, there are approximately 6,000 physicians and another 1,000 administrative and backup support staff; the rest – between 35,000 and 40,000 people, plus part-time helpers and volunteers – fall under the category of what Sangita – like her father – terms 'the unsung heroes of medicine'.

'The Apollo philosophy is very clear: everybody has a crucial role to play in health care – from the housekeeping boy on the ward who helps with the bed pan, to the CSSD technician, to the maintenance staff who ensures everything is working. Every single person has a crucial role to play,' Sangita Reddy says.

The stories and the sagas of courage at Apollo include elevator operators who have revived and resuscitated a visitor who had a cardiac arrest in the elevator when he was visiting a family member, to the maintenance staff and security staff who responded cohesively as a team when a fire broke out, ensuring that not a single life was lost.

'The theme of the "Apollo family" resonates across the system reflecting bravery, training, knowledge, but most importantly passion towards humanity,' Sangita says. 'This golden category understands their power, and lives and breathes to uphold the Apollo credo of touching lives. This is one of the most important facets of Apollo. As Henry Ford said, "You may take away my factories – but give me my people and I will build all over again." I can visualize the Apollo team following the Reddy family – anywhere.'

There are intriguing examples of how members were added to the Apollo family. Dr Reddy was in London one day and read an article in the *International Herald Tribune*[4] about surgeries being conducted on a cruise ship.

He said to himself, 'What a novel idea.'

On reading further, Dr Reddy discovered the influence of Professor Svyatoslav N. Fyodorov of Russia. Fyodorov is an eye surgeon who created not only the concept of the 'conveyor belt' technique of eye surgery[5] but was also able to create a 'seven-star' infrastructure at a

---

4　The name of the *International Herald Tribune*, a daily newspaper wholly owned by the New York Times Company, was changed to *International New York Times* on 15 October 2013 in order to unify the Times's brand globally and also strengthen its digital presence.

5　The conveyor belt system is analogous to the assembly line method used at automobile factories. Individual surgeons attend to one aspect of eye

time when Russia was economically down.

Dr Reddy found out that Professor Fyodorov was in Paris. He went to Paris and checked himself into the same hotel. He found an opportunity to introduce himself to a short, smiling figure that radiated enthusiasm.

'I like your persistence,' Fyodorov said. 'Let's have breakfast tomorrow.'

The two men met the next morning. From that encounter emerged a partnership between the Russian surgeon and Apollo Hyderabad. Professor Fyodorov sent a team to Hyderabad, which soon came to be even more renowned for its eye surgeries.

'When dynamism meets dynamism something special has to emerge,' Sangita Reddy says.

Dr Jairamchander Pingle at Apollo Hospital Hyderabad also symbolizes the dynamism that Sangita Reddy talks about. An orthopaedic surgeon, he's an authority on various hip problems. His team performs cemented primary hip arthroplasty, cementless primary arthroplasty, metal-on-metal hip arthroplasty with anatomical head, total hip resurfacing, ceramic on ceramic uncemented total hip arthroplasty, and revision hip arthroplasty.

I asked Dr Pingle what brought him to Apollo.

'I was working in the Nizam's Institute of Medical Sciences as unit chief in orthopaedics, and when I became a promoter[6] of Apollo in 1984 I knew that there was a great potential as the facilities for hospitals at that time in Hyderabad left much to be desired,' he said.

Dr Pingle left for Saudi Arabia in 1986 when the structure of the Nizam's Hospital changed. He returned to Hyderabad when G. Surender Reddy – then the head of Apollo Hyderabad[7] – came to Saudi Arabia to recruit medical personnel. Dr Pingle arranged a

---

surgery, and robotic techniques are used. The complete surgical procedure takes less time than the conventional method, and has been proven efficient.

6   A 'promoter' is someone who invests in an enterprise.

7   At the twenty-fifth anniversary celebrations of Apollo Hyderabad on 27 August 2013, Dr Reddy fondly recalled the many contributions that Surender Reddy had made to the Group's development.

meeting of potential candidates for Apollo Hyderabad among Indian doctors in Saudi Arabia. Dr Reddy projected a video on the concept of Apollo, after which a fair number of doctors became investors.

'After I joined Apollo my practice and quality of work improved greatly as well as the work satisfaction, thanks to the equipment and infrastructure that Apollo provided,' Dr Pingle said. 'When I look back after spending almost twenty-five years of my life and practice as a family member of Apollo, I have no hesitation in saying that I would not change it for anything else.'

One day Dr Reddy put his arm around Dr Pingle's shoulder and walked him to his office. 'We have created such a wonderful hospital, Jairam,' Dr Reddy said, noting that it had been just three months after President R. Venkataraman had inaugurated Apollo Hyderabad.[8]

'Why don't we see more patients?' Dr Reddy said to Dr Pingle.

Later, Dr Pingle recalled: 'What I do remember was he made me feel that it was my responsibility to look after the hospital. And I have – from that day onwards I have done everything I could to make our institution succeed. Over the years that I have immersed myself in Apollo, I have met so many clinicians – brilliant, committed and capable – some from the finest institutions in the West, some from Australia or even some whose primary training was in India.'

Dr Pingle underscored that Apollo physicians around the country saw themselves as belonging to a 'common family'. The underlying commonality between, say, Dr P.C. Rath in Hyderabad and Dr Murthy in Kakinada was that they were all attracted to Dr Reddy's vision of better health care for Indians. Just as Dr Reddy attracted senior clinicians, they too had begun to become magnets themselves, attracting other talented doctors into the Apollo orbit.

'Multiple atoms were building a larger self-replicating eco-system,'

---

8 President Venkataraman, who'd earlier been finance minister, inaugurated Apollo Hyderabad on 27 August 1988. At the inauguration, he said: 'The Apollo Group has overcome numerous handicaps. Some entrepreneurs break down under pressure. But I can say that Dr Reddy has done more than just "go on". He is an exemplar not only to health care professionals but to all entrepreneurs.'

Dr Pingle said, citing such 'medical stars' as Dr Raja Reddy and others.

'Each one a star in their own way, they together created a constellation,' he said.

One such 'star', Dr Sathyaki Purushotam Nambala, is one of the leading authorities in the country in the treatment of cardio-thoracic and vascular surgery. On 11 May 2013, the Apollo Hospitals Group conducted the Apollo National Cardiology Conference at ITC Gardenia in Bangalore. At the conference more than 250 delegates were in attendance from across India and around the world, and another forty prominent cardiologists and cardiac surgeons were featured speakers. Among the physicians at the conference were other Apollo 'stars' such as Dr Adil Sadiq, Dr Girish Navasundi, Dr B. Ramesh, Dr Yogesh Kothari and Dr K.B. Prasad.

Dr Sathyaki, probably one of the most gifted minimally invasive surgeons in the world, displayed via telemedicine a live surgery repairing four major vessels in the heart with incisions less than three inches long.

As a special invitee His Holiness Sri Sri Ravi Shankar also attended the conference and spoke about the enormous healing power of meditation, which should be used in combination with modern medicine to treat heart disease. He commended the ideology of prevention that Apollo was committed to. According to Dr Umapathy Panyala, CEO, Apollo Hospitals, Karnataka Region, 'His Holiness Sri Sri Ravi Shankar's vision of having a stress-free mind and a violence-free society is essential in combating all diseases on the whole.'

'As a practitioner of modern medicine I know that a stress-free and happy mind is an essential component of a healthy and disease-free body,' Dr Umapathy said.

Sri Sri Ravi Shankar and Dr Reddy have a special relationship, not the least because they are at the forefront of educating the larger public about disease prevention. On 28 June 2010, at the Art of Living Centre in Bangalore, Sri Sri Ravi Shankar launched the Karnataka chapter of the 'Billion Hearts Beating' campaign. Dr Reddy himself discussed the need for a national movement on prevention medicine rather than just curative care to the more than 5,000 people gathered at the ashram. 'The Chairman spoke with the objective to work mainly for promotion, awareness and prevention of heart disease and its contributing risk factors in India,' said Shobana Kamineni. Dr Reddy, in fact, talks frequently about 'Touching a Billion Lives' through Apollo's 'Billion Hearts Beating' Foundation, a not-for-profit organization that came into existence on 28 April 2010.

Shobana recalled that Sri Sri Ravi Shankar attended Dr Reddy's seventy-fifth birthday celebrations. The lobby was packed as usual but a special aura filled the room when he asked everyone to meditate together. 'The individual, the institution and its leader all got recharged and infused with a new energy, a passion and sense of resolve to reach new heights – and so many wonderful things have been achieved in the last few years,' she said. 'Sometimes corporates are shy to invoke religion in a business environment. Dad does it naturally, always telling the team that they can think of any God, their own God, but the idea is to understand that a higher force controls our destiny and then to invoke that very force for the good of mankind.

'This is Dr Reddy's secret weapon, his Brahmastra,' she said.[9]

Like Dr Pingle in Bangalore, Dr Sapna Nangia in New Delhi spoke about her enthusiasm for Apollo. She's a senior consultant on radiation oncology, and had worked earlier at Fortis, Apollo's main competitor.

'What enthused me about joining the Apollo group and Indraprastha Apollo Hospital in particular was the professionalism and vibrant energy of the group. In my initial interactions with the group, I was impressed by the respect that patients and doctors were accorded; I continue to feel the same more than one year after having been a part of the group. The fact that I have access to the

---

9 In Hindu mythology, the Brahmastra is a weapon created by Lord Brahma. As described in a number of the Puranas, it was considered the deadliest weapon.

best facilities as well as fellow professionals makes the pursuit of patient care deeply satisfying,' Dr Nangia told me.

———

All the Reddy daughters are extremely religious and observant. Although born Hindus, they are also deeply secular in their spirituality. 'In medicine as in every sphere of life, knowledge is power; and every day has been a learning experience but nothing as profound as an encounter with His Holiness the Dalai Lama,' Suneeta Reddy said, referring to a health care summit hosted by the CII in New Delhi on 13 November 2007.

'As chairperson of the CII health care conference I was extremely keen to have His Holiness the Dalai Lama address the gathering of doctors, entrepreneurs and health care professionals. I never realized how difficult that would be. It also made me realize the power of intention,' Suneeta said. 'None of us realize the fact that we control our minds. Nothing is easy or difficult. We just magnify the complexity by churning it through our mind which we have lost control on.

'Fortunately I have had the pleasure of meeting and interacting with many positive thinkers. My father being an inspirational one – for him nothing is impossible. When we invited His Holiness the Dalai Lama, we received a response requesting for a year's notice, it seemed impossible. Then suddenly by some quirk of fate or because of our continued hope, he agreed to come. However, the Indian government had a somewhat ambiguous policy on its relations with the Dalai Lama. We were advised that he could have a private meeting with the Reddy family but no public address.

'I could not accept this and decided that with or without permission if he came he would speak.'

At 2.00 p.m. that day the Dalai Lama emerged from his car at the Hyatt Regency hotel where the CII conference was being held.

'My father and mother bent to touch his feet but he held them with his arms around them in a warm embrace,' Suneeta recalled. 'Here was an individual – in fact much more than a mere individual.

Adjectives can't describe the spirituality, the purity of thought and action that are his special trademark – and his complete lack of ego.

'My friend from the US, Rupa, whom I have known for at least forty years, sang a song, and then the Dalai Lama climbed on the stage with an interpreter; waiting for no introduction, he began speaking in his native tongue. But recognizing that the interpreter's translation was a soulless rendition of his words, he switched quickly to simple English and left us with a message which I will never forget.

'As he looked at all those health care professionals, doctors, people from the government and, of course, all of us with huge egos – he touched a special place in all hearts. To the doctors he said that you are blessed because you have the opportunity to serve, not all of us are blessed with the knowledge, but more importantly the opportunity is in recognizing this, and treating each patient as though he is divine. Each person is potentially divine. Even a dog responds to love and affection and human beings, should they not deserve more?'

Suneeta continued: 'I could see that the Dalai Lama's luminosity from the goodness of his heart and the purity of his soul. As he concluded, he honoured my father with a white shawl and the audience spontaneously stood up. Respect for a man who is a leader in every sense of the word, he inspires others to be leaders and for his disciple – my father – who believed it was his divine calling to heal the world.

'Indeed we were touched by the cosmic energy that day – we were truly blessed.'

CHAPTER TWENTY-ONE

The Frontier People

SUCHARITHA REDDY MAY NOT have necessarily imagined how big Apollo Hospitals would become in time but when Prathap Chandra Reddy conjured up his vision for introducing world-class health care in India, he was surely thinking that Indians would be able to get the same care at home that they could get abroad. His dream was that other families would not be left without their husbands or wives or children just because they could not afford to go to the US or Europe. He wanted to develop health care in India for Indians, something that would eventually be available for the rest of the world.

One man's vision, however pristine in its clarity, does not an institution make. Dr Reddy had seen in the United States how well-organized teams generated efficient operations at institutions such as Massachusetts General Hospital. He was determined that Apollo should offer nothing less than the best health care at the most affordable costs to patients. To actualize his vision, he needed not only a superb medical team but also administrators who could handle finances and operations. It was these people who would help deliver international levels of care for various cross-sections of patients with greater access and at low cost.

Dr Reddy had heard of a man in Madras named V.J. Chacko, a chartered accountant. Chacko, a compact man with a deep forehead and shrewd eyes, worked for Spencer's, one of India's biggest distributors of consumer items, including liquor, and he was not at all happy with the way that things were going for him at the company. As the managing director, he supervised more than 500 distributors of Spencer's products around the country. His British superior, a man named John Oakshott, had brought in an ex-officer of the IAS, supposedly to serve as an 'advisor' to Chacko. Moreover, Chacko's mentor, Cooverji Hormusji Bhabha – more popularly known as C.H. Bhabha, a Parsi businessman who'd served as commerce minister in Nehru's first post-Independence cabinet – died suddenly of a heart attack.

When Dr Reddy was talking with John Oakshott at the Madras Club, the doctor described the kind of senior administrator for whom he was searching. Dr Reddy said that he wanted a man of commitment and unquestioned integrity. Oakshott himself was leaving in another six months' time and had just the person in mind.

He told Dr Reddy what a superb administrator Chacko was, that he was a man of tremendous integrity. Dr Reddy went to Chacko's house to convince him to join the fledgling Apollo Hospital.

At that meeting, Dr Reddy said to Chacko, 'I know only medicine; I want someone who knows administration, operations, finance. I want someone who can deal with banks, who can get things done.'

Chacko was shown an audio-visual that Dr Reddy – assisted by his daughters and others – had prepared. 'When I saw the audio-visual, I was very impressed by Dr Reddy's vision to make Apollo one of the best health care organizations in the world,' Chacko, now eighty-seven and living in Bangalore, recalled. 'I instinctively felt that this man was a great motivator. He seemed to have a "never-say-die attitude", and a great driving force. I was also impressed by his message – that in order to set up an institution you needed to have an explicit goal, and that goal had to be very clear. Dr Reddy struck me as absolutely honest and very, very straightforward. I also had the gut feeling that his vision would work.'

An element of doubt had arisen as to whether Chacko would be promoted to succeed Oakshott. 'I was already thinking of getting out of Spencer by that time,' Chacko told me. 'Dr Reddy wanted someone who knew how to work the system. I felt that I could contribute. I thought to myself, "Why don't I join Dr Reddy?" And that's when I told him.'

Dr Reddy's immediate reaction was, 'What a gift you have given me.'

In the event, it was Dr Reddy who wound up giving Chacko a gift of a different sort – an early warning about his health. He'd invited him to come across to HM Hospital, where he personally supervised a four-hour medical examination. At its end, he said to Chacko, 'When would you like the results, later today or tomorrow?'

'Tomorrow,' Chacko said, partly because he was already late for an appointment and partly because he was a bit nervous about what the tests might reveal.

His trepidations weren't quite justified because the next day Dr Reddy told him that Chacko's health was all right. But he warned him that he was at risk for diabetes and perhaps some heart trouble related to stress. Dr Reddy prescribed some medications.

'That was Dr Reddy's gift to me,' Chacko said. 'I'm alive today because of him.'[1]

There was the issue of salary and perquisites, of course. Dr Reddy was surprised by how modest Chacko's requests were. It was a big change coming from the luxurious appointments of Spencer's to the small, no-frills, bare-bones Apollo start-up. He did not ask for a big car, or a fancy house. But he did ask that the company help with the education fees for his three sons and two daughters. They were reasonable requests, and Dr Reddy agreed. In any case, Chacko told me, in those days it would have been pointless to ask for a large salary because the taxation rate was some 80 per cent. Perks such as housing and transportation were taxed at far lower rates, if at all. And so V.J. Chacko became the first managing director of Apollo Hospitals. His small office was adjacent to that of Dr Reddy. His became

---

1   At this point, Chacko did not have much confidence in hospitals. In later years, he underwent angioplasty at Apollo Hospital. He said that he was also treated for pancreatic problems and an enlarged liver.

a very important post for the starting and running of the hospital. He ensured that purchasing contracts were executed. People who bought materials such as hospital supplies and furniture reported to Chacko; he also helped with assessing project evaluations. He oversaw accounting. He dealt with banks. This enabled Dr Reddy to devote more time to the development of Apollo's medical staff, and to negotiate with the powers-that-be in Delhi for the various governmental permissions that were required to make a go of India's first corporate-sector hospital.[2]

Chacko said: 'There were many Doubting Thomases. But Dr Reddy's genius lay in the fact that he was able to overcome many of those doubts. His experience in the West enabled him to put forward to the available niche an entrepreneurial possibility. Our supporters – especially bankers and investors – came around to the view that the hospital was a workable proposition.'

Some politicians suggested that Apollo was building a hotel and not a hospital. According to Dr Reddy, 'fees' were suggested but not a rupee was paid. The license was not approved initially, and construction was stopped.[3]

---

2 The significance of Dr Reddy's dealings with Delhi officials cannot be overstated. In those days of the License Raj, it was extremely difficult for entrepreneurs to obtain permits and permissions. Industrialists typically showered officials with gifts of all kinds. Dr Reddy, in contrast, was never known to spread largesse in such a fashion. A man named Viswanathan, through his PR firm, also helped him at one stage. Perhaps that's why, to this day, Dr Reddy has a reputation of someone who could persuade people through his charm and power of argument, and not through emoluments. Quite a few people have told me that Dr Reddy was the most honest and straightforward man they have ever known.

3 Chacko had some concerns about joining. Construction was at a standstill, and Dr Reddy's office was above a 'palatial garage'. Dr Reddy placed a 'lightning call' to K.T.B. Menon, who was known as the 'king of Kuwait'. Chacko asked him if he thought that Dr Reddy's project would succeed. Menon assured Chacko that Apollo would be a great success – but if not, Menon would give Chacko any job he wanted in the Middle East at three times the salary that Dr Reddy proposed.

Among Chacko's initial recommendations to Dr Reddy was that in order to be sustainable the hospital needed to have an occupancy rate of at least 60 per cent. He also spoke with Dr Reddy about an organization's 'culture': 'I can tell you in a few words: the culture is 95 per cent that of the promoter. It is entirely up to you to set an example for everybody at Apollo. Sir, what is Apollo without you?'

In our conversation years later, Chacko seemed pleased that the value system established by Dr Reddy still flourishes in the Apollo system. Chacko made it a point to tell me how touched he was by that fact that Sucharitha Reddy often brought home-cooked meals for the incipient hospital's staff, and that both she and Dr Reddy would join Apollo colleagues of various stations at mealtimes. [4]

'Chacko's demeanour may have been mild, but his work habits were unflinching,' Dr Reddy said. 'Throughout his career, he has appreciated straight talk; by instinct and upbringing, he isn't a man to be taken in by flattery.'

Chacko said there was an efficient management system in place from the very beginning. 'Even from the initial stages, Dr Reddy

---

4   The initial team that was assembled included Chacko; B. Natarajan, a former IAS official who served as general manager, and who dealt with government officials in Tamil Nadu; Surendra Narayan, the cashier; P.K. Narayan, who worked for Shobana Reddy; S. Narayan, who was general manager for projects; and Nalin Rathod. Those who joined later included Group President K. Padmanabhan and Chief Strategy Officer S.K. Venkataraman. Natarajan was in his way as important as Chacko because he had the delicate task of liaison on permits and reports and dealing with the impulsive behaviour of government officials. B. Natarajan was the Executive Director of Apollo Hospitals, having had thirty-five years' professional experience at the time of joining – he had been Chief Commercial Superintendent, Southern Railways. B. Satya Reddy was the first company secretary cum General Manager, Finance of Apollo Hospitals, having been company secretary of UniLloyds Limited, Hyderabad. K.R. Gangadharan was the first Personnel Manager and General Manager (Operations) of Apollo Hospital Madras. He joined Apollo Hospitals from Lucas TVS with about nine years of experience. U.K. Ananthapadmanaban was the first Materials Manager and General Manager (Technical) of Apollo Hospitals Madras. He joined Apollo from the Rane Engineering group.

clearly segregated the different functions of a corporate hospital – medical services, paramedical services and support services – and structured the organization accordingly.' The early Apollo office was a beehive of activity with construction meetings, and interviews for doctors and other medical personnel.[5]

Meanwhile, his third daughter Shobana Reddy was just twenty-one years old and a fresh college graduate when her father entrusted her with the design and construction of the new hospital in Madras. 'It was a learning space for us all,' she said. 'He said to me, "You're in charge," and so for a year I sat with architects and doctors and suppliers and new staff who would handle everything from housekeeping to medicines to food, everything needed for a physical plant. They talked, I listened and then translated what they needed into what would become a vibrant, thriving hospital.

'Dad empowers people even today, so I really always thought that I could achieve what he wanted. But we really had no idea what it would take and to some it looked like the project would come to an end. There were many issues relating to permissions and cost overruns and equipment that were slow in delivery. We hired an outside hospital administrator from the US to help us open. He took one look and left saying, "You'll never get this hospital off the ground even in three years."

'Dad kept saying, "We are going to build the best hospital in India" and so he brought in his friend and future director Brij Reddy to advise us on how to finish a building and get quality built in.' Shobana later married Brij Reddy's nephew, Anil Kamineni.

'For example, in Delhi we used the best professionals possible,' Shobana said. 'In Madras and Hyderabad we did not have the money to spend. Delhi cost three times more than any hospital we had built and we were "betting the farm", so to speak. Top class engineers, designers, architects and administrative specialists were all used.

---

5 Expenditures of more than $100,000 were presented to the Apollo board so that directors could see the value for money and efficiency. Teams from each department made the necessary presentations.

Thankfully, Delhi broke even faster than any of our other projects.'

'We have a repository of knowledge gathered over the past thirty years. There were some bad situations about which we were very reactive. Now, public relations have been far more pro-active. All of us make mistakes and we've learnt from them. Now we are applying those lessons to our new projects,' Shobana said.

When asked what she thought Dr Reddy's strongest characteristics were, she named two. The first is his absolute belief in meeting his goals and serving patients. The second is his ability to see ahead of the curve. In 1995, the doctor started talking about value travel, what is now known as medical tourism.

'I remember the Swiss ambassador telling me that we were nuts to even consider such a thing. "Why would anyone come to India?" he asked. I replied, "There are big opportunities and India will serve the world." Dad was right. Today, medical tourism is destined to become a big success for the patients and for Apollo.[6] The attitude reflected by the ambassador was one of scepticism, and Apollo proved its worth by actions instead of words,' Shobana said.

When Dr Reddy or any of the Apollo team talks about buying the best, they are serious. Shobana says, 'He always insists on using new equipment, not refurbished ones, even when funds were very tight. Some developing countries used a strategy of used equipment, but Dad insists on new equipment with the latest programmes.' Manufacturers line up in the office reception area daily as decisions are made on equipment for new hospitals. Dr Reddy says that the

---

6 In 2012, India earned revenues of $2.5 billion from health tourism, driven by factors such as affordable prices, shorter waiting period for patients, clinical excellence and a high success rate. Around 1.1 million foreign patients are said to have visited India in 2012. Growing at a compound annual growth rate of 26 per cent, health tourism in India is poised to cross $3 billion by the end of 2013. Tamil Nadu, with its well-known hospitals in Chennai, Coimbatore, Vellore and Madurai, contributes 40 per cent of India's medical tourism industry. 'Lack of uniform pricing among hospitals, lack of insurance coverage for overseas medical care and stringent visa norms are a few stumbling blocks,' says Dr Srinidhi Chidambaram of Apollo Hospitals.

top contenders for providing high-level technology are Phillips, Siemens and GE. Apollo chooses the one that is always updating their capabilities.

Shobana said that Apollo was the first in India to introduce the PET CT, the 124-slice CT scan, and like the rest of the family she reminded me that it is not just technology but the personal touch that makes the difference for Apollo. 'Dad is never afraid to invest in technology if he thinks it will benefit his patient. Our new investment in Proton Therapy is a perfect example,' she said.

Apollo never bought the second-best in equipment or used equipment. Dr Reddy says, 'We didn't buy the best to say that we are the best. We didn't bring the first MRI into India to brag. The same with other technology. We buy the best and most advanced technology to live up to our vision of giving top class care. Just as important as our teams, they need technology, skills and infrastructure.'

The success of Apollo Madras proved to be the tipping point for the health care industry in India. Physicians such as Dr M.R. Girinath established solid records in heart surgeries, and Dr M.K. Mani became a world-renowned nephrologist. The bankers who'd been demanding early repayment of loans softened their stand. And more and more states began to vie to get Apollo to establish a medical facility, making various offers to facilitate construction.

But there were critics, some of them quite vociferous. One of them, Praful Bidwai, an influential columnist, wrote a series of blistering articles for the left-leaning *Economic & Political Weekly*, and for the *Times of India*, the country's biggest English-language newspaper. He acknowledged that along with landlessness, agricultural debt, crop failure, and urban unemployment, health care costs too were contributors to poverty in India. 'But my concern then – as now – is that these private-sector hospitals would be parasitic,' Bidwai told me in a conversation in New Delhi. 'I was concerned that by privatizing health care, a new element of corruption would be introduced – fine doctors from government and charitable hospitals would be wooed away by hospitals like Apollo because of higher salaries and emoluments.'

'And, of course, my concern was – and is – about the access and affordability of these private-sector hospitals,' Bidwai concluded.

The criticisms notwithstanding, the hospital started getting more and more patients from not only India, but from other countries too as news spread of Apollo's accomplishments. One of those accomplishments was that Apollo never denied a patient blood that was needed during surgery. The hospital never bought blood supplies. Instead, it has always met the need by encouraging employees under sixty-five to donate blood. As a matter of fact the Reddy sisters had set an early example by coming forward to donate blood.

Following Apollo's footsteps, a few other corporate hospitals such as Malar Hospital (owned by Fortis) and Devaki Hospital[7] had come up in Madras (Chennai has nearly 400 private hospitals and clinics now). But they could not successfully expand as Apollo did. As K. Padmanabhan, President, Apollo Hospitals, puts it, 'Hospitals in early stages had longer gestation periods and many of them underestimated the capital needs of providing high-tech health care.'

To which Suneeta Reddy adds: 'We had a solid management team that took care of the company while the doctors were given freedom to focus on their work. We carefully leveraged debt to equity and were committed to returns to our shareholders and investors.'[8]

Among those who rejoiced about these developments was a

---

7 Devaki Hospital, headed by Dr V. Krishnamurthy, is now known as Chennai Meenakshi Multispeciality Hospital Limited.

8 Individual and institutional investors have done very well by acquiring shares in Apollo. According to the *Times of India*, private equity giant Apax Partners sold its equity stake in Apollo Hospitals for Rs 2,240 crore in multiple open market transactions, which were completed in mid-June 2013. The London-based investor booked 3.3 times profit on a Rs 680 crore investment, buoying private equity sentiments laid low by the rupee collapse and lack of exit options. Apax entered the Prathap Reddy-controlled health care chain with a primary investment in October 2007 and followed up with secondary deals a year later. 'Our takeaway from this deal is that good returns are to be made in the Indian private equity story for those who are patient and methodical in their approach to investing,' Shashank Singh, MD, Apax Partners India, told the *Times of India*.

young man named C. Sreethar. His father, Sri Krishnamurthy, founder-principal of Andhra Pradesh Agricultural College,[9] presented Dr Reddy with a lovely copy of the Sundara Kanda of the Ramayana (which documents Hanuman's search for Sita). In one of my conversations with Dr Reddy, I got to know that he reads portions from the Sundara Kanda every day.

In early 1981, Sreethar learned that Dr Reddy was looking for people with a commerce background for his new hospital. 'I'm looking for an accountant,' Dr Reddy said.

That was how, on 24 March 1981, Sreethar became an official at Apollo Hospital. His salary: Rs 600 a month. His office was the two-room suite above HM Hospital's garage.

Among his responsibilities was going to the bank every day to deposit cheques. Dr Reddy had started receiving cheques from overseas investors, and it was Sreethar's job to keep track of these revenues. Dr Reddy sought loans totalling Rs 1.3 crore to keep the initial operations going.[10] The banks seemed impressed that Apollo paid off bridge loans on time – sometimes even ahead of time.[11]

At that time Dr Reddy had to go to the high court, where Apollo's acquisition of land for the hospital was being challenged, on a regular basis. 'I marvelled at his energy,' Sreethar told me. 'He spent all those hours in court, then he had his medical practice, and then he had to plan for Apollo. It was surely God's blessings.'

---

9 Andhra Pradesh Agricultural University was renamed Acharya N.G. Ranga Agricultural University on 7 November 1996 in honour and memory of an outstanding parliamentarian Acharya N.G. Ranga, who rendered remarkable selfless service for the cause of farmers and is regarded as an outstanding educationist, kisan leader and freedom fighter.

10 The banks included Indian Bank, Bank of Baroda, Indian Overseas Bank, Union Bank of India and Andhra Bank. Later, loans were given by Indian Overseas Bank, Indian Bank, Andhra Bank, Canara Bank and Syndicate Bank.

11 Dr Reddy especially credits a man named N.J. Yasaswy, who advised him to 'settle short-term sundry creditors' forthwith. Yasaswy said that though Apollo just needed Rs 2 crore, it should borrow Rs 3 crore 'on long-term basis'. 'He gave us a permanent cure,' Dr Reddy told me.

'Dr Reddy would always say, "We have to have the energy of Hanuman. He crossed oceans, he did the impossible. That's what we need to accomplish at Apollo,"' Sreethar recalled.

Sreethar was later given a choice by Shobana as to where he wanted to work, and he asked to join Apollo's pharmacy business. 'I don't know what prompted Dr Reddy to select me originally,' Sreethar said. 'But I look on him as my godfather. He's always guided me throughout my career.'

Another person who expressed similar sentiments was P.B. Ramamoorthy. He joined the Apollo group in 1985 as a store clerk in the pharmacy stores at Madras and was reporting to Sreethar. In 1987, when the expansion programme was being finalized, Ramamoorthy was chosen to lead the initiative and provide the needed inputs for developing the software. A slew of promotions later he was given charge of Andhra Pradesh, West Bengal, Orissa, Chhattisgarh, Goa and Pune regions. He recalls, 'To increase the market share in the pharmacy retail industry, Ms Shobana Kamineni divided the pharmacy operations into Stand Alone Pharmacies (SAP) and Hospital Based Pharmacies (HBP).' Ramamoorthy was made the General Manager, Operations, responsible for SAP, while Sreethar was in charge of HBP.

In the year 2007, under Shobana Kamineni's leadership, an aggressive rollout plan was announced. An average of one outlet a day was opened thereafter till 2010.

In 2010, Apollo's pharmacy business was awarded the Best Healthcare Retail Company for the Year by Frost & Sullivan.

Shobana recalls that a professional management company, Technopak, was brought for three months to share lessons about retailing. Meanwhile, Apollo Pharmacies faced increasing competition. Shobana encouraged colleagues to meet such competition by accelerating their own efforts. Today, the Apollo pharmacy business, led by Sreethar and Ramamoorthy, has grown to 1,517 outlets across 355 cities in seventeen states and employs over 15,000 people.[12] Most of these Apollo pharmacies are open twenty-

---

12 As of October 2013.

four hours a day, seven days a week. Outside of hospitals, there aren't too many other pharmacies that are always open; Dr Reddy often says that Apollo 'owes it to people to provide pharmaceutical services when they seek them'.

Dr N. Satyabhama has observed the rise of Apollo's pharmacy network from its inception. A slim, bespectacled woman who keeps fit through daily exercise, she's the director of medical services at Apollo Chennai. Everyone calls her 'Dr Bhama'.

Dr Bhama had been working with Dr Reddy for over thirty years. When she was asked to take on the position of medical director, she agreed though in her heart as a clinician, she was much more interested in being the primary physician for her patients.

After Apollo Delhi got its JCI accreditation, Dr Reddy wanted Apollo Chennai to be the next, and he made it clear to Dr Satyabhama that it was her responsibility. So she began putting in new systems, scratching deep down to make sure that quality care was thorough. Even simple procedures such as better documentation, new policies, procedures such as disaster drills, site-marking for surgery, met with resistance from some doctors. They said that documenting all procedures was unnecessary, that it was time consuming, and signing the papers was boring. She persevered, intensely training in Chicago for a week and returning with requirements that would set Apollo apart even more in the Indian health care landscape. By the time Apollo Chennai was certified by JCI in 2006 the doctors had accepted the efficiency and benefits of the new procedures.

Dr Satyabhama says, 'Apollo's growth requires the willingness and ability to look at things in a new way. Some staff don't embrace change or they want change for change's sake. It's really got to make sense.'

One morning Dr Reddy reached over and picked up a piece of paper containing an e-mail from Dr Kalpana Dash, a professor and senior consultant in the department of endocrinology and metabolism at

Apollo Hospital, Bilaspur, in the state of Chhattisgarh. Dr Dash – a veteran of eleven years with Apollo – had volunteered to set up a sugar clinic to diagnose and treat those with diabetes. She would continue working in the hospital and also work in the clinic twice a week.

The huge number of people with diabetes is one of the major health issues that India is facing and Dr Reddy is keen to educate, stop diabetes cases from increasing in the population and treat the disease.[13] He gave the go-ahead right away for Dr Dash's suggestion and asked her to find a building for the clinic with room enough for four other physician consultants and a good location to build a 200-bed hospital.

Six months before the meeting with her sugar team, Dr Dash secured the location, and Dr Reddy charged the sugar team with immediately negotiating the space and setting up the clinic.

Yet, on this day, he was not happy because Dr Dash's e-mail was politely asking why nothing had been done and if Dr Reddy was still interested in the project.

'Why have you not done this? What have you been doing? I asked you do to this and nothing has gone forward,' he sternly said to the members of the sugar team that had assembled in his office.

There was silence in the room as Dr Reddy continued, 'We are not asking the impossible. We are asking you to do ordinary things extraordinarily well.'

'Sir,' one man said, 'we have been working with one of the Big Four to set up the entire programme and not stopping at fifty clinics. We are looking at cost and valuations.'

'What does the consultant have to do with setting up this one

---

13 Dr Reddy told me it was at a cardiology conference in California that he discovered he had diabetes. He walked into a stall to have his blood sugar checked and was told that the level was high. He has been extremely careful about his diet since then, and is also particular about keeping fit through walking, meditation and yoga. In the three decades since, Dr Reddy has kept his sugar levels well in control. Similarly, his strict diet and exercise regimen has helped in controlling his blood pressure, and also kept him free of cardiac ailments.

clinic? So many people need this. I asked you to do it. The consultant is not creating a valuation for this clinic. Here we have one good doctor who is going beyond to help others. She did her part and we have not done ours,' Dr Reddy said. 'Do you know how many people could have been treated in the six months since you were told to do this? Do you know how much better health could be for patients with diabetes? For their hearts? Their eyes? Their kidneys?

'Go and come back tomorrow with the results of implementation. We, at Apollo, are not a bureaucracy. We have given our word and we must act. It is for the patients,' Dr Reddy declared.

Dr Kalpana Dash later told me, 'When I was given the task of sharing my view and experience with Dr Reddy, I thought it had come in the form of a golden opportunity. One fine day there came a thought into my mind, that why not the facilities and services provided by Apollo Hospitals be extended to Raipur, the capital city of Chhattisgarh state?

'I expressed my desire to Chairman Reddy in Chennai in October 2012. My thought of starting an Apollo Hospital at Raipur was immediately appreciated and accepted by him. This clearly shows his mindset that nothing is above providing health care services to the people. Without any further delay, Chairman Reddy told me to go ahead with the project and assured that he would help and stand by me in any manner that he could.'

Her colleague, Dr Vinit K. Srivastava – who joined Apollo Hospital Bilaspur as a consultant in neuroanaesthesia in July 2008 – also talked about Dr Reddy's inspirational leadership. 'Dr Reddy never stops encouraging people to stay positive,' Dr Srivastava said.

———

Like Dr Rama Narasimhan and other physicians, Dr D. Vasanthi frequently talks about Dr Reddy's vision of thinking beyond Apollo and looking to how India's health care system might be improved overall. She is senior consultant, obstetrics and gynaecology, and a veteran of nearly thirty years at Apollo Chennai.

When she first began her gynaecology and obstetrics practice, most men did not accompany their wives to exams. Today, that is one of the many changes that she has seen in her practice.

Born in Gudur, Andhra Pradesh – about 80 kilometres from Chennai – Dr Vasanthi received her MBBS from Andhra Medical College and later taught at Sri Venkateswara University in Tirupati. She and her husband, Dr D. Ramachandra Reddy, a general surgeon at Apollo, worked in Jamaica from 1974; in 1980, they decided to try a stint in New York and were accepted at Harlem Hospital in Manhattan.

Regrettably their appointments did not come through in the specialities for which they were trained, and so both worked as paediatricians. After only one year, the couple returned to the West Indies and then moved home to India in December 1983.

Dr Vasanthi's father-in-law, Dr D.J. Reddy, was a pathologist; he and Dr Prathap Reddy were close friends. Dr Vasanthi and her husband met Dr Reddy, and by March 1984 both had joined Apollo.

'More and more patients started coming. As people saw Apollo and the equipment we had, how clean the hospital was and the general experience of being a patient with us, they told their families and friends. It was word of mouth and the good news of better health care spread. Madras had always been a "medical Mecca" for people, but Apollo set a new standard and everyone started knowing about it,' Dr Vasanthi said.

Dr Vasanthi usually sees upwards of thirty patients per day, including walk-ins who either must be seen or want to be seen. For many years she also participated in the medical camps that Apollo runs for poor people. These camps offer free exams and treatments, and some are done with joint sponsorship by the Rotary and Lions Clubs.

One area of concern for women's health care is tuberculosis and how it affects not only the lungs but also the genital tract. This makes it difficult for women to conceive and causes other complications as well. It is seen more in the poorer classes but some women in middle and upper classes had also tuberculosis, according to Dr Vasanthi.

Dr Vasanthi emphasizes the importance of the team in hospital care. She recounts the hospital getting a call that a passenger who had just landed at Chennai airport had gone into labour. The ambulance brought her straight to the hospital where Dr Vasanthi and her team were waiting at the driveway. She jumped into the ambulance and delivered the baby right there. 'Some things just won't wait,' she said.

There is a story that Dr Reddy and his daughters like to tell about the importance of providing prompt service to people in distress.

Two fifteen-year-old girls had completed an English exam for the eleventh grade at the Nasr School, a small private school in Hyderabad's Khairatabad area. They thought that they had done well in the exam and were enjoying the kind of laughter and secrets and friendship that teenagers share. They jumped into one of India's ubiquitous auto-rickshaws, bright yellow and black with open sides and three wheels, one in the front and two in the back. Laveena Arora dropped off her friend at the girl's house near Masab Tank in Hyderabad and proceeded towards her own home in Jubilee Hills. It was 12 December 1996, a bright sunny afternoon.

Road 36 was narrow, only 50 feet wide at the time and busy. If you've ever been on an Indian road, you know how many cars, trucks, three-wheelers and motorbikes try to crowd onto one small area. (Now the road has been widened to 100 feet, a double carriageway in Hyderabad that links Banjara Hills to HiTech city in Madhapur.)

Just as Laveena's auto-rickshaw got to a sharp curve near where there is now Chutneys and Odyssey, a speeding, unladen lorry travelling from the opposite direction smashed into it head-on. The driver of the auto-rickshaw was injured and Laveena had several injuries. Passers-by stopped at the accident scene and pulled Laveena from the auto-rickshaw and put her under the shade of a tree. That area wasn't built up as it is now. The owner of a video rental shop nearby recognized Laveena who was still wearing her dark green school uniform. He knew the girl's family because they were his customers and he ran to a nearby house to call them. Telephone services then were spotty and there were few mobile phones.

Laveena's mother, Meera Kohli, answered the phone and immediately shouted for her husband Yogesh to come downstairs. They rushed to the accident location in their car. Meera says, 'It only took us a few minutes to reach the scene. We were both crying and so worried. When we reached the accident spot, we found Laveena in pain, dazed, confused and covered in blood. Yogesh scooped her up and we drove straight to Apollo Hospital in Jubilee Hills. It took ten or fifteen minutes to reach and Laveena was in such pain and semi-conscious. Apollo was relatively new and it was the only decent hospital in the area so our instant reaction was to take her there.

'When we pulled up, fortunately, Sangita Reddy was standing at the entrance of the emergency room for some reason. She took charge and immediately rang five surgeons to come and examine Laveena. She saved my daughter's life.'

A bolt from the auto-rickshaw had struck Laveena on the side of the head and there was blood everywhere from metal cuts. She had several injuries to her head, neck and spine. Meera says, 'Doctors and nurses rushed to Laveena and began examining her and treating her injuries. She was taken for an MRI and several other tests. Apollo allowed us to stay with Laveena the entire time, we were so worried. I tend to blank out unhappy events and cannot remember too many details of what happened in emergency. I kept saying, "It's unfair." The fact that my beautiful, young talented daughter was in this predicament was heartbreaking and too much for me to bear. Word spread about the accident and friends started arriving to give us support.'

Says Laveena: 'The only thing I remember is semi-waking up in the hospital to see Daddy crying. Then waking up again when they were stitching my head. Mummy was next to me. I asked the doc what needle and thread they were using and Mummy almost fainted. Then I went back to sleep.'

Her mother adds: 'Laveena required a lot of stitches and bandages but no major surgery although she was hospitalized for a month. She wore a neck brace for several months and received physiotherapy. Yogesh and I felt devastated, shattered and helpless.

'Sangita and the hospital team gave us every kindness. She had such a nice touch and comforting way when dealing with a family in distress. She explained everything to us, made sure that the doctors and nurses did, too. I was surprised that she kept coming by Laveena's room to check on her after the initial trauma subsided. You don't usually get that from hospital executives.'

Meera, Laveena's mother, was born in Gurdaspur, Punjab. She and her family emigrated to London from New Delhi when Meera was four. Laveena's father Yogesh was born in Poona but Laveena was born in London and lived there until age eight.

After the accident, Laveena celebrated her sixteenth birthday in Hyderabad, then moved back to England permanently. She is now a banker and lives with her husband James Kerr near London.

'At the time, the service was considered expensive but we knew that Apollo had the best technology and had heard it was clean. We wanted the best for our daughter, of course. Health care at other hospitals in Hyderabad and elsewhere in India was considered dire,' says Meera.

Trained as a lawyer, Meera is active in community and social organizations and does charitable work. She has two other children. Laveena's father is no more.

Meera had met Sangita's husband Vish one time through a friend but her first introduction to Sangita was at the emergency room door. Later the two women would occasionally meet at society events and professional panels. 'Most of my experience with hospitals has been in the UK or Germany and I was so surprised and pleased to see the quality that Apollo brought,' Meera says. It is one thing to hear about it and another to see it for yourself. They have given access to the best technology thus making diagnostics reliable.'

CHAPTER TWENTY-TWO

Dear and Glorious Physicians

THE TWO MEN WERE waiting on a two-wheeler in the fading light of a September day in 1971 outside HM Hospital in Madras. They knew that Dr Prathap Chandra Reddy would come out of the low-slung building soon. It was around 7.30 p.m.

'That's him,' one of the men said speaking in Telugu, pointing to a tall, well-dressed, bespectacled man who strode out of the hospital. 'That's the man from Andhra Pradesh.'[1]

Just as he stepped out of HM Hospital, another man, Dr S.S. Badrinath, joined Dr Reddy. The two men, who were colleagues and friends, walked quickly to Dr Reddy's car, got in and drove off.

The men on the two-wheeler did not have the courage to go up to Dr Reddy.

'In the few minutes that I saw him, his looks and bearing impressed me enormously. Dr Reddy's face was glowing with energy,' one of the men, Dr Prasanna K. Reddy, told me years later.

---

1 Andhra state was formed in October 1953, which catalyzed the formation of other linguistic states. On 1 November 1956 the states of Andhra Pradesh, Kerala, Tamil Nadu and Karnataka were formed, followed by Gujarat and Maharashtra in 1960. The formation of linguistic states is the single most important event in the history of South Indian languages, as it provided an opportunity for these languages to develop independently, each of them having a state to support. Source: Sreenivasarao Vepachedu.

He had come to HM Hospital with a friend, another physician named Dr S.R.K. Rajan with no other purpose than just to get a glimpse of the man he had heard a lot about. At the time, Dr Prasanna Reddy was a house surgeon at Madras General Hospital. Dr Rajan had told him that he'd heard about a young cardiologist who'd returned to India after a stint in the United States, and that celebrities of all sorts were flocking to HM Hospital on account of his expertise, cultivated manner and personal attention to patients.

'I was intrigued,' Dr Prasanna Reddy told me. 'In those days there weren't too many doctors who received training and qualifications in the United States and then came back home to India. America was where the money and opportunities were. I was curious about this man.'

It may not necessarily have been the sight of the confident Dr Reddy stepping out of HM Hospital that September evening in 1971, but after that episode Dr Prasanna Reddy became determined to go abroad for further studies and gain more qualifications. He told me that seeing Dr Reddy reinforced in his own mind the notion that a foreign sojourn would be most helpful professionally.

And so it was that on 7 September 1972 Dr Prasanna Reddy left for Sheffield University in Britain's South Yorkshire region. He stayed in Britain for twelve years and specialized as a gastroenterologist. All the while, however, Dr Prasanna kept thinking of the time when he would return home to India. It was in early 1980 that a physician-friend named Dr M.R. Reddy suggested that perhaps Dr Prasanna might want to get in touch with Dr Prathap Chandra Reddy. Like Dr Prathap, he hailed from Chittoor district. He told Dr Prasanna that Dr Reddy was planning to build a hospital in Madras that would compare favourably with any institution in the West. Dr Prathap Chandra Reddy's vision, Dr M.R. Reddy told Dr Prasanna, was to create a private sector institution where Indians could get the best health care affordably, and with prompt access. Perhaps, Dr Prasanna thought, there was some way that he could play a role in bettering health care in India. He decided to contact Dr Prathap Chandra Reddy: perhaps Dr Reddy, who was already in the arena after spending years in the United States, might have some suggestions. A mutual friend, Dr Pramilla, approached Dr Reddy in Madras on Dr Prasanna's behalf, and Dr Prasanna subsequently wrote to Dr Reddy.

'When I received a letter back from Dr Reddy, I was impressed with the way he assured me that Apollo would provide all the infrastructure and staff that I needed for my practice,' Dr Prasanna recalled. 'He invited me to come and meet him in Madras.'

That meeting took place in mid-1980 during a brief personal visit by Dr Prasanna to India. He showed up at Dr Reddy's office at HM Hospital around 2 o'clock in the afternoon. Dr Reddy was resting at the time.

'But when he heard that I'd come, he got up and came to greet me,' Dr Prasanna said, recalling that Dr Reddy looked as elegant as that evening in September 1971 when he'd first seen him from a distance. 'His manner was very affectionate. Once again he assured me that Apollo very much wanted my expertise and experience.'

The two men met again a few days later for lunch. It was a Sunday, and Dr Prasanna was scheduled to leave for London that very evening. V.J. Chacko came to that meeting to note any particular requirements that Dr Prasanna might have. No agreements were reached that Sunday afternoon. Dr Prasanna boarded his plane to Britain in the evening. He had to return to his job at Leeds University in Birmingham.

Some months later, in early 1981, Dr Reddy happened to be in Birmingham to meet with potential Apollo investors. The two men met again. Had he decided on returning to India, Dr Reddy asked Dr Prasanna.

Dr Prasanna said that he hadn't. He still had some months left on his contract at Leeds University.

'No need to rush,' Dr Reddy said, in his usual comforting manner. 'Complete your contract and then come back.'

Dr Prasanna would later tell me: 'When you're out of your own country for so many years, you always feel insecure. But Dr Reddy somehow gave me enormous confidence to come back and start afresh in India.'

On 5 December 1982, Dr Prasanna Kumar Reddy returned for good to Madras after fulfilling his contract with Leeds University. On 31 December, he formally joined Apollo Hospital, which was still under construction.

'I went straight to Dr Reddy to ask for his blessings,' Dr Prasanna told me.

In time, Dr Prasanna – like his colleague Dr K.R. Palaniswamy – would become one of India's leading surgical gastroenterologists, and the department that he heads at Apollo Chennai is one of the most sought-after in India's health care system.

When Dr Prasanna joined the incipient Apollo Madras Hospital on 31 December 1982, he had no way of knowing the monumental – and often dispiriting – struggles that Dr Reddy had been through for nearly a decade with Delhi's gargantuan bureaucracy to make his dream come true. Later, of course, stories of those struggles became the stuff of legend. But at the time that Dr Reddy was recruiting physicians such as Dr Prasanna, Dr M.K. Mani – a noted nephrologist – and Dr M.R. Girinath, a renowned cardiovascular surgeon, Dr Arcot Gajaraj, and General C.S.V. Subramaniam among others, he was careful not to reveal those struggles.

Dr Reddy had begun privately thinking about the Apollo concept well before a young heart patient at HM Hospital died in 1979 because he – the patient – couldn't raise the $50,000 it would have taken for cardiac surgery in the United States. Dr Reddy would usually refer difficult cases requiring surgery to his friend Dr Denton A. Cooley at the University of Houston's Texas Heart Institute, or to Dr Donald Nixon Ross, a South African-born thoracic surgeon based in London, who led the team that carried out the first heart transplantation in Britain in 1968. He had made his reputation in developing the pulmonary autograft, known as the Ross Procedure, for treatment of aortic valve disease.

Dr Reddy had seen for himself the best that the West had to offer in medicine, and he thought that, with the right vision, the right resources and the right staff, there was no reason why a for-profit model of medical care couldn't be replicated in India. While he was preparing to establish Apollo Madras, he travelled to the United States not only to raise funds but also obtain organizational advice.

While in the United States, Dr Reddy visited Dr Thomas F. Frist Sr, a cardiologist who was widely regarded as the father of the modern for-profit hospital system in the United States; he and his son, Thomas Jr., founded the Hospital Corporation of America in 1968. During the 1970s and 1980s the corporation went through a tremendous growth period acquiring hundreds of hospitals across the United States, which numbered 255 owned and 208 that HCA managed.

Dr Reddy told me of the time when, in 1981, he went on an unannounced visit to Dr Frist in Nashville. He did not carry a business card, and so he wrote out his name on a piece of paper and, exercising his usual charm combined with bravado, persuaded the physician's secretary to give it to Dr Frist. He also wrote on that slip of paper that he wanted to see Dr Frist because he planned to start a hospital in India. Earlier, some friends had cautioned Dr Reddy that it was unlikely that Dr Frist would give him an appointment.

Dr Frist sent a note back: 'I will join you in an hour's time for lunch.' The HCA founder also asked an aide to show Dr Reddy around the premises. And sure enough, Dr Frist came out of his office in an hour and took Dr Reddy to lunch at a nearby Indian restaurant. The eatery served only vegetarian food, which dismayed Dr Reddy slightly because he was a confirmed carnivore.

Their conversation proved highly instructive for Dr Reddy. 'Dr Frist had created the first professional corporate hospital in the world, and he spent a lot of time in building departments, and in corporate planning and human resources. It was a pleasure meeting him and learning from him first-hand to think more clearly on planning various activities,' Dr Reddy said.

That pleasure notwithstanding, Dr Frist did not acquiesce to Dr Reddy's subtly expressed request that perhaps HCA might want to consider assisting him more actively with Apollo Madras. But both men agreed that India needed to accelerate its efforts in providing better health care.

By the time Dr Reddy returned to India, he was fully determined that Apollo would be established.

'Dr Reddy had a very clear vision about the kind of hospital he wanted,' one official, who was familiar with Dr Reddy's early struggles, told me. 'He wanted to see the country improve. He would say to me, "India is going to develop. You have to have the faith." Dr Reddy would fly to Delhi at least three times a week from Madras to meet officials of every variety. From desk officer to department secretary – Dr Reddy met everybody. He had absolutely no ego problems with anyone, even though he was a distinguished doctor. He had the gift of fluently articulating his vision. He never let himself get annoyed or irritated by anything negative that anyone said. Dr Reddy had a goal, and he wanted to achieve his objective. But he was discouraged by so many people.'

One of those who initially expressed his concern about Dr Reddy's plans for Apollo was none other than R. Venkataraman, who was to later become India's finance minister and then President. In 1980, after Indira Gandhi had returned to power, Venkataraman and Dr Reddy had breakfast.

'PC, your plan won't work in India,' Venkataraman said to Dr Reddy, using the initials by which many of his friends called him. 'Poor people prefer going to government hospitals. Where are people going to find the money to come to a private-sector hospital?'

But Prime Minister Indira Gandhi had come to like Dr Reddy's plans. Her closest aide at the time, R.K. Dhawan, told me years later that he would take Dr Reddy to see her. If Mrs Gandhi saw Dr Reddy outside her office in South Block – security in those days was nowhere near as stringent as it is these days – she would nod at Dr Reddy, and say, 'So you want to see me again?'

She would beckon him into her office, where Dr Reddy passionately spelled out his vision for a private-sector hospital.

Dr Reddy would talk about how India's health care needs were far too great for government hospitals alone to tackle and how with some government support the private sector could play a significant role in bringing world-class health care to India.

Another invaluable supporter was B. Venkataraman, secretary of tourism and civil aviation. His minister, A.P. Sharma, was also a supporter of Dr Reddy's plans. Venkataraman said that he would talk to secretaries in different departments.

Eventually, Apollo was allowed to borrow from banks, which had been nationalized by Indira Gandhi. Pranab Mukherjee then succeeded R. Venkataraman as finance minister. It was Mukherjee who signed the order that gave tax exemption for the medical equipment that Apollo needed to import.[2]

In Delhi, as in many capitals, people who informally assist entrepreneurs are sometimes unkindly referred to as 'fixers'. 'I can tell you that Dr Reddy was very honest and above board in his dealings with people,' one such person said to me. 'Apollo never offered money to anyone. Dr Reddy had a very strict code of ethics about this. No payments of any kind. When some high-level people travelled to Madras, he would take them to the Madras Race Club, mainly because his friend Dr Ramaswamy was its steward. But it was nothing more than that. I just cannot imagine Dr Reddy ever tolerating corruption and dishonesty.'

That sentiment was endorsed by Narayanan Vaghul, former chairman of ICICI Bank. 'Dr Reddy possesses great strength of character,' he told me at his modest apartment in Chennai, adding that Dr Reddy's modus operandi was the exception rather than the rule in India.

Vaghul is a legendary figure in Indian banking circles. He worked at the State Bank of India, then was a professor at the National Institute of Bank Management before joining Bank of India. He rose to become chairman of ICICI.

It is impossible to overstate the importance of Vaghul's role in

2 Hospitals were not getting any loans from government-owned banks at the time. Because of Pranab Mukherjee's intervention, a consortium of five institutions led by Indian Overseas Bank – and including Indian Bank, Syndicate Bank, Canara Bank, and Andhra Bank – approved a loan of Rs 3.75 crore to Apollo. Please see Chapter Nineteen.

how Apollo obtained financing from banks. Banks were originally not allowed to lend to hospitals. Prime Minister Rajiv Gandhi's 1986 banking reform changed all that. Dr Reddy was certainly instrumental in engendering ideas in Rajiv's mind about health care reform being included in the prime minister's ambitious plans for transforming India's economy. Indeed, Dr Reddy spelled out some of these ideas in a letter to Rajiv, which the two men subsequently discussed.

Vaghul was forceful in his approach to seeking reform. The prime minister was very pro-market and understood how the power of investment could help India grow. Apollo Hyderabad was the first hospital to be funded after the 1986 Act that changed the contours of the nation's health care industry. Now, of course, there are thousands of hospitals, clinics and other health care facilities in India, and millions of Indians who have benefited from the new policies in banking. No one can imagine what the poor status of health care in India would be today without outside investment.

'Vaghul was willing to support those trying to build the country. When Hyderabad experienced challenges he and his senior management team came to me. There were no roads and it was hard to get to the hospital. That didn't stop them. He said, "Tell me Dr Reddy, do you think that you can turn it around?" I replied, "I have no doubt that it will happen,"' Dr Reddy told me. 'With Vaghul's trust and support Apollo Hyderabad became a medical city where thousands are treated each year. He changed ICICI and the country's banking system, and he certainly helped Apollo at the right time. He is a man of simple tastes and great vision. He is also a man who likes to mentor entrepreneurs. And he's totally intolerant of corruption and dishonesty at all levels of society.'

When I met Mohsina Kidwai, who served as Union health minister in Rajiv Gandhi's government, one of the first things she told me was how impressed she was by Dr Reddy's integrity.

'He's not the kind of man who goes around preaching about morality,' Kidwai, now a member of the Rajya Sabha, said. 'But when you meet him, you know at once that this is a man of high ethics.

He's also a compassionate man. If he gets upset at all, it's over issues such as corruption and dishonesty.'

That intolerance of corruption and dishonesty also seems to be a common trait in the major physicians whom Dr Prathap Chandra Reddy hired from the outset for Apollo. Another trait is the ability to be an exceptional performer – a physician whose 'outcomes' are quantifiable and consistent.

General C.S.V. Subramaniam was one such exceptional performer, and one of the 'pillars' of Apollo – as Dr Reddy puts it – along with Dr M.K. Mani, Dr M.R. Girinath and Dr Arcot Gajaraj. They were also responsible for what Dr Reddy calls the 'culture of excellence' at Apollo.

General Subramaniam was Apollo's first chief of laboratory services, and set international standards that his successors have faithfully followed. Though he was much senior to all his colleagues, he treated them as equals; he would encourage discussion and even dissent from his diagnoses, if the junior could make a convincing argument. 'Whenever one of the other pathologists made a good diagnosis, he would generously give credit to that person openly in clinical meetings,' says Dr Rama Mani, pathologist and chief of lab at Apollo Chennai.

'General Subramaniam would often go to the wards to see patients whose cases came to him for opinions. He was a competent clinician himself, and that added to his abilities. Clinicians were always welcome to walk into his office and discuss their problem cases, and many found it well worthwhile to do so,' she said.

He was always accessible to every member of the department, and would listen to their problems, whether pertaining to the hospital or personal, do his best to solve them, and even offer financial help when needed,' Dr Mani told me.

General Subramaniam was the first Chairman of Apollo's clinical society, and presided over the meetings for years. This was the ideal setting for his great erudition. He was a polymath, a clinician and a pathologist, a scholar in three languages, English, Tamil and Sanskrit, and could quote literature from many sources to enliven the clinical meeting and elucidate a point. He was particularly fond of citing apt quotations from Shakespeare. He took an active part in the inter-hospital pathology meetings in the city.

Another physician Dr Reddy was very keen to invite to Apollo was Dr Sujoy B. Roy, the first head of the cardiology department at AIIMS; but Dr Roy passed away suddenly even as Dr Reddy was discussing the appointment with him.

Rightly recognizing that the need of the hour was as much for carrying forward his vision and training people into that mould, Dr Reddy decided to recruit the registrar of AIIMS rather than a professor of cardiology. Dr Seshagiri Rao joined Apollo Hospitals as its first interventional cardiologist and is a highly respected consultant in the country today.

Dr B.N. Das, a cardio-vascular surgeon at Indraprastha Apollo Hospital in New Delhi, feels the same way.

'I joined Apollo in order to venture into the area of the corporate hospitals and to render my services to a wider range of people, and also to attain more professional success,' Dr Das told me. 'I was also impressed by the fact that the waiting period for heart surgery is much less in corporate hospitals and this is a boon for patients requiring urgent surgery.'

'Apollo has given me the opportunity to operate on many sick patients due to easy availability of extensive modern gadgets, multispeciality infrastructure, trained staff and highly qualified specialists round the clock,' Dr Das said.

———

When I was writing this chapter, I wondered what I should title it. Then the name of a great novel by Taylor Caldwell came to mind, *Dear and Glorious Physician*. It's about Lucanus, a great doctor in ancient Greece, and how he came to write of his experiences with Christ.

Stories of physicians such as Dr Prasanna K. Reddy and Dr Matthew may not offer up instances of their religious experiences.

But in my view, their pursuit of medicine, their loyalty toward Dr Prathap Chandra Reddy, and their dedication to the common good of India's people – all of these things suggest a special spiritual path that each took.

Dr Joseph V. Thachil is one such physician. Born near Cochin in Kerala, he received his medical degree from the University of Zurich, and then moved to Toronto, where he specialized in urology. He made a name for himself in kidney transplants.

He had not expected to join Apollo, but after he'd met Dr Reddy on a visit to India, he was impressed by the fact that Dr Reddy was able to overcome the twin hurdles of indiscipline and red tape that afflicted the practice of medicine in India.

'Dr Reddy, I never thought that this would materialize,' Dr Thachil said, offering to invest in Apollo. 'This is like a dream come true. You have done it – hats off to you!'

'Joe, until we complete establishing the institutions, don't say, "Dr Reddy did it,"' the Apollo founder said. 'Apollo still has a long way to go. We need the involvement of doctors like you.'

Years later, reflecting on his initial meetings with Dr Reddy three decades ago, Dr Thachil told me: 'He wanted to deliver health care to patients that would be accessible in India so that they would not have to go overseas for transplants.'

Dr Thachil was aware that at the time Dr Reddy asked him to establish the renal unit at Apollo, India as a whole simply did not have enough trained medical and paramedical personnel to deliver quality medical care. 'We needed to develop a team, and do it fast,' he said.

Fast enough that by June 1984, Dr Thachil was able to perform the first living kidney transplant at Apollo – just ten months after Apollo Madras opened. Within two years, he and his team had performed 100 transplants. Apollo became the institution where the largest number of living-donor transplants were performed in India; it also ranked among the largest transplant institutions in the world.

After the Indian government approved transplants using organs from cadavers, Dr Thachil did the country's first such transplant at Apollo Madras in October 1995.

By early 2013, Dr Thachil personally had done 3,000 kidney transplants, an accomplishment that has brought him fame in international medical circles. On some days, Apollo did five transplants a day, setting a record.

'This is never a one-man show, but a team effort,' Dr Thachil said, repeating a refrain that I had heard from many top doctors at Apollo. 'It's important to teach our young surgeons and other medical personnel not only up-to-date technology but also to inculcate in them values such as moral respect for the patient. The best ambassador to increase your practice in medicine is your patient.'

'Values begin at home,' Dr Thachil told me. 'At Apollo, we conduct camps where not only sound medical practice but also attitudes towards patients are stressed. Dr Reddy always talks about "compassion, respect and love" – and these are not abstractions. When you spend as much time as I do in the operating theatre, you realize how important it is that the patient's welfare and recovery are based on far more than medicine. It's the way that you deal with the patients. It's the aftercare.

'Dr Reddy believes in continuing education for doctors. In India, doctors are looked upon as demi-gods, or even gods. But the truth is, we are human beings like everyone else. We have our fallibilities. Like everyone else, doctors need to understand that medicine is a lifelong learning process,' Dr Thachil said.

He paused to order more coffee for us in his office, and then told me of a recent episode involving Dr Reddy.

Dr Thachil ran into him in a corridor, and Dr Reddy patted him on the back, more a gesture of affection and appreciation than anything else. 'Then, quite unexpectedly, Dr Reddy said to me, "Is everything all right, Joe? Are you homesick for Canada? Is there anything that you need here?"'

Dr Thachil was clearly touched.

'You know, in how many corporate hospitals does the big boss do something like this?' he said to me. 'Dr Reddy has done India proud. There's no doubt that he started a new era in health care. He created "The Apollo Way" – which, simply put, means that the patient always comes first. That may seem very elementary, but it hadn't been part of the Indian medical ethos until Dr Reddy came along.'

While Dr Reddy isn't above appreciating such praise, he doesn't solicit it. During my conversations with him, I found him more concerned about the roads not taken, about some personal mistakes in business, and about patients who hadn't fared well during their stay at Apollo.

One mistake that he acknowledges concerns an investment that he made in an IT company. On one of his visits to the USA, Dr Reddy had met the senior vice president at Intel, who said that they would be happy to associate with Dr Reddy's group in setting up an IT company in India. Many of his friends advised Dr Reddy that this partnership with a giant like Intel would have huge potential in India and he founded a company in Madras with an investment of $800,000. But what Intel and Dr Reddy had not foreseen were the huge bureaucratic and regulatory delays that a facility in the export zone had to put up with. Intel was partnering with a company in the private sector in India for the first time and it could not understand or condone these delays of several weeks for the movement of any material. This led to their disenchantment and Dr Reddy was forced to close the company. Dr Reddy feels that it was an investment ahead of its time, made well before IT became a favoured sector in India.

One of the main people whom Dr Reddy consulted before he withdrew was Nagarajan Vittal, a prominent member of the IAS, who was to become the central vigilance commissioner (CVC). 'He was secretary in charge of electronics to the Government of India and interested in bringing IT and software to the country. He also was successful in introducing the electronics hardware technology park scheme to boost the manufacture of electronic hardware,' Dr Reddy said.

'Vittal could see what IT could possibly do for India. He realized what an enormous impact it could have for foreign exchange and economic growth. He saw it long before Bangalore became an IT centre and other places, like Hyderabad, followed soon after,' Dr Reddy told me.

'When I told him that I wanted to surrender my interests, he said,

"Then we must have a ceremonial burial for the company." Two years after that IT improvement programmes came about and look what has happened now.'

Dr Reddy added: 'He's a very straightforward man, no ifs and buts. This was very important because he became the central vigilance commissioner and his integrity was never questioned. The CVC has enormous powers and can investigate and arrest anyone for wrongdoing. He was very, very powerful and allowed no nonsense.

'He still comes to Apollo for his check-ups.'

Vittal had spoken to me about Dr Reddy's loyalty to colleagues, particularly those who helped with the founding of Apollo, and with the group's development. Dr Arcot Gajaraj was one such leading light, and Dr Reddy still talks about him with enormous affection and admiration. Dr Gajaraj died in 2005 of lung cancer, choosing not to take any treatments as the cancer had metastasized.

Arcot Gajaraj was one of the four pillars of Apollo and a close friend of Dr Reddy's. He had studied at Stanley Medical College graduating in the early '50s, and that is where he met Prathap Chandra Reddy. After receiving his degree from Stanley Medical College he worked at, among other places, the Government General Hospital in Madras. General Hospital is the affiliate hospital of Madras Medical College.

Dr Gajaraj had always been fascinated with radiographs or X-rays. He would receive his DNB (Diploma of the National Board of India for radiology). He obtained his diploma in radio diagnosis and MD in internal medicine and an FRCR (Fellowship of the Royal College of Radiologists) as well. After his time at General Hospital, he became the director of the Bernard Institute of Radiology at Madras Medical College.

He retired voluntarily from Government General Hospital after a dispute with hospital administrators. His daughter Dr Jaishree Gajaraj – who is an onco-gynaecologist at Apollo – recalls the time that Dr Reddy asked him to join him in building Apollo from the ground up.

Dr Jaishree says, 'I remember Dad coming home and saying

that Dr Reddy had asked him to join him and he was very excited. Dr Reddy gave him a free hand to plan the department, not just the physical arrangement but in determining what services Apollo would offer, purchasing the equipment and hiring staff. He was quite impressed with Dr Reddy's confidence in him.'

There was never any compromise on equipment; only the best would do for Apollo Madras. 'This kind of support was critical to Dad,' says Dr Jaishree.

At home Dr Gajaraj was always talking about the new hospital, and what needed to be done. He would go over the blueprints for the new building and spend hours studying various configurations to see which were the most efficient for patient flow, and use of space.

Dr Gajaraj would discuss with Dr Reddy how he wanted to recruit the very best junior colleagues so that the department would take care of patients in the best way possible. He was very proud of Apollo and quite idealistic about it. When Apollo got the country's first whole-body CT unit (at a very high cost which was a significant portion of the total project value), Dr Reddy told me that Dr Mehta of Jaslok Hospitals, which was the leading private-sector hospital at that time, said it wasn't a worthwhile investment. But later he took Dr Reddy's help in acquiring one for Jaslok. Dr Gajaraj recalls that when the equipment came in there really wasn't the staff to operate it and he sat at the machine and conducted the exam until he was entirely satisfied with the training of the technicians. He also read the test results and made diagnoses. Some people suggested that the new hospital accept radiology candidates who were less qualified but Dr Gajaraj – who, like Dr Reddy, always insisted on getting the best qualified medical talent – wouldn't have any of that.

Dr Gajaraj was an excellent teacher, rigorous in his approach and able to carefully explain the tests and results. He was a workaholic, a no-nonsense kind of man but he loved having parties at home and his wife Kausalya always welcomed colleagues and friends with wonderful dinners. All his old students would come, too.

Kausalya Gajaraj taught math and physics at the Saint Thomas Convent and their home was filled with lively discussions and appreciation of history and culture and, of course, new scientific and medical developments. Dr Jaishree and Dr Gajaraj's former students have started a medical foundation in honour of her father, called TARGET (The Arcot Gajaraj Educational and Training Programme). Each year TARGET sponsors a three-day training at a venue in Chennai. Post-graduate students from all over South India come and the most current techniques, papers and equipment are discussed.

When Apollo Chennai celebrated its twenty-fifth anniversary, Dr Reddy asked Kausalya Gajaraj to come. When she got there, he asked her to sit in the front and later brought her to the stage area with him. He wanted to recognize the contribution that her late husband had made to Apollo and talked about him at the event. Then he gave Kausalya a beautiful silver lamp. She was very moved by this kind gesture.

———

Another physician who is unswervingly loyal to Dr Reddy is Dr Sumana Manohar, who found her true passion, her life's calling, at Apollo. She is one of India's best and brightest who, after years abroad, came home to live and work and prosper. She loves being a surgeon.

After receiving her MBBS from Vellore Medical College in 1989, she and her husband Dr Babu Manohar moved to Chennai. 'Apollo was known to everybody, it was a beacon to us and we visited to see if it was feasible to join. Dr Reddy met us and was looking at my husband's CV,' Dr Sumana recalled.

Then Dr Reddy turned to her and asked, 'Where are you practicing?'

'I haven't started, sir,' Dr Sumana said.

'Come join us,' Dr Reddy said.

'Those two hours changed my life entirely,' Dr Sumana later said.

In a few years she and her husband – an ENT specialist – moved to Britain where she did speciality training in obstetrics and gynaecology and surgery, and then a fellowship in ultrasound at the University of Pennsylvania. After ten years away, the couple and their daughters, one born in Britain, another in the United States, felt the promise of India's future and the pull of her rich past and moved back to Chennai in 2000.

'Dr Reddy was welcoming. The atmosphere was warm and friendly and its facilities excellent. When we left for Britain, Apollo was still relatively new and to see that it had maintained its standards, even improved them, told the future of health care in India,' she says.

She obtained a medical practice immediately at Apollo – as did her husband – and knew that she was making important inroads into women's health care. The number of female surgeons worldwide is a small percentage of the total number of surgeons and in India, that percentage is even lower. In general, women embrace female doctors and Dr Sumana was no exception.

When robotic surgery was introduced, Dr Satyabhama, the director of medical services at Apollo Chennai, asked Dr Sumana to take it up as a speciality. Dr Sumana welcomed the chance and received her first training in endoscopic robotics at the internationally acclaimed IRCAD centre in Strasbourg, France. It was intensive and Dr Sumana knew that she had found a complement to her surgical skills. Later, she studied in Detroit with Dr Rubina Singh who became her mentor.

Robotic surgery is minimally invasive, which usually means that the patient has a shorter hospital stay, fewer complications, and less recovery time. It is one of the accelerators in more efficient health care delivery and Apollo has been at the forefront in adopting robotics.

For example, Apollo Delhi has seven consultants trained in robotic urology which includes one paediatric urologist. The team has operated nearly fifty robotic urology cases, including prostatectomy, nephrectomy and cystectomy. It is accepted that the robotic technique has significantly reduced complications and has dramatically improved clinical outcomes.

Apollo and its surgeons benefited from an alliance with the

PRANAY GUPTE

Vattikuti Foundation which is based in Michigan. Founded in 1997 by Raj and Padma Vattikuti, its mission is to develop centres of excellence in robotic surgery and other minimally invasive techniques and provide better health care to people around the world.

The Vattikuti Foundation funded Dr Rubina Singh and other team members to monitor the launch of the ob-gyn robotic surgery. The Apollo surgical team and the team from the foundation did several surgeries together. After the fifth case, Dr Sumana began doing the surgeries alone.

'When I first started, I would go home and think about the case, and practice in my mind. Then I would rise early and reach the hospital by 5.30 a.m. so that I could practice with the instruments until 6.00. The surgery would start at 6.30 a.m. It was exhilarating to be able to bring this new technology and immediately see the benefits for the patients,' Dr Sumana said.

Dr Sumana was trained in reproductive health and IVF (in-vitro fertilization) and says, 'When you see any baby, but especially those born because of new treatments and procedures, there is always a happiness. That happiness is mostly for the families but for me, my happiness is in surgery.

'Surgery today is not like it was before. We were very pleased to see that at Apollo the teams of doctors and nurses, the entire hospital staff was of the same excellent calibre as in America. The quality of the facilities, too. Apollo made a giant leap and we are continuing to see the effects of the changes that Dr Reddy brought to India.'

Dr Sumana says that one of the joys of her job is seeing the new babies. She remembers a forty-two-year-old woman from Bangalore who had not had children after fourteen years of marriage. The first time her IVF was not successful. The second time she was doing well and came for an appointment in the morning.

'There was a little bleeding and we wanted to keep her in hospital but she insisted on leaving because of an important family function. Suddenly, the bleeding was profuse and she was rushed back to Apollo. We took her straight to the delivery theatre – and now every year on the baby's birthday she brings us sweets from a local shop,' Dr Sumana says.

———

Dr Meenakshi Sundaram was born and reared in Chennai. She comes from an upper middle class family, her father retired from Larsen & Toubro, her mother is a homemaker; an elder sister is a vice principal and her brother a software engineer. Becoming a physician was always her goal and indeed, she is the first doctor in her family.

After schooling, she worked in Mumbai at the Bombay Endoscopy Academy and Centre for Minimally Invasive Surgery and then relocated to Chennai because she wanted to be near her family.

She worked briefly for Meenakshi Multispeciality Hospital. When her views about doing advanced work in her field of specialization were more focused, she decided to explore other alternatives.

She was hesitant to approach Apollo but was attracted by the continual chatter in the medical community that Apollo sought out innovators. Dr Sundaram had two goals: first, to treat women with fibroid tumours, and second, to do so with laparascopic and robotic surgery. She went to Germany and the United States for training in these disciplines. Her speciality is gynaecological surgery, and she wrote to Dr Reddy requesting an appointment.

She was surprised to be summoned to Dr Reddy's office for an interview almost immediately. He had looked at her CV and at the interview discussed her views on women's health care, especially focusing on fibroid treatment.

'He valued my CV and my experience rather than whom I knew. He saw my potential,' Dr Sundaram said.

Dr Reddy also understood how robotic surgery for fibroids would benefit women. Since it is less invasive it is less painful, it does not increase the chance of infertility, it helps improve the chances of getting pregnant. If a woman does get pregnant, she has less complications from scar tissue and the pregnancy is easier. The minimally invasive robotic surgery also results in fewer vascular issues.

'Now, we do patient camps not only in India but in Nigeria, the Maldives, Tanzania, as in these countries the women are often afflicted with fibroid tumours,' she said. 'When you get hope and give hope, then you want to do more. That is why I am at Apollo.'

CHAPTER TWENTY-THREE

A Man Named Rajiv

DR PRATHAP CHANDRA REDDY believes to this day that Rajiv Gandhi was the 'father' of modern health care in India. But in 1986 – less than two years after Rajiv had succeeded his mother, Prime Minister Indira Gandhi, who was assassinated by her Sikh bodyguards in her own garden in New Delhi – Dr Reddy was frustrated. He sent a letter to Rajiv about health care in India. It was dated 10 April 1986.

'I am writing this letter to highlight the urgent need to initiate certain innovative measures and bring about a paradigm shift in quality health care delivery in our country,' Dr Reddy wrote. 'I wish I had set up a beedi factory or beer factory instead of health care.

'If health has to come along with your vision for the twenty-first century, we need: (1) Hospitals to be funded like any other trade or industry; (2) Incentives to be given for health insurance and health plans; and (3) If the expenses for the medical treatment is paid by an employer, it should not be added to the employee's income.'

Some days later, when the two men met, Rajiv jokingly said to Dr Reddy: 'This is how you write a letter to a prime minister, is it?'

That letter set into motion a train of events, some to Dr Reddy's satisfaction, and others not so much. But, perhaps most of all, it could be argued that Dr Reddy succeeded in getting Rajiv's attention – and that of the Indian parliament – focused on health care. Rajiv was to become a staunch supporter of Apollo's founder – as Indira Gandhi had been in her time. Some months after he'd sent the letter to the prime minister, Dr Reddy and Rajiv met again. On that occasion, Dr Reddy told him that it would be important for the health care industry to obtain equity investment – and that foreign investors realized the potential of India's health care opportunities. The prime minister agreed, and authorized 100 per cent FDI in health care. Today, Dr Reddy is even more convinced that because of India's expanding needs in health care, the country offers an even more attractive destination for FDI.[1]

T.K.A. Nair, senior advisor to Prime Minister Manmohan Singh, told me at his office in New Delhi's South Block that Rajiv Gandhi believed that Dr Reddy had a clear and important vision for health care in India. Dr Reddy, in turn, felt that Rajiv would push through reforms that would benefit the entire country. 'Sadly, Rajiv was prime minister for only five years – not enough time to accomplish everything that he envisioned for India,' Nair said.

———

Early in 1991, I met with Rajiv Gandhi at his home in New Delhi. He was no longer India's prime minister; his Indian National Congress had lost the national election in 1989 to the National Front, a jumble of parties of varying ideologies. Chandra Shekhar, a veteran politician who had formed one such grouping, the Samajwadi Janata Party, was prime minister at the time that I visited Delhi from my home in New York.

Although Rajiv hadn't been prime minister for more than a year, he continued to live in a government bungalow at 10 Janpath, a sprawling property that was part of that area of New Delhi known

———

1 The FDI equity inflows received by hospitals and diagnostic centres have been increasing steadily since Rajiv Gandhi's time – Rs 5,417.92 crore between April 2000 and February 2012, accounting for 0.80 per cent of the total FDI in India.

as the Lutyens Zone;[2] Rajiv was still a member of Parliament, which entitled him to free housing – as did the fact that all former prime ministers received accommodations for life.

It was a crisp, cool morning, one of those days that make the capital city so delightful in winter. Hundreds of people were waiting on the lawns to greet Rajiv, but I was speedily ushered into his house by Vincent George, a shrewd Keralite who'd been a long-serving aide to Rajiv Gandhi and, before him, to Rajiv's mother, the late Indira Gandhi. George was Indira's gatekeeper, and he served as one for Rajiv Gandhi as well. He was not a man to cross; it was a safe bet that if George didn't like you for any reason, your chances of getting to meet Indira or Rajiv would be slim.

Mani Shankar Aiyar, a former diplomat who had been close to the Gandhi family, had arranged the meeting with Rajiv.[3] I was meeting with Rajiv for a documentary for public television in the United States. A crew that had flown in from New York accompanied me; it included the veteran TV correspondent Bernard Kalb, a longtime friend and an India admirer, who was to be the documentary's on-screen narrator.

As we waited in Rajiv's living room, I saw that he maintained a large collection of books, including several on Lutyens. They'd been neatly arranged in teak bookcases. I spotted two of my own books, *The Crowded Earth: People and the Politics of Population*, and *Vengeance: India after the Assassination of Indira Gandhi*. I was flattered, to be sure; I had given both books to Rajiv and Sonia Gandhi during their visit to New York in the mid-1980s. But I was also intrigued to see several titles concerning health care. I made a

---

2 The man who had designed 10 Janpath, and scores of other similar houses, was Sir Edwin Landseer Lutyens, a British architect. Along with his partner, Herbert Baker, Lutyens was entrusted with creating New Delhi, the seat of the British Raj.

3 Mani Shankar Aiyar is a prolific author and columnist, and one of the most articulate men I've encountered in public life anywhere. He served in the cabinet of Prime Minister Manmohan Singh, and now is a member of the Rajya Sabha, the Upper House of the Indian parliament.

mental note to myself to ask Rajiv about these books. I could have not imagined that more than twenty years later, his involvement with health care would come up in a book I'd write about Dr Prathap Chandra Reddy.

In the event, the interview on that winter day in Delhi did not offer an opportunity to draw Rajiv out on health care. Today, in hindsight, I very much regret that. Had I asked Rajiv about his views on health care, he would have surely elaborated on the topic – as least as an element of his thinking about sustainable economic development in India. And he would have surely made a reference to Dr Prathap Chandra Reddy – not the least because the plans for Apollo Delhi were finalized while Rajiv was still India's prime minister. In fact, Rajiv's mother, Indira Gandhi, had taken steps to ensure that Apollo Madras would be launched as planned; she even got Dr Reddy to invite the then President Zail Singh to come for the inauguration.[4]

Whenever Dr Reddy talks about Rajiv, a discernible wistful look washes across his visage. I don't think that Dr Prathap Chandra Reddy is a hero-worshipper of any sort, least of all of politicians, but if he were one then Rajiv Gandhi would be the closest that Dr Reddy would consider as an icon.

'He is the politician I admire most,' Dr Reddy says of Rajiv Gandhi.

It wasn't just Rajiv's charm and humility that enthralled Dr Reddy. 'Not only did Rajiv set a precedent for corporate health care in the country,' Dr Reddy says, 'but the Government of India soon recognized his enterprising efforts leading to financial institutions amending their funding legislation to include hospitals.'[5]

---

4 The steps that Prime Minister Indira Gandhi took included writing to Chief Minister M.G. Ramachandran of Tamil Nadu about the significance of Apollo's presence in Madras, and the potential contribution that such a hi-tech hospital would make towards helping the state's people. C.R. Krishnaswamy Rao, Indira's cabinet secretary, sent a letter to the chief minister. Ramachandran had resisted Apollo initially, but eventually acceded to Indira's request. He did not, however, turn up for the inauguration.

5 Quoted in the *Asian Tribune*.

After Dr Reddy had launched his first Apollo Hospital in Madras in September 1983, he felt emboldened to expand to other cities. One of these cities, of course, was New Delhi. By this time, Apollo had already established a thriving hospital in Hyderabad as well.

Rajiv Gandhi, in fact, had wanted Dr Reddy to build an Apollo Hospital in Delhi. Dr Reddy had been in touch with the Delhi administration about this.[6] Rajiv's aides informed Dr Reddy that a multi-speciality hospital might be set up in Players' Hostel, an unfinished building next to the Indira Gandhi Indoor Stadium.[7] The 1982 Asiad Games were being planned at the time, and the Delhi Development Authority (DDA) had obtained large loans from banks to construct the Players' Hostel. But the project was abandoned in November 1980 after it became clear that the building wouldn't be ready in time for the Games. Meanwhile, interest payments on the loans were mounting. Questions were being raised about why the DDA had spent so much money on a building that wouldn't be completed. In the end, the Government of India had to bail out the DDA.

The Parliament's Public Accounts Committee – which is traditionally headed by a member of the Opposition – then resolved that a super-speciality hospital might be raised on the premises. The government accepted this recommendation, and formed a committee to explore the possibility. One prospect seemed to be a facility created by Tata Memorial Hospital, the Bombay-based medical centre that specialized in cancer treatment. One senior IAS official told me that the Sultan of Oman pledged to support such an institution, but then withdrew his pledge when oil prices dropped precipitously and with it, his country's revenues.

Many senior members of the IAS followed this issue. After all, it

---

6 Delhi was designated as a national capital territory in 1991 under the 69th amendment of the Indian Constitution. At the time that Dr Reddy was invited by Rajiv Gandhi to build an Apollo Hospital in Delhi, a lieutenant governor appointed by the federal government administered Delhi.

7 The stadium had been built for the ninth Asian Games, which were held in New Delhi from 19 November to 4 December 1982.

would be the first joint venture in health care between the government and a private-sector entity. Delhi's lieutenant governor H.L. Kapur, a former air marshal, was the chief official who dealt with Apollo at the time. His key advisor was Ajay Shankar. And Delhi's chief secretary was K.K. Mathur. The influence of these three officials was enormous in the governance of Delhi.

Vijai Kapoor took over as chief secretary of Delhi in 1988; he became Delhi's lieutenant governor in 1998, and occupied that important post until 2004. In a conversation at his Delhi home in mid-2012 – long after he had retired from the IAS – Kapoor told me that the Rajiv Gandhi government could have invested in the G.B. Pant Hospital – a decrepit government-run facility – but that Rajiv was convinced that India's capital would benefit from a well-run private-sector medical centre.

Vijai Kapoor also recalls that senior officials such as Vineeta Rai, then the Delhi government's health secretary, discussed Dr Reddy's ideas with government officials in the presence of Rajiv Gandhi.

'At a time when liberalization was still being talked about, Dr Reddy was determined to change the health care landscape of India,' Vineeta Rai said. 'That took guts, but it also needed deep knowledge of how human beings – particularly bureaucrats – behave when confronted with the challenge of making decisions. Dr Reddy knew how to talk to people in a language that was never condescending. And they, in turn, appreciated the respect that he showed them, and the polite manner in which he sought their guidance. All of us were struck by the intensity of his pursuit of excellence, his readiness to take risks, his compassion, his relentless optimism and enthusiasm, his refusal to compromise on quality, and his integrity.'

'The Apollo Delhi venture was the first private–public partnership in India's health care sector. Government hospitals started to realize that competition was coming from the private sector, and that doctors of Indian origin who'd settled abroad were coming back home to join Dr Reddy's Apollo hospitals in Madras and Hyderabad,' Rai said. 'Officials realized that Dr Reddy was creating institutions of quality – and that he embodied the story of positive change in India.'

One of Vineeta Rai's colleagues in the IAS, Dr Vijay S. Madan, agrees with her assessment. A physician by training, he is currently the director general of the powerful Unique Identification Authority of India. Dr Madan understood keenly that access to affordable health care simply wasn't there in India in the late 1970s and early 1980s. 'Dr Reddy offered that access, particularly to those who didn't have the time or resources to get top-class treatment overseas,' Dr Madan told me over tea in New Delhi.

'Dr Reddy brought back doctors who were settled abroad. They found attractive opportunities in private-sector hospitals such as Apollo. By cracking the "code" through his enterprise and sheer endurance, Dr Reddy proved that it was possible for the private sector to flourish in the health care sector.

'A paradigm shift was essential in health care, and Dr Reddy made it happen,' Dr Madan said. Governments usually like to be in the driver's seat in any joint venture, and as a result many companies got into tussles with the government. But Apollo was allowed to take the lead by the Delhi government, and Prime Minister Rajiv Gandhi's support was most critical.

'We started a new platform of health delivery,' Dr Madan – who received his medical training at the University of Delhi's Maulana Azad Medical College – said. 'We were impressed by Dr Reddy, but we went through a process of vetting and checking out various hospitals.'

Both Dr Madan and Vineeta Rai recall that a government committee checked out institutions such as Bombay Hospital. 'But in the end we determined that Apollo offered the best model for the super-speciality hospital in Delhi,' Rai told me.

Until Dr Reddy came along with his Apollo model for a private–public partnership in health care, the shortage of beds in Delhi's existing medical institutions – such as the government-run G.B. Pant Hospital – was acute. Delhi's indigenous population was growing at the rate of 2 per cent annually, and the immigration rate was another 2 per cent each year – for a total population growth of 4 per cent.[8] No government hospital had been built in Delhi since the G.B. Pant Hospital opened in 1964; the next one to open was the Guru Teg Bahadur Hospital in 1987. The average occupancy at Delhi's government hospitals was more than 100 per cent; in the gynaecological wards, the rate was 300 per cent – which translated into three people occupying each bed.

'The available budgets were woefully inadequate, and the Public Works Department didn't have the capacity to build hospitals fast enough in the face of such population growth,' Dr Madan said. 'So our dilemma was: how do we increase the number of beds, and how do we provide access for the poor to good health care?'

The question then arose: was there some other model besides that of a government-run hospital that could be introduced in the health care sector? There were two possibilities: one was to privatize health care entirely, and let corporates build and run hospitals. But such a model wouldn't fly in a country where free enterprise was still frowned on, and where socialism was still official dogma. (In the early 1980s, 'profit' was still considered a dirty word; government officials, even in informal conversations, used the word 'surplus' instead.) A second model was one involving partnerships between government and private entities such as Apollo. These entities would receive land at concessional prices, or perhaps even free, with the proviso that they offer free treatment to a certain number of poor people. It was the adoption of this model that enabled the establishment of Indraprastha Apollo Hospital in New Delhi. 'The two models, however, weren't considered mutually exclusive,' Dr Madan told me.

He was appointed project director for Apollo. 'I was able to bring in my IAS training and experience, and I brought energy and passion to the project because I truly believed that it stood a chance of succeeding. I may not have been a decision maker, but I serviced decision making,' Dr Madan said, particularly citing the important

---

8   The capital's population now is nearly 18 million, making it India's second most populous city after Mumbai.

roles played in the proceedings by two Reddy daughters, Shobana and Sangita.

Talking with top IAS officials such as Keshav Desiraju, Dr Madan and Vineeta Rai gave me an enhanced understanding of how policy-making works in India's government. It isn't enough for an official or a committee to come up with a good idea. There needs to be a 'buy-in' from several departments, as was the case with the Apollo story. The Planning Commission, in fact, put twenty-one questions to the Delhi government about the viability of the project. In the 1980s, you couldn't do anything without the blessings of the Planning Commission.

Listening to Dr Madan, I began to appreciate even more the interplay between officials like him and medical entrepreneurs and visionaries such as Dr Reddy. Dr Reddy's ideas for Apollo Delhi drew influential supporters like Dr Madan and others in government.

The *bhoomi puja* for Apollo Delhi was performed on 30 June 1991. Among those present was Atal Bihari Vajpayee. L.K. Advani was there, too. The day after, Dr Reddy threw a reception at the Oberoi to celebrate the start of construction. That same night, when Dr Vijay Madan returned home, he found a letter waiting for him. He had been transferred to Arunachal Pradesh in the remote North-East.

Vijai Kapoor became Delhi's lieutenant governor in 1998. Many years later, Kapoor would be closely associated with the concept of the Delhi Metro and the capital's flyovers. But in any conversation with him, you'd never realize that Kapoor had accomplished so much in his career. I found his modesty quite touching.

'That Apollo Hospitals could effectively reverse medical brain drain and save valuable foreign exchange for the country had been greatly appreciated by Rajiv's mother, Indira Gandhi,' Kapoor said to me. 'This prompted Rajiv to invite the Apollo Hospitals Group to set up the country's first joint venture hospital in Delhi on the lines of its Madras hospital. Perhaps change would have come anyway in due course – but Dr Reddy was the catalyst of that big change in India's health care sector. He was a dozen years ahead of his time, a time of a highly regulated government regime when things were hard to accomplish for anyone in the private sector.'

Rajiv was very clear in his mind that he wanted not an 'Apollo-like' hospital but an Apollo Hospital itself.

Moreover, he wanted Apollo to be commissioned as part of the Jawaharlal Nehru birth centenary celebrations in November 1989. The hospital, promoted by the government of Delhi and the Apollo Hospitals Group, was incorporated as a public limited company on 16 March 1988. The Delhi government brought in equity and offered land to Apollo at a nominal lease rental of one rupee per year for a period of ninety-nine years. In turn the Apollo Hospitals Group would levy a management consultancy fee of Re 1 per year.

Vineeta Rai told me that, as per the joint venture agreement, 26 per cent of the equity in cash was to be held by the government of Delhi, 25 per cent by the Apollo Hospitals Group, and 49 per cent by the public. Dr Reddy said that Apollo managed to get the country's first foreign direct investment in health care through Schroder Capital Partners, which subscribed to 24 per cent of the equity; the balance of 25 per cent was offered to the public, a large number of whom were retired pensioners.[9]

But neither H.L. Kapur nor Vijai Kapoor nor Vineeta Rai, nor anyone else in the Delhi government had reckoned with the clout of a woman named Margaret Alva, who was Rajiv Gandhi's Union minister for sports. Alva reportedly persuaded Rajiv to rescind his offer to Dr Reddy. There's still some controversy about exactly what happened.

One day, Dr Reddy received a call from Romesh Bhandari, a

---

9   The initial capital of Indraprastha Apollo Hospital was Rs 91.67 crore. But the total cost of the project rose to Rs 160 crore. The government's equity of 26 per cent was Rs 23.83 crore, while that of Apollo's 25 per cent was Rs 22.92 crore.

former secretary of external affairs, and a man close to the Nehru-Gandhi family. He was Delhi's lieutenant governor at the time.

'I have good news for you, and I have bad news,' Bhandari told Dr Reddy. 'Which do you want to hear first?'

'The bad news, of course,' Dr Reddy said.

'Well, the prime minister does not want you to build Apollo near the stadium,' Bhandari said. 'He also doesn't want you to call him about this matter. But he says that you can choose any other piece of land in Delhi.'

In April 1989, Rajiv Gandhi's administration decided to allot the Players' Hostel building to the Sports Authority of India. Although Dr Reddy had already given out contracts worth more than Rs 15 crore – the equivalent of $5 million at the time – to renovate the building, and had employed some 2,000 workers, he had no choice but to halt construction. Construction had begun in February and was stopped in six weeks on account of the prime minister's decision. Apollo was compensated to the tune of the Rs 15 crore that it had already spent on the project.

But Dr Reddy was determined to forge ahead with Apollo. And so, sometimes accompanied by Bhandari, he would drive around the capital, checking out potential sites for the new hospital. Besides being Delhi's lieutenant governor, Bhandari was also chairman of the DDA. Considering that he held two powerful positions, it was most unusual that he would personally accompany Dr Reddy in scouting for sites for Apollo Hospital. This was perhaps an acknowledgment of Rajiv Gandhi's keen interest in getting Apollo to Delhi – and also a sign of how much regard and respect Dr Reddy elicited in Delhi's highest political circles.

They eventually identified fifteen acres of land in Jasola village along Mathura Road. At that time, the property seemed distant from the hustle and bustle of New Delhi. It was surrounded by farms. Bhandari wondered if patients would come to a hospital so far away from the city centre. Dr Reddy, however, says he always believed that if you built a good hospital, the people would come.

The Indraprastha Apollo Hospital – as it was now called – was inaugurated on 27 July 1996 by the President of India, Dr Shankar Dayal Sharma. The ceremony was also attended by the Delhi chief minister Sahib Singh Verma and scores of other dignitaries.

Dr Prathap Chandra Reddy effusively welcomed his guests. They were offered snacks and beverages. There was music. It was a ceremony redolent with the elegance and pomp that characterize Reddy family functions. But in the back of Dr Reddy's mind was the awareness that the delay in opening Apollo Delhi had resulted in the project cost going up to Rs 179.59 crore from the originally budgeted Rs 65 crore.

Rajiv Gandhi was not there at the inauguration. He had been assassinated in a suicide bombing on 21 May 1991 by a Sri Lankan woman named by Thenmozhi Rajaratnam (also known as Dhanu), in the small town of Sriperumbudur in Tamil Nadu, where he had gone to campaign. The attack was blamed on the Liberation Tigers of Tamil Eelam (LTTE), a separatist terrorist organization from Sri Lanka; at the time India was embroiled, through the Indian Peace Keeping Force, in the Sri Lankan civil war.

Some days before the assassination, Rajiv had met with Dr Reddy at Apollo Madras. Farooq Abdullah, now a Union minister and formerly chief minister of Jammu and Kashmir, told me that a couple of friends of Rajiv's had been admitted to Apollo's intensive care unit, and so the former prime minister had decided to pay them a visit. Dr Reddy escorted Rajiv around, and later they chatted for nearly two hours in the chairman's small ground-floor office just off the hospital's crowded lobby.[10]

As Rajiv Gandhi rose to leave, Dr Reddy's oldest daughter, Preetha, walked into her father's office. Preetha and Dr Reddy walked with Rajiv to his car.

As he got into the front seat next to his driver, Rajiv rolled the window down, turned to Preetha, and said: 'You see what your father and I

---

10 Sources: Farooq Abdullah and Dr Prathap Chandra Reddy, in conversations, December 2012, New Delhi.

are going to do. Just see what your father and I will do to completely revolutionize national health care in India. Just wait and see.'

He flew to New Delhi later that day.

A few days later, Rajiv called Dr Reddy to ask if they might meet late in the evening, since he was scheduled to return to Tamil Nadu then.

'How late?' Dr Reddy asked him.

'After 11 o'clock – would that be all right with you?' Rajiv said. 'But campaign rallies can run late, you know.'

Capt. C.P. Krishnan Nair, founder and chairman emeritus of the Leela Group of Palaces, Hotels and Resorts, told me that before flying to Vishakhapatnam – from where he would later go to Madras – Rajiv Gandhi had stopped off at the Leela Hotel near Bombay's Sahar international airport. He met with Murli Deora, then the president of the Bombay Pradesh Congress Committee – and an important fundraiser for the Congress party – and other politicians. Captain Nair rode with Rajiv in an elevator as he headed to the exit, where a car awaited him. It would take him to the airport, where he would board a private aircraft to Vishakhapatnam. Capt. Satish Sharma, Rajiv Gandhi's closest friend, told me in New Delhi in late July 2013 that Rajiv flew the plane himself.

'We'll meet soon,' Rajiv said to Captain Nair.

'God bless you,' Captain Nair said to Rajiv. 'Safe travels.'

By a strange coincidence, my documentary on Rajiv Gandhi and emerging India had been scheduled for broadcast on public television in the United States that very evening. As I sat in my study in New York watching the film, Rajiv Gandhi came across as so real, so endearing. There was that soft smile on his face. But, of course, he was already dead.

Today, seven pillars, each featuring a human value, surround the site of the blast in Sriperumbudur where Rajiv Gandhi was killed. My friends Sunita Kohli and Romesh Chopra, who were very close to Rajiv and Sonia Gandhi, helped design that memorial.

Today, whenever Prathap Chandra Reddy and Preetha Reddy think about that last encounter with Rajiv Gandhi, tears well up in their eyes. They think of a young leader with great aspirations for his country, a man who went away well before his time, at the age of forty-six.

———

For Dr Reddy, it hasn't been an entirely uneventful ride with Apollo Delhi, which was the first public–private partnership enterprise in India. Doubts have been cast about whether the hospital has lived up to its commitment to provide free medical care to poor patients. The Delhi government was originally slated to end its involvement after five years, but the arrangement continues. Moreover, as with any medical institution, there have been some highly publicized cases involving patient complaints.

A high-pressure health care arena where lives are saved and disease is fought on a daily basis is one that is at risk from a variety of sources that might well be beyond a hospital's areas of expertise. While the hospital believes in managing risk with a well-defined strategy, sometimes it overtakes them – as happened in the Rahul Mahajan case.

Rahul Mahajan, son of the late BJP leader Pramod Mahajan, was admitted to Apollo Hospital, Delhi on 1 June 2006 following an alleged drug overdose. The initial toxic screen of Mahajan was negative, but the Central Forensic Sciences Laboratory (CFSL) report established that both Rahul Mahajan and Vivek Moitra, his friend, had consumed morphine (heroin) and cocaine on the fateful night.

While the hospital was attempting to save a young life, the focus unfortunately shifted elsewhere. In the ensuing media circus, doctors and normal hospital protocols were brought under scrutiny; the willingness of the hospital to share information was questioned at best, and misinterpreted at worst. Allegations of tampering and fudging of facts were levied against the hospital.

Dr Reddy lamented, 'Some sections of the media have often not been objective when it comes to the medical fraternity. Accusations of negligence, wrong diagnosis, wrong treatment are flung baselessly.

The fact that doctors render selfless service, attending to emergencies day and night, is just forgotten.'

'We extended every cooperation to the investigating authorities, but the first responsibility of a hospital lies with the patient who comes for the best possible timely treatment,' says Anjali Kapoor Bissell, a senior executive at Indraprastha Apollo Hospital.[11]

Dr Reddy has always maintained that once he enrols physicians, he invests complete trust and confidence in them, offering them authority and privileges. He is confident that the best possible care was extended to Mahajan and his friend. Shobana Kamineni says: 'We sent out for a second opinion for an abundance of caution.'

I think the Mahajan case became a *cause celebre* because of politics, and because of what the Germans call *schadenfreude*, which is pleasure derived from the misery of others. Apollo's success over these past years has surely caused heartburn in certain medical and political circles. I wouldn't at all be surprised if some people in those circles see it as being to their advantage to keep the Rahul Mahajan case running.

Early in 2013, during a trip to New Delhi to attend the sixtieth birthday celebrations of Vasundhara Raje Scindia, the former chief minister of Rajasthan and a member of Gwalior's erstwhile royal family, I ran into two well-wishers of Apollo: L.K. Advani and Jaswant Singh. Like Vasundhara – and the late Pramod Mahajan, who was shot by his brother Pravin on 22 April 2006, and succumbed to his wounds on 3 May – Advani and Singh are doyens of the BJP.[12] I was tempted to ask them about the Rahul Mahajan case. But I desisted from asking them anything. After

---

11 An FIR was registered by Sarita Vihar police station against six doctors and six staff members of the hospital who were involved in the treatment of Rahul Mahajan. The matter is pending before the metropolitan magistrate at the Patiala House Court, New Delhi.

12 L.K. Advani resigned from all leadership positions in the BJP in June 2013 after Gujarat chief minister Narendra Modi was named the party's chief campaigner for the national elections scheduled for 2014. He later rescinded his resignations.

all, I was a guest at a birthday celebration, just as they were, and somehow it didn't seem appropriate to touch on a sensitive issue that was still in the courts.

When I was talking to Dr Reddy about Gwalior's royal family, he recalled a very touching incident. The then Rajmata of Gwalior Vijaya Raje was a patient of Apollo Hospitals. She had to have several admissions to treat chronic renal and cardiac conditions. In her final days at the hospital, her daughters and her son Madhav Rao Scindia would often come visiting her.

'After she passed away, I met Madhav Rao to offer my condolences. He said, "Doctor Reddy, I know you gave her the best care. I am grateful to you for that. But I am even more grateful because you managed to bring us – my sisters and me – back to talking terms,"' Dr Reddy said.

There is general agreement that Dr Reddy has a discernible ability to identify and invite the best of talent to join Apollo in various capacities. One such person whom he requested to become chairman of the Institute Ethics Committee of Indraprastha Apollo in 2003 was Professor Ranjit Roy Chaudhury, who had set up the Delhi Medical Council, and had worked with the World Health Organization for a long time.

Dr Reddy believes that 'research' is one of the three pillars, together with 'service' and 'training', for the efficient functioning of a complete medical institute.

'It was this commitment to research that led to my joining as chairman of Apollo Hospitals Education and Research Foundation [AHERF], and for preparing with the most eminent scientists of the country a road map for research for the Apollo Hospitals,' Professor Roy Chaudhury said. 'Undoubtedly, Apollo is the first corporate hospital to carry out research – basic, clinical and epidemiological – in the country. In a short time we have been able to be recognized nationally and internationally as a centre for carrying out quality research in India.'

Professor Roy Chaudhury added: 'More than my scientific input the Chairman and his immediate family regard me as a member of the family and it is in that spirit that I would continue to work at Apollo as long as I can. It is rare to find a leader with such infectious enthusiasm and high principles as Dr Reddy.'

Because of his strong global reputation, Professor Roy Chaudhury's views about the state of health care in India are taken seriously. 'There are about 400 million people in this country who have inadequate access to health care. They cannot get free medicines – except for a very few – and they cannot afford to buy medicines. Public health measures to prevent diseases are lacking and there are not enough public health experts. There is no referral system. Finally, governance of the doctors is weak and very often patients are exploited. All these can be classed as problems of access, lack of monitoring, lack of accountability, failure to maintain standards, lack of governance and corruption,' he said.

'The government and the private sector and the public need to work immediately and seriously on a health insurance system whereby all Indians are insured for basic health care and emergency care. If Brazil, Thailand and China can do it why can we not do it in India?' the professor said.[13]

Both Professor Roy Chaudhury and Dr Anupam Sibal, Apollo's group medical director, pointed to Apollo's postgraduate programmes.

'We have 600 doctor trainees in thirty-two programmes approved by the National Board of Examinations – more than any other hospital group in India,' Dr Sibal said. 'We opened our first medical college in Hyderabad in 2012. We have our own journal published by Elsiever called *Apollo Medicine*. We have a robust research programme under the Apollo Hospitals Education and Research Foundation.'

All these developments show that Dr Reddy's vision for Apollo as a complete medical institution is constantly evolving. Of course, it goes without saying that no medical institution can afford to remain static. But even so, the velocity of change at Apollo is astonishing.

---

13 Professor Ranjit Roy Chaudhury expressed some of these views in an interview with 'DoctorNDTV'.

No discussion about Indraprastha Apollo Delhi can be complete without mentioning Rajalakshmi Chandru, general manager for patient services. Everyone calls her 'Raji'. She's one of Dr Reddy's most trusted team members.

She stepped into Apollo on 26 December 1986. The Apollo opportunity was suggested to Rajalakshmi Chandru by her then employer K.L. Ramanathan, who in fact mentored her through the four years she had worked for him in Madras soon after she set foot in the city, leaving the small village of Arayapuram in Mayiladuthurai in search of employment.

Sangita Reddy conducted her job interview at Apollo in Madras. Sangita had just then graduated from college and was Dr Reddy's executive assistant; after an initial assessment and a brief meeting, Sangita had Raji draft two letters: a response to a patient complaint and a notice calling for a meeting of the Board of Directors, as that would prove if Raji could draft letters unassisted.

She thought she did well, but did not hear back from Apollo until the second week of the following month, when she was called to meet Chairman Reddy. And the big moment she was actually looking forward to lasted just three minutes.

Dr Reddy said, 'Health care has no holidays. Do you understand that?'

Raji replied, 'Yes, sir.'

Dr Reddy said: 'One does not look at the watch in my office, and go home at five or six o'clock.'

'I know, sir,' Raji said.

That was on 12 January 1987.

Shortly after she joined on 13 January 1987, an executive looked at her and said, 'That girl doesn't look like she's going to last in this place.' How wrong he was.

Dr Reddy had three secretaries: two medical and one for administrative work including all correspondence. The latter had left to join the British legation in Madras, hence the vacancy. In time, Raji would move to New Delhi.

'Chairman Reddy is an institution,' Raji said. 'I have learnt much of life's values just by being at Apollo and working for him. I have learnt never to carry forward emotional baggage from one situation to another; never to lose my temper even under provocation; never to procrastinate; to always treat people with grace and kindness. Most of my training sessions are replete with lessons I have learnt from our Chairman.

'An incident that is etched in his emotional memory has rubbed off on me: when he was working at the Massachusetts General in Boston, a patient slapped him because he was highly offended on being treated by an Indian doctor. Dr Reddy's boss reacted strongly and directed that the patient be discharged forthwith. Dr Reddy prevailed upon his boss and said, "Don't do so; I will visit him again tomorrow, because we need to deal with him with kindness and not react to his behaviour." And yes, it worked wonders, Chairman has said to us. I have learnt such valuable lessons of life from Chairman that perhaps even Harvard or Cornell cannot teach in a century.'

'Dr Reddy encourages his staff to dream and dream boldly, and become entrepreneurs,' Raji said.

She hit upon an initiative that she calls the NeuroAid and Research Foundation, registered with the blessings and patronage of Dr Reddy. Though the foundation was a slow starter, she is very proud that today, the six trustees with herself as chief functionary, have with them a team of four extremely committed physiotherapists who reach out to indigent and deserving patients needing physiotherapy and rehabilitation. The foundation's vision is big and will cost her a lot of money; she is confident she can do it in her lifetime and do her bit as part of the Apollo philanthropy programme.

One July evening in 2013, I went to see Sheila Dikshit, the chief minister of Delhi, at her lovely bungalow in the Lutyens Zone in New Delhi. I waited briefly in a large room where she receives guests. There were bonsai plants there, a metal Ganesh sculpture mounted on a wall, and burnt-orange and light-green sofas, but no carpet on the stone floor. There were paintings of Hanuman, and there were paintings from the Madhubani school. Three miniature Ganesh statues sat next to a phone on a table that seemed too delicate for their weight.

As Delhi's chief minister, Dikshit is also in charge of the union territory's health care, in addition to governance, of course. She told me about the demands on the capital's health care system placed, among other things, by the continuing influx of immigrants – particularly Afghans. She said that some 35 per cent of patients at city hospitals came from outside Delhi.

'Apollo has contributed enormously to health standards,' Dikshit said, at the same time stressing that government hospitals also were upgrading their services.

'I attribute this to the fact that there's now vigorous competition between public-sector and private-sector hospitals,' Dikshit said. 'Such competition creates a much needed challenge of excellence in providing better health care.'

She has been Delhi chief minister since 1998,[14] and has paid particular attention to five issues: health care, education, protection of the environment, empowerment of women and poverty alleviation. She noted that 65 per cent of her government's budget was dedicated to the social sector.

Because of the agreement under which the Delhi government permitted Indraprastha Apollo Hospital to be established, with 26 per cent equity held by the government, a representative of the government – the capital's Chief Secretary – sits on the Delhi Apollo board as chairman.

'But where private hospitals are concerned, we don't interfere,' Dikshit told me, adding that she appreciated Dr Reddy's continuing innovations at Apollo. 'As long as I've known Dr Reddy, he's wanted world class health care not only for Delhi, but for all of India.'

---

14 Sheila Dikshit was engaged in a particularly strenuous re-election campaign towards the end of 2013.

CHAPTER TWENTY-FOUR

Doctors and Devices

ONE DAY IN NEW Delhi I happened to be surfing channels when I saw Apollo's CFO, Krishnan Akhileswaran, on CNBC-TV18. He was talking about a proton therapy project to augment therapy for cancer patients. [1] Proton therapy is the leading radiation therapy available in the world, and Apollo is setting up a new centre on Old Mahabalipuram Road[2] specifically for proton treatment; it is expected to be operational by 2016 at a cost of Rs 400 crore.[3]

The fact that Apollo decided to embark on the proton project is yet another example of Dr Reddy's determination to acquire the

---

1 Proton therapy is a type of external beam radiotherapy using ionizing radiation. During treatment, a particle accelerator is used to target the tumour with a beam of protons. These charged particles damage the DNA of cancerous cells, ultimately causing their death or interfering with their ability to proliferate.
2 Apollo already has strong cancer treatment programmes at Delhi, Chennai, Hyderabad, Ahmedabad, Bangalore and Kolkata.
3 Proton therapy is extraordinarily expensive. A proton facility can cost as much as $100 million to construct, and costs of treatment range up to $50,000 per patient or more, twice as much as contemporary radiation therapy, and up to four times as much as surgery, brachytherapy, and other options.

321

best technology for Apollo patients in India, regardless of the costs.[4]
Dr Reddy told me subsequently that with approximately 3 million
people suffering from cancer in India and 1 million new cases being
detected every year, there was a 'pressing need' for speciality cancer
treatment hospitals. As most patients are diagnosed with advanced
stage cancer, the demand for state-of-the-art cancer treatment is high.

'Apollo's Therapy Centre, with its highly advanced technology,
will be able to provide the best-in-class treatment for patients who
suffer from cancer,' he said. 'Proton therapy is increasingly considered
the most advanced and targeted cancer treatment due to its superior
dose distribution and fewer side effects.'

Dr Reddy says: 'India should become the global health care
destination. That is my vision for the health care domain in India.
And I think it is eminently possible as we have most of the essentials
right: medical and nursing professionals with a very high standard
of skills and talent, infrastructure and technology that matches the
best in the world. Though health care, as an industry, enjoys much
governmental and institutional support today, an intensified focus
from them would really hasten our progress to fulfilment of my vision.'

Technology is obviously a major driver in fulfilling this vision.
Dr Reddy said that Apollo Hospitals utilizes technology in several
forms – for diagnostic and therapeutic purposes, to begin with.
Second, it leverages the benefits of IT in health care: in integrated and
seamless electronic medical records, or telemedicine initiatives for
enhanced access to medical care. Further, he says, automated systems
and processes help in enhancing patient satisfaction, and improving
their experience. Apollo, until recently, before it divested its stake in
Apollo Health Street to another global BPO, was one of the largest
medical business outsourcing companies doing billing, costing and
adjudication for US hospitals, doctors and insurance companies.

While Dr Reddy talks often about incorporating the latest global

---

4   As of September 2012, there were thirty-nine particle therapy facilities in the
    world, representing a total of 106 treatment rooms available to patients on
    a regular basis.

technologies in the Apollo system, he doesn't simply go out and buy such equipment on a whim. He seeks and receives advice from experts, including physicians within the Apollo family. And once the equipment arrives, he takes great pains to ensure that everything works as planned. Moreover, Dr Reddy says, 'From Day One, our doctors accept patients directly. They don't have to have a referral.'

Dr Sajan K. Hegde, a robotics spine surgeon at Apollo Chennai, is a good example of a physician who expected the best technology in his discipline from Apollo. His techniques are widely followed, not only in India but also around the world.

After undergoing advanced training in spine surgery in France and Germany, Dr Hegde was working with a leading orthopaedic surgeon at an institution in Chennai. Dr Hegde's uncle suggested that the surgeon move to Apollo; an introduction was made and Dr Hegde remembers that he was nervous. He bought a tie, which he does not normally wear, for the interview with Dr Reddy: he'd heard that Dr Reddy was always immaculately groomed, and that he always received visitors with his jacket on.

'Why do you want to move to Apollo?' Dr Reddy asked.

Dr Hegde said, 'Sir, I have training in spinal surgery and I want to put it to good use. Arms and legs are not that interesting to me. There is so much need for attention to the spine.'

Dr Reddy readily agreed about the need to focus on spinal surgery, and once more opened the door for innovation at Apollo by bringing Dr Hegde into the family. Asked if ambition played a role in his move to Apollo, Dr Hegde said, 'Totally. Oh yes, I was driven. I wanted the ability to flourish and grow as a top-notch spine surgeon and this was the only facility that could make it possible. I've never looked back.'

Neither has Apollo, whose hospital in Chennai is now the premier centre for spine surgeries in India. Dr Hegde originally did open spine surgeries but was soon captivated by the possibilities of robotic surgery, which he first saw in use in Germany.[5] At the North American

---

5 According to Dr Payam Moazzaz of the University of California, robotic spine surgery is very new, less than ten years old. There are only ten hospitals

Spine Surgery annual meeting he met Dr Samuel Bederman, who pioneered the evolution of robotic techniques and other innovative surgical programmes.

When Dr Hegde told Dr Reddy about a new robotic device developed in Israel that was the size of a cola can, Dr Reddy was immediately interested and asked for a proposal. It was approved and acquired within days. Dr Hegde and his surgical team started using the most advanced robotic guidance device (MAZOR) available for complex spine procedures and within the first ten days, twelve successful surgeries were completed.

Dr Hegde says, 'Dr Reddy has a unique characteristic in that he has an innate ability to gauge a person's knowledge and skill and knows how to incorporate those elements into a long-term vision for Apollo.'

In robotic surgery, the robotic device sits on the patient's back with a small mounting. A CT scan of the patient's spine is fed into a computer and a virtual spine of the patient is created. The surgeon then plans all the elements of the procedure he wants to do on this model in his office. When complete, the new information is fed into the workstation of the robot in the operating room. The robot takes the information from the pre-operative planning and moves to the specific position to help the surgeon to put in the implants to the accuracy of 0.1 mm, even in the most crooked and deformed of spines.[6]

'This technique is truly revolutionizing spinal surgery,' Dr Hegde says. 'The differences between robotic surgery, which is minimally invasive, and open surgeries are monumental.'

Robotics surgery is also a big money saver. It reduces the time in the operating theatre and the overall patient stay in the hospital. It allows patients to be up and walking within days, not confined to a bed for weeks. Most importantly, it gives the patient a new life removed from isolation and dependency.

---

in the US offering it at present. He told writer April Cashin-Garbutt that the technology, based on a CT scan, was developed in Israel.

6 Sources: Dr Hegde and Apollo Hospitals.

Dr Hegde says, 'With the advent of 3D and HD, robotics surgery will be even more game-changing. We are all working together for India.'

He also said that this kind of surgery creates change in ways many don't consider. 'It raises the bar for the medical staff. One can't just be good. The entire staff must be excellent. Stricter quality control, better efficiency in all areas, higher standards of accountability are all-important. Apollo is branded all over India and we have a reputation to uphold and move forward.'

He cited a case where Apollo Hospitals performed a complex spinal surgery on a ten-year-old child. This was the twelfth successful surgery done within ten days of the launch of the 'Renaissance™ Robotic Technology' in 2012 – the only technology specifically designed for spine surgery. Apollo Hospitals Group was the first in the Asia-Pacific region to offer this minimally invasive robotic-guided surgical guidance system for spine surgery, Dr Hegde said.

The ten-year-old from Gujarat, Heema, was born with congenital anomalies that left her with a severely deformed spine. Before being admitted to Apollo Hospitals, the child had already undergone multiple procedures that had failed and left her with rods placed in her back, broken at multiple places, and a spine that was grotesquely deformed, Dr Hegde said.

His team faced several challenges in treating the child. But Renaissance™ Robotic Technology allowed a successful spinal fixation with extreme precision and safety in carrying out the delicate manoeuvre to correct the deformed spine. A child otherwise doomed to go through life with the severe deformity – which could have led to premature death due to cardiopulmonary failure or eventual paralysis – can now lead a normal life like any other ten-year-old.

One of Dr Hegde's patients was the noted industrialist Rahul Bajaj, who called Dr Reddy and asked that a team of surgeons from Apollo come to Breach Candy Hospital in Mumbai to operate on his wife.

'Whatever you want, I will do,' Bajaj said to Dr Reddy.

Dr Reddy had a longstanding policy that patients should come to

Apollo hospitals for treatment, and that Apollo surgeons shouldn't be dispatched to other facilities. But he made an exception for Bajaj. Dr Hegde flew to Mumbai with his team, and successfully performed spinal surgery on Mrs Bajaj.

Dr Reddy told me that foreign patients have also benefited from treatment for spinal problems at Apollo Hospitals. Two young patients from Oman were admitted with severe back pain, which was also affecting both their legs. Both patients had previously taken non-operative treatment in Oman, without any relief whatsoever. Both patients underwent robot-assisted minimally invasive spine surgery. After the surgery, both have been free of pain and are now walking normally.

Another patient, a girl named Stephanie, came from Nigeria. She was brought by her mother, Agatha Amata, who hosts a weekly television programme called *Inside Out*. It is produced in Lagos, where she lives, and broadcast on twenty-two stations in Africa and Western Europe including Britain, Spain, Germany and France.

When her daughter was just fourteen years old, Agatha began noticing that the girl had poor posture. By the time the girl turned fifteen, the poor posture was more pronounced.

Agatha's concern increased and in early 2012 she took her daughter for medical appointments and X-rays in Lagos. Stephanie was diagnosed with adolescent scoliosis. She needed a brace to help correct the condition but the braces were not available in Nigeria.

In the spring of that year, Agatha travelled alone to a scoliosis centre in London. While in London a friend gave Agatha the name of Dr Sajan Hegde. She called the doctor, and he said, 'I can help your daughter.' But Agatha was afraid of complications from surgery. What if something went wrong?

One night, Stephanie came to her mother and said, 'Mommie, I know that you don't want to hear this but I don't want the brace. I want to have the surgery.'

Agatha began a telephone and Internet dialogue with Dr Sajan Hegde. By this time, she realized that she would have to put aside her fear of hospitals. Agatha only wanted a solution for her daughter.

'Dr Sajan was so patient, he explained everything to me and to Stephanie. He put my mind at ease,' Agatha said.

On Sunday, 26 May 2013, Stephanie, her mother Agatha and her aunt Jennifer arrived in Chennai after flying from Nigeria through Dubai. Agatha says, 'I was amazed at the care we received right away. The international staff from Apollo greeted us at the hospital and took care of every detail, even changing money. The next day we had to go to the main hospital and I had never seen so many people in one place. Yet, it was very orderly. We registered and Stephanie had X-rays and others tests. Everything went smoothly.

'Surgery was at the Apollo Speciality Hospital on 28 May, and within four hours, it was done. When Stephanie woke up all she said was, "Mommie, pain, pain, pain." Her pain was intense and it hurt to see her suffering. The hospital, of course, gave her medication to alleviate the pain and within two days, she hardly noticed it at all. Now she wears a low dosage patch.'

Stephanie was a bit tired from the surgery when my colleague Twilla Duncan met her. She would say, 'Yay! I am turning!' Or she would dance a few steps and shout, 'Yay, I am dancing!'

Agatha says, 'I would have done anything to help her. The cost was estimated between $13,000 and $17,000. I can imagine it would be at least three times higher in the United States.'

'Everything at Apollo went so smoothly and we were so well treated that I decided to take a big step for myself. I am hospital-phobic and had not been in a hospital since Stephanie was born. But I felt so at ease with Dr Sajan and the Apollo team that on the fourth day I decided to have a full health physical. Everything was done: EKG, CT, sonogram, pap smear, mammogram, sugar, complete blood workup,' said Agatha.

Apollo Hospitals right from its initial stages had made a name for itself as an organization providing infrastructure matching the best in the world. This along with Dr Reddy's highly supportive and encouraging attitude paved the way for several highly qualified doctors with successful practices outside India to return and take up positions in Apollo Hospitals.

One such physician is Dr Ameet Kishore, a specialist in ear, nose and throat medicine (ENT).

I asked Dr Kishore why he chose to return to India – and why he specifically wanted to join Apollo. This was his response:

'Although I thoroughly enjoyed working in the UK for a number of years, my heart was always in India. I felt that with the skills I had learnt, I could certainly serve a larger number of people, and bring back to our society the much-needed technology and expertise that they deserved. Of course, my wife and I also wanted to be close to our parents, and that our children should know their roots.

'During this phase I would often travel to Delhi and look for the appropriate opportunity and setting where these specialist skills that I had acquired could be put into practice. This necessitated working out of a multi-speciality hospital with good equipment and infrastructure along with like-minded personnel and management who were willing to embrace cutting-edge technology.

'I figured that the Apollo Hospital was indeed one such institution. I had the good fortune of meeting Dr Prathap Chandra Reddy during one of his trips to London, and discussed my idea with him of starting a cochlear implant programme for the hearing impaired. He was extremely excited with the idea and very supportive, and was keen for me to join at the earliest.

'This is when I realized I had found my answer. I decided that the time had come to return to India. I found myself at the Indraprastha Apollo Hospital in Delhi a year later. I had found the place where I was destined to be.'

Another surgeon who joined Apollo Delhi after undergoing surgical and urological training and working in the West for more than a decade was Dr Narasimhan Subramanian, a urologist. He told me that he had apprehensions about the equipment, medical infrastructure and institutional attitudes, and the way these would impact his concept of health care delivery.

'I was truly delighted that well-equipped, excellent-quality infrastructure was being established which would enable me to deliver high-quality and safe health care. I must confess that the setup far exceeded my expectations,' Dr Subramanian said between appointments. 'This could only result from the foresight, enthusiasm and a broad understanding of tertiary health care which Dr Reddy obviously brought to revolutionize health care in India.'

I asked Dr Subramanian why some aspects of urology, especially conditions like incontinence (lack of urine control) and sexual dysfunction have always been kept under wraps in India.

'Comprehensive health care delivery and increasing awareness about patient wellness have resulted in patients coming forward to discuss these issues and it is satisfying to see that most of these can be treated suitably,' he said, adding that there still needs to be a wider campaign of public awareness of male sexual disfunctionality. Part of the reluctance of many Indian males to come forth with their sexual problems, of course, has to do with perceptions of social stigma.

'My recent meeting with Dr Reddy regarding advanced technology like robotic surgery and PET MRI only enhanced my admiration for him,' Dr Subramanian said. 'We must deliver whatever is the best, no matter what it takes. His understanding of current technology, his respect for multi-disciplinary teams, consultation across the globe and most of all, his childlike enthusiasm would be impossible to match. No wonder, he is still the leader of corporate health care in India.'

The use at Apollo Hospitals of some of the best medical technologies available in the world often invites appreciation from patients.[7] A

---

7   As with any leading hospital, on the rare occasion the treatment at Apollo does invite opprobrium as well. In the early days of Apollo Madras, one such instance involved V. Chandrasekhar, three-time national table tennis champion and Arjuna Award winner. In September 1984 he went to Apollo Madras to have a loose cartilage in his knee removed. He reacted to the anaesthesia (a very rare occurrence) and developed severe cardio-pulmonary distress. The enormous efforts put in by the Apollo team saved his life. After being in the ICU for six weeks, Chandrasekhar made a gradual recovery. There was quite a bit of negative publicity in the media and he was awarded

man named Anubhav Tyagi wrote to Dr Reddy: 'If somebody asks us about God, what does he look like, we would definitely say he should be like Dr Subash Gupta.'

Tyagi's daughter Nandini, who was then barely four years old, was battling with jaundice. Her situation was deteriorating and she was becoming unconscious. Tyagi managed to contact a physician named Dr Sarath Gopalan who ensured that Nandini was admitted to Indraprastha Apollo Hospital in Delhi in August 2012. Dr Anupam Sibal's liver-transplant team immediately took over. Dr Sibal – who had joined Apollo in 1997 after training in Britain – is widely known as a paediatric liver specialist, and is often called to deliver papers at medical conferences in India and abroad.

'Once we were in Apollo the doctors were on their toes examining the situation to take the right call,' Tyagi said in his note to Dr Reddy. 'All the doctors were so efficient that our worries came to halt in terms of treatment. We were satisfied that what we were getting was the best. It started from Dr Sarath and then moved to the liver transplant team with Dr Subash Gupta.'

Dr Gupta explained that Nandini was in a state of acute liver failure and told Tyagi and his wife that a liver transplant was recommended. Dr Sibal – an irrepressibly congenial man – told me that one of the great dangers of acute liver failure is the multiplier effect: other organs start failing, and this almost always proves fatal for the patient. 'Time was absolutely of the essence,' he said. 'You just don't have time on your side. Such patients are hard to manage because of the risk of irreversible brain damage.'

The parents agreed to the doctors' recommendation, and the whole process started.[8] Nandini's mother Priya agreed to donate 30

Rs 19 lakh as compensation by the court.

8 Liver transplantation or hepatic transplantation is the replacement of a diseased liver with a healthy liver from another person (the technical term is allograft). The most commonly used technique is orthotropic transplantation, in which the native liver is removed and replaced by the donor organ in the same anatomic location as the original liver. Liver transplantation nowadays is a well-accepted treatment option for end-stage liver disease and acute liver

per cent of her liver. 'As many tests were required to be done as a protocol for the donor as well, all the concerned departments were very cooperative, and the whole process was completed within three hours. The surgery began as planned,' Tyagi said.

Dr Sibal told me that both daughter and mother were able to return home in less than three weeks. He met with them in early April 2013 and was pleased that Nandini and Priya Tyagi were in good shape. What was the satisfaction that even an experienced physician like him gets at times like these? Dr Anupam Sibal didn't need to answer that question. I already knew the answer because I'd read Anubhav Tyagi's letter to Dr Prathap Chandra Reddy, part of which said, 'My daughter and wife are smiling.'

Dr Reddy clearly takes great pride in the organ transplants done at Apollo. He is a great fan of the pioneering work done by Dr Thomas E. Starzl who attempted the first liver transplant in 1963, and then succeeded in 1967 at the University of Colorado Health Sciences Centre.[9] He was also the first to use cyclosporine to combat organ rejection. Dr Reddy – who met with Dr Starzl during his time in the United States – says, 'Millions of people now have hope through Dr Starzl's work.'

'Our work at Apollo shows that we are capable of bettering the best and it inspires those thinking of studying medicine or who are already in medical programmes,' Dr Reddy told me. At Dr Reddy's suggestion, surgeons from Apollo visited Dr Starzl who gave them a lengthy tour of his institute and discussed all the issues related to setting up a liver transplant programme. Upon hearing the issues involved, Dr Reddy agreed to begin a programme at Apollo.

'It will not be easy. But if Pittsburgh can do it, we must do it for

---

failure. The surgical procedure is very demanding and ranges from ten to eighteen hours depending on the outcome.

9 Dr Starzl also performed the first simultaneous heart and liver transplant on six-year-old Stormie Jones in 1984 at the Children's Hospital of Pittsburgh. She died on 11 November 1990.

our people,' Dr Reddy said at the time. It took five years to complete the first ten liver transplants.

Organ donation in India is governed through the Transplantation of Human Organs Act 1994 and the Transplantation of Human Organs Rules 1995. This pathbreaking Act came about through the active work put forth by activists and health care professionals to create an overarching mechanism to control the removal, storage and transplantation of human organs. India, much like the world, faces an acute shortage of organs that can be transplanted to those with end-stage disease requiring a transplantation procedure. By conservative estimates, 175,000 Indians suffer from end-stage renal disease requiring a transplant, while only 6,000-odd receive a transplant in a year. Similarly, 50,000 Indians require a heart transplant while only ten to fifteen surgeries are performed each year. Likewise, some 50,000 Indians require a liver transplant, while only 400 procedures are carried out each year.

While the need for transplantation is acute, India has had the dubious record of having a black market for organs, where the poor and destitute would sell organs for money and those in dire need would pay huge sums to get one. The criminalization of organ availability was prevalent largely due to the lack of a control mechanism through an enabling and controlling law in the country up until the late 1980s and early 1990s.

While initial drafts for a law to control organ donation, transplantation and criminalization of organ markets had been in the works in the Union ministry of health since the early 1980s, it was under the government of Prime Minister Rajiv Gandhi that a final draft was materialized. However, due to the change in the political dispensation in the Centre, the draft law was never approved by the cabinet, nor tabled in Parliament. Regrettably, due to the political instability from 1989 to 1992, the draft law never moved towards approval or enactment.

'India had not had experience in cadaveric transplants. There is a very fine programme at the Minneapolis Heart Institute with which I was familiar. One of the anaesthetists there is from Stanley

Medical College. We took a visit there and it was so impressive. Then we proposed a cadaver organ transplant programme. It took five people to draft the proposal into a bill that would go before the Lok Sabha. We showed it to the health minister who said, "That's nice but will it pass?"' Dr Reddy recalled. This was during the time that his friend – and patient – P.V. Narasimha Rao of Andhra Pradesh was India's prime minister.

Dr Reddy took the onus of not only fine-tuning the various clauses and sections of the draft Act, but also took it upon himself to act as a powerful advocate for its passage in Parliament. The then Union parliamentary affairs minister, V.C. Shukla, was approached and the urgency of the Act needing to be passed in Parliament was pressed upon him. In 1993–94, numerous representations were made by Dr Reddy to pressurize the government on the need for such an Act. Shukla and Dr Reddy also met with the prime minister during the late 1993 parliamentary sessions for the Act to be passed. But due to a political impasse, the Act was held up along with others in Parliament.

However, due to the combined use of pressure led by Dr Reddy and the will to make it pass shown by Prime Minister Rao and Shukla, the Act was finally passed in the Cabinet and in the Parliament and was enacted in 1994.

And it happened in a dramatic way. Members of the Lok Sabha had been called to Delhi to vote on the impeachment of the chief election commissioner, T.N. Seshan.

'One day I got a call from V.C. Shukla, who was then the minister for parliamentary affairs,' Dr Reddy told me. 'He wanted a hospital project for his constituency in Raipur, and was willing to keep us informed of developments on our proposal. Shukla said to me, "They don't have a two-thirds majority to impeach Seshan." I replied, "Since the members are already here in Delhi, this would be a good time to try and get our bill passed." Shukla said, "Why don't we go meet the prime minister?" The rest is history.'

Dr Reddy met with Prime Minister Narasimha Rao and told him: 'This bill is not for you or me. It is for those who desperately need organs so that they can live again and be fulfilled. You can choose to do something about this great gift that otherwise will be burned to ashes.'

Narasimha Rao was not generally perceived as a man of quick action (the standing humorous line about him in the media was, 'When in doubt, pout') but neither was he an obstructionist – he allowed things to happen rather than obstructing them. Pushing through the organ transplant bill was yet another way in which he liberalized policies so that India could have a twenty-first-century economy.[10]

The Human Organ Transplant Bill was passed in Parliament; however, in many years, only a handful of organ donations took place. Tamil Nadu has the highest number of organ donations in the country. The credit for this goes to IAS officer Sheela Priya. Her brother-in-law had a serious liver disease. There was a kidney transplant programme in Gujarat but they did not do liver transplants and he was treated in Delhi. There was a struggle to find a match and the hospital did everything possible for him until a liver was found; now he is alive thanks to Apollo. Sheela Priya told Dr Reddy that it was torturous as they waited indefinitely for a liver. She said that she didn't want other families to go through such an ordeal, and said, 'I must do something for others.'

Two ordinances were drafted to make clear who could be declared as 'brain dead'. First, an EEG must be administered to determine clinical death; if the reading is flat, a second one is administered six hours later to confirm the fact. In doing so, the controversy around brain death and its declaration was laid to rest. The second ordinance made the declaration of brain death mandatory for patients in the ICU, which helped in a larger pool of organ donors being made available for needy recipients. Today, Tamil Nadu and Karnataka lead in cadaveric organ donations; Delhi, Andhra Pradesh and Gujarat

---

10 My own feeling is that Narasimha Rao has not been given sufficient credit for the economic reforms that transformed India from a moribund socialist polity into one of the world's leading economies. The Nehru–Gandhi family did not perceive him as a loyalist.

are also making significant efforts similar to those made in Tamil Nadu and Karnataka to ensure that they also have conducive laws for organ donation. In these states not just the government but the media have been very supportive and helped people understand the importance of cadaveric donations. There is also a strong movement in West Bengal, which Dr Reddy supports vigorously.

Dr Reddy told me that many people die of accidents and so many persons can be helped from just one cadaver: if the heart, liver, kidneys, lungs and corneas are donated. 'It's a waste not to use them,' he said.

The Apollo Group, under the aegis of the 'Gift a Life' initiative, has been active in advocacy and activities to promote the cause of organ donation. India currently ranks abysmally in organ donation rates as compared to the developed and developing world. In Spain, 33 people in a million come forth to donate their organs, while in France the number is 23. In India, this figure is a paltry 0.1 people per million. Various impediments to increasing the number of voluntary organ donations exist. From perceived religious taboos to a lack of social acceptance, all play a part in the number of organ donors being low. The Transplantation Act and the definition of brain death (post which organs from a person can be retreated) have also been highlighted as reasons for low organ donation rates. Coupled with this, India does not have a national registry to match organ donors with recipients, unlike in the United States or the United Kingdom. These reasons compelled the Apollo Group to start the 'Gift a Life' initiative to promote organ donation across the country. Indian cricketer Gautam Gambhir, who decided to support this initiative pro bono, kicked it off in November 2011. The mission of 'Gift a Life' is to ensure that no person in India dies for want of an organ. The aim is to bring together information and awareness on the issue of organ donation and at the same time connect doctors, citizens, hospitals, health care organizations, civil society organizations, governments, NGOs and public sector institutions on a common platform to create awareness on this pressing issue.

Over the last two years, the initiative has tied up with a varied group of like-minded institutions and partners like HCL, Delhi Traffic Police, Chennai Traffic Police, Delhi University and schools and colleges across the country to conduct awareness drives amongst their employees and cadres on organ donation. Taking the lead on this initiative, Dr Reddy pledged his organs in support of 'Gift a Life' on the occasion of his birthday in 2012. This was followed by a similar drive across the Apollo Group of Hospitals where a large number of employees pledged their organs. Going forth, 'Gift a Life' will associate with like-minded partners to further create awareness and focus on the creation of a national registry to help in matching donors with recipients.[11]

After kidneys the most demand is for livers. The liver transplant programme is expensive and it has to sustain itself and grow without continued subsidies from Apollo, according to Dr Reddy. He told me that he is committed to bringing liver transplants to Apollo on a world-class basis. He made it very clear that Apollo would adhere to the highest standards of moral conduct and would not succumb to political or monetary pressure to do wrong things. In India, as in other parts of the world, organ donors are sometimes solicited with what seems like a large amount of money (but which is actually small, since human organs are priceless). This practice of selling organs is illegal and does not adhere to strict medical procedures. Dr Reddy said that he was also determined to bring the transplant programme to India in a cost-effective way.

Liver transplants are very demanding. It's a long surgery. 'Everyone on the team has to be very strong, the doctors, nurses, technicians, all the support staff must be par excellence. We're very, very strict about infection control. In the process, we have brought the success rate up

---

11 While the number of eye donations has increased due to awareness, it is estimated that 4.6 million Indians suffer from corneal blindness. At the same time, India has one of the developing world's highest numbers of road fatalities due to accidents, which could make a large number of cadaveric donations possible. Government estimates state that in 2011 itself, 142,485 persons died in road traffic accidents, a 5.8 per cent compounded increase since 2001.

and the cost down. Infections can bring about many complications. If this happens the patient loses the chance for a normal life and a lot of money is spent combating those,' Dr Reddy said.

'In Delhi we had a talented surgeon but he had a bad temper and no one wanted to work with him. His antics were also bad for the patients. It was a relief when we parted ways. Dr Subash Gupta took over and we have never looked back since,' Dr Reddy said.

When I spoke with Dr Subash Gupta, Apollo's chief liver transplant surgeon, he at once stressed that one of the group's strong points was that 'it lets you develop your skills'.

His skills, in turn, led him to develop two techniques of liver transplantation that have won him worldwide acclaim: middle hepatic vein transplant, by which the surgeon decides which vein drains which part of the liver (which has two lobes and three veins) and applies the transplant accordingly; and portal pressure measurement in donors, which makes donor surgery very safe. Dr Gupta, who came to Apollo in 2006 from Sir Ganga Ram Hospital in Delhi, has done 1,100 living-donor operations, with zero mortality.

'Dr Reddy shows great respect towards doctors,' Dr Gupta said, noting that when he was growing up in West Bengal he had wanted to be an engineer. It was at his mother's behest that he became a physician, training at the All India Institute of Medical Sciences in New Delhi, and later being inspired by veteran surgeon Dr Samiran Nundy to get further training at Queen Elizabeth University Hospital in Birmingham.

And what made him decide to leave Sir Ganga Ram Hospital and join Apollo?

Dr Gupta said, 'The atmosphere at Apollo is very different. They don't interfere with your work. They are extremely encouraging. For instance, Dr Reddy calls us up from time to time, especially when he learns about a particularly difficult surgery that went off well. No matter how experienced and qualified one is as a surgeon, this kind of encouragement is always welcome.'

The programme in Apollo, Delhi has been exceptionally successful: 544 kidney and 269 liver transplants were performed in calendar year 2012, making it the busiest standalone transplant centre in the world. The hospital's state-of-the-art infrastructure and dedicated teams led by Doctors S.N. Mehta, Sandeep Guleria and Vijaya Rajkumari (kidney transplantation) along with Dr Subash Gupta (liver transplantation) have helped the programme overtake the world's leading iconic institutions like University of California at Los Angeles (495 transplants), University of California at San Francisco (458), Cleveland Clinic (416), University of Pittsburgh Medical Centre (296) and the Mayo Clinic Florida (348).

Apollo has a 95 per cent success rate with renal transplants, an impressive number. 'Usually when people come in with kidney or liver disease they are already very sick. It's not a mix of good cases with a few bad cases. Most of the cases are pretty bad. We cannot pick and choose which cases we will accept. It is a general theme at Apollo that we never say "no" to an admission. I ask our team, "Would you say no to a king or queen?" We cannot let a patient brought to us die in a car or an ambulance. We explain the prognosis and treat the patient. All we can promise is that we will do our very best,' Dr Reddy told me. 'There are not enough living donors to provide for all who need them. India has a Central Ethics Committee whose responsibility it is to establish guidelines for the good of all patients and donors. We must encourage compliance with these guidelines.'

The first multi-organ transplant at Apollo Chennai was done from a donor who had died at the hospital. The thirty-two-year-old man had got up from the dinner table to go to the market for a missing spice. He was on his motorcycle and had a head-on collision. After two days, there was no improvement in his condition and his brain was not functioning. His wife and his parents visited him regularly at Apollo.

Recalling the episode, Dr Reddy said: 'I spoke to them in Tamil in the waiting room of the ICU. I explained that the team of doctors had done everything possible but unfortunately the young man was brain dead. "The ventilator is keeping his lungs breathing and medicines are keeping his heart pumping – he is artificially alive, but there is something that you could do to help others," I said. "We could disconnect him from life support and you, the family, could take the body home and burn it. But, you have the opportunity to let him live on in others: for those who are in need, who have no chance at life."

'We spoke for about forty-five minutes. Everyone was devastated. They asked how much time they had to decide. Then they went back to the young patient's room and after about twenty minutes the wife and her parents came to see me and said, "Please let my husband give life and be alive in others." It was a milestone. Her generous and laudable decision enabled the first multi-organ transplant in the country. Dr K.C. Tan came from Singapore to do the liver transplant. The accident victim's organs helped many other people and one recipient would regularly come to the hospital and pay for a three-month supply of cyclosporine to help transplant patients in need. Unfortunately he died in an accident fourteen years after receiving his heart. The donor's wife still comes to the hospital lobby for a little while in the day or night when she is depressed, not to ask for favours but to be reminded of the pleasure of her husband being somewhere on this earth.'

In November 1998 the first successful paediatric liver transplant was performed on an eighteen-month-old child at Apollo Delhi. Today, Sanjay is a sixteen-year-old leading a normal life. 'It is so gratifying to see how Sanjay inspired the establishment of liver transplantation in India,' says Dr Sibal who has been the Group Medical Director of Apollo since 2005. In 2012, the Apollo Transplant Programme became the busiest solid organ transplant programme in the world by performing 1,200 transplants (840 kidney and 360 liver transplants) in a calendar year.

'There was one patient who was registered in the US for a new heart but he was far down the list. The doctors told him that by the time a heart became available he would perhaps not be alive. They suggested he come to India. His wife made the arrangements and Apollo officials told her that they could not guarantee that they would have a heart for him. But he still came. There was a problem in getting a match. His blood type was O negative – yet we had a heart within a week and now he is in his third year of a new life,'

Dr Reddy said. 'It's a very touching thing to think that you can give life to another whose hopes are about to be snuffed out.'

Dr Subhash Kumar Wangnoo, Senior Consultant Endocrinologist and Diabetologist at Indraprastha Apollo Hospital in New Delhi, also talked to me about how physicians viewed practicing medicine at the institution.

'When I came to know about Apollo's foray in the capital, without even thinking twice or batting an eyelid, I decided to be a part of the prestigious venture,' Dr Wangnoo said. 'And when I look back after being associated with the hospital for over two decades, I only have a feeling of profound pride that I have been a part of the organization which has been responsible for transforming health care in our country. Apollo already had its prestige due to its parent hospital in Chennai; in fact, my mamaji underwent a bypass operation under the care of Professor Girinath at Chennai Apollo. I look back at the opportunity that was given to me by the organization to fully develop my skills as an endocrinologist, and I can say with humility that helped me to be counted as one of the foremost in my profession today.'

At Apollo Bangalore, Dr B. Ramesh, an acclaimed cardiologist, told me: 'It is indeed a pleasant and wonderful experience working in an Apollo hospital. You are provided with state-of-the-art technology, highly trained technical and nursing staff, and the best possible cardiac surgical team to back you up. You are confident of meeting any complex clinical situation with ease and with world standards. It is gratifying at the end for saving many precious lives.

'I truly believe that Dr Reddy has a special ability to think ten years ahead. He anticipates health care needs. He introduces the latest technology, he appoints the brightest, most skilled clinicians as consultants, and as a protocol he continually emphasizes compassionate care for the patients. I cannot imagine anyone else like him.'

Dr Sarat Battina is in the business of helping people conceive. He is a specialist in reproductive medicine and operative laparoscopy, and coordinator, department of obstetrics and gynaecology at Apollo Chennai. Through IVF, he and his team of nurses and technicians bring hope and often babies to parents who have been unable to conceive.

The bulletin board in his small office is filled with photos of children and thank-you cards and letters from happy parents. The joy that they symbolize extends beyond the walls and into a visitor's heart. This is what patients see and feel when they meet him.

He is a warm, open man with an expressive face and the kind of personality that lets you relax. Born in Vijayawada, a large city in Andhra Pradesh, he graduated from Kurnool Medical College in 1980. Afterwards, he did his residency and specialist training in gynaecology working at the government hospital affiliated with his medical college.

When Dr Sarat married a woman from Chennai they moved to that city. His father-in-law was a friend of Dr Prathap Reddy who gave Sarat the opportunity to join in the new Indian health care venture. Apollo wasn't yet open so Dr Sarat worked with Dr Reddy in the older doctor's flourishing practice at HM Hospital. He says, 'Everyone wanted to see Dr Reddy, whether they were a cardiology patient or not, so I saw his gynaecological and internal medicine patients to help relieve the patient load. Dr Reddy was very good about welcoming juniors and he was good medical mentor, too.

'I had always been interested in gynaecology and when a friend wrote to me about the developing field of reproductive health, I was intrigued. I had not heard of it or of IVF, but I had seen families that were suffering and upset because they had not had children.

'Dr Reddy always likes to bring new things, new technology and make it available to the common man. He knew of my growing interest in reproductive technology and made an appointment for me to study with Dr S.S. Ratnam at the National University Hospital in Singapore. I was there for two months in the late '80s. Dr Ratnam opened the door to IVF teaching me how to do the testing, prepare the female for the procedures, retrieve eggs, bring forth the embryos and then implant them back into the woman. I was hooked, but we did not begin the IVF programme at Apollo at that time.'

In 1989 Dr Sarat went to the Kings College School of Medicine in London for further study because Apollo was ready to launch its own programme. The IVF procedures require a lot of discipline and training of the staff, and sterile environments.

A prominent – but controversial – gynaecologist from the US, Dr Lakshmi Nadgir, had heard of Apollo's plans and, wanting to help her fellow Indians, brought a team from Philadelphia to help train and open Apollo's new department. Dr Luis Blasco, who is an embryologist, headed the team. Along with Dr Blasco and Dr Nadgir were a nurse and a technician.

Dr Lakshmi Nadgir also brought equipment essential for the new reproductive lab. This included a stereo microscope and a phase contrast microscope needed for examining the eggs, sperm and embryos, an incubator, special small-gauge needles, media in which the embryo can grow and so forth.

'It was essentially a "technology transfer",' says Dr Sarat. 'Dr Blasco did the first procedures and then guided us as we began. It was very exciting.' Dr Nadgir came to Apollo again, this time with an endoscopy team and a pathologist. 'They not only advised us but conducted workshops that doctors from all over India attended.'

There are several causes for infertility: low sperm counts, poor sperm motility, clogged fallopian tubes, ovulation difficulties, sperm or eggs that are not healthy, endometriosis. Nutrition and ages of the mother and father and socio-economic factors are also issues.

Most of the patients who come to see Dr Sarat and his team are in their late twenties or early thirties. He says, 'This is the age when they begin to feel the real pressure and are looking for help. They are often desperate. The process is expensive and couples will sell their jewellery and even houses in order to pay for the IVF. In India as in some other countries, there is a bit of a social stigma when couples don't have children. We have a few patients who are well-off and not only do they pay for their own procedures but they also pay for some of the poor who would not be able to join us otherwise.'

The reproductive team at Apollo Chennai has attended to about 15,000 couples according to Dr Sarat. 'We do have failures and even after an embryo has formed there are instances in which it is not healthy. It is very difficult to face the husband and wife at that particular time. The woman is usually in tears. Compassion is a very important part of our work,' he said.

About 20 per cent of the births that result from the reproductive treatments are twins because of the hormonal injections that the women receive.

Dr Sarat remembers the first successful births that the Apollo team had.

'The mother was a homemaker and the father a dentist. It was in 1990 and she gave birth to twins, a boy and a girl. The boy graduated from IIT and the girl from the Birla Institute of Technology in Hyderabad. They are both engineers. We are all so happy and the children, now adults, come to visit us about once a year. We are still very happy to see them! Helping others is a wonderful gift that we can give,' he said.

———

Dr Reddy also highlighted for me that while the practice of medicine is at the heart of any hospital, administration and management are key components as well. That's why I've often observed him taking the time to meet with Apollo's management team, and to felicitate its members on special occasions such as birthdays.

As it happened, on the 473rd day – 11 May 2013 – after Seshadri Premkumar joined Apollo Hospitals as Group CEO, Dr Reddy hosted a small celebration for him because it was his birthday that day. Senior staff from the various Chennai hospitals was called, as was the corporate staff. They all gathered in the twelfth-floor boardroom of the Apollo corporate office on Greams Road in Chennai.

Dr Reddy wore a broad smile as he faced the gathered colleagues. 'It is our tradition to celebrate each other's successes. We're here today because of Prem's birthday, but, please, if someone else has a birthday in May, do say hello.' Gaurav Khurana, a junior staffer, raised his hand and Dr Reddy asked him to come forward saying, 'We are all a family and we are happy to share this day with you.'

Then Dr Reddy said, 'Everyone here is an integral part of Apollo. We are more than a team; we are a family. You all know that in health care, you can't be 99 per cent good. In business if you are 99 per cent good and have 1 per cent failure, then you throw away the failed part. But we are trusted with the health care of millions and a 1 per cent fail rate is someone's life.

'Last year we became the world number one in transplants. It is not just the surgeons who accomplished this. It is not all because of the doctors' skills. It is because our team is par excellence, because of everyone – doctors, nurses, medical technicians, food, managers, housekeeping.

'I am happy that we are all a part of Apollo and you will see much more of that as we grow. When we grew from here (Chennai) to Hyderabad, it was like we were being powered with automotive fuel; from Hyderabad to Delhi, it was with aviation fuel. From Delhi onwards it is with rocket fuel.'

A large coconut cake with white icing was brought in, along with tea and china cups and plates. Prem and his colleague Gaurav Khurana were given a knife to cut the cake. Dr Reddy led everyone in singing 'Happy Birthday!'

Some days later, I met with Prem at his twelfth-floor corner office at Apollo's headquarters. I wanted to get his thoughts about how Dr Reddy's concept of health care could be dramatically expanded to include the excluded. Although Prem had many accomplishments to his credit in the corporate world, he was a relative newcomer to the health care sector. How did his experience in the world of technology give him an advantage in health care?

Prem said: 'Today, the script is seeking to answer the question, "Can a billion Indians be kept healthy?" Or just to draw a parallel, "How do we continue to enjoy the bloom?" Productivity enhancement is a key theme. Information technology ushered in exponential productivity in similar ways. I feel that technology will play a significant part in health care productivity in access to care, time, cost, clinical outcome, re-visits, efficacy of treatment, integration of primary to secondary to tertiary care, disease management and wellness. This productivity and penetration will provide platforms for innovation of new solutions, segments and customers, given the burden of disease.'

Prem added: 'Interestingly, the vision that Dr Reddy has for health care gathers further potency if we look at the corollary – the absence of addressing the disease burden would cripple the economy in an irrecoverable manner. The good old middle school proverb, "Health is Wealth", simple as it might sound, has great significance but unfortunately is grossly underestimated. The Apollo vision, first formulated thirty years ago, impacted the way health care was delivered; the vision today will impact the way health care impacts India's prosperity.'

Some days later in New Delhi, Dr Anupam Sibal, Apollo's Group Medical Director, noted that Apollo Hospitals developed 'The Apollo Standards of Clinical Care' (TASCC) to establish standards of clinical care that ensure that all its hospitals deliver safe and quality clinical care to its patients, irrespective of the location and size of the hospital.

'TASCC embodies sets of process requirements and sets of outcome measures that underlie the Apollo Hospitals approach to clinical care,' Dr Sibal said. 'TASCC makes up the double helix of the Apollo Group's clinical fabric.' [12]

'Parameters have been benchmarked against the published benchmarks of the world's best hospitals including Cleveland Clinic, Mayo Clinic, National Healthcare Safety Network and Massachusetts General Hospital. The numerators, denominators and inclusions and

---

12 TASCC comprises of six components including Apollo Clinical Excellence @25 (ACE@25), Rocket ACE (RACE), Apollo Quality Plan (AQP), Apollo Mortality Review (AMR), Apollo Incident Reporting System (AIRS) and Apollo Critical Policies, Plans and Procedures (ACPPP). ACE@25 has been written up as a case study by the Ivey School of Business in Canada.

exclusions are defined lucidly and methodology of data collection is standardized. Data is uploaded online every month through a unique login and password,' Dr Sibal said.

Underlying such initiatives is the assumption that Apollo will recruit medical personnel who are the best in their fields. Anupam Sibal is a leading example of an accomplished physician that Dr Reddy recruited. A slim, handsome man, Dr Sibal was born and brought up in Srinagar. He returned from Britain to join Apollo Hospitals, New Delhi in 1997 to fulfil his dream to establish the first successful liver transplant programme in India.

One of his earliest interactions with Dr Reddy was when the team was being felicitated for the first successful liver transplant in the year 1999. The team was elated that they pulled off the first ever liver transplant in India. Dr Reddy said, 'We will hold another party when you reach 1,000 transplants.' A figure of 1,000 at that time seemed unimaginable, but to the visionary that Dr Reddy is, it came spontaneously. Today, Apollo runs the busiest solid organ transplant programme in the world.

Dr Sibal had never thought of getting into management. It was in 2002 that Chairman Reddy asked him if he would like to get involved in the management of the Delhi hospital. In 2003, Dr Sibal became the medical director of Apollo Hospital, New Delhi, and in 2005 he was elevated to the position of group medical director.

Dr Reddy told me: 'I start every recruitment with the assumption that the newcomer is going to be a star. I like to help make our people into real stars. After all, they are the ones who sustain Apollo's reputation. Apollo isn't about Dr Reddy. It's about the people who are part of its system. I hope people realize when they see me that I'm not a guy who wants anything for himself – I'm a guy who wants our people to grow in their jobs, to be men and women with "high-tech" and "high touch". I like to think that even though we all come from different backgrounds, we function as one family.'

Dr Sibal spoke about a programme called MedSkills.

'Dr Reddy has always loved people, been genuinely interested in them and inspired many to follow their dreams. From this missionary zeal and love of people, Apollo MedSkills Limited was conceived to provide training for half a million middle/lower-income youth and make them employable by 2022,' Dr Sibal said.

Apollo MedSkills has partnered with National Skill Development Corporation (NSDC) to support the National Agenda of Skilling Indian Youth by opening forty-seven Apollo Skill Development Centres across the country. The first four centres were scheduled to be operational at Chennai, Patna, Guwahati and Hyderabad in 2013.

———

A few doors down the corridor from Prem's office at the Apollo corporate headquarters in Chennai is a spartan office occupied by a man named S.K. Venkataraman. He is a wiry man with an intense expression that suggests displeasure with anyone who weighs more than him. Notwithstanding this serious image, Venkataraman has a huge – if complicated – sense of humour. He's always quoting aphorisms and poetry, and has a prodigious memory from which he can readily extract titbits of Apollo's record and India's history. He holds the title of Apollo's chief strategy officer.

Venkataraman who joined Apollo in February 1991 as Senior General Manager (Finance) from Shriram Fibres Limited, New Delhi, is another example of the sort of high-level talent that Dr Reddy likes to recruit. He was thirty-one years old at that time, and had a distinguished academic record. He was also a qualified company secretary. When he joined Apollo, he already had rich experience in consulting, auditing, taxation and corporate management, besides working in the Middle East.

'My first meeting with Dr Reddy in the first week of March 1991 was something to remember and cherish,' Venkataraman said. 'Dr Reddy along with Preetha Reddy met me in his office at the Main Hospital and said with his characteristic smile, "Venkat, you will blossom and grow with us, welcome to the Apollo Family."'

Venkataraman's first job was to structurally put Apollo's finances and systems on correct financial principles, as there were classical mismatches between asset and liability cash flows.

'So Apollo had to seek long-term funds to correct the working capital mismatch and infuse more of long-tenure funds. Besides, the hospital sector, being heavily investment-oriented and long-gestation in nature, it was imperative that finances and systems were handled with extreme care and with an acute sense of fiduciary responsibility, as the success of the hospitals services depended on a healthy cash flow and profitability for reinvestment and growth,' Venkataraman said.

Over the years, finances have kept pace with the rapid growth of Apollo's needs with prudent management principles, balancing profitability and growth. Today, he looks back with a deep sense of fulfilment and satisfaction that Apollo is regarded as a financially sound company with a well-earned reputation among both debt and equity holders. The fundamentals of Apollo's finances are reflected in the respectable rating of its debt instruments and as a coveted stock in the equity markets.

'Dr Reddy's vision and passion have been translated into financial success,' Venkataraman said. 'His is a "broaden and build" model of human talent that is rightfully receiving attention in today's current thinking around the world.'

———

Michael Neeb, CEO of HCA International, during his visit to Apollo Hospitals, Delhi in May 2013, after meeting Dr Reddy and Preetha Reddy in Chennai, was keen to learn about the clinical dashboards that Apollo has developed. Dr Sibal shared with Neeb the genesis of ACE@25, and of other programmes. Neeb wanted to know more and asked Dr Sibal as to how the 'quality journey' had started.

The quality journey began way back in early 2003, when a seed of thought germinated in Suneeta Reddy's mind to try and achieve the impossible for Indian health care. Accreditation by the Joint Commission International (JCI) was considered the 'Gold Standard' in health care accreditation; at that time no one believed that an Indian hospital could achieve the hallowed distinction.

That is, except for the Reddy family. Preetha travelled to Oakbrook, Illinois, to meet up with Karen Timmons, the CEO of JCI at that time. Extensive discussions regarding the expectations by JCI took place and Preetha returned with the resolve to make sure that an Apollo hospital became the first hospital in India to achieve JCI accreditation. Indraprastha Apollo Hospital in New Delhi was given the task to become the first hospital in India to receive a JCI accreditation. Getting ready to achieve JCI accreditation for an Indian hospital was no easy matter. Such accreditation would be a first for India. No one knew what the levels of expectations from JCI were to accredit a hospital in India. So Apollo Hospitals went the whole hog.

Dr Mehrotra was given the responsibility and he put together a team which went on full steam from day one. The JCI Standards Manual was dissected. A set of crisp but detailed policies was created. A lot of documentation was introduced by way of plans, medical records and standard operating procedures. The infrastructure was revamped. 'Slab to slab' fire compartmentalization of the buildings, a first for Indian hospitals, was carried out using large numbers of fire and smoke doors. Signages were reinforced. Access to the hospital was ensured for the disabled.

Finally, on 13 June 2005, a team of three JCI surveyors reached India to carry out the first JCI survey for any hospital in India. Five days of feverish activity ensued. Every bit of the facility was covered. All Apollo systems and processes were evaluated. Apollo's medical records were scanned in detail.

On 18 June a preliminary report was handed over to Apollo New Delhi, with a recommendation for the hospital to be accredited based on an assessment of 1,033 measurable elements.

There were, of course, celebrations at Apollo.

But more work lay head for Apollo. Starting from Delhi, the other facilities of Apollo Hospitals got their act together, and underwent JCI accreditations. Apollo hospitals in Chennai, Hyderabad, Kolkata, Ludhiana, Bangalore, Dhaka and finally Apollo-Bramwell in Mauritius were accredited. The stroke programme at Apollo Hospitals Hyderabad became the first JCI accredited stroke programme in the world.

A host of other hospitals beyond the Apollo Group also saw the opportunity and went in for JCI accreditation. Today more than twenty-five hospitals are accredited by JCI in India, including eight within the Apollo system.

But Dr Reddy was not satisfied. His point was that Apollo's bigger hospitals had now proven themselves and got accredited by JCI, but what about the hundreds of smaller hospitals which would find it difficult to achieve JCI accreditation?

'Even while we started instilling quality systems in them, Dr Reddy was thinking far ahead. He wanted an accreditation system for India by India,' Dr Sibal told me.

The idea was floated with the Quality Council of India and other hospital groups and the outcome was the National Accreditation Board for Hospitals (NABH). A think tank was assembled from within the health care industry, comprising of the brightest minds that got together in the boardroom at Apollo New Delhi for the first of many meetings to reach a consensus and finalize the standards for the NABH.

Chacha Nehru Hospital in New Delhi became the first public hospital in India to be accredited by the NABH. The government of Gujarat made a policy decision to get all its public hospitals accredited by NABH. One by one, Apollo Hospitals in the Tier Two and Tier Three cities also started their journey towards NABH accreditation.

NABH generated interest across India, so much so that the Central Government Health Scheme (CGHS) has made it mandatory for hospitals to be accredited to receive compensation for treating patients under this scheme. Today 174 hospitals are accredited by NABH in India even as NABH plans to take its offering to the neighbouring SAARC countries. Dr Reddy has begun to realize his dream of starting a movement to improve the standard of care delivered by Indian hospitals – and not just Apollo – for the country.

Like many others who first joined Apollo, V. Satyanarayana Reddy had no experience working at a large business organization. Generally known as 'Sathi', he was born in Tirupati and began as a trainee at Apollo Chennai in 1988 and came on full-time in the human resources department in 1989.

'I found that Dr Reddy treats patients, what other industries call "customers", not as outsiders but as family. I have heard him say on many occasions, "Think with the brain, act with your hands and feel through the heart,"' Sathi said.

During his induction period, Nageena Ahmed, manager for training and development at Apollo, asked Sathi what he wanted to become in the organization. When she showed him the organizational chart, he pointed to V.J. Chacko's name and title as CEO and said, 'I want to become chief executive.'

Over the years Sathi has served as a 'turn around executive', first at Apollo Gleneagles in Kolkata and then at the Apollo Speciality Hospital in Chennai. He also helped launch the hospitals in Colombo, Mauritius and Bhubaneswar.

In 1992 Sathi received an important lesson from Dr Reddy. Apollo had been the first hospital to reach a wage settlement for employees. At that time, health care didn't have minimum-wage standards, but Dr Reddy wanted to make sure the Apollo team was well taken care of. Shortly after the wage agreement was reached, Ram Murthy – who was chairman of the new Malar Hospital, operated by Apollo's competitor Fortis – called and asked Sathi for a copy of the agreement. Sathi declined to send him a copy.

The next day Sathi received a call from Dr Reddy.

'Did Ram Murthy call you?' Dr Reddy asked.

'Yes, sir, he did,' Sathi said.

'What did you say?'

'I said that the agreement was Apollo's and we couldn't share it.'

Dr Reddy said: 'You've done a great job, and all of the Apollo family will benefit from your work. It's the first of its kind. But believe me, we have to share whatever we do that is good so that health care for Indians will be on a par with international standards. We must not be limited to our own organization but drive down to the people of India. The whole of health care standards will go to a different level. I want you to share the agreement with all hospitals in Chennai.'

India now has a minimum wage act. At Apollo, tipping staff for preferential service is not allowed and Apollo has established the Apollo Hospitals Thrift Society, similar to a credit union, which gives loans to members for various needs.

The late Violet David, the director of nursing at Apollo Indrapastha in Delhi, was another mentor to Sathi's. Each month Sathi would interview 100 nurse candidates and shortlist them to fifty, which he would send to Violet. Invariably, she would only select five of the fifty. After months of this he became furious and went to her office. He was shouting. She listened very quietly and offered him a cup of coffee and said, 'Can I speak for five minutes?'

Sathi nodded.

Violet said: 'When I met Dr Reddy he told me, "Nurses are the torchbearers of Apollo."'

That's why Dr Reddy chose the logo of a nurse holding a torch for Apollo. It is to signify what they mean to Apollo's entire team and how they lead the way for health care.

Then Violet said, 'I will not compromise on who we select for nurses. I will not select anyone who does not match our quality standards and culture.' Today all the nursing directors at Apollo are encouraged to maintain this credo and Sangita has clearly told HR that their authority to exercise a veto is final.

Sathi says, 'Then I understood. She was not against HR but she was very clear in the objective that she had been given by our chairman.'

At that very meeting Violet David and Sathi initiated a solution to the problem of a shortage of qualified nurse candidates. They realized that they could not change the market – but what to do? The solution was obvious in hindsight: on that day in 1991 they realized that Apollo must start its own nursing college. By 1993, the first ten students had graduated and the Indian government had recognized the Apollo programme as a college.

My associate Twilla Duncan asked Sathi, who oversees six hospitals in the Chennai cluster with four new ones opening soon, how Apollo responded to patient complaints and suggestions. 'We are listeners,' he said. 'At one hospital we got feedback that handicapped patients who were sent to radiology for ultrasound exams were not able to use the toilets because none were handicapped-accessible. This was obvious but we had overlooked it. Once we had this in our sights, we built toilets for the handicapped on each floor and in the radiology department. This was much before the JCI standards made it mandatory.'

Sathi's wife Srilatha was previously in the hospitality business so it was a natural fit that she join Apollo in Kolkata as head of housekeeping and food services. Today she is the vice president of Sindoori Hospitality, which provides food service for all Apollo hospitals in Chennai.

CHAPTER TWENTY-FIVE

Tigers

THE TIGER LOOKED AT me, and I stared back. The creature wasn't real, of course, and I wasn't watching *Life of Pi*: it was a black-and-white photograph hanging on a wall in the Chennai office of Dr Subramaniam Arumugam, who's often called the 'father of cosmetic surgery in India'.

'What a stunning photograph,' I said to Dr Arumugam.

'Photograph? Look again,' the grey-haired surgeon said, with a knowing smile.

I looked at the tiger again. Then it struck me that it wasn't a photograph at all but a drawing made from soft pastels and charcoal. Dr Arumugam told me that a twenty-eight-year-old woman named Aishwarya Ramachandran, the daughter of Dr K. Ramachandran – who was among the nearly fifty Indian doctors who had trained under Dr Arumugam in Chicago in the early 1980s – had produced it in two days in 2011. Both surgeons practice at Apollo Hospital in Chennai. Aishwarya is an accomplished artist who started painting since she was four years old; she specializes in tigers. She contracted a serious illness when she was at Arizona State University in the United States, and was treated successfully at Apollo.[1]

---

1 Aishwarya Ramachandran has written a touching memoir which is scheduled for publication in 2014.

Before my meeting with Dr Arumugam I had been told that everybody called him 'Dr Ari'. He has performed nearly 25,000 surgeries in the last thirty years, and has trained more than a thousand surgeons in India. Scores of physicians came to watch his surgeries both in India and abroad. I had expected a stern figure; instead, I found a congenial man who immediately put me at ease with his smile and informal manner.

I had gone to see Dr Ari at Apollo Cosmetic Clinics because he and Dr Prathap Chandra Reddy have been friends for more than four decades. Dr Ari divides his time between Chennai and the Palos Heights suburb of Chicago.[2]

Dr Ari first met Dr Reddy in New York in 1967, when he was at Mercy Douglas Hospital in Philadelphia, and the latter was at Missouri State Chest Hospital in Springfield. Dr Mallikarjuna Rao Anna, a pathologist who practiced medicine in New York at the time, arranged the meeting. Dr Ari recalls that it took place at the Waldorf Astoria Hotel in a suite retained by Dr Reddy's close friends Kumara Raja and Kumara Rani Muthiah Chettiar.

There wasn't much contact between the two men after that meeting in New York. Dr Ari moved to Methodist Hospital in Brooklyn soon afterwards, and then to Northwestern University in Chicago in 1973. Dr Reddy and his family returned to India in January 1970.

The next time that they met was in 1977 in Madras. Dr Reddy was at HM Hospital in 1978, and invited Dr Ari to practice cosmetic surgery there during his two annual sojourns in India. Dr Reddy told him about his plans to build Apollo Hospital and took him to see the site. 'He told me that discussions had already been initiated with architects for the hospital – but then divine fate intervened,' Dr Ari said.

As Dr Reddy puts it: 'I took the plans and went to visit Jagadguru

---

2 Dr Ari focuses these days on his surgeries in India, mainly because of the huge cost of medical indemnity insurance in the United States – $130,000 annually for surgeons. In India, doctors like him pay Rs 7,000 a year, which offers coverage of between Rs 500,000 and Rs 25,000,000.

Kanchi Shankaracharya.[3] He was then camping at Belgaum. I was told that he was in *maunam* – an oath of silence. I was slightly dejected. Later on, when I was about to go for a bath, I was told that he had broken maunam. I thought then that I would now get a chance to meet him before he retreated again into maunam.'

The Shankaracharya listened to Dr Reddy, saw the plans for the hospital, and then told Dr Reddy that the location wasn't appropriate for a hospital.

'I was so disappointed that I told him, "Do you know there is an urban ceiling act, and I'm getting this property for nothing? The balance payment of Rs 24 lakh is to be made at my convenience. The banks have consented." The Shankaracharya heard me out and replied, "That *vaastu* is not for a hospital. If you want to do any other business, that's different." I told him that I would put up a temple there. But he would not say anything more, so that was it,' Dr Reddy said.[4]

Dr Reddy may have been disappointed but he wasn't fazed. He decided to a get a second opinion, as it were, from Swami Jayendra Saraswati Swamigal – who was subsequently to become the sixty-ninth Shankaracharya of Kanchi.[5] He happened to be in Hyderabad, and so Dr Reddy went there. The swami had just completed a puja. He saw Dr Reddy and asked him to wait in a nearby room.

'You want to know if the hotel site you have chosen is appropriate for building the hospital, isn't it?' he said to Dr Reddy.

Dr Reddy was taken aback. How could the swami have known this? In those days there no mobile phones, and it was unlikely that the Shankaracharya in Belgaum would have figured out that Dr Reddy would go to see the swami in Hyderabad.

---

3 The Kanchi Shankaracharya is head of the Kanchi *math*, one of the most revered Hindu institutions.

4 I owe gratitude to Shrinivas Pandit to whom Dr Reddy narrated some of this story well before my interviews with him in 2012–13.

5 Many years later, the sixty-ninth Shankaracharya was involved in a controversy concerning the operations of his temples, and the murder of a temple priest.

'How do you know this?' Dr Reddy said to the swami.

'When a patient goes to a doctor, he must tell him his true complaint. So you have come only for this, am I right?' the swami said. 'When Perival[6] says that . . .'

Dr Reddy interrupted him. 'But how do you know what he said in Belgaum yesterday?'

'If we do not have that much of connectivity, what am I here for?' the swami said.

Dr Reddy asked him some more questions about the viability of the hotel property in Madras.

The swami told him: 'Don't even think of it. Why are you bothered? He has already blessed you, and told you that you will build the hospital.'

Dr Reddy knew that it was pointless to push the matter any further. When he returned to Madras, friends and relatives suggested that he should keep the property and later sell it; it would most certainly have made him a big profit – perhaps as much as Rs 4 crore on a down payment of just Rs 2,500,000. But Dr Reddy declined.

As luck would have it, in just two weeks' time Dr Reddy found out about an auction of a property on Greams Road. He visited the place and felt that it gave off good vibrations. He bought the land, and Apollo Madras eventually rose there.[7]

But well before Apollo Madras started operations, Dr Reddy travelled to the United States several times to raise funds from investors in various cities. In 1979, he looked up Dr Ari, who organized a dinner at his home in Palos Heights for some twenty-five doctors of Indian origin. Several others doctors, such as Dr Rahman in Chicago, Dr Prasad, Dr Kamath, Dr Prem Sagar Reddy, and Dr Reddy in Birmingham also hosted dinners for Prathap Reddy.

'Dr Reddy put on a slide show – it was very well-produced, and

---

6 'Perival', literally meaning 'the elder', is the respectful title that Jagadguru Chandrashekarendra Saraswathi Swami, the sixty-eighth Shanakaracharya of the Kanchi Kamakothi Peetham, was known by.

7 This episode is also covered in an earlier chapter.

it explained his vision for Apollo,' Dr Ari told me. 'I was impressed enough to immediately agree to invest $10,000.'[8]

Some of the other physicians seemed sceptical, however.

'They felt that it would be impossible to build a hospital of world standards in India,' Dr Ari said. 'I will say this for Dr Reddy: he never once was dismissive or defensive. He was always positive in his responses to sceptical questions. His attitude was so positive that a few of us believed he would succeed.'

'There's power in our hands to change India's health care landscape,' Dr Reddy said to Dr Ari, as the two men talked over lunch in Chicago about how Dr Reddy planned to introduce corporate-sector hospitals in India. 'We've got to invest in our future. Why can't we get the best medical treatment in India? Why do Indians have to travel abroad to seek good medical care? Why can't affordable health care be made accessible in India itself?'

Dr Ari found Dr Reddy's arguments so persuasive that he not only invested in Apollo, but also later joined its faculty. [9] 'He hasn't changed in the four decades that I've known him as a friend and colleague,' Dr Ari told me, as an office aide kept bringing me steaming cups of tea thickened with condensed milk and sugar. 'If anything, Dr Reddy's enthusiasm and passion have only increased. I perform surgery for around six or eight hours a day – but he's at his job virtually twenty-four hours. He never seems to get tired. And in all the time that I've known him, I've never once seen Dr Reddy lose his temper. I think his biggest strength is his focus. And it's also his passion for providing great medical care. I'm not

---

8   Dr Ari says that he subsequently also invested $2,000 in Apollo Hospital, Hyderabad. Another US-based physician, Dr Prem Sagar Reddy, also invested $10,000.

9   Apollo Chennai and Apollo Hyderabad are now considered to be the leading centres in India for cosmetic surgery. Until their rise, such surgery was notably performed at Christian Medical College in Vellore, and at the All India Institute of Medical Sciences in New Delhi. Cosmetic surgery centres have also sprung up in China, South Korea and Thailand. The global plastic-surgery industry is estimated at more than $250 billion.

embarrassed to say that Dr Reddy is the single greatest human being I've met in my life.'[10]

That phrase was exactly – and eerily – repeated by Capt. C.K. Krishnan Nair, founder and chairman emeritus of the Leela Group of Hotels, when I met him weeks afterwards at the Leela Palace in Chennai. He had come specifically to join in the eightieth birthday celebrations of Dr Reddy – a testimony to Dr Reddy's ability to make friendships that last. Captain Nair invited me to breakfast in his suite, which was appointed with antiques and tasteful prints. We spoke about his longtime friendship with Dr Reddy.

'We met in New York in 1982, when Dr Reddy was trying to raise funds for Apollo Madras,' Captain Nair said. After a long career in the army, he had become a successful exporter of garments. 'So we went from city to city, meeting people who might be potential investors. My eldest son Vivek – who's now chairman of the Leela Group – was with us.'

Dr Reddy eventually raised $1 million from various investors of Indian origin, a very large amount in those days for a start-up like Apollo to obtain.

One of Dr Ari's colleagues is Dr Nirvikalpa Natarajan of Chennai. She has notched up so many formidable accomplishments that her peers in medicine find it hard to believe that she is only thirty years old. Her career bears testimony to Dr Reddy's willingness to offer opportunities to young doctors.

Her accomplishments include performing hundreds of surgeries, and treating even more hundreds of patients in India, Ireland and

10 Another evangelist was Dr Rahman from Chicago, who hosted at least five dinners and personally ensured that his friends supported their countryman, Dr Reddy, who had the courage to pioneer Apollo. Other early investors included Dr Harinath Reddy and Dr Narasimha Reddy. Dr Prathap Chandra Reddy met more than a thousand doctors across the United States, Britain and the Middle East. He received investment from some 478 doctors of Indian origin. This success ratio is quite unheard of even for the most seasoned fundraisers. And what was Dr Reddy's 'secret'? Says Sangita Reddy: 'Conviction, passion and purity of purpose.'

Britain. Dr Nirvikalpa is a practitioner of oral and maxillofacial surgery, one of only a handful of women in her field.

Dr Nirvikalpa has a simple credo: 'My work speaks for itself.'

That self-confidence is well founded – and she gives full credit to Dr Reddy for his encouragement. Oral and maxillofacial surgery is a unique speciality that deals with conditions, defects and aesthetic aspects of the mouth, jaws and face. It is especially relevant in India, which has the world's largest number of traffic accidents; such accidents often result in severe trauma to the head and face. What sets oral and maxillofacial surgeons apart from other specialists is their in-depth understanding of the skeletal and dental framework of the face. Much as the foundations of a building are made from iron, the foundations of the face are its bones and teeth. Knowing the subtleties of this allows surgeons to deal effectively in areas of cosmetic jaw surgery, facial trauma, craniofacial surgery, oral pathology, temperomandibular joint surgery, oral implantology and oral cancer.

'Oral and maxillofacial surgery is "the next big thing",' Dr Nirvikalpa says. It is a multi-disciplinary field, one that requires surgeons like Dr Nirvikalpa to be deeply familiar with neuroscience, ophthalmology, dentistry and audiology, among other fields of medicine. It is also a field that pays surgeons far more in the West than in India, and Dr Nirvikalpa could have just as easily joined the 400,000 physicians of Indian origin who practice medicine outside India.[11] But she chose to work in her homeland because of the rich diversity of patients, because of patients' needs, and because, ultimately, 'one has to give back to one's own country'. Even more specifically, she wanted to work for Dr Reddy.

Both Dr Reddy and Apollo's director of medical services, Dr N. Satyabhama, serve as her mentors. Another mentor is Dr Vinod Narayanan, who is highly experienced in oral and maxillofacial surgery, and who is a consultant at Apollo Hospital. Dr Nirvikalpa also looks up to Preetha Reddy, whom she considers a role model for women executives.

---

11 Source: Global Association of Physicians of Indian Origin.

Dr Nirvikalpa represents a young generation of physicians that Dr Reddy has been recruiting for Apollo. But the 'pillars' of the system have been physicians such as Dr M.K. Mani – a pioneer in nephrology in the country and chief nephrologist at Apollo Hospitals; the late Dr N. Rangabashyam, who was a top gastrointestinal surgeon until his death in July 2013; Dr Joseph V. Thachil, a urologist; and Dr M.R. Girinath, the chief cardio-vascular surgeon, who has performed more than 50,000 heart operations.

They are all considered 'tigers'.

One evening in Chennai, I went to see Dr Mani at his home. Dr Mani first became famous after he gave a fresh lease of life to Jayaprakash Narayan, who was suffering from a kidney ailment and had a cardiac arrest at the Jaslok Hospital in Bombay.[12]

It had been the end of yet another long day for Dr Mani – he typically rises at 5 a.m. every day and goes for a brisk walk; his work at Apollo rarely ends before 6 p.m. – but the tall, bespectacled man appeared fresh and sprightly. His expression isn't warm, but his manner is welcoming.

Before visiting him, I'd read his autobiography, *Yamaraja's Brother*, and was somewhat startled by his forthright views against the concept of corporate hospitals. His key arguments: that private hospital costs were beyond the reach of the common man in a country where the per capita income was barely Rs 54,000; and that physicians should go beyond the call of duty and perform voluntary work in the field.[13] Dr Mani also believes that there should be an accelerated 'national conversation' about the prevention and

---

12 A veteran freedom fighter, Jayaprakash Narayan led a popular protest against the rule of Prime Minister Indira Gandhi, which led to her defeat in the national elections of 1977. He died in 1979, of complications resulting from diabetes and heart disease.

13 Dr Mani helps the Kidney Help Trust of Chennai with an unusual programme. It involves the screening of the entire population of 43,000 people in fifty-six villages and hamlets, once every year or two, for diabetes and hypertension, using the simplest of methods, a simple questionnaire, a urine test for sugar and albumin, and recording the blood pressure.

treatment of diabetes, including early health check-ups. He cites a method that he developed for patients attending Apollo Hospital for established chronic renal failure; it is aimed at slowing down further deterioration and thereby delaying the need for dialysis.

I asked him why he was opposed to the corporate hospital concept that was promoted by Dr Reddy, and how it was that he could work with Apollo when its very ethos collided with his own anti-corporate philosophy.

'My loyalty is to the hospital,' Dr Mani said. 'I respect Dr Reddy even though I openly disagree with him about charging patients too much. But he still tolerates me – and that is one of his great qualities: he respects you for your work, and he respects dissent, he doesn't mind an honest difference of opinion. Personally, I am very grateful to Dr Reddy. I am therefore able to continue work here though in general I do not approve of the corporate sector and its approach to medicine. There is no doubt that the facilities available for work in hospitals such as this are unrivalled in India, and I have been able to do clinical research of significance here.'

'I'm not pro-profit,' Dr Mani said. '"Profit" to me is wrong. I see no reason why the very wealthy should not pay for their treatment, but we should not impose the same scale of fees on the poor. One problem of corporate hospitals is that they concentrate on the profit motive. The charges are certainly twenty times cheaper than what it would cost in hospitals overseas, but they are far too expensive for the average Indian. The advantage of working in such a hospital is that the facilities provided and the standards maintained make it possible to practice medicine at the most efficient level. It is possible for a caring doctor to reach an agreement with the management of his hospital to provide some relief for those who cannot afford the costs. I work for one of the most expensive of these hospitals, Apollo, but I have been able to ease matters for the poor and the middle class because we have a number of concessional packages of investigations. For end-stage renal disease, we subsidize dialysis for a limited period of three months, so that a patient can have the time to have a donor investigated and go through with a renal transplant.

I have made the sacrifice of working as a full-time salaried employee rather than practicing, which means some restriction of my income, but considerable easing of the burden on my patients since we only charge a consulting fee once in three months, no matter how often we see the patient in that period.'

I later learned that, on 2 November 2009, Dr Mani had spoken about Apollo and Dr Reddy on the occasion of the release of a postage stamp featuring Apollo Hospitals – the first such stamp honouring an Indian hospital issued by the government. As I read his remarks, it occurred to me that Dr Mani was truly articulating the Group's ethos.

'Teamwork is the key to success in modern medicine, and that really has been the key to the success of Apollo Hospitals. Many patients have thanked us for all that we do. One of the questions we often ask them is what makes them come all the way over here when, after all, you have got facilities in every part of the country and you can get all this treatment there – and they say there is something special about this institution, starting from the liftman to the nurse – many patients have commented to me about the quality of the nursing care and say the nurse alone would be worthwhile to come to the hospital for and take treatment over here. This teamwork has really been what has built up and made the hospital what it is today, and the hospital has always driven for excellence in every single aspect of its work. It makes me proud and happy that I too am a part of this and have been able to contribute in some way to this work.'

Not long after my conversation with Dr Mani, his wife Rama also spoke about Apollo Hospitals and the role of medicine in contemporary society. Also a physician, she is chief of laboratory services at Apollo Chennai. Like Dr Reddy, Dr Rama is also a graduate of Stanley Medical College. She was working at Jaslok Hospital when Dr Reddy approached her husband to join Apollo.

'It was very flattering because although Dr Reddy primarily wanted my husband, he also offered me a position,' Dr Rama said. 'Apollo was quite a contrast to other hospitals. Dr Reddy was open to new ideas and he gave a lot of freedom to us. My hospital experience before had come with many restrictions. Now I felt free as a bird. It was wonderful.'

Apollo Chennai stands out in its laboratory services with two excellent pathologists: Dr Rama Mani, of course, and Dr Ashok Parameswaran, chief histopathologist.

Dr Ashok graduated from Christian Medical College in Vellore. He was one of the doctors who knew back in the late 1970s that Dr Prathap Chandra Reddy had big plans for a new health care approach in India. It was 'the talk of the town', he recalls. Dr Ashok was looking for an opening in Madras and went for an interview at the Apollo corporate headquarters in Bishop Garden.

'It was a very small office and the challenges were many,' he says. After a long interview Dr Reddy asked Dr Ashok to join Apollo and he became the first medical employee of the hospital.

'It was a shock that anybody would trust someone so young. Dr Reddy gives a lot freedom when he trusts you,' Dr Ashok said.

Later, his wife, Dr Sarojini Parameswaran, became Apollo's first medical resident, eventually joining the hospital as a consultant in gastroenterology.

'We watched the struggle as the hospital was built. It is difficult to imagine how Indian health care was before and the weight that lifted with Apollo. Dr Reddy's approach creates deep loyalty,' Dr Sarojini said.

Dr Rama Mani and Dr Ashok agreed that the most exciting development of their time in Apollo came in 2012 with an entirely new molecular lab. It was a totally different technology. 'Dr Reddy is always like a tiger. He wants Apollo to be roaring all the time,' Dr Rama said.

During a lunch at the Hotel Imperial in New Delhi with my friend Dilip Cherian, I mentioned that I would be writing about the 'tigers' at Apollo. Dilip, a communications maestro who has a ubiquitous presence on Indian TV talk shows, smiled sagely, and said: 'But what about the tigresses? Apollo has more women than men in executive positions, and quite possibly more women doctors than male doctors. Dr Reddy likes to empower women. Don't forget:

he's been surrounded by strong women all his life, and he trusts their judgement.'

One such tigress is Dr Rupali Basu, chief executive officer of Apollo Gleneagles Hospitals in Kolkata, and chief executive officer, Eastern Region, Apollo Hospitals Group. Dr Basu initially worked for Apollo from 1998 to 2002, after which she joined Wockhardt Hospitals. It was in February 2008, a little before the Wockhardt IPO failed, that Dr Basu decided to rejoin the Apollo Group. 'I approached Managing Director Preetha Reddy about rejoining,' Dr Basu said. 'I had met Chairman Reddy once or twice and felt that Apollo might be open to the idea. The then CEO in Kolkata wanted to move to Chennai, which was perfect since I wanted to move back home.'

In joining Apollo Dr Basu decided to expand her speciality in preventive paediatrics and obstetrics and gynaecology by moving into hospital administration. She felt that she could have more impact on women's health as an administrator than in a medical consultancy. 'She had leadership qualities,' Dr Reddy told me.

Although she was considered a star in Delhi, Pune and Bangalore, she wanted to move from curative care to preventative health care. 'I also wanted to move back to Bengal which is in my blood and I will remain here until my last breath,' Dr Basu told my research associate Twilla Duncan.

She oversees a very large market. Communicating Apollo's quality and skills to doctors and patients alike invigorates her. Many patients in the Kolkata area previously travelled to Apollo Chennai for medical treatment. It was the only nearby location where they trusted the care. Dr Basu's constant emphasis on quality, reaching into neighbourhoods and connecting with doctors, has paid off and the hospital had more than doubled in size with additional growth in the pipeline. Now, patients come to Kolkata for medical tourism from the nearby states, and from Bangladesh and Nepal.

Apollo Gleneagles received its JCI accreditation in 2009 and was reaccredited in 2012. One way to measure the regard for Apollo's work in the Northeast is that the attrition rate is very low. Dr Basu has had no turnover in doctors and senior nurses for nearly three years. The hospital began a nursing college in Kolkata in 2008, with the first class graduating in 2012.

'Keeping our nurses is critical,' Dr Basu says. 'Dr Reddy had the foresight from the beginning to emphasize the role that nurses play. Hospitals in the UAE and new hospitals in Kolkata pay significantly more, sometimes almost double. They are always trying to poach our nurses because they know how well-trained Apollo nurses are and that we adhere to strict international standards. In the past nursing was not considered a prestigious job and middle-class families discouraged their daughters from taking it up. At Apollo we are trying to change that impression.'

Shubhada Sakurikar, Director, Nursing at Apollo Hospitals Hyderabad, adds, 'In the last four years that I have been here, I found that the working environment and culture of Apollo instils a strong sense of belonging in every employee. Everyone feels worthy of the cause and wants to carry forward the mission. We all work together as a team, so that we can achieve a holistic outcome for the patient without worrying about any trivia.'

Mary Jose, Director, Nursing at Apollo Hospitals Bangalore, concurs. 'Every day Chairman used to take rounds, asking all of us what we could do better and about the issues we were facing. He never made us feel he is the chairman of the company and we all are his employees. He made us feel he is the father and we are his children. He kept telling all of us that this place is ours, to make it or break it lies in our hands. Those powerful words got so much into our systems that many of us strongly believe that this is our only place.'

One of the distinguished figures that Dr Reddy invited to join Dr Basu at Apollo Kolkata is Air Marshal Dipankar Ganguly, a physician who is now director of medical service. I asked him how he found the transition from the military's medical service to Apollo's civilian one.

'The transition from being the head of the Medical Services

(Air) after having served thirty-nine years in the defence forces to a completely civilian setup has truly not been easy in spite of all the help and encouragement received,' Dr Ganguly said. 'To learn about the workings of a corporate sector hospital, its rules and its ethos takes some time for a person from a totally different background like myself. Having said that, there are many commonalities between the two, the primary one being that of patient care. To see the satisfaction and gratitude of patients successfully treated in our hospital, at the end of the day, makes everything worthwhile.'

Dr Reddy had earlier told me about the politics involving how Apollo came to acquire its Kolkata property. A major player was the West Bengal chief minister, the redoubtable Jyoti Basu, [14] who told Dr Reddy, 'We want to do a hospital in Kolkata.' A friend of Basu's who ran a chit fund had already written out a cheque for Rs 5 crore, and had told Dr Reddy, 'We assure you that we won't interfere with the working of the hospital.' But Dr Reddy then received a call from Jyoti Basu's office that the chief minister no longer wished the chit fund to be involved with an Apollo Hospital.

Dr Reddy went to see Basu. Present at that meeting was the latter's brother-in-law, Bimal Basu.

'I will get you another person for the hospital,' Bimal Basu said. Dr Reddy recalls that he had no choice at the time but to go along. Because of the Urban Land Ceiling Act, government clearance for the land was needed. A leasing company had acquired the land that had been previously paid for by the chit fund. But the leasing company had got into trouble, and G.P. Goenka, the industrialist, had quickly acquired the property. Meanwhile, the owner of the chit fund had gone to the Parkway Clinic in Singapore and done a deal to form a partnership to build a hospital in Kolkata. Dr Reddy told me that he had no choice but to withdraw from developing the hospital – although his friend and lawyer Habibullah Badsha advised him that

---

14 Jyoti Basu served as the chief minister of West Bengal for the Left Front government from 1977 to 2000 – the longest serving chief minister in the history of India.

he could have stopped the Goenka–Parkway deal because the land lease was in Dr Reddy's name.

When Dr Reddy asked Badsha and his friend P. Obul Reddy, the Chennai industrialist, how long litigation might take to resolve the dispute, they told him in unison, 'At least twenty years.'

That's how G.P. Goenka and Parkway started the Duncan Gleneagles Hospital in Kolkata (Goenka reportedly thought that a 'foreign name' would resonate better with Indian patients). Dr Reddy got minimally compensated for his investment.

In the event, Goenka ran into problems running the new hospital. He had lost $10 million. Dr Reddy was asked again to get involved. Jyoti Basu invited him to visit at the chief minister's residence. Knowing the chief minister's love of *hilsa*, the bony fish favoured by Bengalis, Dr Reddy sent him the fish from Bangladesh. Basu invited Dr Reddy to dinner but the doctor declined saying that he had to catch a flight home. The chief minister replied that it was not a problem to eat early. When Dr Reddy arrived at Basu's home at 5 p.m., the chef had prepared a delicious fish curry with the hilsa. Of the several things said over the meal, one that Dr Reddy clearly remembers is Jyoti Basu's caution.

'Don't compromise on standards in health care,' he said to Dr Reddy during their conversation.[15]

Anil Thadani – who had earlier brought in Apollo's first FDI through Schroeder Capital Partners – explained to me how Apollo-Gleneagles happened.

'When we took effective control of Parkway hospitals in Singapore and I was appointed the chairman of the board, we found that Parkway had a joint venture in Calcutta with a local businessman (Goenka). The purpose of the joint venture was to build a hospital in Calcutta, which would then have been run by Parkway.

---

15 Jyoti Basu was very helpful in settling a labour dispute at Apollo Hyderabad in 1995. Dr Reddy appreciated Basu's decisive actions in settling the dispute. He and Basu had a good relationship where they could speak with each other candidly. Even during the strike Dr Reddy didn't get involved in politics.

'In speaking with Parkway management, we found that they were frustrated with the lack of progress with the joint venture and it looked like the relationship with the joint-venture partner was not ideal. Since we were still invested in Apollo and had an excellent relationship with the company and its founders and management, we approached Dr Reddy to see if Apollo might be interested in taking over the Calcutta joint-venture partner's position and building out the hospital, which would then become an Apollo-Parkway joint-venture.

'After some considerable and skilful negotiation on Suneeta's part, Apollo was finally able to acquire the joint-venture partner's stake in the Calcutta project. The project then proceeded to be completed successfully and was renamed the Apollo-Gleneagles Hospital, Calcutta.

'The investors in this joint venture were Parkway and Apollo. While our fund had a stake in both these businesses, we had no direct investment in the Calcutta joint venture. But I'm delighted that Apollo-Gleneagles has become such a success,' Thadani told me from Singapore, where he is based.

All this, of course, occurred before Dr Rupali Basu's engagement with Apollo Kolkata, an institution that she helped develop well beyond initial expectations.

Like Dr Rupali Basu, Captain Usha Banerjee is another 'tigress' at Apollo Hospitals. She is group director of nursing, and one of the liveliest persons I met during the course of researching this book.

A Keralite by birth and married to a Bengali, Captain Banerjee has always had a nagging thought: 'What can I do to contribute to India?' She joined the Armed Forces Medical College in Pune, and obtained a degree in nursing. She joined Manipal Hospital in Mangalore in 2003. At Mangalore, Banerjee was appalled at the conditions for nurses, which were very different from those at the Armed Forces Medical College. She says that the nurses were treated very poorly; they were intimidated by doctors. After Manipal, Banerjee was headhunted by Max Hospital, Delhi. Although Max – a competitor of Apollo at the time – was considered a fine facility, Captain Banerjee felt its nursing standards needed improvement.

In 2005 the then administrator of Apollo Indraprastha, an American woman named Anne Marie Moncure, recruited Banerjee. Banerjee already knew of Dr Reddy and believed she would have more opportunity for change at Apollo. She was right. Dr Reddy had a larger vision for health care and for nursing. Banerjee saw that the founder treated nurses differently, and he gave her free range to fully develop the nursing programme.

But her first impressions of Apollo Delhi weren't encouraging. She remembers meeting Dr Reddy at his Delhi office; he wore a dark blue suit, a white shirt, and a yellow tie. Captain Banerjee wore a peacock-blue sari.

'What do you see as our problems?' Dr Reddy asked her.

'I'm impressed by the clinical outcomes, and the technical part of the practice of medicine is very good,' Banerjee told Dr Reddy, not giving second thought to whether he would feel offended by her candour. 'What seems to be missing is excellence in hospitality services. It's also important that nurses understand the business aspect of the organization. There's so much to do.'

'Go and do what you think is right,' Dr Reddy said.

So Banerjee implemented 'disruptive programmes' designed to shake up the nursing culture and build stronger relationships with doctors. A richer understanding of super-speciality disciplines was taught. A 'back to basics' programme was implemented and all nurses, old staff or new, were required to spend a month in an Apollo training programme. Banerjee also emphasized good grooming. Medical books and access to computers were provided, and nurses read up on all illnesses, new technology and delivery of health care. At Apollo each nurse is given the task of influencing team members to improve patient care. One of Banerjee's initiatives was 'Each one, teach one'.

'I am told that I'm responsible for changing the culture of nursing in the Apollo organization, and I look at myself as a change agent for nursing,' Captain Banerjee told me. 'The fact that a nurse is depicted on the Apollo logo demonstrates the extent of Dr Reddy's commitment to the nurses' role in health care.'

Along the way, the nurses' self-esteem improved. Even small successes were celebrated at parties and dances that Banerjee organized – she herself is a professional-standard dancer, and sometimes with difficulty persuades Dr Reddy to 'twirl' at staff parties. Dr Reddy obliges as the Apollo family means the world to him.

Captain Banerjee introduced English-language classes at Apollo to improve communication with the patients. As it turned out, the question of speaking English became a political issue. A couple of nurses who disagreed with Captain Banerjee went to a social activist named Usha Krishnakumar; Krishnakumar organized protests against Captain Banerjee. Other nurses spoke anonymously to the Malayalam press in Kerala against Banerjee; critical reports and cartoons about her started appearing in the media. Still other nurses made it seem as though it was all a matter of bias, with Banerjee discriminating against nurses from Kerala; these critics seemed to have missed the fact that Captain Banerjee was a Keralite herself.

Dr Reddy asked Captain Banerjee to meet with him.

'We are in the business of customer service,' she told Dr Reddy. 'People are free to do what they want outside the hospital. But within Apollo, we are obliged to provide the best possible health care to our patients. And that means being able to communicate with patients and physicians in English – a universal language.'

Dr Reddy agreed with her. Not long afterwards, he promoted her to group director of nursing for all Apollo hospitals across India. But both agreed that something needed to be done to stanch the outflow of Apollo nurses to the West. One study showed that hospitals in the United States get nearly 50 per cent of their nurses from various Apollo hospitals. Captain Banerjee's aggressive new approach towards training nurses has been so successful, in fact, that Apollo nurses are vigorously recruited by foreign hospitals. There is about a 20 per cent turnover each year, which creates a huge challenge for Apollo. Pay abroad is higher and the appeal for travel to young nurses is considerable. Of course, hospitals such as Apollo cannot possibly match the salaries offered by counterparts abroad. But both Dr Reddy and Captain Banerjee hope to inculcate institutional loyalty in Apollo nurses through better attention to their requirements, and through other incentives such as creating a more hospitable work environment.

The issue of the physician–nurse partnership also became more important under Captain Banerjee's leadership. Clinical conferencing was developed so that nurses felt free to ask doctors about clinical decisions and make suggestions instead of remaining silent. Previously, nurses had felt far too deferential towards physicians, and rarely spoke up at meetings where doctors were present.

Eventually, the initiatives were accepted. Doctors saw improved clinical outcomes. Patients told others about their experiences, effectively creating a small referral programme.

Banerjee's interaction with Dr Reddy has been limited; he gives staff authority and expects results. In early 2006, she was one of the senior staff from Apollo who travelled to Agra to inaugurate the new hospital there. There was a large crowd of area residents, medical professionals, officials and press.

When Dr Reddy spoke he said, 'It is wonderful to be here so that we can improve health care for all.' He enumerated the many benefits of the new hospital, how it would give better access, higher technology, personalized care. Then, nodding towards Captain Banerjee, he said, 'We are happy to have everyone today but the most important person here is our director of nursing from Delhi.' It was Dr Reddy's way of acknowledging the importance of nurses and the substantive changes that Banerjee had made.

According to Dr Reddy, 'I wanted to unleash the potential of the nurses. From the very beginning and in our logo, nurses were recognized at Apollo. We call them 'sisters' because they are in our family and also close to the patients. We couldn't be the best hospital or provide the best health care without the nurses.'

'I was going to stay at Apollo for two years and then go abroad,' one nurse, Simmi Rajan of Kerala, told me. 'Hospitals abroad were offering as much as $40 an hour. But Captain Banerjee gave us all a special motivation. She has improved the environment for nurses. I've been at Apollo for more than ten years now.'

Another senior nurse, Gracie Philip, left a better-paying job in Muscat, where she'd worked at the Royal Hospital for more than eight years, and came to Apollo Delhi in 1996. Gracie recalls that she first saw Dr Reddy at a large event for Apollo nurses. 'After he spoke from the dais, he stepped down and mingled with us,' she told me. 'When he saw me, he suddenly said, "God bless you." Somehow that touched me instantly. I now often accompany Dr Reddy as he makes his rounds of wards. I have seen for myself how his presence cheers up patients. He really has the power to heal people's souls.'

Another nurse, Savitha Srivastava, said, 'Individually we are a drop, together we are an ocean.'

When you notice that this is the belief that is reflected across, you realize that it's not just one tigress but actually an ethos that is present through the system. The nurses attend clinical conferences outside the hospital and are always recognized as Apollo nurses because of their competence and confidence. Graduates from college and clinical programmes compete now to be accepted by Apollo. With the introduction of nursing specialities the nurses can choose an area of work that fits their interests.

'We have three "Cs": caring for the patient and caring for the caregivers; carving careers; crusading for change,' says Captain Banerjee. 'Our nurses know that emotional well-being is important to healing and they celebrate patient birthdays, recognize special needs for them and their families. It's exciting to see. We get many thank you letters from patients.'

Sister R. Girija also gets thank-you notes from patients, even though she retired from Apollo Chennai not long ago; she'd joined the institution the same month and year that it was established, September 1983. Dr Reddy and Preetha Reddy both asked her to extend her stay several times because of her treasure trove of knowledge and her commitment.

Born in Kerala, she lived in many places since her father was in the Indian Army and had postings around the country. She saw an advertisement in *The Hindu* for a special kind of person needed for a special kind of facility, and came to Apollo. Construction was still going on and there was a lot of activity on every front. 'I told Dr Reddy that I could speak Telugu, Tamil, Hindi, Malayalam, Kannada and English,' she said.

'Dr Reddy set a great example. He has compassion for people who are suffering and that keeps him going. We never saw the sun because we would come early and go home late. During all this time, Dr Reddy would meet the patients and their families and he would meet with us, too, talking with us and giving us all encouragement. He and Mrs Reddy made sure that we were taken care of at the hospital with good food – and our families too,' Girija said. 'We call Chennai the mother hospital and all things flowed from here because the standard of being a family originated with Dr Reddy.'

She added: 'I remember the first time a big change happened for me. There was a patient who had pain in the middle of the night, he came and while he was here in hospital he had a massive heart attack. We had been training in CPR and I used it on him. Our trolley had not been set up and staff ran throughout the hospital to get the necessary items – the emergency drugs, IV lines and other things. Now it is called a cardiac crash cart. It was exciting but it reminded me that in any critical situation, you've got to be ready, to anticipate what will be needed. We do that very well,' she said.

Now the changes that Girija sees are the digitizing of data for all patient information, computer training, organizing patient records for easy retrieval and CNE or Continuous Nursing Education.

'Apollo works hard to retain nurses and was the first to give maternity leave, educational benefits for children, performance appraisals and nursing hostels so that nurses have a safe place to stay,' Girija said.

One woman who worked with Girija is Punitha Singh who graduated from Christian Medical College, Vellore, in nursing and worked on staff there for two years. She worked at Sultan Qaboos University Hospital in Muscat, Oman as an Assistant Nursing Supervisor. Then a friend suggested that she apply to Apollo. By 2011, Punitha was promoted to director of nursing and now, she says, 'There's no turning back.'

'My responsibility, among other things, is to ensure the quality of nurses who are hired are of high standards and no compromise is made on that since they represent Apollo,' she says. 'Part of that is bringing the Apollo culture to every new nurse because each one comes with a different attitude.'

Punitha says that it's more than training that sets Apollo nurses apart. 'We have the latest technology, equipment that other hospitals may not get for years. Apollo nurses are groomed to meet the challenges of today's health care setup,' she says. 'The TLC factor is intertwined in their DNA. They are taught to be passionate about what they are doing. They are global ambassadors of Apollo Hospitals. Apollo is a brand pioneer and the policies and protocols we follow set the standards. Our adherence to JCI requirements ensure quality and safety for our patients and for our Apollo family. They practice this wherever they go.'

All of this leads to her greatest challenge: nurse retention.

Dr Reddy, Apollo and Captain Banerjee recognize that the retention and well-being of nurses is important. There are classes on yoga, nutrition, exercise, sports competitions, and group meals in the nurses' hostels. Not all expenses come from the nursing budget but are provided or supplemented by individuals. One important celebration is the International Nurses' Day in May. Apollo throws a large dinner and dance party for the nurses that also draws doctors and administrators. With a twinkle in her eyes, one young nurse, Sherin, said, 'On that day you won't recognize us. Instead of looking like nurses, we look like models.'

In the emergency department at Indraprastha Apollo, no one appreciates the role of nurses more than Dr Priyadarshini Singh. On any given day, the emergency room overflows with patients. Dr Priya – as everybody calls her – is the director of emergency and trauma services.

Apollo changed the way that emergencies are treated in Indian medical care by actually designating an Emergency department. Previously, even road accidents were just referred to as casualties.

'When Apollo launched this department, emergency medicine was new as a speciality. Patients would come in and be referred to a consultant specialist. It worked okay but did not serve patients in the best way, nor did it use our facilities efficiently. Dr Hariprasad really pushed for this to be recognized as a speciality and it has made all the difference,' Dr Priya told me.

Her reference was to Dr K. Hariprasad, the dynamic CEO of the central region of Apollo Hospitals with additional responsibility of tie-ups and referrals pertaining to all African countries. Trained as an anaesthetist, he has a passion for emergency medicine and was the first person outside of Europe to be given a fellowship by the College of Emergency Medicine in London. In addition, he was the first doctor in India to receive the fellowship of the International Federation of Emergency Medicine based in West Melbourne, Australia.

'It feels really good to see immediate results from the treatment that we offer,' Dr Priya says. 'There is a lot of action and the adrenaline kicks in but it is the results that give us the most satisfaction.'

'No matter what hospital Dr Reddy visits, he always makes morning rounds and includes the emergency room. He has a healing touch, a human touch. It's difficult to explain his gentle awareness but its effect is visible to the patients and their families,' Dr Priya told me.

'Dr Reddy gives one piece of universal advice, "If what you do cannot benefit the patient, do no harm." He never rushes in or out. He has a feeling for every patient, as though that patient is the only one needing care,' Dr Priya said.

'When I came to Apollo I was surprised at how different the atmosphere was in contrast to other hospitals, from the way patient administration is handled to the entire team of housekeeping and nutrition and medical care. We have an excellent triage unit and that has improved patient care for whether the patient has a heart attack or a casualty or a simple illness. Joining Apollo was a dream come true,' she added.

Like Dr Priya, Dr Mahesh Joshi is one of Apollo's rising stars. Dr Reddy has entrusted him with developing emergency medicine. He is a tall man who dresses in dark conservative suits; I'd expected to meet a much older man but Dr Joshi turned out to be barely forty. We were seated at the same table at lunch during the festivities marking the twenty-fifth anniversary of Apollo Hyderabad in August 2013.

It turned out that Dr Joshi headed Apollo's emergency medicine programme, in which Dr Reddy has a special interest. I asked Dr Joshi to define 'emergency medicine'.

'From a physician's perspective you can say that a condition which is life-threatening or has a potential to become life- or limb-threatening is an emergency – for example, road accidents, heart attacks, paralysis, poisoning. However, for a lay person – having severe pain, a fall, vomiting, giddiness, breathing difficulty can all be medical emergencies. For a young mother, a swollen lip of her child after a fall is the biggest emergency,' Dr Joshi said. 'Emergency medicine is therefore an opportunity for hospitals to provide direct access to the community for any kind of medical care.'

According to Dr Joshi, some health care providers in India were known to refuse medico-legal cases or to handle life-threatening emergencies. Dr Reddy recognized this deficiency. Being a cardiologist himself, he understood the importance of door-to-door times and door-to-needle times for thrombolytic therapy. He also understood the vital role that ambulances played in the chain of survival of critical cases, both from mortality and morbidity perspectives.

Dr Reddy spotted talent in the form of a young determined anaesthetist named Dr Hariprasad, who was instrumental in forming the Society of Emergency Medicine in India. The first step was creating a dedicated Accident and Emergency Hospital at Hyderguda in Hyderabad. Thereafter followed a series of pioneering work in this hitherto unknown speciality in India. The 'casualty department' was changed to 'emergency room' with passionate people to drive this key access to the hospital. It was bundled with change in infrastructure, evidence-based protocols and efficient processes. Relatively young physicians like Dr Mahesh Joshi were given a free hand by Dr Reddy to bring about the change in the departments.

Realizing that there was a big disconnect between hospitals and the community in terms of access, efficient transport, en route care and continuum of care, Dr Reddy put his bet on ramping up hospital-based emergency medical services (EMS). Ambulances were designed to deliver advanced life support care – they were termed 'Hospital on Wheels'. For the first time in the history of modern medicine in India, people were transported long distance by ground ambulances with trained paramedics and doctors. A nationwide initiative across all 1,066 locations of Apollo in India, a network of emergency services, was started by Dr Reddy in 2002. This was the basis for the modern-day EMS that India has witnessed. The first use of a helicopter for a medical evacuation in India also happened from Kurnool to Apollo Hyderabad in 1999.

Dr Joshi said: 'Community awareness about common emergencies was a prime focus. "Life Saver", a community-first responder training from Apollo has trained over 100,000 laypersons about common emergencies and their do's and don'ts. The emergency department changed the way medical teams responded to disasters; whether it was an earthquake in Gujarat or floods in Kurnool or bomb blasts in Hyderabad, Apollo Emergency was making its presence felt by its professionalism.'

Dr Joshi pointed out to me that Dr Reddy endorsed and supported various academic activities to promote emergency medicine in collaboration with the American Heart Association and started the first International Training Organization in India. On account of the lack of recognition from the Medical Council of India, there was no formal training programme for emergency medicine physicians in India. Dr Reddy joined hands with the College of General Practitioners and the College of Emergency Medicine, UK, and Stanford Emergency in the US, to create the first emergency medicine physician training programmes in India. He also hosted the first International Emergency Medicine Congress at Hyderabad in 2002. Dr Reddy also did advocacy at various forums about the need for this speciality in India. It took many more years for the Medical Council to take notice of this – and finally in 2009 emergency medicine was recognized as a speciality in its own right.

'It took more than a decade for others to even fathom the importance of this speciality, and now every single hospital in India wants to ramp up its Emergency department,' Dr Joshi said.

Dr Reddy's belief in emergency medicine continues to be as strong – his visit to any of the Apollo hospitals always begins with a round of the Emergency. On days when he has a busy schedule he winds up his day and walks through the Emergency wards before going back home.

I found out during our conversation that Dr Joshi was more than a physician. He was also a singer, and he anchored TV shows. I asked him how these activities were perceived by Dr Reddy.

'He has always been a leader who connects through his heart. He has witnessed some of my performances as a singer, performer or just an anchor for a show. He would always come back and say to me, "Mahesh you have been gifted with a unique power of communication – you must continue to influence people with this." He would mention this many a times in some important meetings too. It is not surprising that communication skills are essential to being an influential emergency physician – most universities incorporate this as a very important piece in leadership development in emergency medicine,' Dr Joshi said.

―――――

One day in late March 2013, Dr Reddy found himself in an unusual role – that of a patient at Apollo Delhi. He was sitting rather uncomfortably in his Delhi office. It is fair-sized, on the first floor of the Indraprastha Delhi Hospital. Both the corporate offices and the hospital are clean and modern. Dr Reddy has no desk in this office, preferring to sit in a low armchair or on one of two couches. A small, rectangular glass table with four cream-coloured rolling chairs serves as a conference table-cum-lunch table. The room is completed by

several pieces of contemporary art, flowers and Hindu deities. Just
beyond the large porthole window is a wall with the bright arrival
of spring announced in a bank of crepe myrtle trees. These trees,
which are popular in the American south, are native to the Indian
subcontinent, Southeast Asia and northern Australia, and have bright
purple or pink flowers.

Dr Reddy was going to have an MRI on this day in the hospital's
new G (Gravity)-Scan Stand-Up or Upright MRI unit. Most MRI
machines require the patient to lie down, with some being semi-open
and others closed, which creates anxiety in those tending towards
claustrophobia. The new machine is the first in India, and Dr Reddy
is particularly proud because it provides diagnostic images of patients
in a variety of positions – sitting, standing, lying down, bending or
at an angle. It's the latest of technological advances, giving a clearer
picture of how the spine and joints actually look during normal
weight-bearing positions.

Because he had constant pain, especially when seated, Dr Reddy
was going to have a scan of both knees and his back. (Some months
later, he would have surgery done on his back.)

Dr Reddy recalled that in 2001 Apollo was the first hospital in
India to introduce a centralized system and an easy-to-remember
phone number for emergency ambulance services. Apollo Hospitals
uses the phone number 1066 and provides specifically trained nurses
for the ambulance, much like EMTs (Emergency Medical Technicians)
abroad.

While India does have common phone numbers for emergencies
(100 for police and 101 for fire), it does not have a unified system
for medical emergencies. Recognizing this, Indraprastha Apollo in
Delhi introduced the number 1066 for ambulance services. These
ambulances primarily serve areas close to Apollo and are busy every
day. As part of the emergency unit, Apollo is relaunching its air
ambulance service. The air ambulances use mostly airplanes, though
there is some helicopter use as well. Like many other areas India was
slow to embrace air ambulances.

Dr Reddy reached for the phone and dialled the 1066 number,

and gave the phone to my research associate, Twilla Duncan. It rang and rang and there was no answer. When she told him, he couldn't believe it and took the phone.

When the call was finally answered he said, 'Dr Reddy here,' listened for a moment and said, 'Chairman.' It was easy to tell that the person on the other end of the line was now paying closer attention. Dr Reddy asked when the person came on duty, how many calls had been received, did Apollo send an ambulance, what was the status of the patients. He said, 'This phone must be answered very, very quickly. Lives are at stake and you are the connection. Our mission is to provide the best health care. They are calling Apollo and we must give the best service. You are doing good work but you must always keep in mind that the patient requires care and response.'

After Apollo's innovation, the government brought up a number for ambulances – 108, currently it is operational in seventeen states across the country.

All of these developments were far in the future when Dr Reddy first met Dr Syed and Gulzar Rahman at customs clearing in Madras in 1970. They were just moving back to Madras from Chicago.

Dr Rahman had graduated from Madras Medical College, and then worked at Government General Hospital. He and some friends decided to go for further training in the United States, and he received a residency and fellowship in cardiology at Mount Sinai Hospital and Medical Centre in New York. Three years seemed long enough in America, and their homeland called. 'I wanted to come back and serve my country,' Dr Rahman said.

'The minute we met the Reddys, they invited us over for dinner,' Mrs Rahman said. 'It was wonderful and a lifelong friendship was made. They are such a wonderful family. We were friends with Prathap and Sucha right away. You don't have to know a person for years and years to know what kind of people they are,' she said.

Dr Rahman had rejoined Government General Hospital but soon became dissatisfied with the state of affairs there. 'After seeing how things were organized in the US, it was discouraging to see that the government hospitals were not entertaining new ideas,' he said. 'The ordinary Indian people were on the outside looking in.'

'There were no adequate supplies, and the equipment was not up to date. The hospital bosses would keep certain supplies for the rich and powerful. If they didn't have adequate medicine, the hospital would borrow to serve the privileged. This kind of activity is very different from Apollo where from day one, all patients have been treated equally, rich and poor alike. This is why people trust Apollo,' Dr Rahman said.

The working conditions deteriorated at the Government General Hospital and Dr and Mrs Rahman decided to go back to Chicago. The Reddy family and the Rahmans stayed in touch. When Dr Reddy decided to open Apollo, Syed and Gulzar Rahman became two of the first investors. They organized fundraising dinners for Dr Reddy in Chicago whenever he visited to entice investors.

Mrs Rahman said, 'Apollo laid the foundation for what modern health care is in India today. It was one family's dream and they all worked very hard, especially Prathap. The Reddy girls have always been involved and each one is equally smart. Prathap proved everybody wrong and now India has modern equipment and procedures.'

Today, the Reddy–Rahman friendship is stronger than ever. When my colleague Twilla Duncan met them, they were in an outer office with Sucharitha Reddy at the Apollo corporate headquarters, visiting after they heard that Dr Reddy had broken his arm. When Dr Reddy learnt that they were present he immediately went outside saying, 'What strangers are these?' Each one was happy to see the others, they all hugged and laughed, and then, of course, they had lunch.

Dr Rahman says, 'He is still the down-to-earth person he always was. Both of them are very loving. They remember each and every person's name, the patients and the employees. Definitely he has charisma and magnetism, but primarily he has a commitment to India. Compared to what Apollo has done, the government has not made any progress, though it has the money, but corruption is a problem in the country – and a lack of will. With Prathap, he used the money to change people's lives. It is like night and day. He genuinely cares about the people. He believes that good health care will make us all as powerful as tigers and India will be much better off for it.'

CHAPTER TWENTY-SIX

Men of Hearts

PRATHAP CHANDRA REDDY IS a man of the heart, and he listens to his. It was not just because he was a cardiologist by training that Dr Reddy visualized Apollo Hospitals as a leading medical institution offering world-class care with a special focus on cardiac care. It was also because cardiac diseases had already become a big cause of concern for India and was growing. Dr Prathap Chandra Reddy must be a 'Renaissance man' by necessity – a doctor who keeps up with the dozens of disciplines in medicine, not to mention fields such as management, human resources and finance. But he's a cardiologist by training, and so it stands to reason that he would take a special interest in the work of Apollo's heart specialists.

This is not the least because Apollo Hospitals has performed among the highest number of heart operations – more than 150,000 since its inception; of these nearly one-third have been done at Apollo Hospitals, Chennai, with results comparable to international standards.[1] Apollo's stellar record includes bypass surgery, complicated coronary artery bypass surgery, and surgery for all types of valvular heart disease and child heart surgery, with success

---

1   In the United States, more than 500,000 heart bypass surgeries are performed each year, according to WebMD.com, the authoritative website.

rates comparable to, or even surpassing, international standards.[2]

In 1977, Dr Reddy went to a meeting of the American Medical Association in Anaheim, California. He presented a paper on eight patients in their thirties with heart disease and the importance of education and changing the pattern in India with factors such as blood pressure. In a conversation with one man who said it would be impossible because Indians didn't know when their birthday was, Dr Reddy responded, 'They not only know their birth date, they also know the star (derived from the celestial configuration at the time of birth) under which they were born.'

'Our initiative "Billion Hearts Beating" has been highly successful. We ask people to take a pledge to stay heart-healthy by just following these five steps – eat right, exercise, put away the death stick (cigarettes), get regular health check-ups done, and practice meditation and yoga,' Dr Reddy said. 'It's important that people realize they need to do a few things themselves for the sake of their own health. You must have your own mission of physical well-being. You can't leave it to others to chart out your life. The popularity of this campaign can be gauged by the fact that over 3,000 cadets signed the pledge when we did this campaign in an NCC camp.'

'Education does work,' Dr Reddy told me. 'Look at what Lieutenant General P.S. Bhalla has done as director general of the National Cadet Corps. Every six months he gives the "Billion Hearts Beating Oath" to 10,000 cadets. By the summer of 2013, 40,000 cadets had taken the oath. Each one is an ambassador for better health. The cadets take pride in themselves, then they tell their parents and also tell their communities. This is the way to spread health awareness.'[3]

---

2 Apollo Chennai performs 5,500 angiograms, 1,200 angioplasties and 1,800 heart surgeries annually.

3 I attended one of General Bhalla's NCC events outside New Delhi in late 2012, and was impressed by the fact that thousands of cadets from all over the country had gathered. They heard Dr Reddy speak, and then took an oath committing themselves to spreading awareness of good health care, particularly the prevention of heart disease.

Dr Reddy's efforts in promoting the concept of wellness has been well appreciated in various forums. The latest is the invitation as the Guest of Honour at the International Conference on Global Health Futures organized by the London College of Medicine and Soukya Foundation in Bangalore in November 2013. HRH Prince Charles and Nobel laureate Archbishop Desmond Tutu are among the galaxy of participants in the conference.

Dr Reddy recalls the 1981 American cardiology meet, when the fact that three doctors who had collapsed in the Duty Room were all Indians led to a major discussion on how as a group, Asian Indians have one of the highest rates of heart disease in the world, four times higher than that of Caucasians. Many Indians have very high levels of the blood fat triglyceride and low levels of HDL (the good cholesterol), as well as a high incidence of diabetes.[4] As in the United States, heart disease has become the biggest cause of deaths in India. Regarding acute heart attacks – not chronic heart disease – that are a major cause of death in urban India, Dr Reddy says it is mainly killing young people in their productive years. A large percentage of these heart attacks are attributed to smoking. Little wonder that Dr Reddy – who was a smoker in his youth and well into middle age before he quit – calls cigarettes 'killer sticks'.

Back in 2005, a team of scholars from Harvard Business School studied the Apollo system, focusing on its heart unit, among other departments. The Harvard team wrote in its report: 'Apollo's record was impressive indeed . . . Apollo hospitals had come to rival the best health care institutions on the globe.'

The Harvard team found that until Dr Reddy pioneered the concept of Apollo as a corporate sector hospital, India's health care sector was dominated by a hodge-podge of government-run institutions and by medical facilities operated by trusts and charities, the latter finding tax advantages in such operations.

---

4   A seminal study by University of Maryland Medical Centre presented in 1999 provided evidence that a genetic abnormality could explain the difference.

One man familiar with the Harvard Business School study is Dr Rana Mehta, who holds a master's degree in hospital administration, and headed Apollo's first overseas venture in Sri Lanka. A physician himself, he was head of operations at Indraprastha Apollo Hospital in New Delhi for a decade, and now heads the India health care section of PriceWaterhouseCoopers.[5]

'There was no accountability with service in most hospitals at the time, and very little innovation,' Dr Mehta said to me. Like education, health care was designated as part of India's social sector since Independence. Indeed, the Nehru government had even talked about establishing a system along the lines of Britain's National Health Service. Primary, secondary and tertiary health care was expected to be provided by the federal and state governments, but it was soon discovered that these entities lacked the necessary resources. Hospitals weren't built as one-stop institutions.

'Dr Reddy was obsessed with ensuring that high quality health care was made available at affordable rates,' Dr Mehta said. 'He brought in a consumer focus. He wanted his doctors and staff to listen to patients – and he himself would talk to patients and their relatives who seemed agitated. That "human touch" offered a lot of reassurance to those who came to Apollo.'

Patients now were given the option of getting a second opinion about critical matters such as surgery. No detail was too minute for Dr Reddy: he even contacted a private-sector company, ITC – which, among other things, runs successful hotels – seeking advice about how food should be arranged on trays so that patients could eat their meals more easily. Dr Reddy continually benchmarked Apollo's performance with those of the world's leading medical institutions such as Johns Hopkins, Mayo Clinic, Cleveland Clinic, Massachusetts General Hospital, and Dr Denton A. Cooley's Texas Heart Institute at the University of Texas in Houston.[6] It is no coincidence that

---

5   Dr Rana Mehta was also CEO of Apollo Colombo.
6   Dr Denton A. Cooley asked his head nurse Shanon Bryson to set up nursing facilities for Apollo. Bryson was a post-operative nurse and in her two stints

these institutions had developed sterling reputations for cardiac care. Dr Reddy was determined that Apollo would match their record – and even surpass it, as it eventually happened.

Dr Mehta was dispatched to the Mayo Clinic in 2001 to study and bring back some of the institution's best health care practices. Dr Anupam Sibal, Apollo's Group Medical Director, told me that by incorporating some of these 'best practices' Apollo Indraprastha received accreditation from the Joint Commission International in 2005 – the first time that JCI gave such an accreditation to a hospital in India.

Dr Mehta told me that Dr Reddy introduced the concept of the checklist to the Apollo system.[7] Dr Mehta said: 'He referred to it as the "bible" for pre-operative, operative and post-operative care. Dr Reddy would say, "Doing repetitively well can be good but it cannot be great; only the checklist can make it great to ensure that no step is missed across the three stages of health care, improving our success rate by another 0.1 per cent."'

Dr Reddy told me that from the anaesthetist to the surgeon to the nurse, the checklist is always followed over the course of treatment at Apollo. 'Apollo has, over the last seven years, benchmarked itself with the best in the world, based on about twenty-five parameters,' he said.[8] Dr Reddy says that Apollo is among the top five hospitals in the world – but owing to its multispeciality orientation, 'it is also unique'.

---

with Dr Reddy in India, she imparted unparalleled post-operative care. The nursing director at Apollo confided to Dr Reddy: 'What my girls do in a year, her girls do at the end of ten years.' It was the result of continuous improvement.

7   The concept of the 'checklist' is generally credited to Dr Atul Gawande of Boston, who also writes on public policy and health care for the *New Yorker*.

8   He was referring to the ACE@25 programme, or Apollo Clinical Excellence, which is dealt with in an earlier chapter.

Among the world-class doctors whom I met at Apollo, names of several heart specialists came up. But invariably the cognoscenti would ask if I'd met Dr M.R. Girinath, Dr Immaneni Sathyamurthy and Dr Matthew Samuel Kalarickal. They certainly qualify to be placed in Dr Reddy's category of 'tigers'. In fact, I would argue that these three men have reached levels of accomplishment so extraordinary that they are beyond classification. In my view, perhaps the only appropriate category in which they belong is the one that Dr Reddy also belongs to: 'men of humility'.

Dr Girinath and Dr Satyamurthy have such demanding schedules that it is difficult for a writer to get to see them. And yet each man made a special effort to give me plenty of time, answering my pesky questions with patience and with a fair degree of elaboration. They were also extremely gracious, which I found touching.

Dr Girinath is a handsome man, and looks every bit as distinguished as the top surgeon that he is. He is the chief cardiothoracic surgeon at Apollo. His office is very tidy, as befitting a surgeon renowned for his meticulous methods in the operating theatre.

His achievements are staggering: He did the first heart transplant as part of the first multi-organ transplant in India. He has been at the forefront of establishing coronary bypass surgery as a standardized and safe procedure in India; he and his team have performed more than 35,000 coronary bypass operations of which 16,000 have been done using the 'beating heart technique', one of the largest series in the world. He has trained more than thirty surgeons who, together, perform 20 per cent of all cardiac surgeries done in the country today. Dr Girinath along with Dr Mathew Samuel Kalarickal was the first to use a heart-lung machine to support coronary angioplasty. Dr Girinath is the recipient of many national awards including the Padma Bhushan.

Dr Girinath considers Sir Brian Gerald Barrett-Boyes of New Zealand, who pioneered the development of the cardiopulmonary bypass, as one of his heroes in medicine. Dr Girinath, in fact, had wanted to go to New Zealand to train under Sir Brian, and when he went there he was startled to find that whereas at AIIMS four to five heart operations were done during the course of a month, Sir Brian's team performed at least that number on any given day in Auckland.

In 1983 Dr Reddy persuaded him to join Apollo Madras. Dr Girinath seemed a bit reluctant at first, something that Dr Reddy sensed at once. 'Why don't you want to join me?' he asked.

'I have certain reservations about the private sector,' Dr Girinath said, noting that 25 per cent of the work he did at his previous employer, Indian Railways, [9] was for poor people not associated with the behemoth.

Then Dr Girinath added: 'Cardiac surgery is not a one-man job – it needs a team.'

'Bring your team over,' Dr Reddy said.

That was just a few months before Apollo Madras opened in September 1983. In February 1984, Dr Girinath brought across five members of his cardiac team from Indian Railways. The day after they arrived at the hospital on Greams Road, Dr Girinath and his team performed their first cardiac surgery. It was done in the gynaecological theatre.

Apollo decided that patients would be charged the equivalent of $3,000 per surgery. That figure, in rupees, stayed constant for nearly thirty years and now of course is even lower in comparison as the rupee continues to plummet against the dollar. Considering the inflation over the last three decades, this surgery should cost around $50,000. Apollo has been able to keep the cost down by improved operations, innovations, better but fewer antibiotics and other medicine. This has resulted in better outcomes and lower morbidity, in patients recovering faster and going home earlier. 'The patient is happy and we are happy. The charges are less and the patient goes home faster,' Dr Reddy said.

'We have tried to always keep our social obligations in mind,' Dr Girinath said, adding that he talked to a Reddy friend, an

---

9   India's Railway Health Services operates 125 hospitals, with nearly 14,000 beds, across the country.

industrialist named V.L. Dutt, about setting up a foundation to assist poor patients.

He has observed with keen interest the evolution of Dr Prathap Chandra Reddy from 'an astute doctor to an astute businessman'.

'I've watched him develop from a struggling businessman to a corporate giant,' Dr Girinath said. 'It is a story to be studied by anyone who wants to know how knowledge, will-power, determination, foresight and intuition can be put to work in the pursuit of an ideal.'

In the early years of Apollo's existence, Dr Girinath and his team performed about 600 surgeries annually in two theatres. Now the figure has risen to 4,000 across the various Apollo hospitals. Paediatric heart surgeries on children are performed at Apollo Children's Hospital. Dr Girinath has trained more than two-thirds of the cardiac surgeons in Gujarat.

'Dr Reddy has been very supportive,' Dr Girinath told me. 'Whatever we asked for, he gave.'

For example, in 1984 Dr Girinath requested a new ventilator at a time when Apollo was just beginning to be financially viable.

'And how much more work would that machine enable you to do?' Dr Reddy asked.

Dr Girinath said, 'Fifteen per cent.'

He got the ventilator.

I asked Dr Girinath whether it took a special temperament in order to be a cardiac surgeon. Other than holding someone's living brain in one's hand, I couldn't imagine that there'd be anything more fraught than holding a living heart.

Dr Girinath smiled. 'What does it take? Cardiac surgery is no different from any other surgery,' he said matter-of-factly. 'That's why I don't spare myself. It takes adequate knowledge, the right skills and a firm commitment to making people well. I really believe that many surgeons abroad don't have the kind of commitment to patients that we do in India. Perhaps that's why we are getting more and more patients who are coming to us from overseas. I personally also believe that it takes a commitment and responsibility to train surgeons. By training scores of surgeons we have put a multiplier effect in operation as these surgeons go out and set up their own units and the number of cardiac operations in the country is thus rapidly increasing.'

But therein lies a problem. As more and more private-sector hospitals spring up in India, their owners have been raiding Apollo.

Does he worry about Apollo's future in the face of such competition?

'Doctors are temperamental – and hospitals are difficult to run,' Dr Girinath said. 'Apollo is in very good hands. But as with all large institutions, you cannot do much more than make an informed prediction. What I can say is that the values that Dr Reddy and his family have injected into Apollo are bound to endure.'

The question really is: Will the vision outlive the visionary?

That question is certainly on the minds of many major physicians at Apollo, but they will seldom, if ever, articulate it for the record. But there are also doctors like Dr Girinath who steadfastly believe that Apollo has grown strong as an institution and that its management will not necessarily be predicated on the hands-on presence of Dr Reddy. They – and outside directors of Apollo's board – say that the Reddy daughters have been remarkably steadfast in adhering to Dr Reddy's vision. And, indeed, the market has given its verdict on Apollo's management: On 17 May 2013, for instance, Apollo's share price rose to a record Rs 1,066, creating a market cap of Rs 14,830 crore, or $2.7 billion.[10] The rise reflected the market's growing confidence in Apollo after the Morgan Stanley Capital Index – which is closely followed by global fund managers – said it that would include the company after 31 May 2013. S.K. Venkataraman, Apollo's chief strategy officer, explained that such inclusion is an indication of a company's growth potential. The market – and those experts who follow it – clearly has faith

---

10 The face value of a share when the first Apollo issue was undertaken in 1983 was Rs 10. The stock split on 10 September 2010, when the face value was Rs 5 on account of the split.

in Apollo's future leadership under Preetha Reddy and her sisters.

Another nationally known physician echoes this view. Prof. K. Srinath Reddy, president of the influential New Delhi-based Public Health Foundation of India, told me: 'Dr Prathap Reddy combines an expansive vision for advanced health care in India with an entrepreneurial ability to execute it to perfection. He is now recognized as a global leader in health care and has inspired the growth of many other institutions modelled after the one created by him.'

The question of Reddy family values came up again some weeks later when I met with Dr Immaneni Sathyamurthy, director and senior interventional cardiologist at Apollo Chennai. Unlike Dr Girinath's sparsely furnished office, Dr Sathyamurthy's wall displayed a mounted picture of him receiving the coveted Padma Shri award from President K.R. Narayanan. There was also a poster with the words, 'The sky is the limit'.

Dr Sathyamurthy turned out to be a tall man with a slight stoop and a professorial look; indeed he once was an academician at Christian Medical College in Vellore. He exuded immense charm and likeability. I asked him about his association with Apollo.

'Its reputation and brand keeps doctors like me at Apollo,' Dr Sathyamurthy said. 'But even more importantly, it's my attachment to the family, my loyalty to Dr Reddy. We've been to each other's homes; we've all attended family events such as weddings and pujas together. It's not just a professional relationship – it's much more a bond. It cannot be broken.'

It's this bond that, perhaps more than anything else, keeps a physician like Dr Satyamurthy at Apollo. In light of his long record of medical accomplishments, almost any major medical institution in the world would be delighted to get him on board – and surely for fees far exceeding what he might get in Chennai.

'Nobody was sure how Apollo would shape up,' Dr Sathyamurthy said. 'The concept of a corporate hospital was so new that one heard more criticism than support, especially in the media.'

He then received a call from Dr Reddy, who'd heard of Dr Sathyamurthy through Dr Girinath. They met for about twenty minutes in mid-1984.

'After talking to him, my scepticism about corporate hospitals turned to enthusiasm,' Dr Sathyamurthy said. 'He told me that he would always be accessible.'

Dr Sathyamurthy joined Apollo Madras in November 1984, shortly after the assassination of Prime Minister Indira Gandhi on 31 October. Earlier in the same month, Mrs Gandhi had visited Apollo Madras to see a famous patient, Chief Minister M.G. Ramachandran. He had suffered a stroke earlier in October. The prime minister had promised to supply an aircraft should doctors decide that he needed to be taken abroad for treatment.

When Indira Gandhi came to visit MGR she asked Dr Reddy whether she would be able to talk with him. He said yes but that the prime minister should move to the patient's left side as the stroke had affected the entire right side. While she was there, MGR was able to respond about 90 per cent of the time.

MGR had been initially against Apollo Hospital, and had stopped construction for eighteen months.

At that time, P.V. Narasimha Rao asked Dr Reddy, 'What can we do for this unique hospital?'

Dr Reddy responded: 'Why is nobody asking what they can do to bring better health care? That is the question that all must ask.'

He said: 'Later, when MGR was still sick we had a good relationship. He didn't want to go to a hospital but said that he would if Dr Reddy was there.

'When I saw him he was absolutely blue from heart failure. His lungs were full of fluid and he was in renal failure. When he saw the room he said, "Do you do this for everyone? You have created an ICU right in this room. This is why everyone loves Apollo. The care that you give is what everybody at Apollo gives and the patients get. That is why Apollo has got into everybody's hearts, because of this care.'

Mrs Gandhi's offer of an aircraft for MGR was accepted by the Tamil Nadu government. A team of American doctors flew in to supervise MGR's transfer from Apollo. But then, Dr Eli Friedman, the leader of the American medical team, decided that MGR was not fit for travel and would have to be kept under observation.

Dr Reddy told me how furious Dr M.K. Mani – Apollo's renowned nephrologist – had been about the importing of the American team; indeed, Dr Mani said as much when Prime Minister Indira Gandhi came to see MGR. Dr Mani said it was a shame on the country that outside doctors were brought in to treat MGR. He was shocked that no one had talked to him and his team about it.

As she left the ICU unit, Indira Gandhi asked Dr Reddy to ride down with her in a separate elevator.

'Is it true that Apollo's doctors could have handled MGR's case by themselves?' Mrs Gandhi said to Dr Reddy.

'Yes, Madam Prime Minister,' Dr Reddy said. 'Dr Mani was right. We have the expertise right here at Apollo. There was no need to get doctors from abroad.'

Indira Gandhi said to Dr Reddy, 'I have been bragging all along about the reversal of brain drain. I've always supported you. Isn't that right?'

Dr Reddy said that MGR's need for a neurologist was urgent but he also had severe damage in his heart and kidneys and the initial problem would be to get him past those issues.

'However, we did need a top-notch person for him and I contacted Fred Plum, the famous neurologist from New York Hospital, to come to India. I knew of him through Dr Denton Cooley. Since MGR was too fragile to move, we brought the doctor to him. I asked Fred if he could immediately come to India. He wanted to know if he had time to go home and I said, "No. Please just go to the airport. Your plane is waiting for you." He immediately left with only a small suitcase,' Dr Reddy recalled.

On 19 October came anxious moments as MGR lapsed into low levels of consciousness because of a tennis ball-sized swelling in the brain. The Tamil Nadu government had summoned Dr Tetsuo

Kanno, a neurosurgeon from Fujita Health University in Japan. He and his assistant Dr Kazuhito Nakamura were booked to fly on Singapore Airlines to Singapore, then connect with an Air India flight to Bombay, and then fly to Madras. The Tamil Nadu government decided to have the aircraft land at Madras en route rather than going to Mumbai. The commander then paged the two doctors through the public address system in the aircraft but no one responded; after forty-five minutes of searching for them, it was discovered that the two Japanese doctors were not on board.

They weren't on board because they had missed the connection in Singapore. The Singapore Airlines flight from Tokyo to Singapore had been late by nearly three hours, by which time the connecting Air India flight had left. There was no direct flight to Madras from Singapore for the next twenty hours.

The Tamil Nadu officials then decided to charter a Boeing 747 plane from Singapore Airlines; the cost was Rs 10 lakh. So Dr Kanno and Dr Nakamura flew to Madras; they were the only passengers, and a crew of six looked after them. They arrived in Madras in about four hours and were driven directly to Apollo Madras.

The decision to ask the Japanese physicians to come across to India was intriguing to Apollo's own highly skilled neurosurgeons. Dr K. Ganapathy, a top neurosurgeon, and Dr Gajaraj, chief of radiology, felt that Apollo was quite capable of handling MGR's case. Indeed, it was a CAT scan performed by Dr Gajaraj that showed that the chief minister had suffered a massive brain haemorrhage. The team of Dr Kanno and Dr Nakamura were categorical in their appreciation of the Apollo team, saying that, 'We could not have done anything more than what they did. The handling over the first seventy-two hours has ensured this man has a chance to recover.'

MGR recovered enough to be flown to New York for further treatment. Sangita, Dr Reddy's youngest daughter, visited him at Downtown Medical Centre in Brooklyn and met MGR's family members. MGR returned to Madras, won the next elections and governed the state for some more time. He would eventually die on 24 December 1987.

For Dr Reddy and Apollo Hospitals, the episode of Apollo Madras receiving MGR as a patient was literally baptism by fire. It was a time of great uncertainty, with no surety whether the hospital would be able to sustain itself. Its occupancy fell from over 100 to under thirty. That wasn't easy for a young institution, with political pressures from everywhere, and different opinions and ringside powerplay. But it was also a time when the hospital got almost daily publicity on account of the presence of MGR. All sorts of rumours were being published in local newspapers, and large crowds gathered near Apollo Hospital. Through it all, Dr Reddy kept his cool, attended to all and, most importantly, evolved.

'That will remain the guiding value for Apollo. Dad told the clinical team, "Just do what's good for the patient and I will ensure everything is OK. Remember to leave no stone unturned. Try everything possible." This remains the value tenet that will always be followed in Apollo. In complex medical decision-making Apollo will always put the patient first,' Sangita Reddy told me.

In recalling the MGR episode, Dr Sathyamurthy said that sometimes fate plays a role in an institution's development – just as it does in the lives of individuals. For example, K.R. Narayanan – who later became India's first Dalit President – visited Christian Medical College in Vellore because his wife needed a check-up. That's when he met Dr Sathyamurthy by chance, who suggested a cardiac examination at Apollo Madras. Just as well, because two vessels in Narayanan's heart were critically blocked. Dr Girinath operated on Narayanan, who lived for another eleven years.

Dr Sathyamurthy believes that the incidence of heart disease in India is on the rise not only because South Asians are genetically and ethnically prone to cardiac problems. 'We seldom exercise, and our children are taught just to study, study and study,' he said. 'Dr Reddy correctly says that India should receive gold medals in three categories: heart disease, diabetes and cancer. In developing countries, 40 per cent of the population either has diabetes or is diabetes prone. And the majority of these populations will develop heart disease. The average age of people in the West who develop heart trouble is sixty-five; in India, it's forty-five. Dr Reddy is absolutely on the right track in sensitizing people about early health check-ups.'

———

Among the most famous patients that Apollo dealt with was Murasoli Maran, then India's minister for commerce and industry, and a nephew of DMK chief and former chief minister of Tamil Nadu M. Karunanidhi; he was admitted in November 2002 with hypertrophic obstructive cardiomyopathy (HOCM). This happens when the heart muscle becomes thick, making it hard for it to pump blood. Maran had congestive heart failure, and his lungs were filled with fluid. In spite of intensive medical therapy, his condition started progressively deteriorating. He was treated by a team of doctors that included Dr M.R. Girinath, Dr K. Subramanian, Dr P. Ramachandran and Dr Sathyamurthy along with Dr Thanikachalam, a senior cardiologist of Sri Ramachandra Medical College and Research Institute in Chennai, who had been attending to him prior to his being admitted to Apollo.

The doctors explained to me that there are several ways to treat HOCM depending on the severity, including medication, open-heart surgery or alcohol septal ablation, which requires alcohol to be injected into an artery and going in to the heart. This is less invasive and usually has a faster recovery time.

Maran became critically ill and was in the ICU. It was at that point that Dr Ramachandran, Senior Interventional Cardiologist at Apollo Chennai, along with Dr Subramanian, did alcohol septal ablation which improved his condition significantly. Meanwhile the Apollo team researched the best doctors for HOCM and settled on Dr Horst J. Kuhn from Nuremberg, Germany. Dr Kuhn flew to Chennai. He did the ablation procedure for the second time for Maran. After these two procedures, Maran significantly improved and became free of symptoms.

A few days later, Maran was discharged. As he was going out of the hospital, he profusely praised the medical care at Apollo to the media who had gathered outside the hospital, a sentiment which was also shared by his wife.

He resumed his official duties soon and began travelling outside India. He went back to Delhi and functioned as a minister. Around this time, he was noted to have a leaking mitral valve impairing the heart function. He decided to have the surgery at AIIMS. Within a month of the operation he developed a severe fungal infection on the prosthetic heart valve, a complication dreaded by every heart surgeon. He was readmitted at Apollo Chennai. This time he had multi-organ failure. He was very ill with life-threatening fungal endocarditis, and the prosthetic valve had to be replaced. Opinions were taken from various centres and a repeat surgery was performed. However the fungal infection could not be controlled. At this point, the doctors at Apollo thought it best to refer Maran to Methodist Hospital in Houston, Texas. Here also the doctors encountered extensive fungal infection and continued antifungal measures. A few weeks later Maran returned to Apollo Chennai to continue the intensive therapy. He started becoming symptomatic with breathlessness. He gradually became worse with multi-organ involvement and finally succumbed to the sepsis.

Years later, Dr Girinath told me: 'Maran is an emotive issue, where we tried our best to salvage a very hopeless situation. But the inevitable had to happen. And it happened.'

'There is another episode that you might like to mention,' he continued. 'Late in 1984 Chairman Reddy's niece Aparajitha (his brother's daughter) needed a double valve replacement and he asked me to do it. Her sisters were living in the US and wanted her to go to the US for surgery. Dr Reddy however called me and said, "I want you to do this operation. I know Apollo and you can do it." Clearly, he did not have different standards for his own family and for other patients. I was greatly touched by the confidence and support that he gave us. She went on to live for twenty-seven years after the operation.'

———

Lieutenant General Mandeep Singh shares Dr Sathyamurthy's viewpoint about the importance of preventive health check-ups. It's not common for a Director General, Hospital Services of the Indian armed forces to join a private corporate hospital, but that's just what General Singh decided to do after a distinguished career serving India.

Several hospitals had approached General Singh; he only knew Dr Reddy incidentally from various medical conferences. 'Even if they don't know him personally, everyone in medicine knows of Dr Reddy,' General Singh said. He knew doctors at Apollo who had also been in the armed forces and one suggested that he meet Dr Reddy.

Like others, General Singh was surprised during the interview when Dr Reddy said, 'Where would you like to serve? We have positions in Hyderabad and Chennai.' There was no talk of money. After talking with his wife, General Singh accepted the position of director of medical services in Hyderabad, and is working closely with Sangita Reddy and Dr K. Hariprasad, CEO of Apollo Hyderabad, to extend Apollo's quality care and services. He says, 'Dr Reddy can discern where a person can make their best contribution.'

One thing that General Singh did know was that there was no inequity in the treatment at Apollo. Even for patients in a general ward, the standard of care is the same as for those who are in private suites. 'This has always been said of Apollo, that Dr Reddy does not tolerate discrimination in treatment. I have found that to be true,' General Singh says.

Good medical care is still manpower-intensive. Apollo is implementing initiatives to keep documentation at the highest level and there is always huge learning going on at the hospital. According to General Singh, 'It's a huge, vibrant experience.'

Such remarks please Dr K. Hariprasad, CEO of Apollo Hyderabad, and of Apollo's central region. His own family runs a 100-bed nursing home in Hyderabad where he was working. In 1996 Dr Reddy called him and said, 'If you continue to work in the nursing home for the rest of your career, you will be touching the lives of a limited number of people. Come join Apollo and set up emergency medical services and you will be touching the lives of millions of people.'

In those days emergency medical services were non-existent in India and Dr Reddy's vision was to bridge this gap in Indian health care with an appropriate solution.

'Chairman's passion to identify gaps in the Indian health care system and bridge these gaps is phenomenal,' Dr Hariprasad told me. 'He does not believe in relaxation or rest. The moment a task is accomplished he is ready with a new task because he believes that there is so much more to be done in health care. His energy levels are unparalleled and difficult to match for people decades younger than him.'

One incident that stands out in Dr Hariprasad's mind took place in Tanzania on 27 May 2011.

'We were in Dar-es-Salaam, where Chairman Reddy was to sign a "joint venture agreement" for a hospital in the presence of President Jakaya Kikwete of Tanzania and Prime Minister Manmohan Singh. Dr Singh introduced Chairman Reddy as the man who changed health care in India and expressed confidence that Tanzania would soon become a destination for global health care, now that Dr Reddy was here. The President of Tanzania followed up saying that the people of Tanzania were fortunate to have Apollo, and requested Chairman Reddy to start five more clinics in different parts of Tanzania in addition to the main hospital.

'It was hot, and with all the security and hustle and bustle of a high-profile event like this we were drained out by the time the event was over. We came back to the hotel. We were extremely happy that the event had gone well and were getting ready to relax. But Chairman had other ideas. He wanted us to negotiate with the Tanzanian authorities and formalize the agreement for the five additional clinics as requested by the President of Tanzania. He wanted it done by the evening – under normal circumstances this would have taken a couple of months. And since he instructed us to do it with so much confidence in our ability, we found a way to get it done.'

Dr Hariprasad told me that Dr Reddy always addresses Apollo Hospitals, Hyderabad with the three 'Bs': 'the big, the beautiful and the best'.

'True to his vision, Apollo Hospital Hyderabad has evolved into the first operational health city in the world,' he said.

The Hyderabad campus has been the innovation factory for health care in the country. A number of innovative products like Telemedicine, Medmantra ('tomorrow's health care management software'), m-health (effectively utilizing the exponentially growing mobile phone penetration in India), the application of Six-Sigma to the health care delivery process, Prism (an online patient health record), Sugar Clinics and Apollo Reach Hospitals are among numerous groundbreaking solutions that were conceptualized at this campus. The first fleet of Apollo's ambulances was launched in Hyderabad by film star K. Chiranjeevi (now the Union minister of state for tourism) way back in 1994. This network of ambulances was controlled from a call centre and wireless sets were used for communication across the network; it paved the path for pre-hospital emergency services in India. Apollo Hospitals, Hyderabad was also the first hospital in the world to receive disease-specific certification for management of acute stroke by the Joint Commission International.

Apollo Health City has also been instrumental in developing and nurturing public–private partnerships. A partnership with NMDC Hospital in Bacheli was the first such initiative which was proposed and nurtured by Dr Yogi Mehrotra, the then director of medical services. 'Dr Mehrotra's contribution to the Hyderabad facility has been tremendous, particularly in creating systems and processes to manage the complex health care environment,' Dr Hariprasad said.

Apollo DRDO Hospital, a partnership with the Defence Research and Development Organization, is another example of a successful public–private partnership. This hospital in Hyderabad was conceptualized by A.P.J. Abdul Kalam, former President of India, and is being operated by Apollo Hospitals. Aarogyabhadrata (a self-funded scheme for police personnel in Andhra Pradesh) and Yesheswani (a self-funded scheme for people below the poverty line in Karnataka) are other examples of innovative health care models that benefited from the think tank at Apollo Health City, Hyderabad.

'Medicine is not a static field,' Dr Reddy told me. 'The needs of patients across the spectrum change. As providers of health care, we need to constantly innovate. People say that I bubble with ideas. Perhaps that's because I constantly think of what more we should be doing in health care. The possibilities are infinite. And while we need to get things done methodically, we also need to get them done in a hurry. Medicine is not a business with a leisurely pace.'

That is one reason Dr Reddy is strenuously pushing to get the Union government to designate health care as an 'infrastructure' sector. Dr Kamalaksha U. Mada, former chairman of IDBI – who once taught me economics at Jai Hind College in Bombay – explained to me why Dr Reddy has a strong case for infrastructure.

'When an industry or economic sector is designated as being in the infrastructure category, that sector gets the benefits of better credit terms – meaning longer term loans and lower interest rates,' Dr Mada said. 'Typically, sectors like hospitality and health care create benefits in the long term. They do not yield profits in the short term. Moreover, infrastructure status helps attract more foreign direct investment to the sector. That in turn usually means more job creation. The hospitality and health care industries in India are already big employers. With more cash infusion that infrastructure would surely fetch, they could easily double the number of people they employ – that means at least 100 million new jobs over the next decade.'

Dr Mada said that IT – which already enjoys infrastructure status – and manufacturing simply cannot generate as much employment.

———

Dr Reddy's original idea for Apollo Chennai was for a heart hospital, mostly because he was a cardiologist and because he'd lost a thirty-eight-year-old patient who needed a bypass but couldn't raise the $50,000 it would have taken to get the operation done at Dr Denton A. Cooley's Texas Heart Institute in Houston. Although the concept of Apollo quickly evolved into that of a world-class multispeciality hospital, the institution continues to be renowned for its cardiac care.

Dr Matthew Samuel Kalarickal, an interventional cardiologist, is a man whose reputation is that of an exceptional performer. In December 1985 Dr Matthew and his wife Bina moved to Bombay after he completed advanced angioplasty training at Emory University Hospital in Atlanta, Georgia. They were very excited to be back in India. Dr Matthew had been approached by several hospitals but he thought that Bombay offered the best opportunity because of the size of the population.

It turned out that he was wrong. Because the angioplasty technique was new and because it was known that most Indians had smaller arteries than other ethnic groups, the medical community did not think angioplasty would be successful.

Dr Matthew and Bina moved in with her parents. He had no work. In February 1986, the couple decided to look for new opportunities and leave Bombay. The doctor had heard of Dr Reddy's vision for a new India in health care and travelled to Madras to meet the visionary. He told Dr Reddy that he had a new procedure that would fit right in with Apollo. It would save lives and cost less. At the time, Dr Reddy was running the entire cardio unit by himself and he asked Dr Matthew to join him on the spot.

'I told him that yes, I would,' Dr Matthew says; he joined Apollo as an independent consultant. Dr Reddy didn't limit him to one hospital. 'He had a bigger view and knew that my success would be Apollo's success,' says Dr Matthew. 'I was so shocked at his ready acceptance that I asked Malathi Manohar if he was serious about me starting immediately.'

Malathi's response was: 'Dr Reddy never says anything that he doesn't mean. Trust me on that.'

Dr Matthew continues, 'It was hard. There were no catheters, no equipment. Everything was difficult to procure. No medical supply companies were bringing these to India. I travelled to the United States and Europe and brought back catheters and balloons and angio wires in my suitcases. I think that I made three trips in that first year and did eighteen procedures. Six were not successful but the twelve that were, marked Apollo as innovative.

'These twelve successes convinced the hospital and the whole country that the angio procedures were viable. Dr Reddy monitored my progress and went all out with his support. He did not hold back.'

In Madras the couple lived in a converted three-bedroom apartment. It was a residence for doctors. Bina supplied the support system for their lives. By 1987, Dr Matthew was in great demand. A trustee from Jaslok Hospital went to Madras and tried to convince the doctor and Bina to move back to Bombay.

Bina says, 'We told the trustee that we would not move from our home in Madras. We both felt, and still feel, a great loyalty to Dr Reddy. Also, we wanted our children to grow up in the south. We wanted them to get the values, and the education system was better in the south.'

Dr Matthew says that the Jaslok representative seemed surprised.

'But he then asked if I would consider spending one week a month in Bombay and I agreed. We could keep the family in place and at the same time work with Apollo,' Dr Matthew says.

The couple feels a genuine attachment not only towards Dr and Mrs Reddy, but even the four daughters. In October 2011, they got word that their youngest grandson had been diagnosed with a cancerous tumour in his kidney. He was just nine months old. 'We were shattered,' said Bina. 'Dr Reddy told us to go abroad immediately, and he kept track of the surgery and treatment and all of our travel.'

When they landed back in Chennai and went to their home, they found Dr and Mrs Reddy waiting for them. It was about 8 o'clock in the evening. Telling the story almost two years later is still emotional for Dr Matthew and Bina. 'They understand the importance of relationships and family. The Reddys go out of their way to help, not just us but all others. Both exude love and passion and concern,' says Dr Matthew.

It wasn't the first time that the Reddys reached out to Dr Matthew and Bina. Now they are neighbours, but it wasn't always so. Dr Matthew wanted to have a nice, large home for his family but the only available land was far from the hospital. He told Dr Reddy, who advised him not to buy. Instead, Dr Reddy sold Matthew and

Bina land next to his own house in Bishop Garden with a no-interest loan saying, 'I'd rather you spend time with your family and not in driving back and forth.'

It is Dr Reddy's continued involvement that still inspires Dr Matthew. And Dr Matthew continually innovates at Apollo. 'Robotic equipment is very costly and it's tough for any institution to keep up financially. The cost is in many multiples of millions, and we ask, "Is it cost effective?" Dr Reddy wants the best technology. We wonder how he manages multiple hospitals and specialities all of which demand so much financially. I always justify it to my conscience before I send a proposal to Dr Reddy or Preetha,' says Dr Matthew.

———

Dr T. Sunder, a cardio-thoracic surgeon at Apollo Chennai, is on the heart transplant team, but most of his time is spent in the operating room doing open-heart surgery, valve replacements, bypasses and various other surgeries relating to the chest. He graduated from Stanley Medical College and then spent ten years training in cardio-thoracic surgery at several hospitals in London, Birmingham, Sheffield, Plymouth and Southampton before joining Apollo Chennai in October 2003.

He tells the story of a man in his fifties who came to the emergency room in Apollo's main hospital with a severe thermal injury. He was a labourer from a poor background and while working, a red hot rod had broken off and lodged itself in his neck, just skirting his brain and missing his carotid artery by a fraction. Instinctively he pulled the rod out. He clearly needed surgery, which was going to be costly, as almost any surgery would have been for the man.

Dr Sunder says he quickly told Dr Satyabhama the story and said, 'I don't think he can self-fund.'

Dr Satyabhama replied, 'What are you waiting for? We must help him now.'

Dr Sunder performed the surgery and repaired torn tissue and stitched up the hole in his neck. 'Ironically,' he says, 'the man saved his own life by pulling the rod out. It was so hot that it cauterized the blood vessels and prevented him from bleeding to death. Just a few days after his surgery, the man left Apollo and walked home.'

These are the kind of stories that delight Dr Reddy. He is, after all, the heart of Apollo – but for him it's always the hearts of patients that matter, both literally and figuratively.

In almost every conversation, he brings up the story of that thirty-eight-year-old patient in Madras who could not afford a trip to the United States for heart surgery. In a twist of fate, Americans and other Westerners are now discovering India as the first resource when affordable and accessible treatment is not available in their home countries.

One such patient was Ron Lemmer, a sixty-five-year-old man from Minnesota.

Ron, a custom glass craftsman with superior creative ability and finely honed skills, had a heart attack in 1998 in Jamaica. It became increasingly clear that he would need a heart transplant. A nurse he knew connected him to Dr Paul Ramesh at Apollo Chennai.

Dr Ramesh explained the rules for transplants in India, talked about Apollo and gave some background on himself and Dr T. Sunder.

Cadaveric transplants are not allowed in all states but Tamil Nadu, where Apollo is headquartered, has an advanced attitude towards life saving, and Dr Reddy was a pioneer in pushing the government for its approval. Dr Sunder says that the cadaveric donor programme by the government of Tamil Nadu is the best in India. Transplant guidelines require that Indian physicians must assess whether the transplant is needed and that eligible Indians have access to the organs first. At that time, there was not a long waiting list for hearts and though there weren't many donors, doctors thought that Ron would get a new heart in less than fifteen months. (There are never enough kidney and liver donors.) Ron's wife had initially been hesitant for him to try India and said, 'You can go but you will come back in a box.' Ron decided to take a chance. He completed all the paperwork and spoke several more times with Dr Ramesh. Travel plans for Ron and his wife were made and a medical visa was secured from the Indian consulate in Chicago. The couple flew from Minnesota to New York, then to Brussels, and reached Chennai on 3 May 2010.

Apollo's international team met Ron and his wife at the airport and took them straight to the hospital where Dr Ramesh met them. They spent the night at the hospital in one of the suites and for the next five days Ron underwent more tests. Dr Jayashree Narasimhan, a pulmonologist, ordered pulmonary tests. It took a month to actually get on the transplant list in India and then approximately six weeks for the transplant. Ron and his wife moved to a guest house only a few blocks from the hospital. (Eventually his wife left India and was not present for the transplant. The couple later divorced.)

'From my very first contact with Dr Ramesh and Apollo I was confident that everything would work out very well. All of the puzzle pieces were falling into place. Later, Dr Ramesh would tell me that I was the calmest person he had ever seen going into heart surgery, much less a transplant,' Ron said.

Time is critical in transplants. A heart needs to be retrieved, transplanted and blood flow restored within four hours. A normal heart transplant procedure requires three cardiac surgeons, three cardiac anaesthetists, three scrub nurses, two circulating nurses, two percussionists, two operating room assistants and, of course, the entire back-up team and those waiting in the ICU to receive the patient with a new lease on life. For Ron's case, Dr Ramesh, Dr Sunder and one other surgeon all scrubbed. All medical procedures are team efforts, nothing more so than heart transplants.

Surgery started at 3 p.m. on 21 July 2010.

And, then, seventy-nine days after arriving in India, Ron had a new heart.

Ron was in intensive care for five days and at Apollo for almost three weeks. He stayed in Chennai for a few more weeks before returning home to Minnesota. He estimates that the total expenses were around $135,000. Heart transplant surgery in the US would have cost between $500,000 and $1,000,000.

Dr Sunder recalls Ron well. 'When he left, he had a spring in his step and a huge smile,' says Dr Sunder.

Dr Sunder, as a fellow graduate of Stanley Medical College, particularly relishes Dr Reddy's success. Dr Sunder graduated from SMC in 1986, nearly three decades after Dr Reddy.

'I have wanted to be a surgeon from my school days. It was mainly due to my father's influence – he would call me "surgeon", probably because he was impressed by some surgeon and he wanted his son to be like that,' Dr Sunder says. 'It is quite ironical because two years ago we admitted him at Apollo with chest pain; he was found to have blocks in his coronaries and I operated on his heart. Of course, while I was willing to operate on him, I also did offer to refer him to Dr M.R. Girinath – but my dad insisted "his surgeon" did the operation. He is doing fine now.'

Dr Sunder then offered an example of Dr Reddy's decision-making:

'Dr Reddy has provided us world-class infrastructure – in terms of ORs, ICU beds, medical equipment and personnel. I remember when Dr Ramesh wanted to meet him – in order to convince him to purchase a portable ECMO machine (an artificial lung for patients who can't be ventilated) which would enable sick patients from peripheral hospitals to be transported to Apollo. Dr Reddy was busy and was just leaving his office and paused for a second when he saw Ramesh. Hurriedly Ramesh explained how useful the machine was. Dr Reddy just lifted the ECMO machine – which weighed 15 kg – agreed it was indeed portable, and approved its purchase. It was all done in about two minutes. It is such support from Chairman Reddy that we cherish.'

Dr Krishnachandra Chandrashankar Mehta – more popularly known as Dr K.C. Mehta – understands completely what Dr Reddy means when he says that he wants to get things done in a hurry. Dr Mehta is arguably one of the world's best-known knee surgeons. He works primarily out of the 234-bed Apollo Ahmedabad, which opened in May 2003.

Dr Mehta first met Dr Reddy at a puja at the Guruvayur Sri Krishna Temple built by the Reddy family in Ahmedabad in 2006.

Dr Mehta had been living in Liverpool and London for nearly a decade at the time, and was visiting India from Britain. He told Dr Reddy that he was considering moving back home. He said that the words of his father Chandrashankar – who died in 1986 – resonated in his mind constantly: 'You must make a difference in other people's lives through your work.' It was his father who had urged Krishnachandra to become a physician. Dr Mehta's words reminded Dr Reddy of what his own father, Raghava Reddy, used to say to him when he was growing up in Aragonda.

He and Dr Reddy exchanged pleasantries and business cards before the puja began. After the hour-long ceremony, Dr Reddy looked around for Dr Mehta.

'Where did that young doctor go?' Dr Reddy said. But Dr Mehta had already left Guruvayur Temple.

Some days later, Dr Mehta received a call from Dr Reddy asking if he wanted to join Apollo Ahmedabad in the former's native state of Gujarat.

'Should I send you my CV?' Dr Mehta said.

'What for? My instinct tells me that you will do well at Apollo. We need skilled joint surgeons. We will give you a very good infrastructure,' Dr Reddy said.

And that's how Dr Mehta came to join Apollo. He has been performing four to six knee surgeries a day – averaging eighty a fortnight – since then. (To put this in perspective, most orthopaedic surgeons in the United States do about eighty knee surgeries a year.)

Dr Mehta represents a younger generation of specialists that Dr Reddy has been able to attract to join the growing Apollo system. His wife, Payal, is a pathologist in Ahmedabad; one son, Sunil, is a dermatologist, and another son, Ansh, is in his second year at medical school. One day, Sunil said to his father, 'I want to become like Dr Reddy. Look at his energy.'

Dr Mehta's own energy is formidable. Besides his year-round surgical schedule and his lectures abroad, he visits small clinics that he's set up in the Himalayas in the name of a foundation he created in memory of his father.

Dr Reddy added, 'Each of our hospitals has strong orthopaedic teams who are doing excellent work. In addition to Chennai, our hospitals in Delhi, Bangalore, Hyderabad, Kolkata and Ahmedabad are recognized as being in the forefront in orthopaedic surgery. I would add that there are many stars in those teams.'

The senior consultants call themselves the Apollo family within the Apollo family. And they pride themselves on the fact that everyone in the Apollo family has a big heart.

The celebrated cardio-vascular surgeon, Dr Naresh Trehan, can also attest to that. I have known Naresh and his wife Madhu – the TV personality and author – for more than three decades, since the time they lived in New York. Naresh returned to India in 1984 and, with the help of the industrialist, the late H.P. Nanda, set up Escorts Heart Institute and Research Centre in New Delhi.

Escorts flourished under Dr Trehan's leadership literally from the day of its opening in 1988. But then Malvinder Singh and Shivinder Singh of Fortis bought over the facility. Disagreements occurred between the brothers and Dr Trehan, and he was asked to leave.

Dr Reddy was in London on that day. When he heard the news, he called up Dr Trehan and invited him to join Indraprastha Apollo Hospital. Dr Trehan agreed, and brought along his team of highly experienced heart surgeons.

'He's a landmark,' Dr Trehan told me about Dr Reddy. 'He's generous to a fault. And he continues to be an interesting combination of a man fiercely dedicated to creating a viable health care delivery system, and to creating an entirely new era where the practice of medicine is world class.'

Dr Trehan worked at Apollo Delhi for more than two years, but he clearly wanted to run his own show again soon. He planned Medanta, a large multi-speciality hospital located in Gurgaon, on the outskirts of Delhi; the 43-acre facility opened in 2009. Dr Trehan told me that Medanta – also known as MediCity – is fashioned after institutions such as Mayo Medical School and Johns Hopkins Hospital in the United States. Collaborating with Siemens and other financial partners, Dr Trehan aims to combine modern medicine with traditional medicine and holistic therapies.

Dr Trehan also told me that the departure from Apollo wasn't easy for him, but that he knew that Dr Reddy recognized that people had their own ambitions and objectives. Dr Reddy wished him well, as he always does to anyone who leaves Apollo. The two men remain friends, and meet at industry conferences. One key member of the Apollo team told me, 'If Dr Reddy had been in Dr Trehan's place – he would have done it differently.' The suggestion was that Dr Trehan could have followed his dream yet nurtured his Apollo cardiac programme as well. Perhaps more importantly, the episode indicated to me that Dr Reddy is not disturbed by the possibility that someone he's helped may one day become a competitor. That, to me, is a sign of his strength of character and magnanimity.

CHAPTER TWENTY-SEVEN

A Bridge to Lanka

IT WAS LATE AFTERNOON on a warm Sunday in April 2002 in the Sri Lankan capital of Colombo. Scores of men and women stood outside a futurist building for a ceremony in the thinning sunshine, expecting two special dignitaries, each of whom would arrive separately by helicopter. They could have chosen to fly together, of course, but neither much liked the other's company, although they had been childhood friends. Each was a scion of political families that had long feuded over the course of development of this island-nation in the Indian Ocean. They had run against each other in a national election, and neither victor nor vanquished had quite got over how vicious the campaign had been. Today would mark the first time that they would be seen together at a public forum.

Prominent among those who waited for them on this day was Dr Prathap Chandra Reddy; he was there for the inauguration of the 350-bed Apollo Hospital Colombo, which he had built in cooperation with local partners, and with the blessings of the government. The hospital was Apollo's first overseas venture; it was set up to serve both as a general hospital and one that offered tertiary acute-care services, including cardio-thoracic surgery, neurology, minimally invasive surgery and internal medicine. The super-speciality hospital had cost $32 million, of which the International Finance Corporation, the private lending arm of the World Bank, had lent $5 million –

the first instance of private direct foreign investment in Sri Lanka's languishing hospital sector.

The building had risen on a seven-acre plot in the Narahenpita section of Colombo, a pleasant if sleepy city that was currently on the edge on account of a civil war that was raging between Sri Lanka's majority Sinhalese and minority Tamils. The land was valued at $4 million, and the hospital was required to only make a down payment of $500,000. The monthly rent would be nominal. The government had originally offered a site on Havelock Road where an abandoned textile mill sat in ruins. But Dr Reddy did not like the property. He opted for the plot in Narahenpita, even though it was mainly a wasteland, with a few shanties. He just had a good feeling about this area. He is, after all, a man who trusts his intuition.

'It's definitely not easy to make changes so profound that they impact an entire country – but that's exactly what Dr Reddy and Apollo did when we opened a hospital in Sri Lanka,' Dr Chandrasekhara Chandilya told me in a lengthy conversation in May 2013. Currently the head of the department of internal medicine at Apollo Chennai, he served as Apollo Colombo's chief physician and helped set up operations there. 'Apollo changed the very culture of health care in Sri Lanka. It created a totally modern environment for patients, and offered them an experience that they would never have got otherwise. Dr Reddy was not only a father figure for all of us at Apollo – he also became a father figure for Sri Lanka's health care sector.'

In many ways Sri Lanka was much like its much bigger neighbour, India: inadequate facilities, poor infrastructure, lack of medical professionals, and very few 'best practices'. The country had been beset by a lack of urgency and attention to detail by government and industry leaders. That's what made it all the more dramatic when Dr Reddy was requested by President Chandrika Bandaranaike Kumaratunga to establish a first-class medical facility in Colombo.

Dr Reddy had been the cardiologist to her mother, the former prime minister, Sirimavo Bandaranaike; he had a personal interest in the outcome. Three other important factors played big roles in Apollo's first international venture. First, the people of Sri Lanka were victims of poor health care. Second – as he often told me – Dr Reddy loves helping those who cannot help themselves. Third, he rises to the occasion – and where it may be darkest and most challenging, he produces results. Those results were easy to see in Sri Lanka. As a matter of fact, the work that Apollo accomplished still echoes throughout Sri Lanka as its people now expect world-class health care.

'Poor health care leads to missed opportunities for national progress,' says Bimal Jalan, the renowned economist and former governor of the Reserve Bank of India. 'Education falters, the spirit of a nation is broken, economic growth stagnates and it is impossible for a country and her people to fully participate on the world stage especially with increasing globalization.'

Dr Reddy subscribes to this view. 'This was the Sri Lanka that Apollo faced and this is why the Apollo team was welcomed and loved,' he says.

The impact of what he and his team accomplished remains in Sri Lanka today. Apollo was very well known and respected for its high standards of care. Its physicians were perceived as exceptionally talented, many known internationally. The nursing staff was seen as the best-trained in South Asia. Apollo came to Sri Lanka in 2002 with nearly two decades of experience; its administrators were viewed as efficient and effective.

Consider Apollo's roster of physicians on opening day, which included a cardiac team headed by Dr Vinay Behl, who now heads the department of cardiology at AIIMS, where one of his most prominent patients is Prime Minister Manmohan Singh; Dr Prasad Krishnan, a cardiothoracic surgeon, who is currently with the Mayo Clinic; Dr Fred Perera, a neurosurgeon, who came from Australia; Dr Shivakumar, a paediatric cardiologist; Dr Nalini Prasad, a gynaecologist, who stayed in Sri Lanka until 2012; Dr B. Krishnamurthy who, says Dr Chandilya, 'set up the best ICU unit that I have ever seen'; and Dr K.C. Prakash, a nephrologist who established a dialysis centre. And then there was Apollo Colombo's first CEO, Brig. Chandra Shukla.

After the opening, Apollo continued to attract top physicians from India. Dr B. Premkumar, Apollo's senior vice president out of Chennai, did the recruiting of physicians from the start.

One of them was Dr Manjeet Singh Dhillon, an orthopaedic surgeon. Also joining was cardiologist Dr Harinder K. Bali. Dr B. Krishnamurthy set up the ICCU, which was very efficiently run by Dr Venkatasalam for more than five years. Presently Dr Venkatasalam is the assistant director of medical services at Apollo Chennai. Dr K.C. Prakash set up the dialysis unit that along with the department of nephrology is till today being run as a successful kidney transplant unit in Sri Lanka by Dr Surjith Somiah, Chief Nephrologist. There was also Dr Rajesh Kapoor, a urologist who later retired as chief of urology, Sanjay Gandhi Institute, Lucknow.

Other physicians who became part of Apollo Colombo included Dr Sanjay Gogoi, a urologist also from SGPM, Lucknow; Dr Surjith Somiah, a nephrologist who'd trained at Apollo Chennai; Dr Tripthi Deb, a cardiologist trained at Apollo Chennai; Dr P.S. Deb, Chief Neurologist; Dr Devendra Jha, an ENT surgeon from AIIMS; Dr Srinivasan and Dr Maheshwari from PGI Chandigarh; and Dr Sunderaman from Apollo Chennai. Also joining Apollo Colombo were Dr Shuba Rao, a dentist from Bombay, and Dr Ashok Kumar, a paediatrician from Chennai. A stellar cast indeed, one that would have brought notice to any hospital in the world.

Notwithstanding Dr Reddy's good feeling about the Narahenpita property, Apollo did not have an easy time at the beginning. Construction suffered delays, but that was to be expected in a city where bombs seemed to go off with some regularity and where workers sometimes failed to show up. Dr Reddy, and the hospital's vice chairman and chief local promoter, Thamby R. Navaratnam, chairman of Singalanka Standard Chemicals Ltd, kept haranguing the builder, Marg Construction. Dr Reddy says that Apollo desired to have a local face in Sri Lanka and chose Navaratnam, as he knew him socially.

Navaratnam told me that he went around government offices in Colombo to obtain a plethora of permissions from various bureaucracies, which Dr Chandilya confirms. Most of the finances to start the hospital were raised by Suneeta Reddy; some 50 per cent of that equity – of the $32 million that was required – came from government institutions such as the Insurance Corporation, and a subsidiary of the Bank of Ceylon called Property Developers Limited. A man named Thilan Wijesinghe, chairman of the government's Board of Investment, proved to be particularly helpful to Apollo.

A week or so before the inauguration, Dr Reddy gathered top hospital executives, physicians and the projects team in the boardroom. Some of them had felt that the inauguration would have to be delayed because the facility was not quite ready. Some expressed dismay that dust still coated the hospital's corridors.

'I have built many hospitals. The inauguration is to take place on 7 April, and it will,' Dr Reddy said, assertively but pleasantly. 'Those of you who think that it won't take place as scheduled should leave this room now. The rest can stay.'

Dr Rana Mehta, a physician who was also CEO of the hospital, was among those who were present at that meeting. He recalls that no one left the room.

The twenty-five doctors who had been seconded from various Apollo hospitals in India, and the local staff, had complete faith in Dr Reddy's ability to make things happen. Apollo had a stake of nearly 33 per cent in the enterprise; other investors included the Sri Lanka Insurance Corporation, technically owned by the government but controlled by tycoon Don Harold Stassen 'Harry' Jayawardene. Sri Lankans invariably referred to the self-made Jayawardene as the country's 'liquor baron'. Harry Jayawardene often boasted that he contributed 5 per cent of the country's GDP, which in 2002 was $17 billion.

Standing with Dr Reddy outside the hospital building on that late Sunday afternoon was Navaratnam. Dr Reddy says: 'We gave him a 3.75 per cent stake.'

Navaratnam says that he knew the Reddys dating back to the 1990s when he began exporting copper scrap to India. He had initially met Dr Reddy's four daughters through Meena Reddy, the sister of the husbands of Preetha and Suneeta Reddy. Navaratnam told me that he still feels moved by how optimistic Dr Reddy was about Apollo's Sri Lanka venture.

Dr Reddy says that the original impetus for entering the Sri Lankan market came from former Prime Minister Sirimavo Bandaranaike – who had been his patient in Chennai – and that her daughter, President Chandrika Bandaranaike Kumaratunga, was 'just like Indira Gandhi' in her determination to encourage the development of good health care in her country.

'She wanted an Apollo hospital, not an Apollo-like hospital,' Dr Reddy says. 'All credit should go to Chandrika.'

This is how it all came about.

The Sri Lankan High Commissioner to India at the time came to Apollo Chennai and contacted Dr Reddy. He said that President Kumaratunga wanted to meet him.

'He gave me two dates and asked which would be suitable. The second time he came we confirmed the dates. We had our visas stamped and were told it was not necessary since we were going because of a presidential invitation, but the visas had already been done,' Dr Reddy recalls. 'We went the day before the presidential appointment, and I visited two existing hospitals just to see what they were like and to get an idea of the health care situation.'

The President had a reputation for making her appointments wait for hours and hours, even days sometimes, to see her. But she only made Dr Reddy wait for two hours.

'When we met the President I told her we would need a good clean place centrally located for the hospital that was easily accessible,' Dr Reddy says. 'One of her aides said, "Dr Reddy, the president already has a site for you." Chandrika did the spadework. I had told her that in India a huge problem had been that the rich and powerful got special treatment and the other people got very poor treatment or none at all.'

Dr Reddy told President Kumaratunga what else, besides land, was needed.

'Zero customs duties,' he said.

'I will give you zero customs duties,' President Kumaratunga said.

'No income tax,' Dr Reddy said.

'I will give you zero income tax,' the President said.

'No local tax,' Dr Reddy said.

'You will have zero local tax,' the President said.

Years later, Dr Reddy would recall: 'If we had had to pay those taxes we could not have opened the hospital. Plus, President Kumaratunga gave us enormous encouragement and did not let others bring down our plans.'

As that meeting with President Kumaratunga drew to a close, Dr Reddy asked, 'How is your mother?'

The president said, 'She is doing well and I want you to see her before you go.'

When Dr Reddy met Sirimavo Bandaranaike, the President told her mother, 'Dr Reddy has agreed to do a hospital here.'[1]

Much later, Dr Reddy said: 'The President's cooperation because of the relationship with her mother was what kept me going during difficult times. We were having difficulties with the local mayor. At the hospital he wanted shelter for 120 ambulances. We said no, we will start with twelve ambulances – three or four at the hospital and others stationed throughout the city. When I told the president about this, she called up the mayor and spoke harshly to him saying, "What is this? Dr Reddy doesn't need 120 ambulances. I told you to keep me informed of the developments – and here is a roadblock."

---

1 In my view, Dr Reddy's special regard for Sri Lanka may have had to do with not only the medical potential there, but also with mythology. 'Lanka' was supposedly the kingdom of Ravana, who kidnapped Lord Rama's wife, Sita. Hanuman, the Hindu monkey god whom Dr Reddy worships daily, was part of the *vanara* (monkey) army who built a bridge across the sea so that Rama could invade Lanka and vanquish Ravana. While Rama's Bridge or Rama Setu is the stuff of legend, there exists an actual 'bridge' – a chain of limestone shoals, between Pamban Island, also known as Rameswaram Island, off the southeastern coast of Tamil Nadu, and Mannar Island, off the northwestern coast of Sri Lanka. Geological evidence suggests that this 'bridge' was a former land connection between India and Sri Lanka.

Chandrika gave me and Apollo an open passage to prepare and run the hospital because we were the ones who knew what was needed. Immediately the next day the land was transferred to the Board of Investment and it was authorized to monitor the building of the hospital. Within twenty-four hours all of the planning permits had been stamped.'

Dr Reddy went to Sri Lanka fourteen times during the planning and construction stages of Apollo Colombo.

Apollo Chennai was already getting a significant number of Sri Lankan patients on account of the poor quality of health care in their own country; perhaps Sri Lanka's national interests would be well served and valuable foreign exchange could be saved if some of those patients received treatment at an Apollo facility in Colombo.

After President Kumaratunga had initially spoken to Dr Reddy about getting Apollo Hospital to Colombo, Suneeta Reddy commissioned a feasibility study. Her assessment was that it would probably take around $20 million to build a 200-bed hospital. Suneeta quickly dispatched an Apollo team to reconnoitre the scene in Sri Lanka. The team's main brief: to understand what Sri Lanka's main needs in health care were, and what would it take to meet those needs.

———

At the opening, the dignitaries were late. The guests chatted cordially as they awaited the two most important members of the government who were about to arrive by helicopter.

The officials they were expecting were President Chandrika Bandaranaike Kumaratunga of the Sri Lanka Freedom Party, and Prime Minister Ranil Shriyan Wickremesinghe of the United National Party. They were to light the traditional lamp, considered auspicious in this part of the world.

The helicopters never came. Instead, Bandaranaike and Wickremesinghe arrived by automobiles that were escorted by armoured vehicles. Security personnel had apparently ruled out flying on account of the possibility of rockets being fired by the Liberation Tigers of Tamil Eelam (LTTE), the rebel group that had been fighting for two decades for a separate Tamil state in the northern and eastern regions of a nation of 20 million people whose land mass was barely 65,000 sq. km.

The prime minister reluctantly greeted the president. He had arrived about five minutes before her. They did not engage in small talk, as politicians – even rival ones – customarily do at public ceremonies. Dr Reddy says that they each lit a torch on the appropriate sides of the dais.

Dr Reddy spoke first, promising the best health care to Sri Lanka and Apollo becoming a superb regional health centre surpassed by none. In his typical inclusive style, he acknowledged the teamwork that had gone into the building of Apollo Colombo.

Then the prime minister spoke and welcomed Apollo and said that he would do everything in his power to make sure that it had the top services and would grow and expand. President Chandrika spoke last and, after welcoming Apollo, brought up medical tourism and the potential that it held for the country. Everyone steered clear of the parlous political climate in the country in their remarks.

Dr Reddy happily showed them around the eleven-storey facility. One of the main decorative features was a thirty-foot atrium with a huge chandelier. Preetha had persuaded the Sri Lankan artist Senaka Senanayake to create a striking work of art; her choice of the artist and approval of his work were yet another indication of Preetha's own artistic sensibilities.[2]

Dr Reddy says that Preetha really came into her own during the building of the hospital in Sri Lanka. She did not have the title of Apollo's managing director then, but she took ownership of the hospital project and later the Apollo response to the December 2004 tsunami. She took all the major decisions and worked carefully to manage both sides so that the project and opening would go

2   Preetha Reddy is modest about her artistic endeavours. Among other things, she is an accomplished photographer.

smoothly. The president and the prime minister both required continuous attention. It was Preetha's idea not to have a ribbon-cutting but instead to tie a bow into the large ribbon with a person standing at each end: when the ends were pulled the ribbon opened. To this day, ribbon-pulling – and not ribbon-cutting – opens all Apollo projects.

The media treated the opening of Apollo as a major event and put the stories and photos of the event on the front page for a week. The inaugural celebrations went on for five days. Six months later, when Dr Reddy visited the hospital, President Kumaratunga called him and said, 'Dr Reddy, I remember your speech that this hospital will not only serve the people of Sri Lanka but will prove to be a medical destination. I believe it is already happening as some people are coming to know that we have excellent facilities in this country.'

Within three years, the hospital was to show a profit, a full year ahead of schedule. A year after that, in 2006, Apollo Hospitals withdrew from the project, a victim of local politics and adverse stock market movements.

———

That development did not surprise me. Outsiders have long found Sri Lanka a difficult place for doing business. The political climate was fraught. And historically Sri Lankans did not trust their big neighbour India. The distrust was mutual. A suicide bomber belonging to the LTTE had assassinated India's former prime minister, Rajiv Gandhi, in May 1991 near Chennai.

I knew Sri Lanka well, having visited it frequently since 1982 for my first book, *The Crowded Earth: People and the Politics of Population*. The long-simmering tensions between Sinhalese and Tamils had yet to escalate into a civil war then. President Junius Richard Jayawardene took me in his helicopter from Colombo to Jaffna, the northernmost city where Tamils were in a majority. I spent two days there with him, not realizing that the wily Jayawardene was secretly making plans to smother an incipient Tamil insurrection.

'We are one people,' Jayawardene told me, 'and there's no question of any one group discriminating against another.'

His priority was politics, not health care. Outside investors perceived the right-leaning Jayawardene as being pro-business.

The tensions between Tamils and Sinhalese were rooted in the island's history. After Ceylon became a crown colony of the British Empire in 1802, the largely Hindu Tamils were given a disproportionate number of well-paying civil service and professional jobs, though they made up just 20 per cent of the island's population. After independence from Britain was won in 1948, the majority Sinhalese – who were Buddhists and Christians – sought to rectify that imbalance, according to the scholar K.P. Mukerji.

When President Kumaratunga's father – Solomon W.R.D. Bandaranaike, an Oxford-educated scion of an elite Sri Lankan family – campaigned for the post of prime minister, for example, he gained political support by calling for an official Sinhalese-only language law. Just after he was elected in 1956, the first street clashes between Sinhalese and Tamils occurred. A Buddhist monk assassinated him in 1959. Chandrika was only fourteen years old at the time, and was in her classroom at a convent school when news of her father's death came. Her mother, Sirimavo Bandaranaike, became prime minister in 1960, the first woman in the world to hold such a position.

Sirimavo Bandaranaike was a patient of Dr Reddy's. She would come to Madras for check-ups at HM Hospital, and referred patients to Dr Reddy at both HM and Apollo Hospitals even after she received a kidney transplant in Vienna. Her loyalty remained with Apollo. The idea that Dr Reddy should bring his expertise to Sri Lanka was spawned during the visits that Mrs Bandaranaike – and her daughter – made to India. Mrs Bandaranaike served as prime minister from 1960 to 1965, and then again from 1970 to 1977. Seventeen years later, she became prime minister again, after her Sri Lanka Freedom Party, along with the People's Alliance coalition, emerged victorious in a 1994 provincial council election in the southern province of the country.

Apollo's withdrawal from its engagement with Sri Lanka was a major disappointment for Dr Reddy.

'In fact, it was not just a disappointment. I was disheartened,' Dr Reddy told me. 'I had put my whole heart into this project. We were also proud of what we accomplished. It was not just idealism. It was action. It was results. I knew, and still know, every inch of the hospital. I was so involved and it is still in my heart.'

In a few short years, Apollo had changed the health care ethos of the country. Where once Sri Lankans travelled to India or the West for medical treatment, they now flocked to Apollo Colombo. Local private hospitals started imitating Apollo by freshening up their facades, and by training receptionists to be more welcoming. The Apollo doctors and staff gained strong reputations. Dr Chandilya told me that at the start, some Sri Lankans perceived Apollo as an 'Indian' or 'Tamil' hospital. 'But very quickly everyone saw how professional and hi-tech we were, that we were really world class,' he said. 'Apollo became the hospital that everyone wanted to come to.'

Dr Reddy told me: 'Apollo brought the concept of intensive care to Sri Lanka. Administrators came. Apollo brought 120 nurses from India and recruited sixty nurses from Sri Lanka. Later, it started a nursing college. Apollo and the nursing director from Delhi brought a super-high standard of nursing care. No one in Sri Lanka was accustomed to such care. Preetha and all of Apollo put in so much when the hospital was created. She and everyone took all the experience from fifteen years to make sure the hospital was top-notch. The systems, the procurements, the clinics were all par excellence. Violet David, the nursing director from Delhi, went to Colombo. She was very strict in training. The housekeeping supervisor, Ann, went as well – and also the CEO from Delhi. It was a major effort from all of Apollo.

'In Sri Lanka they used a system of appointments called channelling. One day I went in and there were fifty patients waiting to see the orthopaedic surgeon. It was impossible. I asked how long the doctor would be there and the response was, two hours. I said, "From this second, there will be no more channelling. It is an insult to the patients."

'Others who came were the face of the hospital, such as the cardiac surgeon, Krishnan Prasad and his wife, a gynaecologist, Nalini Prasad. Apollo brought a neurosurgeon too. The country did not have a cancer hospital. We introduced all of that. All of our doctors were so committed. Some were world-renowned. They would have given their heart for Apollo.'

Dr Reddy empowered the Apollo executives to take critical decisions in the event of public emergencies. For example, when the aftershocks of the December 2004 tsunami off Sumatra hit Sri Lanka, Apollo's ambulances were the first to reach the affected coastal areas. Nearly 40,000 people died in Sri Lanka as the tsunami – which was caused by an earthquake whose magnitude was 9.0 on the Richter scale – and more than 800,000 Sri Lankans were displaced.

Dr Reddy recalls the tsunami vividly.

Apollo's telephone operator in Chennai received a telephone call from the telemedicine centre in the Andaman Islands saying, 'I don't know what's happening. We are under water. I do not think I will be alive after this call.'

Southern India, including Chennai, was also badly affected by the tsunami. Ambulances were airlifted to South India from Delhi and Hyderabad along with three operating theatres. Some 130 people from Chennai went across South India. Apollo, under Preetha Reddy, took the lead in providing medicine and supplies, helping with food and shelter and trying to keep sanitary conditions. 'This was the Apollo spirit in action,' Dr Reddy says.

He was in Hyderabad and received a call about the tsunami. He switched on the television and saw the destruction that was sweeping Sri Lanka. That evening they put out an SOS for medicine and other kinds of aid. Apollo responded with alacrity. The news media, politicians and powerful business leaders all fully acknowledged the role that Apollo played in the tsunami disaster and the services it provided to people.

During the tsunami and just after, Dr Chandilya got together a team of six Apollo doctors with the help of the Rotary Club. They worked hands-on day and night for four days, with the nearly drowned, injured or dead as well as survivors, in and around the district of Batticaloa. The team included Dr P. Radhakrishna, a surgical gastroenterologist, Dr Waheeda Suresh, a gynaecologist, Dr Naveen Ravel, an oncologist – all of whom work at Apollo Chennai to this day.

Dr Reddy says, 'The credit for what we did in India or in Sri Lanka and in other places does not go to me. It goes to all who work ensuring that the very best care is given to all the patients. From conception to the moment the ribbon opens to the daily care of each patient and their families, our team is one. It is one family with the patient and their attendants as part of it. We do our best, nothing less, to make sure that world-class health care that is also tender loving care is delivered. It is our privilege that patients have placed their trust in us.'

———

Apollo Colombo also received plaudits at various other times.

Dr Chandilya recalls that virtually every member of the Sri Lankan cricket team came to Apollo at one time or the other. Dr Dhillon, the orthopaedic surgeon, served as a sports injury consultant to the team.

The celebrated cricketer from the West Indies, Sir Brian Lara, said he was admitted for hepatitis, which he contracted while his team was touring Sri Lanka in 2003. 'This is the best hospital that I've ever seen,' he said. 'There's nothing like this where I come from.' Similar accolades came from President Mahinda Rajapaksa, who came in for a check-up after his election in November 2005. 'World-class hospital,' was how he characterized Apollo. 'And it has world-class doctors.'

It would be difficult to mention all the physicians and surgeons who contributed to the success of Apollo Colombo. There are still nearly twenty Apollo consultants who help out in Sri Lanka. Among these I interviewed Dr Rajesh Fogla, an eye specialist from Apollo Hyderabad who initially spent about two years in Colombo. He had studied under the famous eye specialist Dr S.S. Badrinath – who was associated with Apollo at one time, and remains a great friend of Dr Reddy's – at the Sankara Nethralaya in Chennai.

Dr Fogla took his cornea team to villages to assist those who couldn't make the trip to Colombo. He introduced Lasik surgery to Sri Lanka and brought new techniques in corneal transplantation. Dr Fogla practiced endothelial keratoplasty, which consists of replacing a partial layer of the cornea rather than the entire cornea. 'Apollo brought in a system of specialized care that Sri Lankans simply hadn't experienced before,' he told me. 'People tell me all the time how much Apollo doctors – and Dr Reddy especially – are missed.'[3]

At Apollo Colombo – and at Apollo hospitals generally – the consultants were all told that they could only have four patients per hour. Three patients per hour are recommended.

'I told the doctors that they can charge more but that they should not give less. It is important that each patient have time with the doctor to explain their case and for the doctor to evaluate it,' Dr Reddy said. Among the reasons that Sri Lankans believed that Apollo was a 'gift' was that Dr Reddy helped change the paradigm of health care in their country.

Dr Reddy viewed Apollo as a super-speciality hospital where patients could avail themselves of a range of treatments. It was, in other words, a 'one-stop shop'.

Dr Chandilya, a graduate of Stanley Medical College – like Dr Reddy – spent twenty-five years at Apollo Chennai before coming to Apollo Colombo. He said that the hospital instituted several important rules concerning the treatment of patients. 'One was that patients have to be greeted with smiles,' he said. 'Another was that patients must feel that they were in a place that had warmth and where they would be

---

3 My Sri Lankan friend Edmund Kerner once told me of the courteous treatment he received at Apollo Colombo. Ed suffered from glaucoma and other eye ailments, and hadn't been happy with the medical care he'd got in New York. 'Apollo was one of the biggest gifts that India ever gave Sri Lanka,' Ed said, a sentiment that was echoed by hundreds of his countrymen.

listened to with attention. Dr Reddy was very strict about such rules. In the pre-Apollo days, when I looked around Colombo hospitals, I was surprised that most doctors gave barely two or three minutes to a patient. Many doctors didn't even bother to physically examine patients because the demand for their services was so high that they had to keep seeing patients continuously. I appreciated the medical skills and diagnostic ability that those doctors had, but I noticed that few of them smiled. We changed all that. All our physicians were required to work a full twelve-hour shift, and all our patients were given as much time as required. I dare say that our patients hadn't received such "tender loving care" until Apollo came on the scene.'

Sri Lankans were also impressed by the fact that Apollo Colombo was the only hospital in the capital with a helipad. Dr Reddy had it installed because he knew that soldiers wounded in the civil war would often be taken by helicopter to a medical facility. Apollo achieved the rare distinction of simultaneously treating troops from the Sri Lankan armed forces and rebel combatants from the LTTE.

'I myself treated a number of government ministers, parliamentarians, diplomats, visiting dignitaries, film stars and leading businessmen,' Dr Chandilya told me. 'I treated both Prime Minister Ranil Wickremesinghe and his brother Shan, and their mother Nalini. In fact, Shan – who runs the TV channel TNL – and I became close friends. I brought President Rajapaksa for a nuclear test at Apollo. Apollo also treated his sons Namal, Yoshitha and Rohitha. President Kumaratunga's brother, Anura, who was Speaker of the Sri Lanka Parliament, also received treatment at Apollo. Half the members of Parliament were our patients.

'And then we had as patients many of the top LTTE leaders. This was during the peace period. Each would be accompanied by two policemen, get treated at Apollo, and then leave. We made no distinction with regard to the country's politics. Apollo was neutral territory, everyone was welcome as a patient.'[4]

---

4   The civil war formally ended in 2009. More than 100,000 people, mostly Tamil civilians, were killed in the twenty-six-year-long conflict, and many more wounded

'LTTE leaders treated by me included Tamilselvan, political head and chief administrator; George, his deputy; Pulithevan, a British-trained lawyer; and Paraakrama Singam, chief justice of all the twelve courts of Eelam,' Dr Chandilya said.

'Medicine should have no ideology,' Dr Reddy would tell me years later. 'It's a doctor's moral responsibility to treat anyone who needs medical attention. Medicine should – and can – transcend politics.'

———

Apollo's separation from the hospital that it established in Colombo was less than amicable. The raising by Harry Jayawardene of the stake of Sri Lanka Insurance Corporation (which was formerly owned by the government) in the holding company, Lanka Hospitals, by nearly 15.6 per cent, precipitated Apollo's departure. He did so by buying out a major stakeholder, Dr Senthiverl Thirugnanasambandar. This raised Jayawardene's stake in the company to 35.5 per cent, 2 per cent more than that of Apollo, which had been the biggest shareholder until that point. There were suggestions that the government's Board of Investment (BOI) supported Jayawardene's actions; the BOI had threatened to withdraw tax and import-duty concessions to the Lanka Hospitals Corporation – which would have put Apollo in an untenable position. In effect, the BOI's threat paved the way for Jayawardene to take over the company's control.[5]

---

and maimed. International human rights groups claim that the Sri Lankan military still scours the countryside to flush out unreconstructed rebels. However, during a visit that I made to Sri Lanka in October 2010, Gotabaya Rajapaksa, brother of President Rajapaksa and the country's defence secretary, told me, 'We are a united country now. There is no more fighting or killing.' He said this with an absolutely straight face over a delicious – if hugely spicy – lunch at his heavily guarded home in Colombo. I thought that it was an irony that he was now also chairman of Lanka Hospital, which is under government control.

5   At the time of investment into Apollo, it was owned by the government, But later during the privatization programme, Harry Jayawardene bought the Corporation. Thereafter, the court ruled that there was a flaw in the privatization and the Sri Lanka Insurance Corporation was vested back to the government.

'Harry was a corporate raider,' Thamby Navaratnam told me. 'Apollo Hospital was irresistible to him. He was also helped by the fact that the Insurance Corporation was corporatized – which meant that its shares were readily available to Harry for purchase.'

Dr Rana Mehta, who headed Apollo's operations in Colombo, recalls that Apollo's senior executives appealed to Indian High Commissioner Nirupama Rao to seek the intervention of the government. Nagma Malik, press and information secretary at the Indian High Commission, confirmed to local media that the High Commissioner had taken up the Apollo case with the government.

The United States ambassador was also concerned and spoke to the Lankan prime minister.

When the Apollo Hospital project was initiated, SLI along with the Bank of Ceylon were government entities. Nobody at Apollo anticipated that SLI would be privatized – or that Harry Jayawardene would wind up in control of the hospital. In hindsight, it's clear that Apollo should have taken 51 per cent equity: that way, it would have protected itself from Harry Jayawardene's takeover.

Jayawardene treated Dr Reddy with less than courtesy. He dispatched three young representatives who questioned the Apollo founder with what could only be characterized as rudeness. Said one witness: 'The rug was pulled out from under Apollo. It was a hostile takeover.'

And how did Dr Reddy react to such hostility?

Here is Dr Chandilya's answer: 'When it was time for Apollo to leave Colombo, Dr Reddy said to me, "We cannot leave behind just four walls. We owe continuity in health care to the people of Sri Lanka. I urge those of you who want to stay to do so. Our main business is helping people." So I stayed on in Colombo for another year. I miss the place. Sri Lankans really looked up to Apollo. And Dr Reddy particularly got so much respect, even adoration. He didn't deserve the sort of treatment that Harry Jayawardene gave him. As it turned out, Harry Jayawardene had no clue as to how hospitals should be run. He constituted a board consisting mostly of bean counters. They were more concerned about profits than about how patients were being treated.'

Like Dr Chandilya, Dr Nalini Prasad also stayed on in Colombo after Apollo's formal association with the hospital ended. A gynaecologist, she had become close to Preetha Reddy, whom she also came to admire for her people skills and clear management style.

'Indian doctors may find it difficult because Apollo is leaving – but you can stay on, if you wish,' Dr Nalini recalls Preetha as saying to her. 'But you can return to Apollo any time you want. There will always be a place for you.'

'I always felt an emotional connection to Preetha and to Dr Reddy,' Dr Nalini told me in a telephone interview from her home in Rochester, Minnesota. 'Apollo gave me my first job in medicine – I joined Apollo Chennai on 5 February 1997, which happened to be Dr Reddy's birthday. I went to him for *ashirwad*, and he blessed me. I was really touched by his humility and kindness. He mesmerizes you. To this day I feel the energy that Dr Reddy gave me on my very first day at work.'

In the very first month after Apollo Colombo opened, Dr Reddy expressed the hope that the first child that Dr Nalini helped deliver at the hospital would be on 24 May. He said that it was an astrologically auspicious date.

'I said to myself, "Now how do I make that happen? How can I anticipate which woman would come to deliver her baby on precisely that date?"' Dr Nalini told me.

Serendipitously, a woman named Loretta had come to Apollo Colombo; she was about to deliver a baby. On the morning of 24 May she told the hospital's CEO, Dr Shukla, that she wanted Dr Nalini to perform a Caesarean procedure – what's known as a C-section – and she wanted it done that very day. The baby was a girl; Loretta already had two older daughters – both of whom had been born via a C-section – and had hoped for a son this time. Nonetheless, she was pleased – as any mother would. And Dr Reddy got his wish fulfilled for the first baby to be born at Apollo Colombo on 24 May.

Three days later came another auspicious day. Dr Reddy hoped that Apollo Colombo would do a major heart surgery for the first time on 27 May. Dr Nalini's husband, Dr Prasad Krishnan, had a patient who required a triple heart bypass. Dr Girinath flew in from Chennai to assist Dr Prasad in what was a successful operation. And so it happened that Dr Reddy got his second wish fulfilled too.

'There's always great satisfaction for surgeons in helping a patient with a successful surgery,' Dr Prasad said from Rochester, Minnesota, where he now lives and practices. 'But there was a special joy for us in this particular case because Dr Reddy was so keen that our first heart bypass should take place on 27 May. Over the next several years, Apollo Colombo was able to produce many successes – and I like to think that we not only made Dr Reddy proud, but also served Sri Lanka and our patients well.'

When all of the unpleasant changes came about later, Chandrika Bandaranaike Kumaratunga said to Dr Reddy, 'Apollo opened with great expectations and you have such a wonderful team. This discord should never have happened. You came to give health care and for that everyone must give respect.'

The issue kept attracting headlines in the local press, and also in India. As the situation worsened Dr Reddy talked with the family and said, 'It's not worth it. It is not our business to fight in dirty waters.'

A corporate lawyer in Colombo told the media that irrespective of the parties concerned, it was wrong of the Sri Lankan government to intervene in the market because Apollo Hospital was a publicly quoted firm. 'The government's position is unfair. It is up to the investors to sell their shares or not. The government ethically should not and legally cannot exert pressure on any party to sell their shares or not,' he said, adding, 'the High Commissioner of India cannot interfere either.'

There was a sense among financial analysts that Apollo should have considered a 51 per cent interest in the company from the very start. One newspaper columnist reported that investors and former officials felt the company should have known before it went public that it could be the target of a raid and takeover, an accepted practice. 'If they wanted to retain control, they should have had a 51 per cent stake. If a company needs to retain tight internal control it should not publicly list more than 49 per cent of the company shares. There is no point crying foul after publicly listing majority shares in the open market,' he said.

Harry Jayawardene wasn't able to savour his 'victory' for very long. The Sri Lankan Supreme Court, declaring that the Insurance Corporation was riddled with corruption, ordered it back to government control. And with that loss, Jayawardene found himself losing control of Lanka Hospital as well.

The Sri Lanka story has not quite ended for Dr Prathap Chandra Reddy. His daughter Sangita Reddy – Apollo's group director for Operations – said the company was offering its telemedicine services in Sri Lanka – providing health care and consultative services to patients by using telecommunication technologies that allow transmission of information related to care over distance. In India Apollo has 120 such telemedicine centres; in addition to Sri Lanka Apollo also offers such services in Bangladesh, Africa and the Middle East.

A man like Dr Reddy has a certain kind of special vision about health care. But then you need others to recognize the strength of such a vision – and to honour it. Those who care about these things remain grateful to Dr Reddy and Apollo for having made such positive changes in Sri Lanka's health care landscape. I don't think that Sri Lankans will easily forget his contribution. Apollo's departure was a major loss for their country.

Dr Reddy says, 'Looking back, we made a mistake in not taking 51 per cent interest in the hospital. We thought that equal partnerships would make for less strife but this was not the case in Sri Lanka. The "sharks" were circling in the water and when they realized our success, they wanted it for themselves.

'I don't think we would do the same thing again. It was our first international experience and beyond our control. We learned a big lesson – several big lessons – and we are applying those lessons to all of our new ventures.'

Adds Shobana Reddy: 'We learned our lesson for all our projects. Now we are majority shareholders, or not at all.'

Apollo is still held in high regard for what it did to change health care in Sri Lanka. 'Apollo did not go to establish a hospital in Colombo as an Indian or Sri Lankan hospital,' Dr Reddy says. 'The teams of doctors who went felt that they could make a difference in Sri Lanka – and they did. All of the team members were good-hearted, hard workers. There was such joy for all those who worked on the project, those from Apollo and those from Sri Lanka. It was remarkable how committed everyone was. It gave those in the country a new pride. In just a short three and a half years the medical tourism programme was started. Everything changed, and Apollo was an economic boom for Sri Lanka. Apollo showed Sri Lanka the potential of excellent health care, and till today Apollo stands apart in what it accomplished.'

He adds: 'It is one thing to construct a building. It is another to keep it running for the purposes needed. Most people think of infrastructure as the concrete, the wires and furniture and water. We built all of that for Apollo in Colombo. But we went beyond these because we understood that infrastructure also means the team that runs the buildings and sees the patients and cleans the floors and fixes the food. In that way, we have given to Sri Lanka part of our family, and we are very proud of such a gift.'

The Sri Lanka experience has left its wounds, even in a man who's stoical about the vicissitudes of life.

'We had to leave the country with great sorrow,' Dr Reddy told me. 'A number of other health care facilities have now come up and changed the level of tertiary care for Sri Lankans. I have subsequently had many meetings with President Rajapaksa. His wife Shiranthi told me that she was keen for us to go back. But the President said that his brother, who is in charge of the army, has taken over that hospital – and that he will not be able to help me to get the same hospital. The President said that he would be happy to allot another site for me on similar conditions. But surely, I cannot get back the passion and commitment to create another hospital in Sri Lanka. In any case, I do not get involved in politics. Hospitals and politics are diagonally opposed.'

Be that as it may, the health care sector in India – as in Sri Lanka – is not without its own brand of high-stakes politics either. Government ministers and bureaucrats have to be constantly courted. One has to be continually vigilant about the moves of competitors. The media need to be cultivated. Dr Reddy may not choose to personally play politics, but he knows how the game is played.

CHAPTER TWENTY-EIGHT

Uncomplications

NO ONE AT HM HOSPITAL in Madras had told Antony Jacob about the tall, well-dressed man by his bed, but his stately manner suggested to the thirteen-year-old boy that he was someone important. Everybody around seemed to be deferential towards him. Antony had been brought to the facility almost delirious with fever, eyes yellow and his face pale; he was suffering from jaundice.

The man who examined him was, in fact, a physician; his name was Dr Prathap Chandra Reddy, and he was the boss. He told the boy that his jaundice would be cured and that he would be home in a day or two. For a boy who hadn't slept away from his parents' house for even a night, that prospect might have otherwise seemed intimidating. But Dr Reddy's bedside manner was so pleasant that Antony immediately felt reassured.

'He visited me twice a day. He was always in a smart suit, and he never removed the jacket – which gave him an especially dignified appearance. He made me feel that I was the most important patient for him and he still makes me feel important every time I meet with him,' Antony told me nearly four decades later. 'That's Dr Reddy for you. His presence is soothing. He takes your mind away from whatever it is that afflicts or troubles you.'

Antony was articulating a management and branding practice for which Dr Reddy has gained considerable acclaim in recent years:

serenity – although, in truth, Dr Reddy was practicing it many years ago by carefully and straightforwardly explaining to his patients the nature of their problem. The theory is called 'Let's Uncomplicate', and Antony, chief executive officer of Apollo Munich – India's fastest growing private-sector health insurance company – can rightfully claim the tag for the company.

There is, of course, no such word as 'uncomplicate' in the English dictionary. But if you use it, people will immediately understand that it refers to explication. Health is a complicated subject – no one is immune to thinking about health, and worrying about it. Antony told me: '"Let's Uncomplicate" is not just our positioning, it is our belief and journey.'

Shobana Kamineni, who spearheads the joint venture with partners Munich Re, says: 'We have positioned Apollo Munich as a straightforward, user-friendly and hassle-free health insurance company that will consistently tackle the general concerns faced by people when it comes to health care and health insurance. We focus on the easy uncomplicated process we have for people seeking comprehensive health insurance for themselves and their loved ones. This positioning has enabled us to create a brand identity for the company and differentiate it from the competitors. Of course the halo of Apollo provided instant credibility and trust.'[1]

It was Shobana who brought Antony to Apollo Munich, where he has been for the last four years. After having encountered Dr Reddy as a teenager at HM Hospital – his father is V.J. Chacko – he would meet the founder of Apollo Hospitals on various Indian Airlines flights to New Delhi from Chennai, where he was chief executive officer of Royal Sundaram, a joint venture between Britain's Royal Sun Alliance

---

1   On 23 July 2010, Dr Reddy sent a letter to N. Rangachary, then chairman of India's Insurance Regulatory and Development Authority (IRDA), expressing his appreciation for his role in streamlining the industry. 'As many stars must align appropriately to create the right celestial configuration for success, your alignment of the vital insurance star spurred health reforms in our country. We shall always remember your role and thank God for giving India the right man at the right time,' Dr Reddy wrote, in part.

and Sundaram Finance, which was part of the TVS Group. He was appointed CEO in 1998, when he was just thirty-eight, making him one of the youngest chief executives of any private-sector group in India at the time.

'On those flights, Dr Reddy would always ask me about health insurance, and what my thoughts were,' Antony said. He once told Dr Reddy, 'There's hardly any market penetration.'

Indeed, the health insurance industry reached barely 1.5 per cent of India's population in 1997. Its turnover then was Rs 400 crore,[2] and the industry – despite the recommendations of the Malhotra Committee in 1994 that, among other things, the sector be opened up more to private companies – was dominated by four large government insurance companies, which mainly offered a product called 'Mediclaim': New India, United India, Oriental and National.[3]

By 2008, Antony found himself in Dubai as regional director for Royal Sun Alliance (Asia and Middle East). It was a particularly bad time to be in the United Arab Emirates, and especially in Dubai whose economy had tumbled in the wake of the world financial crisis precipitated by the subprime mortgage scandal in the United States. Questions were being raised about Dubai's ability to service its sovereign debt, which was estimated to be anywhere between $75

---

2 India's health care insurance has a turnover today of Rs 16,000 crore, or roughly $3 billion. This still represents a penetration rate of only 5 per cent. The total spent by the public and private sectors on health care annually in the country is $60 billion. The health care industry is growing by 20 per cent annually, a figure that is expected to rise to 25 per cent by 2020.

3 A committee was set up in 1993 under the chairmanship of Ram N. Malhotra, former governor of the Reserve Bank of India, to make recommendations for reforms in the insurance sector. In its 1994 report, the committee recommended, among other things, that private players be included in the insurance sector; that foreign companies be allowed to enter the insurance sector, preferably through joint ventures with Indian partners; and that the IRDA be constituted as an autonomous body to regulate and develop the insurance sector.

billion and $150 billion.[4] Antony had begun thinking seriously of moving back to India, or perhaps working somewhere else.

One day, Antony's phone rang. It was Shobana Kamineni. Shobana and Antony's wife, Uma, had been at Stella Maris College in Chennai. After exchanging pleasantries, Shobana asked Antony how he felt about being in Dubai.

'Well, things aren't very good here, and I'm not that happy,' Antony told Shobana. 'I'm thinking of moving back to India.'

Shobana told him that Apollo had already launched a health insurance company in cooperation with Munich Re.[5] Would Antony be interested in joining the Apollo Group? (Shobana says that she had actually called him about a colleague but changed tack and threw the offer out to him.)

He subsequently went through tough interviews in Chennai, New Delhi and Munich.

Antony started as chief executive officer on 1 April 2009. His office was in Gurgaon, on the outskirts of New Delhi. Although Apollo was a national and international brand, Nitin Desai – former Secretary in the Department of Economic Affairs, and now head of Oxfam International – told me that there was a lingering perception it was a 'southern company'. Basing the insurance company near the capital in India's north would send a distinct signal that Apollo's expansion would be in all directions. The staff consisted of 400 men and women. Today, some 1,300 people work in the company. Apollo Munich has already become profitable in four years, when the initial expectation

---

4 Dubai eventually worked out a repayment schedule with its creditors, and its economy is flourishing again. I was a witness to the entire financial crisis since I lived in Dubai during those years. The story of the crisis and how it was resolved is told in my 2011 book *Dubai: The Making of a Megapolis*.

5 Munich Re became renowned after the San Francisco earthquake of 1906 as the only insurer that remained solvent after paying out all the claims. In 2010 the company's equity amounted to 23 billion. Munich Re has around 5,000 clients (insurance companies) in about 150 countries. It assumes part of the risk covered by these insurance companies, as well as providing comprehensive advice on insurance business.

had been for five years, and its annual turnover is $112 million with a 25 per cent compounded annual growth rate.

How did Apollo Munich do it? How did it catapult past existing private-sector health insurance companies and build a strong brand – so much so that Apollo Munich's success now seems to be enticing foreign health insurance companies like Blue Cross, Cigna and Aetna to want to enter the huge Indian market?

The first thing was a name change. Somehow, Apollo DKV did not quite resonate with consumers; it was an amalgam of Apollo and the initials of the German arm of Munich Re group that dealt with health insurance.

Apollo didn't just go out and change the brand name arbitrarily or unilaterally. Shobana and the Apollo DKV board decided that the strategic plan be revisited with external expertise. McKinsey & Company were brought in. Antony had worked with the consulting giant during his time at Royal Sundaram, and was pleased with their efforts.

The Apollo DKV–McKinsey joint strategic plan called Project LEAP was presented to Apollo DKV's board in September 2009. The team had drawn up a strategic plan that they promised to fulfil within five years. The brand change required approval from Munich Re, which had hitherto never given approval for any country's insurance company to co-brand itself with the German giant's parent name.

Along with the change in brand name, Apollo initiated an extensive advertising campaign, 'Let's Uncomplicate'.

'We needed to explain in plain language what we stood for,' Antony told me. 'In India and around the world, health insurance is not easily understood. So we launched an ad campaign about our products, and about Apollo's strong record in the health insurance industry. When you are in a customer-facing business it is imperative to hold the right customer perception as a brand. Apollo DKV was changed to Apollo Munich and new brand values were laid down by keeping the customer services at the core. Dr Reddy and Shobana embraced the concept of "Let's Uncomplicate" and worked towards building the brand Apollo Munich.'

Dr Reddy and Shobana Kamineni embraced the concept of 'Let's Uncomplicate' as not just Apollo Munich's positioning, but also their 'belief and journey'. Shobana told me that Munich Re sent fifty officials to work with Apollo when the joint venture started. Apollo Munich now has only Indian officials.

Apollo's entry into the health care insurance business is lauded by Ghyanendra N. Bajpai, former executive chairman of the Life Insurance Corporation of India, and executive chairman of the Securities and Exchange Board of India. He is currently chairman of Siemens in India.

Bajpai met Dr Reddy in Hyderabad in 2000 at a meeting about India's health care infrastructure. 'I was struck by how often he said that he wanted to reach out to the deprived,' Bajpai told me. 'I was greatly impressed by his humility. In a few minutes, I could sense his urge and empathy for health care.'

Underscoring two types of infrastructure – physical, such as roads and ports, and social, such as education and health care – that the state in India had traditionally taken responsibility for, Bajpai said: 'People like me feel that health care provided by the state was inadequate and inefficient. In mature economies, the private sector has to step into education and health care. I particularly consider health infrastructure very significant in any society. It's very simple: when people are healthy, they produce more – and the national economy benefits.

'I see prospects for the health care industry – and the health insurance industry – as very bright in India on account of the size of the population and growing longevity. The state alone cannot take care of the challenges. And while it's true that Dr Reddy alone cannot fill that gap, he's done something remarkable: he's shown that it makes business sense to participate in health care. He's demonstrated that you can make money while doing good, and that you can do good, and still make money. Dr Reddy has created a successful model for health care in India.'

Keshav Desiraju offered another perspective to me. He cited the benefits given to participants in the Central Government Health

Services (CGHS); for the most part, these benefits are free, but even when employees consult empanelled doctors the government pays the cost.

'The insurance debate is important for India,' Desiraju said. 'We need to know more. We're not in a position where we can wholeheartedly embrace private insurance to meet health care needs. Access is a key issue: primary health care should be affordable in an equitable way. Tertiary care is different. The government believes that in tertiary care, the patient pays. As far as private and public health insurance schemes go, the jury is still out on the health outcomes.'

According to McKinsey & Company's India Chairman Adil Zainulbhai, 'Overall, health care services in India are significantly supply-starved across the hierarchy of primary to tertiary health care. Further, while income levels are rising, the private out-of-pocket spend is currently too high for health care access to reach a large population. So, on the one side, there is a strong thrust needed to rapidly scale up health care provision at the right quality and an equal thrust needed to isolate the patients from the cost of care through a combination of private and public insurance.'

Nevertheless, Apollo's leadership in corporate-sector health care has been beneficial for the industry, according to K. Parasaran, India's former Solicitor General. 'Dr Reddy has given more to the country than most people can even begin to imagine,' he told me one evening at his home in Chennai. 'He has applied his healing touch to India.'

Parasaran told me that Dr Reddy also applied his healing touch to him. In November 2010, he checked into Apollo Chennai for a heart bypass that was to be performed by Dr Girinath.

Just before he was taken to the operating theatre, Dr Reddy took his hand and said, 'You are going to be fine.'

Several hours later, when Parasaran woke up, the first person he saw was Dr Reddy, who said: 'The operation is over – and you're fine.'

Parasaran told me: 'I include Dr Reddy in my prayers every day.'

On the business front Apollo Munich has become arguably India's leading private health insurer during the last couple of years. It started to become profitable since the last quarter of 2012.

Says Dr Nikolaus von Bomhard, Chairman of the Board of Management of Munich Re: 'Insurance is all about people, and especially in our international business operations we see that our success in each and every country is highly influenced by the mentality and personality of our business partners. In some cases, we are lucky enough to create joint ventures together with people of great vision and real landmark influence, and so it happened when we were taking our first steps into creating a specialized health insurance company in India. It was Dr Prathap Reddy who really paved the way for the success of our joint endeavour, Apollo Munich Health Insurance, by giving it a clear and solid mission of providing a sustainable solution for the financing of private health care in India.'

With a network of nearly 4,000 hospitals spread across 830 cities, all customers of Apollo Munich can be sure that wherever and whenever they require medical attention, one will be available to him or her on a cashless basis. This network is one of the largest amongst private health insurers. Apollo Munich was the first company to launch a Health Line – a dedicated medical helpline for customers.

When Dr Reddy was informed not long ago that Apollo Munich had been rated among the 25 Best Companies to Work For list in the 2013 edition of the Great Places to Work in India survey, he couldn't but summon a huge smile. The Apollo brand was being reinforced.

The question of branding Apollo is continually important to Dr Reddy. He adds that happy employees lead to happy customers – this twist has enabled the company to catapult itself from being in the top 100 Best Companies to Work For list in 2011 to the top 50 in 2012 and more recently to the elite top 25.

One day in Chennai, I met with a guru of India's advertising industry, Jagannath Ramaswamy,[6] to discuss how brands like Apollo

---

6 Jagannath Ramaswamy holds a degree from the Indian Institute of Management, and is also a chemical engineering graduate of the prestigious

– one of his clients – develop and strengthen their public identity.

'When I look back on my thirty-five years of active involvement in advertising and working on scores of categories and brands, I have found that health care advertising is a bit unique. Cold logic tells you if this product is to be sold in the traditional way, people have to fall ill. While people do fall ill, it is not a nice thing to wish for. A big problem is, no one likes to believe or accept that he or she can have any serious ailment. It is always, "It can happen only to somebody else." And unfortunately most often they seek medical help only when it is a little too late and the cost of treatment is higher and the chances of cure lower,' Jagannath, founder and mentor of Crystal in Chennai, told me. 'So what kind of persuasion can work? Routes like using "fear" can work only up to an extent. Moreover, it is this fear that prevents a lot of people from going in for medical checks, as they are scared of getting a not-so-favourable report.'

I asked: 'So how do private institutions such as Apollo employ the power of persuasion?'

'While government hospitals may not have a profit target, institutions in the private sector have to and do have a business agenda,' Jagannath said. 'Hence, as far as advertising goes, one has to first generate a generic demand – that is, get people to seek timely medical care, and then get them to choose a brand. The Indian Medical Council frowns upon blatant advertising claims with the standard fare of hyperbole and superlatives – almost mandatory today in FMCG products. At Apollo, credibility of any advertisement has not been a problem, because the need for business profit has never overshadowed Dr Reddy's concern to provide the best care. At Apollo Hospitals, advertising was largely restricted to educating the public on the incidence of diseases, risk factors and the emerging treatment options, so the message was never "a sale not to be missed". Their massive investments in technology – many of them firsts in our country – have stood them in good stead. Add to

---

Indian Institute of Technology in Kanpur.

it the universal acknowledgement of some of their pioneering work, both in terms of equipment and procedures. And very importantly the maxim "success begets success" is so true in Apollo's case. One has to just visit any of their hospitals; the huge throng of patients almost throughout the day, does act as an irrefutable proof that it is the preferred health care destination. In turn this motivates so many more to place their trust – nay their life – in the hands of the brand called Apollo.'

During my work on this biography, I met several times with Shailaja Vardhan, vice president of communications at Apollo. Shailaja joined Apollo Hospitals in May 2008, a point in time when the company was gearing up for the twenty-fifth year celebrations. It was just a few weeks after she had joined Apollo that she had to meet Dr Satyabhama at Apollo Chennai. Shailaja said that as she was walking into the hospital, she saw a little boy barely ten years of age, a double amputee, being wheeled in. All around her in the lobby, and as she walked up the floors, she saw many anxious patients and attendants and thought to herself, 'How can one go about being cheerful and positive in such an environment?'

Before the meeting began, she expressed this sentiment to Dr Satyabhama who heard her out and said, 'Shailaja, what you are experiencing is quite a natural emotion for non-medical people, but to feel positive, don't think about the pain and suffering that you see, but think about the lives that Apollo saves each day.'

Shailaja was an integral member of the team that refreshed the Apollo logo in 2009. Every element of the Apollo logo is emblematic of a core value. The flame denotes Light of Hope, which Apollo ignites in millions of patients and their families. The torch denotes the institution's mission as Torch Bearers, the hand represents the Healing Touch and the nurse symbolizes the tender loving care and personalized patient care provided by all the hospitals. That's branding at its very best.

Late one evening about five years ago in Chennai, a twenty-six-year-old man named Kishore Manohar heard his phone ring, and answered it.

'Imagine my surprise when I heard Dr Reddy's voice asking me if I would be interested in doing some work for him,' Kishore told me. 'It wasn't my first time working for Apollo. I had already worked with Preetha Reddy on a few standalone projects for Apollo Hospitals, and so I kind of knew my way around. But being called by Chairman, as the people around him referred to him in awe, was a different ball game altogether.'

Dr Reddy had called young Kishore in the context of an announcement by the government in 2008 that they were going to offer a two-year tax vacation to hospitals that had more than 100 beds. This was a move to address the woeful shortage of hospital beds across the country, a point that Dr Reddy stressed then, and continues to do so now. Dr Reddy had proposed an innovative model which would take tertiary care to Tier Two and Tier Three cities and non-urban areas and at the same time provide added support to the existing health care system in those places.

'I came to recognize that it was classic Dr Reddy – always watchful, always sensitive to health care opportunities. The brand was called Apollo Reach Hospitals and my partner Aravindh and I happily worked in our cocoon, along with the inimitable Dr Hariprasad, the CEO of Apollo Hyderabad, developing an identity and a design language. Dr Reddy listened to us each time. He never criticized anything we presented,' Kishore told me.

Spurred by Dr Reddy's seeming confidence in their work, the two young men went on to develop a comprehensive design manual for the two hospitals being built in Karaikudi, Tamil Nadu and Karimnagar, Hyderabad. Little did they guess that Dr Reddy's dream was to build not just two but 100 such hospitals across the country. They certainly did not know that the project was to be launched by Prime Minister Manmohan Singh. Now Dr Reddy is developing Reach hospitals into one of Apollo's most ambitious ventures.

The first call that Kishore Manohar had received from Dr Reddy, however, was not for the Apollo Reach Hospitals project. It was to help put together a presentation for various state governments for a unified health care emergency service, after Apollo had discovered that another company had bagged the order for emergency services in Hyderabad.

Working with Dr Reddy elicits amazement on the part of people much younger than him. He's irrepressibly enthusiastic. One of his favourite sayings is: 'Medical emergencies don't have Sundays.' With Dr Reddy it's always about being one step ahead of a medical emergency.

That explained Dr Reddy's concern that the powers-that-be had chosen to go with a non-health care player to provide ambulance services across Andhra Pradesh. 'Why would they do that when they have a name like Apollo to go to? Why were we not even informed of this? Anyway, let's move fast now and try and make up in the other states,' Dr Reddy said.

A lot of groundwork was done. Ambulances were lined up. Apollo's emergency service was rebranded. Dr Reddy went through a lot of trouble to ensure the governments got the true picture of Apollo's capabilities and intent. But to no avail. One by one he saw state governments looking beyond Apollo's expertise. Even Tamil Nadu – the Apollo bastion – could not be convinced. For some unfathomable reason the government decided to choose the other player – a software manufacturer – over the architects of modern India's health insurance system.

For Dr Reddy, however, it was another day in the office. He responded by bringing in his grandson Harshad Reddy to revitalize the emergency services. And today's shiny new ambulances with that signature siren and flashing lights resulted from that.

A few years later, while working on the Apollo Children's Hospital project with Preetha Reddy and Sindoori Reddy, and looking at versions of the teddy bear mascot, Sindoori almost casually suggested it be called Paws. It was a great name, and it stuck. It was conceived and driven entirely by Preetha Reddy and Sindoori (Suneeta's daughter). A year later when Sindoori wanted specific pieces of communication in the Children's Hospital, she justified her request saying that staffers should always put patients first and that Apollo always should have brand identification.

That is known as uncomplicating things. Which is another way, I suppose, of also finding the mental and emotional resources to get things done the 'Apollo Way'. And as Dr Reddy defines the 'Apollo Way', it's clear that encouraging young people is part of the Reddy ethos. 'I owe it to them to share my experience, and to give these young people the right opportunities,' Dr Reddy told me.

———

But sometimes, associations with people did get complicated for Dr Prathap Chandra Reddy.

When Dr Reddy first met the controversial guru Chandraswami, the doctor was at a disadvantage because he did not speak Hindi and the guru spoke very little English and Telugu at the time. There was always an interpreter and much of the spontaneity of the conversation was gone.

The guru – whose real name is Nemi Chand Jain – was staying at Adnan Khashoggi's apartment in Olympic Tower, a tall residential building on Fifth Avenue in Manhattan. The doctor was staying at a nearby hotel.

Dr Reddy says, 'He complimented our Apollo standards, and from that day onwards, he had a very special affection for us. I didn't meet with him too many times because I had my own full schedule but he invited me to stop over and meet with him after an appointment. Coincidentally, Donald Trump was there at the same time and we had a nice chat. Trump invited me to go to his casino in Atlantic City that night. Even though I love casinos, I couldn't go because my schedule was entirely booked.'

'Chandraswami came once to Chennai for a festival and we met at the Kali temple. The senior priest introduced us and the teacher said, "I must come and pray for you," and on the third day, he did.

His secretary said that I should call on him in Delhi. Once the guru knows you, he wants to know you very well. Engagement is rapid and often riveting. He's very persuasive in the way he talks,' says Dr Reddy. He continues, 'I went to see Chandraswami in Delhi, and he told me that the government of Rajasthan was going to give him a large piece of land in that state to be used for an ashram and other charitable purposes, possibly even a health clinic. He received many donations for India and abroad for this work. He asked me to join his board and I agreed. There was a problem because the Central government doesn't allow foreign donations to be transferred from one account to the other. Some transfer had been made and it came under investigation. By the time this occurred, I had resigned from the board because nothing was happening and I was so busy that I no longer had time to participate.

'We did take several trips together and once we went to Atlanta, Georgia and met with former President Jimmy Carter and toured his library. We went to the World Expo in Vancouver. In Los Angeles, ordinary people and many celebrities surrounded Chandraswami. One of them, the famous actress Elizabeth Taylor, was so taken by our work at Apollo; she said that she would help raise money for social funds.

'Chandraswami organized several meetings for doctors who were his followers. He wanted them to know about Apollo and either support it or come back and join us. His events always attracted a packed audience, sometimes 250–300 doctors, and he would always introduce me by saying, "My chairman is here." This would get people to pay more attention. Three of the cities where we had meetings were Detroit, Boston and Chicago. Everyone wanted to see the guru and many were curious about Apollo. I worked very hard to get the support of Indian doctors in the US.[7] Often I would have

---

7 Among those who sometimes drove Dr Reddy around was Dr Prem Sagar Reddy, a California-based physician, who also hosted a number of get-togethers for fellow Indian doctors so that Dr Reddy could make his presentations. Dr Prem now owns several medical facilities in the United States.

breakfast in one city and dinner in another so that I could meet as many doctors as possible.[8]

'I took his support. He always has a lively conversation with many entertaining stories. He has friends, and enemies, in government, but they all take his calls.'

'But as for me, I keep out of politics at all times,' Dr Reddy says. 'I am a doctor. As I often like to say, medicine has no ideology. I have sometimes been asked to enter politics. But politics is not my business, medicine is. My concern is for Apollo – and even more overriding is my concern for the development of health care in India. We have not even met the health care challenges of the twentieth century, let alone those of the twenty-first.'

That could explain why it is that leaders across the political spectrum trust Dr Reddy, respect him, and turn to him for medical treatment the 'Apollo Way'.

———

When I met Jaideep Gupta, managing director of the Indraprastha Apollo Hospitals in Delhi, he, too, spoke about the 'Apollo Way'. Naturally, he identifies strongly with Dr Reddy's value system – not the least because Gupta has worked for Apollo for the last twenty-five years.

'One of his biggest strengths is his way with people. Whatever be the age and profile of the guest – be it a twenty-two-year-old new employee, a grateful patient, or a complainant, Dr Reddy will always get up and come forward with a smile and a handshake. On one occasion, we were in a meeting with an associate who had let us down badly, and I was fuming and ready to explode. But Dr Reddy would have none of it. He was as polite, courteous and understanding as he was when he first met them, and never showed

---

8 In India, Dr Reddy travelled to at least fifteen cities. He would meet with doctors between 5 p.m. and 7 p.m., and then members of the public – and potential investors – from 8 p.m. onward.

the slightest sign that he was upset or disappointed with the way we had been treated,' Gupta said, adding, 'For Dr Reddy, it is never just Apollo: it is always for the country, for patients across borders. He is never afraid of competition; in fact, competition is the reason for innovation.'

One of Dr Reddy's oldest friends, B.A. Kodandaraman, spoke to me about his competitiveness, and his continual encouragement of young entrepreneurs. Kodandaraman heads Viveks, one of the biggest retail chains in southern India, and has known Dr Reddy since he returned to India from the United States.

'Many things have changed in Chennai, and in India, but not Dr Reddy's smile, self-assurance, self-confidence,' Kodandaraman said to me over lunch at a dainty restaurant across the street from his Chennai office. 'For any patient, medicines become secondary – what comes first is trust in the doctor. Just by Dr Reddy putting his hand on a patient's shoulder, that person is already 50 per cent cured.'

'The other thing about Dr Reddy is that his success hasn't gone to his head,' Kodandaraman said, echoing comments made to me in New Delhi by leading economist Bimal Jalan and Dr K. Kasturirangan, widely considered to be the father of India's space programme and now a member of the Planning Commission.

Kodandaraman told me of the time when, in 1988, his father was critically ill. His left leg was amputated, but complications developed. Dr Reddy arranged for the older man to be flown to a speciality hospital in Los Angeles, and also dispatched an Apollo doctor to accompany him. 'He personally arranged everything, from a US visa to ambulances to transport my father,' Kodandaraman said. 'How many people would take this kind of trouble for you?'

———

The question of Dr Reddy's foresight has always fascinated Sheela Ketan, vice president of operations at the Apollo Speciality Hospital in Chennai. She has been associated with Apollo for thirty years. Her story echoes that of many in Apollo who started their careers at the institution and today lead departments, divisions, hospitals and businesses within the Apollo system. 'That's the family strength which truly empowers all,' Shobana Kamineni said.

One November day in 1983, Sheela was walking along Greams Road in Madras when she saw the sign for Apollo Hospital. She had heard about the new hospital and decided to go in and take a look. While taking a walk around she met a man who was in human resources and they began talking. Sheela had always wanted to be a doctor but had been unable to follow her passion. As she and the HR man talked, he told her that the hospital was looking for staff and asked her to apply. There were no forms and he gave her a plain piece of white paper and loaned her his pen. He asked her to write down her details, then looked them over and said, 'Go and meet Dr Reddy.'

She went to his small office where he glanced at the sheet. Then he said, 'I would like you to join,' and gave her a piece of paper with her appointment. She was very surprised.

Sheela began work in the office as receptionist, and then went from department to department with each job growing in responsibility. In 1994 Dr Reddy proposed that Sheela shift to the Apollo Speciality Hospital. Most attention had been focused on the main hospital, but the Speciality Hospital needed brushing up. The Apollo Speciality Hospital now has 300 beds, growing from the 100 it had when Sheela took over. It houses the oncology, neurology and orthopaedic departments. A new area for out-patient consulting was added in 2013 so that the hospital could continue to add beds for in-patient care.

When Sheela first joined the Speciality Hospital she found a building needing improvements in infrastructure and an overworked staff that dearly needed an emotional boost. She said to herself, 'How am I going to manage this?' But she set to work.

First, she improved the ambience for both the patients and the staff. The walls were grey and had scratch marks on them from gurneys and supply carts. The entire hospital was repainted a lovely white, brighter and more natural. Immediately she saw a change in attitude.

Then she began soliciting more consultants and nurses to meet the increase in staffing needs. People were eager to join Apollo and this, too, made a big change. World-class doctors form a great nucleus and attract new patients not only from India but also from other countries.

Keeping up with the fast pace of growth was a challenge. Another core element needed an infusion and Sheela presented proposals for new equipment to Dr Reddy and Preetha Reddy. 'They never said no to anything I requested. It was not a struggle to get authorization and we got the best equipment for the Speciality Hospital: an MRI, CT, CyberKnife, Linac Accelerator,' she recalls.

There was not much room to expand so as surrounding buildings became available, Apollo took them, breaking down walls so that four buildings became one.

Today Apollo Speciality Hospital is recognized as a leader in providing comprehensive cancer care. Each case is evaluated individually by the Tumour Board, which plans the treatment strategy, which could be a combination of medical, radiological and surgical programmes.

'Dr Reddy has great faith in people and he and Preetha placed their trust in me. I could not let them down,' Sheela replied.

It was her way of saying that she helped uncomplicate things at Apollo.

———

Throughout his long career, Dr Reddy has had the good fortune of making friends readily. One of them is Grandhi Mallikarjuna Rao of Bangalore, founder and chairman of the GMR conglomerate. Rao's group built the new Rajiv Gandhi International Airport in Hyderabad, and also the Indira Gandhi International Airport in New Delhi. Now he's building a new airport in Istanbul.

Not long ago, he and Dr Reddy agreed to build an Apollo hospital at Hyderabad Airport.

'When we formulated a joint venture, I found him the same person as what he was twenty-five years back when I first got to know Dr Reddy, the same man with the same passion, the same qualities of caring and warmth,' Rao told me. 'The joint venture between Apollo, GMR and the Mayo Clinic is his vision to make India a health care destination of the world by bringing back highly qualified Indian doctors to serve the country – reversing the brain drain. He has always worked with good intentions for creating value to the society.'

Rao paused for a moment, then said: 'Dr Reddy has done more in one lifetime for his country than almost any contemporary figure I can think of.' Perhaps this was his way of saying that Dr Reddy was largely responsible for uncomplicating the way health care was delivered in India.

CHAPTER TWENTY-NINE

The Family Ways

IN MY YEARLONG JOURNEY through the landscape of Dr Prathap Chandra Reddy's life, I met with virtually every member of his immediate family, many of his other relatives and top associates, and numerous friends from across political and social spectrums. It was, nevertheless, too short a journey to traverse through the recollections of all the men and women still living who had witnessed the improbable rise of the man from Aragonda village in Andhra Pradesh.

One day I was in a small private plane in which Dr Reddy and Sucharitha Reddy, along with some family members, were flying. I had been invited as part of that group for a special darshan of Lord Venkateshwara at Tirupati temple. Throughout the one-hour flight from Chennai to Tirupati, Dr Reddy and Sucharitha were teasing each other. It went beyond the banter between husband and wife. There seemed to be a rare kind of deep affection, something indefinable yet discernible. It struck me then that through all the long months that I'd spent with the Reddys, I hadn't asked Dr Reddy directly about his feelings for Sucharitha after so many years of matrimony. Maybe it was the conservative in me, a man brought up not to ask another man how he felt about his wife. Ironically, I'd had no such reservations in asking Sucharitha some months earlier about her husband's career.

Some weeks after our return to Chennai from Tirupati, curiosity trumped conservatism. The marriage of Prathap Chandra and Sucharitha Reddy had been such a celebrated union of two people from different backgrounds that I felt people would want to know about Dr Reddy's innermost feelings. But how much of those feelings would he reveal?

So, with the assistance of my research associate Twilla Duncan, I put some questions to him. Both Twilla – a veteran TV producer and strategic communications specialist – and I were utterly surprised by Dr Reddy's candour. Of course, he seemed more than a trifle embarrassed at times, but he did not hold back.

'Sucha is so much more than my dear wife. She is my best friend. I have many friends but not that many intimates. Right from the beginning I have relied on her. I was lonely at times. Her wise words were always tender and affectionate. I don't take a major decision without talking it over with her,' Dr Reddy said one afternoon at his Chennai corporate office. 'We came from such different backgrounds and somehow we became the ideal match. I was a bit of a brash young man with the entire world before me. You know how boys can be. They say that men mature later than women, even if we are married. Sucha had more appreciation of culture, dance and art. She has passed that along to our four lovely daughters. Fortunately, I have absorbed her interest in culture and beauty too, through osmosis. She was open to new experiences, and that's why she enjoyed London and the US so much. I regret that I didn't do more. I was working all the time and the best I did was on the weekends when we went out as a family.'

What were his expectations when he and Sucharitha got married?

'I didn't know what to expect when we married except that the wives and mothers had always supported their husbands. Even in India, though, times and traditions were changing. When we came back to India from our time in the United States, it was almost constant work. There were many stresses – and whom could I confide in? We did not have the land or the money and people were saying that my vision for Apollo as a corporate-sector hospital was a folly. Some days I would feel burnt out. Sucha understood, and being with her strengthened me. She listened to all of my problems, all of the challenges of starting Apollo, the frustrations, the sick patients, and the poor. She has always been by my side. We are tied together by silken threads.'

Silken threads? I thought that it was an unusual and very classy phrase to use. But that phrase, more than anything I have heard, captures the nature of the bonds between Prathap Chandra and Sucharitha Reddy.

'I didn't want to give out any doubt,' Dr Reddy continued, 'and Sucha supported Apollo and me at each step. In the meantime, she had to deal with the children, grandchildren and all of our families. We have big families, and it is Sucha who keeps us all connected. The girls had school and dance and sports and many friends. They were always busy, and so were Sucha and I. We had a busy family.

'You know how much work it took to build the first Apollo and then Hyderabad and more. It takes even more work to build a family. One thing we did was to take time to talk about how to deal with the stress. She absorbed enormous amounts of exasperation and headaches, enough to make her sick.'

How much did faith help them during those times of stress?

'We have the same values and her faith has always inspired me,' Dr Reddy said. 'Faith sustains us and serves as a bond for our family. Children are more influenced by what you do than by what you say, so the emphasis on spirituality is important for all of us. There were difficult issues in launching all our projects. They could not be allowed to affect the outcome. It was essential to keep focused and move ahead and Sucha allowed me to do so. I could sometimes be difficult but we have give-and-take and I feel like a king around her. It is the unspoken things. I miss her when she is away. We like to share news. It's very fulfilling to share the success of our family and Apollo with her. Our staff, which is really our family, refers to her as "Amma", and the way they say it is with such affection.'

And what about the role that Sucharitha plays at Apollo?

'Everyone knows how generous Sucha is and that she loves to cook and entertain. She doesn't have a formal role at Apollo but she is very observant and knows what is going on,' Dr Reddy said. 'She played a big role when we were setting up Apollo, teaching the staff how to clean, giving instructions to the kitchen and housekeeping staff and helping us create a healing experience for patients and their families. She also taught our staff about behaviour with others, how to greet patients and talk with them tenderly. She still does this today. When I broke my arm recently, Sucha went to the hospital and "made rounds" for me on the days that I did not go. She is often in the hospital visiting patients and encouraging the staff.'

What about Sucharitha's own faith regarding Apollo?

'Here in Chennai we don't get much rain but when we do, it really rains. They say one must give every new building three rainy seasons to see if it is perfect, or determine what is wrong with it. I don't know why the architects cannot plan well ahead for the problems,' Dr Reddy said. 'In the first days of Apollo, the hospital basement would get flooded. I remember getting calls in the middle of the night. Sucha and the girls would get up and go to the hospital. The girls would supervise the bailing of the water and make sure all supplies were dry and had not been damaged. Sucha would go to the kitchen, inspect the food and ensure that it was clean, protected and safe. Then she would inspect housekeeping because she knew that cleanliness and infection control are essential. They would all stay until the job was done, making sure that the hospital could function without interruption or delay. She brings a softer aspect to the hospital and has helped us solve many problems. Her positive energy and affection is endearing and enduring. People remember how close they feel to her years afterwards. She knows what matters most. I read a quote that says love is what you've been through. I've never heard Sucha say a hurtful word although there were many tests in setting up Apollo.'

What about Sucharitha's 'discipline' concerning Dr Reddy and their daughters?

'Sucha has a playful sense of humour and teases the children and me,' Dr Reddy said. 'She is interesting to be around. I like her surprises. She has a strong will and is willing to express it. She will tell you what's on her mind. One day, I had been in meetings on exciting projects and she had been very patient. Suddenly she said, "It is 2.10. Get up and go eat." And that's exactly what I did. My life is richer because of Sucha and Apollo is stronger and richer because of her, too. She is the silent supporter at my back without whom much of Apollo's success would not have happened.'

Dr Reddy is especially proud of Sucharitha's culinary skills – and the fact that she's a published author of cookbooks. During the production of her first book, *Nostalgia Cuisine*, photographers, art directors and technicians would assemble in the morning at the Reddy home in Bishop Garden. Before he left for his office, Dr Reddy would invariably drop by, shake everyone's hands – including the light boys – and wish them good luck.

'On some occasions, when Dr Reddy would come home for lunch, he would find out if all of the production crew had eaten and then insist that some of us join him on the table, if we had not eaten,' Sucharita Varadarajan, an integral member of the team, said. 'One thing he was particular about was the quantity of food; he would often advise – cook enough so that everyone gets enough, but do not waste food. It is a sin.'

On the day that *Nostalgia Cuisine* was launched at the Reddy beach house 'Sindoori' on the outskirts of Chennai, Dr Reddy arrived well ahead of the function. He went through the arrangements, and congratulated all the people involved. He was beaming. He was taking pride in the achievements of Sucharitha Reddy.

———

Their good friend Deepak S. Parekh confirmed my sense of Dr Reddy and Sucharitha as a remarkable couple with their own individual characteristics and also with shared ones. I have known Deepak since our time at St Xavier's High School in Bombay. He was a brilliant student, and our Jesuit teachers openly predicted a bright future for him. They were right. Deepak became one of India's pre-eminent chartered accountants and bankers, and went on to become chairman of the Housing Development Finance Corporation (HDFC). HDFC loaned Apollo money to set up hospitals and other related enterprises.

I ran into Deepak in the lobby of the Leela Palace Hotel in New Delhi's Chanakyapuri area. He was in town to meet government officials, and also attend the annual meeting of the Asian Development Bank in early May 2013.

'Whenever I think of Dr Reddy and Mrs Reddy, what comes to mind is a paean to a couple that is larger than life, personalities that inspire compassion and confidence and a measure of a life lived in service. It is fitting to say that my first interaction with Dr Reddy has left so lasting an impact that I continue to revere his philosophy and his mission to heal,' Deepak told me.

A kinship between the two men grew over the years with Dr Reddy's gentle insistence for a health check annually presided over by him, and his determination to ensure that Deepak was completely inspected by his able team, handpicked by him; Deepak says he has been cajoled and pampered by Apollo's meticulous care. 'For this and more, I will always be indebted,' he told me.

I asked Deepak about his assessment of Apollo's performance as a financial institution under the stewardship of Dr Reddy.

'How do you benchmark perfection? How much reverence can one earn in one lifetime? You need look no further than the mark Dr Reddy makes on the lives of multitudes. Humbly and gently, he wields the baton; he has institutionalized health care, established a blueprint by keeping abreast of the newest and the best, and leads his family and his team to hallmark a brand,' Deepak said. 'The country owes him a monumental debt. Young entrepreneurs, doctors and providers can dip into his treasure trove of expertise to accept nothing but the toughest standards in medical care.'

He added: 'HDFC as a real estate lender has a long and fruitful association with the Apollo Group. The hospital chain has expanded over the decades and has needed institutional finance to acquire real estate in cities across the country. HDFC is proud of this association and feels intrinsically bound to the future of the Group. Apollo has served as a model for other business groups to corporatize health care in India. It has been a successful endeavour and Apollo has been the frontrunner in charting the course for providing affordable and incomparable care in all facets of hospital management.'

Does his wife Smita share Deepak's sentiments about Prathap Chandra and Sucharitha Reddy?

'Of course she does,' Deepak said, seemingly amused that I would even ask a question for which the answer was obvious. 'There is never a moment when my wife and I have hesitated to call and consult him, and there has never been an instance when we have not received his expert advice. The common refrain in our home has been "check with the expert"! This is no other than Dr Prathap Reddy, no other than the doyen of global medicine, no other than the patriarch he is to his four daughters, grandchildren, and ourselves. For, he has adopted us as family and it is to him that we revert for all things big and small. We wish him many more years and the time to hold many a hand through one of the most challenging times in India's economic history.'

As I approached the end of writing this book, I wondered how I should conclude. Dr Prathap Chandra Reddy is still very much at the helm of Apollo, and so it would be premature to offer a 'summing up' when his life is still a journey in progress. I thought that perhaps I might present snapshots of perceptions of some Reddy family members, and some friends. A few of the comments below found their way into earlier chapters, but I thought they seemed worth highlighting because they highlighted the dedication to core values that Dr Reddy had established for Apollo. The perceptions of some might seem to contradict those of others. But underlying all the comments is a fierce loyalty to the Healer, Dr Prathap Chandra Reddy, and his wife Sucharitha.

I was especially intrigued by the thoughts of the third generation of Reddys – the children of the four daughters of Dr Prathap Chandra and Sucharitha Reddy – who are now engaged with expanding to

Dr Reddy's Apollo vision. Adit Reddy was one of them.

I had met Adit Reddy in mid-2012, along with his petite wife Ritika Rai Reddy, over a family lunch at the home of Dr Reddy and Sucharitha. He's the son of Suneeta and Dwarakanath Reddy. He admitted that he had been raucous when younger. 'When I was in high school and college I had a tendency to be rambunctious,' Adit said. 'A few family members were worried but my grandfather said, "Don't worry about it. This is just a phase." His words were always reassuring.'

Adit struck me as a young man with a strong sense of entrepreneurship; at the time, he was seeking funding to launch a power plant. In any environment this would be a big challenge. But now, especially, the banks are not funding power plants because they have too much exposure over non-performing assets.

Adit, a tall, strong man with sharply chiselled features, said that he always takes his grandfather's advice. 'He has some kind of special intuition though he's not dogmatic about things. The afternoons are always a good time to discuss things with him. I have three guidelines from my family: keep close to one another; there is nothing we cannot speak about; and, faith is very important.'

Adit said: 'When we were little we would watch the Mahabharata in the evenings on television over and over. And Amamma [Sucharitha Reddy] would tell us the stories of the epics. It was a wonderful way to drive the imagination. Through my grandparents – and my parents, of course – I've learned how important family is. That's why I want to do well on my own so that I can provide for everyone. My grandfather is smart about money and would advise me to keep my spending in check. He hates it when money is spent on unnecessary things.

'Our family isn't driven by money. You can always get it back. It's important to help others. Apollo and the general health care environment take up so much family time. But it's worth it. My parents also give good advice and my mom is especially strong in finance. We are alike in that we don't lose our tempers easily.'

Does Adit share his grandfather's passion for horse racing?

'No. I don't particularly care for horse racing, I always felt bad for the horse,' Adit said.

His older sister Sindoori Reddy is vice president of Operations at Apollo Children's Hospital. She laughs with delight when asked about her grandparents, Dr Prathap Chandra and Sucharitha Reddy.

'Everything starts with them and they are so close to us. They are constantly teaching and guiding us,' she said, with her trademark broad smile.

She said Dr Reddy excels at leadership skills. 'Whenever my grandfather comes to the hospital, he makes everyone feel wanted and important. He shakes their hand or pats them on the shoulder. It makes all the difference to the patients and their families and also to the workforce. Every industry that is workforce-driven requires people who feel that they are significantly contributing. We don't think of a hospital as an industry but health care surely is. The difference is that we hold the responsibility for a person's health, their lives, and a complete environment is essential for the patient's well-being.'

Sindoori aspires to be like Dr Reddy in her discipline and leadership. For as long as she can remember, he has asked her – and all the daughters and other grandchildren – 'What good thing have you done today?'

'It is his way of getting us to think of others and understanding the true meaning of service at Apollo. He finds time to meet the doctors and nurses and housekeeping and the security, dietary, administrative staff. Many others in his position would not and they would lose touch with the mission of the business,' Sindoori said.

With a degree in international business and finance, she joined Apollo after a stint at the World Bank IFC in Washington, DC. She is the third generation Reddy to become involved at the hospitals. When she returned from the United States, her aunt Preetha Reddy, Apollo's managing director, was just developing the children's hospital concept. Recognizing that Sindoori's strengths were in operations, Preetha assigned Sindoori to the project in mid-construction.

It was Sindoori's combination of discipline and financial models that kept the project on track. In addition, her vision was integral to the interior flow and design of the hospital, which is considered number one in its segment in India. Play areas and bright colours and wallpapers help make the hospital welcoming and child-friendly. The staff is also chosen to be especially aware of the needs of children and families.

Opened in 2009, the hospital serves children and adolescents up to age sixteen with top-of-the-line, multi-speciality care including neonatal and paediatric intensive care, surgical facilities, cardiac, intensive and emergency care. Day surgery is also available, and the ever-important counselling centres are expanding their programmes as Apollo strives to provide comprehensive care at all levels.

Sindoori is a member of the Reddy 'family council'. This small group aims to guide the Reddys in continued Apollo involvement and transition after Chairman Reddy's retirement. She said, 'One thing we want to do is streamline how decisions are made. This will enable projects to move ahead faster and empower the "project manager" and eliminate overlap. It also gives attention to the strength of each person and allows them to excel.'

Sindoori said that Dr Reddy's leadership and management skills are innate. 'He completely understands that everything is about teamwork, from admission to discharge. Every element is important because we are trying to create a different experience for each patient from what they may have heard about hospitals. It should be a pleasant experience even if they are ill. We are all working towards the same vision – for good results, with empathy towards others. If we receive a criticism we truly take it as a way to learn so that things get better. This is how we can improve on what Apollo has to give to the world,' she said.

The Reddy family is exceptionally close, even the ten grandchildren. According to Sindoori, 'Amamma shares the vision for health care and she and Dr Reddy discuss all the major projects. For our family, even the smallest event becomes like a wedding. A lunch becomes a feast. She also loves to design jewellery and has exquisite taste. Her happiness comes from her family and helping others. One of my fondest memories is that before my wedding[1] we had a family dance night and my grandmom danced for me. She is so beautiful and lyrical. I will never forget it.'

Like her brother and cousins, Sindoori gives a lot of thought to Apollo's future.

'The next ten to fifteen years are going to be a dynamic period for health care,' Sindoori said. 'How Apollo anticipates and copes with rapid technological development will define its continued success. We must have mental excellence in our medical team and superb clinical care. The changes are going to be big and we must have a focused way to get there. It's critical that we continue learning – from the rest of the world, from competitors and through our own innovation. The tertiary care model of having all care under one roof is both efficient and comforting to the patients. Every time a patient goes home healthy it is a blessing, and to see their gratefulness to Apollo is tremendously rewarding for all of us from my grandparents to my four moms (the Reddy daughters) and all the way down.'

Sindoori's mother, Suneeta Reddy, is joint managing director of Apollo Hospitals, and the person who looks after finances. 'Perfectionist' is a term that is often bandied around quite easily these days. But one only needs to walk a day in Suneeta Reddy's shoes to know the full manifestation of the term. Zeal defines the woman, which is why she approaches financial planning with the same passion as she does her own fitness regime. Ask any of her colleagues at Apollo and they will tell you that anything short of the best is just not good enough for Suneeta Reddy. With Suneeta, you underperform at your own risk.

Besides her formal role as joint managing director of Apollo, Suneeta sits on the board of several hospitals and corporations. She is a member of the National Committee on Healthcare and the Harvard Business School India Advisory Board. She now has a great affinity

---

1   Sindoori is married to Tarun Reddy; the couple lives in Chennai.

for numbers, but it took a great deal of effort on her part to cultivate that ability and to nurture it. It wasn't always that she was interested in finance and maths. As a matter of fact, she remembers receiving a zero in a maths exam and her father giving her the ultimatum to shape up or pack up.

Suneeta took up the challenge, and decided to conquer the numbers. There came the day when she proudly went up to her father and announced to him that she had scored a 100 in her maths test. That little anecdote is emblematic of Suneeta Reddy's tenacity.

Her job involves a close introspection of numbers that are not always flattering. Sometimes, a hospital is required to take on a lot of risk, which is contrary to Suneeta's cautious instinct. However, at times like these, Dr Reddy often intervenes and says, 'Just do it.' Suneeta says that she trusts this natural instinct completely, and that she is almost in awe of her father's remarkable intuitiveness. More often than not this positive approach works wonders, and unless there are exceptionally strong reasons not to proceed, Dr Reddy's projects move forward. It is Suneeta's job to mix that intuition with facts and find a way to rationalize to the investment community how Apollo can continue to be a successful enterprise.

'India is changing and the macro for the next generation is incredibly significant. Apollo is growing at three times the GDP which surpasses most of the rest of India,' she says.

These developments have led Apollo to re-evaluate the way new facilities are created. The team focuses more now on communication about the type of facilities and how they will help meet health care demands. The 'Mother and Child' birthing centres are one such example, where a specific need is targeted. The demand for health care is huge and complicated deliveries need more specific attention for both the mother and the baby.

Suneeta has strong views on the overall health care ecosystem in India. She is especially concerned about the ominous correlation of health demands and a rising population with high cardio-vascular disease, diabetes, cancer and obesity rates. 'The country needs entrepreneurship and growth in manufacturing, agriculture and the service sector. For growth to be sustainable, we must create vibrant business models. We have every opportunity to manufacture our own consumer goods, which in turn will provide jobs in many sectors from labour to transportation to fuel and even health care. The right kind of entrepreneurship is needed. It's not just about cheap labour and quotas, it's about business opportunities,' she says.

'I attended a Harvard Business School conference where the ex-prime minister of Malaysia said that the key to Malaysia's growth had to be to allow the private sector flexibility in building the country,' Suneeta recalled. 'When the private sector flourishes, the GDP grows. This creates employment and gives people a way upward, and it gives them hope. This is something India needs to emulate.'

Asked what one thing she would change about Apollo's past she replied, 'It would be the way in which we expanded internationally. Our entry into the United Arab Emirates and Sri Lanka were problematic because we were not the majority shareholders. The governments and persons in those countries realized the potential and acquired the majority of stock. They wanted to be involved more extensively on the board and management. We felt that would not work. In the UAE we had a very dominant partner – and we felt that it was essential that the company actually providing the health care intellectual property should be the one who called the shots.'[2]

But Apollo has learned its lessons.

'Now as we expand, a paramount aspect is that we are the majority shareholder in the venture and also that we should have deep local

---

2 The United Arab Emirates has a complex set of laws and regulations concerning institutions and businesses that involve foreign entities or individuals. A joint venture with an Emirati partner, although supported by the government, did not work out for Apollo. Nevertheless, Dr Reddy expects that he will re-enter the lucrative health care market in the Gulf. Apollo has already opened a sugar clinic in Oman. The Asian Business Leaders Forum announced that it has named Dr Reddy as the recipient of its 2013 Lifetime Achievement Award. The ceremony, spearheaded by ABLF founder Malini N. Menon, a Keralite entrepreneur living in Dubai, annually attracts top leaders from various fields.

knowledge before entering the market,' Suneeta says.

When asked, 'What does it take to be successful?' Suneeta replied, 'I am a practical person and I realize that there is always a solution to a problem. We're faced with so many problems each day but if we really focus on them, we can find a solution. The second part is knowledge; there is no substitute for it. And then there is experience. Vision has to have meaning. When my father started Apollo he already had knowledge of health care, it wasn't just a leap of faith. He was already a doctor and knew the challenges and opportunities in the health care field. Today, we are doing well and we are providing things that people want, consumer preferences drive many of our initiatives. In the beginning it was quite challenging so we all pushed on. Three lessons, of many, that I've learned are: not to be limited by your own thinking – the mind is just an instrument, use it that way; always gather as much knowledge as you can before you take a decision; and, experience is a great teacher.'

Apollo recently introduced a new health care immunization programme in less than ten days. I asked Suneeta how that was accomplished.

Her response: 'First, I give all credit to my sister Sangita who understood the programme and what Dad wanted to accomplish. She organized all the key elements. Second, the risk was very small, both in capital outlay and in brand and clinical risks. If it failed, it would not have hurt anyone. If nothing more, it raised consciousness about the risk of cardio disease and simple elements that could make a difference. In the end, it is about teaching people how they can have a good life.'

I asked Suneeta what she had learned from her mother, Sucharitha Reddy. She says, 'My mother taught me that I should be independent. Her independence is clear in that she is a free thinker. She has a deep belief in God. Her ability to show kindness to every human being is always a beacon to me. It is in the Vedas, everything is a part of God and we must respect all human beings.'

She and her husband Dwarakanath Reddy are considered a power couple in Chennai. Both come from strong family backgrounds and are among the top rung of India's business leaders. They both have the sort of looks and deportment that make heads turn when they walk into a room. Whereas Suneeta has a determined intensity about her, Dwarakanath projects an easygoing attitude – although he's as canny a businessman as you'd encounter anywhere.

Dwarakanath – who is fanatical about cricket, and served as president of the Madras Cricket Club – is devoted to his family. When he talks about his father-in-law, Dr Prathap Chandra Reddy, it is always with affection and respect.

'I have seen the way Apollo has grown and know that it is his pure dedicated vision that enabled the health care breakthroughs. He worked as hard as anyone I ever met. Do you know what it takes to cut through red tape, roadblocks, bureaucracy and stubbornness? Dr Reddy was incredibly patient and persistent,' Dwarakanath said. His late father, P. Obul Reddy, was a famed industrialist, and a close friend of Dr Reddy's.[3] Obul Reddy was also an early investor in Apollo. He is perhaps best remembered for the Dyanora television sets that his company manufactured back in the 1970s.

'He had strokes of genius, too,' Dwarakanath said of his father-in-law.' When the Madras hospital was stalled, Dr Reddy went to Hyderabad and the chief minister of Andhra Pradesh promised land for the new hospital. This put pressure on the politicians in Madras to act,' he said.

Even now, Dwarakanath Reddy remembers how people would scoff at Dr Reddy for his vision of better health care for Indians. 'They would laugh and joke and ask, "What is he trying to do? The government does nothing, so what can he do?" Dr Reddy never let that get him down. And he never went back on people and made an ugly fuss. He just kept working. He worked all the time and then the daughters worked all the time. This is what they believe in. I think the thing that built confidence in the hospital was that right from the beginning it had an excellent cardiology unit. People came from

---

3 Dwarakanath's elder brother, P. Vijaykumar Reddy, is married to Suneeta's elder sister, Preetha.

all over India to go there and the word spread.

'And Dr Reddy is a man of impeccable integrity. People recognize this and are attracted to him for it.'

Asked what kind of advice Dr Reddy would give him, Dwarakanath said, 'He never intruded but only asked if it was truly a decision to which I could commit. Of course, he did encourage me to quit smoking and we both celebrated those victories for ourselves.'

Both Dwarakanath Reddy and his father-in-law enjoy time at the family beach house in Chennai; it turns out that the son-in-law has a green thumb and enjoys walking and gardening. He grows mangoes, sweet lime, kumquats, mandarin oranges and flowers. He says that the only times he can remember Dr Reddy really relaxing are at the beach house and at the race course.

Neither Dr Reddy nor Sucharitha is materialistic and buy little for themselves. So, for the celebration of Dr Reddy's eightieth birthday, the daughters and their husbands got together and gifted him a Rolls Royce. 'It is blue and silver,' Dwarakanath said. 'The car was delivered to his total surprise. Immediately he got in and had Mrs Reddy join him and off they drove. He hasn't driven in many years but loved it so much that he couldn't resist on this occasion. He was proving a point that he can still drive. We were all laughing at their delight and actually wondered how long the drive would be. It was great!'

His sister-in-law Preetha Reddy certainly relishes those moments when her parents enjoy themselves.

'When we came back to India, Dad became a man on a mission,' the tall Preetha who is always elegantly attired in saris, said. 'We wanted to do many things and he was focused on health care. Even from the beginning of Apollo, he would often say, "Whatever we do is not enough for the need." Till today he is never satisfied with the care that the majority of Indians receive. When we make a new proposal, he will ask, "Is this a plan for people or is it a plan for a building? Give me a plan for people. Give me a plan for people who are under-served."

'Several private hospitals that have come up since our father started Apollo Chennai have modelled themselves after Apollo. They are looking for an easy, standard approach to success. The difference is that we are always looking at problems, at new ways to serve and in a big way. We want to do what no one else is doing here in India. Just look at our staff. There are no other hospitals with staff like ours. Everyone in our family is so attached to and so proud of the staff. They all have options but very few ever change. It is because of our mission, the environment that Daddy created, which the doctors and nurses want to wholeheartedly support.

'Moreover, our board has been very supportive. They know that we work 24/7. All of our efforts are transparent. I have a very nurturing relationship with our board members – they understand the culture and really go all the way with us.'

Preetha herself is on the board of Medtronic, a prominent medical technology company based in Minneapolis. She likens the Medtronic board to the Apollo board. 'Neither board rubberstamps proposals,' she said. 'Take the example of the decision to sell Health Street. It came down to making choices – whether to focus on our core competency of delivering health care or expand into a related but collateral business. We needed the capital to build more hospitals and had to make a choice. Selling Health Street was hard for us all but it hurt Sangita the most since she had created and shepherded Health Street.[4] Of course, all of our hearts are with

---

4 Apollo Health Street, which was managed by Sangita Reddy, was sold to US-based Sutherland Global Services in December 2012 for Rs 1,000 crore; Apollo had bought the company, formerly a US-based organization called Zapata, in 2007 for Rs 700 crore. Apollo Health Street provided tailor-made IT-based solutions to handle the financial operations of health care organizations, and serviced more than 150 organizations throughout the United States. Of Apollo's total revenue in FY '12, less than 2–3 per cent came from its extended businesses like Health Street. *Forbes India* reports that a large chunk of Apollo's overall revenues, approximately 75 per cent, comes from its hospitals, and the remaining from Apollo Pharmacies, according to Krishnan Akhileswaran, Apollo's CFO. The BPO – or outsourcing – opportunity in the Indian health care sector is $22 billion, out of a global figure of $60 billion. But Apollo Health Street did not work out as hoped

the hospitals and we do get enormous satisfaction from seeing the results of better health care.'

She acknowledges that Apollo faces stiff challenges. One is competition from other hospitals that want to mine the Indian market. The second is retention of talent. Nursing attrition is high, almost 20 per cent annually, because there is a strong draw for foreign travel and significantly higher pay. 'We have very little physician turnover, maybe one or two in five years. Some of the managerial staff leaves quickly. They, too, have a lot of pressure and many want five-day workweeks. We work six days a week. Sickness has no holiday and we are not interested in providing part-time health care,' Preetha said.

Asked how Apollo moved from being a single-hospital-entity entrepreneur to a major national enterprise, Preetha replied, 'Daddy never thought about being a national entrepreneur, although Apollo has that environment. We have a few more beds,' she said with a twinkle in her eye, 'and a few more layers. That's expected. In the beginning Chairman Reddy empowered his CEOs to run their units. We still do that. Out of necessity there are more systems, procedures, more attention to the budgets, which are reviewed every quarter. Dr Reddy continues to place a strong emphasis on recruiting the best talent, those who are innovators and who have a healing touch. That is most important to Apollo.'

The primary responsibility of a health care provider is to offer uncompromised clinical excellence to patients. To achieve that, Apollo Hospitals embarked, about six years ago, on a mission to get accreditation from Joint Commission International (JCI).[5] The accreditation is a beacon for patient safety and quality improvement in the global health care community.

---

because, among other things, 'It grew opportunistically focusing on the US and had US-centric systems, which were not immediately applicable to India,' says Sangita Reddy. By selling Apollo Health Street, Apollo raised additional funds to support Dr Reddy's plans for adding 3,000 new beds in the next three years.

5   As discussed in a previous chapter.

At the time, no other hospital in India had even attempted to get this accreditation. Apollo went for it nevertheless, and it was a big decision. At Apollo, the top management takes such critical decisions jointly. Preetha Reddy had championed this particular policy decision. This was clearly her breakthrough moment.

'The accreditation process required a realignment of many processes and a new training regimen. All the processes moved to a model of outcome measurement,' Preetha said, using the standard lexicon of medical administration. In 2008, Indraprastha Apollo Hospitals, New Delhi, became the first hospital in India and South Asia to get this coveted accreditation. Today, eight Apollo hospitals have this gold standard.

'The accreditation has been pivotal in helping Apollo earn the trust of patients who come from as many as 120 countries. It also helped in our emergence as the foremost integrated health care provider in Asia with over 6,000 owned beds and over 2,000 managed beds across thirty-eight owned and thirteen managed hospitals,' Preetha said.[6] 'The accreditation helped us imbue a culture of rigorous standards of care and in earning the trust of patients well beyond our shores. Today, many hospitals in India have followed us and got themselves accredited. This has been immensely satisfying as a pioneering step taken by Apollo and is once again impacting the standards of health care across India.'

It was instructive to observe Preetha Reddy at a Delphi meeting in Chennai, where the course for Apollo Hospitals was being planned for the next three years. She told Apollo executives that it was decided to call the conference Delphi because in Greek mythology it is the place where the gods meet and she thinks it is where good things happen.

She expressed her appreciation for the Apollo family and her own family: 'I am what I am today because of how my parents brought me up. So many of us have grown into a family, like Malathi and others who were with Apollo from the very beginning. It is good always to acknowledge the wealth of all we have and all that we have built.'

---

6 As of March 2012.

'Like any family, though,' she said, 'our family should never be stagnant. The Chairman doesn't believe in "family planning" and restricting growth. He is always looking for new people with bold ideas – people who can work within teams that are not part of the hospital network but those who can concentrate on building a network. We have expanded to include insurance, IT, branding, clinic and pharmacy teams and the new baby team. We really do have nuggets of gold throughout our system.'

Carefully crafting her words, she explained how bringing beautiful pearls together makes a necklace. Otherwise, a pearl in an oyster is just a pearl. Taking the pearls out and stringing them together is what makes a pearl necklace priceless. 'This is how Apollo has been created – stringing all the pearls together and using all the gold nuggets,' she told the participants.

Preetha said that some people in Apollo were looking over their shoulders at the competition, suggesting that Apollo emulate some of them. Quietly but strongly she said, 'We must not deny the strengths of other groups but it does not mean that Apollo has a problem. We must look at everything we have and use our knowledge well.'

She told the story of three men. The first opens the window and says, 'Oh, God, it's morning!' The second man opens the window and says, 'Thank God, it's morning!' And the third man opens the window and says, 'It's a really wonderful morning. I better run and start my farming so that we can have a much better crop.'

It was as though Preetha was exhorting both new and old Apollo team members to focus on the future, even though there are sceptics. She said, 'We cannot live life by worrying about what others have done. We will never go forward that way. Let's all cultivate the farmer in us and grow.'

She was doing more than indicating. She wanted candid assessments and encouraged the attendees to carefully evaluate what was going wrong and right and not to sweep things under the rug. 'Rather than talking about failure,' she said, 'give me concrete actions we can take. Perhaps our focus got dissipated, we didn't review things properly, not enough attention was given to getting more doctors on board and nurses committed and trained. Perhaps we were too vague in our expectations.'

Discreetly but directly, Preetha told the executives that Apollo wanted open minds, the ability to make course corrections and really work with one another. Her words rang true: 'Perhaps we took the numbers and became defensive about them. We didn't give any suggestions on what would help us get better – the nuts and bolts of success. Strategy is very important, but if it is not backed by tactics, Apollo won't grow. Most importantly, we must never lose contact with the patients. It happens before we realize it. Yet, the best feedback we get is from the patients. Spend time with the patients and their families and clinicians. Spreadsheets and written reports may make a fantastic dashboard but it is not the core Apollo mission.'

She concluded, 'Believe in yourself and remember that we are all here together. If we have a programme and five are supporting it and six speaking against it, we are not unified. I hate that. We are one team. Patients deserve for us to work together. Forgetting the human aspect of why we exist will not help us grow. We owe it to our patients and to our staff to be successful.'

In one of our conversations, I asked Preetha, 'What would you term as your golden moment in Apollo?'

Her reply: 'When we got our first JCI.' She continued: 'It is not just because I was involved in initiating it and following through to its completion. It is more because this heralded a sea change in the health care industry in our country as such – in terms of clinical excellence, patient safety and in the very way health care was delivered. I still recall how some people felt that JCI accreditation would make sense only for foreign patients, but I insisted that every human being whether Indian or otherwise deserves and has the right to quality medical care.

'This passion for quality health care has indeed earned us great wealth. And I am not talking about our market cap, I am talking about the enormous trust that Apollo enjoys today from millions of people. Now one of my primary responsibilities is to ensure that the high standard that Apollo has achieved never gets diluted but in fact is constantly improved. Initiatives like ACE@25, a clinical balanced scorecard focusing on clinical excellence, are steps in this direction.'

I said to Preetha: 'You are said to be the author of TLC or Tender Loving Care, which seems like Apollo's patent. What was in your mind, when you thought up these words?'

'Actually when TLC was initially coined, it stood for "Teamwork, Leadership and Commitment", the ingredients which make our organization tick. Later, I realized to complement medical excellence, one needs the patient to be felt cared for. That led to "Tender Loving Care" or the current TLC. Medical care delivered in an environment of love and concern somehow actually seems to speed up healing. I make sure that not just our nurses but everyone who interfaces with patients follows this maxim,' Preetha said.

'What would you rate as your biggest challenge now?' I asked Preetha in her office in the Prestige Palladium, which is decorated with modern art and also has statues of Lord Ganesha and other deities.

'Scaling up our operations at various locations, without losing out on our service excellence and without compromising on any of our fine values is what I am looking at now. With the support of all our stakeholders, I am confident we will be able to achieve it,' she said.

'As the managing director of a leading health care group, could you give some details of the various bodies and associations you are active in?' I asked Preetha.

'Yes, I am involved in quite a few of them. While in the beginning I thought it was an honour, now I have realized that it is my duty to participate in forums that can help formulate policy decisions on important health care issues. In 2009, I was part of the Indo-US CEOs Forum, a think-tank created to strengthen bilateral cooperation and trade. The meeting with President Barack Obama in Washington was very useful,' she said.

I gathered subsequently that Preetha was the first woman advisor on health care to the Government of India, and is also a member of the National Quality Council, which provides the guidelines on minimum quality standards in Indian hospitals. Preetha is an advisor to the state government of Tamil Nadu for the reorganization of the disaster management programme in Chennai.

'How do you deal with competition?' I asked Preetha.

She had an interesting reply: 'Today for Apollo Hospitals the issue is not about competing but of collaborating. As a matter of fact Apollo has taken the lead to form an association Nathealth on the lines of Nasscom, where we hope to bring all players in health care together. One of the objectives is, as a body we can strongly represent the crying need for policy changes in health care governance in our country. I have been tasked with organizing this meet scheduled in October 2013.'

Once when I met Preetha at her parents' home in Bishop Garden in Chennai, I asked her, 'You had trained in classical dance under Devi Rukmini Arundale at Kalakshetra. Are you still in touch?'

'I am on the governing board of Kalakshetra. And if I can find the time, I certainly do enjoy watching a dance recital. But believe me most of the time I seem to be dancing to everybody's tunes,' she said with a sweet smile.

———

Preetha's husband, P. Vijaykumar Reddy, is a man with a sense of irony and rapier-like wit. One evening in Chennai, I was dining with him at the Chambers Club at the Taj Coromandel. Vijay regaled me with tales of the diversity and evolution of the business and social worlds in Chennai.

He came across as a prudent and agile business strategist and he credits his father, P. Obul Reddy, and father-in-law, Dr Prathap Reddy, with honing his business skills. Both were pioneers in their own ways – Prathap Reddy in health care and Obul Reddy in manufacturing batteries and televisions under foreign collaborations with Japan. Prathap Reddy and Obul Reddy were very close friends and Obul Reddy served on the Apollo board, as did Vijay.

Actually, Vijay feels strongly that the most essential ingredients for his success in his many diversified ventures, including power plants and software, were the robust business advice and the liberal resources that his father-in-law shared with him.

Now quite successful, Vijay's early business experiences were more of an uphill task. He had to tread new paths in business and experiment with ideas that were hard to launch. While each had a strong potential, there was an equal amount of government regulation that stymied business progress.

Vijay remembers the substantial contribution Dr Reddy made to his business. 'I was young and perhaps brash as we are at that age, and Dr Reddy had a clarity in strategic thinking that really guided me,' he said. 'Dr Reddy never wavered in his support and focus and I still learn from him. He has been an amazingly positive and upbeat person, always encouraging me in my personal life and career. Today, he remains chairman of my board of directors.'

Vijay says that he appreciates Dr Reddy's consistent and unconditional support, and he acknowledges that Dr Reddy's example was also instrumental in intensifying and fashioning Vijay's interpersonal skills.

Those skills have made him immensely liked in Chennai social and business circles, and even beyond. Vijay has a huge innate passion and a keen eye for promoting and preserving culture and heritage. Philanthropy has also got its fair share of attention. As of the summer of 2013, he is in his second term as chairman of the board of trustees of the 2,000-year-old Kapaleeshwar Temple in Mylapore.

Much as Preetha helps with the temple's administrative work, Vijay, too, acts as a perfect support system especially in dealing with government agencies. One of Vijay's most satisfying and challenging projects was sprucing up the temple premises and the surrounding areas. Indeed, both areas are clean and orderly despite hosting thousands of daily visitors. The temple has flourished and is also one of the more popular for tourists to visit in Chennai.

More than that, though, Vijay led the board as it revamped the conduct of rituals, reinstating the pristine sanctities of the temple's age-old practices. These rituals require fastidious attention to detail and a complete understanding of not only the rites but also the purpose behind them.

Some of the temple priests were even surprised by Vijay's directness as he gave explicit instructions regarding conduct and maintenance.

One thing reinstated in the temple was the centuries-old tradition of staging music and dance performances by eminent artistes from across India during every festival, all funded through his personal endowments.

His generosity is low-key; it's not in Vijay's nature to be boastful. He promotes Chennai's rich music, dance and other fine arts. Continuing his own father's generous ways, he is a major patron of globally acclaimed traditional music and dance carnivals and festivals that are staged in Chennai the year round.

Vijay is a devout man, hugely inspired by the elders in his family and their focus on tending to others. For example, he provides the unmet needs, including medical care, for persons under the umbrella of many charitable institutions in Chennai. Prominent among them is 'Little Sisters of the Poor', which has sheltered hundreds of desolate and impoverished elderly citizens.

His generosity has benefitted not only residents of Chennai but visitors as well. Vijay handsomely supported the complete restoration of San Thome Cathedral, one of India's oldest churches with beautiful neo-Gothic architecture.

Vijay summed up his feelings about his father-in-law thus: 'Personally, Dr Reddy mentored us generously, shaping our intellect and positively impacting our lives. This, in turn, he allowed us to succeed, and going beyond to reach out to the needy and serve people with compassion.'

He and Preetha raised two sons, Karthik and Harshad, both of whom have studied overseas.

Harshad Reddy was twenty-six years of age in 2013 and already involved in major industries affecting India. He is the executive director of Operations for PPN, a power generating company in Tamil Nadu. He sits on the board of the company with his brother Karthik – who is managing director – his mother and his grandfather.

He has an important role at Apollo, opening doors and negotiating permits, and organizing bids and agreements.

'I've always seen the dedication that my family has to India and to Apollo – and they inspire me. My mom is on call twenty-four hours a day, seven days a week. She's a people person, soft-spoken yet very strong. Things that I might consider intrusive, she does not. Rather, everyone is her family,' Harshad told me. 'Apollo will always have a unique place in health care and certainly in India where it plays a core role in the livelihood, health and well-being of Indians. Occasionally my mom and I speak about productivity and accountability, two elements which will help Apollo continue to grow and lead in the health care field.'

Harshad says that growing up, he played chess with his grandfather. The board itself was elaborately designed and had glass chess pieces. Harshad never won a game but he learned critical thinking and strategic moves from the exercise.

'The best times with my grandfather were sitting at home and sharing a meal with him. Just sitting with him was wonderful. You could always sense his happiness and generosity. All children love him,' Harshad said.

He said that despite the difference in age between him and his grandfather, Dr Reddy was always willing to listen to ideas.

'Looking at what he has done gives him great satisfaction. But, he is also always looking forward to new projects and continued improvements. We had one instance for a project that he wanted to do but on evaluation, it was not a good business model. It wouldn't have achieved the results we all wanted. I remember that he was taken aback in the beginning, then accepted my recommendation,' Harshad said.

'Dr Reddy wrote the rulebook on private health care in India. One thing I admire most is that he always emphasizes doing everything within the law. There is no bending of rules, everything is based on merit,' he added.

The grandson says that, in his mind, three things stand out about Dr Reddy.

'First is his generosity. Second is the way he treats colleagues, the way he treats everyone. He is sensitive to their needs as a person. Third, he enjoys life. He is a great role model for all of us.'

His brother Karthik is one of two third-generation members of the Reddy family who are members of the family council that is guiding the family's transition to a new era. A graduate of the University of Southern California in Los Angeles and City University in London, he specializes in finance.

Although Karthik has had a superb education, he says that some of the most lasting lessons he learned were from his grandfather, Dr Reddy.

One is that vision is important but it's got to be followed by persistence. 'Many people told him that he was going to fail. Instead, Apollo flourished and others failed. It's because of his determination and the fact that he had many supporters – doctors and others – who also adopted his vision,' Karthik said.

'Our grandfather has the ability to motivate. He brightens people rather than berating them. The ability to motivate others and not yell at them is unique in many businesses, even in many families. I hope to develop more of his people skills,' he said.

Karthik and his brother would often go at night and visit Dr and Mrs Reddy at the family home in Bishop Garden in Chennai. He remembers that Dr Reddy would stand the boys up and ask them to give a speech.

Karthik says, 'Our grandfather wanted to know what we had done for others that day, what was the role of Apollo. Some days it was more unnerving than others. I definitely began to learn presentation skills then but I'm allergic to public speaking even today. But I know that Dr Reddy always dispenses sound advice to people so that they can improve their own lives – and in the case of family members, contribute to Apollo's growth.'

CHAPTER THIRTY

Legacy

SHOBANA KAMINENI'S ROLE AT Apollo is particularly interesting because although she is the third of the Reddys' four daughters Shobana was the first to plunge full time into the making of Apollo. She has witnessed Apollo's development from conception to creation to expansion. She has also witnessed the consistency in Dr Reddy's behaviour towards everybody – from ordinary people to high-ranking officials. And she has witnessed how Dr Reddy has made it a point to be a non-political figure, a man who prefers discussion and cooperation to divisiveness.

'One of Dad's principles has been to avoid politics. He doesn't take a stand, he doesn't donate to candidates, he doesn't take favours, nor does he grant any. He feels that doing so would compromise health care, which is counter to everything he has worked for,' Shobana told me. 'When MGR had his stroke, he was in really bad shape, acutely critical. Rumours would spread that he had died, and thousands of people marched to the hospital. Security had to be heightened – but the huge crowds were kept out of the hospital. This was critical in maintaining his care and also of the other patients that we did have. One entire wing was devoted to MGR, and the government, where the ministers and directors would hold meetings and take decisions. Even Prime Minister Indira Gandhi came to see him at Apollo,' Shobana said.

'MGR's illness and the crowds trying to see him disrupted our activities. We devoted just as much medical care to other patients as to MGR. One thing is that we had a decline in patients because the hospital was like a fortress and new patients couldn't even get to the hospital because of the crowds. Because of this we did not get enough patients to meet our expenses that year, which was the first year after we became fully operational. And MGR was the same man who had stopped construction of the hospital for two years,' Shobana recalled, adding that notwithstanding the hostility or animosity of some people in political and administrative circles, Dr Reddy has never believed in trying to retaliate or get even. His unrelenting focus has always been on improving the quality of health care that patients get at Apollo. Medicine, not politics, is his forte.

'Dad was always determined to provide the best medical care possible and make Apollo one of the best medical institutions in the world. The advent of telemedicine helped improve all our services and helped keep medical staff abreast of all new developments. Our multidisciplinary programmes have been validated throughout India as other hospitals adopt our approach,' Shobana said.

'Dad has always been inspiring, bigger than life in some ways. He says that I am fierce – and that is a compliment. He doesn't mind if you ask questions, but he has never entertained foolish questions. He was quite strict. He's more expressive now than he was – early on he was not as outwardly affectionate. He's become more and more so over the years and you can see this when he visits the hospital and talks to patients and staff. His presence calms them, inspires them and gives them hope. He is an early adopter of new ideas and he walks the talk of being patient-centred. One of the intrinsic things about health care is that it allows people to help you. If you're a patient, you take the help. If you're the health care provider, you give help and in turn, take help so that you can continue to provide more services,' she added.

Like her sisters, Shobana is extremely devoted to her mother as well. She told me the story of how Sucharitha Reddy drove in an ambulance to Hyderabad from Chennai after Shobana's car had been hit by a lorry on the road between Bangalore and Hyderabad. Shobana and her husband Anil Kamineni, along with Sangita and her spouse Vishweshwar, had been to Bangalore on a short holiday; Sangita had flown back to Hyderabad, but the others decided to return in their Contessa, with Anil driving. Shobana's neck was broken in six places, and one of her kneecaps was virtually shattered. A doctor later told her that because her athleticism had made her neck strong, she'd been saved from permanent damage.

'Mom has always been there in our lives – during our childhood and during our adulthood. We did have many toys when we were growing up. Dad was cautious with the money. Mom would save from household expenses and from her salary when she was working. She never spent any money on herself but would always buy us gifts and hide them under the bed. We were forbidden from looking under the bed and became very excited whenever she reached under the bed because we knew that a treat was in store,' Shobana said, recalling her childhood in India and the United States.

'Mom always, always encouraged each daughter to be financially independent. She has spent her life fully supporting Dad and that required a lot of attention. He never eats leftovers and she always made fresh food for him. Believe me, he was hard to please. Even in making his tea she has a very careful routine and he knows that each cup is made with loving attention. He doesn't expect to be spoiled by anyone else but her,' Shobana said. 'She worked for a time when we were in the States and enjoyed making her own money. On some level she must have regretted giving that up. Mom is very smart and entirely creative. She was a continuous cheerleader for us, always telling us how capable we are. When she gave up her job it was so that there would be someone at home when we came back from school. Her generosity is legendary but it is her spirit that is the richest. She chose to spend her life giving to others. Each one of us is thankful for her and just as inspired by her actions as Dad's.'

Shobana and her husband Anil Kamineni have two daughters and a son: Upasna, Anushpala and Puansh. I was impressed by how much Upasna shares her mother's excitement and enthusiasm for helping others. This becomes evident as she describes her role at Apollo Hospitals. Upasna is vice president of Apollo Wellness and Apollo Philanthropy. Both are key components in Apollo's move towards preventative health care.

'Education and our new wellness centres are in the forefront of Apollo initiatives to keep India healthy and prosperous,' Upasna said. 'The country has been so focused on providing basic health care for 1.2 billion people that daily health has largely been ignored. We are going to change that,' Upasna said. 'We've launched wellness centres, essentially workout gyms. They're not fancy spas. They are focused on lifestyle improvements. Disease management and keeping people well are our mantras. We provide nutritional information, workout programmes, meditation and yoga with the attitude that these can change India. We have diet plans, heart plans, pregnancy counselling and programmes for smoking cessation. It's important that we focus on prevention and not just cure. We started small with our independent wellness centres and expect to grow slowly and steadily. Now we run occupational wellness programmes for hundreds of major corporations all across India.

'People have confidence in the Apollo brand and really, we're all looking forward to a better India. The young professionals and middle class understand the direction we are going and want to participate. We don't want to see people coming to Apollo as a last resort when they are in bad health. I think my grandfather's vision was not just about curing people – he genuinely doesn't want them to get sick. Apollo one day may become better known for keeping people well rather than only healing them when they are sick.

'I am the perfect example of someone whose life was changed by eating better, exercising and changing my attitude. In college I was chubby, ate too many carbs and was not active. Everyone said I looked fine but it was my dad who changed my direction. He said, "You must get fit. Don't believe what your aunts say because they will always say that you look cute." I'm not obsessed with being a size two or a size zero. I'm just dedicated to keeping a proper weight for my body. Once I began, my metabolism changed and my mind became clearer. It's a wonderful feeling and I can speak honestly now about how healthy choices have helped me. My goal is to help others achieve their wellness potential.'

Upasna directed every detail of the wellness centres, from the exterior construction to the interior design, equipment, furniture and flow. She received advice from her mother and her aunt Sangita – executive director of Apollo – on the direction of the centres.

Her dad gave her stability and discipline by advising, 'Measure a hundred times and cut once.' From her grandfather she got her courage. 'He never let me think small. He says that if you have a big vision, you've got to take big action.'

'Both my grandparents intuitively know how to relate to others,' Upasna said. 'They treat employees and staff like family and think of the patients that way, too. I wanted to join Apollo to support my grandfather. My mom and aunts needed support, too. Our personalities are different but the goal is the same. It gives me a sense of pride to be so active. You know the saying, "An idle mind is the devil's workshop." It's much better to be doing God's work.

'Even though my grandmother doesn't have a formal role at Apollo, she knows everything that is going on. She is really the mother to all, and everyone confides in her. She's got excellent judgement and exudes kindness.'

Sucharitha Reddy also gets high marks from Upasna's brother Puansh, who is known as 'Punch'. He's a tall, confident, articulate and ambitious eighteen-year-old. He recalls that his grandfather really came down hard on him when he found out he and Sangita's son Vishwajith – 'Vivi' – had taken Shobana's sports car for a high-speed jaunt.

Puansh, who's studying in the United States, says that his favourite adages of his father are: 'Don't spend less, earn more', 'Belief is power' and 'The distance from the earth to the sky isn't altitude, it's attitude'. Not long ago, during a visit to India, Puansh impressed Dr Reddy with his knowledge of the world's political geography – particularly Africa.

His father Anil Kamineni is a strict disciplinarian but one who loves to reason with his children. 'It's easy to let our kids get spoilt. The tough job is to keep them grounded and hungry. Punch, like the other kids, idolizes his grandfather but his grandmother found that the way to his heart is through his tummy,' he said.

His younger daughter Anushpala has a stylish, carefree demeanour. For an outsider, it's easy to understand why her father calls her a charmer. She's one of the few kids of her generation of the Reddy family who feel confined by the expectations of being Dr Reddy's grandchild. But Dr Reddy intuitively understands that forcing this one is counter-productive. 'Left to herself she will contribute and define her vision,' he said. Each child has their special place in his heart.

Their elder daughter Upasna also directs Apollo's philanthropic efforts, help that goes to employees and their families as well as community outreach. Among other responsibilities she edits *B Positive* magazine which has a monthly circulation of 200,000. She is devoted to caring for animals, loves horses, especially her pony Daisy, and her new puppy Brat.

In June 2012, she married the actor Ram Charan Teja, the son of actor and politician K. Chiranjeevi. I attended the wedding, whose ceremonies were spread over five days. Thousands of people attended receptions and galas – and everyone was fed in the traditional Reddy style.

Ram Charan's second film *Magadheera* was a blockbuster and he became an overnight sensation. Now with scores of endorsements and film roles, he and his wife are active in many social causes.

Ram Charan remembers that he and Upasna were on-again/off-again dating friends for seven years before they both decided that they missed each other when separated.

His first glimpse of Dr Reddy was when he and Upasna were in an early dating phase, and Ram Charan had gone to the Bishop Garden house to meet Upasna. The actor had ridden his very old red Royal Enfield sports bike to the house. Suddenly he realized that Dr Reddy was on his way home for lunch. Ram Charan bade a quick goodbye to Upasna, jumped on the bike, shut his helmet visor and quickly left. He passed the doctor's car just at the driveway. Dr Reddy said, 'Who was that on the bike that just zoomed past?' Of course, there were general descriptions of the young man, but it was some time later that the two formally met.

Ram Charan says, 'I don't actually remember what he said to me. He shook my hand and it was like an embrace. He is one of the warmest people I have ever met in my life. Our journey started. Each time we see each other it is the same. He has the same laugh and greeting. It is more of a connection than I thought possible. He responds to me and I to him.

'I told him, "After I met you, I do not miss my grandfather any more" – because Dr Reddy provided the same wise bond. He is fifty years my senior and his presence is quite impressive. Sometimes people who have gained such success and are so well known as he is tend to lose their humility. Dr Reddy has his own strength. I have so much to learn from him.'

Before Ram Charan and Upasna married, the young man bought a house on the golf course. When he told Upasna she said, 'Tell me frankly if you are serious. If so, I am not interested. It will be a problem for me. You are a film star and will travel making movies. I will be alone and I won't like that. I come from a very close family with a lot of people around, and it's important for me to have someone to talk and laugh with. If I don't have a mother and father in the home, I will go crazy.'

Ram Charan laughed when he recounted this story. Then he said, 'Well, you know the result. We live with my parents, and Upasna and my mother are very close. Upasna was giving me very good advice even though she said it was for herself.'

'Dr and Mrs Reddy have great compassion and warmth, and are great role models for the family. Every day, Dr Reddy calls all his grandchildren and speaks to them for a few moments. It helps keep the family together. Between them [Prathap Chandra and Sucharitha Reddy] they make sure that the family is connected. That doesn't happen automatically and it is a gift that they give each person,' Ram Charan said. 'When I am feeling low or angry and I step into their house I just forget all of that. It's like going to a spa. Dr Reddy has an aura about his words and his presence. Sometimes I say to him, "I just want to sit with you."'

Upasna and Ram Charan share a commitment to doing good for others. Every other Sunday he goes to a location to take photos with fans who donate to the Chiranjeevi Blood and Eye Banks. This has helped gather more than 64,000 blood donations for people in Andhra Pradesh.

Ram Charan enjoys archery, among other things. In that sport, he has a fellow traveller – his father-in-law, Anil Kamineni, who's served as president of the state archery association. A man possessing movie star looks himself, Anil Kamineni is one of two of Dr Reddy's sons-in-law who actually was part of Apollo at one stage. When Apollo Hyderabad was being conceptualized and constructed, Dr Reddy invited Anil to join him in his efforts. That's one reason that Anil's name appears on the plaque at the entrance of the hospital, along with those of other institutional directors at the time. Anil, a fiercely independent man, left after the operation stabilized, and when asked 'Why?' he told his father-in-law that he, too, wanted to pursue his vision of founding new and innovative businesses.

'Dr Reddy gave the word "family" a new, all-encompassing meaning, effortlessly including all 72,000 employees. Still, blood relatives have played an important role at Apollo,' Anil said.

He told me how much Dr Reddy remembers two relatives in particular, and recalls them with great fondness – G. Surender Reddy, who was CEO of Apollo Hyderabad, and C.D.D. Reddy, the CEO of Apollo Indraprastha in New Delhi.

Sitting in his expansive office set on a 30-acre site in Jubilee Hills overlooking the famous Golconda fort, Dr Reddy said: 'Surender made the Hyderabad campus happen. When we found this land it was just rocks and harsh terrain. Surender engaged hundreds of lorries to move tonnes of fertile mud and planted over a thousand trees. He then nurtured them like they were his babies. As project director he supervised the site, tackled government permissions and even made multiple fund-raising trips to the United States. He was

Sucha's brother and had his share of the Khammam family charm. I could depend on him and he never ever refused me anything. I'm glad he saw Deccan Hospital evolve into Apollo Hyderabad and then to Apollo Health City. Sangita and I miss him.'

Such devotion to family members and family impresses some highly placed people who know Dr Reddy well.

'Aruna and I share his family values. I personally feel that Dr Reddy has been even more successful because of the strength he derives from being such a deeply religious man whose family matters so much to him – I know too many successful businessmen who neglect what should be their first priority, their family,' Lord Swraj Paul of Marylebone, and chairman of Britain's Caparo Group, told me in a conversation at home not far from the House of Lords in London. His wife, Lady Aruna Paul, cited the 'special rapport' between Dr Reddy and Sucharitha Reddy with their grandchildren. 'The Reddys have bridged the generation gap well,' she said. 'In fact, there is no generation gap among the Reddys.'

Dawood A. Rawat, chairman emeritus of the British American Investment Group of Mauritius and London, expressed a similar sentiment. He and Dr Reddy agreed to build Apollo Bramwell Hospital in Mauritius after Prime Minister Manmohan Singh brought up the topic during a state visit by his Mauritian counterpart, Dr Navinchandra Ramgoolam – a physician by training – in 2005. Prime Minister Ramgoolam inaugurated the $70 million 200-bed hospital, a joint venture between Apollo and the British American Investment Group, on 19 August 2009.

Dr Reddy travelled to Mauritius for the inauguration. I happened to be there on a visit unrelated to the hospital, and was invited to the lovely beachside Rawat home for a celebratory dinner. A gentle breeze from the Indian Ocean washed over the gathering. 'Dr and Mrs Reddy share the dedication that my wife Ayesha and I have, to ensuring that people's health and well-being matter,' Rawat said. 'We also share their dedication to the premise that in life one's family should always come first.' Years later, at a retreat outside Rome, Rawat told me: 'It's never easy balancing one's professional life and business life. But Dr Reddy does it. I consider him a friend not the least because of how much of a family man he is.'

———

Upasna had spoken about how closely she worked with her mother Shobana and her aunts, particularly Sangita Reddy. Sangita is the youngest of the Reddy daughters, and lives with her husband, K. Vishweshwar, CEO and managing director of Citadel Research and Solutions Ltd. in Hyderabad, along with their young sons Anindith, Vishwajith and Viraj.

'As Apollo completes thirty years I will as well – professionally – because I formally joined Apollo just three months before the opening. It was an amazing time: hectic activity, the highs and lows of a new enterprise but always a sense of satisfaction. Looking back, one of the most memorable periods was when I was executive assistant to the chairman. We really got things done,' Sangita told me.

'When Dad takes rounds [of the hospitals] it's a 360-degree experience,' she said. 'The patients are seen, met, medically reviewed but more importantly enthused with a fresh sense of reassurance that everything possible is being done. The doctors learn by his example because he really has the greatest bedside manner, and finally support staff and administrative teams know that he sees it all in one glance: are the nurses well informed and up to date, is the ward neat, are the patient rooms comfortable, if there is an empty room, has maintenance used the precious opportunity for repairs – a hundred other things and everything in one blink. Some of our best learning and patient-care decisions have happened with Dr Reddy on rounds.

'I enjoy the connect with patients and their families, and at the end of the day you go home with a sense of satisfaction – that you made a difference. There is no happier moment than seeing a family take a patient home well – and nothing more moving than having a family that has lost their loved one thank us because they know we did everything that we could.'

Sangita continued: 'It is for this reason that we will continue to search for the best doctors, invest in training and in technology, work on continuous improvement at every level from patient safety to process cycle time. We will support research and innovation from our teams and invest in every proven technology that will enable better medicine, all the while remembering that there is more to be done.

'Health care is about people. It's critical to maintain personal interaction with patients. At every level – doctors, nurses and medical personnel – we highlight the power of finding joy in the recovery of our patients. This powerful paradigm changes health care from very tough work to a rewarding mission. As a result of this approach, our teams excel at what they do, and love their jobs. Consequentially our teams have the lowest attrition rates in the industry.

'Apollo will always lead the way. Leadership in health care is part of our mission and it redefines the way we deliver health care. Sometimes it means that we choose to turn over assets (such as Apollo Health Street) so that we can make more of an impact in our health geography. The lessons we learnt at Health Street will be used in Asia: best practices from across the world, some things to emulate and some to avoid. But also importantly the company has moved to good hands and with the foundation we laid I am sure it will grow bigger. One of the new focuses includes philanthropy, growing our foundation so that we can impact more lives. Education and skills development will be another major area of focus. India must double the number of doctors, treble the number of nurses and grow by over four times the number of paramedics. This critical initiative of the foundation will not only help the health care system in India with the much-needed talent but also facilitate "young India" to care for a "greying world".'

'One of the things that we are doing now is to change our orientation from "cure" to include wellness,' Sangita said. 'When a patient is discharged, they will not only receive a discharge summary and prescription for medications but also a "wellness prescription". This is part of Apollo Life. We realize that a cure is great but our interpretation of "Touching Lives" is now deeper and far more pervasive. We're taking a strong look at how all elements of Apollo are integrated – hospitals, clinics, insurance, pharmacies. The synergy is interesting especially from a patient experience perspective as well as the opportunity to optimize the cost of customer acquisition and servicing. I'm most excited about creating an even more satisfying patient experience and new opportunities to achieve that goal.

'Dad's vision is vast and always ahead of everyone else. I've seen that he is delegating more, acting in an advisory capacity (but is still entirely connected). He is definitely preparing for a transition, all the while incubating new concepts. We as an organization will be "Future Ready" because we know the landscape will see change like we never imagined at speeds that we have never seen.

'The outreach efforts being planned in Aragonda are a good example of the future total health. This initiative will be a holistic approach that will use IT like telemedicine to bring access and affordability while empowering the primary care team. The outreach efforts in Aragonda are a good example of expanding from narrow silos to fully integrated health care. Of course, Dad has an emotional attachment to the village and that makes it all the more important. Because he knows it so well, we are able to really see how small changes can make big impacts. Education is so important and we think that the children are the key to this. If we can teach that eating junk leads to childhood obesity, undetected diabetes and high blood pressure, the information will filter from the children upward to the parents. More generations will be touched and there will be less need for curative care. This is an example of our wellness programme.'

'It's one of my goals to establish the Apollo conference as the Davos of health care where innovation in prevention, delivery and care will be shared to create the most effective programmes,' Sangita added. 'We continue to incorporate the Disney principles of satisfied experience with the Indian cultural ethos. We're looking at everything from foot massage to spiritual elements such as faith, yoga and meditation. There are some popular programmes such as subsidized rice that helps make food more accessible. If we can employ a new generation to do that with health care, we will have a stronger economy and a stronger country.'

As Sangita spoke, it occurred to me that it was the first time that I'd heard any of the Reddy daughters refer to a 'transition'.

'Our belief is that health care will change radically in the next decade and we will be prepared for those changes. The upgrades are not just about space and look and feel. It's technology in health care, process innovation, business intelligence and analytics – and it's all real time,' Sangita said.

'The country should be doing critical analyses about population health,' she added. 'We have shifted our data to a private cloud and architected the enterprise in a holistic manner – an ERP-based system for our in-hospital care but also for an improved information flow across the continuum of care with a patient health record at the core. New, wearable devices mean that we will be receiving data from patients and they will be getting coordinated care information from us.'

'Increased computer and technology capacity is essential to keep a well-informed health care team,' Sangita said. 'We are evolving the way that we surround patients and their families. Some of the impact will not be outwardly visible for the patient but will include targeted diagnostics, focused medicine, care guidelines and more detailed planning. It is about more personalized medicine and covers everything from primary to tertiary. We are creating a new era of ubiquitous health care from the cradle through life,' she said, in effect laying out the contours of the global trends of future health care.

Did she ever want to follow in her illustrious father's footsteps and become a physician herself?

'I always wanted to be a doctor and went to a nerdy school,' Sangita said. 'After the tenth year Indian students have to decide what they want to do and I was determined that medicine was my path. I got really good marks and wanted to achieve my goal through merit, not through the connections of my family. At the crucial moment Dad didn't let me join. "You will take all of your patients home at night and on days off and holidays and you will never have a family life," he said.

'Even if he discouraged my dream of becoming a doctor, he

has been very inspiring and extremely supportive of my role in Apollo. It's been an incredible journey working with him. I once shared with him the concept of the three Bs that would change health care – biology, bytes and bandwidth. He gets it. And in the years to come Apollo is poised to not just ride the transformative wave, which is going to sweep health care – but spearhead it. It's not just his vision and perseverance that is the key; it is that he is constantly imbibing new ideas from everywhere. His brain is just wired right to take those ideas and apply them to the health care needs of India,' Sangita said.

She added: 'Over the years I've read and heard many management gurus, and explored multiple management concepts – but I am so often stuck by the fact that Dad applied these principles at Apollo without even reading the books. Is it that good management is common sense or that he is guided by a higher power?

'I travel abroad frequently and I'm often asked how we have achieved everything we did. It really defies some of the management principles of focus and core competence. I think we are where we are today simply because Dad cared enough to put in every effort possible and we achieved what we did because it was his destiny.'

Sangita's husband, Vishweshwar Reddy, also hails from a family with a dominant patriarch. Vishweshwar's father, Konda Madhava Reddy, was chief justice of the Andhra Pradesh High Court, and later also chief justice of the Bombay High Court, and the Governor of Maharashtra; he went on to become the first chairman of the Central Administrative Tribunal (CAT).

Vishweshwar is an engineer and entrepreneur who does extensive social work by educating disadvantaged youth. He set up a foundation in his father's memory that takes students who do not graduate high school, who are from poor homes in small villages, whose parents are not educated and who have little resources, and puts them through a rigorous eighteen-month programme. The Justice Konda Madhava Reddy Foundation guarantees a job for all who stay the entire programme. Vishweshwar says, 'We take fifteen students in each batch and give them work qualifications so that they can have better lives. They have each made phenomenal contributions and grown enormously in their skills.'[1]

As an engineer and the erstwhile CEO and managing director of GE Medical Systems IT, India, he had observed Dr Reddy from close quarters, and even accompanied him for lunch with Jack Welsh, then chairman and CEO of General Electric. He said, 'Even from his school and college days Dr Reddy had many friends. He came from a large family and was very popular, always organizing activities with other boys, playing, hiking and swimming. His extended family became his family. This same attribute crept into his cardiology practice, business activities and Apollo. It doesn't matter who the person is, he is totally comfortable with them. It could be a patient from a rural area, a nurse, a ward boy, a film star or a major industrialist – he relates to all and they recognize in him a kindness that transcends position. This is not something that others can easily do. One thing I noticed is that he pays careful attention to details of a person in the same way that he pays attention to Apollo.'

'It's sometimes difficult to manage situations in which both the bride and groom come from large joint families,' Vishweshwar told me. 'This is where Sucharitha must be given full credit. She finds such joy in getting people together, and organizing things for them. She's a phenomenal person.'

I asked Vishweshwar that, notwithstanding the aristocratic family that he himself belonged to, if he was in any way intimidated by the prospect of marrying Sangita, the youngest daughter of Dr Prathap Chandra Reddy and Sucharitha.

'I was definitely in awe of Dr Reddy,' he said. 'After all, he had made it big in a field that Reddys didn't traditionally enter – medicine. Reddys are known for their business and academic achievements. But

---

1 Vishweshwar Reddy has been exploring the prospects of entering politics. In my conversations with him, I found him to be an astute analyst of national, regional and local politics. I was also struck by his idealism for India, and by his belief that so much more could be done in health care and also in sustainable economic development.

Dr Reddy had become internationally known for his accomplishments in medicine.'

'I was welcomed so warmly into their family,' Vishweshwar said, noting that Sucharitha Reddy and his own mother, Jayalatha, were distantly related. 'Our families had known each other for a long time. I am still in awe of what Dr Reddy has achieved in health care. And it's hard not to be continually impressed by Sucharitha's hospitality and concern for people. Dr Reddy and Sucharitha are the two most caring people I know. They are role models.'

Vishweshwar said that Dr Reddy was 'unrelenting in working for the ordinary person'.

'Many competitors have come up since Dr Reddy introduced Apollo and corporate health care to India,' he said. 'He inspired them and opened an entirely new industry. They can build modern buildings and buy equipment and imitate Apollo's best practices. But, there is one thing that they cannot copy or replicate or transplant to their institutions – and that is the culture that Dr Reddy established when Apollo first opened and that has continued these thirty years. It's the softer touch that he has, things that are difficult to define but are always recognizable. You see it in his management style, in the way he relates to patients and their families and in the regard that he has for ordinary people.

'In the 1990s I realized how open Dr Reddy was to new ideas and how astute he was in sifting through them. Several companies had approached him about collaborations. He listened to each one carefully but did not choose any. I asked, "Why not?" He replied, "They are coming for their own self-interest, not to serve others. They are not adding any value to our outreach." They were looking for an easy entry into India, wanting to capitalize on Apollo's reputation.

'He is not xenophobic at all, willing to listen to others who are different or hold opinions that differ from his. Sometimes those opinions are startlingly different. It's a great lesson: He is absolutely open-minded and objective. He is financially conservative, except when acquiring the latest technology, and yet, willing to take business risks.

'Dr Reddy is the perfect person to approach for advice because of the manner in which he interacts with you. He asks you many questions and the depth of his knowledge is impressive. He will say "You can do it", and you are left to decide. He doesn't say good or bad. You know, of course, that what he is looking for is something that is good for society. Rather than reject something outright, he looks for possibilities — a good idea that can be expanded or adapted, and he looks for a kernel of good.

'He talks about Apollo being a family and working together like family. It sounds good and feels good, but far more importantly, he really means it. He's put it into action throughout Apollo.'

'I'm sure that you've heard about how kind Mrs Reddy is, no words can describe her kindness and generosity: not only to the family but to our staff, to my sister and my sister's household and her family and to people she sees at hospital or temple or wherever she goes,' he added.

———

Vishwajith, Viraj and Anindith, Sangita and Vishweshwar's sons, are the youngest of the grandchildren to embody the characteristics of their grandparents. Like their elder cousins, they describe a relationship with Prathap and Sucharitha Reddy that is unfailingly loving and supportive. It is one that also encourages each child to find his or her own strength and to use it for the good of society.

'Our grandfather always encourages us to be happy and to do good for others. He does say that it would be great if one of us becomes a doctor, but he does not push us,' Vishwajith said.

Both Vishwajith and Viraj are keenly aware of their legacy. Their mother is the executive director for Operations of Apollo Hospitals and the boys have seen up close what it takes to run a major business. Vishwajith said, 'Equally, it is inspiring to see what changes can be made and how people are grateful for their health.'

The boys visited the hospital in Chennai with their grandfather and were impressed not only with his energy and keen empathy with the patients and their families but also with the affection and respect that Dr Reddy receives.

'Seeing how hard he still works and what he has accomplished makes me want to never give up on projects whether it is a book report or something that does good,' said Viraj.

'Patience, persistence and perseverance are the three Ps that our grandfather teaches. Our grandmother is always telling us how intelligent and capable we are. She is the most loving person I know,' added Vishwajith. Viraj, who mentioned the care that Sucharitha always gives, even to those who do not know her, echoed the affection for Mrs Reddy.

Anindith said, 'My grandfather has been called many things by so many people – my label for him is "life changer". He has really changed my life. At eighteen I was having fun, maybe a little too much. My twelfth grade course included an extended essay and somehow I had picked rural health insurance – I knew my mom could help me with it. My study guide insisted I personally conduct the market survey so I left for what I thought would be a brief trip to Aragonda. In the forty-eight hours there, I met more than 170 people, and each one of them told me in different ways how much the Aragonda hospital and the rural insurance scheme meant to them. It had saved somebody's grandchild, snatched from death a young girl's father and repaired many broken bones, while also safely delivering their babies – and it cost them just one rupee a day. Their pride, joy and sense of ownership made me very clear that I must make sure my life has meaning. I am not a doctor or a hospital administrator but as an engineer anything I can do to help grow Apollo or make it stronger I would be proud to. I have definitely learnt that I must ensure I do something significant with my life.'

Yes, it's true that these boys, too, played chess with their grandfather and that he asks each child, 'What good have you done today?'

Among members of the Reddy family with whom I spent time was Rahul Reddy, the eldest son of Sucharitha's younger sister Vijayalakshmi. He lives outside Portland, Oregon, and he and his wife run a software consulting business helping customers maximize online efficiencies. He calls Chairman Reddy 'Pedda Daddy' and refers to the four Reddy daughters as his sisters.

When his mother was about to give birth she went to stay with Prathap and Sucharitha, and Rahul was born in Waltham Hospital in 1967. He was nearly three years old when the Reddys moved back to India and was with them on the return trip. He lived with the Reddys in a house round the corner from their current home in Bishop Garden. He and his family have spent vacations in Chennai with the Reddys and his in-laws.

Asked what impressed him most about Dr Reddy, Rahul replied: 'He was a visionary. He's always had the intelligence and tenacity and ability to get things done. Apollo has treated more than 30 million people, and that is more than three times the population of New York City.'

When the hospital was twenty-five years old there was a great party and everyone was celebrating the huge numbers of people who had been treated by Apollo. Dr Reddy said something to the effect of, 'We haven't done anything yet. There are 1.1 billion left who need care.' That impressed Rahul.

Rahul consults with Apollo on technology issues and is spearheading a pilot project where Apollo will connect with NRIs to provide monitoring and health services for their families back in India. Rahul said the initial testing would be done on twenty NRI families who are yet to be identified. The NRIs would pay a monthly fee. He is also working on ways to grow medical tourism.

'What have you specifically learned from Chairman Reddy, and how have you applied it to your work?' I asked Rahul.

'I learnt how to engage with people by seeing how he interacts with nurses, doctors and executives. He talks at their level,' Rahul said.

'What are some of the characteristics you associate with Chairman and Sucharitha Reddy?'

Rahul's response: 'Diversity and strength; a sense of humour; adventurousness. And that if you don't believe in something there's no point in doing it – it won't work.'

This is how Rahul Reddy summarized his view of Dr Reddy's contribution to post-Independence India: 'It is impressive in the way he improved the quality of life for people. He changed the health care landscape and by doing so, spawned other businesses and attracted new investments to India. His work at Apollo has had a multiplier effect if all you counted was the jobs that were created when the infrastructure was built.'

Some days before I was scheduled to deliver the manuscript of this book to my publishers, I received a note from Dr Ashok Subramaniam, who works with a government hospital in the Andaman Islands (his wife is associated with Apollo Clinics in Port Blair as its medical officer). He's the younger brother of Dr Reddy's longtime associate, Dr N. Uma, and worked for Dr Reddy at HM Hospital in Madras; it was his first job after finishing medical school in 1980.

Dr Subramaniam wrote, in part: 'Today I am respected by all my patients in these beautiful islands because of Dr Reddy's teachings, the bedside manners he taught, and his way of approaching his patients. He used to call me "my boy" – even now when I visit him at Apollo Hospital, Chennai, he will not hesitate to introduce me to others as "my boy". We always used to call him "Doctor", and not "Sir".'

Dr Subramaniam continued: 'There is an incident I will never forget. When we were managing the Madras Race Club intensive coronary care unit, a journalist who was playing jackpot had a heart attack and was brought in. I attended on him and also called Dr Reddy. He immediately came to my help. The patient was going in for ventricular fibrillation following a cardiac arrest. We defibrillated him many times and having little hope, shifted him to our clinic from the club. The patient came through; the next day, during his rounds, Dr Reddy told the patient that it was because of me that he was alive. I was flabbergasted, since I never expected this from him. Actually,

Dr Reddy's timely intervention had saved that patient's life. But he never takes credit for himself – he always praises his associates. This incident left a permanent imprint on my mind.'

———

I asked Shobana Kamineni about her father's place in modern India. Raji Chandru, the general manager of operations at Indraprastha Apollo in New Delhi, had told me of the day-to-day supervision on Shobana's part of the hospital's construction, and her energy.

I spoke to Shobana on a day not long after the celebrations of Dr Reddy's eightieth birthday.

'Ten years from now the real picture of Dr Reddy's vision would have emerged even more clearly,' Shobana said. 'Today the contours of health care are intertwined by hospitals, pharmacies, insurance, research, education, clinics, IT, telemedicine, emergency medicines, encompassing – or blurring into – wellness, predictive health, Ayurveda, pranic healing, music therapy. These have emerged as what Dr Reddy wanted for his patients: a total health care system. Apollo was his enabler.

'What is total health care? Who "owns" it? Is it necessary? These are paradigm-shifting questions, and the answers can be seen in the churn in US health care over the last thirty years (since the time Dr Reddy started Apollo). In the 1980s, the US hospitals were almighty, then in the early 1990s, the HMOs, physician practices and DRG (doctors groups) were encouraged by insurance companies to bring down hospital and health care costs. Then came the extreme churn of the late 1990s when insurance companies started acquiring hospital networks, the mergers of HCA and Columbia and Humana and United Healthcare happened. By the new millennium people were fed up, and the practice of medicine had become commoditized and controlled. The hospital groups demerged and from the ashes a new phoenix emerged – HCA again, Tenet and many other hospitals were back, weakened but wiser. More importantly there came the Democrats' intent to provide universal health care – Bill Clinton's early efforts and Obama's crusade that resulted in Obamacare.

'But in some corners of the globe there emerged success in a model to look after people from the cradle to the grave. Kaiser Permanente – a non-profit health system across the west coast of America – is a great example. Another winner was in Spain where Munich Health was awarded a fixed fee per person to keep them healthy; with the package came hospitals, clinics and pharmacies. The Apollo system is creating this in a larger and more diverse landscape.'

So did this evolve at Apollo, or was it somewhere in Dr Reddy's subconscious that great care came from a responsibility to synergize the system? This is a long way to come from the time when he used to hoard bottles of good intravenous fluid so that his critical patients wouldn't get a reaction.[2] It led to starting Apollo pharmacies three years after the first Apollo Hospital in Chennai. Till date the company and its founder are singularly proud of the fact that they have never sold an expired or spurious medication.

Consider also this: Apollo has fourteen nursing colleges stemming from the challenge of establishing a pipeline and training great nurses for the many Apollo hospitals envisaged by Dr Reddy. Today, there are plans in place to educate and train more than 25,000 people annually in every sphere of health care.

Or consider this: Apollo's championing the cause of financial access to make health care inclusive through health insurance in the '90s and establishing a pilot project in Aragonda. Today Apollo Munich Health Insurance is recognized as the fastest growing specialist health insurance in India and among India's top twenty-five places to work.

'The story is endless – but the point is that this clearly wasn't just the desire of one man or a group to "conquer" the health care space; it stemmed from a need and desire to do better for a person and keep them "well",' Shobana said. 'And the many dimensions of

---

2 This was a common practice in the '70s in India when intravenous fluid-making was prehistoric. Today India has the world's best IV manufacturing facilities.

Dr Reddy include the most powerful one – he is always seeking to do more, create more, heal more. This is the legacy of touching lives.

'So the enduring legacy of Dr Reddy goes beyond creating a chain of hospitals to creating a chain of health care continuity. This ability to traverse the health care universe would have been impossible for anyone except the "Healer".

'That is his true legacy.'

This was the first time that I'd heard anyone from Dr Prathap Chandra Reddy's family use the word 'legacy'. It suggested some sort of finality and closure to an era, but I don't think that Shobana meant it that way.

Still, the questions abound within the Apollo system and well beyond about how long the man who transformed India's health care landscape plans to be a hands-on chairman.

My own view is that Dr Reddy already bequeathed a legacy to India the day that Apollo Hospital opened in Madras, thirty years ago. Health care in India would never be the same again – and all because a fifty-year-old man had a vision in 1983, and the guts to pursue his dreams for his beloved country.

A Life in Full

SINDOORI REDDY, THE FIRST-BORN of Dr Prathap Chandra Reddy and Sucharitha Reddy's ten grandchildren, perhaps summed it up best when I asked her how she viewed her extraordinary grandfather's life.

'He is grateful for the life he has spent, and I think grows stronger every day,' she said. 'He has never lost touch with his small village – and that inspires him to do more so that each person in our country can live a healthier, happier life.'

On balance, how has Dr Reddy led his life? Had he led 'the good life', a philosophical term for the life that one would like to live? He's met with his share of setbacks, but he's also made more than most people do of the opportunities that came his way. Indeed, Dr Reddy saw those opportunities in health care and in national economic development well before anyone else. I don't think that Apollo was built only on a dream: foresight and endurance played as much a role in the story of Dr Prathap Chandra Reddy. And throughout his life, he abided by some things that his parents, Raghava and Shakuntala Reddy, instilled in him. Humility matters. Family matters. People from all stations of life matter. Faith matters. Doing good without expecting anything in return matters. Decency matters. Keeping your word matters. Not complaining matters. And, yes, having a sense of humour matters.

A very long time ago, when I was young and wet behind the

ears and filled with an ambition to be the top newspaperman in the world, my editor and mentor at the *New York Times* told me that the person best qualified to explain the meaning of his – or her – life was that person himself. 'Just ask people about themselves, and they will tell you their story,' the editor, A.M. Rosenthal, memorably said. 'But you must listen carefully. It's not just the text of what they say, it's the subtext that often reveals the truth of a person's life.' Notwithstanding all the things that I knew as a result of researching this book, I thought to myself, 'Who better to ask about his life than Dr Reddy himself as he enters his ninth decade?'

So I decided to ask Dr Reddy how he assessed his life's narrative. How did he see himself after all those accolades, those hagiographies, the business and medical triumphs of Apollo, those adoring headlines that sometimes stretched credulity, those piercing criticisms from competitors and some patients, those wicked whispers from politicians dismayed by his refusal to pay gratuities?

It was late one afternoon in Chennai, and Dr Reddy and I were sitting in his office. A delicious platter of vegetarian sandwiches had been served, along with steaming coffee. The working day had been long for him, as usual, but Dr Reddy appeared remarkably fresh. He'd had a short nap in an adjoining room, and had then bowed before the beautiful statues of Lord Ganesha and Lord Venkateshwara, among other deities, placed on shelves in the office. He leaned back in a chair specially outfitted to accommodate his aching back. He wore a dark blue suit, a light blue shirt, and a tie whose tiny patterns seemed intriguing. He took off his shoes, as he almost always does in his office.

It became clear to me quickly that Dr Reddy wasn't about to launch into a monologue. Rather, this was to be a dialogue – a kind of questioning in which an original question is responded to by a statement as though it were an answer. This in turn forces the questioner to reformulate a new question in light of the progress of the discourse. I thought to myself, 'This is going to be a Socratic dialogue.'

What have been your limitations?

'Whenever you achieve something there will be a limiting factor. You must find a way out – how to get over this limiting factor – if you think that what you want to do is worthwhile. I love to visualize what I want to achieve. There are no limitations to what the mind can come up with. Nothing that can be visualized is insurmountable.'

How do you define 'friendship'?

'It is something you give others without asking. It is an inexpensive gift. It is with love, kind words and a heart-to-heart feeling. Friendship isn't a commodity. You don't trade in it. And you must have no expectations of getting anything back. It is a simple interaction with someone you care about. And friendship always means that you wish the other person well. When they do well, you rejoice. When they suffer, you try and heal them. I have been blessed with the best friend a man could ever expect to have in life – my wife Sucharitha.'

How do you respond to others' selfishness?

'Somebody who works with you suddenly turns around to act as your rival – of course that hurts, even if I don't show it. When top people at Apollo want to leave, I feel bad, as they have given so much that I consider them part of my family. But these things happen in life. I take it as it comes and say, "I appreciate all that you have done, and say thank you." But I also have a policy: if someone leaves Apollo, they can never return to us.'

What explains your faith in Hanuman?

'Rama realized that Hanuman could cross the sea to Lanka, where Ravana was holding Sita hostage. What we understand here is that you need someone to tell you that you have the capability.

That's how Hanuman went off to find Sita, and he finds that he
is superior and second to none in this way. Ravana's younger
brother, Vibhishana, said you should never kill an emissary. What
you can do is punish him by doing something to make him look
ugly. So they decided to burn Hanuman's tail. But Sita prayed to
Agni asking him to spare Hanuman. The tail immediately became
like ice. Hanuman went around burning every single home except
Vibhishana's house. Then he was filled with a sense of recrimination
when he saw the whole place burning. Everything was gone but
Sita remained untouched. He was happy and returned to Rama
and gave Rama what Sita gave to him. All this is narrated very
beautifully with great detail in the Sundara Kanda, which I read
every morning. But what we are really talking about is that each of
us has all these powers within us. Look at the heart. The only thing
is that with power we can get blind. Sometimes our anger blinds
us. What each person needs is patience and persistence. Sometimes
I remind myself of this – if I want to do something even though it's
not going to be easy. Then there's the question of doing something
you never thought of. Obstacles often come your way that you
might not be able to cross. But the way to overcome real obstacles
is through the force of your convictions.'

What do you mean by 'Tender Loving Care'?

'People who come to hospitals, sometimes from great distances, have
this huge anxiety. We need to address that anxiety. That's why I think
compassionate care is important. We must be able to give them that
love, what my daughters call "Tender Loving Care" – TLC. I think
what really happened is that everyone became a Dr Reddy, it is not
just one Dr Reddy who became the leader but we were able to bring
everyone on board in whatever we did. If you ask my housekeeping
boy what would happen if his boiler fails, he will not say, "There will
be no hot water." He will say, "The hospital will come to a standstill
because if the sterilizer stops working there cannot be any surgeries."
Everyone knows that each person is playing a very significant role.

It is because everyone feels they are doing something for the society and to live up to the trust of our patients – and that there are many more things we need to do. "Tender Loving Care" simply means doing for others what you'd have them do for you.'

How do you distinguish between 'Be a human' and 'Be human'?

'I always tell everyone at Apollo, "You can be human or you can be a human, but there is a huge difference between these two. You can be a human and say, "I have done whatever I can," or you can say, "Yes I have done this but I can do more." I think that is a feeling that is continuously being reinforced in all of us at Apollo.'

Do you see yourself as a 'Karmayogi'?

'I believe that one is born to make a difference in other people's lives, particularly those who are less fortunate than you. I could have been anything that I'd wanted – an agriculturist, like my father, or a cardiologist who settled in the United States. But something drove me – I felt deep inside that I had a bigger purpose in life. When you've turned fifty, you start thinking and reflecting about where you've been and where you are going. A lot of people told me that I should return to America and continue my successful medical practice there. One friend told me that India was just not conducive to practicing good medicine. I stayed on because of an inner call that urged me to bring about a change. Call it vision, call it foresight, call it anything you want. I stayed, my family stayed, and here we are today.'

Did you ever imagine that one day you'd preside over an enterprise as large as Apollo?

'As I always say, the loss of that thirty-eight-year-old patient who couldn't raise the funds for a bypass in the United States made me determined to start a world-class hospital in India. I could have built a hospital that catered to 200 patients. But did I think that I had it within me to develop something much bigger? Yes. I always felt that. I wanted to do something in Indian medicine that hadn't been done before. Maybe people had thought about building a corporate-sector hospital. But I was the one who took that leap; I was the one who took the risks. I didn't dismiss the naysayers, but I never listened to them either.'

How do you see yourself as a doctor?

'Doctors are considered demi-gods in our society. People say that you give them hope, that you have the power of life and death. But you cannot let that go to your head. There's only one God – and it isn't you. As a doctor, you need to commit yourself to giving compassion. In the case of some people you give them their life back. For some people you give joy by restoring their health. In all cases, you end up making a difference. As a doctor, you serve. As a doctor, you don't seek to be worshipped. I always want to live up to the trust of the people who come seeking care.'

Do you see yourself as a humanitarian?

'All people are not born equal, at least in their circumstances. But in the medical profession, you are obliged to offer everybody equal care. You can't cut corners just because a patient is poor. To me, being a humanitarian means doing the best that I can – and that means delivering the best health care. I don't covet awards. I don't seek applause. I live every day the way I want to live it – by being a good doctor to as many people as I can through Apollo. Does that make me a "humanitarian"? You decide. You're the writer.'

Do you see yourself as 'The Patriarch'?

'I don't know whether, beyond my immediate family, I'm "The Patriarch" or not. But this I do know: Apollo transformed health care in India by creating the corporate sector in hospitals. It brought about change in the way better health care was delivered. But in the end, I remain disappointed. We still have the old diseases in India, and now we have the twenty-first century challenges – heart problems, diabetes, cancer and infectious diseases. We must put rocket fuel into our efforts so that there's a breakthrough in health care all over the country. And let us not forget the power of Indian innovation. What is right for India is bound to be right for the world.'

Do you see yourself as 'The Visionary'?

'From my childhood, I have tried to do whatever good I could. I gave my friendship freely. I always looked for something good in another person. Being a "visionary" simply means observing your environment and thinking how you can make a difference. In my case, it was through health care. I always tell my grandchildren, "With the access to knowledge that you have, with your intelligence, you can be anything that you want to be. Just be sure whatever that is, it involves doing good." What's the real difference between an everyday person and a Nobel laureate? He or she is focused. I also tell my family members and colleagues that when you succeed at something, people will expect more good things of you. And what is the purpose of all the success we aim for? It is to bring about change in our society. I believe that each one of us has it within us to become transformational figures. As I look at my life, I can say truthfully that I did the best that I could do. But that's not enough for me. There's more to be done – much, much more. I feel blessed by the continuity that my four daughters and their children and the Apollo family offer for Apollo. They are the standard bearers of our brand. They are the keepers of my legacy, and they will all become leaders in their own right. Can a man in my place expect anything more of his family?'

Now that you have mostly achieved what you wanted in life, now that you have built a stable and strong organization, now that you

have a solid succession plan in place, and now that you have crossed
eighty years of age, is it time for you to take it easy?

My answer to that is simple. Between 2013 and 2030, the cumulative
cost of health care and loss in economic productivity due to illness –
largely because of cardiovascular diseases, cancer, chronic pulmonary
ailments and diabetes – is expected to be about $30 trillion. And
quite a significant portion of that would be because of the situation in
India. I like to think that I created a workable ecosystem that would
address India's continuing health care needs. Is this job done? If the
answer is yes, then I would leave my office tomorrow. But I rather
suspect that there's so much more to be done.

———

Our conversation had extended well into the early evening. Behind
Dr Reddy's desk, the lights of Chennai had started to twinkle in the
gloam.

It was time for Dr Prathap Chandra Reddy to leave for the Krishna
Mariamman temple on the hospital premises for his evening prayers.
The priests would be waiting for him. The shrine would be suffused
with the deep fragrance of agarbattis. The deities would be showered
with flowers, and hymns would be chanted. After that, Dr Reddy
would join his friends at the Madras Club for his usual round of
bridge. Then he would go home to Sucharitha for a quiet dinner.

And as for me? I felt a twinge of sudden sadness seeing Dr
Reddy leave his office, greeting all his staff members with folded
hands in the traditional namaskar. I would miss our long hours of
conversation, and I would miss his little courtesies. I would miss his
sense of humour. I would miss his perspectives on Indian history. I
would even miss his physician's advice on how to take better care of
myself. His candour and decency and generosity and patience over
these past months had been overwhelming. I had never met such a
giant of the game, a man relishing the fullness of his life, a man who
had led such a richly accomplished existence caring for so many

people, most of them strangers. I had been one of those strangers, and Dr Reddy and his family had welcomed me with total warmth into their households.

I was tempted to go with the Healer to the temple one last time. But I had a book to write.

Author's Note

ALTHOUGH I CHARACTERIZE MYSELF as a 'secular spiritualist', whenever I start a new book I pray to my primary deities, Lord Ganesha, Sai Baba of Shirdi and Lord Venkateshwara of Tirupati. They have blessed me with wonderful mentors, tutors, role models and supporters – some longtime, others relatively new to my life – in my long writing career, and I would like to cite them here:

Family: Balkrishna Trimbak Gupte (my father); Dr Charusheela Gupte (my mother); Keshav Ramachandra Pradhan (my maternal uncle).

The New York Times: A.M. Rosenthal; Martin Arnold; R.W. 'Johnny' Apple, Jr; George Barrett; Charlotte Curtis; Will Lissner; Richard F. Shepard; Louis A. Silverstein; Arthur Ochs Sulzberger; Harold Gal; Arthur and Barbara Gelb; Warren Hoge; Michael J. Leahy; Joseph Lelyveld; Peter Millones; Sydney H. Schanberg; Marvin Siegel; Sammy Solovitz; Seymour Topping and Audrey Ronning Topping; George and Marianne Vecsey.

Forbes: Jerry M. Flint; James W. Michaels.

Newsweek International: Kenneth Auchincloss; Mathilde Camacho;

Alexis Gelber; Richard Steele.

Brandeis University: Ambassador Morris B. Abram; Professor Robert J. Art; Professor Lawrence H. Fuchs; Professor John Roche; Professor I. Milton Sachs; Lawrence A. Wien.

Columbia University: Professor Richard Baker; Professor Jagdish Bhagwati.

New York: Arthur M. Bergmann; Tina Brown; Sir Harold Evans; Dr Allan E. and Collette Goodman; Judge Bruce J. and Karolyn Gould; David Halberstam; Dr Henry Heinemann; Ann and Theodore W. Kheel; Theodore C. Sorensen; Robert L. and Jan Dilenschneider; Lee E. and Connie Koppelman; Lynn Nesbit; Jon E. and Ellen Deutsch Quint; Nina K. Rosenwald; Howard J. Rubenstein; Timothy Seldes; Helen Silverstein; Allen E. Kaye.

Washington, DC: Berndt Debusmann; Bernard Kalb.

Jai Hind College, Mumbai: Professor K.K. Gajria; Principal T.G. Khubchandani; Professor Vispi Balaporia; Professor S.M. Rai; Dr Kamalaksha U. Mada.

St Xavier's High School, Mumbai: Rev. Leonard Serkis, SJ; Rev. Anthony Bulchand, SJ.

Europe: Ray Moseley; Lord Swraj and Lady Aruna Paul; Hilde and Klaus Schwab; Walter Wells.

India: Shobhaa Dé; Ajai Lal; Anand Mohan Lal; Vijai Kapoor (IAS); Prabhakar Koregaonkar; Dr Rajendra K. Pachauri; N. Ram and Mariam Ram; Khushwant Singh; Ram S. Varma (IAS); Malavika Sangghvi.

Mauritius: Ayesha and Dawood Ajum Rawat.

Pakistan: Dr Mahbub Ul Haq; Dr Nafis Sadik; Sadruddin Hashwani.

Sri Lanka: Edmund Kerner; Varindra Tarzie Vittachi; Professor Ralph Buultjens.

United Arab Emirates: His Highness Sheikh Nahayan Mabarak Al Nahayan; His Excellency Mohammad A. Al Gergawi.

I feel their blessings were particularly important for me during the writing of this difficult book. Most biographies take anywhere from three years to a dozen years from start to finish. This book was a late starter: I was signed on by Penguin in March 2012 to do this biography. This wasn't an easy task, especially given the legendary status of Dr Prathap Chandra Reddy and his peripatetic nature. The book had to be reported, researched and written in less than a year – the publisher wanted it out in time for the thirtieth anniversary of the founding of Apollo Hospitals in late 2013.

   The book began with a suggestion by N. Ram, who had just retired as editor-in-chief of India's national newspaper, *The Hindu*, and who is now chairman of the parent company. He and his wife Mariam have been most encouraging. Disclosure: It was Ram who began running my occasional columns in *The Hindu*, and I am forever grateful to him for the opportunity of being read by millions of Indians and others.

   My thanks go to Dr Prathap Chandra Reddy, his spouse Sucharitha Reddy, and their entire – and extraordinary – family. They couldn't have been more cooperative and forthcoming. A special thanks to Preetha Reddy, Dr Reddy's oldest daughter, for making this book possible, and to her sisters Suneeta, Shobana and Sangita.

   I also wish to acknowledge the next generation of Reddys who are being inducted into the business, the ten grandchildren of Dr and Mrs Reddy: Sindoori Reddy (and her spouse Tarun Reddy); Adithya Reddy (and his spouse Ritika Rai Reddy); Karthik Reddy; Harshad Reddy; Upasna Kamineni (and her spouse Ram Charan Teja); Anindith Konda Reddy; Anushpala Kamineni; Vishwajith

Konda Reddy; Viraj Madhav Konda Reddy; and Puansh Kamineni.

The following CEOs of Apollo Hospitals should also be thanked: Sathyanarayana Reddy in Chennai; Dr K. Hariprasad in Hyderabad; Dr Umapathy Panyala in Bangalore; Sumit Sarkar in Ahmedabad; Dr Rupali Basu in Kolkata; and Jaideep Gupta in New Delhi. A very special thanks, too, to Dr Anupam Sibal in New Delhi; his work as Group Medical Director of Apollo Hospitals is extremely demanding, but Anupam was always prompt in responding to my queries and in making important suggestions.

My special thanks, too, to Malathi Manohar at Apollo Chennai, who has worked closely with Dr Reddy for more than forty years. Malathi helped set up many of the interviews needed for this book. She was herself a source of extraordinary details about Dr Reddy and his life. Thanks to Apollo's Latha Suresh and Sheela Ketan in Chennai for their ever-smiling help; Rajalakshmi Chandru, Anjali Kapoor Bissell and R. Srinivasan in New Delhi; and Zena Brass in Hyderabad.

A special thanks to Sucharitha Reddy's younger sister Vijayalakshmi Reddy in Oregon for reading the manuscript, and to Apollo's Group CEO, S. Premkumar, S.K. Venkatraman, Apollo's Chief Strategy Officer, S. Obul Reddy and L. Lakshmi Narayana Reddy of Apollo Hospitals in Chennai. Jagannath Ramaswamy of Crystal, Chennai, and Shailaja Vardhan of Chennai warrant my enormous appreciation for carefully going through the manuscript – and for putting up with my wacky sense of humour. To Shailaja, in particular, I say: 'Thanks for raising the bar!' (She will know exactly what I mean.) I owe both her and Jagannath a lot.

And a very special thanks to Vanitha Rajkumar (and her husband A. Rajkumar) in Chennai for selecting and assembling archival and contemporary pictures of the Reddy family. Thanks, too, to Srilatha Reddy for her help with logistics and with many other kindnesses. And my gratitude to Aishwarya Ramachandran, a remarkable artist and author of a forthcoming memoir of growing up in Chennai. A special thanks to Kishore Manohar of Chennai for his anecdotes, insights and reading of the manuscript. Special thanks, as well, to

D. Nagarajan and Vimalchand Galada in Chennai for their wise spiritual counsel.

Thanks are due to: V. Parthasarathy, general manager, liaison; Jayashree R. and P. Anuradha of Preetha Reddy's office, and Padmapriya of Suneeta Reddy's office in Chennai, M.P. Singh and Yuvraj and Doss, also in Chennai; Prasad Modali of Shobana Reddy's office in Hyderabad; Mamatha Nallamala, Prashanth Goud, Vijayender Reddy, Mohammed Ali and Dharmendra Nath of Sangita Reddy's office in Hyderabad; Sylvia Thomas, executive assistant to S.K. Venkatraman; K. Padmanabhan, Apollo's Chief Financial Officer and Bindu of Padmanabhan's office; Thabitha David of Dr Umapathy Panyala's office in Bangalore; and Sucharita Varadarajan and Krithika Balasubramaniam of Chennai.

My gratitude also to G. Mani, V. Deenadayalan and Raghunatha Reddy of Chairman Reddy's personal staff in Chennai; S. Parthasarathy and R. Mahesh of the Apollo executive office in Chennai; Farhat Syed and P. Mahesh of Sindoori Travels, also in Chennai; and Shilpee Baxla, Soma Sundar, Sanjay Bharadwaj, and Hari Babu in New Delhi. And thanks to Senthil Kumar in Chennai, and Gurcharan Singh in New Delhi, who drove me around at all odd hours for assorted interviews.

Special thanks to Suresh Kochattil of Hyderabad, one of the most astute and articulate observers of the Indian scene that I know. And also a special thanks to my friends Rajiv Saigal and Dr Rachna Upadhaya of Dubai and London.

Thanks, too, to my researchers: Bhumika Popli, Neha Simlai, Angana Guha Roy and Joydeep Sen Gupta in Delhi. And very warm thanks to my old friend and fellow documentary producer, Twilla Carolyn Duncan of New York, who flew to India to help me complete the research and then carefully scrutinized the manuscript.

I wound up interviewing more than two hundred people for this book in India, Italy, the United Kingdom, the United States, the United Arab Emirates and Mauritius, between March 2012 and August 2013. I thank them for their patience and cooperation.

Surprisingly, however, some associates – whose careers have

prospered on account of their association with Dr Reddy – did not manage to find the time to meet with me. Still others did not bother to respond to my e-mails. A couple of people declined to be interviewed on the grounds that, although they respected him personally, their comments would be perceived as harsh criticisms of Dr Reddy's private-sector orientation. Those few who offered tough assessments of Apollo's record insisted on anonymity because they did not wish to invite opprobrium. (I think that Dr Reddy's critics often misunderstand the man: he actually welcomes criticism, and he follows up on those points that can improve Apollo's performance. He is not a vindictive man, nor one who holds grudges.) Some people who had publicly lauded Dr Reddy seemed to find other things in their schedules that prevented them from being interviewed. I am sure that everyone had his or her reasons, but I like to think that discourtesy towards Dr Reddy was surely not one. I can't but feel disappointed, of course, but as an old occupant of the world of writing I can understand exigencies. I wonder how many more insightful anecdotes about Dr Reddy might have found their way into this book had some of these luminaries made the effort to meet with me.

A number of friends and colleagues read the manuscript prior to publication, including Mohan Guruswamy, former Secretary in the ministry of finance; Dr Ramaswami Venkataswami, a classmate of Dr Reddy's at Stanley Medical College, and one of India's most eminent plastic surgeons; M.R. Sivaraman, a distinguished retired member of the IAS and former director general of Civil Aviation; Dr Vijay Madan and Vineeta Rai, also of the IAS; Sandeep Ahuja, Chief Executive Officer of VLCC in New Delhi; Dr Joseph V. Thachil, Dr Ramesh Nimmagadda, Dr Nirvikalpa Natarajan, Dr C. Chandilya, Dr Vinod Sukhija, Dr Ravi Bhatia, Suganthy Sundararaj, Y.V. Sridhar, Dr Sai Satish and Dr Subramaniam Arumugam of Apollo Hospitals; Dr Shiv Prakash of NMC Hospital in Dubai; and Dr Zain Gulzar of the Dubai Mediclinic. Thanks also to Manveen Sabharwal in Chandigarh for bringing her professorial eye to the manuscript. Also in Chandigarh, my thanks to Kamal Sehgal for his legal counsel.

I thank them for patiently going through the manuscript, and I also hereby absolve them of any errors that may have crept in. These errors – if any – are entirely my responsibility. I would be pleased to make corrections in subsequent editions.

In New Delhi, I must thank Anuj Bahri (who is my literary representative in India, and who worked in a stellar fashion for this book), Rajni Malhotra and Mithilesh Singh of the fabled bookstore in Khan Market, Bahrisons. Thanks, too, to the staffs of the Leela hotels in Chennai, Mumbai and New Delhi, and to the kind folks at the Radisson Blu in Chennai. I suspect that they must think that I've been installed as a permanent piece of furniture in their wonderful facilities.

In Mumbai, my warmest thanks to Capt. C.P. Krishnan Nair, Founder and Chairman Emeritus of the Leela Group of Palaces, Hotels and Resorts; his sons Vivek, Chairman and Managing Director of the Leela; and Dinesh, Co-Chairman and Managing Director. They offered important anecdotes and insights about their longtime friend Dr Reddy.

A huge thanks to Udayan Mitra, publisher of Penguin's Portfolio imprint, to Chiki Sarkar, the editor-in-chief of Penguin India, and to Khozem Merchant. And my thanks to Paloma Dutta. I taxed Udayan's patience during the delivery period of the manuscript. Yet I harbour the audacity to hope that he will edit more of my books. Besides literature, we share a love for canines.

And, as always, I offer my lasting appreciation to my literary agent Lynn Nesbit of Janklow & Nesbit Associates in New York. It has been said before, but it bears repetition: Lynn is a superstar.

The encouragement, and patience, of all my editors, friends and supporters is most appreciated.

One more thought: I confess that all my life I've hated going to hospitals. When I was with the *New York Times* in my younger days, I once covered the hospitals beat – quite possibly the worst journalistic assignment in New York City. But following Dr Reddy around Apollo hospitals in India somehow cured me of this phobia. So I can truthfully report that for this author, Dr Reddy was indeed a healer.

Prathap Chandra Reddy's Family Tree

Aragonda Muniswamy Reddy (*b.* 1875) – Lakshmi

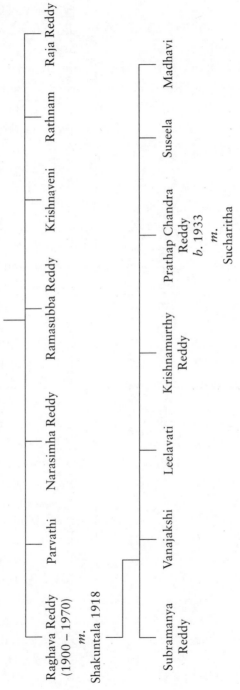

Raghava Reddy (1900 – 1970) *m.* Shakuntala 1918   Parvathi   Narasimha Reddy   Ramasubba Reddy   Krishnaveni   Rathnam   Raja Reddy

Subramanya Reddy   Vanajakshi   Leelavati   Krishnamurthy Reddy   Prathap Chandra Reddy *b.* 1933 *m.* Sucharitha   Suseela   Madhavi

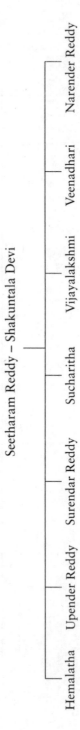

Sucharitha Reddy's Family Tree

Seetharam Reddy – Shakuntala Devi

Hemalatha — Upender Reddy — Surendar Reddy — Sucharitha — Vijayalakshmi — Veenadhari — Narender Reddy

Prathap Chandra Reddy – Sucharitha 1957

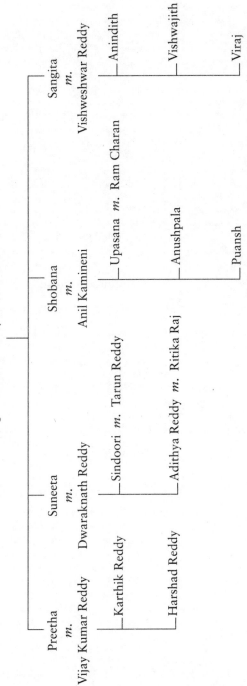

Preetha
m.
Vijay Kumar Reddy

Suneeta
m.
Dwaraknath Reddy

Karthik Reddy

Harshad Reddy

Sindoori *m.* Tarun Reddy

Adithya Reddy *m.* Ritika Raj

Shobana
m.
Anil Kamineni

Upasana *m.* Ram Charan

Anushpala

Puansh

Sangita
m.
Vishweshwar Reddy

Anindith

Vishwajith

Viraj

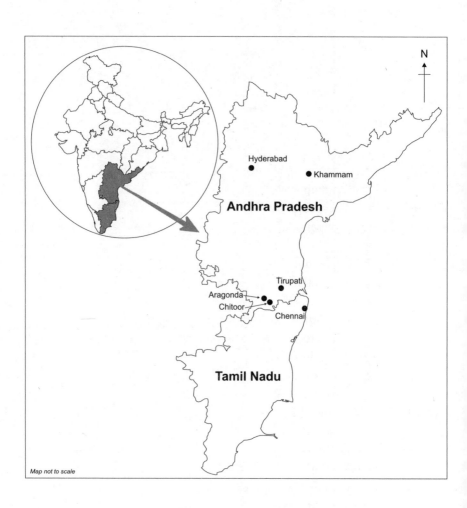

Map not to scale

Timeline

1933 Birth of Prathap Chandra Reddy on 5 February
1938 Birth of Sucharitha Reddy
1947 India becomes independent, Jawaharlal Nehru is India's first prime minister
1948 Mahatma Gandhi is assassinated
1957 Wedding of Prathap C. Reddy and Sucharitha Reddy on 1 February
1963 Dr Reddy leaves India to work in Britain
1964 Dr Reddy named chief resident at Worcester City Hospital, Massachusetts
      Jawaharlal Nehru dies
1965 Dr Reddy receives fellowship at Massachusetts General Hospital; family lives in Waltham
1966 Dr Reddy joins Missouri Chest Hospital; he and family move to Springfield, Missouri
      Indira Gandhi becomes prime minister
1969 The Reddy family leaves the US to return to India
1970 Dr Reddy joins HM Hospital in Madras
      Raghava Reddy, Prathap's father, dies from an aneurysm on 12 March
      Shakuntala Reddy, Prathap's mother, dies of cancer
1975 Emergency declared
1977 Emergency lifted; Prime Minister Indira Gandhi voted out of power
1980 Indira Gandhi returns to power

525

1983   Sri Krishna Mariamman temple at Apollo Hospitals Madras consecrated on 13 June

Apollo Hospitals Madras inaugurated by Giani Zail Singh, President of India on 18 September

Apollo becomes first corporate hospital to list equity shares in Madras Stock Exchange and Bombay Stock Exchange

First hospital-based pharmacy opened in Greames Road, Madras

First Apollo health check on 13 June

First cardiac surgery at Apollo on 17 October

1984   First kidney transplantation at Apollo Madras

100th cardiac surgery case on 30 May

Indira Gandhi assassinated; Rajiv Gandhi becomes prime minister

1985   Cardiac surgery programme at Apollo completes 1000 surgeries with a 98 per cent success rate

1986   Medical Insurance scheme introduced in collaboration with United India Insurance

1987   Apollo Hospitals Madras accredited by National Board of Medicine

1988   Apollo Hospitals Hyderabad inaugurated

First pharmacy retail outlet at Mandaveli, Madras

First of its kind CT scanner (fourth generation) at Apollo Hospitals Hyderabad

First high frequency Cath lab in India at Apollo Hospitals Hyderabad

1989   IVF unit creates medical history with the birth of a baby by 'GIFT' procedure

Telemetry system introduced at Apollo Hospitals Hyderabad, an India first

Rajiv Gandhi and the Congress voted out of power

1990   Revolutionary orthopedic surgery – equalizing of limbs and deformity correction by Lizarov procedure, carried out at Apollo

1991   Dr Reddy and Dr M.K. Mani awarded Padma Bhushan

First international patients – from the Middle East

First Apollo School of Nursing commissioned in Madras

Rajiv Gandhi assassinated; Congress returns to power, P.V. Narasimha Rao becomes prime minister; economic reforms initiated

1992   Apollo Institute of Hospital Management and Allied Sciences established in Madras

1993   24-hour ambulance service with wireless facility launched

362 consecutive coronary bypass surgeries at Apollo Hospitals Hyderabad without mortality or serious complications

1994   Preetha Reddy appointed Managing Director, Apollo Hospitals Group

Teletherapy unit and India's first Dose Rate Micro Selectron installed at Apollo Speciality Hospital

Apollo Hospitals listed in the National Stock Exchange

Apollo Institute of Hospital Administration established in Hyderabad

10,000th heart case on 13 September

Transplantation of Human Organs Act passed

1995   Apollo Speciality Hospital inaugurated in Madras

First bone marrow transplant carried out

First multi-organ transplant in the country at Apollo Hospitals Madras on 25 December

Sangita Reddy appointed Executive Director Operations, Apollo Hospitals Group

First Stereotactic radiosurgery unit in South Asia in May

First successful cadaveric transplant after the Transplantation of Human Organs Act was passed

1996   Harvard Business School introduces case study on Apollo Hospitals

Apollo Indraprastha Hospitals inaugurated in New Delhi

First Apollo College of Nursing commissioned in Madras

Apollo Speciality Hospitals becomes the first hospital in India to get ISO 9002 certification

1000 successful renal transplants completed

First dedicated Linac based stereotactic radio surgery unit outside of USA

First FDI in health care: Schroders Capital

Apollo Cancer Hospital inaugurated in Hyderabad

Madras is officially renamed Chennai

Congress voted out of power

1997   Apollo Hospitals Madurai commences operation

Casualty concept in the country modified to Emergency Medicine concept

1998   First successful Cord Blood Transplant in India

Dr Reddy receives Sir Nilratan Sircar Memorial Oration (JIMA) Award

First successful pediatric and adult liver transplants in India at Apollo Indrapastha Hospital

Apollo Hospitals Vikrampuri inaugurated

First National Democratic Alliance (NDA) government comes to power, Atal Bihari Vajpayee becomes prime minister

1999   Dedicated stroke unit at Apollo with 24 hours neurology cover, spiral CT scanner and Intravascular Neuro lab and Intracranial Doppler, first in India

2000   Apollo Hospitals Aragonda inaugurated

First telemedicine facility in the country inaugurated at Aragonda by Bill Clinton, President of the United States

Apollo Health Street, a customized business outsourcing company, established

Clinical research activities initiated at Apollo Hospitals Chennai

Medvarsity Online Limited, the first medical e-learning venture of Apollo, established

Apollo Speciality Hospitals Madurai inaugurated by K. Karunanidhi, chief minister of Tamil Nadu

Innovative demerger of Sindoori Hotels into AHEL

Emergency medicine course started along with Royal College of Surgeons at Apollo Hospitals Hyderabad

2001   Apollo Speciality Hospital Chennai completes 100 bone marrow transplants

Successful heart surgery on a 2-day-old baby, successful implant of pacemaker in a 97-year-old

Apollo becomes first hospital to receive Grade A rating from CRISIL for health care services and facilities

Dr Reddy along with Dr A.P.J. Abdul Kalam launch DRDO Hospital in Hyderabad

Emergency centres in Hyderabad linked as hub-and-spoke model for the first time in India

2002   Apollo Hospitals introduces nationwide single emergency number
        – 1066
        Dr Reddy receives the Ernst & Young Entrepreneur of the Year
        Award
        Apollo First Med Hospital launched in Chennai
        The first Apollo Clinic inaugurated in Delhi by the chief minister
        Sheila Dikshit
        Air ambulance concept launched at Apollo Hospitals Hyderabad
        Dr A.P.J. Abdul Kalam becomes President of India
2003   American Heart Association appoints Apollo Hospitals as an
        International Training Organization
        Apollo Hospitals launches its first CSR initiative 'Save a Child's
        Heart'
2004   Apollo recognized as 'Super Brand of India' in the Healthcare sector
        Apollo rated the 'Best Private Sector Hospital in India' by the
        Week magazine
        Launch of Apollo Medicine Journal
        Apollo Hospitals Hyderabad becomes first in the world to use
        satellite technology for telemedicine
        United Progressive Alliance (UPA) government comes to power,
        Manmohan Singh becomes prime minister
2005   Dr Reddy becomes the first recipient of the Asia-Pacific Bio-
        Business Leadership Award
        Apollo Hospitals New Delhi becomes the first hospital in India to
        receive accreditation from JCI, USA
        First 3 Tesla MRI in India in Apollo Hospitals New Delhi
        First in Delhi to install a 64 Slice CT Angio Scanner
        First Cradle launched in Gurgaon
        Apollo Speciality Hospitals Madurai wins Good Industrial
        Relations Award from the Government of Tamil Nadu
        First PET CT installed at Apollo Hospitals Hyderabad
        First MCEM course started at Apollo Hospitals Hyderabad
2006   Apollo Hospitals Chennai receives accreditation from JCI, USA
        Apollo Hospitals Group inks a joint venture with DKV of Munich
        Re group to enter Health Insurance in India
        Apollo Hospitals Hyderabad receives accreditation for Acute

Stroke from JCI, USA – the first hospital outside USA to receive a disease-specific certification

Course for paramedics started at Apollo Hospitals Hyderabad in collaboration with Stanford University

2007 First Health City in Asia launched on 15 June in Hyderabad

Dr Reddy awarded Modern Medicare Excellence Award by ICICI Group

Apollo Hospitals inaugurated in Bangalore

2008 Apollo Hospitals featured in the world's top 50 local dynamos list according to a study by Boston Consulting Group

Apollo Hospitals Bangalore becomes the sixth Apollo hospital to receive accreditation from JCI, USA

Prime Minister Manmohan Singh inaugurates Apollo Reach Hospitals at Karim Nagar remotely from Chennai

Apollo Hospitals launches *BPositive*, a health and lifestyle magazine

Apollo Hospitals ranked among India's Top Hospitals in a survey conducted by the *Week* magazine and IMRB

JV for hybrid umbilical cord blood bank along with Cadila Pharmaceuticals and StemCyte Inc. USA

Pediatric liver transplant in Apollo New Delhi on six-month-old baby – a first in India

Apollo Reach and Sugar Clinics win Consumer Health Awards

Apollo Hospitals Hyderabad performs the highest number of cochlear implants in a day

Apollo Hospitals Hyderabad wins Hospital Management Asia Award for CSR

Apollo Hospitals Hyderabad awarded NABL certification

2009 The Apollo Knee Clinic launched at Apollo Hospitals Chennai

Apollo Children's Hospital Chennai inaugurated by A.R. Rahman

Commemorative postage stamp felicitating Apollo Hospitals' pioneering spirit released on 2 November

Asia Pacific's most advanced CyberKnife launched at Apollo Speciality Cancer Hospital, Chennai

ACE@25, a clinical balanced scorecard with international quality benchmarks, launched in all Apollo hospitals

Apollo Speciality Hospitals becomes first hospital in group to receive accreditation from NABH, Quality Council of India

Apollo Health City Hyderabad gets Express Healthcare Award for Sustained Growth and Patient Care

Apollo wins FICCI Healthcare awards for Excellence in Patient Care, Excellence in Healthcare Delivery and Excellence in HR Practices

Apollo Health City performs bypass surgery on a conscious patient

Centre for Bariatric Surgery launched at Apollo Health City, Jubilee Hills

Congress-led UPA government re-elected

2010   Apollo Hospitals recognized as India's Most Preferred Hospital at the India Healthcare Awards

Novalis TX inaugurated at Indraprastha Apollo Hospitals

Apollo's 'Billion Hearts Beating' campaign wins the Best Marketing Campaign of the Year Award at World Brand Congress

Shobana Reddy Kamineni appointed Executive Director of Apollo Hospitals Enterprises

Mobile health services launched

Successful heart transplant at Apollo Hospitals Chennai for the first time

Dr Reddy conferred Padma Vibhushan

Apollo Hospitals Educational and Research Foundation certified by Department of Scientific and Industrial Research

Apollo Indraprastha becomes the first corporate hospital to be named a National Pharmacovigilance Centre by the Government of India

Apollo commences first Research Grants programme by providing grants to twenty-one projects

Apollo Quality Programme detailing methodologies for Clinical Handovers, International Patient Safety Goals, Surgical Care Improvement and Zero Medication Errors launched across the entire Apollo group

Auditory brain implant performed independently for the first time in India

India's first Single Incision Laparoscopic conference and workshop organized by Apollo

Apollo Hospitals launches the fiftieth hospital in the group at

Secunderabad

Apollo Hospitals Hyderabad listed in the top 100 Best Places to Work For

Medicare Excellence Award for being the Safe Practice Hospital of the Year

Sucharitha Reddy publishes cookbook, *Nostalgia Cuisine*

2011   Apollo Reach Hospitals at Karaikudi, Tamil Nadu inaugurated by Prime Minister Manmohan Singh

Suneeta Reddy named Joint Managing Director

'Run for Healthy Heart' ('Apollo Dil Ki Daud'), a mini-marathon, organized by Indraprastha Apollo Hospitals

Cricketer Gautam Gambhir launches 'Gift a Life' Initiative to create awareness about organ donation

Apollo Institute of Robotic Surgery launched in collaboration with the Vattikutti Foundation, USA

Apollo Hospitals opens a critical care unit with ICU facility at Sabarimala

Apollo Pharmacy awarded the Best Healthcare Retail Company of the Year by Frost & Sullivan

Apollo Day Surgery – a dedicated facility for minor surgeries requiring short stay – launched

Apollo Hospitals identified to render specialist health services to Tanzania

World's first iPad Navigation Hip Resurfacing Surgery performed at Apollo Speciality Hospitals Chennai

Apollo becomes the first in India to set up a PET MRI System

Bilateral total knee replacement performed on 93-year-old man at Apollo Indrapastha Hospital

Apollo awarded 'Great Place to Work' – ranked first among hospitals

Apollo achieves Rs 1000-crore pharmacy turnover with 1000 pharmacies

India's first single incision gastric bypass at Apollo Hospitals Chennai

World's first single incision revision bariatric surgery

India's first Robotic Bariatric Programme launched at Apollo Hospitals Chennai

Apollo Hospitals Secunderabad receives NABH accreditation

Apollo Health City Hyderabad recognized as Best Medical Tourism Facility for 2009–10 by the Government of India

Apollo Hospitals Hyderabad gets Hospital Management Asia Award for Clinical Excellence

Dr Reddy launches the four essentials of patient safety at the First International Congress on Patient Safety

First cadaver liver transplant performed at Apollo Hospitals Hyderabad

2012 First of its kind Dental Wellness Centre in India, the White luxury dental spa, launched

Apollo organizes the largest multi-speciality tele-health camp in Ajmer

Apollo Hospitals partners with National Skill Development Corporation to promote skills in health space

Apollo Hospitals Group wins G20 Challenge on Inclusive Business Innovation – the only healthcare organization in the world to do so

More than 130,000 cardiac surgeries performed at Apollo with a 99.6 per cent success rate

Apollo organizes the third International Congress on Transforming Healthcare with Information Technology

Apollo Isha Vidya Rural School launched in Aragonda

AHERF completes 750 clinical trials of which 80 per cent are global multi-centric trials

Apollo performs more than 1000 transplants in the year making it the busiest Solid Organ Transplant programme in the world

Apollo Institute of Medical Sciences and Research starts its first medical college

Bariatric surgery performed on a patient weighing 348 kgs, the heaviest in Asia

Apollo Hospitals Chennai emerges as India's leading Single Incision Laparoscopic centre with over 500 SILS advanced surgeries

Apollo group emerges as the leading corporate hospital with more than 1000 Bariatric surgeries

Apollo Bhubaneshwar's lab accredited by NABL

Apollo Bhubaneshwar completes NABH final assessment within

three years of commissioning

Proton Therapy project gets underway

Apollo Hospitals Hyderabad performs first coronary angioplasty in India using fully absorbable stent

Pranab Mukherjee becomes President of India

2013   Apollo successfully completes 1000 cases of CyberKnife radio surgery

Apollo Hospitals Hyderabad starts first medical college in the group

Apollo Health City Hyderabad performs revolutionary Minimally Invasive Knee Replacement (Resurface) Surgery using OrthoGlide Medial Knee system

Apollo Health City Hyderabad adjudged the Best Medical Tourism Hospital in India by the Government of India

Apollo stock added to MSCI index/Morgan Stanley – the stock value crosses Rs 1000

Dr Reddy delivers Sir Ganga Ram Oration

Apollo Health Street sold to Sutherland Global Initiatives

Dr Reddy receives NDTV Indian of the Year, Lifetime Achievement Award

Apollo wins 21st Global HR Excellence Award for Institution Building

Apollo wins Employer Branding Award for Talent Management and Best HR Strategy in line with Business

Apollo wins AIMA Award for Breakthrough Innovation in Service Delivery

Dr Reddy turns eighty on 5 February

Apollo Hospitals marks its 30th anniversary on 18 September

Dr Reddy sets up Family Council to oversee transition and third generation family involvement in Apollo Hospitals

Bibliography

Aiyar, Mani Shankar. *A Time of Transition: Rajiv Gandhi to the 21st Century*. New Delhi: Penguin Viking, 2009.

Anderson, Perry. *The Indian Ideology*. Gurgaon: Three Essays Collective, 2012.

Bandyopadhyay, Tamal. *A Bank for the Buck: The New Bank Movement and the Untold Story of the Making of India's Most Valued Bank*. Mumbai: Jaico Publishing House, 2013.

Bhagwati, Jagdish, and Panagariya, Arvind. *India's Tryst with Destiny: Debunking Myths That Undermine Progress and Addressing New Challenges*. New Delhi: Collins Business, 2012.

Bhat, Harish. *TataLog: Eight Modern Stories from a Timeless Institution*. New Delhi: Penguin Portfolio, 2012.

Chowdhury, Javid. *The Insider's View: Memoirs of a Public Servant*. New Delhi: Penguin Viking, 2012.

Cooley, Denton A. *100,000 Hearts: A Surgeon's Memoir*. Austin, Texas: University of Texas, 2012.

Das, Gurcharan. *India Grows at Night: A Liberal Case for a Strong State*. New Delhi: Penguin Allen Lane, 2012.

Dehija, Vivek and Subramanya, Rupa. *Indianomix: Making Sense of Modern India*. New Delhi: Random House, 2012.

Gawande, Atul. *Complications: A Surgeon's Notes on an Imperfect Science*. London: Picador, 2003.

————. *Better: A Surgeon's Notes on Performance*. London: Picador, 2008.

Ghosh, Bishwanath. *Tamarind City: Where Modern India Began*. New Delhi: Tranquebar, 2012.

Guha, Ramachandra. *India After Gandhi: The History of the World's Largest Democracy*. London: Pan Books, 2008.

Gupte, Pranay. *Mother India: A Political Biography Of Indira Gandhi*. New Delhi: Penguin, 2010.

Jalan, Bimal. *Emerging India: Economics, Politics and Reforms*. New Delhi: Penguin Viking, 2012.

Kamath, M.V. and Kher, V.B. *Sai Baba of Shirdi: A Unique Saint*. Mumbai: Jaico Publishing House, 2012.

Le Fanu, James. *The Rise and Fall of Modern Medicine*. London: Abacus, 2011.

Mahbubani, Kishore. *The Great Convergence: Asia, the West, and the Logic of One World*. New York: Public Affairs, 2013.

Mani, Dr M.K. *Yamaraja's Brother: The Autobiography of Dr M.K. Mani*. Mumbai: Bharatiya Vidya Bhavan, 1989.

McDonald, Hamish. *Ambani and Sons*. New Delhi: Roli Books, 2010.

Miller, G. Wayne. *King of Hearts: The True Story of the Maverick Who Pioneered Open Heart Surgery*. New York: Three Rivers Press, 2000.

Narayan, Shoba. *Return to India: A Memoir*. New Delhi: Rain Tree, 2012.

Neelima, Kota. *Tirupati: A Guide to Life*. New Delhi: Random House, 2012.

Nuland, Sherwin B. *Doctors: The Biography of Medicine*. New York: Vintage Books, 1995.

Pandit, Shrinivas. *Exemplary CEOs: Insights on Organizational Transformation*. New Delhi: Tata McGraw-Hill, 2005.

Piramal, Gita. *Business Maharajas*. New Delhi: Penguin Portfolio, 1996.

Prasad, Meera, Ranganathan, V.V. and Skaria, George. *In-Sight: Sankara Nethralaya's Passion for Compassion*. Bangalore: Lone Tree Books, 2012.

Rangan, Baradwaj. *Conversations with Mani Ratnam*. New Delhi: Penguin Viking, 2012.

Reddy, Dr Prathap Chandra. *Stay Healthy, India!* New Delhi: Penguin Enterprise, forthcoming.

Reddy, Sucharitha. *Nostalgia Cuisine*. Chennai: privately published, 2008.

Sahgal, Nayantara. *Indira Gandhi: Tryst with Power*. New Delhi: Penguin, 2012.

Sanyal, Sanjeev. *Land of the Seven Rivers: A Brief History of India's Geography*. New Delhi: Penguin Viking, 2012.

Sen, Amartya. *The Argumentative Indian: Writings on Indian Culture, History and Identity*. New Delhi: Penguin, 2005.

Sengupta, Hindol. *The Liberals*. New Delhi: HarperCollins, 2012.

Shetty, Dr Rekha. *Innovate! 90 Days to Transform Your Business*. New Delhi: Penguin Portfolio, 2010.

Varma, Pavan K. *Chanakya's New Manifesto to Resolve the Crisis within India*. New Delhi: Aleph, 2013.

Vittal, N. *Ending Corruption? How to Clean Up India*. New Delhi: Penguin Viking, 2012.

Index